COLLECTING
CHILDREN'S
BOOKS

Published in the United Kingdom 2001
by Diamond Publishing Group Limited,
45 St. Mary's Road, Ealing, London W5 5RQ

Printed in England

ISBN No. 0-9532601-2-7

COLLECTING CHILDREN'S BOOKS

COMPILED BY
BOOK AND MAGAZINE COLLECTOR
BRITAIN'S LEADING PUBLICATION FOR BOOK AND MAGAZINE COLLECTORS

PUBLISHER
Sean O'Mahony

MANAGING EDITOR
John Dean

EDITOR
Crispin Jackson

ART DIRECTOR
Ian Gray

PRODUCTION MANAGER
Peter Phillips

CONSULTANTS
David Adland
John Cowen
Clarissa Cridland
Richard Dalby
June Hopper
Barbara Richardson
David Schutte
Ann F. Smith
David Whitehead
Norman Wright

CONTENTS

EDITOR'S FOREWORD

Welcome to the new edition of 'Collecting Children's Books', the definitive price guide to collectable children's books and annuals.

The new edition has been fully updated and greatly expanded to include 69 new subjects and over 2,000 new entries, making a total of over 12,000 separate items.

The new entries include several modern authors and illustrators whose work has only recently started to attract collectors — people like Quentin Blake, Shirley Hughes, Dick Bruna, Pat Lynch and J.P. Martin. We have also added a number of older writers who we felt could not be left out of the new edition, notably Rumer Godden, Ludwig Bemelmans, W.H.G. Kingston, E.V. Lucas, Spike Milligan, Eileen Soper, Rosemary Sutcliff, Jules Verne and Charlotte Yonge.

The new subjects also include a few names who have established themselves since the first edition of *Collecting Children's Books* appeared in 1995. This is the case with undoubtedly the most successful children's author of modern times, and the most important of our 'new arrivals' — 'Harry Potter' creator, J.K. Rowling. The first of her bestselling children's novels, *Harry Potter and the Philosopher's Stone*, was published in 1997, two years after *Collecting Children's Books*, and since then she has written three more adventures. Such is the popularity of 'Harry Potter' with collectors that all the various 'first issues' of the four books are sought after — not just the first trade editions, but the de luxe editions, the proof copies, and even the first paperbacks. We list *all* of the collectable editions in our Rowling entry. Of course, the 'Holy Grail' for 'Harry Potter' collectors is the first trade edition of *Philosopher's Stone*, which was issued in an edition of just 500 copies. Today, these are worth £8,000 in Very Good condition.

The 'Harry Potter' phenomenon is undoubtedly the major development in children's book collecting over the last six years, but other trends are worth noting here. The first point to make is that the real classics remain as sought-after as ever, with price increases in all cases exceeding inflation. The early and/or rare books of

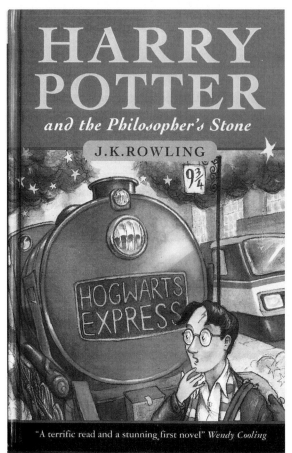

The first edition of **Harry Potter and the Philosopher's Stone** *is already worth over £8,000 in VG condition.*

Beatrix Potter, Lewis Carroll, Edward Lear, Kenneth Grahame, Charles Dickens, J.R.R. Tolkien, Rudyard Kipling and A.A. Milne are the 'blue chip' items in the collectors' market. They have proved their durability, and there will always be demand for exceptional copies of their first editions. Tolkien's *The Hobbit* and *The Lord of the Rings* and Kenneth Grahame's *The Wind in the Willows* have seen a particular increase in value over the past six years.

The picture is more complicated with the 'second division' names. Some have increased in popularity, some have stalled or even declined. Among the 'winners' are Enid Blyton, Arthur Ransome (particularly his 'Swallows and Amazons' books), W.E. Johns, C.S. Lewis, Rupert the Bear and Elsie J. Oxenham. Of these, Oxenham has been the greatest surprise. Her girls' stories are very much of the 'old school', but demand has shot up in recent years, particularly in the case of her popular 'Abbey' series.

Most of Elsie J. Oxenham's books have seen a significant rise in value over the past six years.

There are few surprises on the comics front, with the classic D.C. Thomson titles, *Beano* and *Dandy*, continuing to attract the greatest interest from collectors, although *The Broons* and *Oor Wullie* annuals also remain popular, as does *Eagle*/'Dan Dare' material. TV spin-offs, particularly those relating to Gerry Anderson series like *Thunderbirds* and *Stingray*, have stalled, although *Doctor Who* retains a firm following.

We have pursued an inclusive policy in putting together this guide, and it encompasses every aspect of children's book collecting. It lists *Gulliver's Travels* and *Robinson Crusoe*, and also *The Ladybird Book of Garden Birds* and *Spot's First Walk*. Values range from as little as £3 to as much as £200,000. If a book is collected, then you will find it here.

On pages 10 and 11, you will find a section on 'How to Use the Guide', but I just wanted to offer a brief introduction to new readers who are unfamiliar with its layout. The book provides:

1. A complete list of children's works by over 300 collectable authors and illustrators, arranged alphabetically.
2. Help in identifying the collectable editions of all the works listed.
3. A guide to the value of every first edition.

Each entry begins with a brief biography of the author/illustrator concerned, and then lists all their children's works in chronological order. Major book series are listed separately at the beginning of the entry, and in order of importance. In the case of W.E. Johns, for instance, his 'Biggles' books are considered first, then 'Worrals', 'Gimlet', his science fiction titles, his miscellaneous works and, finally, the handful of volumes by other authors for which he provided the illustrations. All the titles listed are either first editions or first revised editions (i.e. those that have been rewritten, or contain new text or illustrations), but to help you value later editions we've included a brief introduction to reprints on pages 17-21.

Pricing rare books is always a challenge. Top specialist dealers, especially those based in London, will invariably charge more than general booksellers, while, at the other extreme, we all know someone who has paid a couple of pounds for a first of W.E. Johns' *The Camels are Coming* or Edward Lear's *A Book of Nonsense*! Our values reflect those currently charged by non-specialist children's dealers — in other words, those who deal exclusively in children's books, but don't concentrate entirely on one author, series or field, such as 'Biggles' or the nineteenth-century classics. All the entries have been checked by a team of expert consultants, which includes dealers, writers and bibliographers.

One point that needs stressing is that these are *selling* prices. If you

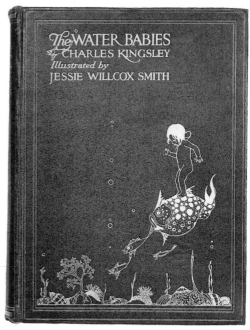

This book is doubly desirable as it contains the work of an important children's author and a collectable illustrator.

Jean de Brunhoff's 'Babar' books have remained firm favourites with children for over seventy years.

walk into your local children's bookshop and offer the owner a Very Good copy of say, *William the Lawless* (our value £750), then he or she would be unlikely to offer you more than half the price listed here. On the other hand, if you were advertising the book in the 'For Sale' section of *Book and Magazine Collector*, then we would recommend that you ask for the full amount, provided of course that the book was in the condition specified (Very Good, in dustjacket).

Children's books are endlessly fascinating, not least from a financial viewpoint. The frailest item can be worth hundreds of pounds, and it is often an author's last — as well as earliest — works which command the highest prices. Sometimes you'll pick up a bargain, at other times you will have to pay the full 'going rate' for a long sought-after title. Whatever the case, *Collecting Children's Books* is here to help you.

THE COLLECTOR'S MARKETPLACE

Book and Magazine Collector is the world's leading marketplace for secondhand books, helping you to find titles you need to complete your collection, or to dispose of anything you want to sell.

Our classified section lists thousands of books wanted and for sale in every issue, offering works of all kinds — from an early 'Biggles' to a De Luxe Arthur Rackham edition — and at all prices. In addition, dealers give details of their latest catalogues, and there are advertisements for new publications, accessories, booksearch services, book fairs and sales all over the country.

Each issue of the magazine also contains a wide selection of fascinating articles by expert contributors on, not just children's books, but modern first editions, crime fiction, Victorian authors, antiquarian books, sports and pastimes, topography, showbusiness, history, biography, comics and magazines — in fact, every sort of collectable publication.

Every feature provides a thorough survey of the lives and works of the author or artist concerned and looks at the details of their careers before going on to assess the merits and collectability of their major titles. *Book and Magazine Collector* is well illustrated, and every feature includes a *complete* list of all their titles, with details of current values, publishers and other important points.

Major writers are featured every couple of years or so, and on each occasion the price guide is updated to reflect current values. Of course, each new article focuses on a different aspect of the subject's work, such as fiction, non-fiction, illustrated editions or other collectable reprints. Major book series, such as the 'Biggles' or 'Sherlock Holmes' stories, have also been given features to themselves.

Another important section of the magazine is the 'Letters' page, in which we answer queries from readers on all sorts of subjects. Sometimes people write in asking for the title of a half-remembered book from childhood; sometimes they want us to value a work in their collection; others are seeking more information about a favourite author. Most of our readers have discovered more than one new area of interest in this fascinating section of the magazine!

In short, if you want to know more about collecting books, or simply want to keep in touch with the market, then *Book and Magazine Collector* is a good place to start every month.

Book and Magazine Collector is published on the third Thursday of every month, and is available from all leading newsagents or direct from the publisher, Diamond Publishing Group Ltd, at: 43-45 St Mary's Road, Ealing, London W5 5RQ.

HOW TO USE THE GUIDE

INTRODUCTION

Collecting Children's Books is designed to be an easy-to-use reference work for the collector and dealer. Its basic layout is simple: the 335 entries are arranged alphabetically by the author or illustrator's surname or by the first word of the book/book series title. The books themselves are listed chronologically, beginning with the major series and ending with a section on miscellaneous titles ('Others'). With illustrators, works both written and illustrated by the artist are listed separately before those for which they simply provided the artwork.

LATER COLLECTABLE EDITIONS

Certain books have, of course, been reprinted many times, often in very desirable illustrated or 'collector's' editions. These are all grouped together immediately after the first edition, in chronological order. Where a single edition is available in both trade and 'De Luxe' formats, then the trade edition is always listed first. Ordinary reprints are not listed.

INDIVIDUAL ENTRIES: BASIC LAYOUT

Each entry has four components:
1) the title (in bold);
2) an opening bracket, which contains details of: i) the book's contents, including any important contributions from other authors and/or illustrators; and, ii) its format, including bindings, dustjackets and — with limited editions — the number of copies printed and whether or not they were signed and/or numbered;
3) a second bracket, which gives the name of the publisher and the date of publication. With undated books, the year of publication is given in square brackets, like this: "(Blackie, [1934])". Where a book has been published before or after the date printed on the title-page, the actual year of publication is given in square brackets: "(Blackie, 1933 [1934])";
4) the current value of the first edition of the book (in bold).

CONDITION AND PRICING

Because of their very nature, most children's books are normally subject to quite a lot of wear and tear, so there are very few around in Fine condition. For this reason, the prices given in this volume are either for books in Good (up to 1900) or Very Good condition (after 1900). The relevant condition category is listed at the beginning of each entry, between the author/illustrator biography and the listings, so do make a point of checking this before you value your book.

GRADING AND VALUING YOUR BOOKS

Although around 75% of children's books advertised today are in Good condition, you will still come across some examples in Fine or Mint condition, plus plenty that are graded as Poor! You can calculate the values for these by turning to our 'Grading Guide' and 'Ready Reckoner' on pages 366 and 367.

ILLUSTRATED BOOKS

Illustrated editions of classic works are listed under both the author's and the artist's name. However, the precise number of illustrations in each edition is given only in the section devoted to the artist — in the first of the two brackets.

GLOSSARY

To help you understand the information given, it is worth knowing the precise meaning of the following words:

1) ILLUSTRATION: this refers to any pictorial decoration that is larger than vignette-size. It can be in either colour or black-and-white.
2) VIGNETTE: a small decorative device normally inserted at the end of a chapter.
3) PLATE: any full-page illustration, in colour or black-and-white. It is often printed on glossier paper than the text itself.
4) TIPPED-IN PLATE: one that is gummed along one edge only. It is often mounted on thicker paper than is used for the pages themselves.

BINDINGS

Unless otherwise stated, the first editions of all the books we've listed were issued in cloth bindings with dustjackets. The other types of binding mentioned are:

1) WRAPPERS: a paper cover, either gummed or sewn onto the pages of the book.
2) PAPERBACK: a modern, small-octavo softcover book, usually with glossy 'wrappers'.
3) BOARDS: covers of unbound, stiff card, often with a cloth spine. 'Laminated' boards are those with a glossy, hard-wearing covering, and are usually found on books and annuals from the mid-1960s onwards.
4) VELLUM: fine, cream or white leather-like material made from the skin of a young animal — usually calf, but sometimes lamb or kid. Note that this 'weathers' very easily and is rarely found in better than Good condition. Some ultra-expensive limited edition giftbooks are actually printed on vellum.
5) JAPANESE VELLUM: a stiff, glossy handmade paper, often used for the pages of De Luxe editions, and sometimes as a substitute for real vellum in bookbinding.

DUSTJACKETS

All dustjackets are printed on matt or glossy paper. 'Glassine' jackets are made from a highly-transparent, almost cellophane-like paper, and are usually entirely plain.

MULTI-VOLUME EDITIONS

Where an edition comprises more than one volume, the exact number is given in the first bracket. In all cases, the value quoted refers to the complete set, as is clearly marked before the price.

INDEX OF ENTRIES

USING THE GUIDE
A BRIEF SUMMARY

ALL PRICES REFER TO BOOKS
IN GOOD OR VERY GOOD CONDITION

The precise grading is specified at the top of each entry, immediately after the biography of the author/illustrator concerned.
(See pages 366 and 367 for Grading System and Ready Reckoner.)

DUSTJACKETS

In some entries, the prices refer to books with dustjackets, in others to copies without them. Once again, check at the head of each entry to find out which condition applies. Where we have stated that prices are for books "with dustjackets where applicable", this means that only some of the books by the author/illustrator concerned were issued in jackets. These are clearly indicated by the inclusion of the words "issued with dustjacket" in the first bracket of the individual listing.

AUTHORS AND ILLUSTRATORS

Authors and illustrators are listed in alphabetical order.

EACH ENTRY

Lists all the children's books by the author or illustrator in chronological order, but not their adult or non-children's titles.

MAJOR BOOK SERIES

These are listed at the beginning of each entry in their own sections.

COLLECTABLE REPRINTS

Always listed in chronological order immediately after the first edition.

LIMITED EDITIONS

Listed immediately after the trade edition of the same book.

ILLUSTRATED EDITIONS

Listed under both the author's and illustrator's names.

REPRINTS
HOW MUCH ARE THEY WORTH?

Most of the 12,000 or so titles listed in *Collecting Children's Books* are first editions. There is a very good reason for this — nothing quite matches the thrill of having the original printing of a classic work, one that the author or illustrator saw through the presses, and which first introduced the title to an eager readership.

But it's in the very nature of a classic that it is reprinted many times, often in a multiplicity of different formats. This inevitably raises something of a problem for the children's book enthusiast: are these later editions collectable, and, if so, how much are they worth?

Needless to say, this is a very complicated subject in which no hard-and-fast rules apply. Nevertheless, here are a few examples which will give you some indication of what reprints are worth.

The first point to clear up is just what is meant by a 'reprint'. Here we

This 'Harry Potter' book is clearly a reprint as it carries a very obvious sticker on the cover announcing that it won the Smarties Prize.

have to draw a distinction between two very important words: 'edition' and 'impression'. For a book to be described as a 'new edition', then the text must have been reset and/or new text or illustrations added. A new *impression*, however, is merely a reprinting of the first edition; apart from the information printed on the reverse of the title-page and, perhaps, the binding, it is identical in every way to the original.

Of course, a famous work like *Alice in Wonderland* has gone through dozens of editions and impressions over the years. The most common variety of new edition is one which features a set of previously unpublished illustrations, but occasionally an author will revise or enlarge the original text. Needless to say, both variations are of considerable interest to collectors, especially if the new illustrations are by a collectable artist like Arthur Rackham or Edmund Dulac.

In addition, there are 'special editions', often published to commemorate an important anniversary or milestone, such as the hundredth printing of the work. These usually feature a special binding and/or slipcase, and may contain new text or illustrations, but, even if they don't, they have an obvious 'symbolic' importance for collectors, which makes them particularly sought after.

The good news is that you won't have any problem valuing 'new editions' like these, for the simple reason that we've included them all in this book. Immediately after the entry for the first edition, you will find a list of all the most collectable reprints, along with details of any new illustrations, bindings, etc. The major illustrated editions are also listed in the section devoted to the relevant artist.

So much for new editions. But what if you have a later *impression* of the first edition, or even of one of the more collectable illustrated editions? Well, here things get a bit more complicated, but it's still possible to lay down a few basic ground rules.

Basically, five factors affect the value of a later impression of a collectable book:

1) the rarity of the first impression;
2) the number of the later impression;
3) its condition;
4) its similarity to the original; and,
5) whether or not it's still in print.

It goes without saying that the rarer the first impression, the more valuable will be the second. Take 'Biggles', for instance. Any 'Biggles' fan will know that the most sought-after titles are the five published by John Hamilton in the 1930s. Needless to say, these are very rare today, particularly in their pictorial dustjackets, and so many collectors are happy to accept a reprint instead of the first impression, providing that it is otherwise identical.

This means that a second or third impression of a book like *"Biggles" of the Camel Squadron* (1934) can sell for as much as £100 even *without* the jacket. A second impression with the jacket might be worth as much as £800.

Compare this with one of the later books, like *Biggles Takes a Holiday*, published by Hodder & Stoughton in 1949. The first impression is now worth £30 (Very Good, in dustjacket), but you'd be lucky to get £8 for a similar copy of a later impression, and more than a pound or two for one without the jacket. This is simply because the first impression is still fairly easy to find, which means that even the earliest reprints are only of value as 'reading copies'.

The second factor to consider is the lateness of the impression. For obvious reasons, collectors who either can't find or afford a first impression of a favourite book would rather have a second impression than, say, an eighth – providing, of course, that they were identical in condition and format — and this, quite naturally is reflected in the values.

Let's take Edward Lear's *A Book of Nonsense* as an example. The enlarged edition was originally published by Routledge in 1861, and this is now worth £700 in Very Good condition. It's such a classic work that you will have still have to pay as much as £60 for a later Routledge reprint, even one from the early 1900s, but this is a relatively small amount when compared with the asking price of an otherwise identical second or third impression: around £250.

Many collectors are happy to buy reprints if they include the illustrations from the first edition.

Nevertheless, although the lateness of the impression *is* important, the condition of the book is also a factor, particularly with less valuable works. The 'Jennings' books are a typical case. A 1959 reprint of *Jennings Goes to School* (1950) in Good condition will fetch less than a Very Good example from 1961 — around £5 and £10 respectively, compared with £60 for the first impression. If we reverse the situation, and hypothetically 'swap' the gradings, then the 1959 book will be worth only slightly more than its 1961 counterpart — £12 at the most — while the 1961 impression will be practically worthless.

But of all the factors that decide the value of a later impression, the most important is the one of format. Put quite simply, if collectors can't have a first edition, then they want their substitute to look as much like the original as possible — the same publisher, binding, illustrations, paper, dustjacket, everything. Even if a reprint dates from ten or twenty years after the first printing, it will still be collectable if it has the same 'feel' as the latter.

For instance, a fourth impression of Helen Bannerman's *Little Black Mingo* would now sell for around £45 — an impressive sum when you consider that it was published nearly a decade after the original (now valued at £250). The important point, though, is that — in all essentials — it is the *same book* as the first. A post-war reprint with laminated boards would be worth just a couple of pounds.

Even the smallest change in format can lower the value of a reprint. In 1919, for instance, Beatrix Potter's publishers, Frederick Warne, became a limited company, with the result that all her books subsequently had the words 'F. Warne & Co. Ltd.' printed on their front boards rather than simply 'F. Warne & Co.'. Although only a minor point, it does lessen the 'authenticity' of post-1919 reprints, with the result that they now sell for £20-£30 (Very Good in dustjacket), compared with £35-£50 for earlier examples.

Of course, not all changes in format are for the worse. For the second impression of *The Hobbit*, J.R.R. Tolkien provided four new colour plates to go with the black-and-white illustrations in the original printing, and these account for its relatively high price of £2,500 (compared with £18,000 for the first).

The situation with E.H. Shepard's much-loved edition of *The Wind in the Willows* is even more complicated. In fact, there are no fewer than *three* important printings to look out for: the original one (1931 — £450), the first to include colour plates (1959 — £125) and the first to be in full-colour (1971 — £60). An inexperienced collector might be forgiven for treating the last two as straight reprints and undervaluing them. We've listed all such major 'issues' in this book.

*The second U.K. edition of **The Cat in the Hat** is now worth £50.*

Needless to say, a crucial component of any twentieth-century children's book — particularly where values are concerned — is the dustjacket. It's a more or less universal rule that reprints with dustjackets hold their value a lot better than those without them. A collector may be willing to pay good money for a first impression of *Just William* (1922) *without* a dustjacket, but if he's got to settle for a later one, then he'll definitely want the jacket. Jacketless reprints of the pre-war 'Williams' titles are now worth £8-£25 depending on condition, but those with jackets can sell for anything up to £100. The later books fetch much less — only £10-£15 with the dustjackets, and just a couple of pounds without.

Of course, if a book is still in print — especially in the original format — then a secondhand copy of a later impression will be of no interest to a collector. Why accept a less-than-perfect reprint when you can buy a Mint one at your local W.H. Smith's or Waterstone's?

Finally, a brief word about illustrated volumes and signed copies. In general, all the rules that apply to other children's books are doubly applicable to illustrated editions, particularly in the matter of format and authenticity. Most of the gift books by Arthur Rackham, Edmund Dulac and the other 'Golden Age' illustrators have gone through several printings, and these have almost invariably been accompanied by a gradual decline in production standards — for instance, the number of illustrations has been reduced, or these have been reproduced directly onto the page rather than being 'tipped-in'. One other point to note is that, with each new impression, the quality of reproduction has tended to drop, so that the colours in the later printings are significantly less bright than in the earlier ones.

Two points, therefore, need to be borne in mind: 1) always inspect the plates very carefully in any reprint you're thinking of buying, above all checking the total against that listed in this book; 2) remember that, as a general rule, the very earliest impressions of classic giftbooks — especially those illustrated by collectable illustrators whose first impressions are particularly rare — hold their value remarkably well, so that for a second impression of, say, Arthur Rackham's *Peter Pan in Kensington Gardens* (1906) or *Alice in Wonderland* (1907) you can expect to pay roughly half the price of the first.

Where signed copies are concerned, the general rule is that an author or illustrator's signature will always increase a book's value, whether it's a first edition or a reprint. The question is, by how much?

Well, two factors affect the size of the increase: 1) the rarity of an author's signature; and 2) the nature of the inscription.

In these days of 'promotional tours', it's quite common for an author to sign literally hundreds of copies of a new book. Even if these include a 'personal message' from the author, they won't increase the book's value by more than five or ten pounds. On the whole, signatures are much rarer in volumes from before the war, and in these cases a plain inscription would raise the value by 25% and, with the most collectable authors, as much as 50%.

The biggest prices are achieved by books that have a personal inscription by the author/illustrator to a friend, relative or collaborator. These are called 'association copies', and are particularly sought-after by collectors. Association copies usually sell for *at least* twice as much as unsigned ones, and where the dedicatee has a particularly close link with the work concerned — maybe they were the original for one of the characters, or designed or illustrated the book — then the price achieved will be three or four times our quoted value.

As I think this brief introduction has shown, it is impossible to lay down any really firm rules on the pricing of reprints — there are just too many factors to consider in a field this vast and varied.

Nevertheless, the following guidelines are worth bearing in mind when valuing books:

1) Reprints that are identical in format to the first impression are usually the most valuable, except where there are later editions illustrated by collectable artists.

2) Where the format is the same, condition is more important than the date of a reprint.

3) Reprints with dustjackets are much more desirable than those without (again, providing that the format is identical).

4) The rarer the book, the greater the parity between the price of the first impression and those of early reprints. This is particularly the case with illustrated books.

ADAMS, Richard

British author. Born: Richard George Adams in Berkshire, 1920. Studied at Bradfield College and Worcester College, Oxford. Worked for the Civil Service between 1948 and 1974. Won Guardian Award and Carnegie Medal for *Watership Down*. Past President of the RSPCA.

Prices are for books in Very Good condition with dustjackets where applicable.

WATERSHIP DOWN (Rex Collings, 1972) £350
WATERSHIP DOWN (first illustrated edition; in slipcase) (Penguin/Kestrel, 1976)..£40
SHARDIK (Lane/Rex Collings, 1974) £15
NATURE THROUGH THE SEASONS (non-fiction; science texts by Max Hooper) (Kestrel, 1975) £10
THE TYGER VOYAGE (verse; illustrated by Nicola Bayley) (Cape, 1976) £20
THE SHIP'S CAT (verse; illustrated by Alan Aldridge) (Cape, 1977) £20
THE PLAGUE DOGS (illustrated by A. Wainwright) (Lane, 1977) £15
NATURE DAY AND NIGHT (non-fiction; illustrated by David Goddard; science texts by Max Hooper) (Kestrel, 1978)...£10
THE WATERSHIP DOWN FILM PICTURE BOOK (Lane, 1978) £15
THE IRON WOLF and Other Stories (illustrated by Yvonne Gilbert and Jennifer Campbell) (Lane, 1980) £10
THE BUREAUCATS (illustrated by Robin Jacques) (Viking, 1985) £20

AESOP'S 'FABLES'

Collection of moral tales reputedly written by the Greek storyteller, Aesop, who lived on the island of Samos in the middle years of the sixth century BC. First printed in England by Caxton in 1484, and reissued many times since.

Prices are for books in Very Good condition.

AESOP'S FABLES. Retold by Rev Thomas James (illustrated by John Tenniel) (Murray, 1852)..............................£75
AESOP'S FABLES. Revised and rewritten by J.B. Rundell (illustrated by Ernest Griset) (Cassell, Peter & Galpin, [1869])..........£75
SOME OF AESOP'S FABLES (illustrated by Randolph Caldecott; translated by Alfred Caldecott) (Macmillan, 1883) £25
THE BABY'S OWN AESOP. Being the Fables condensed in rhyme by W.J. Linton
    (illustrated by Walter Crane) (Routledge, 1887 [1886]) £50
AESOP'S FABLES (illustrated by Charles Robinson) (Dent: 'Banbury Cross' series, 1895) £100
THE FABLES OF AESOP (illustrated by E.J. Detmold) (Hodder & Stoughton, 1909) £100
THE FABLES OF AESOP (illustrated by E.J. Detmold; limited to 750 copies, signed by the artist)
    (Hodder & Stoughton, 1909) £500
AESOP'S FABLES. Preface by Gordon Home (illustrated by Charles Folkard) (A. & C. Black, 1912) £35
AESOP'S FABLES. A new translation by V.S. Vernon Jones, with an introduction by G.K. Chesterton.
    (illustrated by Arthur Rackham) (Heinemann, 1912) £300
AESOP'S FABLES. A new translation by V.S. Vernon Jones, with an introduction by G.K. Chesterton.
    (illustrated by Arthur Rackham; limited to 1,450 copies, signed by the artist) (Heinemann, 1912) £1,500
AESOP'S FABLES. Retold by Blanche Winder (illustrated by Harry Rountree) (Ward Lock, [1924]) £35
AESOP'S FABLES (illustrated by Louis Rhead) (Harper, U.S., [1927]) £40
THE FABLES OF ESOPE. Translated out of Frensshe into Englysshe by William Caxton
    (illustrated by Agnes Miller Parker; limited to 250 copies) (Gregynog Press, 1931) £1,250
AESOP'S FABLES. Edited by Michael Hague (Holt, U.S., 1985)..£30

AHLBERG, Allan and Janet

British husband-and-wife author/illustrator team. Born in 1938 and 1944 respectively, Allan and Janet Ahlberg met at Sunderland Teacher Training College, and were married in 1969. They collaborated on many books for young readers, although not all Allan's 100+ titles were illustrated by Janet. Janet died in November 1994.

Prices are for books in Very Good condition with dustjackets where applicable.

HERE ARE THE BRICK STREET BOYS by Allan Ahlberg (illustrated by Janet Ahlberg) (Collins, 1975)....................£15
A PLACE TO PLAY by Allan Ahlberg (illustrated by Janet Ahlberg) (Collins, 1975)..£15
SAM THE REFEREE by Allan Ahlberg (illustrated by Janet Ahlberg) (Collins, 1975) £15
THE OLD JOKE BOOK by Allan and Janet Ahlberg (Kestrel, 1976) £25
FRED'S DREAM by Allan Ahlberg (illustrated by Janet Ahlberg) (Collins, 1976)..£15
THE GREAT MARATHON FOOTBALL MATCH by Allan Ahlberg (illustrated by Janet Ahlberg) (Collins, 1976) £15
BURGLAR BILL by Allan and Janet Ahlberg (Heinemann, 1977)..£20
THE VANISHMENT OF THOMAS TULL by Allan and Janet Ahlberg (A. & C. Black, 1977) £20
JEREMIAH IN THE DARK WOODS by Allan and Janet Ahlberg (Kestrel, 1977)..£15
EACH, PEACH, PEAR, PLUM by Allan and Janet Ahlberg (Kestrel, 1978) £30
COPS AND ROBBERS by Allan and Janet Ahlberg (Heinemann, 1978)..£20
THE LITTLE WORM BOOK by Allan and Janet Ahlberg (Granada, 1979 [1981]) £12
THE ONE AND ONLY TWO HEADS by Allan and Janet Ahlberg (Collins, 1979) £12
TWO WHEELS, TWO HEADS by Allan and Janet Ahlberg (Collins, 1979) £20

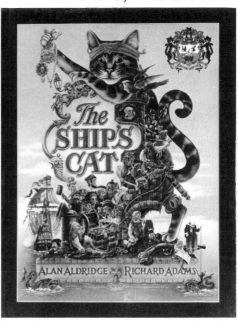

*The Tyger Voyage contains illustrations by Nicola Bayley and verses by **Watership Down** author, Richard Adams.*

*Alan Aldridge illustrated Adams' later verse-tale **The Ship's Cat**. Both books are worth £20 in Very Good Condition.*

SON OF A GUN by Allan and Janet Ahlberg (Heinemann, 1979) £20
FUNNYBONES by Allan and Janet Ahlberg (Heinemann, 1980) £20
A PAIR OF SINNERS by Allan Ahlberg and John Lawrence (Granada, 1980) £15
MR BIFF THE BOXER by Allan Ahlberg (illustrated by Janet Ahlberg) (Viking, 1980)....................£10
MR COSMO THE CONJURER by Allan Ahlberg (illustrated by Joe Wright) (Viking, 1980)..............£10
MRS PLUG THE PLUMBER by Allan Ahlberg (illustrated by Joe Wright) (Viking, 1980) £10
MRS WOBBLE THE WAITRESS by Allan Ahlberg (illustrated by Janet Ahlberg) (Viking, 1980).......£10
MASTER SALT THE SAILOR'S SON by Allan Ahlberg (illustrated by André Amstutz) (Kestrel, 1980)...£10
MISS JUMP THE JOCKEY by Allan Ahlberg (illustrated by André Amstutz) (Viking, 1980) £10
PEEPO! by Allan and Janet Ahlberg (Kestrel, 1981) £30
MASTER MONEY THE MILLIONAIRE by Allan Ahlberg (illustrated by André Amstutz) (Viking, 1981) ...£10
MISS BRICK THE BUILDER'S BABY by Allan Ahlberg (illustrated by Colin McNaughton) (Viking, 1981)...£10
MR AND MRS HAY THE HORSE by Allan Ahlberg (illustrated by Colin McNaughton) (Viking, 1981) ...£10
MR BUZZ THE BEEMAN by Allan Ahlberg (illustrated by Faith Jaques) (Viking, 1981) £10
MR TICK THE TEACHER by Allan Ahlberg (illustrated by Faith Jaques) (Viking, 1981) £10
MRS LATHER'S LAUNDRY by Allan Ahlberg (illustrated by André Amstutz) (Viking, 1981)............£10
THE BABY'S CATALOGUE by Allan and Janet Ahlberg (Kestrel, 1982)...£30
THE BABY'S CATALOGUE FRIEZE by Allan and Janet Ahlberg (Kestrel, 1982) £15
DOUBLE DUCK by Allan Ahlberg and Eric Hill (Granada: 'Help Your Child To Read' series, 1982) £8
SILLY SHEEP by Allan Ahlberg and Eric Hill (Granada: 'Help Your Child To Read' series, 1982) £8
POORLY PIG by Allan Ahlberg and Eric Hill (Granada: 'Help Your Child To Read' series, 1982) £8
RUBBER RABBIT by Allan Ahlberg and Eric Hill (Granada: 'Help Your Child To Read' series, 1982)..........£8
FAST FROG by Allan Ahlberg and Eric Hill (Granada: 'Help Your Child To Read' series, 1982) £8
BAD BEAR by Allan Ahlberg and Eric Hill (Granada: 'Help Your Child To Read' series, 1982) £8
THE HA-HA BONK BOOK by Allan and Janet Ahlberg (Kestrel, 1982)...£8
HIP-HIPPO-RAY by Allan Ahlberg and André Amstutz (Granada: 'Help Your Child To Read' series, 1983)......£8
MISTER WOLF by Allan Ahlberg and André Amstutz (Granada: 'Help Your Child To Read' series, 1983)........£8
KING KANGAROO by Allan Ahlberg and André Amstutz (Granada: 'Help Your Child To Read' series, 1983) £8
SPIDER SPY by Allan Ahlberg and André Amstutz (Granada: 'Help Your Child To Read' series, 1983) £8
TELL-TALE TIGER by Allan Ahlberg and André Amstutz (Granada: 'Help Your Child To Read' series, 1983) ...£8
TRAVELLING MOOSE by Allan Ahlberg and André Amstutz (Granada: 'Help Your Child To Read' series, 1983) ...£8
TEN IN A BED by Allan Ahlberg and André Amstutz (Granada, 1983) £10
WHICH WITCH? by Allan and Janet Ahlberg (Heinemann: 'Daisychain' series, 1983) £20
THAT'S MY BABY by Allan and Janet Ahlberg (Heinemann: 'Daisychain' series, 1983) £10
SUMMER SNOWMAN by Allan and Janet Ahlberg (Heinemann: 'Daisychain' series, 1983) £10
READY, TEDDY, GO by Allan and Janet Ahlberg (Heinemann: 'Daisychain' series, 1983)...............£20
PLEASE MRS BUTLER by Allan Ahlberg (verse; illustrated by Fritz Wegner) (Kestrel, 1983) £15
CLOWNING ABOUT by Allan and Janet Ahlberg and André Amstutz (Heinemann, 1984) £20

AHLBERG, Allan and Janet

*A plate from **Peepo!** by husband-and-wife team, Allan and Janet Ahlberg. Their works are becoming increasingly collectable.*

MONSTER MUNCH by Allan and Janet Ahlberg and André Amstutz (Heinemann, 1984) £20
THE GOOD OLD DOLLS by Allan and Janet Ahlberg and André Amstutz (Heinemann, 1984) £20
RENT-A-ROBOT by Allan and Janet Ahlberg and André Amstutz (Heinemann, 1984) £20
YUM YUM by Allan and Janet Ahlberg (Viking Kestrel, 1984)...£5
PLAYMATES by Allan and Janet Ahlberg (Viking Kestrel, 1984) £5
BEAR'S BIRTHDAY by Allan Ahlberg (Walker: 'Red Nose Readers' series, 1985) £8
JUMPING by Allan Ahlberg (illustrated by Colin McNaughton) (Walker: 'Red Nose Readers' series, 1985) £5
SO CAN I by Allan Ahlberg (illustrated by Colin McNaughton) (Walker: 'Red Nose Readers' series, 1985) £5
BIG BAD PIG by Allan Ahlberg (Walker: 'Red Nose Readers' series, 1985) £5
FEE FI FO FUM by Allan Ahlberg (illustrated by Colin McNaughton) (Walker: 'Red Nose Readers' series, 1985) £5
HAPPY WORM by Allan Ahlberg (illustrated by Colin McNaughton) (Walker: 'Red Nose Readers' series, 1985) £5
HELP! by Allan Ahlberg (illustrated by Colin McNaughton) (Walker: 'Red Nose Readers' series, 1985) £5
MAKE A FACE by Allan Ahlberg (illustrated by Colin McNaughton) (Walker: 'Red Nose Readers' series, 1985) £5
PUSH THE DOG by Allan Ahlberg (illustrated by Colin McNaughton) (Walker: 'Red Nose Readers' series, 1986)........£5
CRASH! BANG! WALLOP! by Allan Ahlberg (illustrated by Colin McNaughton) (Walker: 'Red Nose Readers' series, 1986) £5
SHIRLEY'S SHOPS by Allan Ahlberg (illustrated by Colin McNaughton) (Walker: 'Red Nose Readers' series, 1986) £5
ME AND MY FRIEND by Allan Ahlberg (illustrated by Colin McNaughton) (Walker: 'Red Nose Readers' series, 1986)................£5
THE CINDERELLA SHOW by Allan and Janet Ahlberg (Viking, 1986) £10
THE JOLLY POSTMAN by Allan and Janet Ahlberg (Heinemann, 1986) £25
THE JOLLY POSTMAN'S LETTERS (Heinemann, 1986) £20
THE CLOTHES HORSE and Other Stories by Allan and Janet Ahlberg (Viking Kestrel, 1987) £12
WOOF! by Allan Ahlberg (Viking, 1987) £15
TELL US A STORY by Allan Ahlberg (illustrated by Colin McNaughton) (Walker, 1987)........................£15
ONE, TOW, FLEA! by Allan Ahlberg (illustrated by Colin McNaughton) (Walker, 1987).........................£15
MASTER BUN THE BAKER'S SON by Allan Ahlberg (illustrated by Fritz Wegner) (Viking, 1988) £8
MISS DOSE THE DOCTOR'S DAUGHTER by Allan Ahlberg (illustrated by Faith Jaques) (Viking, 1988) £8
MR CREEP THE CROOK by Allan Ahlberg (illustrated by André Amstutz) (Viking, 1988) £8
MRS JOLLY'S JOKE SHOP by Allan Ahlberg (illustrated by Colin McNaughton) (Viking, 1988) £8
THE MIGHTY SLIDE by Allan Ahlberg (Viking, 1988) £10
STARTING SCHOOL by Allan Ahlberg (Viking, 1988) £12
BYE BYE BABY by Allan and Janet Ahlberg (Heinemann, 1989) £20
HEARD IT IN THE PLAYGROUND by Allan Ahlberg (Viking, 1989) £10
BLACK CAT by Allan Ahlberg (Heinemann, 1990) £10

MYSTERY TOUR by Allan Ahlberg (Heinemann, 1990) £10
BLOW ME DOWN by Allan Ahlberg (illustrated by Colin McNaughton) (Walker, 1990) £10
LOOK OUT FOR THE SEALS! by Allan Ahlberg (illustrated by Colin McNaughton) (Walker, 1990)..£10
THE JOLLY CHRISTMAS POSTMAN by Allan Ahlberg (illustrated by Janet Ahlberg) (Heinemann, 1991) £30
MRS BUTLER SONGBOOK by Allan Ahlberg and Colin Matthews (illustrated by Fritz Wegner) (Viking, 1992) £12
THE BEAR NOBODY WANTED by Allan and Janet Ahlberg (Viking, 1992) £35
PET SHOP by Allan Ahlberg (illustrated by André Amstutz) (Little Mammoth, 1992)..£12
SKELETON CREW by Allan Ahlberg (illustrated by André Amstutz) (Heinemann, 1992) £12
BUMPS IN THE NIGHT by Allan Ahlberg (illustrated by André Amstutz) (Heinemann, 1993) £7
GIVE THE DOG A BONE by Allan Ahlberg (illustrated by André Amstutz) (Heinemann, 1993) £10
IT WAS A DARK AND STORMY NIGHT by Allan Ahlberg (illustrated by Janet Ahlberg) (Viking, 1993) £15
THE GIANT BABY by Allan Ahlberg (illustrated by Fritz Wegner) (Viking, 1994) £8
THE JOLLY POCKET POSTMAN by Allan Ahlberg (illustrated by Janet Ahlberg) (Heinemann, 1995) £10

AIKEN, Joan

British author. Born: Sussex, 1924, the daughter of the American poet, Conrad Aiken. Joined *Argosy* magazine as features editor in 1955. As well as her children's books, she has written a large number of adult works, notably several volumes of horror and fantasy stories.
Prices are for books in Very Good condition with dustjackets where applicable.

'James III' Books

THE WOLVES OF WILLOUGHBY CHASE (illustrated by Pat Marriott) (Cape, 1962) £60
BLACK HEARTS IN BATTERSEA (illustrated by Robin Jacques) (Cape, 1965)..£50
NIGHTBIRDS ON NANTUCKET (illustrated by Pat Marriott) (Cape, 1966) £45
THE CUCKOO TREE (illustrated by Pat Marriott) (Cape, 1971) £40
THE STOLEN LAKE (illustrated by Pat Marriott) (Cape, 1981) £30
DIDO AND PA (illustrated by Pat Marriott) (Cape, 1986) £25
IS (illustrated by Pat Marriott) (Red Fox, 1993) £10

Others

ALL YOU'VE EVER WANTED and Other Stories (illustrated by Pat Marriott) (Cape, 1953) £45
MORE THAN YOU BARGAINED FOR and Other Stories (illustrated by Pat Marriott) (Cape, 1955)..£45
THE KINGDOM AND THE CAVE (novel; illustrated by Dick Hart) (Abelard Schuman, 1960) £40
A NECKLACE OF RAINDROPS and Other Stories (illustrated by Jan Pienkowski) (Cape, 1968) £30
THE WHISPERING MOUNTAIN (illustrated by Pat Marriott) (Cape, 1968) £45
A SMALL PINCH OF WEATHER and Other Stories (illustrated by Pat Marriott) (Cape, 1969)..£20
ALL AND MORE (contains 'All You've Ever Wanted' and 'More Than You Bargained For'; illustrated by Pat Marriott) (Cape, 1971) £20
THE KINGDOM UNDER THE SEA and Other Stories (illustrated by Jan Pienkowski) (Cape, 1971) £25
A HARP OF FISHBONES and Other Stories (illustrated by Pat Marriott) (Cape 1972)..£20
ARABEL'S RAVEN (illustrated by Quentin Blake) (BBC, 1972) £15
THE ESCAPED BLACK MAMBA (illustrated by Quentin Blake; paperback) (BBC, 1973) £15
ALL BUT A FEW (paperback) (Puffin, 1974) £5
THE BREAD BIN (illustrated by Quentin Blake; paperback) (BBC, 1974) £5
MIDNIGHT IS A PLACE (novel) (Cape, 1974) £20
MORTIMER'S TIE (illustrated by Quentin Blake; paperback) (BBC, 1976) £5
ANGEL INN (Cape, 1976) £10
A BUNDLE OF NERVES: Stories of Horror, Suspense and Fantasy (Gollancz, 1976) £10
THE FAITHLESS LOLLYBIRD and Other Stories (illustrated by Pat Marriott) (Cape, 1977)..£20
TALE OF A ONE-WAY STREET and Other Stories (illustrated by Jan Pienkowski) (Cape, 1978) £25
MICE AND MENDELSON (illustrated by Babette Cole; music by John Sebastian Brown) (Cape, 1978) £15
GO SADDLE THE SEA (novel; illustrated by Pat Marriott) (Cape, 1978) £25
MORTIMER AND THE SWORD EXCALIBUR (illustrated by Quentin Blake; paperback) (BBC, 1979) £5
THE SPIRAL STAIR (illustrated by Quentin Blake; paperback) (BBC, 1979) £5
A TOUCH OF CHILL: Stories of Horror, Suspense and Fantasy (Gollancz, 1979) £10
ARABEL AND MORTIMER (contains 'Mortimer's Tie', 'Mortimer and the Sword Excalibur' and 'The Spiral Stair'; illustrated by Quentin Blake) (Cape, 1980) £15
MORTIMER'S PORTRAIT ON GLASS (illustrated by Quentin Blake) (BBC, 1980) £5
MR JONES'S DISAPPEARING TAXI (illustrated by Quentin Blake; paperback) (BBC, 1980)..£5
THE SHADOW GUESTS (novel) (Cape, 1980) £15
A WHISPER IN THE NIGHT: Stories of Horror, Suspense and Fantasy (Gollancz, 1982)..£15
MORTIMER'S CROSS (illustrated by Quentin Blake) (Cape, 1983)..£15
THE KITCHEN WARRIORS (BBC, 1983) £15
BRIDLE THE WIND (novel; illustrated by Pat Marriott) (Cape, 1983) £20
UP THE CHIMNEY DOWN and Other Stories (illustrated by Pat Marriott) (Cape, 1984) £15
MORTIMER SAYS NOTHING (illustrated by Quentin Blake) (Cape, 1985) £15
THE LAST SLICE OF RAINBOW (Cape, 1985)..£15
PAST EIGHT O'CLOCK (illustrated by Jan Pienkowski) (Cape, 1986) £15
THE MOON'S REVENGE (illustrated by Alan Lee) (cape, 1987) £15

AIKEN, Joan

THE TEETH OF THE GALE (novel) (Cape, 1988) £20
A FOOT IN THE GRAVE (illustrated by Jan Pienkowski) (Cape, 1989) £20
A FIT OF SHIVERS (short stories) (Gollancz, 1990) £10
A CREEPY COMPANY (short stories) (Gollancz, 1993) £10
THE WINTER SLEEPWALKER (illustrated by Quentin Blake) (Cape, 1994).......£10
COLD SHOULDER ROAD (Cape, 1995) £10
A HANDFUL OF GOLD (illustrated by Wayne Anderson; paperback) (Hodder, 1998) £10
MOON CAKE (illustrated by Wayne Anderson; paperback) (Hodder, 1998) £2

AINSLIE, Kathleen

British author-illustrator. Her work covers a period from 1900 to 1910. Her stocking-sized children's books with hand-written texts and Dutch doll characters were influenced by Florence K. Upton's slightly earlier 'Golliwog' series.

Prices are for books in Good condition.

OH! POOR AMELIA JANE! (Castell, [1900]) £40
CATHERINE SUSAN'S LITTLE HOLIDAY (Castell, [1900]).......£50
ME AND CATHERINE SUSAN (Castell, [1903]).......£50
AT GREAT-AUNT MARTHA'S (Castell, [1904]).......£40
ME AND CATHERINE SUSAN EARNS AN HONEST PENNY (Castell, [1905]) £40
LADY TABITHA AND US (Castell, [1905]) £40
CATHERINE AND ME'S COMING OUT (Castell, [1905]) £40
CATHERINE AND ME'S GOES ABROAD (Castell, [1905]) £40
SAMMY GOES A `HUNTING (Castell, [1905]) £35
CATHERINE SUSAN'S CALENDAR 1906 (Castell, [1905]) £50
"WHAT I DID" (Castell, [1906]) £35
MOPS VERSUS TAILS (Castell, [1907]) £40
DEAR DIRTY DOLLY (Castell, [1908]) £50
CATHERINE SUSAN'S CALENDAR 1910 (Castell, [1909]) £50
CATHERINE SUSAN IN HOT WATER (Castell, [1910]) £35
VOTES FOR CATHERINE SUSAN AND ME (Castell, [1910]) £35

ALCOTT, Louisa M.

American author. Born: Louisa May Alcott in Pennsylvania in 1832, but lived most of her life in Boston. Published her first novel, *Moods*, in 1866, and achieved immediate and lasting fame with the follow-up, *Little Women* (1868). Died: 1888.

Prices are for books in Very Good condition.

FLOWER FABLES (Briggs, U.S., 1855) £175
MOODS (Routledge, [1866]) £100
LITTLE WOMEN, or Meg, Jo, Beth and Amy (Sampson Low, 1868) £300
LITTLE WOMEN (illustrated by H.M. Brock) (Seeley, 1908) £30
LITTLE WOMEN (illustrated by M.V. Wheelhouse) (Bell, 1909) £30
LITTLE WOMEN. Introduction by Flora Klickmann (illustrated by Harold Copping) (R.T.S., 1912) £30
LITTLE WOMEN (illustrated by Jessie Willcox Smith) (Little Brown, U.S., 1915) £50
LITTLE WOMEN (illustrated by Millicent E. Gray) (Hodder & Stoughton, 1922).......£30
LITTLE WOMEN (illustrated by Percy Tarrant) (Harrap, 1922) £30
LITTLE WOMEN (illustrated by S. Van Abbe) (Dent, 1948) £20
LITTLE WOMEN (illustrated by Rene Cloke) (Gawthorn [1949]) £25
GOOD WIVES (Sampson Low, 1869) £200
GOOD WIVES (illustrated by H.M. Brock) (Seeley, 1905) £30
GOOD WIVES (illustrated by M.V. Wheelhouse) (G. Bell, 1911) £30
GOOD WIVES (illustrated by Harold Copping) (R.T.S., 1913).......£30
GOOD WIVES (illustrated by S. Van Abbe) (Dent, 1953) £20
ON PICKET DUTY (James Redpath, U.S., [1864]).......£145
HOSPITAL SKETCHES AND CAMP AND FIRESIDE STORIES (Sampson Low, 1870) £100
AN OLD FASHIONED GIRL (Sampson Low, 1870) £85
AN OLD FASHIONED GIRL (illustrated by Jessie Willcox Smith) (Little Brown, U.S., 1902).......£40
LITTLE MEN: Life at Plumfield with Jo's Boys (Sampson Low, 1871) £200
MY BOYS (Volume One of 'Aunt Jo's Scrapbag'; precedes first U.S. edition) (Sampson Low, 1871) £75
SHAWL STRAPS (Volume Two of 'Aunt Jo's Scrapbag') (Sampson Low, 1873 [1872]).......£75
CUPID AND CHOW CHOW (Volume Three of 'Aunt Jo's Scrapbag') (Sampson Low, 1873).......£75
SOMETHING TO DO (Ward Lock, [1873]).......£60
FIRESIDE AND CAMP STORIES (Ward Lock, 1873) £60
WORK: A Story of Experience (precedes first U.S. 'Experience'; two volumes) (Sampson Low, 1873) £130
EIGHT COUSINS, or The Aunt Hill (Sampson Low, 1875) £85
BEGINNING AGAIN: Being a Continuation of 'Work' (Sampson Low, 1875) £85
SILVER PITCHERS and Other Stories (Sampson Low, 1876) £70
A MODERN MEPHISTOPHELES (Sampson Low, 1877) £40

*Kathleen Ainslie's **Lady Tabitha and Us** now sells for £40 in Good condition. It was published by Castell in 1905.*

ROSE IN BLOOM: A Sequel to 'Eight Cousins' (Sampson Low, 1877 [1876]) £65
ROSE IN BLOOM (illustrated by Rodney Shackell; issued with dustjacket) (Hart-Davis, 1967)...............................£15
UNDER THE LILACS (precedes first U.S. appearance; issued in eleven monthly parts; illustrated) (Sampson Low, 1877-78) £80
UNDER THE LILACS (first one-volume edition) (Sampson Low, 1878) £50
JIMMY'S CRUISE IN THE 'PINAFORE' (Volume Five of 'Aunt Jo's Scrapbag') (Sampson Low, 1879)....................£45
JACK AND JILL (Sampson Low, 1880) £50
AN OLD FASHIONED THANKSGIVING and Other Stories (Volume Six of 'Aunt Jo's Scrapbag') (Sampson Low, 1882) £35
PROVERB STORIES (Sampson Low, 1882)...£30
SPINNING WHEEL STORIES (Sampson Low, 1884)...£30
LULU'S LIBRARY (Sampson Low, 1886 [1885]) £30
JO'S BOYS: And How They Turned Out (Sampson Low, 1886)...£100
JO'S BOYS (illustrated by Harry Toothill) (Dent, 1960)...£15
A GARLAND FOR GIRLS (Blackie, 1888) £30
RECOLLECTIONS OF MY CHILDHOOD DAYS (Sampson Low, 1890) £25
COMIC TRAGEDIES: Written by 'Jo' and 'Meg' (Sampson Low, 1893) £40

ALDIN, Cecil

British illustrator. Born: Slough, 1870. Studied at South Kensington School of Art. Worked as a comic illustrator in the 1890s before achieving great success as a sporting artist. Contributed to the *Boy's Own Paper* and *Oxford Annual*. Retired to Majorca in 1930. Died: 1935.

Prices are for books in Very Good condition.

SPOT, AN AUTOBIOGRAPHY (fourteen mono illustrations by Cecil Aldin) (Houlston, 1894) £100
WONDERLAND WONDERS by Rev. John Isabell (mono frontispiece and nineteen illustrations by Cecil Aldin;
    also includes contributions by Louis Wain) (Home Words, 1895) £65
TWO LITTLE RUNAWAYS by James Buckland (Longman, 1898) £80
TWO WELL-WORN SHOE STORIES (contains 'The Old Woman Who Lived in a Shoe' illustrated by John Hassall, and
    'Cock-a-doodle-do, My Dame Has Lost Her Shoe' illustrated by Cecil Aldin) (Sands, 1899) £200
TEN LITTLE PUPPY DOGS (Sands, [1902]) £175
FAITHFUL FRIENDS (includes two illustrations by Arthur Rackham) (Blackie, 1902) £80
BUBBLE AND SQUEAK by P. Robinson (Isbister, 1902)..£300
A DOG DAY, or The Angel in the House by Walter Emanuel (28 tinted full-page colour illustrations by Cecil Aldin)
    (Heinemann, 1902) £100
THE HOUSE ANNUAL (Gale & Polden, 1902) £75
THE YOUNG FOLKS' BIRTHDAY BOOK (Hills, 1902)..£50
THE SNOB: Some Episodes in a Mis-spent Youth by Walter Emanuel (nineteen colour plates by Cecil Aldin)
    (Lawrence & Bullen, 1904)..£100
A GAY DOG: The Story of a Foolish Year by Walter Emanuel (24 colour plates by Cecil Aldin) (Heinemann, 1905) £150
THE DOGS OF WAR by Walter Emanuel (Bradbury Agnew, [1906]) £100
THE HAPPY ANNUAL (with John Hassall) (Heinemann, 1907)..£60

*Aldin has long been a favourite with collectors. His **Jack and Jill** (above) is now worth £300 in Very Good Condition.*

OLD CHRISTMAS by Washington Irving (27 colour plates, six mono plates and decorations by Cecil Aldin)
(Hodder & Stoughton, 1908) £125
FARM FRIENDS FOR LITTLE FOLK (with other illustrators, including Arthur Rackham) (Blackie, 1908) £75
THE PLAYTIME PICTURE BOOKS. With verses by Richard Waylett (series; includes 'The Doggie Book')
(Lawrence & Jellicoe, 1909) ....each £150
PUSSY AND HER WAYS (Henry Frowde/Hodder & Stoughton, [1909]) £200
DOGGIE AND HIS WAYS (Henry Frowde/Hodder & Stoughton, [1909]) £200
THE BLACK PUPPY BOOK (Henry Frowde/Hodder & Stoughton, [1909]) £200
THE WHITE PUPPY BOOK (Henry Frowde/Hodder & Stoughton, [1909]) £200
THE WHITE KITTEN BOOK (eleven colour plates by Cecil Aldin) (Henry Frowde/Hodder & Stoughton, [1909]) £200
PICKLES, A PUPPY DOG'S TALE (24 colour illustrations by Cecil Aldin) (Henry Frowde/Hodder & Stoughton, [1909])..........£300
ROUGH AND TUMBLE (Henry Frowde/Hodder & Stoughton, [1909]) £300
FIELD BABIES (24 colour plates by Cecil Aldin) (Henry Frowde/Hodder & Stoughton, [1910]) £175
THE TWINS (24 full-page colour plates by Cecil Aldin) (Henry Frowde/Hodder & Stoughton, [1910])......................£300
THE RED PUPPY BOOK (twelve colour plates) (Henry Frowde/Hodder & Stoughton, [1910])...............................£175

MY PETS (Henry Frowde/Hodder & Stoughton, [1910]) £75
AN OLD-FASHIONED CHRISTMAS EVE by Washington Irving (Hodder & Stoughton, 1910) £35
AN OLD-FASHIONED CHRISTMAS DAY by Washington Irving (Hodder & Stoughton, 1910) £35
THE POSTHUMOUS PAPERS OF THE PICKWICK CLUB (two volumes; Vol. 1 has thirteen colour plates,
   Vol. II has eleven colour plates) (Chapman & Hall/Lawrence & Jellicoe, 1910) £200
MY BOOK OF DOGGIES: Stories and Pictures for Little Folk (with other artists, including Arthur Rackham)
   (Blackie, [1910]) £100
PUPPY TAILS by Richard Waylett (Lawrence & Jellicoe, [1910]) £125
FARM BABIES by May Byron (24 full-page colour illustrations by Cecil Aldin) (Henry Frowde/Hodder & Stoughton, [1911]) £300
FARMYARD PUPPIES (twelve colour illustrations by Cecil Aldin) (Henry Frowde/Hodder & Stoughton, [1911]) £150
MERRY AND BRIGHT (24 full-page colour illustrations by Cecil Aldin) (Henry Frowde/Hodder & Stoughton, [1911]) £300
MAC: A Story of a Dog (Henry Frowde/Hodder & Stoughton, [1912]) £320
THE MONGREL PUPPY BOOK (twelve colour plates by Cecil Aldin) (Henry Frowde/Hodder & Stoughton, [1912]) £175
BLACK BEAUTY by Anna Sewell (eighteen plates in colour and endpapers especially drawn for this edition by Cecil Aldin)
   (Jarrold, [1912]) £125
WHITE-EAR AND PETER: The Story of a Fox and a Fox-Terrier by Neils Heiberg (sixteen colour plates by Cecil Aldin)
   (Macmillan, 1912) £175
CECIL ALDIN'S HAPPY FAMILY by May Byron (six parts; illustrated in colour by Cecil Aldin;
   also issued in a single volume edition) (Henry Frowde/Hodder & Stoughton, [1912]) ....each £75
CECIL ALDIN'S MERRY PARTY by May Byron (six parts; illustrated with many full-page pictures in colour by Cecil Aldin;
   also issued as a single-volume edition) (Henry Frowde/Hodder & Stoughton, 1913) ....each £75
MY DOG by Maurice Maeterlinck. Translated by A. Teixeira de Mattos (six colour plates by Cecil Aldin) (Allen, 1913)................£75
ZOO BABIES by G.E. Farrow (Frowde/Hodder & Stoughton, 1913)...£135
THE MERRY PUPPY BOOK (36 colour plates by Cecil Aldin) (Milford, 1913) £300
THE UNDERDOG by Sidney Trist (four illustrations by Cecil Aldin) (Animals' Guardian, 1913) £75
CECIL ALDIN'S RAG BOOK, THE ANIMALS' SCHOOL TREAT by Clifton Bingham (24 colour illustrations by Cecil Aldin)
   (Dean: 'Rag Book' series No. 70, [1913]) £150
THE BOBTAIL PUPPY BOOK (verse) (Henry Frowde/Hodder & Stoughton, [1914]) £200
JACK AND JILL by May Byron (illustrated by Cecil Aldin) (Henry Frowde/Hodder & Stoughton, [1914]) £300
THE DOG WHO WASN'T WHAT HE THOUGHT HE WAS by Walter Emanuel (24 colour plates by Cecil Aldin)
   (Raphael Tuck, [1914]) £300
ANIMAL REVELS by May Byron (Henry Frowde/Hodder & Stoughton, [1914]) £75
ANIMAL FROLICS by May Byron (Henry Frowde/Hodder & Stoughton, [1914]) £75
MOUFLOU by Ouida (T.C. & E.C. Jack, 1915) £100
THE CECIL ALDIN PAINTING BOOKS (contains 'The Puppy Book', 'The Normandy', 'The Cat and Dog Book' and
   'The Pied Piper of Hamelin') (Lawrence & Jellicoe, [1915]) ....each £100
JOCK AND SOME OTHERS by Richard Waylett (sixteen full-page colour illustrations and
   fifteen black-and-white illustrations by Cecil Aldin) (Gale & Polden, [1916]) £250
THE MERRY PARTY (Humphrey Milford, [1918]) £150
BUNNYBOROUGH (Humphrey Milford, [1919]) £275
GYP'S HOUR OF BLISS by Gladys Davidson (Collins, 1919) £200
THE GREAT ADVENTURE (seventeen colour plates by Cecil Aldin) (Humphrey Milford, [1920]) £200
CECIL ALDIN LETTER BOOKS (Humphrey Milford, [1920])...£100
US (Humphrey Milford, [1922]) £150
DOGS OF CHARACTER (Eyre & Spottiswoode, 1927)..£75
A DOZEN DOGS OR SO by P.R. Chalmers (thirteen colour plates by Cecil Aldin) (Eyre & Spottiswoode, 1927) £120
SLEEPING PARTNERS: A Series of Episodes (twenty colour plates by Cecil Aldin) (Eyre & Spottiswoode, [1929])............£250
JERRY: The Story of an Exmoor Pony by Eleanor E. Helme and Nance Paul
   (eleven full-page black-and-white illustrations by Cecil Aldin) (Eyre & Spottiswoode, [1930]) £45
AN ARTIST'S MODELS (twenty colour plates by Cecil Aldin) (Witherby, 1930) £200
MRS TICKLER'S CARAVAN (with Pat Wood) (Eyre & Spottiswoode, 1931) £50
LOST, STOLEN OR STRAYED by Marion Ashmore (thirty black-and-white illustrations and colour frontispiece by Cecil Aldin)
   (Eyre & Spottiswoode, 1931) £45
FLAX, POLICE DOG by Svend Fleuron. Translated from Danish by E. Gee Nash
   (ten black-and-white illustrations by Cecil Aldin) (Eyre & Spottiswoode, [1931]).....................£35
THE BUNCH BOOK by James Douglas (51 black-and-white illustrations and coloured frontispiece by Cecil Aldin)
   (Eyre & Spottiswoode, 1932) £35
THE JOKER, AND JERRY AGAIN by Eleanor E. Helme and Nance Paul (Eyre & Spottiswoode, 1932) £45
THE CECIL ALDIN BOOK (eight colour plates and 95 black-and-white illustrations by Cecil Aldin)
   (Eyre & Spottiswoode, 1932) £45
SCARLET, BLUE AND GREEN by Duncan Fife (four colour plates, seven half-tone and 25 mono illustrations by Cecil Aldin)
   (Macmillan, 1932) £75
HIS APOLOGIES by Rudyard Kipling (Doubleday Doran, U.S., 1932)..£45
DOGS OF EVERY DAY by Patrick Chalmers (twelve full-page mono plates by Cecil Aldin) (Eyre & Spottiswoode, 1933)...........£75
WHO'S WHO IN THE ZOO (four colour plates and 35 full-page black-and-white illustrations by Cecil Aldin)
   (Eyre & Spottiswoode, 1933) £50
HOTSPUR THE BEAGLE by John Vickerman (Constable, 1934)...£50
JUST AMONG FRIENDS (Eyre & Spottiswoode, 1935) £175
HOW TO DRAW DOGS (47 pages of sketches by Cecil Aldin; foreword by Gwen Aldin) (John Lane: The Bodley Head, 1935) £150
SMUGGLERS' GALLOWS by Stanton Hope (Eyre & Spottiswoode, 1936) £30
BUNNYBOROUGH (reissue of 1919 edition; fifteen colour plates by Cecil Aldin; issued in dustjacket)
   (Eyre & Spottiswoode, 1946) £45

'ALICE' BOOKS

Lewis Carroll's *Alice's Adventures in Wonderland* (1865) and *Through the Looking-Glass* (1872 [1871]) have been illustrated by countless artists. What follows is a list of the most collectable editions.

Prices are for books in Very Good condition (with dustjackets after 1940).

'Alice's Adventures Under Ground'

ALICE'S ADVENTURES UNDER GROUND (red binding) (Macmillan, 1886) £175
ALICE'S ADVENTURES UNDER GROUND (variant binding) (Macmillan, 1886) £1,750

'Alice's Adventures in Wonderland'

FIRST [WITHDRAWN] EDITION (illustrated by John Tenniel) (Macmillan, 1865) £200,000
FIRST U.S. EDITION (illustrated by John Tenniel) (Appleton, U.S., 1865)......................................£5,000
FIRST U.K. EDITION (illustrated by John Tenniel) (Macmillan, 1866 [1865]) £3,000
JOHN TENNIEL: 'PEOPLE'S EDITION' (Macmillan, 1887) £50
GERTRUDE THOMSON EDITION ('The Nursery Alice') (Macmillan, 1889) £150
PETER NEWELL EDITION (Harper, U.S., 1901) £150
BLANCHE McMANUS EDITION (Mansfield, U.S., 1896; U.K.: Ward Lock, 1907).........................£80
CHARLES ROBINSON EDITION (illustrated by Charles Robinson) (Cassell, 1907)........................£150
ARTHUR RACKHAM EDITION (with poem by Austin Dobson; green cloth binding) (Heinemann, [1907]) £300
ARTHUR RACKHAM EDITION (with poem by Austin Dobson; De Luxe edition:
    limited to 1,130 copies; white vellum binding) (Heinemann, [1907])...£1,750
THOMAS MAYBANK EDITION (Routledge, [1907])...£100
MILLICENT SOWERBY EDITION (Chatto & Windus, 1907) £120
HARRY ROUNTREE EDITION (Nelson, 1908)...£100
THOMAS HEATH ROBINSON EDITION (illustrated by Thomas Heath Robinson and Charles Pears) (William Collins, London, 1908) ..£30
MABEL LUCIE ATTWELL EDITION (Raphael Tuck, [1910]) £200
FRANK ADAMS EDITION (Blackie, 1912) £35
ALICE B. WOODWARD EDITION (Bell, 1913) £90
A.E. JACKSON EDITION (Hodder & Stoughton, U.S., 1914; U.K.: Frowde, [1915]) £150
MARGARET TARRANT EDITION (Ward Lock, 1916) £110
A.L. BOWLEY EDITION (Raphael Tuck, 1921)..£50
GWYNEDD HUDSON EDITION (Hodder & Stoughton, [1922]) £125
WILLY POGANY EDITION (Dutton, U.S., 1929)..£50
WILLY POGANY EDITION (signed, limited edition) (Dutton, U.S., 1929).......................................£250
CHARLES FOLKARD EDITION (A. & C. Black, 1929)..£40

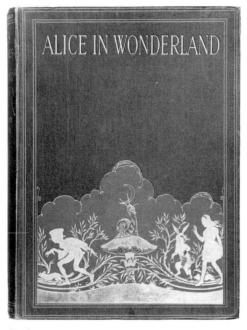
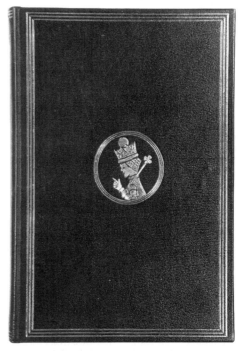

*The Gwynedd Hudson edition of **Alice in Wonderland** (left) and the first edition of **Through the Looking-Glass** (right).*

The 1887 **Ally Sloper Summer Number** (left) and **Ally Sloper's Christmas Holidays** from the same year (right).

MARIE LAURENCIN EDITION (Black Sun Press, Paris, 1930) £2,000
MARIE LAURENCIN EDITION (with extra plates) (Black Sun Press, Paris, 1930)................................£5,000
RENE CLOKE EDITION (P.R. Gawthorn, [c.1943]) £30
ANTHONY RADO EDITION (Newman Wolsey, [c.1944]) £40
EILEEN SOPER EDITION (Harrap, 1947) £40
RALPH STEADMAN EDITION (Dobson, 1967) £70
SALVADOR DALI EDITION (Random House, U.S., 1969) £3,000
MICHAEL HAGUE EDITION (Holt, U.S., 1985) £30
MICHAEL HAGUE EDITION (Methuen, 1985) £25

'Through the Looking-Glass'

JOHN TENNIEL EDITION (Macmillan, 1872 [1871]) £300
JOHN TENNIEL: 'PEOPLE'S EDITION' (Macmillan, U.S., 1887)..£50
BLANCHE McMANUS EDITION (Mansfield, U.S., 1899)..£50
PETER NEWELL EDITION (Harper, U.S., 1902) £100
HELEN MUNRO EDITION (Nelson, 1937) £30
RALPH STEADMAN EDITION (MacGibbon & Kee, 1972)..£60

Combined Editions

JOHN TENNIEL EDITION (92 illustrations by John Tenniel, including sixteen in colour) (Macmillan, 1911) £75
MERVYN PEAKE EDITION (Continental, Sweden, 1946) £150
MERVYN PEAKE EDITION (Wingate, 1954) £60

'ALLY SLOPER' ANNUALS

The best-known of the early British comics, featuring the world's first regular strip cartoon character, Ally Sloper, an accident-prone, gin-drinking misfit originally created by Charles Henry Ross. He first appeared on 14th August 1867 in the pages of the weekly magazine, *Judy*, achieving his own comic, *Ally Sloper's Half Holiday*, on 3rd May 1884. The title continued in various incarnations until 1923, but it is the early 'special numbers' that are most collected today.

Prices are for numbers in Very Good condition.

ALLY SLOPER'S HALF HOLIDAY (W.J. Sinkin, 3rd May 1884) £40
ALLY SLOPER'S CHRISTMAS HOLIDAYS (W.J. Sinkin, December 1884) £40
ALLY SLOPER'S CHRISTMAS HOLIDAYS (W.J. Sinkin, 1885-1914) ....each £35
ALLY SLOPER'S SUMMER NUMBER (W.J. Sinkin, 1880) £35
ALLY SLOPER'S SUMMER NUMBER (W.J. Sinkin, 1881-1887) ....each £30

ANDERSEN, Hans

Danish author. Born: Hans Christian Andersen in Odense, Denmark, 1805. Had little formal education. Began his literary career with a novel, *The Improvisatore* (1835), but achieved his greatest success with his *Eventyr fortalte for Børn* (*Tales Told for Children*) of the same year. His stories were first published in English in 1846, and their popularity in Britain brought him the friendship of Charles Dickens, amongst others. Died: 1875.

Prices are for books in Good condition.

Early Editions

WONDERFUL STORIES FOR CHILDREN (translated by Mary Howitt) (Chapman & Hall, 1846) £600
A DANISH STORY BOOK (illustrated by Count Pocci; translated by Charles Boner) (Joseph Cundall, 1846) £400
DANISH FAIRY LEGENDS AND TALES (translated by Caroline Peachey) (W. Pickering, 1846) £300
THE SHOES OF FORTUNE and Other Tales (illustrated by Otto Speckter; translated by Charles Boner)
   (Chapman & Hall, 1847) £120
A PICTURE BOOK WITHOUT PICTURES (translated by Meta Taylor) (Bogue, 1847) £120
TALES FOR THE YOUNG (illustrated by the Dalziel Bros) (Burns, 1847) £100
A CHRISTMAS GREETING TO MY ENGLISH FRIENDS (translated by Lockmeyer; dedicated to Charles Dickens)
   (R. Bentley, 1847)...£100
THE DREAM OF LITTLE TUK and Other Tales (illustrated by Count Pocci; translated by Charles Boner)
   (Grant & Griffiths, 1848)..£300
TALES AND FAIRY STORIES (illustrated by H. Warren; translated by Madame de Chatelain) (Routledge 1853) £120
THE ICE MAIDEN (illustrated by Pearson after Zwecker; translated by Bushby) (R. Bentley, 1853) £90
THE WILD SWANS (J. Haddock, 1863) £120
STORIES AND TALES (illustrated by the Dalziel Bros after A.W. Bayes; translated by H.W. Dulken) (Routledge, 1864) £120
WHAT THE MOON SAW and Other Tales (illustrated by the Dalziel Bros after A.W. Bayes; translated by H.W. Dulken)
   (Routledge, 1866 [1865]) £90
OUT OF THE HEART: Spoken to the Little Ones (illustrated by the Dalziel Bros; translated by H.W. Dulken)
   (Routledge, 1867) £80
THE WILL O' THE WISPS ARE IN TOWN and Other Tales (illustrated by Swain; translated by A. Plesner and
   S. Rugeley-Powers) (Strahan, 1867) £55
FAIRY TALES AND SKETCHES (illustrated by Otto Speckter, Cooper and others; translated by Caroline Peachey,
   A. Plesner, H. Ward and others) (Bell & Daldy, 1870) £120
THE WOOD NYMPH (translated by A.M. and A. Plesner) (Sampson Low, 1870) £55
THE WHITE SWAN and Other Tales (illustrated by Alice Havers; translated by Mrs H.B. Paull)
   (Hildesheimer & Faulkner, 1873) £70
STORIES AND FAIRY TALES (illustrated by Gaskin; translated by Oskar Sommer; two volumes)
   (George Allen, 1893) ....the set £175

Important Illustrated Editions (with dustjackets where applicable)

MABEL LUCIE ATTWELL
HANS ANDERSEN'S FAIRY TALES (Raphael Tuck, [1914]) £150
EDWARD ARDIZZONE
ARDIZZONE'S HANS ANDERSEN (Deutsch, 1978) £25
E.V.BOYLE
FAIRY TALES (quarto) (Sampson Low, 1872) £500
FAIRY TALES (with two extra colour plates by E.V. Boyle; small folio) (Sampson Low, 1872) £800
HARRY CLARKE
FAIRY TALES (Harrap 1916) £400
FAIRY TALES (limited edition, signed by the artist) (Harrap 1916)..£850
A. DUNCAN CARSE
FAIRY TALES (limited edition, signed by the publishers and the artist) (A. & C. Black, 1912) £180
EDMUND DULAC
STORIES (issued with dustjacket) (Hodder & Stoughton, [1911]) £300
STORIES (De Luxe edition: limited to 750 copies, signed by the artist) (Hodder & Stoughton, [1911]) £1,300
ARTHUR GASKIN
STORIES AND FAIRY TALES (limited edition; two volumes) (George Allen, 1893)..the set £150
MICHAEL HAGUE
MICHAEL HAGUE'S FAVOURITE HANS ANDERSEN FAIRY TALES (Holt, U.S., 1981) £30
WILLI HARWERTH
THE RED SHOES (limited edition, signed by the artist) (Cleverdon, 1928) £60
CHRISTINE JACKSON
HANS ANDERSEN: FORTY STORIES (translated by M.R. James) (Faber, 1930) £30
FRITZ KREDEL
FAIRY TALES (translated by Jean Hersholt; signed by the artist and the translator) (New York Limited Editions, U.S., 1942) £80
THE COMPLETE ANDERSEN (translated by Jean Hersholt; signed by the artist and
   the translator) (New York Limited Editions, U.S., 1949) £140
KAY NIELSEN
FAIRY TALES (in box) (Hodder & Stoughton, [1924]) £800
FAIRY TALES (limited to 500 copies, signed by the artist; blue cloth [issued with dustjacket] or white vellum binding)
   (Hodder & Stoughton, [1924])...£2,000

*The 1927 Boots edition of **Hans Andersen's Fairy Tales**, with illustrations by W. Heath Robinson.*

ARTHUR RACKHAM
FAIRY TALES (Harrap, 1932) £400
FAIRY TALES (limited to 525 copies, signed by the artist) (Harrap, 1932) £2,000
CHARLES ROBINSON
FAIRY TALES (illustrated by Charles, William and W. Heath Robinson; translated by Mrs E. Lucas) (Dent, 1899) £100
W. HEATH ROBINSON
DANISH FAIRY TALES AND LEGENDS (Sands, 1897)..£100
FAIRY TALES (Constable, 1913)..£600

ANDERSEN, Hans

FAIRY TALES (De Luxe edition: limited to 100 copies, signed by the artist; vellum binding) (Constable, 1913)......................**£3,000**
FAIRY TALES (new edition) (Hodder & Stoughton, [1923]) **£100**
FAIRY TALES (Boots edition; reissue of 1923 edition) (Hodder & Stoughton, [1927]) **£40**
<u>E.H. SHEPARD</u>
FAIRY TALES (translated by L.W. Kingland) (OUP, 1961)...**£30**
<u>HELEN STRATTON</u>
FAIRY TALES (Newnes, 1899) **£50**

The Sleepy-Song Book, illustrated by Anne Anderson, is currently valued at £100 in Very Good condition.

MARGARET TARRANT
FAIRY STORIES (Ward Lock, 1917) £60
REX WHISTLER
FAIRY TALES AND LEGENDS (Cobden-Sanderson, 1935) £40
FAIRY TALES AND LEGENDS (limited edition, signed by the artist) (Cobden-Sanderson, 1935) £300

ANDERSON, Anne

Scottish illustrator. Born: Scotland, 1874, but lived in Argentina, then Berkshire. Married the illustrator Alan Wright, with whom she collaborated on several children's books.

Prices are for books in Very Good condition with dustjackets where applicable.

AUCASSIN AND NICOLETE. Translated and edited with introduction by Harold Child (A. & C. Black, 1911) £80
THE DANDY ANDY BOOK (twelve colour plates by Anne Anderson) (Nelson, [1911])...............................£100
THE FUNNY BUNNY ABC: A Book of Bunnies and Bairnies with Pictures for Painting (Nelson, [1912])...........£85
THE GATEWAY TO CHAUCER (sixteen colour plates by Anne Anderson) (Nelson, 1912)............................£65
THE DARING-DUCKIE BOOK (with Alan Wright) (twelve colour plates by Anne Anderson) (Nelson, 1914) £85
OLD FRENCH NURSERY SONGS by Horace Mansion (Harrap, [1915]) £100
OLD ENGLISH NURSERY SONGS (eight plates by Anne Anderson) (Harrap, [1915])..............................£100
THE BUSY BUNNY BOOK (illustrated by Anne Anderson and Alan Wright) (Nelson, [1916]) £85
THE NAUGHTY NEDDY BOOK (with Alan Wright) (Nelson, [1916]) £85
THE GILLY FLOWER GARDEN BOOK (Nelson, [c.1916]) £100
THE ROSIE POSY BOOK (Nelson, [c.1917]) £100
TWO BOLD SPORTSMEN (with Alan Wright) (Nelson, 1918) £70
RIP by E.W. Garrett (Humphrey Milford, 1919) £60
THE PATSY BOOK: Being the Adventures of Patsy, Patty and Pat (Nelson, [1919]) £70
HOP O'MY THUMB (Nelson, [c.1920]) £70
TUB TIME TALES by Madeline Barnes (Blackie, 1920) £90
THE JACKIE JACKDAW BOOK (Nelson, 1920) £80
THE JACKY HORNER ABC (Dean, [c.1920]) £60
THE HOUSE ABOVE THE TREES by Ethel Eliot (Thornton Butterworth, 1921) £130
FIRESIDE STORIES by Madeline Barnes (Blackie, 1922) £70
GRIMM'S FAIRY TALES (Collins, [1922]) £75
SING-SONG STORIES by Agnes Grozier Herbertson (illustrated by Anne Anderson and Alan Wright) (Milford, [1922]).............£70
COSY-TIME TALES by Natalie Joan (Nelson, [1922]) £80
THE ANNE ANDERSON FAIRY-TALE BOOK (Nelson, [1923])...£70
HANS ANDERSEN'S FAIRY TALES (Collins, [1924]) £100
COSY CHAIR STORIES by Peggy Morrison (Collins, [1924]) £70
THE ISLE OF WIRRAWOO by A.L. Purse (illustrated by Anne Anderson and Alan Wright) (Humphrey Milford/OUP, 1924) £60
HEIDI by Johanna Spyri (translated by Helene S. White) (Harrap, 1924) £75
WANDA AND THE GARDEN OF THE RED HOUSE (Humphrey Milford, 1924) £60
THE WATER BABIES by Charles Kingsley (T.C. & E.C. Jack, [1924]) £130
LITTLE RHYMES FOR LITTLE FOLKS by Mrs H. Strang (Humphrey Milford, 1925) £50
THE OLD MOTHER GOOSE NURSERY RHYME BOOK (Nelson, [1926]) £85
MR PICKLES AND THE PARTY by Constance Heward (Warne, [1926])..£50
THE CUDDLY KITTY AND THE BUSY BUNNY (illustrated by Anne Anderson and Alan Wright) (Nelson, 1926) £80
THE PODGY-PUPPY (illustrated by Anne Anderson and Alan Wright) (Nelson, [1927]) £100
A SERIES OF FAIRY TALES (six parts; written by Anne Anderson) (Nelson, [1928]) ....each £30
A SERIES OF FAIRY TALES (three parts; written by Anne Anderson) (Collins, [1929])......................each £30
PLAYTIME ABC (written by Anne Anderson) (Collins, 1930) £45
MERRY FOLK (written by Anne Anderson) (Collins, 1930) £70
THE ANNE ANDERSON PICTURE BOOK (fairy tales by Hans Andersen and the Grimm brothers accompanied by numerous coloured and black-and-white illustrations by Anne Anderson) (Collins, [1943]) £100
THE COSY CORNER BOOK (Collins, [1943]) £80
PRETENDER PEGGY by Violet Methley (T.C. & E.C. Jack, no date) £40
THE SLEEPY-SONG BOOK by Horace Mansion (Harrap, no date) £100

ANDERSON, Gerry

British TV producer. Born: 1929. Creator of some of the most popular children's TV shows of the 1960s and '70s, including *Stingray* and *Thunderbirds*. These series inspired a number of collectable spin-off novels and annuals.

Prices are for books in Very Good condition.

Annuals and Large Hardbacks

TWIZZLE ADVENTURE STORIES (Birn Brothers, 1959)..£15
MORE TWIZZLE ADVENTURE STORIES (Birn Brothers, 1960) £15
TWIZZLE STORY BOOK (Birn Brothers, 1960) £15
TV PLAYLAND 1965 (with three 'Twizzle' stories) (TV Publications, 1965) £12
TORCHY AND HIS TWO BEST FRIENDS STORY BOOK (Daily Mirror, 1962) £15
TORCHY GIFTBOOK (Daily Mirror, 1960) £15

TORCHY GIFTBOOK (Daily Mirror, 1961) £15
TORCHY GIFTBOOK (Daily Mirror, 1962) £15
TORCHY GIFTBOOK (Daily Mirror, 1963) £15
TORCHY GIFTBOOK (Daily Mirror, 1964) £15
FOUR FEATHER FALLS ANNUAL (Collins, 1960) £40
TEX TUCKERS FOUR FEATHER FALLS (Collins, 1961) £15
FOUR FEATHER FALLS (Collins, 1961) £40
MIKE MERCURY IN SUPERCAR (Collins, 1961)..£35
SUPERCAR — A LITTLE GOLDEN BOOK (Golden Press, 1962) £20
SUPERCAR ANNUAL (Collins, 1962) £30
SUPERCAR ANNUAL (Collins, 1963) £30
GIRL TELEVISION AND FILM ANNUAL 1963 (with 'Supercar' feature) (Odhams, 1963)................£10
FIREBALL XL5 — A LITTLE GOLDEN BOOK (Golden Press, 1963) £15
ATV TELEVISION SHOWBOOK (with 'Fireball XL5' feature) (Purnell, 1963)...................................£8
FIREBALL XL5 ANNUAL (Collins, 1963) £40
FIREBALL XL5 ANNUAL (Collins, 1964) £30
FIREBALL XL5 ANNUAL (Collins, 1965) £20
FIREBALL XL5 ANNUAL (Collins, 1966) £20
ITV ANNUAL 1964 (with 'Fireball XL5' feature) (TV Publications, 1964) £10
STINGRAY TELEVISION STORY BOOK (PBS, 1965) £12
STINGRAY ANNUAL (City Magazines, 1965)...£25
STINGRAY ANNUAL (City Magazines, 1966)...£15
STINGRAY — THE DEADLY ALLIANCE (World Distributors, 1965) £10
STINGRAY IN 'DANGER IN THE DEEP' (World Distributors, 1966) £10
THUNDERBIRDS — THE TARGET (large storybook) (World Distributors, 1966) £10
THUNDERBIRDS TELEVISION STORY BOOK (PBS, 1966) £10
THUNDERBIRDS ANNUAL (City Magazines, 1966) £30
THUNDERBIRDS ANNUAL (Century 21, 1967)...£20
THUNDERBIRDS ANNUAL (Century 21, 1968)...£12
CAPTAIN SCARLET AND THUNDERBIRDS ANNUAL (Century 21, 1969) £25
THUNDERBIRDS ANNUAL 1971 (Century 21, 1970) £10
THUNDERBIRDS ANNUAL (Purnell, 1972) £12
LADY PENELOPE IN 'THE CITY OF DARKNESS' (World Distributors, 1966) £20

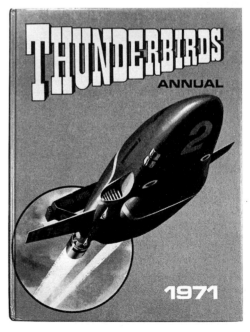

*The **Stingray Annual** was one of many spin-off publications inspired by Gerry Anderson's hit TV shows of the Sixties.*

*The 1971 **Thunderbirds Annual** features 'Thunderbird 2' on the cover and now sells for £8 in Very Good Condition.*

LADY PENELOPE ANNUAL (City Magazines, 1966) £25
LADY PENELOPE ANNUAL (Century 21, 1967) £20
LADY PENELOPE ANNUAL (Century 21, 1968) £15
LADY PENELOPE ANNUAL (Century 21, 1969) £10
PENELOPE 1971 (IPC Magazines) £5
PENELOPE 1972 (IPC Magazines) £5
TV21 ANNUAL (City Magazines, 1965) £10
TV21 ANNUAL (City Magazines, 1966) £10
TV21 ANNUAL (Century 21, 1967) £10
TV21 ANNUAL (Century 21, 1968) £10
TV21 ANNUAL (Century 21, 1969) £10
CANDY AND ANDY (features Thunderbirds) (Century 21, 1967) £8
CANDY AND ANDY STORYBOOK: The Duck Who Could Not Swim (Century 21, 1968) £8
CANDY AND ANDY (Century 21, 1968) £8
CANDY AND ANDY (Century 21, 1969) £8
CAPTAIN SCARLET ANNUAL (Century 21, 1967) £25
CAPTAIN SCARLET ANNUAL (Century 21, 1968) £15
THE ANGELS ANNUAL (Century 21, 1967) £20
THE ANGELS STORYBOOK 1 (Century 21, 1967) £8
THE ANGELS STORYBOOK 2 (Century 21, 1968) £8
JOE 90 ANNUAL (Century 21, 1968) £20
JOE 90 ANNUAL (Century 21, 1969) £20
JOE 90 TOP SECRET (Century 21, 1969) £15
JOE 90 DOSSIER (large paperback) (Century 21, 1969) £8
JOE 90 STORYBOOK — JOSEPH NINESKI (Century 21, 1968) £12
JOE 90 STORYBOOK — APPOINTMENT WITH DEATH (Century 21, 1968) £12
JOE 90 STORYBOOK — DOUBLE AGENT (Century 21, 1968) £12
JOE 90 STORYBOOK — THE CRACKSMAN (Century 21, 1969) £12
UFO ANNUAL (Century 21, 1971) £10
COUNTDOWN (features 'UFO', 'Captain Scarlet' and 'Thunderbirds') (Purnell, 1972) £15
COUNTDOWN 1973 (features 'UFO', 'Captain Scarlet' and 'Thunderbirds') (Purnell, 1973) ...£10
TV ACTION 1974 (features 'UFO' and 'Protectors') (Purnell, 1974) £10
PROTECTORS 1974 (Polystyle, 1974) £10
SPACE 1999 ANNUAL (World Distributors, 1975) £10
SPACE 1999 ANNUAL (World Distributors, 1976) £8
SPACE 1999 ANNUAL (World Distributors, 1977) £8
SPACE 1999 ANNUAL (World Distributors, 1978) £8
SPACE 1999 ANNUAL (World Distributors, 1979) £12
TERRAHAWKS ANNUAL (World Distributors, 1983) £6
TERRAHAWKS ANNUAL (World Distributors, 1984) £6
TERRAHAWKS ANNUAL (World Distributors, 1985) £6

Novels (all paperback unless otherwise indicated)

SUPERCAR — BLACK DIAMOND TRAIL (hardback) (World Distributors, 1961) £20
STINGRAY by John Theydon (illustrated by Peter Archer) (Armada, 1965) £8
STINGRAY AND THE MONSTER by John Theydon (Armada, 1966) £8
THUNDERBIRDS by John Theydon (illustrated by Peter Archer) (Armada, 1966) £8
THUNDERBIRDS by John Theydon (reissue) (Titan, 1989) £5
THUNDERBIRDS ARE GO by Angus P. Allan (Armada, 1966) £8
CALLING THUNDERBIRDS by John Theydon (Armada, 1966) £8
CALLING THUNDERBIRDS (reissue) (Titan, 1990) £4
THUNDERBIRDS — RING OF FIRE by John Theydon (Armada, 1966) £7
THUNDERBIRDS — OPERATION ASTEROIDS by Angus P. Allan (hardback) (World Distributors, 1966) £15
THUNDERBIRDS — LOST WORLDS by John W. Jennison (hardback) (World Distributors, 1966) £18
LADY PENELOPE IN 'A GALLERY OF THIEVES' by Kevin McGarry (hardback)
(World Distributors, 1966) £25
LADY PENELOPE IN 'COOL FOR DANGER' by Kevin McGarry (hardback) (World Distributors, 1966) £25
LADY PENELOPE AND THE ALBANIAN AFFAIR by John Theydon
(illustrated by Chris Highton) (Armada, 1966) £8
CAPTAIN SCARLET AND THE MYSTERONS by John Theydon (Armada, 1967) £7
CAPTAIN SCARLET AND THE MYSTERONS (reissue) (Titan, 1989) £4
CAPTAIN SCARLET AND THE SILENT SABOTEUR by John Theydon (Armada, 1967) £7
CAPTAIN SCARLET AND THE SILENT SABOTEUR by John Theydon (reissue) (Titan, 1990) £4
THE ANGELS AND THE CREEPING ENEMY by John Theydon (Armada, 1968) £8
JOE 90 AND THE RAIDERS by Tod Sullivan (Armada, 1968) £3
JOE 90 IN REVENGE by Howard Elson (Armada, 1969) £3
THE SECRET SERVICE — THE DESTROYER by John Theydon (Armada, 1969) £3
THE SECRET SERVICE — THE V.I.P. by John Theydon (Armada, 1969) £3
UFO by Robert Miall (Pan, 1970) £5

ANDERSON, Gerry

UFO by Robert Miall (Piccolo, 1971) £5
UFO 2 by Robert Miall (Pan, 1971) £5
THE PROTECTORS by Robert Miall (Pan, 1973) £3
SPACE 1999: Breakaway by E.C. Tubb (Orbit, 1975)..£5
SPACE 1999: Breakaway by E.C. Tubb (hardback) (Dobson, 1975) £8
SPACE 1999: Moon Odyssey by John Rankine (Orbit, 1975) £5
SPACE 1999: Moon Odyssey by John Rankine (hardback) (Dobson, 1975) £8
SPACE 1999: The Space Guardians by Brian Ball (Orbit, 1975) £5
SPACE 1999: The Space Guardians by Brian Ball (hardback) (Dobson, 1975) ..£8
SPACE 1999: The Collision Course by E.C. Tubb (Orbit, 1975) £5
SPACE 1999: The Collision Course by E.C. Tubb (hardback) (Dobson, 1975)...£8
SPACE 1999: Lunar Attack by John Rankine (Orbit, 1975) £5
SPACE 1999: Lunar Attack (hardback) (Dobson, 1975) £8
SPACE 1999: Astral Quest by John Rankine (Orbit, 1975) £5
SPACE 1999: Astral Quest by John Rankine (hardback) (Dobson, 1975) £8
SPACE 1999: Alien Seed by E.C. Tubb (Orbit, 1976).......................................£5
SPACE 1999: Alien Seed (hardback) (Arthur Barker, 1976) £8
SPACE 1999: Android Planet by John Rankine (Orbit, 1976) £5
SPACE 1999: Android Planet by John Rankine (hardback) (Arthur Barker, 1976) ..£8
SPACE 1999: Rogue Planet by E.C. Tubb (Orbit, 1977) £5
SPACE 1999: Rogue Planet by E.C. Tubb (hardback) (Arthur Barker, 1077) ...£8
SPACE 1999: Earthfall by E.C. Tubb (Orbit, 1977)...£5
SPACE 1999: Planets of Peril by Michael Butterworth (Star, 1977) £5
SPACE 1999: Planets of Peril by Michael Butterworth (hardback) (Wingate, 1977) ..£8
SPACE 1999: Mind-Breaks of Space by Michael Butterworth and J. Jeff Jones (Star, 1977) £5
SPACE 1999: Mind-Breaks of Space by Michael Butterworth and J. Jeff Jones
    (hardback) (Wingate, 1978) £8
SPACE 1999: The Space-Jackers by Michael Butterworth (Star, 1977) £5
SPACE 1999: The Psychomorph by Michael Butterworth (Star, 1977)..............£5
SPACE 1999: The Time Fighters by Michael Butterworth (Star, 1977) £5
TERRAHAWKS by Jack Curtis (Sparrow, 1984)..£3
TERRAHAWKS STORYBOOK (Purnell, 1984) £2
TERRAHAWKS (8 novels) (Purnell, 1984/5) ....each £2

Joe 90 never quite enjoyed the success of *Thunderbirds* and *Stingray*, but the tie-in annuals still sell for up to £8.

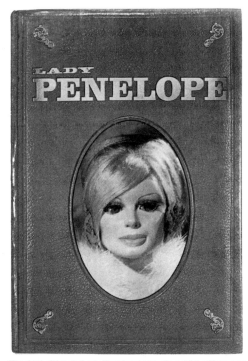

The third of the six 'Lady Penelope' annuals published between 1966 and 1972. She also featured in three spin-off novels.

APPLETON, Honor C.

British illustrator. Born: 1879. Best known for her illustrations to Mrs H.C. Cradock's 'Josephine' books. Also contributed to *Blackie's Annuals*. Died: 1951.

Prices are for books in Very Good condition.

Books Written and Illustrated by Honor C. Appleton

THE BAD MRS GINGER (Grant Richards: 'Dumpy Books for Children' series No. 16, 1902) £80
DUMPY PROVERBS (Grant Richards: 'Dumpy Books for Children' series No. 24, 1903) £90
BABIES THREE (Nelson, [1921]) £90
ME AND MY PUSSIES (Nelson, 1924)..£75

Books by Mrs H.C. Cradock Illustrated by Honor C. Appleton

JOSEPHINE AND HER DOLLS (Blackie, 1916 [1915]) £120
JOSEPHINE'S HAPPY FAMILY (Blackie, 1917 [1916]) £80
JOSEPHINE IS BUSY (Blackie, 1918) £90
WHERE THE DOLLS LIVED (ten illustrations by Honor C. Appleton) (SPCK, [1919]) £90
THE BIG BOOK OF JOSEPHINE (contains 'Josephine and her Dolls', 'Josephine's Happy Family' and 'Josephine is Busy')
 (Blackie, [1919]) £175
JOSEPHINE'S BIRTHDAY (Blackie, 1920 [1919]) £90
JOSEPHINE, JOHN AND THE PUPPY (Blackie, [1920]) £85
PEGGY'S TWINS (SPCK, [1920])·...£60
THE HOUSE OF FANCY (O'Connor, 1922) £60
PEGGY AND JOAN (Blackie, [1922]) £60
JOSEPHINE KEEPS SCHOOL (Blackie, [1925]) £70
THE BONNY BOOK OF JOSEPHINE (contains 'Josephine,'John and the Puppy', 'Josephine's Birthday' and
 'Josephine Keeps School') (Blackie, [1926]) £150
JOSEPHINE GOES SHOPPING (Blackie, [1926]) £70
THE BEST TEDDY BEAR IN THE WORLD (Nelson, [1926]) £45
PAMELA'S TEDDY BEARS (Jack, [1927]) £50
JOSEPHINE'S CHRISTMAS PARTY (Blackie, [1927])...£70
THE WORLD'S BEST STORIES FOR CHILDREN (Blackie, 1930) £35
JOSEPHINE KEEPS HOUSE (Blackie, 1931) £60
THE JOSEPHINE DOLLY BOOK (contains 'Josephine's Happy Family', 'Josephine, John and the Puppy' and
 'Josephine is Busy') (Blackie, [1934]) £150
JOSEPHINE'S PANTOMIME (Blackie, 1939) £60
JOSEPHINE GOES TRAVELLING (Blackie, 1940) £60
JOSEPHINE KEEPS HOUSE (Blackie: 'Josephine Miniatures' series, [1953]) £35
JOSEPHINE'S PANTOMIME (Blackie: 'Josephine Miniatures' series, [1953]) £35
JOSEPHINE GOES TRAVELLING (Blackie: 'Josephine Miniatures' series, [1953])..£35
JOSEPHINE'S CHRISTMAS PARTY (Blackie: 'Josephine Miniatures' series, [1953])...£35
JOSEPHINE KEEPS SCHOOL (Blackie: 'Josephine Miniatures' series, [1953]) £35
JOSEPHINE, JOHN AND THE PUPPY (Blackie: 'Josephine Miniatures' series, [1953]) £35

Other Books Illustrated by Honor C. Appleton

TOWLOCKS AND HIS WOODEN HORSE by Alice Appleton
 (Grant Richards: 'Dumpy Books for Children' series No. 20, 1903) £75
PERRAULT'S FAIRY TALES (twelve colour illustrations by Honor C. Appleton; translated by S.R. Littlewood)
 (Herbert Daniel, [1911]) £65
SONG OF INNOCENCE by William Blake (twelve colour illustrations by Honor C. Appleton; preface by Thomas Secombe)
 (Herbert Daniel, [1911]) £55
OUR NURSERY RHYME BOOK. Edited by L. and F. Littlewood
 (Herbert & Daniel, [1912]) £40
CHILDREN IN VERSE. Edited by Thomas Burke (Duckworth, 1913)...£80
BETTY'S DIARY by Dorothy Russell (Blackie, 1914) £45
HOW I TAMED THE WILD SQUIRRELS by Eleanor Tyrrell (Nelson, 1914) £55
THOSE MYSTERIOUS CHILDREN by Dorothy Russell (Blackie, [1915]) £55
THE CHILD OF THE SEA. Retold by S.R. Littlewood
 (Simpkin, Marshall, Hamilton & Kent, 1915) £35
BETTY AND THE BOYS by Dorothy Russell (T.C. & E.C. Jack, [1917])...£50
THE SECRET PASSAGE by Dorothy Russell (T.C. & E.C. Jack, [1917]) £40
ST GEORGE FOR ENGLAND by Basil Hood (Harrap, 1919) £20
A CHRISTMAS CAROL by Charles Dickens (eight colour illustrations by Honor C. Appleton)
 (Simpkin, Marshall, Hamilton, Kent, 1920) £45
FAIRY TALES by Hans Christian Andersen (Nelson, [1920]) £200
THE THIRTEENTH ORPHAN by Christine Chaundler (Nisbet, 1920) £30
SNUFFLES FOR SHORT by Christine Chaundler (Nisbet, [1921]) £25
BROTHER RABBIT and Other Stories by Sara Cone Bryant
 (with others) (Harrap, 1926)...£30
MARJORY'S WHITE RAT by Penelope Leslie (Blackie, 1926)..£25
WEE WILLIE WINKIE by Ada M. Marzials (Harrap, 1932) £25

THE BOOK OF FAIRY STORIES (with Nora Fry) (Harrap, 1935) £25
THE BOOK OF ANIMAL TALES by S. Southwold (Harrap, 1936) £35
HEATHER THE SECOND by May Wynne (Nelson, 1938) £20
THE CHILDREN'S SWISS FAMILY ROBINSON. Adapted by F.H. Lee (Harrap, 1938)...................£25
THE CHILDREN'S KING OF THE GOLDEN RIVER. Adapted by F.H. Lee from John Ruskin (Harrap, 1940) £25

Peggy and Joan ([1922]) was one of the many collaborations between author, Mrs. H.C. Cradock, and illustrator, Honor C. Appleton.

'THE ARABIAN NIGHTS'

Collection of popular tales from the Middle East dating from the eighth century and afterwards. Among the best known are 'Aladdin', 'Ali Baba' and 'Sinbad the Sailor'. First published in France between 1704 and 1717, and in England from 1706 onwards, originally in chapbooks.

Prices are for books in Very Good condition.

THE ARABIAN NIGHTS (four volumes; illustrated with engravings from designs by R. Westall) (Booker, 1819) £300
DALZIELS' ILLUSTRATED ARABIAN NIGHTS' ENTERTAINMENTS. Text revised by H.W. Ducken (published in parts; illustrated by various eminent artists, engraved by the Brothers Dalziel) (Ward, Lock & Tyler, [1864 & 1865]) £450
ALADDIN, or The Wonderful Lamp; Sinbad The Sailor; Ali Baba. Revised by M.E. Braddon (illustrated by Gustave Doré) (Maxwell, [1880]) £100
FAIRY TALES FROM THE ARABIAN NIGHTS. Edited and arranged by E. Dixon (illustrated by J.D. Batten) (Dent, 1893) £30
THE ARABIAN NIGHTS' ENTERTAINMENTS (illustrated by W. Heath Robinson, Helen Stratton, A.D. McCormick, A.L. Davis and A.E. Norbury) (Newnes/Constable, 1899) £100
THE CHILD'S ARABIAN NIGHTS (illustrated by W. Heath Robinson) (Grant Richards, 1903)......................£250
THE ARABIAN NIGHTS' ENTERTAINMENTS. Selected and retold for children by Gladys Davidson (illustrated by Helen Stratton) (Blackie, [1906]) £35
THE ARABIAN NIGHTS. Edited with an introduction by W.H.D. Rouse (illustrated by Walter Paget) (Nister, [1907])......................£30
FAIRY TALES FROM THE ARABIAN NIGHTS. Edited and arranged by E. Dixon (illustrated by John D. Batten; reprint of 1893 edition) (Dent, 1907) £20
STORIES FROM THE ARABIAN NIGHTS. Retold by Laurence Housman (illustrated by Edmund Dulac) (Hodder & Stoughton, 1907) £220
STORIES FROM THE ARABIAN NIGHTS. Retold by Laurence Housman (illustrated by Edmund Dulac) (limited to 350 copies, signed by the artist) (Hodder & Stoughton, 1907) £1,250
THE ARABIAN NIGHTS. Their best-known tales retold by Kate Douglas Wiggin and Nora Smith (illustrated by Maxfield Parrish) (Werner Laurie, [1909]) £40
THE ARABIAN NIGHTS (illustrated by René Bull) (Constable, 1912) £150
THE ARABIAN NIGHTS (illustrated by Charles Folkard; preface by Gordon Home) (A. & C. Black, 1913) £45
MORE TALES FROM THE ARABIAN NIGHTS (illustrated by Willy Pogány) (Holt, U.S., 1915) £45
TALES FROM THE ARABIAN NIGHTS (illustrated by A.E. Jackson) (Ward Lock, 1920) £30
THE ARABIAN NIGHTS' ENTERTAINMENTS (illustrated by Louis Rhead) (Harper, U.S., [1923]) £40
THE ARABIAN NIGHTS: Tales from the Thousand and One Nights (illustrated by E.J. Detmold) (Hodder & Stoughton, [1924]) £250
THE ARABIAN NIGHTS: Tales from the Thousand and One Nights (illustrated by E.J. Detmold; limited to 100 copies, signed by the artist) (Hodder & Stoughton, [1924]) £750
STORIES FROM THE ARABIAN NIGHTS. Edited by Frances J. Olcott (illustrated by Monro S. Orr) (Harrap, 1934) £30
TALES FROM THE ARABIAN NIGHTS (illustrated by Frank C. Papé) (Hutchinson, [1934])......................£20

ARDIZZONE, Edward

British illustrator. Born: Haiphong, China, in 1900, although brought up in England. Studied at Claysmore School and Westminster School of Art. Married in 1929. Served as an official war artist during the Second World War. As well as his many children's books, he illustrated a large number of classics, including the works of Dickens, Trollope and Thackeray. Contributed to *Radio Times*, *Punch*, the *Strand* and the *London Magazine*. Died: 1979.

Prices are for books in Very Good condition with dustjackets where applicable.

Books Written and Illustrated by Edward Ardizzone

LITTLE TIM AND THE BRAVE SEA CAPTAIN (OUP, [1936]) £350
LITTLE TIM AND THE BRAVE SEA CAPTAIN (revised edition) (OUP, 1955) £25
LUCY BROWN AND MR GRIMES (OUP, [1937])......................£275
LUCY BROWN AND MR GRIMES (revised edition) (The Bodley Head, 1970) £40
TIM AND LUCY GO TO SEA (OUP, [1938]) £275
TIM AND LUCY GO TO SEA (revised edition) (OUP, 1958) £25
NICHOLAS THE FAST-MOVING DIESEL (Eyre & Spottiswoode, [1947]) £250
PAUL, THE HERO OF THE FIRE (paperback) (Puffin, 1948) £40
PAUL, THE HERO OF THE FIRE (revised edition) (Constable, 1962) £20
TIM TO THE RESCUE (OUP, 1949)......................£200
TIM AND CHARLOTTE (OUP, 1951) £170
TIM IN DANGER (OUP, 1953)......................£125
TIM ALL ALONE (OUP, 1956) £50
JOHNNY THE CLOCKMAKER (OUP, 1960) £50
TIM'S FRIEND TOWSER (OUP, 1962) £50
PETER THE WANDERER (OUP, 1963)......................£50
DIANA AND HER RHINOCEROS (The Bodley Head, 1964) £40
SARAH AND SIMON AND NO RED PAINT (Constable, [1965]) £45
TIM AND GINGER (OUP, 1965) £35
THE LITTLE GIRL AND THE TINY DOLL by Aingelda and Edward Ardizzone (Constable, [1966]) £35
TIM TO THE LIGHTHOUSE (OUP, 1968) £35
JOHNNY'S BAD DAY (The Bodley Head, 1970) £25

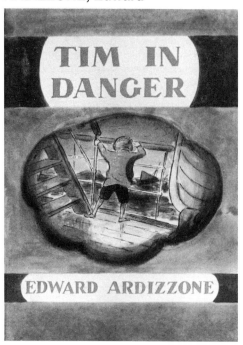

Amongst the most collectable of Edward Ardizzone's many works are those featuring the redoubtable boy hero, Tim.

*Another book both written and illustrated by Ardizzone: **Peter the Wanderer**, published in 1963 and now worth £50.*

TIM'S LAST VOYAGE (The Bodley Head, 1972) £30
SHIP'S COOK GINGER: Another Tim Story (The Bodley Head, 1977) £25
THE ADVENTURES OF TIM (The Bodley Head, 1985) £20

Books Illustrated by Edward Ardizzone

TOM, DICK AND HARRIET by Albert N. Lyons (Cresset Press, 1937) £250
GREAT EXPECTATIONS by Charles Dickens (Limited Editions Club, U.S., 1939) £350
MIMFF by H.J. Kaeser (OUP, 1939) £50
PEACOCK PIE by Walter de la Mare (Faber, 1946) £75
THE PILGRIM'S PROGRESS by John Bunyan (Faber, 1947) £60
THREE BROTHERS AND A LADY by Margaret Black (Acorn Press, 1947) £45
A TRUE AND PATHETIC HISTORY OF DESBAROLLDA, THE WALTZING MOUSE by Noel Langley
   (Lindsay Drummond, 1947) £45
HEY NONNY YES: Passions and Conceits from Shakespeare. Edited by Hallam Fordham (John Lehmann, 1947) £35
CHARLES DICKENS' BIRTHDAY BOOK. Edited by Enid Dickens Hawksley (Faber, 1948)..........£40
THE OTTERBURY INCIDENT by Cecil Day Lewis (Putnam, 1948) £40
THE ROSE AND THE RING by W.M. Thackeray (Guilford Press/Wilfrid David, 1948) £30
MIMFF IN CHARGE by H.J. Kaeser (translated by David Ascoli) (OUP, 1949) £35
THE TALE OF ALI BABA. Translated by J.C. Mardrus and E. Powys Mathers (Limited Editions Club, U.S., 1949) £200
SOMEBODY'S ROCKING MY DREAMBOAT by Noel Langley and Hazel Pynegar (Arthur Barker, 1949)...................................£30
THE HUMOUR OF DICKENS (News Chronicle, 1952) £15
THE BLACKBIRD IN THE LILAC by James Reeves (OUP, 1952) £45
MIMFF TAKES OVER by H.J. Kaeser (OUP, 1954)..£30
THE FANTASTIC TALE OF THE PLUCKY SAILOR AND THE POSTAGE STAMP by Stephen Corrin (Faber, 1954) £25
THE LITTLE BOOKROOM by Eleanor Farjeon (OUP, 1955) £45
THE SUBURBAN CHILD by James Kenward (CUP, 1955) £35
MINNOW ON THE SAY by Philippa Pearce (OUP, 1955) £60
DAVID COPPERFIELD by Charles Dickens (abridged by S. Wood) (OUP, 1955) £30
BLEAK HOUSE by Charles Dickens (abridged by S. Wood) (OUP, 1955) £30
SUN SLOWER, SUN FASTER by Meriol Trevor (Collins, 1955) £30
PIGEONS AND PRINCESSES by James Reeves (Heinemann, 1956) £40
ST LUKE'S LIFE OF CHRIST (translated by J.B. Phillips) (Collins, 1956)...............................£25
WANDERING MOON by James Reeves (Heinemann, 1957)...£35
A STICKFUL OF NONPAREIL by George Scurfield (limited to 500 copies; issued without dustjacket) (CUP, 1956) £70
HUNTING WITH MR JORROCKS by Robert Surtees. Edited by Lionel Gough (OUP, 1956) £45
PREFABULOUS ANIMILES by James Reeves (Heinemann, 1957) £35

THE SCHOOL IN OUR VILLAGE by Joan M. Goldman (Batsford, 1957) £30
THE BOY DOWN KITCHINER STREET by Leslie Paul (Faber, 1957)..£30
LOTTIE by John Symonds (The Bodley Head, 1957)..£30
MIMFF-ROBINSON by H.J. Kaeser (translated by Ruth Michaelis and Jena & Arthur Ratcliff) (OUP, 1958) £30
THE STORY OF JOSEPH by Walter de la Mare (Faber, 1958) £30
JIM AT THE CORNER by Eleanor Farjeon (OUP, 1958)..£40
PINKY PYE by Eleanor Estes (Constable, 1959) £30
THE NINE LIVES OF ISLAND MACKENZIE by Ursula Moray Williams (Chatto & Windus, 1959) £25
TITUS IN TROUBLE by James Reeves (The Bodley Head, 1959)..£40
EXPLOITS OF DON QUIXOTE (abridged by James Reeves) (Blackie, [1959])...£30
STORY OF MOSES by Walter de la Mare (Faber, 1959) £30
ELFRIDA AND THE PIG by John Symonds (Harrap, 1959) £35
HOLIDAY TRENCH by Joan Ballantyne (Nelson, 1959) £20
THE GODSTONE AND THE BLACKYMOR by T.H. White (Cape, 1959) £40
THE STORY OF SAMUEL AND SAUL by Walter de la Mare (Faber, 1960) £30
KIDKNAPPERS AT COOMBE by Joan Ballantyne (Nelson, 1960) £25
THE RIB OF THE GREEN UMBRELLA by Naomi Mitchison (Collins, 1960) £30
ELEANOR FARJEON'S BOOK. Edited by Eleanor Graham (paperback) (Puffin, 1960) £15
MERRY ENGLAND by Cyril Ray (Vista Books, 1960) £35
ITALIAN PEEPSHOW by Eleanor Farjeon (OUP, 1960) £30
THE PENNY FIDDLE: Poems for Children by Robert Graves (Cassell, 1960) £80
BOYHOODS OF THE GREAT COMPOSERS (two volumes) (OUP, 1960 & 1963) ....the set £40
HURDY GURDY by James Reeves (Heinemann, 1961) £40
NO MYSTERY FOR THE MAITLANDS by Joan Ballantyne (Nelson, 1961) £35
DOWN IN THE CELLAR Nicholas Gray (Dobson, 1961) £30
THE ADVENTURES OF HUCKLEBERRY FINN by Mark Twain (Heinemann, 1961) £35
THE ADVENTURES OF TOM SAWYER by Mark Twain (Heinemann, 1961)...£35
STORIES FROM THE BIBLE by Walter de la Mare (Faber, 1961)...£35
THE WITCH FAMILY by Eleanor Estes (Constable, 1962) £35
NAUGHTY CHILDREN by Christianna Brand (Gollancz, 1962) £45
SAILOR RUMBELOW AND BRITANNIA by James Reeves (Heinemann, 1962) £40
PETER PAN by J.M. Barrie (Brockhampton Press, 1962)..£50
A RING OF BELLS by John Betjeman (John Murray, 1962) £45
THE STORY OF LET'S MAKE AN OPERA by Eric Crosier (OUP, 1962) £20
THE SINGING CUPBOARD by Dana Farralla (Blackie, 1962) £35
MRS MALONE by Eleanor Farjeon (OUP, 1962) £40
STIG OF THE DUMP by Clive King (paperback) (Puffin Original, 1963) £30
KALEIDOSCOPE by Eleanor Farjeon (OUP, 1963) £40
SWANHILDA-OF-THE-SWANS by Dana Faralla (Blackie, [1964])...£30
ANN AT HIGHWOOD HALL by Robert Graves (Cassell, 1964)..£80
THREE TALL TALES by James Reeves (Abelard-Schumann, 1964) £30
THE ALLEY by Eleanor Estes (Harcourt Brace, U.S., 1964) £25
NURSE MATILDA by Christianna Brand (Brockhampton Press, 1964) £35
ISLAND OF FISH IN THE TREES by Eva-Lis Wuorio (Dobson, 1964)..£35
THE LAND OF RIGHT UP AND DOWN by Eva-Lis Wuorio (Dobson, 1965) £35
OPEN THE DOOR. Edited by Margery Fisher (Brockhampton Press, 1965) £30
THE STORY OF JACKIE THIMBLE by James Reeves (Chatto & Windus, 1965) £30
OLD PERISHER by Diana Ross (Faber, 1965)...£30
THE OLD NURSE'S STOCKING BASKET by Eleanor Farjeon (OUP, 1965) £30
THE TRUANTS and Other Poems for Children by John Walsh (Heinemann, 1965) £30
THE GROWING SUMMER by Noel Streatfeild (Collins, 1966) £35
LONG AGO WHEN I WAS YOUNG by E. Nesbit (Whiting & Wheaton, 1966) £35
DADDY LONGLEGS by Jean Webster (Brockhampton Press, 1966) £40
THE LAND OF GREEN GINGER by Noel Langley (paperback) (Puffin, 1966) £15
THE DRAGON by Archibald Marshall (Hamish Hamilton, 1966) £25
THE SECRET SHOEMAKER and Other Stories by James Reeves (Abelard-Schumann, 1966) £40
TIMOTHY'S SONG by W.J. Lederer (Lutterworth Press, 1966) £25
THE YEAR ROUND by Leonard Clark (Hart-Davis, 1966) £25
RHYMING WILL by James Reeves (Hamish Hamilton, 1967) £25
MIRANDA THE GREAT by Eleanor Estes (Harcourt Brace, U.S., 1967) £20
A LIKELY PLACE by Paula Fox (Macmillan, [1967]) £20
KALI AND THE GOLDEN MIRROR by Eva-Lis Wuorio (World Publishing, 1967) £30
THE STUFFED DOG by John Symonds (Arthur Barker, 1967) £25
NURSE MATILDA GOES TO TOWN by Christianna Brand (Brockhampton Press, 1967) £25
ROBINSON CRUSOE by Daniel Defoe (Nonesuch Press, 1968)..£45
UPSIDE-DOWN WILLIE by Dorothy Clewes (Hamish Hamilton, 1968) £20
SPECIAL BRANCH WILLIE by Dorothy Clewes (Hamish Hamilton, 1969) £20
THE ANGEL AND THE DONKEY by James Reeves (Hamish Hamilton, 1969) £20
DICK WHITTINGTON. Retold by Kathleen Lines (The Bodley Head, 1970)..£15

ARDIZZONE, Edward

Ardizzone provided the illustrations for Cecil Day Lewis's classic children's novel, **The Otterbury Incident** (1948).

Even a less familiar title like Cyril Ray's **Merry England** (1960) is worth £35 thanks to its Edward Ardizzone illustrations.

FIRE BRIGADE WILLIE by Dorothy Clewes (Hamish Hamilton, 1970) £25
HOW THE MOON BEGAN by James Reeves (Abelard-Schumann, 1971) £20
THE OLD BALLAD OF THE BABES IN THE WOOD (The Bodley Head, 1972) £15
THE SECOND BEST CHILDREN IN THE WORLD by Mary Lavin (Longmans, 1972) £15
THE TUNNEL OF HUGSY GOODE by Eleanor Estes (Harcourt Brace, U.S., 1972)..£15
THE LITTLE FIRE ENGINE by Graham Greene (The Bodley Head, 1973)...£85
THE LITTLE TRAIN by Graham Greene (The Bodley Head, 1973) £85
COMPLETE POEMS FOR CHILDREN by James Reeves (Heinemann, 1973)..£25
THE NIGHT RIDE by Aingelda Ardizzone (The Bodley Head, 1973) £15
THE LITTLE HORSE BUS by Graham Greene (The Bodley Head, 1974)..£85
THE LITTLE STEAM ROLLER by Graham Greene (The Bodley Head, 1974) £85
THE LION THAT FLEW by James Reeves (issued without dustjacket) (Chatto & Windus, 1974) £25
NURSE MATILDA GOES TO HOSPITAL by Christianna Brand (Brockhampton Press, 1974) £25
MORE PREFABULOUS ANIMILES by James Reeves (Heinemann, 1975) £25
ARDIZZONE'S KILVERT (Cape, 1976)..£25
ARCADIAN BALLADS by James Reeves (Heinemann, 1977) £20
ARDIZZONE'S HANS ANDERSEN (Deutsch, 1978) £25
A CHILD'S CHRISTMAS IN WALES by Dylan Thomas (Dent, 1978) £35
THE JAMES REEVES STORY BOOK (Heinemann, 1978) £25
ARDIZZONE'S ENGLISH FAIRY TALES (Deutsch, 1980) £25

ARTHURIAN LEGENDS

The legend of King Arthur has been retold in countless stories and poems, many of them presented in beautiful illustrated editions. Caxton's edition of Sir Thomas Malory's *Le Morte D'Arthur* (1469-70) was particularly influential, attracting the attention of Spenser and Milton and later, Tennyson.

Prices are for books in: (i) Good condition in a contemporary leather binding (pre-1850); (ii) Good condition in the original binding (1851-1900); (iii) Very Good condition in the original binding without dustjackets (1901-20) or with dustjackets (1921 to present).

Original Romances, Translations and Renditions

LE MORTE D'ARTHUR (reprint of 1498 De Worde edition on vellum; two volumes; boxed)
  (Shakespeare Head Press, 1933) ....the set £6,000
LE MORTE D'ARTHUR (William Stansby, 1634)...£5,000

LE MORTE D'ARTHUR (edited by Robert Southey) (Longman, 1817) **£600**
LE MORTE D'ARTHUR (illustrated by Aubrey Beardsley; two volumes; publisher's binding)
(Dent, 1893 & 1894)..the set **£600**
LE MORTE D'ARTHUR (illustrated by W. Russell Flint; four volumes)
(Riccardi Press, 1910-1911) ....the set **£500**
LE MORTE D'ARTHUR (illustrated by Charles Gere) (Ashendene Press, 1913) **£2,000**
HISTORIA REGUM BRITANNIAE by Geoffrey of Monmouth (Paris, 1508) ....**n/a**
HISTORIA REGUM BRITANNIAE (as 'The British History'; translated by Aaron Thompson)
(Bohn, 1842) **£50**
THE MABINOGION. Edited by Lady Charlotte Guest (three volumes) (London, 1849).............the set **£100**
THE MABINOGION. Edited by Gwyn and Thomas Jones
(Golden Cockerel Press, 1948) **£300**
THE LEGENDS OF KING ARTHUR AND HIS KNIGHTS by James Knowles (Griffith and Farran, 1862) **£60**
THE LEGENDS OF KING ARTHUR AND HIS KNIGHTS (illustrated by Lancelot Speed)
(Frederick Warne, 1912) **£15**
IDYLLS OF THE KING by Alfred Lord Tennyson (Moxon, 1859) **£500**
IDYLLS OF THE KING (illustrated by Gustave Doré) (Moxon, 1868) **£200**
THE BOY'S KING ARTHUR by Sidney Lanier (Scribner's, U.S., 1880) **£50**
THE BOY'S KING ARTHUR (illustrated by N.C. Wyeth) (Scribner's, U.S., 1917)..........................**£40**
THE BOOK OF ROMANCE by Andrew Lang (Longman, 1902)...**£20**
TALES OF KING ARTHUR AND THE ROUND TABLE by Andrew Lang (Longman, 1905)...............**£15**
THE STORY OF KING ARTHUR AND HIS KNIGHTS by Howard Pyle (Scribner's, U.S., 1903) **£40**
THE STORY OF THE CHAMPIONS OF THE ROUND TABLE by Howard Pyle (Scribner's, U.S., 1905) **£40**
THE STORY OF SIR LAUNCELOT AND HIS COMPANIONS by Howard Pyle (Scribner's, U.S., 1907) **£40**
THE STORY OF THE GRAIL AND THE PASSING OF ARTHUR by Howard Pyle (Scribner's, U.S., 1911) **£40**
STORIES OF KING ARTHUR by A.L. Haydon (illustrated by Arthur Rackham) (Cassell, 1910) **£75**
KING ARTHUR'S KNIGHTS by Henry Gilbert (illustrated by Walter Crane) (T.C. & E.C. Jack, 1911)...........**£50**
ERIC AND ENID by Chretien de Troyes. Edited by W.W. Comfort (Dent: 'Everyman's Library', 1914)......**£5**
THE ROMANCE OF KING ARTHUR AND HIS KNIGHTS OF THE ROUND TABLE by Alfred W. Pollard (illustrated by
Arthur Rackham; De Luxe Edition : limited to 500 copies on vellum, signed by the author) (Macmillan, 1917) ....**£1,500+**
SIR GAWAIN AND THE GREEN KNIGHT. Edited by J.R.R. Tolkien and E.V. Gordon (OUP, 1925).......**£75**
KING ARTHUR AND THE KNIGHTS OF THE ROUND TABLE by Roger Lancelyn Green
(paperback) (Penguin, 1953) **£8**
KING ARTHUR AND THE ROUND TABLE by Alice M. Hadfield (Dent, 1953) **£10**
THE ACTS OF KING ARTHUR AND HIS NOBLE KNIGHTS by John Steinbeck
(Farrar, Straus & Giroux, U.S., 1976)..**£15**

Modern Arthurian Fiction

A CONNECTICUT YANKEE AT THE COURT OF KING ARTHUR by Mark Twain (illustrated by Daniel Beard)
(Chatto & Windus, 1889) **£100**
CIAN OF THE CHARIOTS by William H. Babcock (Lothrop, U.S., 1898) **£30**
SIR MARROK by Allan French (Century, U.S., 1902)..**£30**
UTHER AND IGRAINE by Warwick Deeping (Outlook, 1903) **£25**
THE LIFE OF SIR AGLOVALE DE GALIS by Clemence Housman (Methuen, 1905)......................**£35**
THE CLUTCH OF CIRCUMSTANCE by Dorothy Senior (Black, 1908) **£25**
THE BOY APPRENTICED TO AN ENCHANTER by Padriac Colum (Macmillan, 1920) **£30**
THE FAMOUS TRAGEDY OF THE QUEEN OF CORNWALL AT TINTAGEL IN LYONESSE by Thomas Hardy (play)
(Macmillan, 1923)..**£50**
PERRONIK THE FOOL by George Moore (Boni & Liveright, U.S., 1924) **£30**
GALAHAD: Enough of His Life to Explain His Reputation by John Erskine (Bobbs-Merrill, U.S., 1926)......**£15**
LAUNCELOT : A ROMANCE AT THE COURT OF KING ARTHUR by Ernest Hamilton (Methuen, 1926)................**£20**
LAUNCELOT AND THE LADIES by Will Bradley (Harper, U.K./U.S.,1927) **£20**
THE GRAVE OF ARTHUR by G.K. Chesterton (poem; wrappers) (Faber: 'Ariel Poems' series, 1930)........**£10**
THE GRAVE OF ARTHUR by G.K. Chesterton (De Luxe Edition; poem; limited to 350 copies, signed by the author;
illustrated by Celia Fiennes) (Faber: 'Ariel Poems' series, 1930)...**£250**
PENDRAGON by W. Barnard Faraday (Methuen, 1930)..**£30**
TRISTON AND ISOLDE : RESTORING PALAMEDE by John Erskine (Bobbs-Merrill, U.S., 1932) **£15**
THE LITTLE WENCH by Philip Lindsay (Nicholson & Watson, 1935) **£20**
THE SWORD IN THE STONE by T.H. White (Collins, 1938)...**£250**
THE WITCH IN THE WOOD by T.H. White (Collins, 1940) **£300**
THE ILL-MADE KNIGHT by T.H. White (Collins, 1941) **£150**
THE BEAR OF BRITAIN by Edward Frankland (Macdonald, 1944) **£30**
PORIUS by John Cowper Powys (Macdonald, 1951) **£30**
THE ENCHANTED CUP by Dorothy James Roberts (Appleton-Century-Crofts, U.S., 1953) **£20**
LAUNCELOT MY BROTHER by Dorothy James Roberts (Appleton-Century-Crofts, U.S., 1954)........**£20**
THE ENCHANTED CUP by Dorothy James Roberts (Hutchinson, 1954) **£20**
THE QUEEN'S KNIGHT by Marvin Borowsky (Random House, U.S., 1955) **£20**
TO THE CHAPEL PERILOUS by Naomi Mitchison (Allen & Unwin, 1955) **£30**
GARETH OF ORKNEY by E.M.R. Ditmas (Faber, 1956) **£25**
BIRTH OF A LEGEND by Mary Mitchell (Methuen, 1956) **£30**
THE GREAT CAPTAINS by Henry Treece (The Bodley Head, 1956) **£25**

ARTHURIAN LEGENDS

THE ONCE AND FUTURE by TH White (omnibus edition; contains 'The Sword in the Stone',
' The Witch in the Wood', 'The Ill-Made Knight' and 'The Candle in the Wind') (Collins, 1958)............£100
THE PAGAN KING by Edison Marshall (Doubleday, U.S., 1959) £15
THE LANTERN BEARERS by Rosemary Sutcliff (illustrated by Charles Keeping) (OUP, 1959) £25
SWORD AT SUNSET by Rosemary Sutcliff (Hodder & Stoughton, 1963) £20
KINSMEN OF THE GRAIL by Dorothy James Roberts (Little Brown, U.S., 1963) £20
KING OF THE WORLD'S EDGE by H. Warner Munn (paperback) (Ace Books, U.S., 1967) £10
THE DUKE OF WAR by Walter O'Meara (Harcourt, Brace & World, U.S., 1966)..........................£15
THE GREEN MAN by Henry Treece (The Bodley Head, 1966) £20
THE SHIP FROM ATLANTIS by H Warner Munn (paperback) (Ace Books, U.S., 1967) £10
THE EMPEROR ARTHUR by Godfrey E Turton (Doubleday, U.S., 1968) £12
THE CRYSTAL CAVE by Mary Stewart (Hodder & Stoughton, 1970) £12
TRISTAN AND ISEULT by Rosemary Sutcliff (The Bodley Head, 1971) £12
DRUSTAN THE WANDERER by Anna Taylor (Longman, 1971) £10
KING OF THE LORDLESS COUNTRY by Roy Turner (Dobson, 1971) £12
THE HOLLOW HILLS by Mary Stewart (Hodder & Stoughton, 1973) £12
MERLIN'S RING by H. Warner Munn (paperback) (Ballantine Books, U.S., 1974) £8
THE GREEN KNIGHT by Vera Chapman (Rex Collings, 1975) £15
THE BRIGHT-HELMED ONE by Jayne Viney (Robert Hale, 1975) £15
THE CRIMSON CHALICE by Victor Canning (Heinemann, 1976) £15
KING ARTHUR'S DAUGHTER by Vera Chapman (Rex Collings, 1976) £15
THE KING'S DAMOSEL by Vera Chapman (Rex Collings, 1976) £15
THE CIRCLE OF THE GODS by Victor Canning (Heinemann, 1977) £15
PENDRAGON by Douglas Carmichael (Blackwater Press, U.S., 1977) £75
ARTORIUS REX by John Gloag (Cassell, 1977) £15
PARSIVAL, or A KNIGHT'S TALE by Richard Monaco (Macmillan, 1977) £15
THE BOOK OF MERLIN by T.H. White (University of Texas Press, US, 1977) £20
ARTHUR REX by Thomas Berger (Delacorte Press, U.S., 1978).......................................£20
THE IMMORTAL WOUND by Victor Canning (Heinemann, 1978) £15
THE SWORD AND THE FLAME by Catherine Christian (Macmillan, 1978) £12
THE SWORD AND THE FLAME (as 'The Pendragon') (Knopf, U.S., 1979) £10
PERCIVAL AND THE PRESENCE OF GOD by Jim Hunter (Faber, 1978) £30
MERLIN by Robert Nye (Hamish Hamilton, 1978) £30
LANCELOT by Peter Vansittart (Peter Owen, 1978)..£20
THE MAGIC CUP by Andrew M Greeley (McGraw-Hill, U.S., 1979)...................................£20
THE GRAIL WAR by Richard Monaco (paperback) (Pocket Books, U.S., 1979) £8
THE LAST ENCHANTMENT by Mary Stewart (Hodder & Stoughton, 1979).............................£12
THE LIGHT BEYOND THE FOREST by Rosemary Sutcliff (The Bodley Head, 1979) £12
HAWK OF MAY by Gillian Bradshaw (Simon & Schuster, U.S., 1980) £15
THE CRIMSON CHALICE by Victor Canning (omnibus edition: 'The Crimson Chalice',
'The Circle of the Gods' and 'The Immortal Wound') (Heinemann, 1980) £10
FIRELORD by Parke Godwin (Doubleday, U.S., 1980) £20
THE FINAL QUEST by Richard Monaco (Putnam, U.S., 1980).......................................£12
KINGDOM OF SUMMER by Gillian Bradshaw (Simon & Schuster, U.S., 1981) £15
GUINEVERE by Sharan Newman (St Martin's Press, U.S., 1981) £15
THE ROAD TO CAMLANN by Rosemary Sutcliff (The Bodley Head, 1981) £12
THE SWORD AND THE CIRCLE by Rosemary Sutcliff (The Bodley Head, 1981) £12
THE MISTS OF AVALON by Marion Zimmer Bradley (Knopf, U.S., 1982)..............................£120
IN WINTER'S SHADOW by Gillian Bradshaw (Simon & Schuster, U.S., 1982) £15
THE IDYLLS OF THE QUEEN by Phyllis Ann Karr (paperback) (Ace Books, U.S., 1982)..................£8
THE CHESSBOARD QUEEN by Sharan Newman (St Martin's Press, U.S., 1983) £15
THE WICKED DAY by Mary Stewart (Hodder & Stoughton, 1983)....................................£10
BELOVED EXILE by Parke Godwin (paperback) (Bantam Books, U.S., 1984) £8
SIR AGRAVAINE by P.G. Wodehouse (Blandford Press, 1984) £15
THE LAST RAINBOW by Parke Godwin (paperback) (Bantam Books, U.S., 1985) £8
BLOOD AND DREAMS by Richard Monaco (paperback) (Ace Books, U.S., 1985) £8
GUINEVERE EVERMORE by Sharan Newman (St Martin's Press, U.S., 1985) £15
MERLIN'S BOOKE by Jane Yolen (Ace Books, U.S., 1986)...£20
TALIESIN by Stephen Lawhead (Crossway, U.S., 1987) £15
CHILD OF THE NORTHERN SPRING by Persia Woolley (Poseidon, U.S., 1987)........................£15
DOWN THE LONG WIND by Gillian Bradshaw (omnibus edition: contains 'Hawk of May',
'Kingdom of Summer' and 'In Winter's Shadow'; paperback) (Methuen, 1988) £8
MERLIN DREAMS by Peter Dickinson (Gollancz, 1988) £15
MERLIN by Stephen Lawhead (Crossway, U.S., 1988)...£15
THE WHITE RAVEN by Diana L Paxson (Morrow, U.S., 1988) £20
THE COMING OF THE KING by Nikolai Tolstoy (Bantam, 1988) £15
PARSIFAL by Peter Vansittart (Peter Owen, 1988) £15
THE ROAD TO AVALON by Joan Wolf (New American Library, U.S., 1988) £15
ARTHUR by Stephen Lawhead (Crossway, U.S., 1989) £15
WHITE NUN'S TELLING by Fay Sampson (paperback) (Headline, 1989) £3

WISE WOMAN'S TELLING by Fay Sampson (paperback) (Headline, 1989) £3
BLACK SMITH'S TELLING by Fay Sampson (paperback) (Headline, 1990)...£3
QUEEN OF THE SUMMER STARS by Persia Woolley (Poseidon, 1990) £15
GUINEVERE : THE LEGEND IN AUTUMN by Persia Woolley (Poseidon, 1991).................................£15
TALIESIN'S TELLING by Fay Sampson (paperback) (Headline, 1991) £3
DAUGHTER OF TINTAGEL by Fay Sampson (omnibus edition : contains 'Morgan' series; paperback)
(Headline, 1992)..£5
HERSELF by Fay Sampson (paperback) (Headline, 1992) £3
THE SKY STONE by Jack Whyte (trade paperback) (Viking, Canada, 1992) £15
THE FOREST HOUSE by Marion Zimmer Bradley (Michael Joseph, 1993) £15
DRUID SACRIFICE by Nigel Tranter (Hodder & Stoughton, 1993)..£15
THE SINGING SWORD by Jack Whyte (trade paperback) (Viking, Canada, 1993)...................£15
THE KINGMAKING by Helen Hollick (Heinemann, 1994) £10
PENDRAGON by Stephen Lawhead (Morrow, U.S., 1994)...£12
THE EAGLES' BROOD by Jack Whyte (trade paperback) (Viking, Canada, 1994) £12
THE WINTER KING by Bernard Cornwell (Michael Joseph, 1995) £10
PENDRAGON'S BANNER by Helen Hollick (Heinemann, 1995) £10
THE KING'S EVIL by Haydn Middleton (Little Brown, U.S., 1995) £10
THE PRINCE AND THE PILGRIM by Mary Stewart (Hodder & Stoughton, 1995)....................£10
THE SAXON SHORE by Jack Whyte (trade paperback)
(Viking, Canada, 1995) £12
ENEMY OF GOD by Bernard Cornwell (Michael Joseph, 1996) £10
BLACK HORSES FOR THE KING by Anne McCaffrey (Harcourt Brace, U.S., 1996)...............£15
THE KNIGHT'S VENGEANCE by Haydn Middleton (Little Brown, U.S., 1996) £8
THE QUEEN'S CAPTIVE by Haydn Middleton (Little Brown, U.S., 1996) £10
LADY OF AVALON by Marion Zimmer Bradley (Viking, 1997)..£10
THE ENCHANTRESSES by Vera Chapman (Gollancz, 1997) £10
EXCALIBUR by Bernard Cornwell (Michael Joseph, 1997) £10
SHADOW OF THE KING by Helen Hollick (Heinemann, 1997) £10
GRAIL by Stephen Lawhead (Avon, U.S., 1997) £10
THE SORCEROR by Jack Whyte (trade paperback; two volumes) (Viking, Canada, 1997) ....the set £10

This Arthurian tale by 'Blandings' author, P.G. Wodehouse, was published in 1984 and now sells for £15 in Very Good condition.

ASHFORD, Daisy

British author. Born: 1890. Best known for her story, *The Young Visiters* (1919), written when she was nine. Died: 1972.

Price is for books in Very Good condition with dustjackets.

THE YOUNG VISITERS, or Mr Salteena's Plan. Preface by J.M. Barrie (Chatto & Windus, 1919) £125

ATKINSON, Mary Evelyn

British author. Born: Mary Evelyn Atkinson in 1899. Wrote several Arthur Ransome-style children's stories featuring the Lockett family. Died: 1974.

Prices are for books in Very Good condition with dustjackets.

AUGUST ADVENTURE (illustrated by Harold Jones) (Cape, 1936) £45
MYSTERY MANOR (illustrated by Harold Jones) (John Lane: The Bodley Head, 1937).........................£35
THE COMPASS POINTS NORTH (illustrated by Harold Jones) (John Lane: The Bodley Head, 1938) £35
SMUGGLERS' GAP (illustrated by Harold Jones) (John Lane: The Bodley Head, 1939) £25
GOING GANGSTER (illustrated by Harold Jones) (John Lane: The Bodley Head, 1940) £25
CRUSOE ISLAND (illustrated by Harold Jones) (John Lane: The Bodley Head, 1941).........................£25
CHALLENGE TO ADVENTURE (illustrated by Stuart Tresilian) (John Lane: The Bodley Head, 1942).........................£20
THE MONSTER OF WIDGEON WEIR (illustrated by Stuart Tresilian) (John Lane: The Bodley Head, 1943) £20
THE NEST OF THE SCARECROW (illustrated by Stuart Tresilian) (John Lane: The Bodley Head, 1944) £20
PROBLEM PARTY (illustrated by Stuart Tresilian) (John Lane: The Bodley Head, 1945) £20
CHIMNEY COTTAGE (illustrated by Dorothy Craigie) (The Bodley Head, 1947) £15
THE HOUSE ON THE MOOR (illustrated by Charlotte Hough) (The Bodley Head, 1948).........................£15
THE 13TH ADVENTURE (illustrated by Charlotte Hough) (The Bodley Head, 1949) £15
STEEPLE FOLLY (illustrated by Charlotte Hough) (The Bodley Head, 1950) £15
CASTAWAY CAMP (illustrated by Charlotte Hough) (The Bodley Head, 1951) £15
HUNTER'S MOON (illustrated by Charlotte Hough) (The Bodley Head, 1952) £15
THE BARNSTORMERS (illustrated by Charlotte Hough) (The Bodley Head, 1953) £15
RIDERS AND RAIDS (illustrated by Sheila Rose) (The Bodley Head, 1955) £15
UNEXPECTED ADVENTURE (illustrated by Sheila Rose) (The Bodley Head, 1955) £15
HORSESHOES AND HANDLE BARS (illustrated by Sheila Rose) (The Bodley Head, 1958) £15
WHERE THERE'S A WILL (illustrated by Wendy Marchant) (Nelson, 1961) £15

ATTWELL, Mabel Lucie

British illustrator. Born: East London, 4th June 1879. Married the illustrator, Harold Cecil Earnshaw, in 1908. As well as illustrating such children's classics as *Peter Pan* and *Alice in Wonderland*, Attwell produced her own series of postcards, annuals and 'midget books'. She also drew a comic-strip for the magazine, *The Passing Show*, and contributed to *Pearsons*, the *Strand* and other magazines. Died: 1964.

Prices are for books in Very Good condition.

'Bunty and the Boo Boos' Books

BUNTY AND THE BOO BOOS (Valentine, [1921-22]) £125
THE BOO BOOS AND BUNTY'S BABY (Valentine, [1921-22]) £125
THE BOO BOOS AT SCHOOL (Valentine, [1921-22]) £125
THE BOO BOOS AT THE SEASIDE (Valentine, [1921-22]).........................£125
THE BOO BOOS AT HONEYSWEET FARM (Valentine, [1921-22]) £125
THE BOO BOOS AND SANTA CLAUS (Valentine, [1921-22]) £125

Annuals

THE LUCIE ATTWELL ANNUAL NO. 1 (Partridge, 1922) £175
THE LUCIE ATTWELL ANNUAL NO. 2 (Partridge, 1923) £150
THE LUCIE ATTWELL ANNUAL NO. 3 (Partridge, 1924) £150
LUCIE ATTWELL'S CHILDREN'S BOOK (Partridge, 1925-32) ....each £150
LUCIE ATTWELL'S ANNUAL (Dean, 1934-35, 1937-1941) ....each £100
LUCIE ATTWELL'S ANNUAL (Dean, 1942) ....each £75
LUCIE ATTWELL'S ANNUAL (Dean, 1945-1968) ....each £50
LUCIE ATTWELL'S ANNUAL (Dean, 1969-1974) ....each £40

Other Books Written and Illustrated by Mabel Lucie Attwell

PEGGY: The Lucie Attwell Cut-Out Dressing Doll (Valentine, [1921]) £150
STITCH STITCH (Valentine, [1922]) £100
COMFORTING THOUGHTS (Valentine, [1922]) £45
BABY'S BOOK (Raphael Tuck, [1922]) £75
ALL ABOUT BAD BABIES (John Swain, [c.1925]) £50
ALL ABOUT THE SEASIDE (John Swain, [c.1925]) £45
ALL ABOUT FAIRIES (John Swain, [c.1925]) £50
ALL ABOUT THE COUNTRY (John Swain, [c.1925]).........................£45
ALL ABOUT SCHOOL (John Swain, [c.1925]).........................£45

Mabel Lucie Attwell produced more than forty annuals between 1922 and 1976, and these are now worth from £50 to £175.

ALL ABOUT FIDO (John Swain, [c.1925]) £75
LUCIE ATTWELL'S RAINY-DAY TALES (with other authors) (Partridge, [1931]) £100
LUCIE ATTWELL'S ROCK-AWAY TALES (with other authors) (London, 1931) £80
LUCIE ATTWELL'S FAIRY BOOK (Partridge, 1932) £150
LUCIE ATTWELL'S HAPPY-DAY TALES (Partridge, [1932]) £80
LUCIE ATTWELL'S QUIET TIME TALES (Partridge, [1932]) £80
LUCIE ATTWELL'S PAINTING BOOK (Dean, [1934]) £50
LUCIE ATTWELL'S GREAT BIG MIDGET BOOK (Dean, [1934]) £80
LUCIE ATTWELL'S GREAT BIG MIDGET BOOK (different from above) (Dean, [1935]) £80

ATTWELL, Mabel Lucie

LUCIE ATTWELL'S PLAYTIME PICTURES (Carlton Publishing Co, 1935) £60
LUCIE ATTWELL'S STORY BOOK (Dean, [1943]) £50
LUCIE ATTWELL'S STORY BOOK (different from above) (Dean, [1945]) £50
LUCIE ATTWELL'S JOLLY BOOK (Dean, [1953]) £40
LUCIE ATTWELL'S NURSERY RHYMES POP-UP BOOK (Dean, 1958) £35
LUCIE ATTWELL'S STORYTIME TALES (Dean, [1959]) £35
LUCIE ATTWELL'S BOOK OF VERSE (Dean, 1960) £35
LUCIE ATTWELL'S BOOK OF RHYMES (Dean, 1962) £35
STORIES FOR EVERYDAY (Dean, 1964) £20
A LITTLE BIRD TOLD ME (Dean, 1964) £20
A LITTLE BIRD TOLD ME ANOTHER STORY (Dean, 1966) £20
TINIES' BOOK OF PRAYERS (Dean, 1967) £20
LUCIE ATTWELL'S TINY RHYMES POP-UP BOOK (Dean, 1967) £25
LUCIE ATTWELL'S TELL ME A STORY POP-UP BOOK (Dean, 1968) £25
LUCIE ATTWELL'S BOOK OF RHYMES (Dean, 1969) £15

Books Illustrated by Mabel Lucie Attwell

THAT LITTLE LIMB by May Baldwin (Chambers, 1905) £50
THE AMATEUR COOK by K. Burrill (Chambers, 1905) £75
TROUBLESOME URSULA by Mabel Quiller-Couch (Chambers, 1905) £50
DORA: A High School Girl by May Baldwin (Chambers, 1906) £50
TURQUIOSE AND RUBY by L.T. Meade (Chambers, 1906) £50
A BOY AND A SECRET by Raymond Jacberns (Chambers, 1908) £40
THE LITTLE TIN SOLDIER by Graham Mar (Chambers, 1909) £40
THE FEBRUARY BOYS by Mrs Molesworth (Chambers, 1909) £60
OLD RHYMES (Raphael Tuck, 1909) £35
THE OLD PINCUSHION by Mrs Molesworth (Chambers, 1910) £60
MOTHER GOOSE (Raphael Tuck, 1910) £150
ALICE IN WONDERLAND by Lewis Carroll (twelve colour plates by Mabel Lucie Attwell) (Raphael Tuck, [1910]) £200
MY DOLLY'S HOUSE ABC ('untearable' pages) (Raphael Tuck, [c.1910]) £125
GRIMM'S FAIRY TALES (four full-page illustrations by Mabel Lucie Attwell) (Cassell, [1910]) £120
TABITHA SMALLWAYS by Raymond Jacberns (Chambers, 1911) £50
GRIMM'S FAIRY STORIES (twelve colour plates by Mabel Lucie Attwell) (Raphael Tuck, 1912) £140
TROUBLESOME TOPSY AND HER FRIENDS by May Baldwin (Chambers, 1913) £40
HANS ANDERSEN'S FAIRY TALES (twelve colour plates by Mabel Lucie Attwell) (Raphael Tuck, [1914]) £150
A BAND OF MIRTH by L.T. Meade (Chambers, 1914) £50
THE WATER BABIES by Charles Kingsley (twelve colour plates by Mabel Lucie Attwell)
    (Raphael Tuck, [1915]) £160
CHILDREN'S STORIES FROM FRENCH FAIRY TALES by Doris Ashley (Raphael Tuck, 1917) £140
PEEPING PANSY by Marie, Queen of Roumania (issued with dustjacket) (Hodder & Stoughton, [1919]) £350
WOODEN by Archibald Marshall (Collins, [1920]) £60
PETER PAN AND WENDY by J.M. Barrie (Hodder & Stoughton, [1921]) £275
THE LOST PRINCESS: A Fairy Tale by Marie, Queen of Roumania (Partridge, 1924) £100
CHILDREN'S STORIES (Whitman Publishing Co., [c.1930]) £200

'AUNT JUDY'S' CHRISTMAS VOLUMES

Spin-offs from *Aunt Judy's Magazine*, one of the most popular children's periodicals of the nineteenth century. Launched in 1866, it was originally edited by Mrs Margaret Gatty and featured serials, poems, articles and readers' letters. Among the illustrators who contributed to the title were George Cruikshank and Randolph Caldecott.

Prices are for volumes in Very Good condition.

AUNT JUDY'S CHRISTMAS VOLUME (annual; contributors include Lewis Carroll, Hans Andersen; artists include George
    Cruikshank, Randolph Caldecott, etc.; collated from 'Aunt Judy's Magazine') (Bell & Daldy, 1866-1885) £45
AUNT JUDY'S MAGAZINE (monthly) (Bell & Daldy, 1866) ....each £8

'AUNT LOUISA' BOOKS

Pseudonym of Laura B.J. Valentine. Born: 1814. Died: 1899. Best known as a compiler of toy books for children.

Prices are for books in Very Good condition.

AUNT LOUISA'S LONDON GIFT BOOK (Warne, 1867) £150
AUNT LOUISA'S NURSERY FAVOURITES (illustrated by K. Greenaway) (Warne, 1870) £300
AUNT LOUISA'S LONDON TOY BOOKS (series of titles) (Warne, c.1870-1880) ....each £45
AUNT LOUISA'S BIRTHDAY GIFT (Warne, 1875) £150
AUNT LOUISA'S SUNDAY BOOK (Warne, c.1878) £150
AUNT LOUISA'S BOOK OF NURSERY RHYMES (Warne, 1880) £70
AUNT LOUISA'S BOOK OF ANIMAL STORIES (Warne, [1899]) £65
AUNT LOUISA'S FIRST BOOK FOR CHILDREN (Warne, 1902) £40
AUNT LOUISA'S BOOK OF COMMON THINGS (Warne, c.1910) £30

AVERY, Gillian

British author. Born: Gillian Elise Avery in Reigate, Surrey, 1929. Worked as a reporter and as an illustration editor before publishing her first story, *The Warden's Niece*, in 1957. Many of her books are set in the Victorian era.

Prices are for books in Very Good condition with dustjackets.

THE WARDEN'S NIECE (illustrated by Dick Hart) (Collins, 1957) £50
TRESPASSERS AT CHARLCOTE (illustrated by Dick Hart) (Collins, 1958) £40
JAMES WITHOUT THOMAS (illustrated by John Verney) (Collins, 1959) £40
THE ELEPHANT WAR (illustrated by John Verney) (Collins, 1960) £40
TO TAME A SISTER (illustrated by John Verney) (Collins, 1961)..£40
THE GREATEST GRESHAM (illustrated by John Verney) (Collins, 1962) £30
THE PEACOCK HOUSE (illustrated by John Verney) (Collins, 1963) £30
THE ITALIAN SPRING (illustrated by John Verney) (Collins, 1964)..£25
CALL OF THE VALLEY (illustrated by Laszlo Acs) (Collins, 1966) £20
A LIKELY LAD (illustrated by Faith Jaques) (Collins, 1971)...£20
ELLEN'S BIRTHDAY (illustrated by Krystyna Turska) (Hamish Hamilton, 1971) £10
ELLEN AND THE QUEEN (illustrated by Krystyna Turska) (Hamish Hamilton, 1971) £10
JEMIMA AND THE WELSH RABBIT (illustrated by J. Lawrence) (Hamish Hamilton, 1972)..........................£10
FREDDIE'S FEET (illustrated by Krystyna Turska) (Hamish Hamilton, 1976) £10
HUCK AND HER TIME MACHINE (Collins, 1977) £10
MOULDY'S ORPHAN (illustrated by Faith Jaques) (Collins, 1978) £10
SIXPENCE! (illustrated by Antony Maitland) (Collins, 1979)..£10
THE LOST RAILWAY (Collins, 1980) £10
ONLOOKERS (Collins, 1983) £10

AWDRY, The Rev W.

British author/illustrator, creator of Thomas the Tank Engine. Born Wilbert Vere Awdry in Ampfield, Hampshire, in 1911. Studied at Dauntsey's School, St. Peter's Hall, Oxford, and Wycliffe Hall, Oxford. Served as Rector of Elsworth and Vicar of Elmneth in Norfolk. As well as the 'Thomas the Tank Engine' books, has written several books for adults on steam railways. Died: 1997.

Prices are for books in Very Good condition with dustjackets where applicable.

THE THREE RAILWAY ENGINES (illustrated by William Middleton) (Ward, 1945) £45
THOMAS THE TANK ENGINE (illustrated by Reginald Payne) (Ward, 1946) £75
JAMES THE RED ENGINE (illustrated by C. Reginald Dalby) (Ward, 1948) £35
TANK ENGINE THOMAS AGAIN (illustrated by C. Reginald Dalby) (Ward, 1949) £30
TROUBLESOME ENGINES (illustrated by C. Reginald Dalby) (Ward, 1950) £30
HENRY THE GREEN ENGINE (illustrated by C. Reginald Dalby) (Ward, 1951) £30
TOBY THE TRAM ENGINE (illustrated by C. Reginald Dalby) (Ward, 1952) £30
GORDON THE BIG ENGINE (illustrated by C. Reginald Dalby) (Ward, 1953) £30
EDWARD THE BLUE ENGINE (illustrated by C. Reginald Dalby) (Ward, 1954) £30
FOUR LITTLE ENGINES (illustrated by C. Reginald Dalby) (Ward, 1955)...£30
PERCY THE SMALL ENGINE (illustrated by C. Reginald Dalby) (Ward, 1956)...£25
THE EIGHT FAMOUS ENGINES (illustrated by John Kenney) (Ward, 1957) £25
DUCK AND THE DIESEL ENGINE (illustrated by John Kenney) (Ward, 1958) £20
BELINDA THE BEETLE (illustrated by Ionicus) (Brockhampton Press, 1958)..£25
RAILWAY MAP OF THE ISLAND OF SODOR (illustrated by C. Reginald Dalby) (Ward, 1958) £25
THE LITTLE OLD ENGINE (illustrated by John Kenney) (Ward, 1959) £20
THE TWIN ENGINES (illustrated by John Kenney) (Ward, 1960) £20
BRANCH LINE ENGINES (illustrated by John Kenney) (Ward, 1961) £20
BELINDA BEATS THE BAND (illustrated by John Kenney) (Brockhampton Press, 1961) £20
GALLANT OLD ENGINE (illustrated by John Kenney) (Ward, 1962)...£20
STEPNEY THE 'BLUEBELL' ENGINE (illustrated by Gunvor and Peter Edwards) (Ward, 1963) £20
MOUNTAIN ENGINES (illustrated by Gunvor and Peter Edwards) (Ward, 1964)..£20
VERY OLD ENGINES (illustrated by Gunvor and Peter Edwards) (Ward, 1965) £20
MAIN LINE ENGINES (illustrated by Gunvor and Peter Edwards) (Ward, 1966) £15
SMALL RAILWAY ENGINES (illustrated by Gunvor and Peter Edwards) (Kaye & Ward, 1967) £15
ENTERPRISING ENGINES (illustrated by Gunvor and Peter Edwards) (Kaye & Ward, 1968) £15
OLIVER THE WESTERN ENGINE (illustrated by Gunvor and Peter Edwards) (Kaye & Ward, 1969) £15
DUKE THE LOST ENGINE (illustrated by Gunvor and Peter Edwards) (Kaye & Ward, 1970)..........................£15
TRAMWAY ENGINES (illustrated by Gunvor and Peter Edwards) (Kaye & Ward, 1972) £15
SURPRISE PACKET (illustrated by Peter Edwards) (Kaye & Ward, 1972) £15
BERTIE THE BUS AND THOMAS THE TANK ENGINE (pop-up book) (Kaye & Ward, 1983)............................£15
THE FLYING KIPPER AND HENRY THE GREEN ENGINE (pop-up book) (Kaye & Ward, 1983) £15
HENRY THE GREEN ENGINE GETS OUT (pop-up book) (Kaye & Ward, 1983) £15
THOMAS THE TANK ENGINE GOES FISHING (pop-up book) (Kaye & Ward, 1983).....................................£15
HENRY THE GREEN ENGINE AND THE ELEPHANT (pop-up book; originally published in 'Henry the Green Engine')
(Kaye & Ward, 1984) £15

This montage of classic 'Thomas the Tank Engine' titles gives some idea of the range of covers to be found in the series.

JAMES THE RED ENGINE AND THE TROUBLESOME TRUCKS (pop-up book; originally published in 'James the Red Engine')
(Kaye & Ward, 1984) £12
PERCY THE SMALL ENGINE TAKES THE PLUNGE (pop-up book) (Kaye & Ward, 1984) £12
THOMAS AND BERTIE (Octopus, 1984) £12
THOMAS AND THE TRUCKS (Octopus, 1984) £12
MORE RAILWAY STORIES (illustrated by C. Reginald Dalby and John T. Kenney) (Kaye & Ward, [1984]) £10
THOMAS GOES FISHING (Octopus, 1984) £10
THOMAS, TERENCE AND THE SNOW (Octopus, 1984)..£10
THOMAS THE TANK ENGINE AND THE TRACTOR (pop-up book; originally published in 'Thomas the Tank Engine')
(Kaye & Ward, 1984) £10
THOMAS'S CHRISTMAS PARTY (pop-up book; illustrated by Clive Spong) (Kaye & Ward, 1984) £10

'Thomas the Tank Engine' Books by Christopher Awdry (son of Rev W. Awdry)
REALLY USEFUL ENGINES (illustrated by Clive Spong) (Kaye & Ward, 1983) £10
JAMES AND THE DIESEL ENGINES (illustrated by Clive Spong) (Kaye & Ward, 1984) £10
GREAT LITTLE ENGINES (illustrated by Clive Spong) (Kaye & Ward, 1985) £10
MORE ABOUT THOMAS THE TANK ENGINE (illustrated by Clive Spong) (Kaye & Ward, 1986) £10
GORDON THE HIGH-SPEED ENGINE (illustrated by Clive Spong) (Kaye & Ward, 1987) £10

B

'BB'

British author-illustrator. Born: Denys James Watkins-Pitchford in Northamptonshire in 1905. Studied at Royal College of Art, subsequently working for many years as art master at Rugby School. Also wrote many works for adults, notably on wildlife and field sports, and illustrated most of his own titles. Awarded an MBE in 1989. Died: 1990.

Prices are for books in Very Good condition with dustjackets.

Books Written and Illustrated by 'BB'

WILD LONE: The Story of a Pytchley Fox (Eyre & Spottiswoode, 1938) £100
SKY GIPSY (Eyre & Spottiswoode, 1939)...£90
THE LITTLE GREY MEN: A Story for the Young in Heart (Eyre & Spottiswoode, 1942) £85
BRENDON CHASE (Hollis & Carter, 1944) £60
THE LITTLE GREY MEN: A Story for the Young in Heart (eight colour plates by 'BB') (Eyre & Spottiswoode, 1946)............£150
DOWN THE BRIGHT STREAM (Eyre & Spottiswoode, [1948]) £60
MEETING HILL: BB's Fairy Book (Hollis & Carter, 1948)...£80
THE WIND IN THE WOOD (Hollis & Carter, 1952) £40
FAIRY TALES OF LONG AGO (Dent, 1952)...£25
THE FOREST OF BOLAND LIGHT RAILWAY (Eyre & Spottiswoode, 1955) £40
MONTY WOODPIG'S CARAVAN (Ward, 1957) £80
BEN THE BULLFINCH (Hamish Hamilton, 1957) £40
WANDERING WIND (Hamish Hamilton, 1957) £40
BILL BADGER AND THE WANDERING WIND (Methuen, 1981) £70
ALEXANDER (Blackwell, 1957 [1958]) £65
MONTY WOODPIG AND HIS BUBBLEBUZZ CAR (Ward, 1958) £100
MR BUMSTEAD (Eyre & Spottiswoode, 1958) £60
THE WIZARD OF BOLAND (Ward, 1959) £40
BILL BADGER'S WINTER CRUISE (Hamish Hamilton, 1959) £55

The splendid 'scraperboard' dustjacket of the first edition of 'BB's' classic adventure story, **Brendon Chase** (1944). Like all of the illustrations in the book, it is signed with his real name.

'BB' also wrote a number of children's stories featuring fairies and other fantastic creatures. **Meeting Hill** was published by Hollis & Carter in 1948 and is now worth £80.

BILL BADGER AND THE PIRATES (Hamish Hamilton, 1960) £50
BILL BADGER'S FINEST HOUR (Hamish Hamilton, 1961) £50
BILL BADGER'S WHISPERING REEDS ADVENTURE (Hamish Hamilton, 1962) £50
LEPUS THE BROWN HARE (Benn, 1962) £40
BILL BADGER'S BIG MISTAKE (Hamish Hamilton, 1963) £45
BILL BADGER AND THE BIG STORE ROBBERY (Hamish Hamilton, 1967) £40
THE WHOPPER (Benn, 1967) £200
AT THE BACK O'BEN DEE (Benn, 1968) £65
BILL BADGER'S VOYAGE TO THE WORLD'S END (Kaye & Ward, 1969) £50
THE TYGER TRAY (Methuen, 1971) £45
THE POOL OF THE BLACK WITCH (Methuen, 1974) £30
LORD OF THE FOREST (Methuen, 1975) £40
STORIES OF THE WILD (with A.L.E. Fenton and A. Windsor Richards) (Benn, 1975) £30
MORE STORIES OF THE WILD (with A. Windsor Richards) (Benn, 1977) £30
A CHILD ALONE (Joseph, 1978) £35

Books Illustrated by 'BB'

THE LONG NIGHT by William Mayne (Blackwell, 1957 [1958]) £45
THIRTEEN O'CLOCK by William Mayne (Blackwell, 1959) £35
THE BIRDS OF THE LONELY LAKE by A. Windsor Richards (Benn, 1961)...£20
PRINCE PRIGIO AND PRINCE RICARDO by Andrew Lang (Dent, 1961) £20
THE ROGUE ELEPHANT by A.R. Channel (Dobson, 1962) £40
GRANNY'S WONDERFUL CHAIR by Frances Browne (Dent, 1963) £30
THE LOST PRINCESS by George MacDonald (Dent, 1967) £50

BAGNOLD, Enid

British author. Born: Rochester, Kent, in 1889. Studied art in London before serving as a nurse in the Great War. Had her greatest success with *National Velvet* (1935), but also wrote several adult novels and plays, notably the drama, *The Chalk Garden* (1956). Died: 1981.

Prices are for books in Very Good condition with dustjackets.

ALICE AND THOMAS AND JANE (Heinemann, 1930) £45
NATIONAL VELVET (Heinemann, 1935) £175

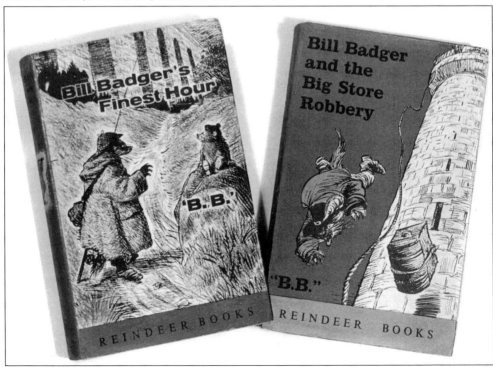

*Two of the titles in 'BB's' popular 'Bill Badger' series, which was launched in 1957 with **Wandering Wind** and concluded twelve years later with **Bill Badger's Voyage to the World's End**. Very Good copies of the former are now worth £50 in the dustjacket.*

BALLANTYNE, R.M.

Scottish author. Born: Robert Michael Ballantyne, 1825. Apprenticed to the Hudson Bay Company at the age of sixteen and sent off to Canada, where he worked as a fur trader. Returned to Scotland where, in 1848, he published an account of his life in Canada, followed, in 1856, by his first adventure novel, *Snowflakes and Sunbeams, or The Young Fur-Traders*. Amongst his many other works are *The Coral Island* (1858) and *The Gorilla Hunters* (1861). Also an accomplished painter and lecturer, and an Elder of the Free Kirk of Scotland. Described by Stevenson in the dedicatory poem to *Treasure Island* as "Ballantyne the brave". Died: 1894.

Prices are for books in Good condition.

SNOWFLAKES AND SUNBEAMS, or The Young Fur-Traders (illustrated by the author) (Nelson, 1856) £1,500
THREE LITTLE KITTENS by 'Comus' (verses and music) (Nelson, [1856]) £60
MY MOTHER by 'Comus' (Nelson, 1857) £60
THE BUTTERFLY'S BALL by 'Comus' (Nelson, 1857)..£75
MISTER FOX by 'Comus' (Nelson, 1857) £60
UNGAVA: A Tale of Esquimaux Land (Nelson, 1858 [1857]) £60
THE CORAL ISLAND: A Tale of the Pacific Ocean (illustrated by the author) (Nelson, 1858 [1857])....................£6,000
THE ROBBER KITTEN by 'Comus' (Nelson, 1858) £75
MARTIN RATTLER, or A Boy's Adventures in the Forests of Brazil (Nelson, 1858) £75
MEE-A-OW! or Good Advice to Cats and Kittens (Nelson, 1859) £75
THE WORLD OF ICE, or Adventures in the Polar Regions (Nelson, 1860 [1859]) £75
THE DOG CRUSOE: A Tale of the Western Prairies (Nelson, 1861 [1860])...£100
THE GOLDEN DREAM, or Adventures in the Far West (Shaw, 1861 [1860])..£100
THE GORILLA HUNTERS: A Tale of the Wilds of Africa (Nelson, 1861)..£1,500
THE RED ERIC, or The Whaler's Last Cruise: A Tale (illustrated by William Coleman) (Routledge, 1861) £75
MAN ON THE OCEAN: A Book for Boys (Nelson, 1863 [1862]) £75
THE WILD MAN OF THE WEST: A Tale of the Rocky Mountains (illustrated by Johann Zwecker) (Routledge, 1863 [1862])..£100
BALLANTYNE'S MISCELLANY (fifteen volumes) (Nisbet, 1863-1886) ....each £50
GASCOYNE, THE SANDAL-WOOD TRADER: A Tale of the Pacific (Nisbet, 1864 [1863])....................................£75
THE LIFEBOAT: A Tale of Our Coast Heroes (Nisbet, 1864) £60
FREAKS ON THE FELLS, or Three Months' Rustication: And Why I did not Become a Sailor (Routledge, 1865 [1864]).....£75
THE LIGHTOUSE: Being the Story of a Great Fight Between Man and the Sea (Nisbet, 1865) £60
SHIFTING WINDS: A Tough Yarn (Nisbet, 1866) £60
SILVER LAKE, or Lost in the Snow (Jackson, 1867) £60
FIGHTING THE FLAMES: A Tale of the London Fire Brigade (Nisbet, 1868) £75
AWAY IN THE WILDERNESS, or Life Among the Red-Indians and Fur-Traders of North America
   (Porter & Coates, U.S., 1869) £100
DEEP DOWN: A Tale of the Cornish Mines (Nisbet, 1869) £60
ERLING THE BOLD: A Tale of the Norse Sea-Kings (illustrated by the author) (Nisbet, 1869) £60
THE FLOATING LIGHTS OF THE GOODWIN SANDS: A Tale (illustrated by the author) (Nisbet, 1870)...............£60
THE IRON HORSE, or Life on the Line: A Tale of the Grand National Trunk Railway (Nisbet, 1871) £100
THE NORSEMEN IN THE WEST, or America Before Columbus (Nisbet, 1872)..£75
THE PIONEERS: A Tale of the Western Wilderness (Nisbet, 1872) £75
BLACK IVORY: A Tale of Adventure among the Slavers of East Africa (Nisbet, 1873) £75
LIFE IN THE RED BRIGADE: A Story for Boys (Routledge [1873])..£50
THE OCEAN AND ITS WONDERS (Nelson, 1874) £30
THE PIRATE CITY: An Algerine Tale (Nisbet, 1875)...£75
RIVERS OF ICE: A Tale Illustrative of Alpine Adventure and Glacier Action (Nisbet, 1875)...............................£50
UNDER THE WAVES, or Diving In Deep Waters: A Tale (Nisbet, 1876) £50
THE SETTLER AND THE SAVAGE: A Tale of Peace and War in South Africa (Nisbet, 1877) £75
IN THE TRACK OF THE TROOPS: A Tale of Modern War (Nisbet, 1878) £50
JARWIN AND CUFFY: A Tale (Warne, [1878])...£50
SIX MONTHS AT THE CAPE, or Letters to Periwinkle from South Africa (Nisbet, 1879 [1878]) £75
POST HASTE: A Tale of Her Majesty's Mails (Nisbet, 1880 [1879]) £75
PHILOSOPHER JACK: A Tale of the Southern Seas (Nisbet, 1880)...£60
THE LONELY ISLAND, or the Refuge of the Mutineers (Nisbet, 1880) £60
THE REDMAN'S REVENGE: A Tale of the Red River Flood (Nisbet, 1880)..£75
THE COLLECTED WORKS OF ENSIGN SOPHT, LATE OF THE VOLUNTEERS (Nisbet, 1881) £150
MY DOGGY AND I (Nisbet, [1881]) £60
THE GIANT OF THE NORTH, or Pokings Round the Pole (Nisbet, 1882 [1881])..£75
THE KITTEN PILGRIMS, or Great Battles and Grand Victories (illustrated by the author) (Nisbet, [1882]) £75
THE BATTERY AND THE BOILER, or Adventures in the Laying of Submarine Cable (Nisbet, 1883 [1882]) £75
THE MADMAN AND THE PIRATE (Nisbet, 1883) £60
BATTLES WITH THE SEA, or Heroes of the Lifeboat and Rocket (Nisbet, 1883) £60
THE YOUNG TRAWLERS: A Story of Life and Death and Rescue on the North Sea (Nisbet, 1884) £60
DUSTY DIAMONDS CUT AND POLISHED: A Tale of City-Arab Life and Adventure (Nisbet, 1884 [1883]) £60
TWICE BOUGHT: A Tale of the Oregon Gold Fields (Nisbet, 1885 [1884]) £60
THE ROVER OF THE ANDES: A Tale of Adventure in South America (Nisbet, 1885) £60
THE ISLAND QUEEN: A Tale of the Southern Hemisphere (Nisbet, 1885) £60

RED ROONEY, or Last of the Crew (Nisbet, 1886)..£60
THE BIG OTTER: A Tale of the Great Nor'West (Routledge, 1887 [1886]) £60
BLUE LIGHTS, or Hot Work in the Soudan: A Tale of Soldier Life (Nisbet, 1888) £60
THE MIDDY AND THE MOORS: An Algerine Story (Nisbet, 1888) £60
THE CREW OF THE WATER WAGTAIL: A Story of Newfoundland (Nisbet, [1889]) £60
THE GARRETT AND THE GARDEN, or Low Life High Up; and JEFF BENSON, or The Young Coastguardsmen
(Nisbet, [1890])...£60
CHARLIE TO THE RESCUE: A Tale of the Sea and the Rockies (illustrated by the author) (Nisbet, 1890)...............£60
THE COXSWAIN'S BRIDE, or The Rising Tide and Other Tales (illustrated by the author) (Nisbet, 1891) £60
THE HOT SWAMP: A Romance of Old Albion (Nisbet, 1892) £60
HUNTED AND HARRIED: A Tale of the Scottish Covenanters (Nisbet, [1892]) £50
THE WALRUS HUNTERS: A Romance of the Realms of Ice (Nisbet, 1893) £50
FIGHTING THE WHALES (Blackie, [1915]) £20
THE JOLLY KITTEN BOOK (Blackie, [1925])...£30
BALLANTYNE OMNIBUS FOR BOYS (Collins, [1932])...£10

BANNERMAN, Helen

Scottish author. Born: Helen Brodie Cowan Watson in Edinburgh in 1863. Married an army doctor and settled in India, where she wrote *Little Black Sambo* (1899) to amuse her children. The success of this little picture book — the copyright of which she sold for £5 — prompted her to produce several more in the same style and format. She died in her native Scotland in 1946.

Prices are for books in Very Good condition.

THE STORY OF LITTLE BLACK SAMBO (anonymous)
(Grant Richards: 'Dumpy Books for Children' series No. 4, 1899) £6,000
THE STORY OF LITTLE BLACK MINGO (anonymous) (Nisbet, 1901).......................................£250
THE STORY OF LITTLE BLACK QUIBBA (anonymous) (Nisbet, 1902) £250
LITTLE DEGCHIE-HEAD: An Awful Warning to Bad Babas (anonymous) (Nisbet, 1903) £200
PAT AND THE SPIDER: The Biter Bit (anonymous) (Nisbet, 1904) £175
THE STORY OF THE TEASING MONKEY (anonymous) (Nisbet, 1906) £100
THE STORY OF LITTLE BLACK QUASHA (anonymous) (Nisbet, 1908) £120
THE STORY OF LITTLE BLACK BOBTAIL (anonymous) (Nisbet, 1909) £100
THE STORY OF SAMBO AND THE TWINS (Nisbet, [1937])...£60
THE STORY OF LITTLE WHITE SQUIBBA (Chatto & Windus, 1966)..£30

BARKER, Cicely Mary

British author-illustrator. Born: 1895. Best known for her 'Flower Fairies' books, in which fairy children are shown dressed as different types of flowers. Died: 1973.

Prices are for books in Very Good condition.

THE CHILDREN'S BOOK OF HYMNS (Blackie & Son, [c.1920]) £50
FLOWER FAIRIES OF THE SPRING (poems and pictures by C.M. Barker) (Blackie, [1923])...............£80
FLOWER FAIRIES OF THE SUMMER (poems and pictures by C.M. Barker) (Blackie, [1925]) £70
FLOWER FAIRIES OF THE AUTUMN: With the Nuts and Berries they Bring (poems and pictures by C.M. Barker)
(Blackie, [1926]) £60
THE BOOK OF FLOWER FAIRIES (contains the above three books) (Blackie, [1927]) £250
FLOWER FAIRIES OF THE WINTER (Warne, [1925]) £125
AUTUMN SONGS WITH MUSIC (from 'Flower Fairies of the Autumn'; music by Olive Linnell; twelve coloured plates)
(Blackie, [1926]) £125
SPRING SONGS WITH MUSIC (from 'Flower Fairies of the Spring'; music by Olive Linnell; twelve coloured plates)
(Blackie, [1926]) £125
SUMMER SONGS WITH MUSIC (from 'Flower Fairies of the Summer'; music by Olive Linnell; twelve coloured plates)
(Blackie, no date) £125
OLD RHYMES FOR ALL TIMES (collected, edited and illustrated by C.M. Barker) (Blackie, [1928]) £100
FLOWER SONGS OF THE SEASONS (music by Olive Linnell; twelve coloured plates) (Blackie, [c.1930])...............£125
BEAUTIFUL BIBLE PICTURES (six cards painted by C.M. Barker) (Blackie, [1932])................£30
A LITTLE BOOK OF RHYMES NEW AND OLD (collected, edited and illustrated by C.M. Barker) (Blackie, [1933]) £45
THE LITTLE PICTURE HYMN BOOK (illustrated and decorated by C.M. Barker) (Blackie, [1933])...........£50
A FLOWER FAIRY ALPHABET (poems and pictures by C.M. Barker) (Blackie, [1934]).............£90
A LITTLE BOOK OF OLD RHYMES (collected, edited and illustrated by C.M. Barker) (Blackie, [1936])...............£40
HE LEADETH ME: A Book of Bible Stories by Dorothy O. Barker (illustrated by C.M. Barker) (Blackie, [1936]) £40
THE LORD OF THE RUSHIE RIVER (story and pictures by C.M. Barker) (Blackie, [1938]) £45
FAIRIES OF THE TREES (poems and pictures by C.M. Barker) (Blackie, 1940) £50
WHEN SPRING CAME IN AT THE WINDOW: A One-Act Play (with songs from 'Flower Fairies of the Spring';
music by Olive Linnell) (Blackie, 1942) £65
FLOWER FAIRIES OF THE GARDEN (poems and pictures by C.M. Barker) (Blackie, [1944])...............£60
GROUNDSEL AND NECKLACES (story and pictures by C.M. Barker) (Blackie, [1946]) £40
FLOWER FAIRIES OF THE WAYSIDE (poems and pictures by C.M. Barker) (Blackie, [1948])...............£60
FAIRIES OF THE FLOWERS AND TREES (contains 'Flower Fairies of the Wayside', '
Flower Fairies of the Garden' and 'Fairies of the Trees') (Blackie, [1950]) £200

LIVELY STORIES (five books: 'The Little House', 'Do You Know?', 'The Click-Clock Man', 'The Why Girl' and 'Hutch the Peg Doll') (Macmillan, 1954-1955) ....each £40
CICELY BARKER'S FLOWER FAIRY PICTURE BOOK (Blackie, [1955])...£75
LIVELY NUMBERS (three books: 'The Little Man', 'The Little Boats' and 'The Lazy Giant') (Macmillan, 1960-1962) ....each £40
THE RHYMING RAINBOW (Blackie, 1977) £20
THE FAIRIES' GIFT (Blackie, 1977) £20
FLOWER FAIRIES MINIATURE LIBRARY (poems and illustrations from the 1920s Flower Fairies series; four miniature books: 'Spring Flower Fairies', 'Summer Flower Fairies', Blossom Flower Fairies' and 'Berry Flower Fairies'; in slipcase) (Blackie & Son Intervisual, 1981) ....the set £35
SIMON THE SWAN (Blackie, 1988) £40

*A selection of books by Helen Bannerman, including a very early issue of **The Story of Little Black Sambo** (bottom right)*

*A plate from Arthur Rackham's **Peter Pan in Kensington Gardens**, a particularly popular edition of Barrie's story.*

BARKLEM, Jill

British author-illustrator. Born: Epping, 1951. She studied illustration with Fritz Wegner at St Martin's College of Art in London. Her 'Brambly Hedge' series began in 1980.

Prices are for books in Very Good condition with dustjackets where applicable.

Books Written and Illustrated by Jill Barklem

SPRING STORY (Collins, 1980)	£25
SUMMER STORY (Collins, 1980)	£20
AUTUMN STORY (Collins, 1980)	£20
WINTER STORY (Collins, 1980)	£20
BRAMBLY HEDGE: The Seasons — Summer, Winter, Autumn, Spring (in decorative slipcase) (Collins, 1981)	£70
THE SECRET STAIRCASE (Collins, 1983)	£20
THE HIGH HILLS A Brambly Hedge story (Collins, 1986)	£20

SEA STORY (Collins, 1990) £20
THE BRAMBLY HEDGE TREASURY (Harper Collins, 1991) £10
POPPY'S BABIES A Brambly Hedge story (Collins, 1994) £25
BRAMBLY HEDGE Sliding Picture Books (four little volumes : 'Wilfred's Birthday', 'Poppy & Dusty's Wedding',
  'Primrose's Adventure' and 'The Snow Ball') (Collins, 1995) £25
WINTER STORY Colouring Book (from the 'Brambly Hedge' stories) (Collins, 1996) £5
SPRING STORY Sticker Book (from the 'Brambly Hedge' stories) (Collins, 1997) £5
BABY MICE IN BRAMBLY HEDGE (illustrated boards; contains 'Summer Story' and 'Poppy's Babies') (Collins, 1999) £10

BARRIE, J.M.

Scottish author. Born: James Matthew Barrie in Kirriemuir ('Thrums'), Scotland, in 1860. Barrie's favourite reading as a child were 'penny dreadfuls' and the works of R.M. Ballantyne, James Fenimore Cooper and Robert Louis Stevenson. After studying in Edinburgh, he became a journalist on the *Nottingham Journal* before moving to London in 1885, where he worked as a freelance. Enjoyed success with the plays *Quality Street* and *The Admirable Crichton*, before achieving lasting fame with *Peter Pan*, first produced in 1904. Became a baronet in 1913. Died: 1937.

Prices are for books in Very Good condition with dustjackets where applicable.

THE LITTLE WHITE BIRD (issued without dustjacket) (Hodder & Stoughton, 1902) £65
PETER PAN IN KENSINGTON GARDENS (illustrated by Arthur Rackham) (Hodder & Stoughton, [1906]) £1,000
PETER PAN IN KENSINGTON GARDENS (illustrated by Arthur Rackham; limited to 500 copies, signed by the artist)
  (Hodder & Stoughton, [1906]) £3,750
PETER PAN IN KENSINGTON GARDENS (illustrated by Arthur Rackham; new edition) (Hodder & Stoughton, 1912) £1,500
PETER PAN IN KENSINGTON GARDENS (illustrated by Arthur Rackham;
  facsimile of the 1912 Rackham De Luxe edition; limited to 500 numbered copies) (Hodder & Stoughton, 1983) £150
THE PETER PAN PICTURE BOOK. Edited by D. O'Connor (illustrated by Alice B. Woodward)
  (Hodder & Stoughton, 1907) £90
PETER AND WENDY (illustrated by F.D. Bedford) (Hodder & Stoughton, [1911]) £145
PETER AND WENDY (illustrated by Arthur Rackham; enlarged edition) (Hodder & Stoughton, [1912]) £1,250
PETER AND WENDY (illustrated by Arthur Rackham; limited to 500 copies,
  numbered 101 to 600, signed by the publisher, engravers and printers) (Hodder & Stoughton, [1912]) £1,750
THE PETER PAN PORTFOLIO (illustrated by Arthur Rackham; edition limited to twenty copies,
  each plate signed by the artist) (Hodder & Stoughton, 1912) £6,000
THE STORY OF PETER PAN (illustrated by Alice B. Woodward) (Hodder & Stoughton, 1914) £40
THE PETER PAN PAINTING BOOK (illustrated by John Hassall) (Hodder & Stoughton, [1915]).................£40
PETER PAN AND WENDY (illustrated by Mabel Lucie Attwell; issued with dustjacket) (Hodder & Stoughton [1921]) £275
PETER PAN, or The Boy Who Would Not Grow Up (play) (Hodder & Stoughton, 1928) £60
PETER PAN AND WENDY (illustrated by Gwynedd Hudson; issued with dustjacket) (Hodder & Stoughton, 1931) £150
THE BLAMPIED EDITION OF PETER PAN (issued with dustjacket) (Hodder & Stoughton, 1939) £100
PETER PAN (illustrated by Nora S. Unwin; issued with dustjacket) (Hodder & Stoughton, 1951) £35
PETER PAN CHILDREN'S ALBUM (Walt Disney, 1952) £40
PETER PAN (Walt Disney, 1953) £40
WHEN WENDY GREW UP: An Afterthought (play; issued with dustjacket) (Nelson, 1957) £20
PETER PAN (illustrated by Edward Ardizzone) (Brockhampton Press, 1962) £50
PETER PAN (illustrated by Trina Schart Hyman) (Hodder & Stoughton, 1980) £20
PETER PAN (illustrated by Michael Hague) (Holt, U.S., 1987) £35

BATES, H.E.

British author. Born: Herbert Ernest Bates in Higham Ferrers, Northants, in 1905. Best known for his adult novels, including *The Purple Plain*, *Love for Lydia* and the 'Larkins Family' series, but also wrote a handful of children's titles. Died: 1974.

Prices are for books in Very Good condition with dustjackets.

ACHILLES AND THE DONKEY (illustrated by Carol Barker) (Dobson, 1962).......................................£40
ACHILLES AND DIANA (illustrated by Carol Barker) (Dobson, 1963)..£40
ACHILLES AND THE TWINS (illustrated by Carol Barker) (Dobson, 1964)...£40
THE WHITE ADMIRAL (illustrated by P. Chapman) (Dennis Dobson, 1968) £40

BAUM, L. Frank

American author. Born: Lyman Frank Baum in Chittenago, New York, in 1856. Launched his career as a children's writer with *Mother Goose in Prose* (1897), following this three years later with *The Wonderful Wizard of Oz* (1900). Many more 'Oz' books followed, along with several other children's fantasies. After his death in 1919, the series was continued by Ruth Plumly Thompson and John R. Neill.

Prices are for books in Very Good condition.

MOTHER GOOSE IN PROSE (illustrated by Maxwell Parrish) (Way & Williams, U.S., [1897])................£2,750
MOTHER GOOSE IN PROSE (illustrated by Maxwell Parrish) (Duckworth, 1899) £1,000
FATHER GOOSE, HIS BOOK (illustrated by W.W. Denslow and R.F. Seymour) (George M. Hill, U.S., 1899) £2,500
FATHER GOOSE, HIS BOOK (illustrated by W.W. Denslow and R.F. Seymour) (Werner, 1899) £1,000
A NEW WONDERLAND (illustrated by Frank Berbeck) (Russell, U.S., 1900)..£1,000

BAUM, L. Frank

THE WONDERFUL WIZARD OF OZ (illustrated by W.W. Denslow) (Hill, U.S., 1900) £15,000
AMERICAN FAIRY TALES (George M. Hill, U.S., 1901) £1,000
DOT AND TOT OF MERRYLAND (illustrated by W.W. Denslow) (Hill, U.S., 1901) £1,000
THE MASTER KEY: An Electrical Fairy Tale (Bobbs-Merrill, U.S., 1901) £600
THE MASTER KEY: An Electrical Fairy Tale (Stevens & Brown, [1902])...£500
THE LIFE AND ADVENTURES OF SANTA CLAUS (illustrated by Mary Cowles Clark) (Bobbs-Merrill, U.S., 1902)................£600
THE LIFE AND ADVENTURES OF SANTA CLAUS (illustrated by Mary Cowles Clark) (Stevens & Brown, 1902) £500
THE SURPRISING ADVENTURES OF THE MAGICAL MONARCH OF MO AND HIS PEOPLE
    (illustrated by F. Verbeck) (Bobbs-Merrill, U.S., [1903]) £750
THE ENCHANTED ISLAND OF YEW (illustrated by Fanny Cory) (Bobbs-Merrill, U.S., [1903]) £600
THE NEW WIZARD OF OZ (illustrated by W.W. Denslow) (Bobbs-Merrill, U.S., [1903]) £550
THE MARVELOUS LAND OF OZ (illustrated by John R. Neill) (Reilly & Britton, U.S., 1904) £4,000
THE MARVELOUS LAND OF OZ (illustrated by John R. Neill) (Revell, 1904) £1,000
THE WOGGLE-BUG BOOK (Reilly & Britton, U.S., 1905) £1,000
QUEEN ZIXI OF IX (illustrated by Frederick Richardson) (Century, U.S., 1905) £1,000
QUEEN ZIXI OF IX (same as U.S. edition, except with different title page) (Hodder & Stoughton, 1906) £750
THE WONDERFUL WIZARD OF OZ (illustrated by W.W. Denslow) (Hodder & Stoughton, 1906) £1,000
JOHN DOUGH AND THE CHERUB (illustrated by John R. Neill) (Reilly & Britton, U.S., 1906) £600
JOHN DOUGH AND THE CHERUB (illustrated by John R. Neill) (Constable, 1906) £500
OZMA OF OZ (illustrated by John R. Neill) (Reilly & Britton, U.S., 1907) £3,000
OZMA OF OZ (illustrated by John R. Neill) (Hutchinson, 1942) £75
THE LAST EGYPTIAN: A Romance of the Nile (illustrated by Francis P. Wightman) (Reilly & Britton, U.S., 1908) £300
DOROTHY AND THE WIZARD IN OZ (illustrated by John R. Neill) (Reilly & Britton, U.S., 1908) £1,200
THE ROAD TO OZ (illustrated by John R. Neill) (Reilly & Britton, U.S., 1909) £3,000
THE EMERALD CITY OF OZ (illustrated by John R. Neill) (Reilly & Britton, U.S., 1910).....................£3,000
THE SEA FAIRIES (illustrated by John R. Neill) (Reilly & Britton, U.S., 1911).....................................£500
SKY ISLAND (illustrated by John R. Neill) (Reilly & Britton, U.S., 1912) £400
THE PATCHWORK GIRL OF OZ (illustrated by John R. Neill) (Reilly & Britton, U.S., 1913) £3,000
TIK-TOK OF OZ (illustrated by John R. Neill) (Reilly & Britton, U.S., 1914) £1,500
THE SCARECROW OF OZ (illustrated by John R. Neill) (Reilly & Britton, U.S., 1915) £1,000
RINKITINK IN OZ (illustrated by John R. Neill) (Reilly & Britton, U.S., 1916)....................................£800
THE LOST PRINCESS OF OZ (illustrated by John R. Neill) (Reilly & Britton, U.S., 1917).................£1,500
THE TIN WOODMAN OF OZ (illustrated by John R. Neill) (Reilly & Britton, U.S., 1918) £1,500
THE MAGIC OF OZ (illustrated by John R. Neill) (Reilly & Lee, U.S., 1919) £700

Nicola Bayley wrote and illustrated **One Old Oxford Ox**.
This book now sells for £15 in Very Good condition.

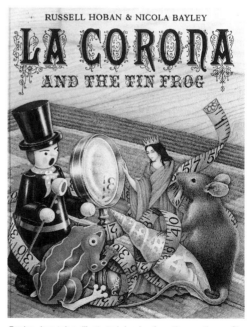

Bayley has also illustrated books for other authors. She
collaborated with Russell Hoban on this volume from 1979.

GLINDA OF OZ (illustrated by John R. Neill) (Reilly & Lee, U.S., 1920) £700
THE LAND OF OZ STORY BOOK (Hutchinson, [1941]) £100
THE WONDERFUL WIZARD OF OZ (illustrated by L. Frank Baum) (Dent, 1965) £30
THE WIZARD OF OZ (illustrated by Michael Hague) (Holt, U.S., 1982)...£40

BAWDEN, Nina

British author. Born: London, 1925. A high reputation in books for adults and children, and notable for and *Carrie's War* (1973) and *The Peppermint Pig* (1975).

Prices are for books in Very Good condition with dustjackets where applicable.

DEVIL BY THE SEA (Collins, 1957) £40
THE SECRET PASSAGE (Gollancz, 1963) £35
ON THE RUN (Gollancz, 1964) £25
THE WHITE HORSE GANG (Gollancz, 1966) £25
THE WITCH'S DAUGHTER (illustrated by Shirley Hughes) (Gollancz, 1966) £25
A HANDFUL OF THIEVES (Gollancz, 1967) £15
THE RUNAWAY SUMMER (Gollancz, 1969) £15
SQUIB (illustrated by Shirley Hughes) (Gollancz, 1971)..£15
CARRIE'S WAR (Gollancz, 1973) £25
THE PEPPERMINT PIG (illustrated by Alexy Pendle) (Gollancz, 1975)..£25
REBEL ON A ROCK (sequel to 'Carrie's War') (Gollancz, 1978) £15
THE ROBBERS (illustrated by Charles Keeping) (Gollancz, 1979) £15
WILLIAM TELL (illustrated by Pascale Allamand) (Cape, 1981) £15
KEPT IN THE DARK (Gollancz, 1982) £15
THE FINDING (Gollancz, 1985) £15
PRINCESS ALICE (illustrated by Phillida Gili) (Deutsch, 1985) £15

BAYLEY, Nicola

British illustrator. Born: 1949. Produced *Nicola Bayley's Book of Nursery Rhymes* in 1975 and illustrations for books by Richard Adams, Russell Hoban and William Mayne.

Prices are for books in Very Good condition with dustjackets where applicable.

Books Written and Illustrated by Nicola Bayley

BOOK OF NURSERY RHYMES (Cape, 1973)..£45
NICOLA BAYLEY'S BOOK OF NURSERY RHYMES (eight volumes; pictorial boards) (Cape, 1975) ....the set £60
PUSS IN BOOTS (pop-up book) (Cape, 1976) £25
ONE OLD OXFORD OX (pictorial boards) (Cape, 1977) £15
PUSS IN BOOTS (pop-up) (Greenwillow, 1977) £15
ELEPHANT CAT (Walker, 1984) £15
CRAB CAT (Walker, 1984) £15
SPIDER CAT (Walker, 1984) £15
POLAR BEAR CAT (Walker, 1984)..£15
BEDTIME & MOONSHINE (Walker, 1987) £20
HUSH-A-BYE-BABY (eight volumes; pictorial boards) (Sainsbury's, 1985) ....the set £20
AS I WAS GOING UP AND DOWN (eight volumes; pictorial boards) (Sainsbury's/Walker Books, 1985) ....the set £20
THE NECESSARY CAT (Walker, 1998) £10

Books Illustrated by Nicola Bayley

THE TYGER VOYAGE by Richard Adams (Cape, 1976)..£20
LA CORONA AND THE TIN FROG by Russell Hoban (Cape, 1979)...£25
THE PATCHWORK CAT by William Mayne (Cape, 1981) £30
THE MOULDY by William Mayne (Cape, 1983) £25
BOY by Paul Manning (Macmillan, 1987) £15
TAIL FEATHERS FROM MOTHER GOOSE by Iona Opie (illustrated by Maurice Sendak, Janet Ahlberg,
    Nicola Bayley, Quentin Blake, John Burningham and Anthony Browne) (Walker, 1988)...........£25
THE MOUSEHOLE CAT by Antonia Barber (Walker, 1990) £20
FUN WITH MRS THUMB by Jan Mark (Walker, 1993) £10

BEAMAN, S.G. Hulme

British author-illustrator. Born: Sydney George Hulme Beaman in London in 1886. Began as a toymaker, but then turned to drawing strips in which the characters were all represented as toys. His popular 'Toytown' stories, featuring Larry the Lamb, were later adapted for BBC Radio's *Children's Hour*, remaining firm favourites until the programme's demise in 1964. Beaman died in 1932.

Prices are for books in Very Good condition with dustjackets where applicable.

ALADDIN (retold and illustrated by S.G. Hulme Beaman) (The Bodley Head, 1924) £60
THE ROAD TO TOYTOWN (1925) £90
THE SEVEN VOYAGES OF SINBAD THE SAILOR (retold and illustrated by S.G. Hulme Beaman) (The Bodley Head, 1926) £60
'OUT OF THE ARK' BOOKS (six books) (Warne, [1927])..each £25
TALES OF TOYTOWN (written and illustrated by S.G. Hulme Beaman) (Humphrey Milford, 1928)............£120

As this photograph clearly shows, S.G. Hulme Beaman's famous 'Toytown' books were issued in a wide variety of formats.

JOHN TRUSTY (written and illustrated by S.G. Hulme Beaman) (Collins, [1929]) £40
WIRELESS IN TOYTOWN (written and illustrated by S.G. Hulme Beaman) (Collins, 1930) £60
THE SMITH FAMILY by H.C. Craddock (illustrated by S.G. Hulme Beaman) (Nelson, [1931]) £30
THE TOYTOWN MYSTERY (written and illustrated by S.G. Hulme Beaman) (Collins, [1932]) £60
STORIES FROM TOYTOWN (written and illustrated by S.G. Hulme Beaman) (OUP, 1938) £55
TOY TOWN SERIES (also known as 'The Adventures of Larry the Lamb'; illustrated by Ernest Noble)
(Lapworth, [1942-1947]) ....each £25
LARRY THE LAMB (illustrated by S.G. Hulme Beaman) (Collins, 1946) £50
TOY TOWN TALES (illustrated by George Moreno) (News of the World, [1952]) £35
THE CRUISE OF THE TOYTOWN BELLE (play; adapted by Hendrik Baker) (Samuel French, [1953]) £25
TOYTOWN SERIES (Oldbourne, 1957-1961)...each £20

'BEANO' ANNUALS
Probably the best-known of all British comic annuals, published by D.C. Thomson of Dundee. The comic itself first appeared on 30th July 1938. Among the title's most popular characters are Dennis the Menace, Biffo the Bear, Beryl the Peril and the Bash Street Kids.

Prices are for annuals in Very Good condition (with cover description in brackets).

THE BEANO BOOK 1940 (Pansy Potter holding see-saw for Big Eggo and other 'Beano' characters)...................£3,000
THE BEANO BOOK 1941 (Big Eggo and other 'Beano' characters appearing from large eggs) £1,000
THE BEANO BOOK 1942 (Lord Snooty playing bagpipes) £900

THE MAGIC BEANO BOOK 1943 (Big Eggo and others in three-legged race) £700
THE MAGIC BEANO BOOK 1944 ('Beano' characters in pillow fight)..£550
THE MAGIC BEANO BOOK 1945 (Big Eggo and others playing leap-frog) £450
THE MAGIC BEANO BOOK 1946 (Big Eggo pulling others along in a cart)..£400
THE MAGIC BEANO BOOK 1947 ('Beano' characters gathered around Big Eggo; quarto) £300
THE MAGIC BEANO BOOK 1948 (Big Eggo and others playing musical instruments; quarto) £250
THE MAGIC BEANO BOOK 1949 (Biffo, Big Eggo and others around a taxi; quarto) £200
THE MAGIC BEANO BOOK 1950 (Biffo, painting portrait of Big Eggo; quarto) £150
THE BEANO BOOK 1951 (Biffo riding on mechanical horse) £100
THE BEANO BOOK 1952 (Biffo nailing pictures of 'Beano' characters to cover)..£75
THE BEANO BOOK 1953 (Jack Flash carrying 'Beano' characters on trips to the moon) £70
THE BEANO BOOK 1954 (Biffo hangs from a tree; Dennis holding lobster)..£65
THE BEANO BOOK 1955 (Policeman stopping Dennis and Biffo from fishing)..£55
THE BEANO BOOK 1956 (Biffo looking at Bash Street Kids) £55
THE BEANO BOOK 1957 (Dennis kicking ball which rebounds off various characters) £55
THE BEANO BOOK 1958 (Biffo juggling; Dennis freeing bees from hive)...£55
THE BEANO BOOK 1959 (Dennis playing leapfrog with a goat)..£55
THE BEANO BOOK 1960 (Biffo completing Bash Street Kids jigsaw)..£45
THE BEANO BOOK 1961 ('Beano' in large letters; with characters at top and bottom of cover) £45
THE BEANO BOOK 1962 (Jonah dancing on mast of sinking ship) £45
THE BEANO BOOK 1963 (Bash Street Kids on large swing) £45
THE BEANO BOOK 1964 (Buster tickling Biffo with feather) £45
THE BEANO BOOK 1965 (two children blowing up a Biffo balloon) £40
THE BEANO BOOK 1966 (dated '1966' on cover)..£30
THE BEANO BOOK 1967-69 ....each £25
THE BEANO BOOK 1970 ....each £15
THE BEANO BOOK 1971-72 ....each £12
THE BEANO BOOK 1973-74 ....each £10
THE BEANO BOOK 1975-77 ....each £8
THE BEANO BOOK 1978-80 ....each £5
THE BEANO BOOK 1981-Present ....each £5

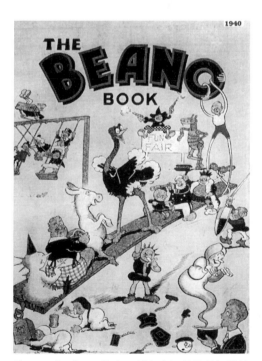

The very first Beano Book, published in 1940. This highly sought-after item sells for £3,000 in Very Good condition.

The **Beano Book** from 1952, worth £75 in Very Good condition. Like all the early annuals, this book wasn't dated on the cover.

*The first edition of Hilaire Belloc's **More Beasts (for Worse Children)**, featuring a cover illustration by Basil Blackwood.*

'BEEZER' ANNUALS

Popular British comic annual, published by D.C. Thomson. The comic itself was launched on 21st January 1956, the first *Beezer Book* appearing the following year. Among the title's best-known characters were Ginger, Baby Crocket and 'Pop, Dick and Harry'.

Prices are for annuals in Very Good condition.

THE BEEZER BOOK 1958	£90
THE BEEZER BOOK 1959	£25
THE BEEZER BOOK 1960-65	each £20
THE BEEZER BOOK 1966-69	each £15
THE BEEZER BOOK 1970-74	each £8
THE BEEZER BOOK 1975-77	each £6
THE BEEZER BOOK 1978-91	each £4

BELLOC, Hilaire

British author. Born: Joseph Hilaire Pierre René Belloc in 1870. Educated at the Oratory School in Birmingham and Balliol College, Oxford. Belloc wrote a large number of adult works, many of them reflecting his Catholic faith, as well as some very popular collections of humorous verses for children. Died: 1953.

Prices are for books in Very Good condition.

VERSES AND SONNETS (Ward & Downey, 1896)	£150
THE BAD CHILD'S BOOK OF BEASTS (illustrated by Basil Blackwood) (Alden Press, [1896])	£90
MORE BEASTS (FOR WORSE CHILDREN) (illustrated by Basil Blackwood) (Arnold, [1897])	£75
A MORAL ALPHABET (illustrated by Basil Blackwood) (Arnold, 1899)	£75
CAUTIONARY TALES FOR CHILDREN (illustrated by Basil Blackwood) (Eveleigh Nash, [1908])	£50
MORE PEERS (illustrated by Basil Blackwood) (Stephen Swift, [1911])	£45
NEW CAUTIONARY TALES (illustrated by Nicolas Bentley) (Duckworth, 1930)	£50
NEW CAUTIONARY TALES (illustrated by Nicolas Bentley; De Luxe edition: limited to 110 copies, signed by the author) (Duckworth, 1930)	£130
CAUTIONARY VERSES: The Collected Humorous Verses of Hilaire Belloc (Duckworth, 1939)	£40

BEMELMANS, Ludwig

Austrian author. Born in 1898 and emigrated to America in 1914. Notable for his 'Madeline' picture books, with verse texts. *Madeline's Rescue* (1953) won the Caldecott Medal. Died: 1962.

Prices are for books in Very Good condition with dustjackets where applicable.

'Madeline' Books

MADELINE (Simon & Schuster, U.S., 1939) £120
MADELINE (Derek Verschoyle, 1952) £60
MADELINE'S RESCUE (Viking Press, U.S., 1953) £100
MADELINE'S RESCUE (Derek Verschoyle, 1953) £60
MADELINE AND THE BAD HAT (limited to 985 copies, signed by the author) (Viking Press, U.S., 1956) £150
MADELINE AND THE BAD HAT (trade edition) (Viking Press, U.S., 1957)...£100
MADELINE AND THE BAD HAT (Deutsch, 1958) £40
MADELINE AND THE GYPSIES (Viking Press, U.S., 1959) £80
MADELINE AND THE GYPSIES (Deutsch, 1961) £40
MADELINE IN LONDON (Viking Press, U.S., 1961) £80
MADELINE IN LONDON (Deutsch, 1962) £40
MADELINE'S CHRISTMAS (completed by Madeline and Barbara Bemelmans) (Viking Kestrel, U.S., 1985) £15
MADELINE'S CHRISTMAS (completed by Madeline and Barbara Bemelmans) (Deutsch, 1985) £15

Others

HANSI (Viking Press, U.S., 1934) £80
HANSI (Lovat Dickson, 1935) £50
THE GOLDEN BASKET (Viking Press, U.S., 1936) £50
THE CASTLE NUMBER 9 (Viking Press, U.S., 1937) £50
QUITO EXPRESS (Viking Press, U.S., 1938) £50
ROSEBUD (Random House, U.S., 1942) £40
A TALE OF TWO GLIMPS (CBS, U.S., 1947)..£20
THE HAPPY PLACE (Little Brown, U.S., 1952) £20
THE HIGH WORLD (Harper, U.S., 1954) £20
THE HIGH WORLD (Hamish Hamilton, 1958) £15
PARSLEY (Harper, U.S., 1955) £20

*The very first **Beezer Book** of 1958 (left) and the 1977 annual (right). They are now worth £90 and £8 respectively.*

BERESFORD, Elisabeth

British author and creator of the Wombles. Born: Paris in 1926, the daughter of the popular novelist, J.D. Beresford. Educated at Brighton and Hove High School, and served in the WRNS during the war. Married the TV presenter, Max Robertson, in 1949, and subsequently wrote extensively for television, which provided the subject for her first book. Best known for *The Wombles* (1968) and its many sequels, but has also written children's fantasies and adult romances.

Prices are for books in Very Good condition with dustjackets where applicable.

'Wombles' Books

THE WOMBLES (illustrated by Margaret Gordon) (Benn, 1968) £50
THE WANDERING WOMBLES (illustrated by Oliver Chadwick) (Benn, 1970) £45
THE INVISIBLE WOMBLE and Other Stories (illustrated by Ivor Wood) (Benn, 1973) £45
THE WOMBLES IN DANGER (Benn, 1973) £20
THE WOMBLES AT WORK (illustrated by Barry Leith) (Benn, 1973) £15
THE WOMBLES GO THE SEASIDE (World Distributors, 1974)...£18
THE WOMBLES GIFT BOOK (illustrated by Margaret Gordon and Derek Collard) (Benn, 1975)............£12
THE SNOW WOMBLE (illustrated by Margaret Gordon) (Benn, 1975) £12
TOMSK AND THE TIRED TREE (illustrated by Margaret Gordon) (Benn, 1975) £18
WELLINGTON AND THE BLUE BALLOON (illustrated by Margaret Gordon) (Benn, 1975) £14
ORINOCO RUNS AWAY (illustrated by Margaret Gordon) (Benn, 1975) £10
THE WOMBLES MAKE A CLEAN SWEEP (illustrated by Ivor Wood) (Benn, 1975) £14
THE WOMBLES TO THE RESCUE (illustrated by Margaret Gordon) (Benn, 1975) £10
THE WOMBLES OF WIMBLEDON (contains 'The Wombles at Work' [illustrated by Barry Leith] and
'The Wombles to the Hescue' [illustrated by Margaret Gordon]) (Benn, 1976) £10
THE MACWOMBLE'S PIPE BAND (illustrated by Margaret Gordon) (Benn, 1976) £10
MADAME CHOLET'S PICNIC PARTY (illustrated by Margaret Gordon) (Benn, 1976) £10
BUNGO KNOWS BEST (illustrated by Margaret Gordon) (Benn, 1976) £14
TOBERMORY'S BIG SURPRISE (illustrated by Margaret Gordon) (Benn, 1976) £10
THE WOMBLES GO ROUND THE WORLD (illustrated by Margaret Gordon) (Benn, 1976)....................£10

The Wombles

Elisabeth Beresford

Illustrated by MARGARET GORDON

The book that introduced the world to the Wombles. Jacketed copies in Very Good condition are now worth £50.

The Television Mystery (1957) was Elisabeth Beresford's first book. It sells for £25 in Very Good condition with the jacket.

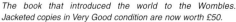

THE WORLD OF THE WOMBLES (illustrated by Edgar Hodges) (World Distributors, 1976) £10
WOMBLING FREE (illustrated by Edgar Hodges) (Benn, 1978) £10

Others

THE TELEVISION MYSTERY (Parrish, 1957)..£25
THE FLYING DOCTOR MYSTERY (Parrish, 1958) £20
TROUBLE AT TULLINGTON CASTLE (Parrish, 1958) £20
COCKY AND THE MISSING CASTLE (illustrated by Jennifer Miles) (Constable, 1959).......................................£20
GAPPY GOES WEST (Parrish, 1959)...£20
THE TULLINGTON FILM-MAKERS (Parrish, 1960)...£10
TWO GOLD DOLPHINS (illustrated by Peggy Fortnum) (Constable, 1961)..£10
DANGER ON THE OLD PULL'N PUSH (Parrish, 1962) £8
STRANGE HIDING PLACE (Parrish, 1962) £8
DIANA IN TELEVISION (Collins, 1963)..£8
THE MISSING FORMULA MYSTERY (Parrish, 1963) £8
THE MULBERRY STREET TEAM (illustrated by Juliet Pannett) (Friday Press, 1963) £10
AWKWARD MAGIC (illustrated by Judith Valpy) (Hart-Davis, 1964) £8
THE FLYING DOCTOR TO THE RESCUE (Parrish, 1964)..£8
HOLIDAY FOR SLIPPY (illustrated by Pat Williams) (Friday Press, 1964)..£10
GAME, SET AND MATCH (Parrish, 1965) £15
KNIGHTS OF THE CARDBOARD CASTLE (illustrated by C.R. Evans) (Methuen, 1965)......................................£8
TRAVELLING MAGIC (illustrated by Judith Valpy) (Hart-Davis, 1965) £8
THE HIDDEN MILL (illustrated by Margery Gill) (Benn, 1965) £8
PETER CLIMBS A TREE (illustrated by Margery Gill) (Benn, 1966) £8
FASHION GIRL (Collins, 1967) £8
THE BLACK MOUNTAIN MYSTERY (Parrish, 1967)..£8
LOOKING FOR A FRIEND (illustrated by Margery Gill) (Benn, 1967) £8
THE ISLAND BUS (illustrated by Robert Hodgson) (Methuen, 1968) £8
SEA-GREEN MAGIC (illustrated by Ann Tout) (Hart-Davis, 1968) £8
DAVID GOES FISHING (illustrated by Imre Hofbauer) (Benn, 1969) £8
GORDON'S GO-KART (illustrated by Margery Gill) (Benn, 1970) £8
STEPHEN AND THE SHAGGY DOG (illustrated by Robert Hales) (Methuen, 1970) £5
VANISHING MAGIC (illustrated by Ann Tout) (Hart-Davis, 1970)..£5
DANGEROUS MAGIC (illustrated by Oliver Chadwick) (Hart-Davis, 1972) £5
THE SECRET RAILWAY (illustrated by James Hunt) (Methuen, 1973) £5
INVISIBLE MAGIC (illustrated by Reg Gray) (Hart-Davis, 1974) £5
SNUFFLE TO THE RESCUE (illustrated by Gunvor Edwards) (Kestrel, 1975)..£5
TOBY'S LUCK (illustrated by Doreen Caldwell) (Methuen, 1978) £5
SECRET MAGIC (illustrated by Caroline Sharpe) (Hart-Davis, 1978) £5
THE HAPPY GHOST (illustrated by Joanna Carey) (Methuen, 1979) £5
THE TREASURE HUNTERS (illustrated by Joanna Carey) (Methuen, 1980) £5
CURIOUS MAGIC (illustrated by Jayel Jordan) (Granada, 1980) £5
THE FOUR OF US (illustrated by Trevor Stubley) (Hutchinson, 1981) £5
THE ANIMALS NOBODY WANTED (illustrated by Joanna Carey) (Methuen, 1982)..£5
THE TOVERS (illustrated by Geoffrey Beitz) (Methuen, 1982) £5
JACK AND THE MAGIC STOVE. Retold by Elisabeth Beresford (illustrated by Rita van Bilsen) (Hutchinson, 1982) £5
THE ADVENTURES OF POON (illustrated by Dinah Shedden) (Hutchinson, 1984) £5
THE MYSTERIOUS ISLAND (illustrated by Joanna Carey) (Methuen, 1984) £5
ONE OF THE FAMILY (illustrated by Barry Thorpe) (Hutchinson, 1985) £5
THE GHOSTS OF LUPUS STREET SCHOOL (illustrated by Oliver Chadwick) (Methuen, 1986) £5
STRANGE MAGIC (illustrated by Judith Valpy) (Methuen, 1986)..£5
ONCE UPON A TIME STORIES (illustrated by Alice Englander) (Methuen, 1987) £5
EMILY AND THE HAUNTED CASTLE (illustrated by Kate Rogers) (Hutchinson, 1987) £5
THE SECRET ROOM (Methuen, 1987) £5
THE ARMADA ADVENTURE (Methuen, 1988) £5
THE ISLAND RAILWAY (Hamish Hamilton, 1988) £5
ROSE (Hutchinson, 1989) £5
THE WOODEN GUN (Hutchinson, 1989) £5
CHARLIE'S ARK (Methuen, 1989)...£5
TIM THE TRUMPET (Blackie, 1992) £5
JAMIE AND THE ROLLA POLA BEAR (Blackie, 1993) £5
LIZZY'S WAR (Simon & Schuster, 1993) £5

'BERYL THE PERIL' ANNUALS

Popular spin-offs from the *Beano* comic and annuals. Published biennially by D.C. Thomson, but irregularly in later years (post-1981).

Prices are for annuals in Very Good condition.

BERYL THE PERIL 1959 ....£75
BERYL THE PERIL 1961 ....£30
BERYL THE PERIL 1963 ....£25

BERYL THE PERIL 1965 .... £20
BERYL THE PERIL 1967 .... £15
BERYL THE PERIL 1969 .... £15
BERYL THE PERIL 1971 .... £12
BERYL THE PERIL 1973 .... £12
BERYL THE PERIL 1975 .... £10
BERYL THE PERIL 1977 .... £8
BERYL THE PERIL 1979 .... £5
BERYL THE PERIL 1981-Present ....each £3

BESTALL, Alfred

British author-illustrator. Born: Alfred Edmeads Bestall in Mandalay, Burma, on 14th December 1892.
Studied at Rydal School and Central School of Art, London, subsequently contributing work to *Blighty*,
Punch and the *Tatler*, as well as illustrating works by Blyton, Dumas and other children's authors. Took over
the *Daily Express*'s 'Rupert' strip from Mary Tourtel in 1935, and continued with the character until 1973.
Awarded an MBE in 1985. Died: 1986.
Prices are for books in Very Good condition with dustjackets where applicable.
THE PLAY'S THE THING! by Enid Blyton (Home Library Book Co., [1927]) £90
MYTHS AND LEGENDS OF MANY LANDS. Retold by Evelyn Smith (Nelson, 1930) £75
THE SPANISH GOLD-FISH by Dudley Glass (Warne, [1934])..£75
MOTHER GOOSE (Warne, 1937) £75
SCHOOLGIRL'S OWN ANNUALS (illustrated by Alfred Bestall and others) (1923 onwards)......each £20
SCHOOLGIRL'S ALBUM (illustrated by Alfred Bestall and others) (1925-27) ....each £20
PLAYS FOR OLDER CHILDREN by Enid Blyton (Newnes, 1940)...£30
PLAYS FOR YOUNGER CHILDREN by Enid Blyton (Newnes, [1940]) £30
THE BOY NEXT DOOR by Enid Blyton (Newnes, 1944) £40
THE LAND OF THE CHRISTMAS STOCKING by Mabel Buchanan (Latimer House, 1948) £30

BETJEMAN, John

British poet and architectural historian. Born: North London, 1906. Educated at Marlborough and Oxford
University. Wrote many volumes of poetry and prose, but produced only two children's titles. Knighted in
1969, and appointed Poet Laureate in 1972. Died: 1984.
Prices are for books in Very Good condition with dustjackets.
A RING OF BELLS. Introduced and selected by Irene Slade (new version of 'Summoned by Bells',
    revised for children; illustrated by Edward Ardizzone) (John Murray, 1962) £45
ARCHIE AND THE STRICT BAPTISTS (illustrated by Phillida Gili) (John Murray, 1977) £40

BIRO, Val

British author-illustrator. Born: Balint Stephen Biro in Budapest, Hungary, on 6th October 1921. Came to
Britain in July 1939 to study art, subsequently working as a freelance illustrator and producing his first
solo work, *Bumpy's Holiday*, in 1943. He is best known for the 'Gumdrop' series featuring an old Austin
motor-car.
Prices are for books in Very Good condition with dustjackets where applicable.
BUMPY'S HOLIDAY (Sylvan Press, [1943]) £60
THE WONDERFUL WIZARD OF OZ by L. Frank Baum (Dent, 1965) £30
GUMDROP: The Adventures of a Vintage Car (Brockhampton Press, 1966) £60
GUMDROP AND THE FARMER'S FRIEND (Brockhampton Press, 1967) £30
GUMDROP ON THE RALLY (Brockhampton Press, 1968) £30
GUMDROP ON THE MOVE (Brockhampton Press, 1969) £30
GUMDROP GOES TO LONDON (Brockhampton Press, 1971) £25
THE HONEST THIEF: A Hungarian Folk Tale (Brockhampton Press, 1972) £10
GUMDROP FINDS A FRIEND (Brockhampton Press, 1973) £25
BUSTER IS LOST (Macmillan, 1974) £10
GUMDROP IN DOUBLE TROUBLE (Brockhampton Press, 1975) £20
A DOG AND HIS BONE (Macmillan, 1975) £10
BRER RABBIT AND THE TAR BABY by Enid Blyton (Hodder & Stoughton, 1975) £10
GUMDROP AND THE STEAMROLLER (Hodder & Stoughton, 1976)...£18
GUMDROP POSTS A LETTER (Knight Books, 1976) £18
GUMDROP ON THE BRIGHTON RUN (Hodder & Stoughton, 1976)...£15
GUMDROP HAS A BIRTHDAY (Hodder & Stoughton, 1977) £10
THE DEVIL'S CUT by Clive King (Hodder & Stoughton, 1978) £20
GUMDROP GETS HIS WINGS (Hodder & Stoughton, 1979)...£10
HUNGARIAN FOLK-TALES (OUP, 1980)...£10
GUMDROP FINDS A GHOST (Hodder & Stoughton, 1980) £10
JUNGLE SILVER by H.E. Todd (Hodder & Stoughton, 1981)...£8
GUMDROP AND THE SECRET SWITCHES (Hodder & Stoughton, 1981) £10
GUMDROP AT SEA (Hodder & Stoughton, 1982) £10

GUMDROP ON THE MOVE

Story and Pictures by Val Biro

BROCKHAMPTON PRESS

Gumdrop on the Move (1969) was the fourth book to feature the little car. It is now worth £30 in Very Good condition.

THE MAGIC DOCTOR (OUP, 1982) £10
GUMDROP MAKES A START (Hodder & Stoughton, 1982) £8
GUMDROP AND HORACE (Hodder & Stoughton, 1982)..£8
GUMDROP RACES A TRAIN (Hodder & Stoughton, 1982)...£8
GUMDROP GOES TO SCHOOL (Hodder & Stoughton, 1983) £8
THE WIND IN THE WILLOWS (Purnell, 1983) £20
GUMDROP GETS A LIFT (Hodder & Stoughton, 1983)..£8
GUMDROP AT THE ZOO (Hodder & Stoughton, 1983) £8
GUMDROP IN A HURRY (Hodder & Stoughton, 1983) £8
FABLES FROM AESOP (eighteen volumes) (Ginn & Wright, 1983-1988)..the set £125
GUMDROP'S MAGIC JOURNEY (Hodder & Stoughton, 1984) £8
GUMDROP FISHING (Hodder & Stoughton, 1984) £8
GUMDROP HAS A TUMMY-ACHE (Hodder & Stoughton, 1984) £8
GUMDROP IS THE BEST CAR (Hodder & Stoughton, 1984) £8
GUMDROP ON THE FARM (Hodder & Stoughton, 1984) £8
GUMDROP AND THE MONSTER (Hodder & Stoughton, 1985) £8
THE HOBYAHS (OUP, 1985) £10
THE PIED PIPER OF HAMELIN (OUP, 1985) £10
TALES FROM HANS ANDERSEN (eighteen volumes) (Ginn & Wright, 1985-1989) ....the set £75
THE DONKEY THAT SNEEZED (OUP, 1986)..£10
GUMDROP TO THE RESCUE (Hodder & Stoughton, 1986) £5
GUMDROP AT SEA (Hodder & Stoughton, 1987) £5
GUMDROP AND THE DINOSAUR (Hodder & Stoughton, 1988) £5
DRANGO DRAGON (Ladybird, 1989)..£4
PETER CHEATER (Ginn, 1989) £5
JACK AND THE BEANSTALK (OUP, 1989) £10
TOBIAS AND THE DRAGON: A Folk Tale from Hungary (Blackie, 1989)...£10
GUMDROP AND THE PIRATES (Hodder & Stoughton, 1989)..£5
THE THREE LITTLE PIGS (OUP, 1990) £10
LOOK AND FIND A.B.C. (Hippo Books, 1990)...£5
MIRANDA'S UMBRELLA (Blackie, 1990) £5
GUMDROP AND THE ELEPHANT (Hodder & Stoughton, 1990)...£5
GUMDROP AND THE BULLDOZERS (Hodder & Stoughton, 1991) £5
GUMDROP FOR EVER! (paperback) (Puffin, 1991)...£5
GUMDROP'S MERRY CHRISTMAS (Hodder & Stoughton, 1992) £8
THREE BILLY GOATS GRUFF (OUP, 1992) £5
BOASTING MONSTERS (Longman, 1994) £5
MONSTER FEAST (Longman, 1994) £5
MONSTER PACK (Longman, 1994) £5

Black Bob, the 'Dandy Wonder Dog', featured in no fewer than eight D.C. Thomson annuals between 1950 and 1965.

'BLACK BOB' ANNUALS

Popular series of spin-off annuals, published by D.C. Thomson, featuring the Dandy's 'wonder dog', Black Bob. Note that the books were published biennially between 1951 and 1965, and that there was no edition for 1963.

Prices are for annuals in Very Good condition.

BLACK BOB 1950 ....£75
BLACK BOB 1951 ....£40
BLACK BOB 1953 ....£30
BLACK BOB 1955 ....£30
BLACK BOB 1957 ....£25
BLACK BOB 1959 ....£20
BLACK BOB 1961 ....£20
BLACK BOB 1965 ....£20

BLAKE, Quentin

British author-illustrator. Born: Sidcup, Kent, in 1932. Illustrated his own work and that of many others, notably Roald Dahl. He was a tutor at the Royal College of Art from 1965 to 1988. He won the Kate Greenaway Medal for *Mr Magnolia*, the Kurt Maschler Award for *All Join In* and the international Bologna Ragazzi Prize for *Clown*. He was awarded the OBE in 1988. He was appointed the first Children's Laureate in May 1999.

Prices are for books in Very Good condition with dustjackets where applicable.

Books Written and Illustrated by Quentin Blake

PATRICK (Cape, 1968) £30
JACK AND NANCY (Cape, 1969)...£30
BAND OF ANGELS (Gordon Fraser, 1969) £15
ANGELO (Cape, 1970) £30
THE ADVENTURES OF LESTER (BBC, 1971) £30
THE PUFFIN BOOK OF IMPROBABLE RECORDS (with John Yeoman; paperback) (Puffin, 1975) £15
HORSESHOE HARRY AND THE WHALE (Dobson, 1976) £25

THE BED BOOK (Faber, 1976)..£45
THE ADVENTURES OF LESTER ('Jackanory Stories') (BBC, 1977) £50
MR MAGNOLIA (Cape, 1980)..£20
ACE DRAGON LTD (Cape, 1980)..£15
QUENTIN BLAKE'S NURSERY RHYME BOOK (Cape, 1983) £20
THE STORY OF THE DANCING FROG (Cape, 1984) £20
A LAMP FOR THE LAMB CHOPS (Methuen, 1985) £20
DON'T PUT MUSTARD ON THE CUSTARD (Deutsch, 1985) £20
MRS ARMITAGE ON WHEELS (Cape, 1987) £20
ABC (Cape, 1989)..£15
QUENTIN BLAKE BOOK OF NONSENSE VERSE (Viking, 1994) £30
CLOWN (Cape, 1995) £15
THE GREEN SHIP (Cape, 1998) £15
FANTASTIC DAISY ARTICHOKE (Cape, 1999)..£10

Books Illustrated by Quentin Blake

PUNKY, MOUSE FOR A DAY by John Moreton (Faber, 1962) £15
UNCLE by J.P. Martin (Cape, 1964) £45
UNCLE CLEANS UP by J.P. Martin (Cape, 1965) £45
UNCLE AND HIS DETECTIVE by J.P. Martin (Cape, 1966)..£45
UNCLE AND HIS TREACLE TROUBLE by J.P. Martin (Cape, 1967)..£45
ALBERT THE DRAGON AND THE CENTAUR by Rosemary Weir (Abelard-Schuman, 1968) £20
UNCLE AND CLAUDIUS THE CAMEL by J.P. Martin (Cape, 1969) £45
MR HORROX AND THE GRATCH by James Reeves (Abelard-Schuman, 1969) £25
CARLSON by Natalie Savage (Blackie, 1972) £15
ARABEL'S RAVEN by Joan Aiken (BBC, 1972) £15
MOUSE TROUBLE by John Yeoman (Macmillan, 1972)..£15
MCBROOM'S ONE-ACRE FARM by S. Fleischman (Chatto & Windus, 1972) £15
THE ESCAPED BLACK MAMBA by Joan Aiken (BBC, 1973) £15
UNCLE AND THE BATTLE FOR BADGERTOWN by J.P. Martin (Cape, 1973)..................................£45
HOW TOM BEAT CAPTAIN NAJORK AND HIS HIRED SPORTSMEN by Russell Hoban (Cape, 1974)....£25
THE BREAD BIN by Joan Aiken (paperback) (BBC, 1974) £5

Clown (1995) is one of Quentin Blake's most popular works. The first edition is now worth £15 in Very Good condition.

Blake provided the illustrations for several Roald Dahl books, including **Matilda***. You can expect to pay £60 for a first edition.*

MIND YOUR OWN BUSINESS by Michael Rosen (Deutsch, 1974)	£15
A NEAR THING FOR CAPTAIN NAJORK by Russell Hoban (Cape, 1975)	£25
A GREAT DAY FOR UP! by Dr Seuss (Collins, 1975)	£15
MORTIMER'S TIE by Joan Aiken (paperback) (BBC, 1976)	£5
THE HUNTING OF THE SNARK by Lewis Carroll (in slipcase) (Folio Society, 1976)	£30
THE HUNTING OF THE SNARK by Lewis Carroll (facsimile edition; issued with dustjacket) (Windward, 1980)	£10
THE ENORMOUS CROCODILE by Roald Dahl (Cape, 1978)	£35
MORTIMER AND THE SWORD EXCALIBUR by Joan Aiken (BBC, 1979)	£15
THE SPIRAL STAIR by Joan Aiken (paperback) (BBC, 1979)	£5
ARABEL AND MORTIMER by Joan Aiken (contains 'Mortimer's Tie', 'Mortimer and the sword Excalibur' and 'The Spiral Stair') (Cape, 1980)	£15
MORTIMER'S PORTRAIT ON GLASS by Joan Aiken (paperback) (BBC, 1980)	£5
MR JONES'S DISAPPEARING TAXI by Joan Aiken (paperback) (BBC, 1980)	£5
THE TWITS by Roald Dahl (Cape, 1980)	£35
ACE DRAGON LTD by Russell Hoban (Cape, 1980)	£15
GEORGE'S MARVELLOUS MEDICINE by Roald Dahl (Cape, 1981)	£45
THE BFG by Roald Dahl (Cape, 1982)	£50
ROALD DAHL'S REVOLTING RHYMES by Roald Dahl (Cape, 1982)	£50
MORTIMER'S CROSS by Joan Aiken (BBC/Cape, 1983)	£15
THE WITCHES by Roald Dahl (Cape, 1983)	£50
HOW THE CAMEL GOT HIS HUMP by Rudyard Kipling (Macmillan, 1984)	£15
DIRTY BEASTS by Roald Dahl (Cape, 1984)	£30
MORTIMER SAYS NOTHING by Joan Aiken (Cape, 1985)	£15
THE GIRAFFE, THE PELLY AND ME by Roald Dahl (Cape, 1985)	£45
SMELL JELLY SMELL FISH by Michael Rosen (Walker, 1986)	£15
ASK DR PETE by Doctor Peter Rowan (Cape, 1986)	£15
THE RAIN DOOR by Russell Hoban (Gollancz, 1986)	£20
THE MARZIPAN PIG by Russell Hoban (Cape, 1986)	£20
SPOLLJOLLY-DIDDLY-TIDDLYITIS by Michael Rosen (Walker, 1987)	£15
MATILDA by Roald Dahl (Cape, 1988)	£60
TAIL FEATHERS FROM MOTHER GOOSE by Iona Opie (illustrated by Quentin Blake and others) (Walker, 1988)	£30
RHYME STEW by Roald Dahl (Cape, 1989)	£25
ALPHABEASTS by Dick King-Smith (Gollancz, 1990)	£15
ESIO TROT by Roald Dahl (Cape, 1990)	£20
VICAR OF NIBBLESWICKE by Roald Dahl (Century,1991)	£20
ROALD DAHL'S GUIDE TO RAILWAY SAFETY by Roald Dahl (pamphlet) (British Rail, 1991)	£15
A HANDFUL OF GOLD by Joan Aiken (Cape, 1995)	£10
FANTASTIC MR FOX by Roald Dahl (Viking, 1996)	£15
BREAKFAST WITH DOLLY by John Hedgecoe (Collins, 1996)	£15
CHARLIE AND THE CHOCOLATE FACTORY by Roald Dahl (Puffin hardback, 1997)	£20
UP WITH THE BIRDS by John Yeoman (Hamilton, 1998)	£10

'BLUE PETER' ANNUALS

The BBC's hugely popular twice-weekly magazine programme for children was launched in 1958 and has inspired a number of spin-off books and annuals.

Prices are for annuals in Very Good condition.

BLUE PETER NO. 1 (BBC, 1964)	£100
BLUE PETER NO. 2 (BBC, 1965)	£35
BLUE PETER NO. 3 (BBC, 1966)	£20
BLUE PETER NO. 4 to No. 9 (BBC, 1967-72)	£10
BLUE PETER NOS. 5 to Present (BBC, 1973 to present)	each £6

BLYTON, Enid

The most successful British children's author of the twentieth century. Born: Enid Mary Blyton in London on 11th August 1897, and spent her childhood in the suburb of Beckenham. After school, studied to be a kindergarten teacher, at the same time submitting verses and stories to various magazines, including *Teachers' World*. Her first book, a volume of poems entitled *Child Whispers*, was published in 1922, and was followed by *The Enid Blyton Book of Fairies* (1924), *Sunny Stories for Little Folk* (1926) and countless other works. Best known for the 'Famous Five' (1942 onwards) and 'Secret Seven' (1949 onwards) series, and the phenomenally popular 'Noddy' books (1949 onwards). Died: 1968.

Prices are for books in Very Good condition with dustjackets where applicable.

'Famous Five' Books

FIVE ON A TREASURE ISLAND: An Adventure Story (illustrated by Eileen Soper) (Hodder & Stoughton, 1942)	£500
FIVE GO ADVENTURING AGAIN (illustrated by Eileen Soper) (Hodder & Stoughton, 1943)	£250
FIVE RUN AWAY TOGETHER (illustrated by Eileen Soper) (Hodder & Stoughton, 1944)	£200
FIVE GO TO SMUGGLERS' TOP (illustrated by Eileen Soper) (Hodder & Stoughton, 1945)	£300

One of the eight collectable 'Adventure' books which the hugely-prolific Enid Blyton wrote between 1944 and 1955.

*The second book in the series, **The Castle of Adventure** (1946), is now worth £75 in its colourful Stuart Tresilian dustjacket.*

FIVE GO OFF IN A CARAVAN (illustrated by Eileen Soper) (Hodder & Stoughton, 1946) £200
FIVE ON KIRRIN ISLAND AGAIN (illustrated by Eileen Soper) (Hodder & Stoughton, 1947) £150
FIVE GO OFF TO CAMP (illustrated by Eileen Soper) (Hodder & Stoughton, 1948).......................................£120
FIVE GET INTO TROUBLE (illustrated by Eileen Soper) (Hodder & Stoughton, 1949) £100
FIVE FALL INTO ADVENTURE (illustrated by Eileen Soper) (Hodder & Stoughton, 1950) £75
FIVE ON A HIKE TOGETHER (illustrated by Eileen Soper) (Hodder & Stoughton, 1951)....................................£55
FIVE HAVE A WONDERFUL TIME (illustrated by Eileen Soper) (Hodder & Stoughton, [1952]) £55
FIVE GO DOWN TO THE SEA (illustrated by Eileen Soper) (Hodder & Stoughton, 1953) £45
FIVE GO TO MYSTERY MOOR (illustrated by Eileen Soper) (Hodder & Stoughton, 1954) £45
FIVE HAVE PLENTY OF FUN (illustrated by Eileen Soper) (Hodder & Stoughton, 1955) £40
FIVE ON A SECRET TRAIL (illustrated by Eileen Soper) (Hodder & Stoughton, 1956) £40
FIVE GO TO BILLYCOCK HILL (illustrated by Eileen Soper) (Hodder & Stoughton, 1957) £40
FIVE GET INTO A FIX (illustrated by Eileen Soper) (Hodder & Stoughton, [1958])..£35
THE FAMOUS FIVE SPECIAL (contains 'Five Go Off to Camp', 'Five Go Off in a Caravan' and
  'Five Have a Wonderful Time'; illustrated by Eileen Soper) (Hodder & Stoughton, 1959)...............................£35
FIVE ON FINNISTON FARM (illustrated by Eileen Soper) (Hodder & Stoughton, [1960]) £35
FIVE GO TO DEMON'S ROCKS (illustrated by Eileen Soper) (Hodder & Stoughton, 1961) £35
FIVE HAVE A MYSTERY TO SOLVE (illustrated by Eileen Soper) (Hodder & Stoughton, 1962) £35
FIVE ARE TOGETHER AGAIN (illustrated by Eileen Soper) (Hodder & Stoughton, 1963) £35
THE FAMOUS FIVE BIG BOOK (contains 'Five on a Treasure Island', 'Five Go Adventuring Again' and
  'Five Run Away Together'; illustrated by Eileen Soper) (Hodder & Stoughton, 1964).....................................£35
FIVE HAVE A PUZZLING TIME & OTHER STORIES (paperback) (Red Fox 1995) £5

'Adventure' Books

THE ISLAND OF ADVENTURE (illustrated by Stuart Tresilian) (Macmillan, 1944) £100
THE CASTLE OF ADVENTURE (illustrated by Stuart Tresilian) (Macmillan, 1946)..£75
THE VALLEY OF ADVENTURE (illustrated by Stuart Tresilian) (Macmillan, 1947) £75
THE SEA OF ADVENTURE (illustrated by Stuart Tresilian) (Macmillan, 1948) £75
THE MOUNTAIN OF ADVENTURE (illustrated by Stuart Tresilian) (Macmillan, 1949) £75
THE SHIP OF ADVENTURE (illustrated by Stuart Tresilian) (Macmillan, 1950)..£60
THE CIRCUS OF ADVENTURE (illustrated by Stuart Tresilian) (Macmillan, 1952) £55
THE RIVER OF ADVENTURE (illustrated by Stuart Tresilian) (Macmillan, 1955) £55

'Secret Seven' Books

THE SECRET SEVEN (illustrated by George Brook) (Brockhampton Press, 1949)..£60
SECRET SEVEN ADVENTURE (illustrated by George Brook) (Brockhampton Press, 1950) £35
WELL DONE, SECRET SEVEN (illustrated by George Brook) (Brockhampton Press, 1951) £30
SECRET SEVEN ON THE TRAIL (illustrated by George Brook) (Brockhampton Press, 1952) £30
GO AHEAD SECRET SEVEN (illustrated by Bruno Kay) (Brockhampton Press, 1953) £30
GOOD WORK, SECRET SEVEN! (illustrated by Bruno Kay) (Brockhampton Press, 1954) £30
SECRET SEVEN WIN THROUGH (illustrated by Bruno Kay) (Brockhampton Press, 1955) £30
THREE CHEERS SECRET SEVEN (illustrated by Burgess Sharrocks) (Brockhampton Press, 1956) £30
SECRET SEVEN MYSTERY (illustrated by Burgess Sharrocks) (Brockhampton Press, 1957)...........................£25
PUZZLE FOR THE SECRET SEVEN (illustrated by Burgess Sharrocks) (Brockhampton Press, 1958) £25
SECRET SEVEN FIREWORKS (illustrated by Burgess Sharrocks) (Brockhampton Press, 1959) £25
GOOD OLD SECRET SEVEN (illustrated by Burgess Sharrocks) (Brockhampton Press, 1960) £25
SHOCK FOR THE SECRET SEVEN (illustrated by Burgess Sharrocks) (Brockhampton Press, 1961) £25
LOOK OUT SECRET SEVEN (illustrated by Burgess Sharrocks) (Brockhampton Press, 1962)......................£25
FUN FOR THE SECRET SEVEN (illustrated by Burgess Sharrocks) (Brockhampton Press, 1963) £25

'Mystery' Books

THE MYSTERY OF THE BURNT COTTAGE (illustrated by J. Abbey) (Methuen, 1943) £200
THE MYSTERY OF THE DISAPPEARING CAT (illustrated by J. Abbey) (Methuen, 1944).................................£150
THE MYSTERY OF THE SECRET ROOM (illustrated by J. Abbey) (Methuen, 1945) £100
THE MYSTERY OF THE SPITEFUL LETTERS (illustrated by J. Abbey) (Methuen, 1946) £60
THE MYSTERY OF THE MISSING NECKLACE (illustrated by J. Abbey) (Methuen, 1947) £55
THE MYSTERY OF THE HIDDEN HOUSE (illustrated by J. Abbey) (Methuen, 1948)..£55
THE MYSTERY OF THE PANTOMIME CAT (Methuen, 1949) £50
THE MYSTERY OF THE INVISIBLE THIEF (Methuen, 1950) £40
THE MYSTERY OF THE VANISHED PRINCE: Being the Ninth Adventure of the Five Find-Outers and Dog
   (illustrated by Treyer Evans) (Methuen, 1951) £40
THE MYSTERY OF THE STRANGE BUNDLE (illustrated by Treyer Evans) (Methuen, 1952) £40
THE MYSTERY OF HOLLY LANE (illustrated by Treyer Evans) (Methuen, 1953)..£40
THE MYSTERY OF TALLY-HO COTTAGE (illustrated by Treyer Evans) (Methuen, 1954) £40
THE MYSTERY OF THE MISSING MAN (illustrated by Lilian Buchanan) (Methuen, 1956)..............................£40
THE MYSTERY OF THE STRANGE MESSAGES (illustrated by Lilian Buchanan) (Methuen, 1957) £40
THE MYSTERY OF BANSHEE TOWERS (illustrated by Lilian Buchanan) (Methuen, 1961)............................£40

'Barney Junior Mystery' Books

THE ROCKINGDOWN MYSTERY (illustrated by Gilbert Dunlop) (Collins, [1949]) £35
THE RILLOBY FAIR MYSTERY (illustrated by Gilbert Dunlop) (Collins, [1950]) £30
THE RING O'BELLS MYSTERY (illustrated by Gilbert Dunlop) (Collins, 1951)..£25
THE RUBADUB MYSTERY (illustrated by Gilbert Dunlop) (Collins, 1952) £25
THE RAT-A-TAT MYSTERY (illustrated by Gilbert Dunlop) (Collins, 1956) £25
THE RAGAMUFFIN MYSTERY (illustrated by Gilbert Dunlop) (Collins, 1959) £25

'St. Clare's School' Books

THE TWINS AT ST. CLARE'S (Methuen, 1941) £45
THE O'SULLIVAN TWINS: Another School Story about St. Clare's (Methuen, 1942).....................................£45
SUMMER TERM AT ST. CLARE'S (Methuen, 1943) £40
CLAUDINE AT ST. CLARE'S (Methuen, 1944) £35
THE SECOND FORM AT ST. CLARE'S (illustrated by W. Lindsay Cable) (Methuen, 1944) £35
FIFTH FORMERS AT ST. CLARE'S (illustrated by W. Lindsay Cable) (Methuen, 1945) £35

'Malory Towers' Books

FIRST TERM AT MALORY TOWERS (illustrated by Stanley Lloyd) (Methuen, 1946) £40
THE SECOND FORM AT MALORY TOWERS (illustrated by Stanley Lloyd) (Methuen, 1947) £35
THIRD YEAR AT MALORY TOWERS (illustrated by Stanley Lloyd) (Methuen, 1948) £35
THE UPPER FOURTH AT MALORY TOWERS (illustrated by Stanley Lloyd) (Methuen, 1949) £35
IN THE FIFTH AT MALORY TOWERS (illustrated by Stanley Lloyd) (Methuen, 1950) £35
LAST TERM AT MALORY TOWERS (illustrated by Stanley Lloyd) (Methuen, 1951).......................................£35

Numbered 'Noddy' Books

NO. 1: NODDY GOES TO TOYLAND (Sampson Low, 1949) £75
NO. 2: HURRAH FOR LITTLE NODDY (Sampson Low, 1950) £50
NO. 3: NODDY AND HIS CAR (Sampson Low, 1951) £45
NO. 4: HERE COMES NODDY AGAIN! (Sampson Low, 1951) £40
NO. 5: WELL DONE, NODDY! (Sampson Low, 1952) £40
NO. 6: NODDY GOES TO SCHOOL (Sampson Low, 1952) £40
NO. 7: NODDY AT THE SEASIDE (Sampson Low, 1953) £40
NO. 8: NODDY GETS INTO TROUBLE (Sampson Low, 1954) £40
NO. 9: NODDY AND THE MAGIC RUBBER (Sampson Low, 1954)...£40
NO. 10: YOU FUNNY LITTLE NODDY (Sampson Low, 1955) £40
NO. 11: NODDY MEETS FATHER CHRISTMAS (Sampson Low, 1955) £40

Noddy Goes to Toyland (1949) was the first of 24 books featuring the popular characters, Noddy and Big Ears.

The third book in the series, *Noddy and his Car* (1951), is now worth £45 in Very Good condition with the dustjacket.

NO. 12: NODDY AND TESSIE BEAR (Sampson Low, 1956) £40
NO. 13: BE BRAVE, LITTLE NODDY! (Sampson Low, 1956) £40
NO. 14: NODDY AND THE BUMPY-DOG (Sampson Low, 1957) £40
NO. 15: DO LOOK OUT, NODDY! (Sampson Low, 1957) £40
NO. 16: YOU'RE A GOOD FRIEND, NODDY! (Sampson Low, 1958) £40
NO. 17: NODDY HAS AN ADVENTURE (Sampson Low, 1958) £40
NO. 18: NODDY GOES TO SEA (Sampson Low, 1959) £40
NO. 19: NODDY AND THE BUNKEY (Sampson Low, 1959) £40
NO. 20: CHEER UP, LITTLE NODDY! (Sampson Low, 1960) £40
NO. 21: NODDY GOES TO THE FAIR (Sampson Low, 1960)...£40
NO. 22: MR PLOD AND LITTLE NODDY (Sampson Low, 1961) £40
NO. 23: NODDY AND THE TOOTLES (Sampson Low, 1962) £40
NO. 24: NODDY AND THE AEROPLANE (Sampson Low, 1964) £40

Other 'Noddy' Books

NODDY'S HOUSE OF BOOKS ('The Tiny Noddy Book Nos. 1-6'; pictorial wraps; in cardboard case;
    issued without dustjackets) (Sampson Low, [1951]) ....the set £125 (each £12)
THE BIG NODDY BOOK (illustrated by Beek; issued without dustjacket) (Sampson Low, 1952) £40
ENID BLYTON'S NODDY PAINTING BOOKS (Robinson, [1952])..£20
ENID BLYTON'S NODDY COLOUR STRIP BOOK (illustrated by Beek) (Sampson Low, [1952]) £20
ENID BLYTON'S NODDY'S ARK OF BOOKS (five books; in ornamental cardboard case;
    issued without dustjackets) (Sampson Low, [1952]) ....the set £125 (each £12)
THE NEW BIG NODDY BOOK (Sampson Low, 1953) £30
NODDY CUT-OUT MODEL BOOK (Sampson Low, 1953) £75
NODDY'S GARAGE OF BOOKS (five books; illustrated by Beek; pictorial wraps; in cardboard case;
    issued without dustjackets) (Sampson Low, [1953])...the set £125 (each £12)
ENID BLYTON'S NODDY GIANT PAINTING BOOK (issued without dustjacket) (Sampson Low, [1954]) £20
ENID BLYTON'S NODDY POP-UP BOOK (issued without dustjacket) (Sampson Low, [1954]) £35
NODDY STRIP BOOKS (pictorial wraps; issued without dustjackets) (Sampson Low, [1954])............each £20
NODDY'S CASTLE OF BOOKS (five books; illustrated by Beek; pictorial wraps;
    in ornamental cardboard case; issued without dustjackets) (Sampson Low, [1954]) ....the set £125 (each £12)
A DAY WITH NODDY (Sampson Low, [1956]) £25
ENID BLYTON'S BOOK OF HER FAMOUS PLAY 'NODDY IN TOYLAND' (Sampson Low, [1956]) £60
ENID BLYTON'S NODDY PLAY DAY PAINTING BOOK (issued without dustjacket) (Sampson Low, [1956]) £20
NODDY AND HIS FRIENDS (pop-up picture book; issued without dustjacket) (Sampson Low, [1956]) £30
THE NODDY TOY STATION BOOK NOS. 1-5 (in cardboard case) (Sampson Low, [1956]) ....the set £125 (each £12)
NODDY'S NEW BIG BOOK (Sampson Low, 1957) £25
MY BIG EARS PICTURE BOOK (Sampson Low, [1958]) £25

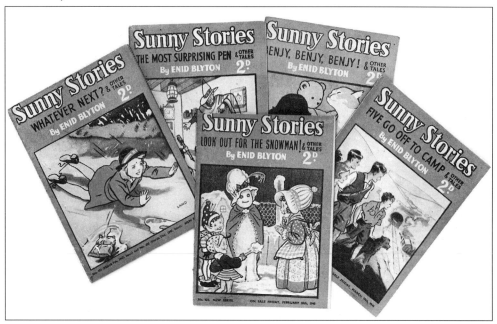

*Five issues of the 'new series' **Sunny Stories**, a twopenny story paper published by Newnes and written entirely by Enid Blyton.*

MY NODDY PICTURE BOOK (Sampson Low, [1958]) £25
NODDY'S SHOP OF BOOK NOS. 1-5 (in cardboard case) (Sampson Low, [1958]).....................the set **£125** (each **£12**)
NODDY'S OWN NURSERY RHYMES (Sampson Low, [1958]) £25
A.B.C. WITH NODDY (Sampson Low, [1959]) £20
NODDY'S CAR PICTURE BOOK (Sampson Low, 1959) £15
NODDY'S TALL BLUE (GREEN-ORANGE-PINK-RED-YELLOW) BOOK (set of six books) (Sampson Low, [1960])..........each **£25**
NODDY AND THE TUBBY BEARS (rag book) (Dean, 1960) £20
NODDY'S ONE, TWO, THREE BOOK (Sampson Low, [1961]) £15
NODDY'S TOYLAND TRAIN PICTURE BOOK (Sampson Low, [1961]) £15
A DAY AT SCHOOL WITH NODDY (Sampson Low [1962])...£15
ENID BLYTON'S NODDY (board book) (Purnell, [c.1963])...£15
NODDY TREASURE BOX (Sampson Low, [1965])...£20
LEARN TO COUNT WITH NODDY (Sampson Low, [1965]) £15
LEARN TO GO SHOPPING WITH NODDY (Sampson Low, [1965]) £15
LEARN TO READ ABOUT ANIMALS WITH NODDY (Sampson Low, [1965]) £15
LEARN TO TELL THE TIME WITH NODDY (Sampson Low, [1965]) £15
NODDY AND HIS FRIENDS: A Nursery Picture Book (Sampson Low, 1965) £15
NODDY AND BIG-EARS (Sampson Low, [1967])...£15
NODDY AND HIS PASSENGERS (Sampson Low, [1967]) £15
NODDY AND THE MAGIC BOOTS: With 'Noddy's Funny Kite' (the cover bears the title 'Noddy's Funny Kite')
   (Sampson Low, [1967]) £15
NODDY AND THE NOAH'S ARK ADVENTURE PICTURE BOOK (Sampson Low, [1967]) £15
ENID BLYTON'S NODDY (board book) (Purnell, 1967) £15
NODDY IN TOYLAND PICTURE BOOK (Sampson Low, 1967)..£15
NODDY'S TOYLAND ABC PICTURE BOOK (Sampson Low, [1967]) £15
NODDY'S AEROPLANE PICTURE BOOK (Sampson Low, [1967]) £15

Strip Books (all in pictorial wraps, and issued without dustjackets)
MARY MOUSE AND THE DOLLS HOUSE (Brockhampton Press, [1942]) £15
MORE ADVENTURES OF MARY MOUSE (Brockhampton Press, [1943]) £15
LITTLE MARY MOUSE AGAIN (Brockhampton Press, [1944]) £15
HALLO, LITTLE MARY MOUSE (illustrated by Olive F. Openshaw) (Brockhampton Press, [1945]) £15
MARY MOUSE AND HER FAMILY (illustrated by Olive F. Openshaw) (Brockhampton Press, [1946]) £15
HERE COMES MARY MOUSE AGAIN (Brockhampton Press, 1947) £15
HOW DO YOU DO, MARY MOUSE (Brockhampton Press, 1948) £15
WELCOME MARY MOUSE (illustrated by Olive F. Openshaw) (Brockhampton Press, [1950])...............£15
WE DO LOVE MARY MOUSE (Brockhampton Press, 1950) £15
A PRIZE FOR MARY MOUSE (Brockhampton Press, [1951]) £15
HURRAH FOR MARY MOUSE (Brockhampton Press, 1951) £15

MARY MOUSE AND HER BICYCLE (illustrated by Olive F. Openshaw) (Brockhampton Press, [1952]) £15
MANDY, MOPS AND CUBBY AGAIN (Sampson Low, 1952) £15
MANDY, MOPS AND CUBBY FIND A HOUSE (Sampson Low, 1952) £15
MR TUMPY PLAYS A TRICK ON SAUCEPAN (Sampson Low, 1952)...................£15
MARY MOUSE AND THE NOAH'S ARK (illustrated by Olive F. Openshaw) (Brockhampton Press, [1953]) £15
CLICKY THE CLOCKWORK CLOWN (Brockhampton Press, 1953)...................£15
MANDY MAKES CUBBY A HAT (Sampson Low, 1953) £15
MR TUMPY IN THE LAND OF WISHES (Sampson Low, 1953) £15
MARY MOUSE TO THE RESCUE (Brockhampton Press, [1954]) £15
MANDY, MOPS AND CUBBY AND THE WHITEWASH (Sampson Low, [1955]) £15
GOBO IN THE LAND OF DREAMS (Sampson Low, [1955]) £15
MARY MOUSE IN NURSERY RHYME LAND (Brockhampton Press, [1955]) £15
MR TUMPY IN THE LAND OF BOYS AND GIRLS (Sampson Low, [1955]) £15
BOM BOOK (Brockhampton Press, 1956) £15
A DAY WITH MARY MOUSE (illustrated by Frederick White) (Brockhampton Press, [1956]) £15
BOM THE LITTLE TOY DRUMMER (Brockhampton Press, 1956) £15
MARY MOUSE AND THE GARDEN PARTY (illustrated by Frederick White) (Brockhampton Press, [1957]) £15
BOM AND HIS MAGIC DRUMSTICK (Brockhampton Press, 1957) £15
BOM GOES ADVENTURING (illustrated by R. Paul Höye) (Brockhampton Press, 1958) £15
CLICKY GETS INTO TROUBLE (illustrated by Molly Brett) (Brockhampton Press, [1958]) £15
MARY MOUSE GOES TO THE FAIR (illustrated by Frederick White) (Brockhampton Press, [1958]) £15
BOM AND THE RAINBOW (illustrated by R. Paul Höye) (Brockhampton Press, 1959)...................£15
HELLO BOM AND WUFFY DOG (illustrated by R. Paul Höye) (Brockhampton Press, [1959])...................£15
MARY MOUSE HAS A WONDERFUL IDEA (illustrated by Fred White) (Brockhampton Press, [1959])...................£15
BOM AND THE CLOWN (Brockhampton Press, 1959) £15
CLICKY AND TIPTOE (illustrated by Molly Brett) (Brockhampton Press, 1960) £15
HERE COMES BOM (illustrated by R. Paul Höye) (Brockhampton Press, [1960])...................£15
MARY MOUSE GOES TO SEA (illustrated by Fred White) (Brockhampton Press, [1960]) £15
BOM GOES TO MAGIC TOWN (Brockhampton Press, 1960) £15
BOM AT THE SEASIDE (illustrated by R. Paul Höye) (Brockhampton Press, 1961) £15
BOM GOES TO THE CIRCUS (illustrated by R. Paul Höye) (Brockhampton Press, [1961]) £15
HAPPY BIRTHDAY CLICKY (illustrated by Molly Brett) (Brockhampton Press, [1961]) £15
MARY MOUSE GOES OUT FOR THE DAY (illustrated by Fred White) (Brockhampton Press, [1961]) £15
HAPPY HOLIDAY, CLICKY (illustrated by Molly Brett) (Brockhampton Press, 1961) £15
FUN WITH MARY MOUSE (illustrated by R. Paul Höye) (Brockhampton Press, 1962) £15
MARY MOUSE AND THE LITTLE DONKEY (illustrated by R. Paul Höye) (Brockhampton Press, [1964]) £15

Miscellaneous and Related Titles

NASH & PALL MALL MAGAZINE (March 1917, August 1917 and September 1918 issues; in original covers)...................each £15
TEACHER'S WORLD MAGAZINE (issues including Blyton contributions, from 1922 onwards)...................each £10
CHILD WHISPERS (poems; pictorial card covers) (J. Saville, [1922]) £225
CHILD WHISPERS (poems; issued with dustjacket) (J. Saville, 1923) £225
RESPONSIVE SINGING GAMES (card covers; issued without dustjacket) (J. Saville, 1923) £100
REAL FAIRIES (poems; issued with dustjacket) (J. Saville, 1923) £225
REAL FAIRIES (poems; pictorial card covers) (J. Saville, 1923) £225
SONGS OF GLADNESS (words by Enid Blyton; music by Alec Rowley; card wraps; issued without dustjacket)
    (J. Saville, 1924)...................£100
THE ZOO BOOK (Newnes, [1924])...................£30
THE ENID BLYTON BOOK OF FAIRIES (Newnes, [1924]) £60
SPORTS AND GAMES (illustrated by Richard Ogle; boards) (Birn, 1924) £150
SONGS OF GLADNESS (large format; card covers) (J. Saville, 1924) £100
SILVER AND GOLD (poems; illustrated by Lewis Baumer) (Nelson, [1925]) £100
THE ENID BLYTON BOOK OF BUNNIES (Newnes, [1925]) £60
READING PRACTICE NOS. 1-5, 8, 9 & 11 (others not published; issued without dustjackets) (Nelson, [1925-1926]) ....each £15
THE ENID BLYTON BOOK OF BROWNIES (illustrated by Ernest Aris) (Newnes, [1926]) £60
TALES HALF TOLD (Nelson, 1926) £75
THE BIRD BOOK (illustrated by Ronald Green; plates) (Newnes, [1926])...................£25
THE TEACHER'S TREASURY. Edited by Enid Blyton (three volumes) (Newnes, [1926]) ....each £15
SUNNY STORIES FOR LITTLE FOLKS MAGAZINES. Edited by Enid Blyton (240 issues) (Newnes, [1926-1936]) ....each £8
THE ANIMAL BOOK (illustrated by K. Nixon) (Newnes, [1927]) £20
A BOOK OF LITTLE PLAYS (Nelson, 1927) £25
THE PLAY'S THE THING: Musical Plays for Children (music by Alec Rowley; illustrated by Alfred E. Bestall)
    (Home Library Book Co., [1927]) £100
LET'S PRETEND (illustrated by I. Bennington Angrave) (Nelson, [1928]) £45
AESOP'S FABLES RETOLD (Nelson, 1928) £25
OLD ENGLISH TALES RETOLD (Nelson, 1928) £25
PINKITY'S PRANKS and Other Nature Fairy Stories: Retold (Nelson, 1928) £25
TALES OF BRER RABBIT RETOLD (Nelson, 1928) £25
ENID BLYTON'S NATURE LESSONS (Evans, 1929) £15
TARRYDIDDLE TOWN (Nelson, 1929) £25

THE KNIGHTS OF THE ROUND TABLE (Newnes, [1930]) £30
TALES FROM THE ARABIAN NIGHTS. Retold By Enid Blyton (Newnes, [1930]) £30
TALES OF ANCIENT GREECE (Newnes, [1930]) £30
TALES OF ROBIN HOOD (Newnes, [1930])...£30
PICTORIAL KNOWLEDGE (Enid Blyton was assistant editor and contributed the verse section; ten volumes)
   (Newnes, 1930) ....the set £40
MY FIRST READING BOOK (Birn, [1933])...£30
CHEERIO! A Book for Boys and Girls (Birn, [1933]) £60
FIVE MINUTE TALES: Sixty Short Stories for Children (Methuen, 1933) £30
LET'S READ (Birn, [1933])...£25
READ TO US (Birn, 1933) £25
THE ADVENTURES OF ODYSSEUS: Stories from World History Retold (Evans, 1934) £20
THE STORY OF THE SIEGE OF TROY: Stories from World History Retold (Evans, 1934)......£20
TALES OF THE ANCIENT GREEKS AND PERSIANS: Stories from World History Retold (Evans, 1934) £20
TALES OF THE ROMANS: Stories from World History Retold (Evans, 1934).......................£20
THE ENID BLYTON POETRY BOOK (Methuen, 1934) £35
THE RED PIXIE BOOK (issued with dustjacket) (Newnes, [1934]) £75
ROUND THE YEAR WITH ENID BLYTON: A Year's Nature Study for Children (four books: 'Spring', 'Summer',
   'Autumn' and 'Winter'; issued without dustjackets) (Evans, [1934]).........................the set £20
TEN-MINUTE TALES: Twenty-Nine Varied Stories for Children (Methuen, 1934) £25
THE OLD THATCH SERIES (eight volumes; issued without dustjackets) (W. & A.K. Johnston, 1934-1935) ......each £12
TREASURE TROVE READERS ('Junior' series only compiled by Enid Blyton ['Senior' series complied by Cyril Midgley];
   issued without dustjackets) (A. Wheaton, 1934-1935) ....each £12
THE STRANGE TALE OF MR WUMBLE (pictorial wraps; issued without dustjacket) (Coker, [1935]) £20
HOP, SKIP AND JUMP (pictorial wraps; issued without dustjacket) (Coker, [1935]) £20
THE TALKING TEAPOT and Other Tales (Coker, [1935]) £20
BRER RABBIT. Retold by Enid Blyton ([1935]) £20
THE CHILDREN'S GARDEN (Newnes, [1935]) £25
THE GREEN GOBLIN BOOK (Newnes, [1935])..£80
HEDGEROW TALES (illustrated by Vere Temple) (Methuen, 1935) £20
NATURE OBSERVATION PICTURES (32 pictures from 'The Birds of the British Isles' by T.A. Coward;
   selected by and with footnotes by Enid Blyton; in four folders) (Warne, 1935) £40
BIRDS OF THE WAYSIDE AND WOODLAND by Thomas A. Coward.
   Edited and with introductory chapters by Enid Blyton (Warne, 1936) £20
FIFTEEN-MINUTE TALES: Nineteen Stories for Children (Methuen, 1936) £25
THE FAMOUS JIMMY (illustrated by Benjamin Rabier) (Muller, 1936) £25
SIX ENID BLYTON PLAYS (Methuen, 1936) £20
THE YELLOW FAIRY BOOK (Newnes, [1936]) £45
ADVENTURES OF THE WISHING-CHAIR (illustrated by Hilda McGavin) (Newnes, [1937])......£150
ENID BLYTON'S SUNNY STORIES (new series) (Newnes, 1937-1953) ....each £4
THE ADVENTURES OF BINKLE AND FLIP (illustrated by Kathleen Nixon) (Newnes, [1938]) £30
BILLY-BOB TALES (illustrated by May Smith) (Methuen, 1938) £30
HEYO, BRER RABBIT! Tales of Brer Rabbit and His Friends. Retold by Enid Blyton (Newnes, 1938)......£40
MR GALLIANO'S CIRCUS (Newnes, [1938])..£100
THE SECRET ISLAND (Blackwell, 1938) £200
THE OLD THATCH (second series; eight volumes) (W. & A.K. Johnston, 1938-1939) ....each £10
HURRAH FOR THE CIRCUS! Being the Further Adventures of Mr Galliano and his Famous Circus
   (illustrated by E.H. Davie) (Newnes, 1939) £100
NAUGHTY AMELIA JANE! (Newnes, 1939) £75
THE WISHING BEAN and Other Plays (Blackwell, 1939) £20
THE ENCHANTED WOOD (Newnes, 1939) £150
THE BLYTON-SHARMAN MUSICAL PLAYS FOR JUNIORS (words by Enid Blyton; six books) (Wheaton, 1939) ....each £12
CAMEO PLAYS BOOK NO. 4. Edited by George H. Holroyd (only Book No. 4 is by Enid Blyton) (Arnold, 1939) £12
HOW THE FLOWERS GROW and Other Musical Plays (Wheaton, 1939) £12
SCHOOL PLAYS: Six Plays for School (Blackwell, 1939) £15
NEWS CHRONICLE BOYS' AND GIRLS' CIRCUS BOOK (News Chronicle, [1940]) £40
BOYS' AND GIRLS' CIRCUS BOOK (illustrated by Hilda McGavin) (Newnes, [1940]) £35
BOYS' AND GIRLS' STORY BOOK (Newnes, 1940) £35
NEWS CHRONICLE BOYS' AND GIRLS' BOOK (News Chronicle, 1940) £25
THE SECRET OF SPIGGY HOLES (Blackwood, [1940])...£100
BIRDS OF OUR GARDENS (illustrated by Roland Green and Ernest Aris) (Newnes, 1940) £20
THE CHILDREN OF CHERRY-TREE FARM (illustrated by Harry Rountree) (Country Life, 1940) £40
THE LITTLE TREE-HOUSE: Being the Adventures of Josie, Bun and Click (illustrated by Dorothy M. Wheeler)
   (Newnes, [1940]) £45
MISTER MEDDLE'S MISCHIEF (illustrated by Joyce Mercer and Rosalind M. Turvey) (Newnes, 1940) £40
THE NAUGHTIEST GIRL IN THE SCHOOL (Newnes, 1940) £60
PLAYS FOR OLDER CHILDREN (from 'The Play's the Thing'; illustrated by Alfred Bestall) (Newnes, [1940])...........£30
PLAYS FOR YOUNGER CHILDREN (from 'The Play's the Thing'; illustrated by Alfred Bestall) (Newnes, [1940]) £30
TWENTY-MINUTE TALES (Methuen, 1940) £20
TALES OF BETSY-MAY (illustrated by J. Gale Thomas) (Methuen, 1940) £25

*The dustjacket (left) and decorative front board of Blyton's **Mr Tumpy and his Caravan** (1949), illustrated by Dorothy M. Wheeler.*

THE TREASURE HUNTERS (illustrated by E. Wilson and Joyce Davies) (Newnes, 1940) £75
CHILDREN OF KIDILLIN (first published under the pseudonym 'Mary Pollock') (Newnes, 1940)................................£25
THREE BOYS AND A CIRCUS (first published under the pseudonym 'Mary Pollock') (Newnes, 1940) £25
THE ADVENTURES OF MR PINK-WHISTLE (Newnes, 1941) £75
FIVE O'CLOCK TALES: Sixty Five-Minute Stories for Children (Methuen, 1941) £15
THE FURTHER ADVENTURES OF JOSIE, CLICK AND BUN (illustrated by Dorothy M. Wheeler) (Newnes, [1941]) £35
THE SECRET MOUNTAIN: Being the Third Story of the Strange Adventures of the Secret Island Children
    (Blackwell, 1941) £75
THE ADVENTUROUS FOUR (Newnes, 1941) £50
THE BABAR STORY BOOK. Told by Enid Blyton (Methuen, 1941)..£60
A CALENDAR FOR CHILDREN (Newnes, 1941) £100
ENID BLYTON'S BOOK OF THE YEAR (Evans, 1941)..£15
THE CHILDREN OF WILLOW FARM: A Tale of Life on a Farm (illustrated by Harry Rountree) (Country Life, 1942) £35
THE NAUGHTIEST GIRL AGAIN (Newnes, 1942)..£50
MORE ADVENTURES ON WILLOW FARM (Country Life, 1942) £30
SIX O'CLOCK TALES: Thirty-Three Short Stories for Children (illustrated by Dorothy M. Wheeler) (Methuen, 1942)..........£20
SHADOW, THE SHEEP-DOG (Newnes, 1942)..£40
THE LAND OF FAR-BEYOND (Methuen, 1942)..£30
I'LL TELL YOU A STORY (illustrated by Eileen A. Soper) (Macmillan, 1942) £15
I'LL TELL YOU ANOTHER STORY (Macmillan, 1942) £25
ENID BLYTON'S HAPPY STORY (Hodder & Stoughton, 1942) £25
HELLO, MR TWIDDLE! (illustrated by Hilda McGavin) (Newnes, 1942) £30
THE FURTHER ADVENTURES OF BRER RABBIT. Retold By Enid Blyton (Newnes, 1942)................................£30
ENID BLYTON'S LITTLE BOOKS (pictorial wraps; issued without dustjacket) (Evans, [1942]) ....each £15
CIRCUS DAYS AGAIN (Newnes, 1942) £30
ENID BLYTON'S READERS (Books 1-3; issued without dustjackets) (Macmillan, 1942)......................................each £10
JOHN JOLLY AT CHRISTMAS TIME (Evans, 1942) £50
THE CHILDREN'S LIFE OF CHRIST (Methuen, 1943) £15
THE SECRET OF KILLIMOOIN (Blackwell, 1943) £60
SEVEN O'CLOCK TALES: Thirty Short Stories for Children (Methuen, 1943) £20
DAME SLAP AND HER SCHOOL (illustrated by Dorothy M. Wheeler) (Newnes, [1943])....................................£30
THE MAGIC FARAWAY TREE (illustrated by Dorothy M. Wheeler) (Newnes, 1943) £150
ENID BLYTON'S MERRY STORY BOOK (illustrated by Eileen A. Soper) (Hodder & Stoughton, 1943)......................£30
BIMBO AND TOPSY (illustrated by Lucy Gee) (Newnes, 1943)..£25

THE JOLLY FAMILY PICTURE STORY BOOKS (Evans, [1943]) £25
THE ADVENTURES OF SCAMP (published under the pseudonym 'Mary Pollock') (Newnes, 1943) £25
JOHN JOLLY BY THE SEA (Evans, 1943) £50
JOHN JOLLY ON THE FARM (Evans, 1943) £50
SMUGGLER BEN (published under the pseudonym 'Mary Pollock') (Laurie, 1943) £20
THE TOYS COME TO LIFE (illustrated by Eileen A. Soper) (Brockhampton Press, [1944]) £30
BILLY AND BETTY AT THE SEASIDE (Valentine, [1944]) £60
THE BOY NEXT DOOR (illustrated by A.E. Bestall) (Newnes, 1944) £75
ENID BLYTON'S NATURE LOVER'S BOOK (illustrated by Donin Nachshen and Noel Hopkin) (Evans, 1944) £15
THE CHRISTMAS BOOK (illustrated by Treyer Evans) (Macmillan, 1944) £20
COME TO THE CIRCUS (illustrated by Eileen A. Soper) (Brockhampton Press, [1944]) £30
EIGHT O'CLOCK TALES (illustrated by Dorothy M. Wheeler) (Methuen, 1944) £20
ENID BLYTON'S JOLLY STORY BOOK (illustrated by Eileen Soper) (Hodder & Stoughton, 1944) £25
POLLY PIGLET (illustrated by Eileen A. Soper) (Brockhampton, [1944]) £35
RAINY DAY STORIES (illustrated by Nora S. Unwin) (Evans, [1944]) £30
TALES FROM THE BIBLE (illustrated by Eileen A. Soper) (Methuen, 1944) £25
TALES OF TOYLAND (illustrated by Hilda McGavin) (Newnes, 1944) £30
AT APPLETREE FARM (Brockhampton Press, 1944) £30
A BOOK OF NAUGHTY CHILDREN (Methuen, 1944) £30
THE DOG THAT WENT TO FAIRYLAND (Brockhampton Press, 1944) £25
JOLLY LITTLE JUMBO (Brockhampton Press, 1944) £30
ENID BLYTON READERS BOOKS 4-6 (Macmillan, 1944) .... each £8
THE THREE GOLLIWOGS (Newnes, 1944) £40
THE BLUE STORY BOOK (illustrated by Eileen A. Soper) (Methuen, 1945) £25
ROUND THE CLOCK STORIES (illustrated by Nora S. Unwin) (National Magazine Co., 1945) £20
THE CARAVAN FAMILY (illustrated by William Fyffe) (Lutterworth Press, 1945) £20
THE BROWN FAMILY (illustrated by E. and R. Buhler) (News Chronicle, [1945]) £20
THE CONJURING WIZARD and Other Stories (illustrated by Eileen A. Soper) (Macmillan, 1945) £25
THE ENID BLYTON NATURE READERS NOS. 1-20 (Macmillan, [1945]) .... each £8
THE FAMILY AT RED ROOFS (illustrated by W. Spence) (Lutterworth Press, 1945) £30
THE FIRST CHRISTMAS (photographs by Paul Henning) (Methuen, 1945) £15
HOLLOW TREE HOUSE (illustrated by Elizabeth Wall) (Lutterworth Press, 1945) £20
THE NAUGHTIEST GIRL IS A MONITOR (Newnes, 1945) £30
THE RUNAWAY KITTEN (illustrated by Eileen A. Soper) (Brockhampton Press, [1945]) £30
THE TWINS GO TO NURSERY-RHYME LAND (illustrated by Eileen A. Soper) (Brockhampton Press, [1945]) £30
ENID BLYTON'S SUNNY STORY BOOK (Hodder & Stoughton, 1945) £20
THE TEDDY BEAR'S PARTY (illustrated by Eileen A. Soper) (Brockhampton Press, [1945]) £30
JOHN JOLLY AT THE CIRCUS (Evans, 1945) £50
AMELIA JANE AGAIN (Newnes, 1946) £35
THE BAD LITTLE MONKEY (illustrated by Eileen A. Soper) (Brockhampton Press, [1946]) £30
THE CHILDREN AT HAPPY HOUSE (illustrated by Kathleen Gell) (Blackwell, 1946) £25
CHIMNEY CORNER STORIES (illustrated by Pat Harrison) (National Magazine Co., 1946) £25
THE ENID BLYTON HOLIDAY BOOK (Sampson Low, [1946]) £25
ENID BLYTON'S GAY STORY BOOK (illustrated by Eileen Soper) (Hodder & Stoughton, 1946) £30
JOSIE, CLICK AND BUN AGAIN (illustrated by Dorothy M. Wheeler) (Newnes, [1946]) £35
THE LITTLE WHITE DUCK and Other Stories (illustrated by Eileen A. Soper) (Macmillan, 1946) £25
THE PUT-EM-RIGHTS (illustrated by Elizabeth Wall) (Lutterworth Press, 1946) £15
THE RED STORY BOOK (Methuen, 1946) £25
TALES OF GREEN HEDGES (illustrated by Gwen White) (National Magazine Co., 1946) £20
THE SURPRISING CARAVAN (illustrated by Eileen A. Soper) (Brockhampton Press, 1946) £30
THE TRAIN THAT LOST ITS WAY (illustrated by Eileen A. Soper) (Brockhampton Press, [1946]) £30
ENID BLYTON NATURE READERS NOS. 21-30 (Macmillan, 1946) .... each £8
THE FOLK OF THE FARAWAY TREE (illustrated by Dorothy M. Wheeler) (Newnes, 1946) £75
THE ADVENTUROUS FOUR AGAIN (Newnes, 1947) £40
AT SEASIDE COTTAGE (illustrated by Eileen A. Soper) (Brockhampton Press, [1947]) £30
THE GREEN STORY BOOK (illustrated by Eileen A. Soper) (Methuen, 1947) £20
THE HAPPY HOUSE CHILDREN AGAIN (illustrated by Kathleen Gell) (Blackwell, 1947) £30
HOUSE-AT-THE-CORNER (illustrated by Elsie Walker) (Lutterworth Press, 1947) £25
JINKY NATURE BOOKS (four books) (Arnold, [1947]) .... each £8
MORE ABOUT JOSIE, CLICK AND BUN (illustrated by Dorothy M. Wheeler) (Newnes, 1947) £30
ENID BLYTON'S LUCKY STORY BOOK (illustrated by Eileen Soper) (Hodder & Stoughton, 1947) £25
RAMBLES WITH UNCLE NAT (illustrated by Nora S. Unwin) (National Magazine Co., [1947]) £20
THE SAUCY JANE FAMILY (illustrated by Ruth Gervis) (Lutterworth Press, 1947) £25
A SECOND BOOK OF NAUGHTY CHILDREN: Twenty-Four Short Stories (illustrated by Kathleen Gell) (Methuen, 1947) £25
THE SMITH FAMILY (Books 1-3 by Enid Blyton [Books 4-6 by Rose Fyleman]) (Arnold, [1947]) .... each £10
ENID BLYTON'S TREASURY (published for Boots) (Evans, 1947) £25
BEFORE I GO TO SLEEP: A Book of Bible Stories and Prayers for Children at Night
      (illustrated by Grace Lodge) (Latimer House, 1947) £30
THE VERY CLEVER RABBIT (Brockhampton Press, 1947) £25

LITTLE GREEN DUCK and Other Stories (Brockhampton Press, 1947) £25
MISCHIEF AT ST. ROLLO'S (published under the pseudonym 'Mary Pollock') (Newnes: 'Tower House' series, 1947) £25
THE SECRET OF CLIFF CASTLE (published under the pseudonym 'Mary Pollock') (Newnes: 'Tower House' series, 1947) £25
MISTER ICEY-COLD (Blackwell, 1948) £25
THE ADVENTURES OF PIP (Sampson Low, [1948])...£25
THE BOY WITH THE LOAVES AND FISHES (illustrated by Elsie Walker) (Lutterworth Press, 1948) £12
ENID BLYTON'S BRER RABBIT BOOK (first of a series, followed by 2nd-8th 'Brer Rabbit Books')
   (Latimer House, 1948) ....each £15
JUST TIME FOR A STORY (illustrated by Grace Lodge) (Macmillan, 1948) £20
LET'S GARDEN (illustrated by William McLaren) (Latimer House, 1948) £25
LET'S HAVE A STORY (illustrated by George Bowe) (Pitkin, [1948]) £20
THE LITTLE BUTTON-ELVES (Coker, [1948]) £20
THE LITTLE GIRL AT CAPERNAUM (illustrated by Elsie Walker) (Lutterworth Press, 1948)....................£10
BRER RABBIT AND HIS FRIENDS. Retold by Enid Blyton (Coker, 1948) £16
ENID BLYTON'S BEDTIME SERIES (two parts) (Brockhampton Press, 1948) ....each £12
CHILDREN OF OTHER LANDS (Coker, [1948]) £16
COME TO THE CIRCUS! (a different work from the 1944 Brockhampton book; illustrated by Joyce M. Johnson)
   (Newnes, 1948) £20
MORE ADVENTURES OF PIP (Marston, [1948]) £20
NOW FOR A STORY (illustrated by Frank Varty) (Harold Hill, 1948) £15
THE RED-SPOTTED HANDKERCHIEF and Other Stories (illustrated by Kathleen Gell) (Brockhampton Press, [1948]) £25
SECRET OF THE OLD MILL (illustrated by Eileen A. Soper) (Brockhampton Press, [1948]) £25
SIX COUSINS AT MISTLETOE FARM (illustrated by Peter Beigel) (Evans, 1948) £20
TALES OF OLD THATCH (Coker, 1948)...£20
TALES OF THE TWINS (illustrated by Eileen A. Soper) (Brockhampton Press, [1948]) £15
THEY RAN AWAY TOGETHER (illustrated by Jeanne Farrar) (Brockhampton Press, [1948]) £15
WE WANT A STORY (illustrated by George Bowe) (Pitkin, [1948]) £25
ENID BLYTON READERS BOOK NO. 7 (Macmillan, 1948) £7
NATURE TALES (Johnston, 1948) £10
TALES AFTER TEA (Werner Laurie, 1948) £20
ENID BLYTON'S BLUEBELL STORY BOOK (Gifford, [1949]) £30
HUMPTY DUMPTY AND BELINDA (Collins, [1949]) £30
A BOOK OF MAGIC (Macmillan, 1949) £16
BUMPY AND HIS BUS (illustrated by Dorothy K. Wheeler) (Newnes, 1949) £25
ENID BLYTON'S DAFFODIL STORY BOOK (Gifford, [1949]) £30
THE DEAR OLD SNOWMAN (Brockhampton Press, [1949])...£25
THE ENID BLYTON BIBLE STORIES: OLD TESTAMENT (Macmillan, 1949) £20

*Individual issues of the fortnightly **Enid Blyton's Magazine** from the 1950s (above) are now worth £4 in Very Good condition.*

THE ENID BLYTON PICTURES: OLD TESTAMENT by John Turner (Macmillan, 1949)......................£20
JINKY'S JOKE and Other Stories (illustrated by Kathleen Gell) (Brockhampton Press, [1949])......................£20
MR TUMPY AND HIS CARAVAN (illustrated by Dorothy M. Wheeler) (Sidgwick & Jackson, 1949) £30
MY ENID BLYTON BEDSIDE BOOK (first of a series, followed by Enid Blyton's 2nd-12th 'Bedside Books')
    (Arthur Barker, 1949) ....each £20
A STORY PARTY AT GREEN HEDGES (illustrated by Grace Lodge) (Hodder & Stoughton, 1949)......................£20
TALES AFTER SUPPER (Werner Laurie, 1949) £10
A CAT IN FAIRYLAND (Pitkin, 1949)......................£25
CHUFF THE CHIMNEY SWEEP (Pitkin, 1949)......................£25
THE CIRCUS BOOK (Latimer House, 1949) £20
DON'T BE SILLY, MR TWIDDLE (Newnes, 1949) £25
THOSE DREADFUL CHILDREN (illustrated by Grace Lodge) (Lutterworth Press, 1949)......................£25
ENID BLYTON'S GOOD MORNING BOOK (illustrated by Don & Ann Goring) (National Magazine Co., 1949)......................£20
OH, WHAT A LOVELY TIME (Brockhampton Press, 1949)......................£20
ROBIN HOOD BOOK (Latimer House, 1949)......................£20
TINY TALES (Littlebury, 1949)......................£20
THE STRANGE UMBRELLA and Other Stories (Pitkin, [1949]) £25
THE ENCHANTED SEA and Other Stories (Pitkin, [1949]) £25
A RUBBALONG TALE SHOWBOOK (devised by Jack Chambers; complete with all cut-outs; boards) (Werner Laurie, 1950)..£250
MARY MOUSE SHOWBOOK (devised by Jack Chambers; complete with all cut-outs; boards) (Werner Laurie, 1950)......................£250
THE ASTONISHING LADDER and Other Stories (illustrated by Eileen A. Soper) (Macmillan, 1950)......................£25
THE MAGIC KNITTING NEEDLES and Other Stories (Macmillan, 1950) £25
THE MAGIC SNOW-BIRD and Other Stories (Pitkin, [1950]) £25
THE THREE NAUGHTY CHILDREN and Other Stories (illustrated by Eileen A. Soper) (Macmillan, 1950) £20
THE WISHING CHAIR AGAIN (Newnes, 1950) £25
SIX COUSINS AGAIN (illustrated by Maurice Tulloch) (Evans, 1950) £20
SMUGGLER BEN (Werner Laurie, 1950) £15
TRICKY THE GOBLIN and Other Stories (illustrated by Eileen A. Soper) (Macmillan, 1950) £25
RUBBALONG TALES (illustrated by Norman Meredith) (Macmillan, 1950) £30
THE POLE STAR FAMILY (illustrated by Ruth Gervis) (Lutterworth Press, 1950)......................£20
ENID BLYTON'S POPPY STORY BOOK (Gifford, [1950])......................£20
THE SEASIDE FAMILY (illustrated by Ruth Gervis) (Lutterworth Press, 1950) £20
MR PINK-WHISTLE INTERFERES (illustrated by Dorothy M. Wheeler) (Newnes, 1950) £25
ENID BLYTON'S BOOK OF THE YEAR (illustrated by Eileen Soper; music by Alec Rowley) (Evans, 1950) £20
MISTER MEDDLE'S MUDDLES (illustrated by Rosalind M. Turvey and Joyce Mercer) (Newnes, 1950) £25
ENID BLYTON LITTLE BOOK NO. 1 (first of a series, followed by Nos. 2-6) (Brockhampton, [1950]) ....each £10
THE ENID BLYTON PENNANT SERIES (thirty books) (Macmillan, 1950) ....each £7
ENID BLYTON READERS BOOKS NOS. 10-12 (Macmillan, 1950) ....each £7
ROUND THE YEAR WITH ENID BLYTON (Evans, 1950)......................£10
ROUND THE YEAR STORIES (Coke, 1950)......................£15
TALES ABOUT TOYS (Brockhampton Press, 1950)......................£20
WHAT AN ADVENTURE (Brockhampton Press, 1950) £20
THE YELLOW STORY BOOK (illustrated by Kathleen Gell) (Newnes, 1950) £20
PIPPY AND THE GNOME and Other Stories (Pitkin, 1951) £15
THE PROUD GOLLIWOG (Brockhampton Press, 1951) £15
THE QUEEN ELIZABETH FAMILY (illustrated by Ruth Gervis) (Lutterworth Press, 1951) £15
BENJY AND THE PRINCESS and Other Stories (Pitkin, [1951]) £15
THE BOOK OF BROWNIES (illustrated by Ernest Aris) (Newnes, [1951]) £25
THE BUTTERCUP FARM FAMILY (illustrated by Ruth Gervis) (Lutterworth Press, 1951) £20
ENID BLYTON'S BUTTERCUP STORY BOOK (Gifford, [1951]) £20
THE FLYING GOAT and Other Stories (Pitkin, [1951]) £25
ENID BLYTON'S GAY STREET BOOK (illustrated by Grace Lodge) (Latimer House, [1951]) £25
JOSIE, CLICK AND BUN, AND THE LITTLE TREE HOUSE (reprint of 'The Little Tree House' [1940];
    illustrated by Dorothy M. Wheeler) (Newnes, [1951])......................£25
A PICNIC PARTY WITH ENID BLYTON (illustrated by Grace Lodge) (Hodder & Stoughton, 1951) £20
THE RUNAWAY TEDDY BEAR and Other Stories (Pitkin, [1951]) £25
THE SIX BAD BOYS (illustrated by Mary Gernat) (Lutterworth Press, 1951) £25
'TOO-WISE' THE WONDERFUL WIZARD and Other Stories (Pitkin, [1951]) £25
UP THE FARAWAY TREE (illustrated by Dorothy M. Wheeler) (Newnes, 1951) £40
TALES OF ANCIENT GREECE (reissue; illustrated by Anne and Janet Johnstone) (Latimer House, [1951]) £12
DOWN AT THE FARM (Sampson Low, 1951) £20
FATHER CHRISTMAS AND BELINDA (Collins, 1951) £20
FEEFO, TUPPENY AND JINKS (abridged edition of the 'Green Goblin Book' [1935]) (Staples Press, 1951)......................£20
THE LITTLE SPINNING MOUSE and Other Stories (Pitkin, 1951) £25
ENID BLYTON'S ANIMAL LOVER'S BOOK (Evans, 1952)......................£15
ENID BLYTON'S BRIGHT STORY BOOK (illustrated by Eileen Soper) (Brockhampton Press, 1952) £20
THE ENID BLYTON BIBLE PICTURES: NEW TESTAMENT (Macmillan, [1952])......................£20
THE QUEER ADVENTURE (illustrated by Norman Meredith) (Staples Press, 1952) £20
THE STORY OF MY LIFE (Pitkin, [1952])......................£30

Enid Blyton was one of the most prolific children's authors of all time, and this selection represents just a fraction of her output.

WELCOME, JOSIE, CLICK AND BUN! (illustrated by Dorothy M. Wheeler) (Newnes, 1952)..............................£25
THE VERY BIG SECRET (illustrated by Ruth Gervis) (Lutterworth Press, 1952) £20
ENID BLYTON'S SNOWDROP STORY BOOK (Gifford, [1952]) £25
ENID BLYTON'S OMNIBUS! (illustrated by Jessie Land) (Newnes, 1952) £20
ENID BLYTON TINY STRIP BOOKS (first of a series) (Sampson Low, [1952]) ....each £12
MY FIRST ENID BLYTON BOOK (first of a series, followed by the 2nd and 3rd 'Enid Blyton Books')
(Latimer House, 1952) ....each £20
MY FIRST NATURE BOOK (first of a series, followed by the 2nd and 3rd 'Nature Books'; illustrated by Eileen A. Soper)
(Macmillan, 1952) ....each £7
THE CHILDREN'S JOLLY BOOK (with W.E. Johns and others) (Odhams, 1952) £15
COME ALONG TWINS (Brockhampton Press, 1952)..............................£12
THE MAD TEAPOT (Brockhampton Press, 1952)..............................£12
THE TWO SILLIES and Other Stories. Retold By Enid Blyton (Coker, 1952)..............................£20
THE SECRET OF MOON CASTLE (Blackwell, 1953) £40
SNOWBALL THE PONY (illustrated by Iris Gillespie) (Lutterworth Press, 1953)..............................£15
THE STORY OF OUR QUEEN (illustrated by F. Stocks May) (Muller, 1953)..............................£15
WELL REALLY, MR. TWIDDLE! (illustrated by Hilda McGavin) (Newnes, 1953)..............................£25
THE CHILDREN'S BOOK OF PRAYERS. Chosen by Enid Blyton (Muller, [1953])..............................£15
ENID BLYTON'S CHRISTMAS STORY (advent calendar; illustrated by Fritz Wegner) (Hamilton, [1953]) £30

THE ENID BLYTON BIBLE STORIES: NEW TESTAMENT (fourteen books) (Macmillan, 1953 [1954]) ....each £6
ENID BLYTON'S MAGAZINE (1953-) ....each £4
GOBO AND MR FIERCE (Sampson Low, 1953) £12
HERE COME THE TWINS (Brockhampton Press, 1953) £12
LITTLE GIFT BOOKS. Translated by Enid Blyton (first of a series; illustrated by Pierre Probst) (Hackett, 1953) ....each £20
PLAYWAYS ANNUAL by Enid Blyton and others (Lutterworth Press, 1953) £10
VISITORS IN THE NIGHT (Brockhampton Press, 1953)...£12
THE ADVENTURE OF THE SECRET NECKLACE (illustrated by Isabel Veevers) (Lutterworth Press, 1954) £15
THE CASTLE WITHOUT A DOOR and Other Stories (Pitkin, [1954]) £15
THE CHILDREN AT GREEN MEADOWS (illustrated by Grace Lodge) (Lutterworth Press, 1954)..................................£20
ENID BLYTON'S FRIENDLY STORY BOOK (illustrated by Eileen Soper) (Brockhampton Press, 1954) £20
ENID BLYTON'S GOOD MORNING BOOK (illustrated by Willy Schermelé) (Juvenile Productions, [1954]) £20
THE GREATEST BOOK IN THE WORLD (illustrated by Mabel Peacock) (British & Foreign Bible Society, [1954]) £15
THE LITTLE TOY FARM and Other Stories (Pitkin, 1954) £15
ENID BLYTON'S MARIGOLD STORY BOOK (Gifford, [1954]) £25
MERRY MISTER MEDDLE! (illustrated by Rosalind M. Turvey and Joyce Mercer) (Newnes, 1954) £25
MORE ABOUT AMELIA JANE! (illustrated by Sylvia I. Venus) (Newnes, 1954) £30
ENID BLYTON'S MAGAZINE ANNUAL (first of a series of four) (Evans, [1954])..each £15
LITTLE STRIP PICTURE BOOKS (Sampson Low, 1954)..each £10
ENID BLYTON'S AWAY GOES SOOTY (illustrated by Pierre Probst) (Collins [printed in the Netherlands], [1955]) £20
BENJY AND THE OTHERS (illustrated by Kathleen Gell) (Latimer House, 1955)..£20
BIBLE STORIES FROM THE OLD TESTAMENT (illustrated by Grace Lodge) (Muller, [1955]) £10
ENID BLYTON'S BOBS (illustrated by Pierre Probst) (Collins [printed in the Netherlands], [1955]) £20
FINDING THE TICKETS (play) (Evans, 1955) £15
ENID BLYTON'S FOXGLOVE STORY BOOK (Gifford, [1955]) £25
HOLIDAY HOUSE (illustrated by Grace Lodge) (Evans, [1955]) £15
ENID BLYTON'S LITTLE BEDTIME BOOKS (series of eight books) (Sampson Low, [1955])......................................each £12
MISCHIEF AGAIN! (photographs by Paul Kaye) (Collins, 1955) £15
MORE CHIMNEY CORNER STORIES (illustrated by Pat Harrison) (Macdonald, 1955) £20
THE MOTHERS' MEETING (play) (Evans, 1955) £12
MR PINK-WHISTLE'S PARTY (illustrated by Dorothy M. Wheeler) (Newnes, 1955) £22
MR SLY-ONE AND THE CATS (play) (Evans, 1955) £15
ENID BLYTON'S NEDDY THE LITTLE DONKEY (illustrated by Romain Simson) (Collins [printed in the Netherlands], [1955]) ...£20
PLAYING AT HOME: A Novelty Book (story by Enid Blyton; devised and illustrated by Sabine Schweitzer) (Methuen, 1955) £160
RUN-ABOUT'S HOLIDAY (illustrated by Lilian Chivers) (Lutterworth Press, 1955)..£20
ENID BLYTON'S CHRISTMAS WITH SCAMP AND BIMBO (Collins, [1955])..£20
ENID BLYTON'S SOOTY (illustrated by Pierre Probst) (Collins [printed in the Netherlands], [1955])............................£20
THE TROUBLESOME THREE (illustrated by Leo) (Sampson Low, [1955]) £15
ENID BLYTON'S 'WHAT SHALL I BE?' (illustrated by Pierre Probst) (Collins [printed in the Netherlands], [1955]) £15
WHO WILL HOLD THE GIANT? (play) (Evans, 1955) £15
BIBLE STORIES FROM THE NEW TESTAMENT (illustrated by Grace Lodge) (Muller, 1955) £10
BIMBO AND BLACKIE GO CAMPING (illustrated by Pierre Probst) (Collins, 1955) £20
ENID BLYTON'S FAVOURITE BOOK OF FABLES, from the Tales of La Fontaine (Collins, 1955) £25
GOLLIWOG GRUMBLED (Brockhampton Press, 1955) £20
LAUGHING KITTEN (photographs by Paul Kave) (Harvill, 1955)..£15
ENID BLYTON'S ANIMAL TALES (illustrated by Romain Simson) (Collins [printed in the Netherlands], [1956])......................£20
THE CLEVER LITTLE DONKEY (illustrated by Romain Simon) (Collins [printed in the Netherlands], [1956])..............................£20
COLIN THE COW-BOY (illustrated by R. Caillé) (Collins [printed in the Netherlands], [1956]) £20
FOUR IN A FAMILY (illustrated by Tom Kerr) (Lutterworth Press, 1956) £15
LET'S HAVE A PARTY (photographs by Paul Kaye) (Harvill Press, 1956) £15
SCAMP AT SCHOOL (illustrated by Pierre Probst) (Collins [printed in the Netherlands], [1956]) £20
A STORY BOOK OF JESUS (illustrated by Elsie Walker) (Macmillan, 1956) £10
ENID BLYTON'S BOM PAINTING BOOK (Dean, [1957]) £15
CHILDREN'S OWN WONDER BOOK (containing contributions by Enid Blyton and others) (Odhams, 1957) £10
NEW TESTAMENT PICTURE BOOKS NOS. 1-2 (Macmillan, 1957) ....each £5
THE BIRTHDAY KITTEN (illustrated by Grace Lodge) (Lutterworth Press, 1958) £35
ENID BLYTON'S LITTLE BEDTIME BOOK (four books; all different work from the earlier book of the same title)
   (Sampson Low, [1958]) ....each £12
MR PINK WHISTLE'S BIG BOOK (Evans, 1958)...£20
RUMBLE AND CHUFF (illustrated by David Walsh) (Juvenile Productions, [1958]) £20
TALES AFTER TEA (Collins, 1958) £10
ENID BLYTON'S MYSTERY STORIES (contains 'The Secret of Cliff Castle' and 'Smuggler Ben') (Collins, 1959) £10
ENID BLYTON'S DOG STORIES (contains 'Three Boys and a Circus' [1940] and 'The Adventures of Scamp' [1943])
   (Collins, 1959) £10
ADVENTURE STORIES (Collins, 1960)...£10
ADVENTURE OF THE STRANGE RUBY (illustrated by Roger Payne) (Brockhampton Press, 1960) £15
HAPPY DAY STORIES (illustrated by Marcia Lane) (Evans, 1960) £15
WILL THE FIDDLER (illustrated by Grace Lodge) (Instructive Arts, [1960]) £20
OLD TESTAMENT PICTURE BOOKS (Macmillan, 1960) ....each £5

TALES AT BEDTIME (illustrated by Hilda McGavin) (Collins, 1960) £15
THE BIG ENID BLYTON BOOK (Hamlyn, 1961) £15
THE MYSTERY THAT NEVER WAS (illustrated by Gilbert Dunlop) (Collins, 1961)...........................£20
CIRCUS DAYS AGAIN (May Fair Books, 1962) £10
THE FOUR COUSINS (illustrated by Joan Thompson) (Lutterworth Press, 1962)...........................£15
STORIES FOR MONDAY (issued without dustjacket) (Oliphants, 1962) £20
STORIES FOR TUESDAY (Oliphants, 1962)..£20
THE BOY WHO WANTED A DOG (illustrated by Sally Michel) (Lutterworth Press, 1963) £10
TALES OF BRAVE ADVENTURE. Retold by Enid Blyton (stories about Robin Hood and King Arthur) (Dean, [1963]) £12
BRER RABBIT AGAIN (Dean, 1963) £8
THE ENID BLYTON STORYBOOK FOR FIVES TO SEVENS (illustrated by Dorothy Hall and Grace Shelton) (Parrish, [1964])..£25
HAPPY HOURS STORY BOOK (Dean, [1964]) £15
ENID BLYTON'S SUNSHINE PICTURE STORY BOOK (first of a series) (World Distributors [printed in the Netherlands], [1964])..£15
STORYTIME BOOK (Dean, 1964) £15
TELL-A-STORY BOOKS (World Distributors, 1964) ....each £6
TROUBLE FOR THE TWINS (Brockhampton Press, 1964) £12
ENID BLYTON'S SUNSHINE BOOK (Dean, [1965]) £12
THE BOY WHO CAME BACK (illustrated by Elsie Walker) (Lutterworth Press, 1965) £10
THE MAN WHO STOPPED TO HELP (illustrated by Elsie Walker) (Lutterworth Press, 1965) £10
EASY READER (first of a series; issued without dustjacket) (Collins, 1965) £8
ENID BLYTON'S BRER RABBIT'S A RASCAL (Dean, 1965) £12
TALES OF LONG AGO. Retold by Enid Blyton (Dean, 1965) £12
ENID BLYTON'S PIXIE TALES (Collins, 1966)..£12
ENID BLYTON'S PIXIELAND STORY BOOK (Collins, 1966) £12
ENID BLYTON'S PLAYBOOK (first of a series) (Collins, [1966]) £12
ENID BLYTON'S FIRESIDE TALES (Collins, 1966) £12
THE HAPPY HOUSE CHILDREN (Collins, 1966) £15
ENID BLYTON'S BEDTIME ANNUAL (Manchester, 1966) £15
THE FAIRY FOLK STORY BOOK (Collins, 1966) £15
ENID BLYTON'S GIFT BOOK (Purnell, 1966) £15
STORIES FOR BEDTIME (Dean, 1966) £12
STORIES FOR YOU (Dean, 1966) £12
JOHN AND MARY (series of nine books; illustrated by Fromont) (Brockhampton Press, 1966-68) ....each £8
HOLIDAY ANNUAL STORIES (Low Marston, 1967) £12
HOLIDAY MAGIC STORIES (Low Marston, 1967) £12
HOLIDAY PIXIE STORIES (Low Marston, 1967) £12
HOLIDAY TOY STORIES (Low Marston, 1967) £12
THE PLAYTIME STORY BOOK NOS. 1-14 (World Distributors, 1967)....................................each £6
ADVENTURES ON WILLOW FARM (Collins, 1968)..£10
BROWNIE TALES (Collins, 1968) £10
ONCE UPON A TIME (Collins, 1968) £10
THE BEAR WITH BOOT-BUTTON EYES and Other Stories (Purnell, 1975)...................................£5
DAME ROUNDY'S STOCKINGS and Other Stories (Purnell, 1975) £5
THE DOG WITH THE LONG TAIL and Other Stories (Purnell, 1975) £5
THE GOBLIN AND THE DRAGON and Other Stories (Purnell, 1975)..£5
THE GOOD OLD ROCKING HORSE and Other Stories (Purnell, 1975) £5
THE LITTLE SUGAR MOUSE and Other Stories (Purnell, 1975) £5
BRER RABBIT AND THE TAR BABY (illustrated by Val Biro) (Hodder & Stoughton, 1975)...........£10

BOND, Michael

British author. Born: 1926. Worked as a cameraman for the BBC during the 1950s, before turning to writing following the success of *A Bear Called Paddington* (1958). As well as Paddington, Bond has created several other popular children's characters, including Thursday, Parsley the Lion and Olga da Polga.

Prices are for books in Very Good condition with dustjackets where applicable.

'Paddington' Story Books

A BEAR CALLED PADDINGTON (illustrated by Peggy Fortnum) (Collins, 1958) £100
MORE ABOUT PADDINGTON (illustrated by Peggy Fortnum) (Collins, 1959) £65
PADDINGTON HELPS OUT (illustrated by Peggy Fortnum) (Collins, 1960) £50
PADDINGTON ABROAD (illustrated by Peggy Fortnum) (Collins, 1961) £50
PADDINGTON AT LARGE (illustrated by Peggy Fortnum) (Collins, 1962) £50
PADDINGTON MARCHES ON (illustrated by Peggy Fortnum) (Collins, 1964) £50
THE ADVENTURES OF PADDINGTON (contains 'A Bear Called Paddington' and 'More About Paddington') (Collins, 1965)......£25
PADDINGTON AT WORK (illustrated by Peggy Fortnum) (Collins, 1966) £35
PADDINGTON GOES TO TOWN (illustrated by Peggy Fortnum) (Collins, 1968) £35
PADDINGTON TAKES THE AIR (illustrated by Peggy Fortnum) (Collins, 1970) £30
PADDINGTON 'BLUE PETER' STORYBOOK (Collins, 1973) £20
PADDINGTON TAKES A BATH (illustrated by Barry Wilkinson) (Collins, 1976) £12
PADDINGTON GOES TO THE SALES (illustrated by Barry Wilkinson) (Collins, 1976) £12

BOND, Michael

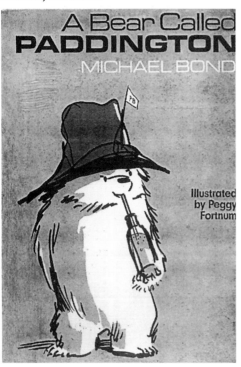

*The very first 'Paddington' book of them all: **A Bear Called Paddington**, published by Collins in 1958 and now worth £100.*

__Paddington Helps Out__ (1960) was the third book in the series. Like all the early titles, it was illustrated by Peggy Fortnum.

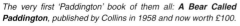

PADDINGTON'S NEW ROOM (illustrated by Barry Wilkinson) (Collins, 1976) £12
PADDINGTON TAKES THE TEST (illustrated by Peggy Fortnum) (Collins, 1979) £30
PADDINGTON AT HOME (Collins, 1980) £12
PADDINGTON GOES OUT (Collins, 1980) £12
PADDINGTON ON SCREEN: A Second Blue Peter Storybook (illustrated by Barry Macey) (BBC, 1981) £12
PADDINGTON'S STORYBOOK (anthology; illustrated by Peggy Fortnum) (Collins, 1983) £10

Paddington 'Young Set' Books
PADDINGTON BEAR (illustrated by Fred Banbery) (Collins, 1972) £15
PADDINGTON'S GARDEN (illustrated by Fred Banbery) (Collins, 1972) £12
PADDINGTON AT THE CIRCUS (illustrated by Fred Banbery) (Collins, 1973) £10
PADDINGTON GOES SHOPPING (illustrated by Fred Banbery) (Collins, 1973) £10
PADDINGTON AT THE SEASIDE (illustrated by Fred Banbery) (Collins, 1975) £10
PADDINGTON AT THE TOWER (illustrated by Fred Banbery) (Collins, 1975) £10
PADDINGTON'S PICTURE BOOK (anthology; contains 'Paddington Bear', 'Paddington's Garden', 'Paddington at the Circus',
   'Paddington Goes Shopping', 'Paddington at the Tower' and 'Paddington at the Seaside') (Collins, [1978]) £10

Paddington 'First' Picture Books
PADDINGTON AND THE KNICKERBOCKER RAINBOW (illustrated by David McKee) (Collins, 1984)..................£10
PADDINGTON AT THE ZOO (illustrated by David McKee) (Collins, 1984)...£10
PADDINGTON AT THE FAIR (illustrated by David McKee) (Collins, 1985) £10
PADDINGTON'S PAINTING EXHIBITION (illustrated by David McKee) (Collins, 1985) £10
PADDINGTON AT THE PALACE (illustrated by David McKee) (Collins, 1986) £10
PADDINGTON MINDS THE HOUSE (illustrated by David McKee) (Collins, 1986) £10
PADDINGTON AND THE MARMALADE MAZE (illustrated by David McKee) (Collins, 1987) £10
PADDINGTON'S BUSY DAY (illustrated by David McKee) (Collins, 1987) £10
PADDINGTON'S MAGICAL CHRISTMAS (illustrated by David McKee) (Collins, 1988) £10

Picture Books Written with Karen Bond
PADDINGTON'S LONDON (David Booth/Hutchinson, 1986) £8
PADDINGTON AT THE AIRPORT (illustrated by Toni Goffe) (David Booth/Hutchinson, 1986) £8
PADDINGTON POSTS A LETTER (Crocodile, 1987)..£8
PADDINGTON'S COLOURS (Crocodile, 1986) £8
PADDINGTON'S BUS RIDES (Hutchinson, 1986) £8
PADDINGTON'S CLOCK BOOK (Hutchinson, 1986)..£8

Paddington 'Pop-Up' Books
PADDINGTON'S POP-UP BOOK (Collins, 1977) £25
PADDINGTON'S SHOPPING ADVENTURE (Collins, 1981) £18
PADDINGTON'S BIRTHDAY TREAT (Collins, 1981) £18
PADDINGTON AND THE SNOWBEAR (Collins, 1981) £18
PADDINGTON AT THE LAUNDERETTE (Collins, 1981) £18

Other 'Paddington' Titles
PADDINGTON'S BIRTHDAY BOOK. Compiled by Brenda Bond (illustrated by Peggy Fortnum) (Collins, 1969) £15
THE GREAT BIG PADDINGTON BOOK (illustrated by Ivor Wood) (Collins, 1976) £10
PADDINGTON'S LOOSE-END BOOK: An ABC of Things to Do (illustrated by Ivor Wood) (Collins, 1976) £8
PADDINGTON'S PARTY BOOK (illustrated by Ivor Wood) (Collins, 1976) £8
FUN AND GAMES WITH PADDINGTON (with Lesley Young) (Collins, 1977) £8
PADDINGTON'S CARTOON BOOK (illustrated by Ivor Wood) (Collins, 1979) £8
PADDINGTON BEAR RAG BOOK: DRESSING (Dean's Rag Book Co., 1982) £10
PADDINGTON'S DAY OF ACTION (illustrated by Barry Macey) (Paddington & Co., 1983) £8
PADDINGTON'S FIRST PUZZLE BOOK (Crocodile, 1987) £8
PADDINGTON'S SECOND PUZZLE BOOK (Crocodile, 1987) £8

'Thursday' Books
HERE COMES THURSDAY (illustrated by Daphne Rowles) (Harrap, 1966) £18
THURSDAY RIDES AGAIN (illustrated by Beryl Sanders) (Harrap, 1968) £15
THURSDAY AHOY! (illustrated by Leslie Wood) (Harrap, 1969) £15
THURSDAY IN PARIS (illustrated by Leslie Wood) (Harrap, 1971) £15

'Parsley' Books
PARSLEY'S GOOD DEED (illustrated by Esor) (BBC, 1969)...£10
THE STORY OF PARSLEY'S TAIL (illustrated by Esor) (BBC, 1969) £10
PARSLEY'S LAST STAND (BBC, 1970) £10
PARSLEY'S PROBLEM PRESENT (BBC, 1970) £10
PARSLEY THE LION (illustrated by Ivor Wood) (Collins, 1972) £10
PARSLEY PARADE (illustrated by Ivor Wood) (Collins, 1972) £10

'Olga Da Polga' Books
THE TALES OF OLGA DA POLGA (illustrated by Hans Helweg; paperback) (Puffin, 1971) £10
OLGA MEETS HER MATCH (illustrated by Hans Helweg) (Longman, 1973) £12
THE FIRST BIG OLGA DA POLGA BOOK (illustrated by Hans Helweg) (Longman, 1975).............................£10
THE SECOND BIG OLGA DA POLGA BOOK (illustrated by Hans Helweg) (Longman, 1975) £10
OLGA CARRIES ON (illustrated by Hans Helweg) (Kestrel, 1976) £5

'J.D. Polson' Books
J.D. POLSON AND THE LIBERTY HEAD DIME (illustrated by Roger Wade-Walker) (Octopus, 1980) £15
J.D. POLSON AND THE DILLOGATE AFFAIR (illustrated by Roger Wade-Walker) (Hodder & Stoughton, 1981).......................£15
J.D. POLSON AND THE GREAT UNVEILING (illustrated by Roger Wade-Walker) (Hodder & Stoughton, 1982) £15

Others
THE DAY THE ANIMALS WENT ON STRIKE (illustrated by Jim Hodgson) (Studio Vista, 1972) £15
MICHAEL BOND'S BOOK OF MICE (Purnell [printed in Holland], [1972]) £10
MR CRAM'S MAGIC BUBBLES (illustrated by Gioia Fiammenghi; paperback) (Puffin, 1975) £5
WINDMILL (illustrated by Tony Cattaneo) (Studio Vista, 1975)...£15
THE CARAVAN PUPPETS (illustrated by Vanessa Julian-Ottie) (Collins, 1983) £12

'BONZO' BOOKS AND ANNUALS
A popular series of books and annuals featuring Bonzo the Dog, the creation of the British artist George E. Studdy (1878-1948). Bonzo first appeared in 1912 and, as well as books, inspired postcards, toys and a series of silent animated films.

Prices are for annuals in Very Good condition (with cover description in brackets).

'Bonzo' Annuals
BONZO LAUGHTER ANNUAL [1935] £140
BONZO'S ANNUAL [1936] (Bonzo sitting on throne)...£125
BONZO'S ANNUAL [1937] (Bonzo dressed as clown with balloon)..£120
BONZO'S ANNUAL [1938] (Bonzo skipping)..£120
BONZO'S ANNUAL [1947] (Bonzo and jack-in-the-box) £50
BONZO'S ANNUAL [1948] (Bonzo with a donkey and cart) £50
BONZO'S ANNUAL [1949] (Bonzo wearing a fez and firing a peashooter) £50
BONZO'S ANNUAL [1950] (Bonzo with parrot) £50
BONZO'S ANNUAL [1951] (Bonzo as a cowboy)..£45
BONZO'S ANNUAL [1952] (Bonzo on a moon rocket)...£40
THE BONZO PORTFOLIO (1-10) ....the set £250

'Bonzo' Books

BONZO'S HAPPY DAY (Dunlop Press, no date) £150
BONZO'S LEAP YEAR (Dunlop Press, no date) £150
BONZO'S HAPPY FAMILY (Dunlop Press, no date) £150
BONZO'S LITTLE HOLIDAY (Dunlop Press, no date) £150
BACHELOR BONZO (Dunlop Press, no date) £150
BONZO'S BRAN PIE (Dunlop Press, no date) £150
MR BONZO COMES TO TOWN (Thomas Allen, Toronto, 1923-1927) £150
BAD BOY BONZO (Thomas Allen, Toronto, 1923-1927) £150
BONZO'S SEASIDE HOLIDAY (Thomas Allen, Toronto, 1923-1927) £150
BONZO'S COUNTRY HOLIDAY (Thomas Allen, Toronto, 1923-1927) £150
THE GOOD DEEDS OF BONZO (Thomas Allen, Toronto, 1923-1927) £150
THE ADVENTURES OF BONZO (Thomas Allen, Toronto, 1923-1927) £150
BONZO PAINTING BOOK (Swain, [1924]) £150
THE BONZO BOOK (Partridge, [1925]) £200
THE NEW BONZO BOOK (Partridge, [1927]) £200
THE BONZOOLOO BOOK (Partridge, [1929]) £200
BONZO AND US (Partridge, 1931) £160
BONZO: The Great Big Holiday Book (cover shows Bonzo on rocking horse) (Dean, 1934) £75
BONZO: The Great Big Holiday Book (cover shows Bonzo's head) (Dean, 1934) £75
BONZO COLOURING BOOK (Dean, [1934]) £70

'BOOKANO' BOOKS

Popular series of pop-up books designed and published by S.L. Giraud under the Strand Publications imprint between 1934 and 1951. Note that during the war years (Nos. 7-13) the books were compiled from previously used material. In the mid-Thirties (probably 1936), the title was changed from *Bookano Annual* to *Bookano Stories*.

Prices are for books in Very Good condition.

BOOKANO STORIES: With Pictures that Spring Up in Model Form (edited by S.L. Giraud)
    (Strand Publications: 'Bookano Living Pictures' series, [1936-]) £70
BOOKANO ZOO: Animals in Fact, Fancy and Fun (edited and produced by S.L. Giraud) (Strand Publications, [1939]) £65
BOOKANO NO. 1: Goblins in a Carpenter's Shop, with Sound Effects of Sawing Wood! (Strand Publications, 1934) £90
BOOKANO NO. 2: Cottage, with Semi-Transparent Fairy (Strand Publications, 1935) £80
BOOKANO NO. 3 (Strand Publications, 1936) £70
BOOKANO NO. 4 (Strand Publications, 1937) £70
BOOKANO NO. 5 (Strand Publications, 1938) £60
BOOKANO NO. 6 (Strand Publications, 1939) £60
BOOKANO NO. 7 (Strand Publications, 1940) £60
BOOKANO NO. 8 (Strand Publications, 1941) £60
BOOKANO NO. 9 (Strand Publications, 1942) £60
BOOKANO NO. 10 (Strand Publications, 1943) £55
BOOKANO NO. 11 (Strand Publications, 1944) £55
BOOKANO NO. 12 (Strand Publications, 1945) £55
BOOKANO NO. 13 (Strand Publications, 1946) £55
BOOKANO NO. 14 (Strand Publications, 1947) £55
BOOKANO NO. 15 (Strand Publications, 1948) £55
BOOKANO NO. 16: Tower Bridge (Strand Publications, 1949) £80
BOOKANO STORIES NO. 17 (Strand Publications, 1950) £90

BOSTON, Lucy M.

British author. Born Lucy Maria Wood in Southport, Lancashire, in 1892. Studied at Somerville College, Oxford, before training as a nurse and serving in France during the Great War. In 1935, she bought the 800-year-old Hemingford Grey Manor in Cambridgeshire, which inspired *The Children of Green Knowe* (1954) and five sequels, all illustrated by her son, Peter. Died: 1990.

Prices are for books in Very Good condition with dustjackets.

'Green Knowe' Books

THE CHILDREN OF GREEN KNOWE (illustrated by Peter Boston) (Faber, 1954) £45
THE CHIMNEYS OF GREEN KNOWE (illustrated by Peter Boston) (Faber, 1958) £25
THE RIVER AT GREEN KNOWE (illustrated by Peter Boston) (Faber, 1959) £25
A STRANGER AT GREEN KNOWE (illustrated by Peter Boston) (Faber, 1961) £25
AN ENEMY AT GREEN KNOWE (illustrated by Peter Boston) (Faber, 1964) £25
THE STONES OF GREEN KNOWE (illustrated by Peter Boston) (The Bodley Head, 1976) £20

Others

YEW HALL (Faber, 1954) £30
THE CASTLE OF YEW (illustrated by Margery Gill) (The Bodley Head, 1965) £15
THE SEA-EGG (illustrated by Peter Boston) (Faber, 1967) £15

George E. Studdy's Bonzo the Dog featured in a number of annuals between 1936 and 1952. This one dates from 1949.

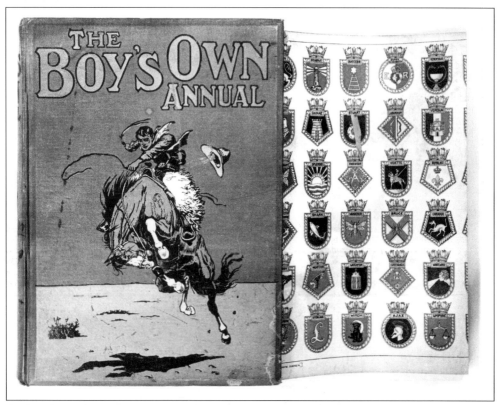

This ***Boy's Own Annual*** *features a pull-out chart showing the badges of a number of Royal Navy vessels.*

'BOY'S OWN' ANNUALS

Bestselling British story annual, described by its publisher, the Religious Tract Society, as "an illustrated volume of pure and entertaining reading". The paper itself was launched on 18th January 1879, the first annual appearing later that year. Although the paper survived until February 1967, the last annual was published in 1940.

Prices are for annuals (bound volumes) in Very Good condition (from Volume 37: with dustjackets where applicable).

VOLUMES 1 (with colour plates) (January-September 1879)..£75
VOLUMES 2-36 (with double-page sporting prints and special supplements where issued)
    (October 1879-September 1914) ....each £40
VOLUMES 37-58 (with colour plates) (October 1914-September 1935) ....each £45
VOLUMES 59-63 (with colour plates) (October 1935-September 1940) ....each £30

BRADLEY, Helen

British author-illustrator. Born: Lancashire, 1900. Began painting in her sixties, producing a series of distinctive Lowryesque scenes reminiscent of her Edwardian childhood that were collected in four books.

Prices are for books in Very Good condition with dustjackets.

AND MISS CARTER WORE PINK: Scenes from an Edwardian Childhood (Cape, 1971) £25
MISS CARTER CAME WITH US (Cape, 1973) £25
'IN THE BEGINNING' SAID GREAT-AUNT JANE (Cape, 1975) £20
THE QUEEN WHO CAME TO TEA (Cape, 1978)...£20

BRAZIL, Angela

British author. Born: Preston, 1868. Attended Manchester High School, Ellerslie College and finally Heatherly's, where she studied art. Her first school story, *The Fortunes of Philippa* (1907), was followed by many others, including *The Jolliest Term on Record* (1915) and *A Patriotic Schoolgirl* (1918). Died: 1947.

Prices are for books in Very Good condition with dustjackets where applicable.

A TERRIBLE TOMBOY (illustrated by Angela and Amy Brazil) (Gay & Bird, 1904) £100
THE FORTUNES OF PHILIPPA (Blackie, 1907 [1906]) £75

THE THIRD CLASS AT MISS KAYE'S (Blackie, 1909 [1908]) £75
THE NICEST GIRL IN THE SCHOOL (Blackie, 1910) £65
BOSOM FRIENDS: A Seaside Story (Nelson, [1910]) £50
THE MANOR HOUSE SCHOOL (illustrated by F. Moorsom) (Blackie, 1911) £45
A FOURTH FORM FRIENDSHIP (Blackie, 1912)...£45
THE NEW GIRL AT ST. CHAD'S (Blackie, 1912)..£45
A PAIR OF SCHOOLGIRLS (Blackie, [1912]) £45
THE MISCHIEVOUS BROWNIE (play) (Paterson: 'Children's Plays' series No. 1, [1913]).......................£45
THE FAIRY GIFTS (play) (Paterson: 'Children's Plays' series No. 2, [1913]) £45
THE ENCHANTED FIDDLE (play) (Paterson: 'Children's Plays' series No. 3, [1913]) £45
THE WISHING PRINCESS (play) (Paterson: 'Children's Plays' series No. 4, [1913]) £40
THE LEADER OF THE LOWER SCHOOL (Blackie, [1914]) £45
THE YOUNGEST GIRL IN THE FIFTH (Blackie, [1914])..£45
THE GIRLS OF ST. CYPRIAN'S (Blackie, [1914]) £45
THE SCHOOL BY THE SEA (Blackie, [1914]) £45
THE JOLLIEST TERM ON RECORD (illustrated by Balliol Salmon) (Blackie, [1915])..............................£40
FOR THE SAKE OF THE SCHOOL (Blackie, [1915]) £40
THE LUCKIEST GIRL IN THE SCHOOL (illustrated by Balliol Salmon) (Blackie, [1916]) £40
THE SLAP-BANG BOYS (T.C. & E.C. Jack, [1917]) £40
THE MADCAP OF THE SCHOOL (illustrated by Balliol Salmon) (Blackie, [1918]) £40
A PATRIOTIC SCHOOLGIRL (illustrated by Balliol Salmon) (Blackie, [1918])..£40
FOR THE SCHOOL COLOURS (illustrated by Balliol Salmon) (Blackie, [1918]) £40
A HARUM-SCARUM SCHOOLGIRL (illustrated by John Campbell) (Blackie, [1919]) £40
THE HEAD GIRL AT THE GABLES (illustrated by Balliol Salmon) (Blackie, [1919]).................................£40
TWO LITTLE SCAMPS AND A PUPPY (illustrated by E. Blampied) (Nelson, [1919]) £45
A GIFT FROM THE SEA (illustrated by A.E. Jackson) (Nelson, [1920])...£75
A POPULAR SCHOOLGIRL (illustrated by Balliol Salmon) (Blackie, [1920]) £75
THE PRINCESS OF THE SCHOOL (illustrated by Frank Wiles) (Blackie, [1920]) £75
A FORTUNATE TERM (illustrated by Treyer Evans) (Blackie, [1921]) £75
LOYAL TO THE SCHOOL (illustrated by Treyer Evans) (Blackie, [1921])...£75
MONITRESS MERLE (illustrated by Treyer Evans) (Blackie, [1922]) £75
THE SCHOOL IN THE SOUTH (illustrated by W. Smithson-Broadhead) (Blackie, [1922])........................£75

A very late work by Angela Brazil: **The School on the Moor**, published by Blackie in 1939 and now worth £35 in its jacket.

Even without their colourful dustjackets, many of Angela Brazil's books are still very handsome and desirable volumes.

BRAZIL, Angela

THE KHAKI BOYS and Other Stories (Nelson, [1923]) £75
SCHOOLGIRL KITTY (illustrated by W.E. Wightman) (Blackie, [1923]) £75
CAPTAIN PEGGIE (illustrated by W.E. Wightman) (Blackie, [1924]) £50
MY OWN SCHOOLDAYS (autobiography) (Blackie, [1925]) £80
JOAN'S BEST CHUM (illustrated by W.E. Wightman) (Blackie, [1926]) £50
QUEEN OF THE DORMITORY and Other Stories (illustrated by P.B. Hickling) (Cassell, 1926) £50
RUTH OF ST. RONAN'S (illustrated by F. Oldham) (Blackie, [1927]) £45
AT SCHOOL WITH RACHEL (illustrated by W.E. Wightman) (Blackie, [1928]) £45
ST CATHERINE'S COLLEGE (illustrated by Frank Wiles) (Blackie, [1929]) £40
THE LITTLE GREEN SCHOOL (illustrated by Frank Wiles) (Blackie, [1931]) £40
NESTA'S NEW SCHOOL (illustrated by J. Dewar Mills) (Blackie, [1932]) £40
JEAN'S GOLDEN TERM (Blackie, [1934]) £40
THE SCHOOL AT THE TURRETS (Blackie, [1935]) £40
AN EXCITING TERM (Blackie, [1936]) £35
JILL'S JOLLIEST SCHOOL (Blackie, 1937) £35
THE SCHOOL ON THE CLIFF (illustrated by F.E. Hiley) (Blackie, [1938]) £35
THE SCHOOL ON THE MOOR (illustrated by Henry Coller) (Blackie, [1939]) £35
THE NEW SCHOOL AT SCAWDALE (illustrated by M. Mackinlay) (Blackie, [1940]) £35
FIVE JOLLY SCHOOLGIRLS (Blackie, [1941]) £25
THE MYSTERY OF THE MOATED GRANGE (Blackie, [1942]) £25
THE SECRET OF THE BORDER CASTLE (illustrated by Charles Willis) (Blackie, [1943]) £25
THE SCHOOL IN THE FOREST (illustrated by J. Dewar Mills) (Blackie, [1944]) £25
THREE TERMS AT UPLANDS (illustrated by D.L. Mays) (Blackie, [1945]) £25
THE SCHOOL ON THE LOCH (illustrated by W. Lindsay Cable) (Blackie, [1946]) £25

BREARY, Nancy

British author who started to write her school stories for girls in the 1940s, concentrating on separate stories rather than series, with mystery strongly featured.

Prices are for books in Very Good condition with dustjacket.

GIVE A FORM A BAD NAME (Newnes, 1943) £35
TWO THRILLING TERMS (Blackie, 1943) £35
NO PEACE FOR THE PREFECTS (Newnes, 1944) £30

*Two of Elinor M. Brent-Dyer's 'Chalet School' books, including the very collectable **The Chalet School Reunion** fron 1963 (right).*

THE LOWER FOURTH EXCELS ITSELF (Newnes, 1945) £30
A SCHOOL DIVIDED (Newnes, 1945) £30
THIS TIME NEXT TERM (Blackie, 1945)..£30
JUNIOR CAPTAIN (illustrated by D.L. Mays) (Blackie, 1946) £30
THE SNACK BOAT SAILS AT NOON ! (illustrated by Alfred Sindall) (Newnes, 1946) £30
THE IMPOSSIBLE PREFECT (illustrated by Leo Bates) (Blackie, 1947).................................£30
JUNIORS WILL BE JUNIORS (Newnes, 1947) £30
THE FORM THAT LIKED TO BE FIRST (illustrated by W. Spence) (Blackie, 1948) £30
IT WAS FUN IN THE FOURTH (illustrated by Joan Martin May) (Newnes, 1948) £30
RACHEL CHANGES SCHOOLS (illustrated by D.L. Mays) (Blackie, 1948)..............................£25
MAINLY ABOUT THE FOURTH (Newnes, 1949) £25
FIVE SISTERS AT SEDGEWICK (illustrated by W. Spence) (Blackie, 1950)...........................£25
DIMITY DREW'S FIRST TERM (Newnes, 1951) £20
THE RELUCTANT SCHOOLGIRL (illustrated by Louis Ward) (Blackie, 1951) £20
HAZEL HEAD GIRL (illustrated by W. Spence) (Blackie, 1952)..£20
AT SCHOOL WITH PETRA (illustrated by Newton Whittaker) (Blackie, 1953)..........................£20
FOURTH FORM DETECTIVES (illustrated by Newton Whittaker) (Blackie, 1954).......................£20
THE RIVAL FOURTHS (illustrated by Frank Haseler) (Blackie, 1955) £20
STUDY NUMBER SIX (illustrated by Betty Ladler) (Blackie, 1957) £20
THE MYSTERY OF THE MOTELS (illustrated by Victor Bertoglio) (Blackie, 1958) £20
SO THIS IS SCHOOL! (illustrated by Drake Brookshaw) (Blackie, 1959)................................£20
THE AMAZING FRIENDSHIP (illustrated by Drake Brookshaw) (Blackie, 1960) £20
THE FOURTH WAS FUN FOR PHILIPPA (illustrated by Drake Brookshaw) (Blackie, 1961) £20

BRENT-DYER, Elinor M.

British author. Born: Gladys Eleanor May Dyer in South Shields in 1894. Studied at the City of Leeds Training College during the Great War, working as a teacher for the next thirty years. Submitted stories to various magazines and anthologies before publishing her first book, *Gerry Goes to School*, in 1922. This was followed three years later by *The School at the Chalet* (1925), the first of her long-running series of novels set at a chalet school in the Tyrol. Died: 1969.

Prices are for books in Very Good condition with dustjackets.

'Chalet School' Books

THE SCHOOL AT THE CHALET (Chambers, [1925]) £300
JO OF THE CHALET SCHOOL (Chambers, [1926]) £200
THE PRINCESS OF THE CHALET SCHOOL (Chambers, [1927]) £200
THE HEAD-GIRL OF THE CHALET SCHOOL (Chambers, 1928) £200
THE RIVALS OF THE CHALET SCHOOL (Chambers, 1929) £200
EUSTACIA GOES TO THE CHALET SCHOOL (Chambers, 1930) £200
THE CHALET SCHOOL AND JO (Chambers, 1931)...£200
THE CHALET GIRLS IN CAMP (Chambers, 1932) £200
THE EXPLOITS OF THE CHALET GIRLS (Chambers, 1933) £200
THE CHALET SCHOOL AND THE LINTONS (Chambers, 1934) £200
THE NEW HOUSE AT THE CHALET SCHOOL (Chambers, 1935)..£150
JO RETURNS TO THE CHALET SCHOOL (Chambers, 1936) £100
THE NEW CHALET SCHOOL (Chambers, 1938) £100
THE CHALET SCHOOL IN EXILE (with Brisley dustjacket) (Chambers, 1940) £350
THE CHALET SCHOOL IN EXILE (with non-Brisley dustjacket) (Chambers, 1940) £50
THE CHALET SCHOOL GOES TO IT (Chambers, 1941) £75
THE HIGHLAND TWINS AT THE CHALET SCHOOL (Chambers, 1942) £75
LAVENDER LAUGHS IN THE CHALET SCHOOL (Chambers, 1943)....................................£75
GAY FROM CHINA AT THE CHALET SCHOOL (Chambers, 1944) £75
JO TO THE RESCUE (Chambers, 1945)..£75
THREE GO TO THE CHALET SCHOOL (Chambers, 1949) £70
THE CHALET SCHOOL AND THE ISLAND (Chambers, 1950) £50
PEGGY OF THE CHALET SCHOOL (Chambers, 1950) £50
CAROLA STORMS THE CHALET SCHOOL (Chambers, 1951) £60
THE CHALET SCHOOL AND ROSALIE (paperback) (Chambers, 1951) £150
THE WRONG CHALET SCHOOL (Chambers, 1952)..£65
SHOCKS FOR THE CHALET SCHOOL (Chambers, 1952)..£65
THE CHALET SCHOOL IN THE OBERLAND (Chambers, 1952) £75
BRIDE LEADS THE CHALET SCHOOL (Chambers, 1953) £75
CHANGES FOR THE CHALET SCHOOL (Chambers, 1953) £70
JOEY GOES TO THE OBERLAND (Chambers, 1954) £75
THE CHALET SCHOOL AND BARBARA (Chambers, 1954) £60
TOM TACKLES THE CHALET SCHOOL (Chambers, 1955) £65
THE CHALET SCHOOL DOES IT AGAIN (Chambers, 1955) £75
A CHALET GIRL FROM KENYA (Chambers, 1955) £70

BRENT-DYER, Elinor M.

Prices for the 'Chalet School' books range from £50 to £350. These two late titles are worth £65 and £75 respectively.

MARY-LOU OF THE CHALET SCHOOL (Chambers, 1956) £65
A GENIUS AT THE CHALET SCHOOL (Chambers, 1956) £60
A PROBLEM FOR THE CHALET SCHOOL (Chambers, 1956)..£60
THE NEW MISTRESS AT THE CHALET SCHOOL (Chambers, 1957) £55
EXCITEMENTS AT THE CHALET SCHOOL (Chambers, 1957) £55
THE COMING OF AGE OF THE CHALET SCHOOL (Chambers, 1958)..£55
THE CHALET SCHOOL AND RICHENDA (Chambers, 1958)..£55
TRIALS FOR THE CHALET SCHOOL (Chambers, 1959) £50
THEODORA AND THE CHALET SCHOOL (Chambers, 1959) £55
JOEY AND CO IN TIROL (Chambers, 1960) £65
RUEY RICHARDSON — CHALETIAN (Chambers, 1960)..£65
A LEADER IN THE CHALET SCHOOL (Chambers, 1961) £60
THE CHALET SCHOOL WINS THE TRICK (Chambers, 1961) £50
A FUTURE CHALET SCHOOL GIRL (Chambers, 1962)..£75
THE FEUD IN THE CHALET SCHOOL (Chambers, 1962) £55
THE CHALET SCHOOL TRIPLETS (Chambers, 1963)..£65
THE CHALET SCHOOL REUNION (with identification key) (Chambers, 1963) ....£100 (with original yellow band: £120)
JANE AND THE CHALET SCHOOL (Chambers, 1964) £75
REDHEADS AT THE CHALET SCHOOL (Chambers, 1964) £55
ADRIENNE AND THE CHALET SCHOOL (Chambers, 1965) £70
SUMMER TERM AT THE CHALET SCHOOL (Chambers, 1965) £70
CHALLENGE FOR THE CHALET SCHOOL (Chambers, 1966) £70
TWO SAMS AT THE CHALET SCHOOL (Chambers, 1967) £70
ALTHEA JOINS THE CHALET SCHOOL (Chambers, 1969)..£70
PREFECTS OF THE CHALET SCHOOL (Chambers, 1970) £70

Related Titles
THE CHALET BOOK FOR GIRLS (issued without dustjacket) (Chambers, [1947]) £60
THE SECOND CHALET BOOK FOR GIRLS (issued without dustjacket) (Chambers, 1948) £60
THE THIRD CHALET BOOK FOR GIRLS (Chambers, 1949) £75
THE CHALET GIRLS' COOKBOOK (Chambers, 1953)..£90

'La Rochelle' Books
GERRY GOES TO SCHOOL (illustrated by Gordon Browne) (Chambers, [1922])......................................£200
GERRY GOES TO SCHOOL (Lippincott, U.S., 1923) £200

A HEAD GIRL'S DIFFICULTIES (Chambers, [1923]) £175
THE MAIDS OF LA ROCHELLE (Chambers, [1924]) £175
SEVEN SCAMPS (Chambers, [1927]) £175
HEATHER LEAVES SCHOOL (Chambers, 1929) £175
JANIE OF LA ROCHELLE (Chambers, 1932) £175
JANIE STEPS IN (Chambers, 1953) £50

'Chudleigh Hold' Books
CHUDLEIGH HOLD (Chambers, 1954) £40
THE CONDOR CRAGS ADVENTURE (Chambers, 1954) £40
TOP SECRET (Chambers, 1955) £40

Others
A THRILLING TERM AT JANEWAY'S (Nelson, [1927]) £120
THE NEW HOUSE MISTRESS (Nelson, [1928]) £30
JUDY THE GUIDE (Nelson, [1928]) £120
THE SCHOOL BY THE RIVER (Burns, Oates & Washbourne, [1930]) £500
THE FEUD IN THE FIFTH REMOVE (Girl's Own Paper, [1932]) £80
THE LITTLE MARIE-JOSÉ (Burns, Oates & Washbourne, 1932) £500
CARNATION OF THE UPPER FOURTH (Girl's Own Paper, [1934]) £80
ELIZABETH THE GALLANT (Thornton Butterworth, 1935) £350
MONICA TURNS UP TRUMPS (Girl's Own Paper, [1936]) £80
CAROLINE THE SECOND (Girl's Own Paper, [1937]) £350
THEY BOTH LIKED DOGS (Girl's Own Paper, [1938]) £350
THE LITTLE MISSUS (Chambers, 1942) £100
THE LOST STAIRCASE (Chambers, 1946) £75
LORNA AT WYNYARDS (Lutterworth Press, 1947) £120
STEPSISTERS FOR LORNA (illustrated by John Bruce) (Temple, 1948) £120
FARDINGALES (Latimer House, 1950) £120
VERENA VISITS NEW ZEALAND (Chambers, 1951) £150
BESS ON HER OWN IN CANADA (Chambers, 1951) £150
A QUINTETTE IN QUEENSLAND (Chambers, 1951) £150
SHARLIE'S KENYA DIARY (Chambers, 1951) £150
THE 'SUSANNAH' ADVENTURE (Chambers, 1953) £60
NESTA STEPS OUT (Oliphants, 1954) £100
KENNELMAID NAN (Lutterworth Press, 1954) £100
BEECHY OF THE HARBOUR SCHOOL (Oliphants, 1955) £85
LEADER IN SPITE OF HERSELF (Oliphants, 1956) £85
THE SCHOOL AT SKELTON HALL (Parrish, 1962) £120
TROUBLE AT SKELTON HALL (Parrish, 1963) £120

Books Containing Stories by Elinor M. Brent-Dyer
SUNDAY AND EVERYDAY READING FOR THE YOUNG (contains Elinor M. Brent-Dyer's 'Jack's Revenge')
(Wells Gardner Darton, 1914) £20
THE BIG BOOK FOR GIRLS (contains Elinor M. Brent-Dyer's 'The Lady in the Yellow Gown') (Humphrey Milford/OUP, 1925) ..£25
THE GOLDEN STORY BOOK FOR GIRLS (contains Elinor M. Brent-Dyer's 'The Lady in the Yellow Gown')
(Humphrey Milford/OUP, 1931) £20
STORIES OF THE CIRCUS, BOOK 4 (magazine; contains Elinor M. Brent-Dyer's 'Carlotta to the Rescue') ([c.1931]) £10
THE CHILDREN'S CIRCUS BOOK (contains Elinor M. Brent-Dyer's 'Carlotta to the Rescue') (Associated Newspapers, [c.1934]) ..£30
COME TO THE CIRCUS (contains Elinor M. Brent-Dyer's 'Carlotta to the Rescue') (P.R. Gawthorn, [c.1938]) £15
THE SECOND CORONET BOOK FOR GIRLS (contains Elinor M. Brent-Dyer's 'Cavalier Maid') (Sampson Low, no date) £10
MY FAVOURITE STORY (contains Elinor M. Brent-Dyer's 'Rescue in the Snows') (Thames, no date) £10
SCEPTRE GIRLS' STORY ANNUAL (contains Elinor M. Brent-Dyer's 'House of Secrets') (Purnell, no date) £10
GIRL'S OWN ANNUAL VOL. 57 (contains Elinor M. Brent-Dyer's 'The Robins Makes Good') (Girl's Own, no date) £50
MY TREASURE HOUR BUMPER ANNUAL (contains Elinor M. Brent-Dyer's 'The Chalet School Mystery')
(Murrays Sales & Service Co., 1970) £15

BRIGGS, Raymond

British author-illustrator. Born: Raymond Redvers Briggs in Wimbledon in 1934. Studied at the Wimbledon School of Art and the Slade School of Fine Art, subsequently working on advertisements and book covers before producing his first solo work, *Midnight Adventure*, in 1961. His distinctive 'comic strip' style was first seen in *Father Christmas* (1973), and has been used to great effect in *Fungus the Bogeyman* (1977), *The Snowman* (1978) and other books.

Prices are for books in Very Good condition with dustjackets where applicable.

'Father Christmas' Books
FATHER CHRISTMAS (Hamish Hamilton, 1973) £60
FATHER CHRISTMAS GOES ON HOLIDAY (Hamish Hamilton, 1975) £50
THE COMPLETE FATHER CHRISTMAS (contains 'Father Christmas' and 'Father Christmas Goes on Holiday')
(Hamish Hamilton, 1978) £40
THE FATHER CHRISTMAS MINI BOOK (Hamish Hamilton, 1989) £10

*The first edition of Raymond Briggs' **Fungus the Bogeyman** (above) is now worth £40 in Very Good condition.*

THE FATHER CHRISTMAS BOOK OF THE FILM (paperback) (Puffin, 1992) £5
THE FATHER CHRISTMAS BLOOMING DIARY 1994 (paperback) (Puffin, 1992) £5
FATHER CHRISTMAS HAVING A WONDERFUL TIME: A Story Book with Postcards (Hamish Hamilton, 1993) £10

'Fungus the Bogeyman' Books
FUNGUS THE BOGEYMAN (Hamish Hamilton, 1977)..£40
FUNGUS THE BOGEYMAN PLOP-UP BOOK (Hamish Hamilton, 1982) £30

'Snowman' Books

THE SNOWMAN (Hamish Hamilton, 1978) £45
THE SNOWMAN: The Party (board book) (Hamish Hamilton, 1985)...£7
THE SNOWMAN: Dressing-Up (board book) (Hamish Hamilton, 1985)..£7
THE SNOWMAN: Walking in the Air (board book) (Hamish Hamilton, 1985) £7
THE SNOWMAN: Building the Snowman (board book) (Hamish Hamilton, 1985) £7
THE SNOWMAN: A Pop-up Book with Music (with Ron Van Der Meer) (Hamish Hamilton, 1986) £35
THE SNOWMAN: Address Book (Hamish Hamilton, 1987) £10
THE SNOWMAN BOOK OF THE FILM (paperback) (Puffin, 1988) £5
THE SNOWMAN MINI BOOK (Hamish Hamilton, 1989) £5
THE SNOWMAN STORY BOOK (Random House, 1990) £5
THE SNOWMAN CHRISTMAS BOOK (Ladybird, 1990) £4
THE SNOWMAN FLAP BOOK (Random House, 1991)...£5
THE SNOWMAN CLOCK BOOK (Random House, 1991) £5
THE SNOWMAN TELL THE TIME BOOK (Hamish Hamilton, 1991) £5
THE SNOWMAN SOFT AND SMALL BABY BOOK (Hamish Hamilton, 1993) £5

Other Books Written and Illustrated by Raymond Briggs

MIDNIGHT ADVENTURE (Hamish Hamilton, 1961)...£40
THE STRANGE HOUSE (Hamish Hamilton, 1961) £40
RING-A-RING O'ROSES (Hamish Hamilton, 1962) £45
SLEDGES TO THE RESCUE (Hamish Hamilton, 1963)..£40
THE WHITE LAND: A Picture Book of Traditional Rhymes and Verses (Hamish Hamilton, 1963)............£40
FEE FI FO FUM: A Picture Book of Nursery Rhymes (Hamish Hamilton, 1964) £35

A typically exuberant spread from the pop-up version of Briggs' **The Snowman** *(1986), which includes music by Ron van der Meer.*

THE MOTHER GOOSE TREASURY (Hamish Hamilton, 1966) £60
JIM AND THE BEANSTALK (Hamish Hamilton, 1970) £20
GENTLEMAN JIM (Hamish Hamilton, 1980) £25
WHEN THE WIND BLOWS (Hamish Hamilton, 1982) £20
THE TIN-POT GENERAL AND THE OLD IRON WOMAN (Hamish Hamilton, 1984) £20
UNLUCKY WALLY (Hamish Hamilton, 1987) £20
UNLUCKY WALLY TWENTY YEARS ON (Hamish Hamilton 1989) £15
THE MAN (Random Century/Julia MacRae Books, 1992) £15
THE BEAR (Hamish Hamilton, 1994) £12
ETHEL AND ERNEST: A True Story (Cape, 1998) £10

Books Illustrated by Raymond Briggs

PETER AND THE PISKIES: Cornish Folk and Fairy Tales by Ruth Manning-Sanders (OUP, 1958) £25
THE ONION MAN by Alan Ross (Hamish Hamilton: 'Antelope' series, 1959) £20
DANGER ON GLASS ISLAND by Alan Ross (Hamish Hamilton: 'Antelope' series, 1963) £20
THE WRECK OF MONI by Alan Ross (Hamish Hamilton: 'Antelope' series, 1963) £20
MYTHS AND LEGENDS. Edited by Jacynth Hope-Simpson (Hamish Hamilton, 1964) £25
WHISTLING RUFUS by William Mayne (Hamish Hamilton, 1964) £25
THE DAY THE TOWN WENT SILENT by Friedrich Feld (Blackie, 1965) £25
THE FLYING 19 by James Aldridge (Hamish Hamilton, 1966) £20
JIMMY MURPHY AND THE WHITE DUESENBERG by Bruce Carter (Hamish Hamilton, 1968) £25
LINDBERGH THE LONE FLIER by Nicholas Fisk (Hamish Hamilton, 1968) £25
RICHTOVEN THE RED BARON by Nicholas Fisk (Hamish Hamilton, 1968) £25
THE CHRISTMAS BOOKS. Edited by James Reeves (Heinemann, 1968) £30
FIRST UP EVEREST by Showell Styles (Hamish Hamilton, 1969) £25
SHACKLETON'S EPIC VOYAGE by Michael Brown (Hamish Hamilton, 1969) £25
THE ELEPHANT AND THE BAD BABY by Elfrida Vipont (Hamish Hamilton, 1969) £20
FESTIVALS by Ruth Manning-Sanders (Heinemann, 1970) £25
THE TALE OF THREE LANDLUBBERS by Ian Serraillier (Hamish Hamilton, 1970) £20
THE FAIRY TALE TREASURY. Selected by Virginia Haviland (Hamish Hamilton, 1972) £40
THE FORBIDDEN FOREST by James Reeves (Heinemann, 1973) £25
THIS LITTLE PUFFIN — FINGER PLAYS AND NURSERY GAMES. Edited by Elizabeth Matterson (Viking, 1975) £10
ALL IN A DAY by Mitsumasa Anno (Hamish Hamilton, 1986) £8

BRISLEY, Joyce Lankester

British author-illustrator. Born: Joyce Lankester Brisley in 1896. Creator of 'Milly-Molly-Mandy' (Millicent Margaret Amanda), who featured in a long-running series of books, beginning in 1928 with *Milly-Molly-Mandy Stories* and continuing until 1967. Brisley died in 1978.

Prices are books in Very Good condition with dustjackets.

MILLY-MOLLY-MANDY STORIES (Harrap, 1928) £100
MORE OF MILLY-MOLLY-MANDY (Harrap, 1929) £75
LAMBS'-TAILS AND SUCHLIKE: Verses and Sketches (Harrap, 1930) £50
FURTHER DOINGS OF MILLY-MOLLY-MANDY (Harrap, 1932) £60
THE DAWN SHOPS and Other Stories (Harrap, 1933) £40
MARIGOLD IN GODMOTHER'S HOUSE (Harrap, 1934) £60
BUNCHY (Harrap, 1937) £45
THREE LITTLE MILLY-MOLLY-MANDY PLAYS FOR CHILDREN (Harrap, 1938) £50
MY BIBLE-BOOK (Harrap, 1940) £35
THE ADVENTURES OF PURL AND PLAIN (Harrap, 1941) £45
MILLY-MOLLY-MANDY AGAIN (Harrap, 1948) £50
ANOTHER BUNCHY BOOK (Harrap, 1951) £30
MILLY-MOLLY-MANDY & CO (Harrap, 1955) £45
MILLY-MOLLY-MANDY AND BILLY BLUNT (Harrap, 1967) £30
CHILDREN OF BIBLE DAYS (Harrap, 1970) £10
THE JOYCE LANKESTER BRISLEY BOOK. Edited by Frank Walters (anthology) (Harrap, 1981) £10

BROOKE, L. Leslie

British author-illustrator. Born: Leonard Leslie Brooke in Liverpool in 1862. Began work as an artist in 1889, illustrating books by Mrs Molesworth, Andrew Lang and Edward Lear. Also wrote/illustrated his own series of 'picture books', beginning with *Johnny Crow's Garden* (1903). Father of Henry Brooke, who became British Home Secretary. Died: 1940.

Prices are for books in Very Good condition.

THE LIGHT PRINCESS and Other Stories by George MacDonald (Blackie, [1890]) £125
NURSE HEATHERDALE'S STORY by Mrs Molesworth (Macmillan, 1891) £35
THE GIRLS AND I: A Veracious History by Mrs Molesworth (Macmillan, 1892) £30
MARY: A Nursery Story for Very Little Children by Mrs Molesworth (Macmillan, 1893) £30
MY NEW HOME by Mrs Molesworth (Macmillan, 1894) £30

The first annual featuring "Scotland's happy family", the Broons. This is now valued at £2,000 for a Very Good copy.

The title-page from this book, featuring artwork from the regular 'Broons' and 'Oor Wullie' artist, Dudley Watkins.

THE CARVED LIONS by Mrs Molesworth (Macmillan, 1895) £30
SHEILA'S MYSTERY by Mrs Molesworth (Macmillan, 1895) £30
THE ORIEL WINDOW by Mrs Molesworth (Macmillan, 1896) £30
MISS MOUSE AND HER BOYS by Mrs Molesworth (Macmillan, 1897) £30
THE NURSERY RHYME BOOK. Edited by Andrew Lang (Warne, 1897) £75
A SPRING SONG by Thomas Nash (Dent, 1898) £35
THE JUMBLIES and Other Nonsense Verses (Warne, [1900]) £75
THE PELICAN CHORUS and Other Nonsense Verses (Warne, 1900) £75
NONSENSE SONGS AND STORIES (Warne, 1900) £75
JOHNNY CROW'S GARDEN: A Picture Book (Warne, 1903) £100
THE STORY OF THE THREE LITTLE PIGS (Warne, [1904])..£60
TOM THUMB (Warne, [1904]) £45
THE GOLDEN GOOSE BOOK (Warne, [1905]) £100
JOHNNY CROW'S PARTY: Another Picture Book (Warne, 1907)...£75
LESLIE BROOKE'S CHILDREN'S BOOKS (seven books) (Warne, [1907-1922]) ....each £30
THE HOUSE IN THE WOOD and Other Old Fairy Stories (Warne, [1909])..£35
THE TAILOR AND THE CROW: An Old Rhyme with New Drawings by L.L. Brooke (Warne, [1911]) £50
THE MAN IN THE MOON: A Nursery Rhyme Picture Book (Warne, [1913]) £40
ORANGES AND LEMONS: A Nursery Rhyme Picture Book (Warne, [1913]) £30
A NURSERY RHYME PICTURE BOOK (two books) (Warne, [1913 & 1922]) ....the pair £50
NURSERY RHYMES (Warne, [1916]) £60
RING O'ROSES: A Nursery Rhyme Picture Book (Warne, [1922])..£60
JOHNNY CROW'S NEW GARDEN (Warne, 1935) £45

'THE BROONS' ANNUALS

Long-running cartoon strip drawn by Dudley Watkins and featuring a 'typical' Scottish family. Launched in the 'Fun' section of the *Sunday Post* on 8th March 1936, the first annual — published by D.C. Thomson — appearing at Christmas 1939. They were subsequently issued biennially, although there were no editions for 1944 and 1946 because of paper shortages. Note that the annuals were undated before 1968.

Prices are for annuals in Very Good condition (with cover description in brackets for undated annuals).

THE BROONS 1940 (portraits of the Broon family with names below) £1,800
THE BROONS 1942 (head and shoulders profile of Maw and Paw in oval frame) £900
THE BROONS 1948 (Paw in a chair with newspaper and Maw with tea tray; this cover was also used on the 1974 annual) £650

The Windmill Family (1954) is one of several children's novels written by the Essex-born author, Pamela Brown (1924-89).

*Her 1974 novel, **Looking After Libby**, is now valued at £15 in Very Good condition with the pictorial dustjacket.*

THE BROONS 1950 (Broons family standing smiling at reader) **£500**
THE BROONS 1952 (Broons family sitting around a table smiling at the reader) **£400**
THE BROONS 1954 (Maw and Paw dancing the highland fling) **£150**
THE BROONS 1956 (Broons family sitting in front of a window) **£150**
THE BROONS 1958 (Broons family playing board games on a table and the floor) **£80**
THE BROONS 1960 (Broons family at the dinner table; calendar in background reads 'Jan 25') **£60**
THE BROONS 1962 (Broons family at home; two boys playing board games, Maw standing) **£50**
THE BROONS 1964 (Broons family on a mountain top) **£35**
THE BROONS 1966 (Broons family crossing a road)...**£30**
THE BROONS 1968 ....**£20**
THE BROONS 1970 ....**£15**
THE BROONS 1972-74 ....each **£15**
THE BROONS 1976-80 ....each **£15**
THE BROONS 1982-Present ....each **£5**

BROWN, Pamela

British author. Born: Colchester, Essex, in 1924. Having trained for the stage herself, she frequently brought this interest to her novels whether historical or contemporary, notably *The Swish of the Curtain*. Died: 1989.

Prices are for books in Very Good condition with dustjackets where applicable.

THE SWISH OF THE CURTAIN (illustrated by Newton Whittaker) (Nelson, 1941) **£40**
THE SWISH OF THE CURTAIN (revised edition, Brockhampton Press, 1971) **£25**
THE SWISH OF THE CURTAIN (revised edition, Goodchild, 1984)..**£20**
MADDY ALONE (illustrated by Newton Whittaker) (Nelson, 1945)..**£25**
GOLDEN PAVEMENTS (illustrated by Newton Whittaker) (Nelson, 1947)...**£20**
BLUE DOOR ADVENTURE (illustrated by Newton Whittaker) (Nelson, 1949) **£20**
TO BE A BALLERINA AND OTHER STORIES (illustrated by Marcia Lane Foster)
  (Nelson, 1950) **£20**
FAMILY PLAYBILL (illustrated by Marcia Lane Foster) (Nelson, 1951) **£20**
THE TELEVISION TWINS (illustrated by Marcia Lane Foster) (Nelson, 1952).....................................**£20**
HARLEQUIN CORNER (illustrated by Marcia Lane Foster) (Nelson, 1953) **£20**
THE WINDMILL FAMILY (illustrated by Marcia Lane Foster) (Nelson, 1954).......................................**£20**

LOUISA (illustrated by Sax) (Nelson, 1955) £20
MADDY AGAIN (illustrated by Drake Brookshaw) (Nelson, 1956) £20
THE BRIDESMAIDS (illustrated by Peggy Beetles) (Brockhampton Press, 1956)....................................£20
SHOWBOAT SUMMER (illustrated by Charles Paine) (Brockhampton Press, 1957) £20
BACK-STAGE PORTRAIT (illustrated by Drake Brookshaw) (Nelson, 1957)..£20
UNDERSTUDY (illustrated by Drake Brookshaw) (Nelson, 1958) £20
FIRST HOUSE (illustrated by Drake Brookshaw) (Nelson, 1959)..£20
AS FAR AS SINGAPORE (illustrated by Peggy Beetles) (Brockhampton Press, 1959) £20
THE OTHER SIDE OF THE STREET (illustrated by Nathan Mayer) (Brockhampton Press, 1965) £15
THE GIRL WHO RAN AWAY (illustrated by Nathan Mayer) (Brockhampton Press, 1968) £15
A LITTLE UNIVERSE (illustrated by Faith Jaques) (Brockhampton Press, 1970) £15
SUMMER IS A FESTIVAL (Brockhampton Press, 1972) £15
LOOKING AFTER LIBBY (Brockhampton Press, 1974) £15
EVERY DAY IS MARKET DAY (Hodder & Stoughton, 1977) £15
THE MGM GIRLS Behind the Velvet Curtain by Peter Harry Brown and Pamela Ann Brown
    (Harrap, 1984) £15
THE FINISHING SCHOOL (Goodchild, 1984) £15

BRUCE, Dorita Fairlie
British author. Born Dorita Morris Fairlie Bruce in Spain on 20th May 1885. Her happy years at a boarding school in Roehampton inspired a whole series of girls' stories, the best-known featuring the character 'Dimsie', who appeared in her first book, *The Senior Prefect* (1921). She also wrote four historical novels. Died: 1970.
Prices are for books in Very Good condition with dustjackets.

'Dimsie' Books
THE SENIOR PREFECT (OUP, 1921) £200
DIMSIE MOVES UP (OUP, 1921) £100
DIMSIE MOVES UP AGAIN (OUP, 1922) £95
DIMSIE AMONG THE PREFECTS (OUP, 1923)..£80
DIMSIE GROWS UP (OUP, 1924) £70
DIMSIE, HEAD-GIRL (OUP, 1925) £60
DIMSIE GOES TO SCHOOL (reissue of 'The Senior Prefect') (OUP, 1925)..£40
DIMSIE GOES BACK (OUP, 1927) £50
THE DIMSIE OMNIBUS (contains 'Dimsie Goes to School', 'Dimsie Moves Up' and 'Dimsie Moves Up Again';
    'Dimsie Goes to School' was originally published under the title 'The Senior Prefect') (OUP, 1932) £45
THE NEW DIMSIE OMNIBUS (contains 'The New House-Captain', 'The Best House in the School' and
    'Captain of Springdale') (OUP, 1935)..£40
DIMSIE INTERVENES (OUP, 1937) £45
DIMSIE CARRIES ON (OUP, [1942]) £50

'Nancy' Books
THE GIRLS OF ST. BRIDE'S (OUP, 1923)..£180
THAT BOARDING SCHOOL GIRL (OUP, 1925) £75
THE NEW GIRL AND NANCY (OUP, 1926) £75
NANCY TO THE RESCUE (OUP, [1927]) £60
THE BEST BAT IN THE SCHOOL (OUP, 1931) £70
NANCY AT ST. BRIDE'S (OUP, 1933) £50
NANCY IN THE SIXTH (OUP, 1935) £75
THE DORITA BRUCE OMNIBUS (contains 'Nancy at St. Bride's', 'That Boarding School Girl' and
    'The New Girl and Nancy') (OUP, 1937) £40
NANCY RETURNS TO ST. BRIDE'S (OUP, 1938) £50
NANCY CALLS THE TUNE (illustrated by Margaret Horder) (OUP, 1944)..£50

'Springdale' Books
THE NEW HOUSE-CAPTAIN (OUP, 1928)..£100
THE BEST HOUSE IN THE SCHOOL (OUP, 1930) £100
CAPTAIN OF SPRINGDALE (OUP, 1932) £100
THE NEW HOUSE AT SPRINGDALE (OUP, 1934) £100
PREFECTS AT SPRINGDALE (OUP, 1936)..£100
CAPTAIN ANNE (OUP, 1939) £100

'School on the Moor' Books
THE SCHOOL ON THE MOOR (OUP, 1931) £80
THE SCHOOL IN THE WOODS (OUP, 1940) £250
TOBY AT TIBBS CROSS (illustrated by Margaret Horder) (OUP, 1942) £70

'Sally' Books
SALLY SCATTERBRAIN (illustrated by Margaret Horder) (Blackie, 1956) £65
SALLY AGAIN (illustrated by Betty Ladler) (Blackie, 1959) £65
SALLY'S SUMMER TERM (illustrated by Joan Thompson) (Blackie, 1961)..£65

Historical Novels
THE KING'S CURATE (John Murray, 1930) £300
MISTRESS-MARINER (John Murray, 1932) £300
A LAVEROCK LILTING (OUP, 1945) £40
THE BEES ON DRUMWHINNIE (illustrated by Margaret Horder) (OUP, 1952) £40

Others
WILD GOOSE QUEST (Lutterworth Press, 1945) £70
THE SERENDIPITY SHOP (illustrated by Margaret Horder) (OUP, 1947) £75
TRIFFENY (illustrated by Margaret Horder) (OUP, 1950) £90
THE DEBATABLE MOUND (illustrated by Patricia M. Lambe) (OUP, 1953) £70
THE BARTLE BEQUEST (illustrated by Sylvia Green) (OUP, 1955) £90

BRUNA, Dick

Dutch author-illustrator. Born: Holland, 1927. Creator of an outstandingly successful series of small picture books for very young children. The now-familiar square format appeared from 1959 onwards, and include the 'Miffy' and 'Snuffy' books.

Prices are for books in Very Good condition with dustjackets where applicable.

Books Written and Illustrated by Dick Bruna
THE LITTLE BIRD (Methuen, 1962) £15
TILLY AND TESSA (Methuen, 1962) £15
THE FISH (Methuen, 1962) £5
CIRCUS (Methuen, 1963) £5
LITTLE BIRD TWEET (Methuen, 1963) £5
THE EGG (Methuen, 1964) £5
THE KING (Methuen, 1964) £5
MIFFY (Methuen, 1964)...£10
MIFFY AT THE SEASIDE (Methuen, 1964) £10
THE CHRISTMAS BOOK (Methuen, 1964) £10
MIFFY IN THE SNOW (Methuen, 1965) £10
MIFFY AT THE ZOO (Methuen, 1965) £10
THE SAILOR (Methuen, 1966) £5
THE SCHOOL (Methuen, 1966) £5
THE APPLE (Methuen, 1966) £5
PUSSY NELL (Methuen, 1966)...£5
LITTLE RED RIDING HOOD (Methuen, 1967) £5
TOM THUMB (Methuen, 1967) £5
CINDERELLA (Methuen, 1968) £5
SNOW WHITE AND THE SEVEN DWARFS (Methuen, 1968) £5
B IS FOR BEAR (Methuen, 1967) £5
A STORY TO TELL (Methuen, 1968) £5
I CAN COUNT (Methuen, 1968) £5
I CAN READ (Methuen, 1969) £5
I CAN READ MORE (Methuen, 1969) £5
SNUFFY (Methuen, 1970) £5
SNUFFY AND THE FIRE (Methuen, 1970) £5
MIFFY'S BIRTHDAY (Methuen, 1971) £5
MIFFY GOES FLYING (Methuen, 1971) £5
ABC (frieze) (Methuen, 1971) £5
MY VEST IS WHITE (Methuen, 1973)...£5
I CAN COUNT MORE (Methuen, 1973) £5
123 (frieze) (Methuen, 1974) £5
ANIMAL (frieze) (Methuen, 1975 ....£5
ANOTHER STORY TO TELL (Methuen, 1976) £5
LISA AND LYNN (Two Continents, U.S., 1975) £5
MIFFY AT THE PLAYGROUND (Methuen, 1976) £5
DICK BRUNA'S ANIMAL BOOK (Methuen, 1976) £5
I AM A CLOWN (Methuen, 1976) £5
MIFFY IN HOSPITAL (Methuen, 1976) £5
I CAN READ DIFFICULT WORDS (Methuen, 1977) £5
I CAN DRESS MYSELF (Methuen, 1977) £5
POPPY PIG (Methuen, 1978) £5
POPPY PIG'S GARDEN (Methuen, 1978) £5
MIFFY'S DREAM (Methuen, 1979) £5
MY TOYS (Methuen, 1980) £5
READ WITH MIFFY (frieze) (Methuen, 1980) £5
POPPY PIG GOES TO MARKET (Methuen, 1981) £5
WHEN I'M BIG (Methuen, 1981)...£5

This book launched the career of Babar the elephant, creation of the French author/artist, Laurent de Brunhoff.

The first edition of **Babar the King** was published by Methuen in 1936. Very Good copies are now valued at £150.

I KNOW ABOUT NUMBERS (Methuen, 1981) £5
DICK BRUNA'S WORD BOOK (Methuen, 1982) £5
MIFFY'S BICYCLE (Methuen, 1984) £5
MIFFY AT SCHOOL (Methuen, 1984) £5
I KNOW ABOUT SHAPES (Methuen, 1984) £5
I CAN MAKE MUSIC (Methuen, 1984) £5
FARMER JOHN (Methuen, 1984) £5
THE LIFEBOAT (Methuen, 1984) £5
FIND MY HAT (Methuen, 1984) £5
BACK TO FRONT (Methuen, 1984) £5
MY SPORT BOOK (Methuen, 1984)..£5
BLUE BOAT (with Peter Jones) (Methuen, 1984)..£5
MY HOUSE (Methuen, 1984) £5
PLAYING IN WINTER (Methuen, 1984) £5
MY PLAYTIME (Methuen, 1985) £5
MY STREET (Methuen, 1985)..£5
MY GARDEN (Methuen, 1985) £5
MY ANIMALS (Methuen, 1985)...£5
MIFFY'S BOOK OF COLOUR (Methuen, 1986)..£5
POPPY PIG'S BOOK (Methuen, 1987) £5
SNUFFY'S PUPPY (Methuen, 1987) £5
BEAR'S SPRINGTIME (Methuen, 1987) £5

de BRUNHOFF, Jean

French author-illustrator, best known as the creator of Babar the Elephant. Born in Paris in 1899, de Brunhoff studied at the École Alsacienne. His first 'Babar' book, *L'Histoire de Babar, le petit eléphant*, was published in 1931, appearing in Britain three years later under the title *The Story of Babar, the Little Elephant*. Following de Brunhoff's death in 1937, the series was continued by his son, Laurent.

Prices are for U.K. editions in Very Good condition.

THE STORY OF BABAR, THE LITTLE ELEPHANT (Methuen, 1934)..£175
BABAR'S TRAVELS (Methuen, 1935) £160
BABAR THE KING (Methuen, 1936)..£150
BABAR'S ABC (Methuen, 1937) £160

BABAR'S FRIEND ZEPHIR (Methuen, 1937)..£100
BABAR AT HOME (Methuen, 1938) £150
BABAR AND FATHER CHRISTMAS (Methuen, 1940) £120

'Babar' Books by Laurent de Brunhoff (son of Jean de Brunhoff)

BABAR AND THAT RASCAL ARTHUR (Methuen, 1948) £70
PICNIC AT BABAR'S (Methuen, 1950) £70
BABAR'S VISIT TO BIRD ISLAND (Methuen, 1952) £50
BABAR'S CASTLE (Methuen, 1962) £35
SERAFINA THE GIRAFFE (illustrated by Laurent de Brunhoff) (Methuen, 1964 [1965]) £30
BABAR'S FRENCH LESSONS (Cape, 1965) £30
SERAFINA'S LUCKY FIND (illustrated by Laurent de Brunhoff) (Methuen, 1967) £25
BABAR AND THE PROFESSOR (Methuen, 1972) £20
BABAR'S BOOK OF COLOUR (Methuen, 1985)..£15

BUCKERIDGE, Anthony

British author. Born: London, 1912. Taught in a prep school, having his first success as a writer with a handful of adult plays broadcast on BBC Radio. These were followed by a series of radio scripts featuring the schoolboy, Jennings, who subsequently featured in two dozen books, beginning with *Jennings Goes to School* (1950). Buckeridge has also written four novels featuring the grammar schoolboy, Rex Milligan.

Prices are for books in Very Good condition with dustjackets.

'Jennings' Books

JENNINGS GOES TO SCHOOL (Collins, 1950)..£60
JENNINGS FOLLOWS A CLUE (Collins, 1951)..£45
JENNINGS' LITTLE HUT (Collins, 1951) £40
JENNINGS AND DARBISHIRE (Collins, 1952) £40
JENNINGS' DIARY (Collins, 1953) £40
ACCORDING TO JENNINGS (Collins, 1954) £35
OUR FRIEND JENNINGS (Collins, 1955)...£35

Jennings and Darbishire, published by Collins in 1952, was the fourth book in Anthony Buckeridge's popular series of novels.

Although published as recently as 1970, The Jennings Report is now the most sought-after title in the series, selling for £75.

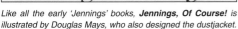

*Like all the early 'Jennings' books, **Jennings, Of Course!** is illustrated by Douglas Mays, who also designed the dustjacket.*

Buckeridge's four 'Rex Milligan' books are also collectable, this one from 1961 selling for £25 in its Mazure dustjacket.

THANKS TO JENNINGS (Collins, 1957)..£30
TAKE JENNINGS, FOR INSTANCE (illustrated by Mays) (Collins, 1958) £25
JENNINGS, AS USUAL (illustrated by Mays) (Collins, 1959)..£25
THE TROUBLE WITH JENNINGS (illustrated by Mays) (Collins, 1960)...................................£25
JUST LIKE JENNINGS (illustrated by Mays) (Collins, 1961) £25
LEAVE IT TO JENNINGS (illustrated by Mays) (Collins, 1963) £25
JENNINGS, OF COURSE! (illustrated by Mays) (Collins, 1964)...£25
ESPECIALLY JENNINGS! (illustrated by Mays) (Collins, 1965)..£25
A BOOKFUL OF JENNINGS (anthology) (Collins, 1966)..£25
JENNINGS ABOUNDING (illustrated by Mays) (Collins, 1967) £30
JENNINGS IN PARTICULAR (illustrated by Mays) (Collins, 1968) £30
TRUST JENNINGS! (illustrated by Mays) (Collins, 1969) £30
THE JENNINGS REPORT (Collins, 1970) £75
TYPICALLY JENNINGS! (Collins, 1971)...£30
THE BEST OF JENNINGS (anthology; revised reissue of 'A Bookful of Jennings' [1966])
     (Collins, 1972) £25
SPEAKING OF JENNINGS (Collins, 1973) £30
JENNINGS AT LARGE (paperback original) (Armada, 1977) £15
JENNINGS AT LARGE (first hardback edition) (Severn House, 1980) £35
JENNINGS ABOUNDING!: A Comedy with Music (play; paperback) (Samuel French, 1980) £5
JENNINGS AGAIN! (Macmillan, 1991) £15
THAT'S JENNINGS (Macmillan, 1994) £15

'Bligh Family' Books
A FUNNY THING HAPPENED! (Lutterworth Press, [1953]) £25

'Rex Milligan' Books
REX MILLIGAN'S BUSY TERM (illustrated by Mazure) (Lutterworth Press, 1953) £25
REX MILLIGAN RAISES THE ROOF (illustrated by Mazure) (Lutterworth Press, 1955)..........£25
REX MILLIGAN HOLDS FORTH (illustrated by Mazure) (Lutterworth Press, 1957) £25
REX MILLIGAN REPORTING (illustrated by Mazure) (Lutterworth Press, 1961) £25

Others
STORIES FOR BOYS. Edited by Anthony Buckeridge (Faber, 1957) £10
IN AND OUT OF SCHOOL. Edited by Anthony Buckeridge (Faber, 1958) £10
STORIES FOR BOYS 2. Edited by Anthony Buckeridge (Faber, 1965) £10

BURNETT, Frances Hodgson
Anglo-American author. Born: Frances Eliza Hodgson in Manchester in November 1849. Following the death of her father, the family emigrated to America in 1865, where Frances remained until 1898, supporting her family through her writing. She produced a number of adult novels before enjoying huge success with her children's stories, *Little Lord Fauntleroy* (1886) and *The Secret Garden* (1911), the latter inspired by her nine-year residence at Maytham Hall in Rolvenden, Kent. She moved back to the United States in 1908, where she died in 1924.

Prices are for books in Very Good condition.

SURLY TIM and Other Stories (Armstrong, U.S., 1877) £100
SURLY TIM and Other Stories (Ward Lock, [1877]) £70
OUR NEIGHBOUR OPPOSITE (stories) (Routledge, [1878]) £60
NATALIE and Other Stories (Warne, [1879]) £60
LINDSAY'S LUCK (stories) (Scribner, U.S., [1878]) £60
LINDSAY'S LUCK (stories) (Routledge, 1879) £50
THE TIDE ON THE MOANING BAR and A QUIET LIFE (stories) (Routledge, [1879]) £45
LITTLE LORD FAUNTLEROY (Warne, 1886) £100
SARA CREWE, or What Happened at Miss Minchin's (Unwin, 1887) £65
SARA CREWE, or What Happened at Miss Minchin's and Editha's Burglar
(Warne, 1888) £60
LITTLE SAINT ELIZABETH and Other Child Stories (Warne, 1890) £20
CHILDREN I HAVE KNOWN: And Giovanni and the Other
(Osgood McIlvaine, 1892 [1891]) £30

*John Burnigham is best known for his illustrations for **Chitty-Chitty Bang-Bang**, but he also produced his own pictures books.*

THE ONE I KNEW THE BEST OF ALL (illustrated by Reginald Birch) (Warne, 1893) £20
THE CAPTAIN'S YOUNGEST, PICCINO and Other Child Stories (illustrated by R.B. Birch) (Warne, 1894) £15
TWO LITTLE PILGRIMS' PROGRESS: A Story of the City Beautiful (Warne, 1895) £25
IN THE CLOSED ROOM (illustrated by Jessie Willcox Smith) (McClure Philips, U.S., 1904) £75
A LITTLE PRINCESS: Being the Whole Story of Sara Crewe Now Told for the First Time (illustrated by Harold Pifford)
     (Warne, 1905) £100
RACKETTY-PACKETTY HOUSE by Queen Crosspatch. Spelled by F.H. Burnett (Warne, 1907)........................£75
THE TROUBLES OF QUEEN SILVER-BELL (Warne, 1907) £75
THE COZY LION told by Queen Crosspatch (illustrated by Harison Cady) (Century, U.S., 1907) £45
THE COZY LION (issued with dustjacket) (Tom Stacey, 1972)..£10
THE SPRING CLEANING told by Queen Crosspatch (illustrated by Harrison Cady) (Century, U.S., 1908) £45
THE SPRING CLEANING (issued with dustjacket) (Tom Stacey, 1973)...£10
THE SECRET GARDEN (illustrated by Charles Robinson) (Heinemann, 1911) £350
THE SECRET GARDEN (illustrated by E.H. Shepard) (1956) £40
THE SECRET GARDEN (illustrated by Michael Hague) (Holt, U.S., 1987) £30
THE LAND OF THE BLUE FLOWER (Putnam, 1912) £15
MY ROBIN (illustrated by Alfred Brennan) (Stokes, U.S., 1912)...£40
MY ROBIN (Putnam, 1913) £15
THE LOST PRINCE (Hodder & Stoughton, 1915) £50
THE LITTLE HUNCHBACK ZIA (illustrated by Charles Robinson) (Heinemann, 1916) £60

BURNINGHAM, John

British author-illustrator. Born: Farnham, Surrey, in 1936. Studied at the Central School of Art, London, 1956-59. Married the illustrator Helen Oxenbury in 1964. Won the Kate Greenway Medal in 1964 and 1971 and the Kurt Maschler Award in 1984. Illustrated the three volumes of Ian Fleming's *Chitty-Chitty-Bang-Bang* (1964-65).

Prices are for books in Very Good condition with dustjackets where applicable.

Books Written and Illustrated by John Burningham

BORKA: THE ADVENTURES OF A GOOSE WITH NO FEATHERS (Cape, 1963) £35
THE MOUSE WHO WANTED TO PLAY THE BALALA!KA (Cape, 1964) £30
ABC (illustrated by John Burningham and Leigh Taylor) (Cape, 1964)...£30
HUMBERT, MISTER FIRKIN AND THE LORD MAYOR OF LONDON (Cape, 1965) £20
CANONBALL SIMP (Cape, 1966) £20
HARQUIN, THE FOX WHO WENT DOWN TO THE VALLEY (Cape, 1967) £25
SEASONS (Cape, 1969) £35
MR GUMPY'S OUTING (Cape, 1970)...£30
MR GUMPY'S MOTOR CAR (Cape, 1973)..£25
COME AWAY FROM THE WATER, SHIRLEY (Cape, 1977) £20
TIME TO GET OUT OF THE BATH, SHIRLEY (Cape, 1978) £20
WOULD YOU RATHER (Cape, 1978) £25
THE SHOPPING BASKET (Cape, 1980) £20
AVOCADO BABY (Cape, 1982) £15
GRANPA (Cape, 1984) £15
WHERE'S JULIUS? (Cape, 1986) £15
JOHN PATRICK NORMAN McHENNESSY: The Boy Who Was Always Late (Cape, 1987).........................£15

Books Illustrated by John Burningham

CHITTY-CHITTY-BANG-BANG, THE MAGICAL CAR: ADVENTURE NUMBER 1 by Ian Fleming (Cape, 1964) £100
CHITTY-CHITTY-BANG-BANG, THE MAGICAL CAR: ADVENTURE NUMBER 2 by Ian Fleming (Cape, 1964) £100
CHITTY-CHITTY-BANG-BANG, THE MAGICAL CAR: ADVENTURE NUMBER 3 by Ian Fleming (Cape, 1965) £100
THE WIND IN THE WILLOWS by Kenneth Grahame (pictorial slipcase) (Viking, 1983) £80

Others

BIRDLAND (wall frieze) (Cape, 1966)..£10
LIONLAND (wall frieze) (Cape, 1966)..£10
STORYLAND (wall frieze) (Cape, 1966)...£10
JUNGLELAND (wall frieze) (Cape, 1968)...£10
WONDERLAND (wall frieze) (Cape, 1968) £10
AROUND THE WORLD (two wall friezes) (Cape, 1972) £10
AROUND THE WORLD IN EIGHTY DAYS (Cape, 1972) £20
LITTLE BOOKS (readers, eight books: 'The Baby' 'The Rabbit', 'The School', 'The Snow', 'The Blanket',
     'The Cupboard', 'The Dog' and 'The Friend' (Cape, 1984)..the set £10
NUMBER PLAY (six books: 'Count Up', 'Read One', 'Ride off', 'Pigs Plus', 'Just Cats' and 'Five Down')
     (Walker, 1983) ....the set £10
FIRST WORDS (six books: 'Cluck Baa', 'Skip Trip', 'Slam Bang', 'Sniff Shout', 'Wobble Pop' and 'Jangle Twang')
     (Walker, 1984) ....the set £10
PLAY AND LEARN (three books: '123', 'Opposites' and 'Colours') (Sainsbury-Walker, 1985)....................the set £10
TAIL FEATHERS FROM MOTHER GOOSE by Iona Opie (illustrated by Maurice Sendak, Janet Ahlberg,
     Nicola Bayley, Quentin Blake, John Burningham and Anthony Browne) (Walker, 1988)............................£25

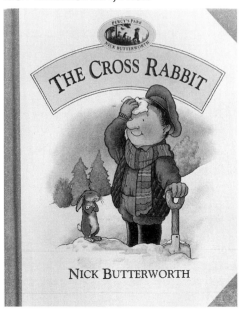

Nick Butterworth is a comparatively recent arrival on the collecting scene. This title first appeared in 1995.

This omnibus from 1996 brings together several tales featuring Butterworth's best-known creation, Percy the park keeper.

BUTTERWORTH, Nick

British author-illustrator. Born: Kingsbury, London, in 1946. Worked as a freelance graphics artist and as a TV-AM children's programme presenter. He produced a regular illustrated story, 'Upney Junction', for the *Sunday Express.*

Prices are for books in Very Good condition with dustjackets where applicable.

Books Written and Illustrated by Nick Butterworth

B.B.BLACKSHEEP AND FAMILY: A Collection of Nursery Rhymes (Macdonald, 1981) £15
TREASURE TROVE AT UPNEY JUNCTION (Macdonald, 1983)..£10
INVASION AT UPNEY JUNCTION (Macdonald, 1983) £10
A MONSTER AT UPNEY JUNCTION (Macdonald, 1983) £10
A WINDY DAY AT UPNEY JUNCTION (Macdonald, 1983) £10
JACK THE CARPENTER AND HIS FRIENDS (Sainsbury's/Walker, 1986) £10
TOM THE GREENGROCER AND HIS FRIENDS (Sainsbury's, 1986)..£10
JULIE THE PAPER GIRL AND HER FRIENDS (Sainsbury's, 1986) £10
ONE SNOWY NIGHT (HarperCollins, 1989)..£7
THE SECRET PATH (HarperCollins, 1990)...£7
AFTER THE STORM (HarperCollins, 1993) £7
THE RESCUE PARTY (HarperCollins, 1983) £7
THE CROSS RABBIT (HarperCollins, 1995) £5
THE FOX'S HICCUPS (HarperCollins, 1996) £5
A YEAR IN PERCY'S PARK (HarperCollins, 1995) £8
THE HEDGEHOG'S BALLOON (HarperCollins, 1996)..£7
THE BADGER'S BATH (HarperCollins, 1996) £7
TALES FROM PERCY'S PARK (omnibus) (HarperCollins, 1996) £7
THE OWL'S LESSON (HarperCollins, 1997) £5

Others

TALES FOR A PRINCE (illustrated by Mick Inkpen, M Ursell and Krystyna Turska) (Hodder & Stoughton, 1988).......................£10
JAKE AGAIN by Annette Butterworth (Hodder & Stoughton, 1996)...£6

CALDECOTT, Randolph

British illustrator. Born: Chester, 1846. Worked as a bank clerk before moving to London at the age of 26, where he studied at the Slade School of Art. His work for *London Society* magazine led to a fruitful partnership with the printer, Edmund Evans, with whom he produced a series of popular picture books, notably *The Diverting History of John Gilpin* (1878) and *Ride a Cock Horse* (1884). Also contributed to the *Graphic* and other magazines. Caldecott was an important influence on Beatrix Potter. Died: 1886.

Prices are for Books in Very Good condition.

Randolph Caldecott's 'Picture Books'
(all printed by Edmund Evans and issued in sewn stiff card covers)

THE DIVERTING HISTORY OF JOHN GILPIN (Routledge, [1878]) £30
THE HOUSE THAT JACK BUILT (Routledge, [1878]) £30
ELEGY ON THE DEATH OF A MAD DOG by Oliver Goldsmith (Routledge, [1879]) £70
THE BABES IN THE WOOD (Routledge, [1879]) £30
THE THREE JOVIAL HUNTSMEN (Routledge, [1880]) £30
SING A SONG FOR SIXPENCE (Routledge, [1880]) £30
THE QUEEN OF HEARTS (Routledge, [1881]) £30
THE FARMER'S BOY (Routledge, [1881]) £30
THE MILKMAID (Routledge, [1882]) £30
HEY DIDDLE DIDDLE and BYE BABY BUNTING (Routledge, [1882]) £30
THE FOX JUMPS OVER THE PARSON'S GATE (Routledge, [1883]) £30
A FROG HE WOULD A-WOOING GO (Routledge, [1883]) £30
COME LASSES AND LADS (Routledge, [1884]) £30

This Frederick Warne collection from 1895 contains no fewer than eight of Randolph Caldecott's very popular picture books.

RIDE A-COCK HORSE TO BANBURY CROSS and A FARMER WENT TROTTING UPON HIS GREY MARE
(Routledge, [1884]) £30
AN ELEGY ON THE GLORY OF HER SEX, MRS MARY BLAIZE by Oliver Goldsmith (Routledge, [1885]) £30

The most sought-after of Katharine Cameron's illustrated books: **The Enchanted Land**, *published by T.C. & E.C. Jack in 1906.*

THE GREAT PANJANDRUM HIMSELF (Routledge, [1885]) £30
R. CALDECOTT'S PICTURE BOOK (Volume One, containing the first four 'Picture Books')
(Routledge, [1879]) £55
R. CALDECOTT'S PICTURE BOOK (Volume Two, containing the second four 'Picture Books')
(Routledge, [1881]) £55
R. CALDECOTT'S COLLECTION OF PICTURES & SONGS (single-volume reissue of
'R. Caldecott's Picture Book' Volumes One and Two) (Routledge, [1881]) £50
THE HEY DIDDLE DIDDLE PICTURE BOOK (contains four 'Picture Books') (Routledge, [1883])......£50
THE PANJANDRUM PICTURE BOOK (contains four 'Picture Books') (Routledge, [1885]) £50
THE COMPLETE COLLECTION OF RANDOLPH CALDECOTT'S PICTURES AND SONGS
(contains all sixteen 'Picture Books', with a preface by Austin Dobson; limited to 800 copies; engraved,
printed and signed by Edmund Evans) (Routledge, U.K./U.S., 1887) £250
R. CALDECOTT'S PICTURE BOOKS (contains the first four 'Picture Books') (Routledge, [1889 & 1892]) £50
R. CALDECOTT'S SECOND COLLECTION OF PICTURES AND SONGS (a one-volume reissue of
'The Hey Diddle Diddle Picture Book' and 'The Panjandrum Picture Book') (Warne, [1895])..........£50
R. CALDECOTT'S COLLECTION OF PICTURES AND SONGS (reissue of 1881 edition) (Warne, [1896]) £50
R. CALDECOTT'S PICTURE BOOK NO. 1 (four volumes; together contain fourteen 'Picture Books')
(Warne: U.K./U.S., [1906-1907]) ....each £50
MINIATURE PICTURE BOOKS (miniature editions of each 'Picture Book';
four volumes containing four 'Picture Books' each were also published) (Warne, U.K./U.S., [1906-1907]) ....each £25

Other Books Illustrated by Randolph Caldecott

FRANK MILDMAY, or The Naval Officer by Captain Marryat (six full-page black-and-white illustrations by
Randolph Caldecott; engraved by Edmund Evans; with a memoir by F. Marryat) (Routledge, U.K./U.S., [1873]) £45
BARON BRUNO, or The Unbelieving Philosopher and Other Fairy Stories by Louisa Morgan
(eight black-and-white illustrations by Randolph Caldecott) (Macmillan, 1875) £45
OLD CHRISTMAS. From the Sketch Book of Washington Irving (second edition; 120 black-and-white illustrations by
Randolph Caldecott; arranged and engraved by J.D. Cooper) (Macmillan, 1876)....................£30
BRACEBRIDGE HALL, or The Humorists by Washington Irving (116 black-and-white illustrations by Randolph Caldecott;
arranged and engraved by J.D. Cooper) (Macmillan, 1877 [1876]) £35
WHAT THE BLACKBIRD SAID: A Story in Four Chirps by Mrs Frederick Locker
(four full-page black-and-white illustrations of birds by Randolph Caldecott) (Routledge, 1881) £45
JACKANAPES by Juliana Horatia Ewing (SPCK, 1884 [1883]) £20
SOME OF AESOP'S FABLES WITH MODERN INSTANCES (Macmillan 1883)..................................£30
DADDY DARWIN'S DOVECOTE: A Country Tale by Juliana Horatia Ewing (SPCK, [1884]) £20
LOB LIE-BY-THE-FIRE by Juliana Horatia Ewing (SPCK, [1885])...£20
FABLES DE LA FONTAINE (selected and introduced by Louis M. Moriarty) (Macmillan, 1885) £30
JACK AND THE BEANSTALK by Hallam Tennyson (Macmillan, 1886)...£30
THE OWLS OF OLYNN BELFRY by A.Y.D. (Field & Tuer, [1886])..£30
JACKANAPES by Juliana Horatia Ewing (contains 'Daddy Darwin's Dovecote' and 'Lob Lie-By-The-Fire')
(SPCK, [1892])..£25
RANDOLPH CALDECOTT'S PAINTING BOOK (SPCK, [1895]) £45
RANDOLPH CALDECOTT'S PAINTING BOOK (first series) (Warne, U.K/U.S., [1902]) £35

CAMERON, Katharine

Scottish illustrator. Born: Glasgow, 1874. Studied at the Glasgow School of Art and in Paris. Illustrated many children's books, and was a contributor to *The Yellow Book*. Married the artist, Arthur Kay, in 1928. Died: 1965.

Prices are for books in Very Good condition.

IN FAIRYLAND: Tales Told Again by Louey Chisholm (T.C. & E.C. Jack, 1904) £75
THE WATER BABIES by Charles Kingsley (T.C. & E.C. Jack, [1905]) £50
STORIES OF KING ARTHUR'S KNIGHTS by Mary MacGregor (T.C. & E.C. Jack, [1905]) £35
THE ENCHANTED LAND by Louey Chisholm (T.C. & E.C. Jack, 1906) £90
LEGENDS AND STORIES OF ITALY FOR CHILDREN by Amy Steedman (T.C. & E.C. Jack, [1909])...........£45
'IN FAIRYLAND' SERIES by Louey Chisholm (T.C. & E.C. Jack, [1910]) £30
CELTIC TALES by Louey Chisholm (T.C. & E.C. Jack, [1910])..£40
IN A CITY GARDEN by James R. Aitken (Foulis, 1913)..£30
WHERE THE BEE SUCKS: A Book of Flowers. Poems chosen by Iola A. Williams (Medici Society, [1929]) £30
IAIN THE HAPPY PUPPY: Being the Autobiography of a West Highland White Terrier
(written and illustrated by Katherine Cameron) (Moray Press, 1934) £30

THE 'CAPTAIN' MAGAZINE

British boys' magazine, published by Newnes between 1899 and 1924. Its best-known contributor was P.G. Wodehouse, who submitted many of his early school stories to the title.

Prices are for volumes in Very Good condition.

THE CAPTAIN MAGAZINE: A Magazine for Boys and Old Boys. Vol. 1 (April-September 1899) £45
THE CAPTAIN MAGAZINE Vols. 2-25 (October 1899-September 1911) ....each £35
THE CAPTAIN MAGAZINE Vols. 26-46 (October 1911-March 1922) ....each £30
THE CAPTAIN MAGAZINE Vols. 47-50 (April 1922-March 1924)..each £25

CARROLL, Lewis

British author. Born: Charles Lutwidge Dodgson in Daresbury, Cheshire, in 1832. Educated at Rugby School and Christ Church College, Oxford. Received Studentship of the college in 1852 and appointed Sub-Librarian in 1855. His first humorous pieces appeared in the *Comic Times* in that year. Inspired by his friendship with the young Alice Liddell, he wrote *Alice Adventures Under Ground* in 1864, the book appearing under the title *Alice's Adventures in Wonderland* the following year. The sequel, *Through the Looking-Glass, and What Alice Found There*, was published in 1871. As well as his various books of nonsense, he also wrote several pamphlets and was an accomplished photographer. Died: 1898.

Prices are for books in Very Good condition (with dustjackets after 1940).

'ALICE' BOOKS

'Alice's Adventures Under Ground'

ALICE'S ADVENTURES UNDER GROUND (red cloth binding) (Macmillan, 1886) £175
ALICE'S ADVENTURES UNDER GROUND (variant binding) (Macmillan, 1886) £1,750

'Alice's Adventures in Wonderland'

FIRST [WITHDRAWN] EDITION (illustrated by John Tenniel) (Macmillan, 1865)..............................£200,000
FIRST U.S. EDITION (illustrated by John Tenniel) (Appleton, U.S., 1865) £5,000
FIRST U.K. EDITION (illustrated by John Tenniel) (Macmillan, 1866 [1865]) £3,000
PETER NEWELL EDITION (Harper, U.S., 1901) £150
BLANCHE McMANUS EDITION (Mansfield, U.S., 1896; U.K.: Ward Lock, 1907)...............................£80
CHARLES ROBINSON EDITION (Cassell, 1907) £150
ARTHUR RACKHAM EDITION (with a poem by Austin Dobson; green cloth binding) (Heinemann, [1907]) £300
ARTHUR RACKHAM EDITION (with a poem by Austin Dobson; De Luxe edition: limited to 1,130 copies;
    white vellum binding) (Heinemann, [1907])...£1,750
THOMAS MAYBANK EDITION (Routledge, 1907)...£100
MILLICENT SOWERBY EDITION (Chatto & Windus, 1907) £120
HARRY ROUNTREE EDITION (Nelson, 1908) £100
THOMAS HEATH ROBINSON EDITION (illustrated by Thomas Heath Robinson and Charles Pears) (William Collins, 1908) £30
MABEL LUCIE ATTWELL EDITION (Raphael Tuck, [1910]) £200
FRANK ADAMS EDITION (Blackie, 1912) £35
ALICE B. WOODWARD EDITION (Bell, 1913) £90
A.E. JACKSON EDITION (Frowde, 1915)..£150
MARGARET TARRANT EDITION (Ward Lock, 1916) £110
A.L. BOWLEY EDITION (Raphael Tuck, 1921)..£50
GWYNNED HUDSON EDITION (Hodder & Stoughton, 1922) £125
WILLY POGANY EDITION (Dutton, U.S., 1929)..£50
WILLY POGANY EDITION (signed, limited edition) (Dutton, U.S., 1929)...................................£250
CHARLES FOLKARD EDITION (A. & C. Black, 1929)...£40
MARIE LAURENCIN EDITION (Black Sun Press, Paris, 1930) £2,000
MARIE LAURENCIN EDITION (with extra plates) (Black Sun Press, Paris, 1930)...........................£5,000
RENE CLOKE EDITION (P.R. Gawthorn, [1944]) £30
ANTHONY RADO EDITION (Newman Wolsey, [1944]) £40
EILEEN SOPER EDITION (Harrap, 1947) £40
MARAJA EDITION (W.H. Allen, 1958) £40
RALPH STEADMAN EDITION (Dobson, 1967) £70
SALVADOR DALI EDITION (Random House, U.S., 1969) £3,000
MICHAEL HAGUE EDITION (Holt, U.S., 1985) £30
MICHAEL HAGUE EDITION (Methuen, 1985) £25
JUSTIN TODD EDITION (Gollancz, 1988) £30
ANTONY BROWNE EDITION (Julia MacRae Books, 1988)...£30
HELEN OXENBURY EDITION (Walker, 1999) £20

'Through the Looking-Glass'

JOHN TENNIEL EDITION (Macmillan, 1872 [1871]) £300
BLANCHE McMANUS EDITION (Mansfield, U.S., 1899)..£50
PETER NEWELL EDITION (Harper, U.S., 1902) £100
HELEN MUNRO EDITION (Nelson, 1937) £30
RALPH STEADMAN EDITION (MacGibbon & Kee, 1972)..£60

Combined Editions

JOHN TENNIEL EDITION (92 illustrations by John Tenniel, including sixteen in colour) (Macmillan, 1911) £75
MERVYN PEAKE EDITION (Continental, Sweden, 1946) £150
MERVYN PEAKE EDITION (Wingate, 1954) £60

Other Children's Books

PHANTASMAGORIA and Other Poems (Macmillan, 1869) £200
PHANTASMAGORIA and Other Poems (illustrated by Arthur B. Frost; miniature edition) (Macmillan, 1911) £20
THE HUNTING OF THE SNARK: An Agony in Eight Fits (Macmillan, 1876) £350

THE HUNTING OF THE SNARK: An Agony in Eight Fits (illustrated by Mervyn Peake) (Chatto & Windus, 1941) £60
THE HUNTING OF THE SNARK (illustrated by Helen Oxenbury) (Heinemann, 1970) £15
THE HUNTING OF THE SNARK (illustrated by Harold Jones; De Luxe edition: limited to 900 copies;
  morocco binding and slipcase) (Whittington Press, 1975)....................£80
THE HUNTING OF THE SNARK (illustrated by Ralph Steadman) (Dempsey, 1975) £45
THE HUNTING OF THE SNARK (illustrated by Quentin Blake; in slipcase) (Folio Society, 1976) £30
THE HUNTING OF THE SNARK (facsimile edition; issued with dustjacket) (Windward, 1980)....................£10
RHYME? AND REASON? (illustrated by Arthur B. Frost and Henry Holiday) (Macmillan, 1883) £150

A plate from Arthur Rackham's 1907 edition of **Alice in Wonderland**. *Unusually, the De Luxe copies of this book were not signed.*

A TANGLED TALE (illustrated by Arthur B. Frost) (Macmillan, 1885) £100
THE NURSERY ALICE (standard edition) (Macmillan, 1890) £120
THE NURSERY ALICE ('Peoples Edition') (Macmillan, 1889) £150
SYLVIE AND BRUNO (illustrated by Harry Furniss) (Macmillan, 1889) £50
SYLVIE AND BRUNO CONCLUDED (illustrated by Harry Furniss) (Macmillan, 1893) £50
THREE SUNSETS AND OTHER POEMS (illustrated by Gertrude B. Thomson) (Macmillan, 1898) ...£40
THE LEWIS CARROLL PICTURE BOOK (illustrated by the author) (Unwin, 1899) £125
FEEDING THE MIND (preface by William H. Draper) (Chatto & Windus, 1907)................................£40
FURTHER NONSENSE, VERSE AND PROSE (photographs by the author; one illustration by H.M. Bateman) (Unwin, 1926)....£35
THE COLLECTED VERSE OF LEWIS CARROLL (illustrated by John Tenniel, Frost, Holiday, Furniss and the author)
    (Macmillan, 1932)..£60
FOR THE TRAIN (illustrated by C.H. Bennett and W. McConnell) (Denis Archer, 1932) £40
THE RECTORY UMBRELLA AND MISCHMASCH (Cassell, 1932) £40

'CHATTERBOX' ANNUALS

Long-running British children's annual. The magazine itself was founded in 1866 as a rival to the 'penny dreadfuls' of the time, and contained both serials and factual/religious articles. It ceased publication in 1948.

Prices are for annuals in Very Good condition.

CHATTERBOX 1866 (William Mackintosh, [1866]) £45
CHATTERBOX 1867-1929 (William Mackintosh/Wells Gardner & Darton) ....each £35
CHATTERBOX 1930-1956 (Wells Gardner & Darton/Dean) ....each £10

CHRISTOPHER, John

British author. Born: Christopher Samuel Youd in 1922. An accomplished science fiction writer for adults, he is one of the few authors to write successfully in the field for children. Many of his works are grouped together in trilogies.

Prices are for books in Very Good condition with dustjackets.

THE WHITE MOUNTAINS (Hamish Hamilton, 1967) £30
THE CITY OF LEAD AND GOLD (Hamish Hamilton, 1967) £30
THE POOL OF FIRE (Hamish Hamilton, 1968) £30
THE LOTUS CAVES (Hamish Hamilton, 1969) £15
THE GUARDIANS (Hamish Hamilton, 1970) £15
THE PRINCE IN WAITING (Hamish Hamilton, 1970) £15
BEYOND THE BURNING LANDS (Hamish Hamilton, 1971) £15
THE SWORD OF THE SPIRITS (Hamilton Hamilton, 1972)..£15
DOM AND VA (Hamish Hamilton, 1973) £15
A FIGURE IN GREY (written under the pseudonym 'Hilary Ford') (World's Work, 1973) £10
WILD JACK (Hamish Hamilton, 1974) £10
IN THE BEGINNING (Longman, 1975) £10
EMPTY WORLD (Hamish Hamilton, 1977) £10
FIREBALL (Gollancz, 1981) £10
NEW FOUND LAND (Gollancz, 1983) £10
DRAGONDANCE (Viking Kestrel, 1986) £10

'CHUMS' ANNUALS

British boys' annual, published between 1892 and 1941. It was a less popular rival to the *Boy's Own Paper*. Vols. 1-34 published by Cassell, Vol. 35 onwards published by Amalgamated Press.

Prices are for annuals (bound volumes) in Very Good condition.

VOLUME 1 (1892-1893) £35
VOLUMES 2-22 (1893-1914) ....each £25
VOLUMES 23-26 (1914-1918) ....each £25
VOLUMES 27-42 (1918-1935) ....each £25
VOLUMES 43-48 (1935-1941) ....each £20

COLLODI, Carlo

Italian author. Born: Carlo Lorenzini in Florence in 1826. Took his pseudonym from the name of his mother's home town. Worked as a journalist and founded his own satirical magazine, before turning to children's writing. Best known for *Pinocchio*, which was first serialised in 1881. Also translated Perrault's tales. Died: 1890.

Prices are for books in Very Good condition.

LE AVVENTURE DI PINOCCHIO (first edition in book form; illustrated by E. Mazzanti) (Florence, 1883)............................£20,000
THE STORY OF A PUPPET, or The Adventures of Pinocchio (translated by M.A. Murray) (Unwin, 1892) £4,000
ADVENTURES EVERY CHILD SHOULD KNOW: The Marvellous Adventures of Pinocchio. Edited by Mary E. Burt,
    from an original translation by A.G. Capriani (illustrated by Emily Hall Chamberlin) (Doubleday, U.S., 1909) £200
PINOCCHIO: The Tale of a Puppet (illustrated by Charles Folkard; translated by M.A. Murray) (Dent, 1911) £75

This edition of **Pinocchio** was published by Collins in 1939 and is now valued at £25 in Very Good condition with the jacket.

This American paperback was published in 1939 to coincide with the Disney film. Very Good copies are valued at £800.

PINOCCHIO (illustrated by Maria L. Kirk) (Lippincott, U.S., 1920) £65
PINOCCHIO (illustrated by Jack Tinker) (Lippincott, U.S., [1930]) £50
PINOCCHIO (illustrated by K. Wiese; translated by M.A. Murray) (Nelson, 1938) £25
THE ADVENTURES OF PINOCCHIO (illustrated by A.H. Watson) (Collins, 1939) £25
WALT DISNEY'S PINOCCHIO (limited to 100 numbered copies; comb-bound) (Collins, [1939]) £150
WALT DISNEY TELLS THE STORY OF PINOCCHIO (paperback) (Whitman No 556, U.S., 1939) £800
WALT DISNEY'S VERSION OF PINOCCHIO (pictorial boards) (Collins, 1940) £50
PINOCCHIO (illustrated by Charles Folkard; translated by M.A. Murray, revised by G. Tassinari) (Dent, 1951) £35
THE ADVENTURES OF PINOCCHIO AND PIP, or The Little Rose-Coloured Monkey
   (illustrated by Will Nickless; introduction by David Davis) (Collins, 1954) £20
PINOCCHIO. Adapted by Allen Chafee (illustrated by Lois Lenski) (Publicity Products, [1954]) £20
THE ADVENTURES OF PINOCCHIO (illustrated by Roberto Innocenti) (Cape, 1988) £10

COOLIDGE, Susan
American author. Born: Sarah Chauncy Woolsey in Cleveland, Ohio, in 1845. Spent most of her childhood in New Haven, Connecticut, and worked as a nurse during the Civil War. Her first children's book, *The New-Year's Bargain* (1872), was quickly followed by *What Katy Did*. She also wrote several volumes of verse and edited the letters of Fanny Burney and Jane Austen. Died: 1905.

Prices are for books in Very Good condition.

THE NEW YEAR'S BARGAIN (illustrated by Addie Ledyard) (Roberts Brothers, U.S.,1872) £65
THE NEW YEAR'S BARGAIN (illustrated by Addie Ledyard) (Warne, [1872]) £25
WHAT KATY DID (illustrated by Addie Ledyard) (Roberts Brothers, U.S., 1873) £175
WHAT KATY DID (illustrated by Addie Ledyard) (Ward & Lock, [1873]) £125
WHAT KATY DID AT SCHOOL (Roberts Brothers, U.S., 1874) £150
WHAT KATY DID AT SCHOOL (Ward & Lock, 1874) £90
LITTLE MISS MISCHIEF and Other Stories (illustrated by Addie Ledyard) (Roberts Brothers, U.S., 1874) £60
LITTLE MISS MISCHIEF and Other Stories (illustrated by Addie Ledyard) (Ward & Lock, [1874]) £30
MISCHIEF'S THANKSGIVING and Other Stories (illustrated by Addie Ledyard) (Roberts Brothers, U.S., 1874) £60
MISCHIEF'S THANKSGIVING and Other Stories (illustrated by Addie Ledyard) (Routledge, [1875]) £30
NINE LITTLE GOSLINGS (Roberts Bros, U.S., 1875) £40

FOR SUMMER AFTERNOONS (Roberts Brothers, U.S., 1876) £15
EYEBRIGHT (Roberts Brothers, U.S., 1879) £50
EYEBRIGHT (Routledge, [1879]) £25
CROSS PATCH and Other Stories (illustrated by Ellen Oakford) (Roberts Brothers, U.S., 1881) £30
CROSS PATCH and Other Stories (illustrated by Ellen Oakford; same as above, but with different title-page) (Bogue, 1881)....£30
A GUERNSEY LILY (Roberts Brothers, U.S., 1881 [1880]) £50
A GUERNSEY LILY (Bogue, 1881)...£50
A ROUND DOZEN (Roberts Brothers, U.S., 1883)...£30
A LITTLE COUNTRY GIRL (Roberts Brothers, U.S., 1885) £25
WHAT KATY DID NEXT (illustrated by Jessie McDermot) (Roberts Brothers, U.S., 1886) £150
WHAT KATY DID NEXT (illustrated by Jessie McDermot) (Ward & Lock, [1887]) £150
WHAT KATY DID NEXT (illustrated by Jessie McDermot) (Blackie, 1903 [1902]) £90
CLOVER (Roberts Brothers, U.S., 1888) £50
JUST SIXTEEN (Roberts Brothers, U.S., 1889) £20
IN THE HIGH VALLEY (Roberts Brothers, U.S., 1890) £60
IN THE HIGH VALLEY (Blackie, 1959) £20
THE BARBERRY BUSH (Roberts Brothers, U.S., 1893) £20
NOT QUITE EIGHTEEN (Roberts Brothers, U.S., 1894) £20
AN OLD CONVENT SCHOOL IN PARIS (Roberts Brothers, U.S., 1895) £20
CURLY LOCKS (Little Brown, U.S., 1899) £20
A LITTLE KNIGHT OF LABOR (Little Brown, U.S., 1899) £20
LITTLE TOMMY TUCKER (Little Brown, U.S., 1900) £20
TWO GIRLS (Little Brown, U.S., 1900) £20
UNCLE AND AUNT (Little Brown, U.S., 1901) £20
LITTLE BO-PEEP (Little Brown, U.S., 1901) £20
THE RULE OF THREE (Henry Altemus, U.S., 1904) £15
A SHEAF OF STORIES (Little Brown, U.S., 1906) £15

CORKRAN, Alice

British author. Wrote several children's works, but is best known for *Down the Snow Stairs* (1887), a fantasy partly inspired by the works of Lewis Carroll. Died: 1916.

Prices are for books in Very Good condition.

THE ADVENTURES OF MRS WISHING-TO-BE and Other Stories (Blackie, 1883 [1882]) £25
DOWN THE SNOW STAIRS or From Good-Night to Good-Morning (illustrated by Gordon Browne) (Blackie, 1887 [1886]) £50
MARGERY MERTON'S GIRLHOOD (illustrated by Gordon Browne) (Blackie, 1888 [1887]) £40
MEG'S FRIEND (illustrated by Robert Fowler) (Blackie, 1889 [1888]) £25
JOAN'S ADVENTURES AT THE NORTH POLE AND ELSEWHERE (Blackie, 1889 [1888])...................£35

CRADOCK, Mrs H.C.

British author of the 'Josephine' series and other children's books, many of them illustrated by Honor C. Appleton. Also wrote the 'Teddy Bear' series.

Prices are for books in Very Good condition.

THE CARE OF BABIES: A Reading Book for Girls (Bell, 1908) £60
JOSEPHINE AND HER DOLLS (illustrated by Honor C. Appleton) (Blackie, 1916 [1915]) £120
JOSEPHINE'S HAPPY FAMILY (illustrated by Honor C. Appleton) (Blackie, 1917 [1916]) £80
JOSEPHINE IS BUSY (illustrated by Honor C. Appleton) (Blackie, 1918) £90
EVERYDAY STORIES TO TELL TO CHILDREN (Harrap, 1919) £40
THE BIG BOOK OF JOSEPHINE (contains 'Josephine and her Dolls', 'Josephine's Happy Family' and
    'Josephine is Busy'; illustrated by Honor C. Appleton) (Blackie, [1919]) £175
WHERE THE DOLLS LIVED (illustrated by Honor C. Appleton) (SPCK, [1919]) £90
JOSEPHINE'S BIRTHDAY (illustrated by Honor C. Appleton) (Blackie, 1920 [1919]) £90
JOSEPHINE, JOHN AND THE PUPPY (illustrated by Honor C. Appleton) (Blackie, [1920]) £85
PEGGY'S TWINS (illustrated by Honor C. Appleton) (SPCK, [1920])..£60
THE HOUSE OF FANCY (illustrated by Honor C. Appleton) (O'Connor, 1922) £60
PEGGY AND JOAN (illustrated by Honor C. Appleton) (Blackie, [1922]) £60
THE STORY OF PAT (SPCK, [1923]) £25
JOSEPHINE KEEPS SCHOOL (illustrated by Honor C. Appleton) (Blackie, [1925]) £70
THE BONNY BOOK OF JOSEPHINE (contains 'Josephine, John and the Puppy',
    'Josephine's Birthday' and 'Josephine Keeps School'; illustrated by Honor C. Appleton) (Blackie, [1926])..........£150
JOSEPHINE GOES SHOPPING (illustrated by Honor C. Appleton) (Blackie, [1926]) £70
THE BEST TEDDY BEAR IN THE WORLD (illustrated by Honor C. Appleton) (Nelson, [1926]) £45
PAMELA'S TEDDY BEARS (illustrated by Honor C. Appleton) (Jack, [1927]) £50
JOSEPHINE'S CHRISTMAS PARTY (illustrated by Honor C. Appleton) (Blackie, [1927]) £70
ELIZABETH (illustrated by Doris Burton) (Nelson, [1930]) £25
JOSEPHINE KEEPS HOUSE (illustrated by Honor C. Appleton) (Blackie, 1931) £60
THE SMITH FAMILY (illustrated by S.G. Hulme Beaman) (Nelson, [1931]) £30
BARBARA AND PETER (illustrated by Doris Burton) (Nelson, [1931]) £25

THE JOSEPHINE DOLLY BOOK (contains 'Josephine's Happy Family', 'Josephine, John and the Puppy' and 'Josephine is Busy'; illustrated by Honor C. Appleton) (Blackie, [1934]) £150

ADVENTURES OF A TEDDY BEAR (illustrated by Joyce L. Brisley) (Harrap, 1934) £55

MORE ADVENTURES OF A TEDDY BEAR (illustrated by Joyce L. Brisley) (Harrap, 1935) £40

IN TEDDY BEAR'S HOUSE (illustrated by Joyce L. Brisley) (Harrap, 1936) £40

JOSEPHINE'S PANTOMIME (illustrated by Honor C. Appleton) (Blackie, 1939) £60

TEDDY BEAR'S SHOP (illustrated by Joyce L. Brisley) (Harrap, 1939) £35

JOSEPHINE GOES TRAVELLING (illustrated by Honor C. Appleton) (Blackie, 1940) £60

TEDDY BEAR'S FARM (illustrated by Joyce L. Brisley) (Harrap, 1941) £35

THE JOSEPHINE MINIATURES (six books: 'Josephine Keeps House', 'Josephine's Pantomime', 'Josephine Goes Travelling', 'Josephine's Christmas Party', 'Josephine Keeps School' and 'Josephine, John and the Puppy'; illustrated by Honor C. Appleton) (Blackie, [1953]) ....each £35

CRANE, Walter

British illustrator. Born: Liverpool, 1845. Formed a successful partnership with the printer, Edmund Evans, for whom he illustrated many 'yellowback' novels and a long-running series of children's 'picture books', published by Warne and Routledge. Died: 1915.

Prices are for books in Very Good condition.

Warne's 'Sixpenny Toybooks' Illustrated by Walter Crane

THE HOUSE THAT JACK BUILT (Warne, 1865) £100

THE COMICAL CAT (Warne, 1865) £75

THE AFFECTING STORY OF JENNY WREN (Warne, 1865) £75

THE RAILROAD ALPHABET (Warne, 1865) £75

THE FARMYARD ALPHABET (Warne, 1865) £75

COCK ROBIN (Warne, 1866) £75

A GAPING-WIDE-MOUTH WADDLING FROG (Warne, [1866]) £75

Routledge's 'Sixpenny' and 'Shilling Toybooks' Illustrated by Walter Crane

THE OLD COURTIER (Routledge, 1867) £75

MULTIPLICATION TABLE IN VERSE (Routledge, [1867]) £75

CHATTERING JACK'S PICTURE BOOK (Routledge, [1867]) £75

HOW JESSIE WAS LOST (Routledge, [1868]) £75

GRAMMAR IN RHYME (Routledge, [1868]) £75

ANNIE AND JACK IN LONDON (Routledge, [1869]) £75

ONE, TWO, BUCKLE MY SHOE (Routledge, [1869]) £75

THE FAIRY SHIP (Routledge, 1870) £75

THE ADVENTURES OF PUFFY (Routledge, 1870) £75

THIS LITTLE PIG WENT TO MARKET (Routledge, [1871]) £75

KING LUCKIEBOY'S PARTY (Routledge, [1871]) £75

KING LUCKIEBOY'S PICTURE BOOK (contains 'King Luckieboy's Party', 'This Little Pig Went to Market' and 'The Old Courtier') (Routledge, 1871) £125

ROUTLEDGE'S BOOK OF ALPHABETS (contains 'The Railroad Alphabet' and 'The Farmyard Alphabet') (Routledge, 1871)....£125

NOAH'S ARK ALPHABET (Routledge, 1872) £75

MY MOTHER (Routledge, 1873) £75

ALI BABA AND THE FORTY THIEVES (Routledge, 1873) £75

CINDERELLA (Routledge, 1873) £75

WALTER CRANE'S NEW TOY BOOK (contains eight previously published titles) (Routledge, 1873) £250

WALTER CRANE'S PICTURE BOOK (contains eight previously published titles) (Routledge, 1874) £250

VALENTINE AND ORSON (Routledge, 1874) £75

PUSS IN BOOTS (Routledge, 1874) £75

OLD MOTHER HUBBARD (Routledge, 1874) £75

THE MARQUIS OF CARABAS' PICTURE BOOK (Routledge, [1874]) £75

THE ABSURD ABC (Routledge, 1874)...£60

THE FROG PRINCE (Routledge: 'Walter Crane Shilling' series, 1874) £75

GOODY TWO SHOES (Routledge: 'Walter Crane Shilling' series, 1874) £75

BEAUTY AND THE BEAST (Routledge: 'Walter Crane Shilling' series, 1874)................................£75

THE ALPHABET OF OLD FRIENDS (Routledge: 'Walter Crane Shilling' series, 1874) £75

LITTLE RED RIDING HOOD (Routledge, 1875) £75

JACK AND THE BEANSTALK (Routledge, 1875) £75

THE BLUEBEARD PICTURE BOOK (Routledge, [1875]) £75

BABY'S OWN ALPHABET (Routledge, 1875) £75

THE YELLOW DWARF (Routledge: 'Walter Crane Shilling' series, 1875) £75

THE HIND IN THE WOOD (Routledge: 'Walter Crane Shilling' series, 1875) £75

PRINCESS BELLE ETOILE (Routledge: 'Walter Crane Shilling' series, 1875) £75

ALADDIN'S PICTURE BOOK (Routledge: 'Walter Crane Shilling' series, 1875 [1876]) £75

SONG OF SIXPENCE TOY BOOK (Warne, [1876]) £75

THE THREE BEARS PICTURE BOOK (Routledge, [1876])..£75

THE SLEEPING BEAUTY IN THE WOOD (Routledge, 1876) £75

CRANE, Walter

*One of the illustrations from Walter Crane's **The Baby's Opera** (1877), a book which had a great influence on Kate Greenaway.*

WALTER CRANE'S PICTURE BOOKS VOL. 1: The Little Pig: His Picture Book (John Lane, 1895) £50
WALTER CRANE'S PICTURE BOOKS VOL. 2: Mother Hubbard: Her Picture Book (John Lane, 1897) £50
WALTER CRANE'S PICTURE BOOKS VOL. 3: Cinderella's Picture Book (John Lane, 1897) £50
WALTER CRANE'S PICTURE BOOKS VOL. 4: Red Riding Hood's Picture Book (John Lane, 1898) £50
BEAUTY AND THE BEAST PICTURE BOOK (John Lane: 'Large' series Vol. 1, 1901) £40
GOODY TWO SHOES PICTURE BOOK (John Lane: 'Large' series Vol. 2, 1901) £40
THE SONG OF SIXPENCE PICTURE BOOK (John Lane: 'Large' series Vol. 3, 1909)......................................£40
THE BUCKLE MY SHOE PICTURE BOOKS (John Lane: 'Large' series Vol. 4, 1910) £40
PUSS IN BOOTS and THE FORTY THIEVES (John Lane, 1914) £40
THE SLEEPING BEAUTY and BLUEBEARD (John Lane, 1914) £40
THE THREE BEARS and MOTHER HUBBARD (John Lane, 1914) £40

Other Books Illustrated by Walter Crane

ROUTLEDGE'S COLOURED PICTURE BOOK (contains 'King Grisly Beard', 'The Fairy Ship' and
'The Adventures of Puffy'; illustrated by Walter Crane and others) (Routledge, [1871]) £200
OUR OLD UNCLE'S HOME by Mother Carey (1872) £75
MRS MUNDI AT HOME by Walter Crane (Marcus Ward, 1875) £75
TELL ME A STORY by Mrs Molesworth (Macmillan 1875)......................................£65
CARROTS by Mrs Molesworth (Macmillan, 1876) £65
THE QUIVER OF LOVE: A Collection of Valentines (illustrated by Walter Crane and Kate Greenaway) (Marcus Ward, 1876) £90
THE BABY'S OPERA: Old Rhymes With New Dresses by Walter Crane (Routledge, 1877) £75
THE CUCKOO CLOCK by Mrs Molesworth (Macmillan, 1877) £65

MOTHER GOOSE'S JINGLES (illustrated by Walter Crane, H. Weir and others) (London, 1878 [1877]) £75
GRANDMOTHER DEAR by Mrs Molesworth (Macmillan, 1878) £45
THE BABY'S BOUQUET by Walter Crane (Routledge, 1878) £75
THE TAPESTRY ROOM by Mrs Molesworth (Macmillan, 1879) £45
A CHRISTMAS CHILD by Mrs Molesworth (Macmillan, 1880)...£45
THE NECKLACE OF PRINCESS FIORIMONDE by Mary de Morgan (Macmillan, 1880) £60
THE FIRST OF MAY: A Fairy Masque by John R. Wise (limited to 300 copies, signed by the artist) (Sotheran, 1881) £500
THE FIRST OF MAY: A Fairy Masque (folio; limited to 200 copies, signed by the artist) (Sotheran, 1881) £500
THE ADVENTURES OF HERR BABY by Mrs Molesworth (Macmillan, 1881) £30
ROSY by Mrs Molesworth (Macmillan, 1882) £35
HOUSEHOLD STORIES by the Brothers Grimm (Macmillan, 1882) £80
PAN PIPES: A Book of Old Songs by Theodore Marzials (Routledge, 1883) £150
TWO LITTLE WAIFS by Mrs Molesworth (Macmillan, 1883) £35
CHRISTMAS-TREE LAND by Mrs Molesworth (Macmillan, 1884)...£35
THE GOLDEN PRIMER Parts 1 and 2 by Professor J.M.D. Meiklejohn (two volumes) (Blackwood, [1884]) ....the set £60
FOLK AND FAIRY TALES by Constance C. Harrison (Ward & Downey, 1885) £60
SLATEANDPENCILVANIA: Being the Adventures of Dick on a Desert Island by Walter Crane (Marcus Ward, 1885) £150
US by Mrs Molesworth (Macmillan, 1885)...£35
LITTLE QUEEN ANNE by Walter Crane (Marcus Ward, 1886) £150
POTHOOKS AND PERSEVERANCE, or The ABC Serpent by Walter Crane (Marcus Ward, 1886) £175
A ROMANCE OF THE THREE Rs by Walter Crane (Marcus Ward, 1886) £150
LEGENDS FOR LIONEL IN PEN AND PENCIL by Walter Crane (Cassell, 1887) £50
THE BABY'S OWN AESOP by Walter Crane (Routledge, 1887 [1886]) £125
FOUR WINDS FARM by Mrs Molesworth (Macmillan, 1887) £35
LITTLE MISS PEGGY by Mrs Molesworth (Macmillan, 1887) £35
A CHRISTMAS POSY by Mrs Molesworth (Macmillan, 1888) £40
THE HAPPY PRINCE and Other Tales by Oscar Wilde (illustrated by Walter Crane and G. Jacomb-Hood) (David Nutt, 1888)..£750
FLORA'S FEAST: A Masque Of Flowers by Walter Crane (Cassell, 1889) £100
THE RECTORY CHILDREN by Mrs Molesworth (Macmillan, 1889)..£35
THE CHILDREN OF THE CASTLE by Mrs Molesworth (Macmillan, 1890) £35
QUEEN SUMMER, or The Tourney of the Lilly and the Rose by Walter Crane (Cassell, 1891)...............................£125
A WONDER BOOK FOR BOYS AND GIRLS by Nathaniel Hawthorne (sixty designs by Walter Crane) (Osgood, McIlvaine, 1892)..£175
STUDIES AND STORIES by Mrs Molesworth (A.D. Innes, 1893) £35
THE HISTORY OF REYNARD THE FOX by F.S. Ellis (David Nutt, 1894) £75
THE STORY OF THE GLITTERING PLAIN by William Morris (limited to 250 copies) (Kelmscott Press, 1894) £2,000
THE MERRY WIVES OF WINDSOR by William Shakespeare (George Allen, 1894) £60
TWO GENTLEMEN OF VERONA by William Shakespeare (Dent, 1894) £60
THE FAERIE QUEEN by Edmund Spenser (issued in nineteen parts) (George Allen, 1894-97) ....the set £500
THE FAERIE QUEEN by Edmund Spenser (issued in six volumes; limited to 1,000 sets) (George Allen, 1897) ....the set £750
CARTOONS FOR THE CAUSE (Twentieth Century Press, 1896) £500
A FLORAL FANTASY IN AN OLD ENGLISH GARDEN by Walter Crane (Harper, 1898) £125
THE SHEPHERD'S CALENDAR by Edmund Spenser (Harper, 1898) £80
TRIPLETS by Walter Crane (limited to 750 numbered copies) (Routledge, 1899) £250
THE BOOK OF WEDDING DAYS (Longmans Green, 1889) £175
DON QUIXOTE. Translated by Judge Parry (Blackie, 1900) £60
WALTER CRANE'S PICTURE BOOK (contains 'The Baby's Opera', 'The Baby's Bouquet' and
    'The Baby's Own Aesop'; limited to 750 copies; vellum binding) (Warne, 1900)..£300
A MASQUE OF DAYS by Charles Lamb (Cassell, 1901) £200
FLOWERS FROM SHAKESPEARE'S GARDEN by Walter Crane (Cassell, 1906)...£125
THE CHILD'S SOCIALIST READER by A.A. Watts (Methuen, 1907) £50
THE ROSEBUD and Other Tales by Arthur Kelly (Fisher & Unwin, 1909) £75
KING ARTHUR'S KNIGHTS by H. Gilbert (T.C. & E.C. Jack, 1911) £50
RUMBO RHYMES by Alfred C. Calmour (Harper, 1911) £150
ROBIN HOOD by H. Gilbert (T.C. & E.C. Jack, 1912) £50
THE STORY OF GREECE by M. MacGregor (T.C. & E.C. Jack, [1913]) £40
THE KNIGHTS OF THE ROUND TABLE by H. Gilbert (T.C. & E.C. Jack, [1915]) £40

CROMPTON, Richmal

British author. Born: Richmal Crompton Lamburn in Lancashire in 1890. Studied at London University, subsequently becoming Classics mistress at Bromley High School before being compelled to retire because of illness. Best known for the enormously popular 'William' books, although she also wrote several novels for adults. Died: 1969.

Prices are for books in Very Good condition with dustjackets.

'William' Books

JUST WILLIAM (illustrated by Thomas Henry; this book's first edition is smaller than the usual Crown 8vo size, measuring 7"x 4.5"; the
    first edition is also identified by the unnumbered pages of adverts at the rear of the volume; red boards) (Newnes, [1922]) £1,500
MORE WILLIAM (illustrated by Thomas Henry; red boards) (Newnes, 1922) £500
WILLIAM AGAIN (illustrated by Thomas Henry; red boards) (Newnes, 1923) £500
WILLIAM THE FOURTH (illustrated by Thomas Henry; red boards) (Newnes, 1924) £300

CROMPTON, Richmal

More William (1922), the second book in Richmal Crompton's popular series, is now worth £500 in Very Good condition.

William the Gangster (1934) was issued in blue boards and this splendid dustjacket by regular illustrator, Thomas Henry.

STILL WILLIAM (illustrated by Thomas Henry; red boards) (Newnes, [1925])..£300
WILLIAM THE CONQUEROR (illustrated by Thomas Henry; red boards) (Newnes, [1926])..............................£300
WILLIAM THE OUTLAW (illustrated by Thomas Henry; red boards) (Newnes, [1927])..................................£300
WILLIAM IN TROUBLE (illustrated by Thomas Henry; red boards) (Newnes, [1927])....................................£300
WILLIAM THE GOOD (illustrated by Thomas Henry; red boards) (Newnes, [1928]) £300
WILLIAM (illustrated by Thomas Henry; blue boards) (Newnes, [1929]) £400
WILLIAM THE BAD (illustrated by Thomas Henry; blue boards) (Newnes, 1930) £400
WILLIAM'S HAPPY DAYS (illustrated by Thomas Henry; blue boards) (Newnes, [1930])..............................£400
WILLIAM'S CROWDED HOURS (illustrated by Thomas Henry; blue boards) (Newnes, [1931])..........................£400
WILLIAM THE PIRATE (illustrated by Thomas Henry; blue boards) (Newnes, 1932) £400
WILLIAM THE REBEL (illustrated by Thomas Henry; buff boards) (Newnes, [1933]) £400
WILLIAM THE GANGSTER (illustrated by Thomas Henry; blue boards) (Newnes, [1934])..............................£400
WILLIAM THE DETECTIVE (illustrated by Thomas Henry; brown boards) (Newnes, 1935) £400
SWEET WILLIAM (illustrated by Thomas Henry; green boards) (Newnes, [1936]) £400
WILLIAM THE SHOWMAN (illustrated by Thomas Henry; green boards) (Newnes, [1937]) £400
WILLIAM THE DICTATOR (illustrated by Thomas Henry; green boards) (Newnes, [1938])............................£400
WILLIAM AND A.R.P. (illustrated by Thomas Henry; green boards) (Newnes, 1939) £300
JUST WILLIAM: The Story of the Film (stories selected from six of the 'William' books, together with the script of the film)
    (Newnes, 1939) £80
WILLIAM AND THE EVACUEES (illustrated by Thomas Henry; green boards) (Newnes, 1940) £500
WILLIAM DOES HIS BIT (illustrated by Thomas Henry; green boards) (Newnes, 1941) £300
WILLIAM CARRIES ON (illustrated by Thomas Henry; green boards) (Newnes, 1942) £200
WILLIAM AND THE BRAINS TRUST (illustrated by Thomas Henry; green boards) (Newnes, 1945) £100
JUST WILLIAM'S LUCK (illustrated by Thomas Henry; green boards) (Newnes, 1948) £85
WILLIAM THE BOLD (illustrated by Thomas Henry; green boards) (Newnes, 1950) £75
WILLIAM AND THE TRAMP (illustrated by Thomas Henry; green boards) (Newnes, 1952) £50
WILLIAM AND THE MOON ROCKET (illustrated by Thomas Henry; green boards) (Newnes, 1954) £50
WILLIAM AND THE SPACE ANIMAL (illustrated by Thomas Henry; green boards) (Newnes, 1956)....................£50
WILLIAM'S BAD RESOLUTION (reissue of 'William and A.R.P.') (Newnes, 1956) £25
WILLIAM THE FILM STAR (reissue of 'William and the Evacuees') (Newnes, 1956) £25
WILLIAM AND THE ARTIST'S MODEL: A Play in One Act (pamphlet) (J. Garnet Miller, 1956)........................£15
WILLIAM'S TELEVISION SHOW (illustrated by Thomas Henry; green boards) (Newnes, 1958) £60

WILLIAM THE EXPLORER (illustrated by Thomas Henry; green boards) (Newnes, 1960) £60
WILLIAM'S TREASURE TROVE (illustrated by Thomas Henry; green boards) (Newnes, 1962).............................£60
WILLIAM AND THE WITCH (illustrated by Thomas Henry and Henry Ford; green boards) (Newnes, 1964) £80
WILLIAM AND THE MONSTER (illustrated by Peter Archer and Thomas Henry; paperback) (Armada, 1965) £10
WILLIAM THE ANCIENT BRITON (illustrated by Peter Archer and Thomas Henry; paperback) (Armada, 1965) £10
WILLIAM THE CANNIBAL (illustrated by Peter Archer and Thomas Henry; paperback) (Armada, 1965) £10
WILLIAM THE GLOBETROTTER (illustrated by Peter Archer and Thomas Henry; paperback) (Armada, 1965) £10
WILLIAM AND THE POP SINGERS (illustrated by Henry Ford; green boards) (Newnes, 1965) £75
WILLIAM AND THE MASKED RANGER (illustrated by Henry Ford; green boards) (Newnes, 1966)........................£85
WILLIAM THE SUPERMAN (illustrated by Henry Ford; green boards) (Newnes, 1968) £150
WILLIAM THE LAWLESS (illustrated by Henry Ford; red boards) (Newnes, 1970)..£750

'Jimmy' Books
JIMMY (Newnes, 1949)...£40
JIMMY AGAIN (illustrated by Lunt Roberts) (Newnes, 1951) £40
JIMMY THE THIRD (illustrated by Lunt Roberts; paperback) (Armada, 1965) £10

CUNLIFFE, John
British author Born: Lancashire, 1933. Creator of 'Postman Pat' in 1981, and also notable for his 'Giant' and 'Farmer Barnes' stories.
Prices are for books in Very Good condition with dustjackets where applicable.

'Farmer Barnes' Books
FARMER BARNES BUYS A PIG (illustrated by Carol Barker) (Deutsch, 1964) £25
FARMER BARNES AND BLUEBELL (illustrated by Carol Barker) (Deutsch, 1965)...£15
FARMER BARNES AT THE COUNTY SHOW (illustrated by Jill McDonald) (Deutsch, 1969).............................£15
FARMER BARNES AND THE GOATS (illustrated by Jill McDonald) (Deutsch, 1971) £10
FARMER BARNES GOES FISHING (illustrated by Jill McDonald) (Deutsch, 1972) £10
FARMER BARNES AND THE SNOW PICNIC (illustrated by Joan Hickson) (Deutsch, 1974) £10
FARMER BARNES FELLS A TREE (illustrated by Joan Hickson) (Deutsch, 1977)..£8
FARMER BARNES AND THE HARVEST DOLL (illustrated by Joan Hickson) (Deutsch, 1977)...............................£8
FARMER BARNES' GUY FAWKES DAY (illustrated by Joan Hickson) (Deutsch, 1978)..£8

'Giant' Books
THE GIANT WHO STOLE THE WORLD (illustrated by Faith Jaques) (Deutsch, 1971)..£5
THE GIANT WHO SWALLOWED THE WIND (illustrated by Faith Jaques) (Deutsch, 1972)....................................£5
GIANT KIPPERNOSE AND OTHER STORIES (illustrated by Fritz Wegner) (Deutsch, 1972) £5
GIANT BROG AND THE MOTORWAY (illustrated by Alexy Pendle) (Deutsch 1976) £5

'Postman Pat' Books
POSTMAN PAT AND THE MYSTERY THIEF (illustrated by Celia Berridge) (Deutsch, 1981)..................................£8
POSTMAN PAT'S TREASURE HUNT (illustrated by Celia Berridge) (Deutsch, 1981) £8
POSTMAN PAT'S SECRET (illustrated by Celia Berridge) (Deutsch, 1981) £8
POSTMAN PAT'S RAINY DAY (illustrated by Celia Berridge) (Deutsch, 1982) £8
POSTMAN PAT'S DIFFICULT DAY (illustrated by Celia Berridge) (Deutsch, 1982) £8
POSTMAN PAT'S FOGGY DAY (illustrated by Celia Berridge) (Deutsch, 1982) £8
POSTMAN PAT'S TRACTOR EXPRESS (illustrated by Celia Berridge) (Deutsch, 1983) £8
POSTMAN PAT TAKES A MESSAGE (illustrated by Celia Berridge) (Deutsch, 1983) £8
POSTMAN PAT'S THIRSTY DAY (illustrated by Celia Berridge) (Deutsch, 1984) £8
POSTMAN PAT GOES SLEDGING (illustrated by Celia Berridge) (Deutsch, 1984) £8
POSTMAN PAT'S LETTERS ON ICE (illustrated by Celia Berridge) (Deutsch, 1985) £5
POSTMAN PAT'S BREEZY DAY (illustrated by Celia Berridge) (Deutsch, 1985) £5
POSTMAN PAT TO THE RESCUE (illustrated by Celia Berridge) (Deutsch, 1986) £5
POSTMAN PAT'S SUMMER STORYBOOK (illustrated by Celia Berridge) (Deutsch, 1987) £5
POSTMAN PAT'S PARCEL OF FUN (illustrated by Stuart Trotter) (Deutsch, 1987) £5
POSTMAN PAT'S WINTER STORYBOOK (illustrated by Celia Berridge) (Deutsch, 1987).....................................£5
POSTMAN PAT MAKES A SPLASH (illustrated by Joan Hickson) (Deutsch, 1987) £5
POSTMAN PAT'S ZODIAC STORYBOOK (illustrated by Celia Berridge) (Deutsch, 1989).....................................£5
POSTMAN PAT'S THREE WISHES (Deutsch, 1990) £5

'Beginners' Books
POSTMAN PAT'S ABC STORY (illustrated by Joan Hickson) (Deutsch, 1986)..£4
POSTMAN PAT'S 123 STORY (illustrated by Joan Hickson) (Deutsch, 1986)...£4

'Easy Reader' Books
POSTMAN PAT'S WET DAY (illustrated by Joan Hickson) (Deutsch, 1986) £4
POSTMAN PAT'S MESSY DAY (illustrated by Joan Hickson) (Deutsch, 1986) £4
POSTMAN PAT ON SAFARI (illustrated by Joan Hickson) (Deutsch, 1986) £4
POSTMAN PAT AND THE GREENDALE GHOST (illustrated by Joan Hickson) (Deutsch, 1987) £4
POSTMAN PAT AND THE CHRISTMAS PUDDING (illustrated by Joan Hickson) (Deutsch, 1987) £4
POSTMAN PAT PLAYS FOR GREENDALE (illustrated by Joan Hickson) (Deutsch, 1988) £4

CUNLIFFE, John

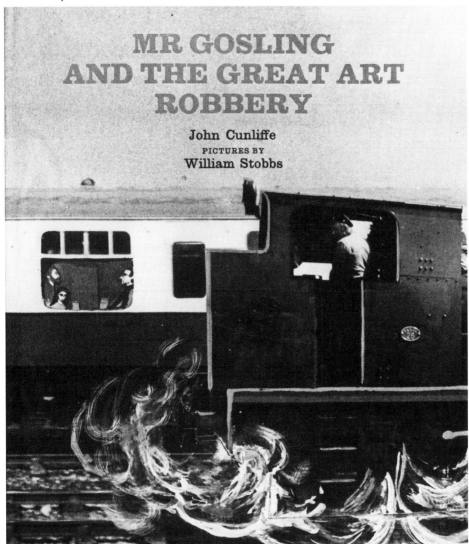

Mr Gosling and the Great Art Robbery (1979) is the work of John Cunliffe, best known for his 'Postman Pat' titles.

'Baby' Books

A DAY WITH POSTMAN PAT (illustrated by Celia Berridge) (Deutsch, 1985) £3
POSTMAN PAT AND THE SUMMER SHOW (illustrated by Celia Berridge) (Deutsch, 1985) £3

Others

THE ADVENTURES OF LORD PIP (illustrated by Robert Hales) (Deutsch, 1970) £10
RIDDLES AND RHYMES AND RIGMAROLES (illustrated by Alexy Pendle) (Deutsch, 1971) £10
THE KING'S BIRTHDAY CAKE (illustrated by Faith Jaques) (Deutsch, 1973) £10
THE GREAT DRAGON COMPETITION AND OTHER STORIES (illustrated by Alexy Pendle) (Deutsch, 1973) £10
THE FARMER, THE ROOKS AND THE CHERRY TREE (illustrated by Prudence Seward) (Deutsch, 1974) £10
SMALL MONKEY TALES (illustrated by Gerry Downes) (Deutsch, 1974) £10
MR GOSLING AND THE RUNAWAY CHAIR (illustrated by William Stobbs) (Deutsch, 1978) £10
MR GOSLING AND THE GREAT ART ROBBERY (illustrated by William Stobbs) (Deutsch, 1979) £10
SARA'S GIANT AND THE UPSIDE-DOWN HOUSE (illustrated by Hilary Abrahams) (Deutsch, 1980) £8
OUR SAM: THE DAFTEST DOG IN THE WORLD (illustrated by Maurice Wilson) (Deutsch, 1980) £8
THE MINISTER'S CAT (illustrated by David Parkins) (Deutsch, 1989) £8
ROSIE AND JIM AND THE GLASS BLOWERS (illustrated by Celia Berridge) (Deutsch, 1993) £5

D

DAHL, Roald

British author. Born: Llandaff, Wales, in 1916, of Norwegian parents. Educated at Repton School, and worked for the Shell Oil Company before serving with the RAF in North Africa during the Second World War. His first children's book, *The Gremlins* (1943), came out of his wartime experiences, and was followed by several other classic works, including *James and the Giant Peach* (1961) and *Charlie and the Chocolate Factory* (1964), most of which were first published in America. Died: 1990.

Prices are for books in Very Good condition with dustjackets where applicable.

THE GREMLINS. From the Walt Disney Production 'A Royal Air Force Story' (Random House, U.S., [1943]).........................£1,250
THE GREMLINS. From the Walt Disney Production 'A Royal Air Force Story' (boards; issued without dustjacket)
(Collins, [1944]) £700
JAMES AND THE GIANT PEACH (illustrated by Nancy Ekholm Burket) (Knopf, U.S., 1961)....................................£175
JAMES AND THE GIANT PEACH (illustrated by Michael Simeon; boards; issued without dustjacket) (Allen & Unwin, 1967) ..£100
CHARLIE AND THE CHOCOLATE FACTORY (illustrated by Joseph Schindelman) (Knopf, U.S., 1964)....................................£250
CHARLIE AND THE CHOCOLATE FACTORY (illustrated by Faith Jaques; boards; issued without dustjacket)
(Allen & Unwin, 1967) £100
CHARLIE AND THE CHOCOLATE FACTORY (illustrated by Quentin Blake; hardback) (Puffin, 1997) £20
THE MAGIC FINGER (Harper, U.S., 1966)...£100
THE MAGIC FINGER (boards; issued without dustjacket) (Allen & Unwin, 1968) £60
FANTASTIC MR FOX (boards) (Allen & Unwin, 1970)...£60
CHARLIE AND THE GREAT GLASS ELEVATOR (Knopf, U.S., 1972) £150
CHARLIE AND THE GREAT GLASS ELEVATOR (illustrated by Faith Jaques; boards) (Allen & Unwin, 1973) £65
DANNY, THE CHAMPION OF THE WORLD (illustrated by Jill Bennett) (Cape, 1975) £60
THE WONDERFUL STORY OF HENRY SUGAR and Six More (Cape, 1977)...£50
THE ENORMOUS CROCODILE (illustrated by Quentin Blake) (Cape, 1978) £35
THE TWITS (Cape, 1980) £35
GEORGE'S MARVELLOUS MEDICINE (illustrated by Quentin Blake) (Cape, 1981) £45
THE BFG (illustrated by Quentin Blake) (Cape, 1982) £50
ROALD DAHL'S REVOLTING RHYMES (illustrated by Quentin Blake; issued without dustjacket) (Cape, 1982)......................£50

The book that properly launched Roald Dahl's hugely successful career as a writer for children: *James and the Giant Peach*.

Like all of Dahl's early children's books, **Charlie and the Chocolate Factory** was first published in the United States.

DAHL, Roald

A less well-known work by Roald Dahl: *Fantastic Mr Fox*, published by Allen & Unwin in 1970 and now worth £60.

Charlie and the Great Glass Elevator was a sequel to Dahl's bestselling *Charlie and the Chocolate Factory*.

DIRTY BEASTS (illustrated by Rosemary Fawcett; issued without dustjacket) (Cape, 1983) £50
DIRTY BEASTS (illustrated by Quentin Blake; issued without dustjacket) (Cape, 1984) £30
THE WITCHES (illustrated by Quentin Blake) (Cape, 1983) £50
BOY: Tales of Childhood (memoir) (Cape, 1984) £20
THE GIRAFFE, THE PELLY AND ME (illustrated by Quentin Blake) (Cape, 1985)..£45
GOING SOLO (memoir; illustrated by Quentin Blake) (Cape, 1986) £15
MATILDA (illustrated by Quentin Blake) (Cape, 1988) £60
RHYME STEW (illustrated by Quentin Blake) (Cape, 1989) £30
ESIO TROT (illustrated by Quentin Blake) (Cape, 1990)..£20
ROALD DAHL'S GUIDE TO RAILWAY SAFETY (illustrated by Quentin Blake; pamphlet) (British Rail, 1991) £15
THE VICAR OF NIBBLESWICKE (illustrated by Quentin Blake) (Random Century, 1991)..£20
THE MIN PINS (Cape, 1991)..£25

'DAN DARE' BOOKS AND ANNUALS

Popular British comic character, originally featured in the *Eagle* (1950-69) and later in *Lion*. Inspired many spin-off publications and items of ephemera.

Prices are for books and annuals in Very Good condition.

DAN DARE SPACE BOOK (1953) £100
DAN DARE: PILOT OF THE FUTURE. With Realistic Pop-Up Pictures (1953) £80
DAN DARE (pop-up) (1954) £60
DAN DARE PICTURE CARD ALBUM (with cards) (1954)..£80
DAN DARE PICTURE CARD ALBUM (without cards) (1954) £50
DAN DARE'S ANASTASIA JET PLANE ('Presso Book')..£45
DAN DARE'S SPACESHIP ('Presso Book') £60
THE HORLICKS SPACEMAN'S HANDBOOK £75
DAN DARE ON MARS ('Eagle Novel', 1956) £60
DAN DARE INTERPLANETARY STAMP FOLDER (1950s) £50
DAN DARE'S SPACE ANNUAL (1963) £25
DAN DARE ANNUAL 1974 ....£15
DAN DARE: PILOT OF THE FUTURE (novelisation of the first 'Dan Dare' serial; paperback)
   (New English Library, 1977)..£5
THE MAN FROM NOWHERE (Dragons Dream, 1979) £12
DAN DARE ANNUAL 1979 ....£4
DAN DARE ANNUAL 1980 ....£4
ROGUE PLANET (Dragons Dream, 1980) £12

REIGN OF THE ROBOTS (Dragons Dream, 1981) £12
DAN DARE: PILOT OF THE FUTURE (illustrated by Frank Hampson and others; softcover)
    (Hamlyn, 1981) £15
DAN DARE: PILOT OF THE FUTURE (Hawk, 1987) £25
DAN DARE ANNUAL 1987 ....£3
RED MOON MYSTERY/MAROONED ON MERCURY (Hawk, 1988) £25
OPERATION SATURN (Hawk, 1989) £15
PRISONERS OF SPACE (Hawk, 1990) £15
DAN DARE DOSSIER (1990) £25
DAN DARE HOLIDAY SPECIAL 1990 ....£3
DAN DARE HOLIDAY SPECIAL 1991 ....£3
MAN FROM NOWHERE (Hawk, 1991) £15
DAN DARE ANNUAL 1991 ....£3
DARE by Grant Morrison and Rian Hughes (softcover; 1991) £6
ROGUE PLANET (Hawk, 1992) £15
REIGN OF THE ROBOTS/THE SHIP THAT LIVED (Hawk, 1993) £15
THE PHANTOM FLEET (Hawk, 1993) £15
TERRA NOVA TRILOGY (Hawk, 1993) £15
PROJECT NIMBUS AND OTHER STORIES (Hawk, 1994) £15
SOLID SPACE MYSTERY AND OTHER STORIES (Hawk, 1995) £15
DARE: THE FINAL VOLUME (Hawk, 1995) £15
DAN DARE 3D BOOK OF JET PLANES (given free with 'Eagle'; in original envelope) £40
DAN DARE STAMP ALBUM £50

'DANDY' ANNUALS

Popular British comic annual, published by D.C. Thomson of Dundee. The comic itself was launched on 4th December 1937, the first annual, entitled *The Dandy Monster Comic*, appearing in 1939. Among the title's many well-known characters are Desperate Dan and Korky the Cat. Note that the annuals were undated before 1966, after which they were dated on the cover.

Prices are for annuals in Very Good condition (with cover description in brackets for undated annuals).

'The Dandy Monster Comic'

1939 (Korky, Desperate Dan, monkeys and other characters holding the 'y' of 'Dandy') £2,750
1940 (Korky the Cat hanging from a trapeze) £1,250
1941 (Korky leading others in band) £750
1942 (Desperate Dan towing others in boat)..£750
1943 (Korky leading others in boat)..£550
1944 (Korky on football kicked by Desperate Dan) £550
1945 (Korky on skis and Desperate Dan on logs)..£400
1946 (Korky and others in stars)..£300
1947 (Korky being tossed in blanket) £300
1948 (Korky and others as puppets) £250
1949 (Korky in top hat with cigar, and Desperate Dan; quarto) £200
1950 (Korky with kettle on beach, pouring hot water into the sea; quarto)..............................£150
1951 (Korky as ringmaster in circus, and Desperate Dan holding an elephant; quarto)............£100
1952 (Korky's toyshop, with toy Desperate Dan pushing tin of red paint onto Korky; quarto) £75

'The Dandy Book'

1953 (six sets of Korky with mice and dinner table) £75
1954 (four sets of Korky hiding a fish under top hat) £60
1955 (four sets of Korky fishing by 'no fishing' sign) £60
1956 (four sets of Korky in front of 'Korky's Joke Shop')..£60
1957 (three sets of Korky stealing fish from train) £50
1958 (three sets of Korky catching fish with magnet in rowing boat) £45
1959 (three sets of Korky sitting in an umbrella, in a canoe) £40
1960 (three sets of Korky eating meal, with chained letter box) £40
1961 (three sets of Korky balancing an egg on his nose) £40
1962 (three sets of Korky leaning on a lamp-post) £40
1963 (four sets of Korky wearing sailor suit and looking through porthole) £40
1964 (Korky in a deckchair eating a pie) £40
1965 (two sets of Korky with pantomime horse) £40
1966 (dated '1966' on cover)..£30
1967-69 ....each £25
1970 ....£15
1971-72 ....each £10
1973-74 ....each £10
1975-77 ....each £8
1978-80 ....each £8
1981-Present ....each £5

DARCH, Winifred

British author. Born: Brighton, 1884. Worked as a High School Mistress before writing popular school stories for girls.

Prices are for books in Very Good condition.

CHRIS AND SOME OTHERS (illustrated by Savile Lumley) (OUP, 1920) £20
JEAN OF THE FIFTH (OUP, 1923) £20
POPPIES AND PREFECTS (illustrated by Charles E. Brock) (OUP, 1923) £20
CECIL OF THE CARNATIONS (illustrated by Mary Strange Reeve) (OUP, 1924) £20
HEATHER AT THE HIGH SCHOOL (illustrated by C.E. Brock) (OUP, 1924) £15
KATHERINE GOES TO SCHOOL (illustrated by M.D. Johnston) (OUP, 1925) £15
GILLIAN OF THE GUIDES (illustrated by M.D. Johnston) (OUP, 1925) £15
THE NEW SCHOOL AND HILARY (illustrated by Mary Strange Reeve) (OUP, 1926) £15
VARVARA COMES TO ENGLAND (illustrated by M.D. Johnston) (OUP, 1927) £15
CICELY BASSETT, PATROL LEADER (illustrated by M.D. Johnston) (OUP, 1927)...................................£15
THE UPPER FIFTH IN COMMAND (illustrated by M.D. Johnston) (OUP, 1928) £15
FOR THE HONOUR OF THE HOUSE (illustrated by M.D. Johnston) (OUP, 1929) £15
THE FIFTH FORM RIVALS (OUP, 1930) £15
THE LOWER FOUTH AND JOAN (illustrated by M.D. Johnston) (OUP, 1930) £15
MARGARET PLAYS THE GAME (illustrated by E. Brier) (OUP, 1931) £15
THE GIRLS OF QUEEN ELIZABETH'S (OUP, 1932) £15
THE SCHOOL ON THE CLIFF (illustrated by M.D. Johnston) (OUP, 1933) £15
THE NEW SCHOOLGIRL OMNIBUS (contains 'Chris and Some Others', 'Heather at the High School' and 'Jean of the Fifth') (OUP, 1934)..£20
THE HEAD GIRL AT WYNFORD (illustrated by Reginald Mills) (OUP, 1935) £15
SUSAN'S LAST TERM (illustrated by Margaret Horder) (OUP, 1936) £15
THE WINIFRED DARCH OMNIBUS (contains 'For the Honour of the School', 'Cicely Bassett,
   Patrol Leader' and 'Margaret Plays the Game') (OUP, 1936) £20
ELINOR IN THE FIFTH (illustrated by Margaret Horder) (OUP, 1937) £15
ALISON TEMPLE – PREFECT (illustrated by Gilbert Dunlop) (OUP, 1938) £15
THE SCHOLARSHIP AND MARGERY (OUP, 1938) £15
THE NEW GIRL AT GRAYCHURCH (illustrated by Gilbert Dunlop) (OUP, 1939) £15

DE LA MARE, Walter

British author. Born: Walter John de la Mare in London in 1873, of Huguenot descent. Studied at St. Paul's School, leaving at the age of sixteen to work for the Anglo-American Oil Company. His first book was a volume of poems entitled *Songs of Childhood* (1902), and this was followed by several more verse collections — notably *Peacock Pie* (1913) — as well as novels, of which the best-known is *Memoirs of a Midget* (1921). Received a Civil List pension in 1908. Died: 1956.

Prices are for books in Very Good condition (with dustjackets after 1940).

SONGS OF CHILDHOOD by Walter Ramal (verse) (Longmans Green, 1902) £300
SONGS OF CHILDHOOD (verse; enlarged, revised edition; illustrated by Estella Canziani) (Longmans, 1923) £35
SONGS OF CHILDHOOD (verse; illustrated by Marion Rivers-Moore) (Faber, 1942) £20
THE THREE MULLA-MULGARS (Duckworth, 1910) £35
THE THREE MULLA-MULGARS (illustrated by Dorothy Lathrop) (Duckworth, 1921)................................£20
THE THREE MULLA-MULGARS (illustrated by J.A. Shepherd) (Selwyn & Blount, 1924)..........................£20
A CHILD'S DAY: A Book of Rhymes (verse; illustrated by Carine and Will Cadby) (Constable, 1912) £120
PEACOCK PIE: A Book of Rhymes (verse) (Constable, 1913) £30
PEACOCK PIE (verse; illustrated by W. Heath Robinson) (Constable, [1916]) £75
PEACOCK PIE (verse; illustrated by C. Lovat Fraser) (Constable, [1924])...£30
PEACOCK PIE (verse; illustrated by Jocelyn Crowe) (Faber, 1936) £20
PEACOCK PIE (verse; illustrated by Rowland Emett) (Faber, 1941) £20
PEACOCK PIE (verse; illustrated by Edward Ardizzone) (Faber, 1946)..£75
CROSSINGS: A Fairy Play (illustrated by Randolph Schwabe; music by C. Armstrong Gibbs) (Beaumont Press, 1921) £35
DOWN-ADOWN-DERRY: A Book of Fairy Poems (verse; illustrated by Dorothy P. Lathrop) (Constable, 1922) £100
BROOMSTICKS and Other Tales (illustrated by Bold) (Constable, 1925)..£45
MISS JEMIMA (illustrated by Alec Buckels) (Blackwell, [1925]) £25
LUCY (illustrated by Hilda T. Miller) (Blackwell, [1927])..£25
OLD JOE (illustrated by C.T. Nightingale) (Blackwell, [1927]) £25
TOLD AGAIN: Traditional Tales (illustrated by A.H. Watson) (Blackwell, 1927) £25
STORIES FROM THE BIBLE (illustrated by Theodore Nadajen) (Faber, 1929) £15
STORIES FROM THE BIBLE (illustrated by John Farleigh) (Faber, 1933) £25
STORIES FROM THE BIBLE (illustrated by Edward Ardizzone) (Faber, 1961) £35
DESERT ISLANDS AND ROBINSON CRUSOE (illustrated by Rex Whistler; issued with dustjacket) (Faber, 1930) £40
DESERT ISLANDS AND ROBINSON CRUSOE (illustrated by Rex Whistler; De Luxe edition:
   limited to 650 copies, signed by the author) (Faber/Fountain Press, 1930) £250
POEMS FOR CHILDREN (verse; contains 'Songs of Childhood', 'Peacock Pie' and other poems) (Constable, [1930]) £30
TOM TIDDLER'S GROUND: A Book of Poetry for the Junior and Middle Schools.
   Edited by Walter de la Mare (verse) (Collins, [1932]) £10
THE LORD FISH and Other Tales (illustrated by Rex Whistler; issued with dustjacket) (Faber, 1933)........£40

The Book of Penny Toys was one of Mabel Dearmer's earliest successes. It was published by Macmillan in 1899.

The combined names of Laurence Housman and Mabel Dearmer make this a particularly sought-after book, now worth £150.

THE LORD FISH and Other Tales (illustrated by Rex Whistler; limited to sixty copies) (Faber, 1933) £250
THE THREE ROYAL MONKEYS, or The Three Mulla-Mulgars (illustrated by J.A. Shepherd) (Faber, 1935) £15
THIS YEAR: NEXT YEAR (verse; illustrated by Harold Jones) (Faber, 1937) £140
ANIMAL STORIES: Chosen, Arranged and in Some Part Rewritten (verse) (Faber, 1939) £20
BELLS AND GRASS: A Book of Rhymes (verse; illustrated by Rowland Emett) (Faber, 1941) £20
THE OLD LION and Other Stories (illustrated by Irene Hawkins) (Faber, 1942) £20
MR BUMPS AND HIS MONKEY (originally published in 'The Lord Fish' under the title 'The Old Lion';
    illustrated by Dorothy P. Lathrop) (J.C. Winston, U.S., [1942]) £20
THE MAGIC JACKET and Other Stories (illustrated by Irene Hawkins) (Faber, 1943) £25
COLLECTED RHYMES AND VERSES (verse; illustrated by Berthold Wolpe) (Faber, 1944) £15
THE SCARECROW and Other Stories (illustrated by Irene Hawkins) (Faber, 1945) £25
THE THREE ROYAL MONKEYS (illustrated by Mildred Eldridge) (Faber, 1946) £10
THE DUTCH CHEESE and Other Stories (illustrated by Irene Hawkins) (Faber, 1946)...£15
COLLECTED STORIES FOR CHILDREN (illustrated by Irene Hawkins) (Faber, 1947) £15
COLLECTED STORIES FOR CHILDREN (illustrated by Robin Jacques) (Faber, 1957)...£15
RHYMES AND VERSES: Collected Poems for Children (verse; illustrated by Elinore Blaisdell) (Holt, U.S., [1947])................£20
JACK AND THE BEANSTALK (adapted from 'Told Again') (Hulton Press, 1951) £10
DICK WHITTINGTON (adapted from 'Told Again'; illustrated by Ionicus) (Hulton Press, 1951) £10
SNOW-WHITE (adapted from 'Told Again'; illustrated by David Walsh) (Hulton Press, 1952) £10
CINDERELLA (adapted from 'Told Again'; illustrated by Ionicus) (Hulton Press, 1952)...£10
SELECTED STORIES AND VERSE (paperback) (Puffin, 1952) £3
THE STORY OF JOSEPH (illustrated by Edward Ardizzone) (Faber, 1958) £30
THE STORY OF MOSES (illustrated by Edward Ardizzone) (Faber, 1959) £30
THE STORY OF SAMUEL AND SAUL (illustrated by Edward Ardizzone) (Faber, 1960) £30
A PENNY A DAY (illustrated by Paul Kennedy) (Knopf, U.S., 1960) £15
POEMS. Edited by Eleanor Graham (verse; paperback) (Puffin, 1962) £4

DEARMER, Mabel

British illustrator. Born: Mabel White in 1872. Studied art at the Herkomer School, Bushey, subsequently illustrating a number of children's books, many of them written by herself. Died: 1915.

Prices are for books in Very Good condition.

Books Written and Illustrated by Mabel Dearmer

ROUND-ABOUT-RHYMES by Mrs Percy Dearmer (Blackie, [1898]) £200
THE BOOK OF PENNY TOYS (Macmillan, 1899)..£175
THE NOAH'S ARK GEOGRAPHY (Macmillan, 1900) £175
THE COCKYOLLY BIRD (Hodder & Stoughton, 1914)..£150
BRER RABBIT AND MR FOX (Joseph Williams, [1914])...£200

Books Written by Mabel Dearmer

A CHILD'S LIFE OF CHRIST (illustrated by Eleanor Fortescue-Brickdale) (Methuen, 1906) £40
THE PLAYMATE: A Christmas Mystery Play (illustrated by Helen Stratton) (Mowbray, 1910) £60

Books Illustrated by Mabel Dearmer

WYMPS and Other Fairy Tales by Evelyn Sharp (John Lane, 1897) £100
ALL THE WAY FAIRYLAND by Evelyn Sharp (John Lane, 1898) £100
THE STORY OF THE SEVEN YOUNG GOSLINGS by Laurence Housman (Blackie, [1899]) £150

DEFOE, Daniel

British author. Born: Daniel Foe in London in 1660/61, the son of Noncomformist parents. Following a disastrous attempt to establish himself as a merchant, he became a prolific writer of political tracts and 'novels', publishing his best-known work, *Robinson Crusoe*, in 1719. Although not intended for young readers, it has long been established as a children's classic. Died: 1731.

Prices are for books in Good condition, rebound (pre-1850) or in original cloth.

ROBINSON CRUSOE (as 'The Life and Strange Surprizing Adventures of Robinson Crusoe'; anonymous;
   first edition, first issue) (W. Taylor, 1719) £12,000
ROBINSON CRUSOE (as 'The Life and Strange Surprizing Adventures of Robinson Crusoe';
   anonymous; later impressions) (W. Taylor, 1719) £1,500
ROBINSON CRUSOE (illustrated by E. McKnight Kauffer; limited to 525 copies) (Etchells & MacDonald, 1929).......................£500
ROBINSON CRUSOE (illustrated by Edward Ardizzone) (Nonesuch Press, 1968) £45
ROBINSON CRUSOE (illustrated by Edward Gordon Craig; limited to 500 copies; morocco-backed cloth binding; in slipcase)
   (Basilisk Press, 1979) £500
THE FARTHER ADVENTURES OF ROBINSON CRUSOE (anonymous) (W. Taylor, 1719)...£1,500
SERIOUS REFLECTIONS DURING THE LIFE AND SURPRISING ADVENTURES OF ROBINSON CRUSOE
   (anonymous) (W. Taylor, 1720) £1,500
ROBINSON CRUSOE (first joint edition of the first two novels; made up of the [abridged] seventh edition of
   'The Life and Strange Adventures of Robinson Crusoe' and the fifth edition of
   'The Farther Adventures of Robinson Crusoe'; two volumes) (W. Mears/T. Woodward, 1726) ....the set £500

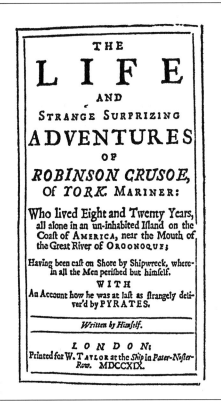

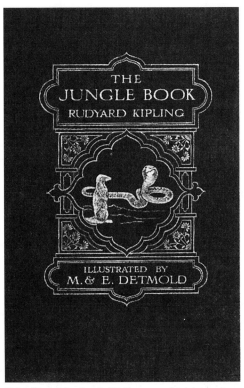

*The first edition of **Robinson Crusoe** is Daniel Defoe's most expensive work, regularly fetching five-figure sums.*

*This edition of **The Jungle Book** was one of only two works on which the Detmolds collaborated before Maurice's tragic death.*

ROBINSON CRUSOE (as 'The Life and Strange Surprising Adventures of Robinson Crusoe';
  illustrated by Thomas Stothard; introduction by George Chalmers; two volumes) (John Stockdale, 1790) ....the set **£500**
ROBINSON CRUSOE (first joint edition of all three novels; as 'The Life and Adventures of Robinson Crusoe';
  includes 'The True-Born Englishman, a Satire' and 'The Original Power of the People of England Examined and
  Asserted'; three volumes) (Printed at the Logographic Press; sold by J. Walter, 1790) ....the set **£500**
ROBINSON CRUSOE (illustrated by George Cruikshank and Thomas Stothard;
  introductory verses by Bernard Barton; two volumes) (John Major, 1831) ....the set **£500**
ROBINSON CRUSOE (illustrated by J. Ayton Symington) (Dent, 1903) **£30**
ROBINSON CRUSOE (as 'The Life and Strange Surprising Adventures of Robinson Crusoe'; illustrated by
  Thomas Stothard; introduction by Charles Whibley; limited to 775 copies; three volumes) (Constable, 1925)..........the set **£300**

'DENNIS THE MENACE' ANNUALS
Popular spin-offs from the *Beano* **comics and annuals. Published biennially by D.C. Thomson.**

Prices are for annuals in Very Good condition (with cover description in brackets).

DENNIS THE MENACE 1956 (Dennis holding a tin of paint) **£120**
DENNIS THE MENACE 1958 (Dennis on go-cart speeding down a hill,
  knocking down a policeman, sweep and painter) **£60**
DENNIS THE MENACE 1960 (Dennis underwater using pincers on swimmer's foot) **£35**
DENNIS THE MENACE 1962 (Dennis holding a large caricature head of himself over his own head) **£30**
DENNIS THE MENACE 1964 (Dennis's head bursting through a black and white paper sheet) **£25**
DENNIS THE MENACE 1968 ....**£20**
DENNIS THE MENACE 1970 & 1972   ....each **£15**
DENNIS THE MENACE 1974 & 1976 ....each **£12**
DENNIS THE MENACE 1978 ....**£10**
DENNIS THE MENACE 1980 ....**£6**
DENNIS THE MENACE 1982 ....**£5**
DENNIS THE MENACE 1984-Present   ....each **£4**

'DESPERATE DAN' ANNUALS
Popular spin-offs from the *Dandy* **comics and annuals, published by D.C. Thomson.**

Prices are for annuals in Very Good condition.

DESPERATE DAN 1954 ....**£140**
THE DESPERATE DAN BOOK 1979 ....**£8**

DETMOLD, Maurice and Edward
**British illustrators. Born: Charles Frederick and Edward Barton Detmold on 21st November 1883,
subsequently changing their middle names to 'Maurice' and 'Julius' respectively. Both brothers excelled at
representing animals, having studied them at London's Zoological Gardens. Collaborated on an edition of**
The Jungle Book, **before Charles committed suicide in 1908. Edward continued to illustrate books until the
late 1920s. Died: 1957.**

Prices are for books in Very Good condition.

Books Illustrated by Maurice and Edward Detmold
PICTURES FROM BIRDLAND (Dent, 1899) **£300**
SIXTEEN ILLUSTRATION OF SUBJECTS FROM KIPLING'S 'JUNGLE BOOK'
  (in portfolio) (Macmillan, 1903) **£800**
THE JUNGLE BOOK (Macmillan, 1908)..**£100**

Books Illustrated by Edward Detmold
THE FABLES OF AESOP (Hodder & Stoughton, 1909) **£100**
THE FABLES OF AESOP (limited to 750 copies, signed by the artist) (Hodder & Stoughton, 1909) **£500**
BIRDS AND BEASTS by Camille Lemonnier (George Allen, 1911)..**£50**
THE BOOK OF BABY BEASTS by Florence E. Dugdale (Henry Frowde/Hodder & Stoughton, [1911]) **£75**
THE LIFE OF THE BEE by Maurice Maeterlinck (George Allen, 1911) **£150**
HOURS OF GLADNESS by Maurice Maeterlinck (George Allen, 1912) **£125**
THE BOOK OF BABY BIRDS by Florence E. Dugdale (Henry Frowde/Hodder & Stoughton, [1912]) **£75**
THE BOOK OF BABY PETS by Florence E. Dugdale (Henry Frowde/Hodder & Stoughton, [1915]) **£75**
THE BOOK OF BABY DOGS by Charles J. Kaberry (Henry Frowde/Hodder & Stoughton, [1915]) **£75**
TWENTY-FOUR NATURE PICTURES (in portfolio) (Dent, [1919]) **£450**
BIRDS IN TOWN AND VILLAGE by W.H. Hudson (Dent, 1919)...**£45**
OUR LITTLE NEIGHBOURS by Charles J. Kaberry (Henry Frowde/Hodder & Stoughton, [1921])......................**£80**
FABRE'S BOOK OF INSECTS by J.H.C. Fabre (Hodder & Stoughton, [1921])..**£150**
RAINBOW HOUSES FOR BOYS AND GIRLS by Arthur Vine Hall (Cape, 1923) **£60**
THE ARABIAN NIGHTS — TALES FROM THE THOUSAND AND ONE NIGHTS
  (Hodder & Stoughton, [1924]) **£250**
THE ARABIAN NIGHTS — TALES FROM THE THOUSAND AND ONE NIGHTS (limited to 100 copies, signed by the artist)
  (Hodder & Stoughton, [1924]) **£750**
THE FANTASTIC CREATURES OF EDWARD JULIUS DETMOLD (paperback) (Pan, 1976) **£10**

DICKENS, Charles

British author. Born: Portsmouth, 1812. The great novelist wrote few works specifically for young readers, but his 'Christmas Books' — notably *A Christmas Carol* (1843) — are of equal appeal to both children and adults. Died: 1870.

Prices are for books in Very Good condition with dustjackets where applicable.

A CHRISTMAS CAROL: Being a Ghost Story of Christmas (trial issue [proof stage];
    illustrated by John Leech) (Chapman & Hall, 1843) £10,000
A CHRISTMAS CAROL (first edition, first issue; first chapter headed 'Stave 1'; illustrated by John Leech)
    (Chapman & Hall, 1843) £3,000
A CHRISTMAS CAROL (first edition, second issue; first chapter headed 'Stave One'; illustrated by John Leech)
    (Chapman & Hall, 1843) £2,000
A CHRISTMAS CAROL (second edition; illustrated by John Leech) (Chapman & Hall, 1843) £750
A CHRISTMAS CAROL (illustrated by Charles E. Brock) (Dent, 1905) £30
A CHRISTMAS CAROL (illustrated by Arthur Rackham; issued with dustjacket) (Heinemann, 1915) £350
A CHRISTMAS CAROL (illustrated by Arthur Rackham; limited to 530 copies, signed by the artist) (Heinemann, 1915).......£1,500
A CHRISTMAS CAROL (illustrated by Honor C. Appleton) (Simpkin, Marshall, Hamilton, Kent, 1920) £45
A CHRISTMAS CAROL (illustrated by John Leech; issued without dustjacket) (King Penguin, 1946) £10
A CHRISTMAS CAROL (with stills from the film 'Scrooge'; issued with dustjacket) (Ward Lock, 1951) £15
A CHRISTMAS CAROL (illustrated by Ronald Searle; issued with dustjacket) (Perpetua, 1961) £20
THE CHIMES: A Goblin Story of Some Bells that Rang an Old Year Out and a New Year In (first edition, first issue;
    illustrated by Daniel Maclise, Richard Doyle, John Leech and William C. Stanfield) (Chapman & Hall, 1845 [1844]) £300
THE CHIMES (first edition, second issue; illustrated by Daniel Maclise, Richard Doyle,
    John Leech and William C. Stanfield) (Chapman & Hall, 1845 [1844]) £175
THE CHIMES (illustrated by Hugh Thomson) (Hodder & Stoughton, [1913]) £35
THE CRICKET ON THE HEARTH: A Fairy Tale of Home (first edition, with 'Daily News' advert pink slip inserted; illustrated
    by Daniel Maclise, Richard Doyle, William C. Stanfield, John Leech and Edwin Landseer) (Bradbury & Evans, 1846 [1845]) £600
THE CRICKET ON THE HEARTH: A Fairy Tale of Home (first edition, without pink slip inserted; illustrated by
    Daniel Maclise, Richard Doyle, William C. Stanfield, John Leech and Edwin Landseer) (Bradbury & Evans, 1846 [1845]) £150
THE CRICKET ON THE HEARTH: A Fairy Tale of Home (illustrated by Hugh Thomson) (Golden Cockerel Press, 1933)..........£60
THE BATTLE OF LIFE: A Love Story (first edition, first issue; illustrated by Daniel Maclise, Richard Doyle,
    William C. Stanfield and John Leech) (Bradbury & Evans, 1846) £2,250
THE BATTLE OF LIFE: A Love Story (first edition, second issue; illustrated by Daniel Maclise, Richard Doyle,
    William C. Stanfield and John Leech) (Bradbury & Evans, 1846) £300
THE BATTLE OF LIFE: A Love Story (first edition, third issue; illustrated by Daniel Maclise, Richard Doyle,
    William C. Stanfield and John Leech) (Bradbury & Evans, 1846) £1,200
THE BATTLE OF LIFE: A Love Story (first edition, fourth issue; illustrated by Daniel Maclise, Richard Doyle,
    William C. Stanfield and John Leech) (Bradbury & Evans, 1846) £200
THE HAUNTED MAN AND THE GHOST'S BARGAIN: A Fancy for Christmas Time (illustrated by John Tenniel,
    William C. Stanfield, Frank Stone and John Leech) (Bradbury & Evans, 1848) £200
CHRISTMAS BOOKS (Chapman & Hall, 1852) £60
CHRISTMAS BOOKS (illustrated by H. M. Brock) (Harrap, 1932) £25
A CHILD'S HISTORY OF ENGLAND (frontispiece by F.W. Topham; three volumes) (Bradbury & Evans, 1852-54)..................£300
THE MAGIC FISHBONE (illustrated by S.B. Pearse) (Saint Catherine Press/Nisbet, [1912]) £30
THE HOLLY TREE and Other Christmas Stories (illustrated by E.H. Shepard) (Partridge, [1926]) £50
A LIFE OF OUR LORD: Written for his Children (Associated Newspapers, 1934).....................................£10

DICKINSON, Peter

British author. Born: Zambia, 1927. Awarded Carnegie Medal in 1980. His first three highly successful 'Changes' books were followed by others with distant and exotic settings.

Prices are for books in Very Good condition with dustjackets where applicable.

THE WEATHERMONGER (Gollancz, 1968) £35
HEARTSEASE (illustrated by Robert Hales) (Gollancz, 1969)..£25
THE DEVIL'S CHILDREN (illustrated by Robert Hales) (Gollancz, 1970) £25
EMMA TUPPER'S DIARY (Gollancz, 1971) £20
THE DANCING BEAR (illustrated by David Smee) (Gollancz, 1972)...£20
THE IRON LION (illustrated by Marc Brown) (Allen & Unwin, 1973) £20
THE GIFT (illustrated by Gareth Floyd) (Gollancz, 1973) £20
PRESTO! (Hutchinson, 1975) £20
THE CHANGES (Gollancz, 1975) £45
THE BLUE HAWK (illustrated by David Smee) (Gollancz, 1976) £20
KING AND JOKER (Hodder & Stoughton, 1976) £20
ANNERTON PIT (Gollancz, 1977)..£20
WALKING DEAD (Hodder & Stoughton, 1977) £20
HEPZIBAH (illustrated by Sue Porter) (Eel Pie, 1978) £20
TULKA (Gollancz, 1979) £20
THE FLIGHT OF DRAGONS (illustrated by Wayne Anderson) (Gollancz,1979) £20
CITY OF GOLD (illustrated by Michael Foreman) (Gollancz, 1980) £20
THE SEVENTH RAVEN (Gollancz, 1981)..£20

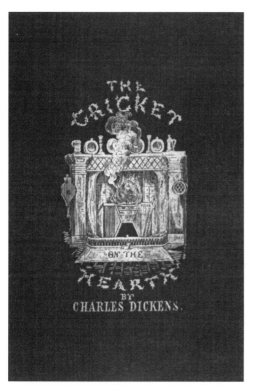

PETER DICKINSON

GIANT COLD

ILLUSTRATED BY ALAN E. COBER

*The first edition of **The Cricket on the Hearth** (1846), the third of Charles Dickens' very popular Christmas books.*

*Peter Dickinson's **Giant Cold** was published in 1984, four years after the author won the coveted Carnegie Medal.*

A SUMMER IN THE TWENTIES (Hodder & Stoughton, 1981) £20
HEALER (Gollancz, 1983)..£10
HINDSIGHT (The Bodley Head, 1983) £10
GIANT COLD (illustrated by Alan Cober) (Gollancz, 1984) £10
A BOX OF NOTHING (illustrated by Ian Newsham) (Gollancz, 1985) £10
DEATH OF A UNICORN (paperback) (Hamlyn, 1985) £10
MOLE HOLE (illustrated by Jean Claverie) (Blackie, 1987) £10
EVA (Gollancz, 1988) £10
MERLIN DREAMS (illustrated by Alan Lee) (Gollancz, 1988) £15
SKELETON-IN-WAITING (The Bodley Head, 1989)...£10
AK (Gollancz, 1990) £10
PLAY DEAD (The Bodley Head, 1991) £10
THE YELLOW ROOM CONSPIRACY (London : Little Brown, 1994) £10

DISNEY, Walt

The American film-maker, Walt Disney (1901-66), adapted many classic children's stories for the screen, notably *Snow White and the Seven Dwarfs* (1937), *Alice in Wonderland* (1951), *Peter Pan* (1953), *The Sword in the Stone* (1963) and *The Jungle Book* (1967). These, and original works featuring Mickey Mouse, Donald Duck and the studio's other characters, prompted a number of spin-off publications.

Prices are for books in Very Good condition.

MICKEY MOUSE BOOK by B. Bobette (Bibo & Lang, 1930) £500
MICKEY CHERCHEUR D'OR (Hachette, France, 1931) £150
MICKEY MOUSE MOVIE STORIES (Dean, 1931) £225
MICKEY MOUSE STORY BOOK (David McKay, 1931) £325
THE ADVENTURES OF MICKEY MOUSE: Book 1 (David McKay, 1931) £350
MORE ADVENTURES OF MICKEY MOUSE (Dean, 1932)..£200
MICKEY MOUSE (Dean: 'Great Big Midget Books' series, [1933])..£175
MICKY MAUS IM ZIRKUS (German version of 'Mickey Mouse at the Circus'; three pop-up pictures)
(Verlag Bollmann, [c.1933]) £550
MINNI MAUS UND DAS ENTLEIN (German version of 'Minnie Mouse and the Little Duck'; three pop-up pictures)
(Verlag Bollmann, [c.1933]) £550

THE POP-UP MICKEY MOUSE (three pop-up pictures) (Whitman, 1933) £550
THE POP-UP MINNIE MOUSE (Whitman, U.S., 1933) £550
THE POP-UP SILLY SYMPHONIES: Babes in the Woods and King Neptune (Whitman, U.S., 1933) £450
THREE LITTLE PIGS (Whitman, U.S., 1933) £120
WHO'S AFRAID OF THE BIG BAD WOLF: The Three Little Pigs (David McKay, 1933) £80
MICKEY IN KING ARTHUR'S COURT (four pop-up pictures) (Dean, [1934]) £450
MICKEY MOUSE AND HIS HORSE TANGLEFOOT (Whitman, U.S., 1934) £80
MICKEY MOUSE IN GIANT LAND (Collins, 1934) £160
MICKEY MOUSE WINS THE RACE (Whitman, U.S., 1934) £80
SANTA'S WORKSHOP: From 'Silly Symphony' (Collins, [c.1934]) £80
THE PIED PIPER (John Lane: The Bodley Head, 1934) £160
DONALD DUCK (Whitman, U.S., 1935) £100
MICKEY MOUSE AND THE MAGIC CARPET (Whitman, U.S., [1935]) £130
MICKEY MOUSE CRUSOE (Collins, [1935]) £150
MICKEY MOUSE MOVIE STORIES BOOK 2 (Dean, [1935]) £400
THE THREE ORPHAN KITTENS (Whitman, U.S., 1935) £100
THE TORTOISE AND THE HARE (Dean, 1935)...£75
THE WALT DISNEY SILLY SYMPHONY OMNIBUS (John Lane: The Bodley Head, 1935) £150
PRINCESS ELIZABETH GIFT BOOK (includes two Mickey Mouse colour plates and Disney endpapers)
      (Hodder & Stoughton, [1935]) £30
MICKEY MOUSE AT THE CARNIVAL (Collins: 'Wee Little Books' series, 1936)...................................£120
THE THREE ORPHAN KITTENS (Dean, 1936) £75
MICKEY MOUSE'S MISFORTUNE (Collins: 'Wee Little Books' series, 1936) £120
DONALD DUCK AND HIS MISADVENTURES (Whitman: 'The Better Little Books' series, U.S., 1937) £80
SNOW WHITE AND THE SEVEN DWARFS. Adapted from Grimm's Fairy Tales (Whitman, U.S., 1937) £120
FERDINAND THE BULL (Whitman, U.S., 1938)...£35
MICKEY MOUSE IN THE RACE FOR RICHES (Whitman: 'The Better Little Books' series, U.S., 1938) £80
PLUTO'S PLAYTIME (Juvenile Productions, [1938]) £100
SNOW WHITE ANNUAL (Dean, [1938]) £100
THE STORY OF CLARABELLE COW (Whitman, U.S., 1938)...£40
WALT DISNEY'S SNOW WHITE SKETCH BOOK (Collins, [1938])..£400
SCHOOL DAYS IN DISNEYVILLE (Heath, 1939)...£20
SNOW WHITE AND THE MAGIC MIRROR (3-D plates; with special spectacles) (Dean, [1939]) £80
SNOW WHITE AND THE SEVEN DWARFS (Collins, [c.1939]) £100

The Cinderella Magic Wand Book (1950), included 3-D pictures plus a pair of special spectacles through which to view them!

WALT DISNEY'S 'PINOCCHIO' (film scenario with illustrations; adapted from 'Adventures of Pinocchio';
  limited to 100 numbered copies; comb-bound) (Collins, [1939]) £150
WALT DISNEY TELLS THE STORY OF 'PINOCCHIO' (paperback) (Whitman, U.S., 1939) £800
WALT DISNEY'S VERSION OF 'PINOCCHIO' (pictorial boards) (Collins, 1940) £50
BAMBI (Collins, [c.1940]) £75
DONALD DUCK GETS FED UP (Whitman: 'The Better Little Books' series, U.S., 1940) £75
DUMBO PAINTING BOOK (Collins, [c.1940])...£25
FATHER NOAH'S ARK. From the film 'Silly Symphony' (small format; without colour plates) (Birn, [c.1940]) £50
FATHER NOAH'S ARK (quarto; with colour plates) (Birn, [c. 1940]) £150
THE PINOCCHIO STORY BOOK (Collins, 1940) £50
THE DISNEYLAND OMNIBUS (Dean, 1940) £50
WALT DISNEY WONDER BOOK (Sunshine Press, [c.1940]) £50
WALT DISNEY'S 'FANTASIA' by Deems Taylor (Simon & Schuster, U.S., 1940) £450
MICKEY MOUSE AND THE DUDE RANCH BANDIT (Whitman, U.S., 1943) £200
THE NUTCRACKER SUITE (Collins, 1943) £75
BAMBI (Heath, 1944) £20
DONALD DUCK AND HIS FRIENDS: As Told by Jean Ayer (Heath, 1944) £45
MICKEY SEES THE USA (Heath, 1944)...£25
MICKEY'S VOYAGE (Hachette, France 1948) £40
POOR PLUTO (Whitman, U.S., 1948)...£35
THE CINDERELLA MAGIC WAND BOOK (3-D; with special spectacles) (Dean 1950) £75
WALT DISNEY'S TREASURE ISLAND (Collins, 1950) £20
WALT DISNEY'S THUMPER ANNUAL (Odhams, 1952) £25
PETER PAN CHILDREN'S ALBUM (Walt Disney, 1952) £40
PETER PAN (Walt Disney, 1953) £40
PLUTO'S PAINTING BOOK (Adprint, 1953)...£20
MICKEY MOUSE ALPINISTE (Hachette, France, 1954) £120
LADY AND THE TRAMP AT THE ZOO (Adprint, 1955) £15
WALT DISNEY'S LADY AND THE TRAMP. Based on the Story by Ward Greene (Dean, [1955]) £35
WALT DISNEY'S CROSSWORD PUZZLE BOOK (Birn, 1960) £12
DONALD DUCK'S POP-UP CIRCUS (Purnell, 1970) £30
THE DISNEY POSTER BOOK (introduction by Maurice Sendak; 22 large colour plates; card covers)
  (Academy Editions, [1977]) £25
PINOCCHIO (pop-up book) (Walt Disney, 1981)...£20
WALT DISNEY'S TREASURY OF CARTOON CLASSICS (Abrams, 1981)..£10
WALT DISNEY'S MOVIE POSTER BOOK (Walt Disney, 1989)..£12
SNOW WHITE TEACHES THE SEVEN DWARFS TO KNIT (Walt Disney, no date)...................................£75
THE ROBBER KITTEN (Whitman, U.S., no date) £100
THE STORY OF CASEY JNR THE LITTLE ENGINE WHO SAVED A CIRCUS AND ALL THE ANIMALS
  (Collins, no date) £40

'Mickey Mouse' Annuals
MICKEY MOUSE ANNUAL 1931 (Dean, 1930) £325
MICKEY MOUSE ANNUAL 1932-40 (Dean) ....each £200
MICKEY MOUSE ANNUAL 1941-45 (Dean) ....each £100
MICKEY MOUSE ANNUAL 1946-49 (Dean) ....each £50
MICKEY MOUSE ANNUAL 1950-59 (Dean) ....each £30
MICKEY MOUSE ANNUAL 1960-65 (Dean) ....each £15

'Donald Duck' Annuals
DONALD DUCK'S ANNUAL 1939 (Collins) £250
DONALD DUCK'S ANNUAL 1940 (Collins) £200
DONALD DUCK'S ANNUAL 1941 (Collins) £150
DONALD DUCK'S ANNUAL 1942 (Collins) £130

DIXON, Franklin W.
House name, under which the 'Hardy Boys' novels, featuring Frank and Joe Hardy, were written.

Prices are for U.K. editions in Very Good condition with dustjackets where applicable.

'Hardy Boys' Books
HUNTING FOR HIDDEN GOLD (Harold Hill, 1951) £20
THE MARK ON THE DOOR (Harold Hill, 1957) £10
THE MYSTERY OF THE DISAPPEARING FLOOR (Low Marston, 1961) £15
THE MYSTERY OF THE FLYING EXPRESS (Low Marston, 1961) £15
THE MYSTERY OF THE DESERT GIANT (Low Marston, 1963) £15
THE MYSTERY AT DEVIL'S PAW (Low Marston, 1963) £15
THE FLICKERING TORCH MYSTERY (Low Marston, 1963)...£15
THE MYSTERY OF THE CHINESE JUNK (Low Marston, 1963) £15
THE CLUE OF THE BROKEN BLADE (Low Marston, 1963)...£15
THE GHOST AT SKELETON ROCK (Low Marston, 1964) £15

THE VIKING SYMBOL MYSTERY (Low Marston, 1964) £15
THE CLUE IN THE EMBERS (Low Marston, 1965) £15
THE HOODED HAWK MYSTERY (Low Marston, 1965) £15
THE YELLOW FEATHER MYSTERY (Low Marston, 1965) £15
THE SECRET OF PIRATE'S HILL (Low Marston, 1965) £15
THE CRISSCROSS SHADOW (Low Marston, 1965) £15
THE HAUNTED FORT (Low Marston, 1966) £15
THE WAILING SIREN MYSTERY (Low Marston, 1966) £15
SECRET OF THE WILD CAT SWAMP (Low Marston, 1966) £15
THE MYSTERY OF THE MELTED COINS (Low Marston, 1967) £12
THE MYSTERY OF THE SPIRAL BRIDGE (Low Marston, 1967) £12
THE TWISTED CLAW (Macdonald, 1968) £12
THE SINISTER SIGNPOST (Macdonald, 1969) £12
THE SECRET AGENT ON FLIGHT 101 (Macdonald, 1969) £12
THE CLUE OF THE SCREECHING OWL (Macdonald, 1969) £12
THE MYSTERY OF THE AZTEC WARRIOR (Collins, 1971) £12
THE SECRET OF THE OLD MILL (Collins, 1972) £12
THE SHORE ROAD MYSTERY (Collins, 1972) £12
THE GREAT AIRPORT MYSTERY (Collins, 1972) £10
THE MYSTERY OF THE WHALE TATTOO (paperback) (Armada, 1973) £4
MISSING CHUMS (Collins, 1974) £10
SIGN OF THE CROOKED ARROW (paperback) (Armada, 1975) £4
THE SECRET OF SKULL MOUNTAIN (Collins, [1977]) £10
DANGER ON VAMPIRE TRAIL (Collins, [1977])..£10
THE MYSTERIOUS CARAVAN (1977) £10
THE SECRET OF THE CAVES (paperback) (Armada, 1977)...£4
WHILE THE CLOCK TICKED (paperback) (Armada, 1979) £4
THE SHORT-WAVE MYSTERY (Collins, 1980)...£10
THE SECRET PANEL (Collins, 1980) £10
THE SECRET WARNING (Collins, 1980) £10

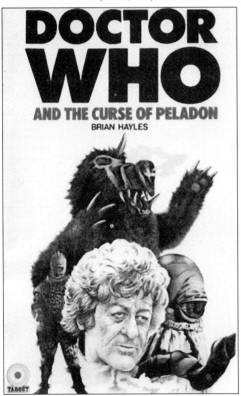

The Target paperback edition of **Doctor Who and the Curse of Peladon** (1974), featuring Jon Pertwee on the cover.

The Daleks are probably Doctor Who's most famous adversaries, and have appeared in many novels over the years.

A FIGURE IN HIDING (Collins, 1980) £8
THE SECRET OF THE LOST TUNNEL (Collins, 1980) £8
THE WITCHMASTER'S KEY (Collins, 1980) £8
THE STING OF THE SCORPION (Collins, 1980) £8
THE MYSTERY OF THE SAMURAI SWORD (illustrated by Leslie Morrill) (Angus & Robertson, 1980).......£8
NIGHT OF THE WEREWOLF (illustrated by Leslie Morrill) (Angus & Robertson, 1980) £8
THE APEMAN'S SECRET (illustrated by Leslie Morrill) (Angus & Robertson, 1980) £8
THE PENTAGON SPY (illustrated by Leslie Morrill) (Angus & Robertson, 1980) £8
THE MUMMY CASE (Angus & Robertson, 1981)...£8
THE STONE IDOL (illustrated by Leslie Morrill) (Angus & Robertson, 1982)..£8
THE VANISHING THIEVES (illustrated by Leslie Morrill) (Angus & Robertson, 1982) £8
THE OUTLAW'S SILVER (illustrated by Leslie Morrill) (Angus & Robertson, 1982) £8
THE SUBMARINE CAPER (illustrated by Leslie Morrill) (Angus & Robertson, 1982) £8
THE MYSTERY OF SMUGGLER'S COVE (Angus & Robertson, 1982) £4
THE TOWER TREASURE (Angus & Robertson, 1982) £4
TRACK OF THE ZOMBIE (Angus & Robertson, 1983) £4
THE BILLION DOLLAR RANSOM (illustrated by Leslie Morrill) (Angus & Robertson, 1983).........................£8
THE VOODOO PLOT (Angus & Robertson, 1983) £8
THE TIC-TAC TERROR (Angus & Robertson, 1983) £8
'SUPER SLEUTHS' SERIES (by Carolyn Keene and Franklin W. Dixon; seven books) (Angus & Robertson, 1983)............each £5
CAVE-IN (Angus & Robertson, 1984) £8
THE CRIMSON FLAME (Angus & Robertson, 1984) £8
TRAPPED AT SEA (Angus & Robertson, 1984)..£8
GAME PLAN FOR DISASTER (Angus & Robertson, 1984) £8
THE BLACKWING PUZZLE (Angus & Robertson, 1985) £6
THE DEMON'S DEN (Angus & Robertson, 1985) £6
THE SKYFIRE PUZZLE (Angus & Robertson, 1986) £6
THE SWAMP MONSTER (Angus & Robertson, 1986) £7
REVENGE OF THE DESERT PHANTOM (Angus & Robertson, 1986) £7

'DOCTOR WHO' BOOKS AND ANNUALS

The BBC's hugely popular children's science fiction drama series was launched in 1963 and inspired a number of spin-off books and annuals.

Prices are for books and annuals in Very Good condition.

'Doctor Who' Annuals

1966 (William Hartnell as 'Doctor Who') (World Distributors) £35
1967 (William Hartnell as 'Doctor Who') (World Distributors) £60
1968 (Patrick Troughton as 'Doctor Who') (World Distributors) £70
1969 (Patrick Troughton as 'Doctor Who') (World Distributors) £60
1970 (Patrick Troughton as 'Doctor Who') (World Distributors) £30
1971 (Jon Pertwee as 'Doctor Who') (World Distributors) £70
1973 (Jon Pertwee as 'Doctor Who') (World Distributors) £15
1974 (Jon Pertwee as 'Doctor Who') (World Distributors) £15
1975 (Jon Pertwee as 'Doctor Who') (World Distributors) £15
1976 (Tom Baker as 'Doctor Who') (World Distributors) £8
1977 (Tom Baker as 'Doctor Who') (World Distributors) £8
1978 (Tom Baker as 'Doctor Who') (World Distributors) £8
1979 (Tom Baker as 'Doctor Who') (World Distributors) £8
1980 (Tom Baker as 'Doctor Who') (World Distributors) £8
1981 (Tom Baker as 'Doctor Who') (World Distributors) £8
1982 (Tom Baker and Peter Davison as 'Doctor Who'; with cover date) (World Distributors) £8
1983 (Peter Davison as 'Doctor Who'; without cover date) (World Distributors) £8
1984 (Peter Davison as 'Doctor Who', with Peter Davison) (World Distributors)...£8
1985 (Colin Baker as 'Doctor Who') (World Distributors)...£8
1986 (Colin Baker as 'Doctor Who') (World Distributors)...£8

'Dalek' Books

THE DALEK BOOK 1964 (Souvenir/Panther) £75
THE DALEK WORLD1965 (Souvenir/Panther) £65
THE DALEK OUTER SPACE BOOK 1966 (Souvenir/Panther) £75
TERRY NATION'S DALEK 1976 (World Distributors) £15
TERRY NATION'S DALEK 1977 (World Distributors)...£15
TERRY NATION'S DALEK 1978 (World Distributors)...£10
TERRY NATION'S DALEK 1979 (World Distributors)...£10

Other Annuals

DOCTOR WHO AND THE INVASION FROM SPACE (World Distributors, 1966) £50
THE AMAZING WORLD OF DOCTOR WHO (World Distributors, 1976) £10

'DOCTOR WHO' BOOKS AND ANNUALS

DOCTOR WHO — ADVENTURES IN TIME AND SPACE (compilation from previous annuals) (World Distributors, 1981) **£8**
K9 ANNUAL (World Distributors, 1983) **£5**

Target Novels
DOCTOR WHO NOVELS (Wingate/W.H. Allen, 1974-1988) ....each **£8**
DOCTOR WHO NOVELS (with black logo; paperback) (Target, 1973-1975)..each **£5**
DOCTOR WHO NOVELS (with diamond crescent logo; paperback) (Target, 1975-1981)..........................each **£2**
DOCTOR WHO NOVELS (with neon logo; paperback) (Target, 1981-1988)..each **£2**
DOCTOR WHO NOVELS (with asteroid logo; paperback) (Target, 1987-Present) ....each **£2**
JUNIOR DOCTOR WHO AND THE GIANT ROBOT by Terrance Dicks (W.H. Allen, 1979)...........................**£8**
JUNIOR DOCTOR WHO AND THE GIANT ROBOT by Terrance Dicks (paperback) (Target, 1980) **£3**
JUNIOR TARGET AND THE BRAIN OF MORBUS by Terrance Dicks (W.H. Allen, 1980) **£8**
JUNIOR TARGET AND THE BRAIN OF MORBUS by Terrance Dicks (paperback) (Target, 1980)............**£3**
THE FIVE DOCTORS by Terrance Dicks (paperback) (Target, 1983)..**£3**
THE TWO DOCTORS by Robert Holmes (paperback) (Target, 1985) **£4**
THE COMPANIONS OF DOCTOR WHO (paperback) (Target, 1986-1987) ....each **£2**

Other Novels
DOCTOR WHO IN AN EXCITING ADVENTURE WITH THE DALEKS by David Whitaker (Muller, 1964).......................**£20**
DOCTOR WHO IN AN EXCITING ADVENTURE WITH THE DALEKS by David Whitaker (paperback) (Armada, 1965) **£6**
DOCTOR WHO IN AN EXCITING ADVENTURE WITH THE DALEKS by David Whitaker (paperback) (Avon, U.S. 1967) **£10**
DOCTOR WHO AND THE CRUSADERS by David Whitaker (Muller, 1965) **£10**
DOCTOR WHO AND THE CRUSADERS by David Whitaker (paperback) (Dragon, 1967) **£6**
DOCTOR WHO AND THE ZARBI by Bill Strutton (Muller, 1965) **£10**
K9 AND THE TIME TRAP by Dave Martin (Sparrow, 1980) **£3**
K9 AND THE BEAST OF VEGA by Dave Martin (Sparrow, 1980) **£3**
K9 AND THE ZETA RESCUE by Dave Martin (Sparrow, 1980) **£3**
K9 AND THE MISSING PLANET by Dave Martin (Sparrow, 1980) **£3**
SEARCH FOR THE DOCTOR by David Martin (Severn House, 1986) **£2**
CRISIS IN SPACE by Michael Holt (Severn House, 1986) **£2**
THE GARDEN OF EVIL by David Martin (Severn House, 1986) **£2**
RACE AGAINST TIME by Pip and Jane Baker (Severn House, 1986) **£2**
MISSION TO VENUS by William Emms (Severn House, 1986) **£2**
INVASION OF THE ORMAZOIDS by Philip Martin (Severn House, 1986)..**£2**

Non-Fiction Titles
THE DALEK POCKET BOOK AND SPACE TRAVELLER'S GUIDE by Terry Nation (paperback) (Panther, 1965) **£20**
THE DOCTOR WHO MONSTER BOOK by Terrance Dicks (paperback) (Target, 1975) **£6**
THE SECOND DOCTOR WHO MONSTER BOOK by Terrance Dicks (paperback) (Target, 1976).................**£6**
THE ADVENTURES OF K9 AND OTHER MECHANICAL CREATURES by Terrance Dicks (paperback) (Target, 1975) **£3**
TERRY NATION'S DALEK SPECIAL (paperback) (Target, 1979) **£3**
THE DOCTOR WHO QUIZ BOOK by Nigel Robinson (paperback) (Target, 1981) **£2**
THE DOCTOR WHO CROSSWORD BOOK by Nigel Robinson (paperback) (Target, 1982) **£2**
DOCTOR WHO QUIZ BOOKS by Michael Holt (paperback) (Magnet, 1982-83) ....each **£1**
THE SECOND DOCTOR WHO QUIZ BOOK by Nigel Robinson (paperback) (Target, 1983) **£2**
DOCTOR WHO: BRAIN-TEASERS AND MIND BENDERS by Adrian Heath (paperback) (Target, 1984) **£2**
THE DOCTOR WHO PUZZLE BOOK by Michael Holt (paperback) (Magnet, 1985) **£1**
THE THIRD DOCTOR WHO QUIZ BOOK by Nigel Robinson (paperback) (Target, 1985) **£2**

'Doctor Who' Reference Books: Large-Format
DOCTOR WHO: THE MAKING OF A TELEVISION SERIES by Alan Road (Deutsch, 1982) **£10**
DOCTOR WHO: THE MAKING OF A TELEVISION SERIES by Alan Road (paperback) (Puffin, 1983) **£4**
THE DOCTOR WHO TECHNICAL MANUAL by Mark Harris (Severn House, 1983)..**£10**
THE DOCTOR WHO TECHNICAL MANUAL by Mark Harris (paperback) (Sphere, 1983) **£2**
DOCTOR WHO: A CELEBRATION by Peter Haining (W.H. Allen, 1983)..**£10**
DOCTOR WHO: A CELEBRATION by Peter Haining (limited to 500 copies; leather binding) (W.H. Allen, 1983) **£35**
DOCTOR WHO: THE KEY TO TIME by Peter Haining (W.H. Allen, 1984) **£10**
DOCTOR WHO: THE KEY TO TIME by Peter Haining (limited to 500 copies; leather binding) (W.H. Allen, 1984) **£35**
DOCTOR WHO: THE KEY TO TIME by Peter Haining (paperback) (Comet, 1987) **£4**
THE DOCTOR WHO PATTERN BOOK by Joy Gammon (W.H. Allen, 1984) **£3**
THE DOCTOR WHO PATTERN BOOK by Joy Gammon (paperback) (W.H. Allen, 1986)...............................**£2**
DOCTOR WHO: THE TARDIS INSIDE OUT by John Nathan-Turner (Piccadilly, 1985) **£5**
DOCTOR WHO: THE TARDIS INSIDE OUT by John Nathan-Turner (paperback) (Piccadilly, 1985) **£3**
THE DOCTOR WHO COOKBOOK by Gary Downie (W.H. Allen, 1985) **£4**
THE DOCTOR WHO COOKBOOK by Gary Downie (paperback) (Star, 1986) **£2**
THE DOCTOR WHO ILLUSTRATED A-Z by Lesley Standring (W.H. Allen, 1985) **£10**
THE DOCTOR WHO ILLUSTRATED A-Z by Lesley Standring (paperback) (Star, 1987) **£4**
TIMEVIEW: THE COMPLETE DOCTOR WHO ILLUSTRATIONS OF FRANK BELLAMY.
    Text by David Bellamy (Who Dares Publishing, 1985)...**£8**
TIMEVIEW: THE COMPLETE DOCTOR WHO ILLUSTRATIONS OF FRANK BELLAMY.
    Text by David Bellamy (paperback) (Who Dares Publishing, 1985) **£5**

*Peter Haining's **Doctor Who: A Celebration** (1983) is one of the most comprehensive books ever written about the Doctor.*

*Another important large-format work from the prolific Peter Haining: **Doctor Who: The Time-Travellers' Guide** (1987).*

DOCTOR WHO: THE EARLY YEARS by Jeremy Bentham (W.H. Allen, 1986) £10
DOCTOR WHO: THE EARLY YEARS by Jeremy Bentham (limited to 500 copies; leather binding) (W.H. Allen, 1986) £60
DOCTOR WHO: THE EARLY YEARS by Jeremy Bentham (paperback) (Comet, 1988) £6
THE DOCTOR WHO FILE by Peter Haining (W.H. Allen, 1986) £6
THE DOCTOR WHO FILE by Peter Haining (paperback) (W.H. Allen, 1992) £3
DOCTOR WHO: THE COMPANIONS by John Nathan-Turner (Piccadilly, 1986) £5
DOCTOR WHO: THE COMPANIONS by John Nathan-Turner (paperback) (Piccadilly, 1986) £3
DOCTOR WHO: SPECIAL EFFECTS by Mat Irvine (Hutchinson, 1986) £6
DOCTOR WHO: SPECIAL EFFECTS by Mat Irvine (paperback) (Beaver, 1986) £3
DOCTOR WHO: THE TIME-TRAVELLERS' GUIDE by Peter Haining (W.H. Allen, 1987) £6
DOCTOR WHO: THE TIME-TRAVELLERS' GUIDE by Peter Haining (paperback) (Comet, 1989) £3
DOCTOR WHO: 25 GLORIOUS YEARS by Peter Haining (W.H. Allen/Planet, 1988) £10
DOCTOR WHO: 25 GLORIOUS YEARS by Peter Haining (paperback) (Virgin, 1990) £5
DOCTOR WHO: CYBERMEN by David Banks (Who Dares Publishing, 1988) £10
DOCTOR WHO: THE CYBERMEN by David Banks (silver leather binding) (Who Dares Publishing, 1988) £90
DOCTOR WHO: THE CYBERMEN by David Banks (paperback) (Virgin, 1990) £5
DOCTOR WHO YEARBOOK (boards; issued without dustjacket) (Marvel, 1991) £3
DOCTOR WHO: THE GALLIFREY CHRONICLES by John Peel (Doctor Who, 1991) £12
DOCTOR WHO YEARBOOK 1993 (boards; issued without dustjacket) (Marvel, 1992)..£3
DOCTOR WHO: THE MONSTERS by Adrian Rigleford and Andrew Skilleter (Doctor Who, 1992) £12
DOCTOR WHO: THE SIXTIES by David J. Howe, Mark Stammers and Stephen James Walker (Doctor Who, 1992) £12
DOCTOR WHO: THE SIXTIES by David J. Howe, Mark Stammers and Stephen James Walker (Doctor Who, 1993) £10
DOCTOR WHO YEARBOOK 1994 (boards; issued without dustjacket) (Marvel, 1993)..£4
DOCTOR WHO — TIMEFRAME: THE ILLUSTRATED HISTORY by David J. Howe (Doctor Who, 1993) £12

'Doctor Who' Reference Books: Small-Format

THE MAKING OF DOCTOR WHO by Malcolm Hulke and Terrance Dicks (paperback) (Piccolo, 1972) £10
THE MAKING OF DOCTOR WHO by Malcolm Hulke and Terrance Dicks (revised edition; paperback) (Target/Wyndham, 1976)..£5
A DAY WITH A TV PRODUCER by Graham Rickard (Wayland, 1980) £6
THE DOCTOR WHO PROGRAMME GUIDE — VOLUME ONE by Jean-Marc Lofficier (W. H. Allen, 1981)....................£4
THE DOCTOR WHO PROGRAMME GUIDE — VOLUME ONE by Jean-Marc Lofficier (paperback) (Target, 1981) £2
THE DOCTOR WHO PROGRAMME GUIDE — VOLUME TWO by Jean-Marc Lofficier (W.H. Allen, 1981) £4
THE DOCTOR WHO PROGRAMME GUIDE — VOLUME TWO by Jean-Marc Lofficier (paperback) (Target, 1981) £2
DOCTOR WHO: THE UNFOLDING TEXT by John Tulloch and Manuel Alvarado (Macmillan, 1983) £6
DOCTOR WHO: THE UNFOLDING TEXT by John Tulloch and Manuel Alvarado (paperback) (Macmillan, 1983) £3
DOCTOR WHO: TRAVEL WITHOUT THE TARDIS by Jean Airey and Laurie Haldeman (paperback) (Target, 1986) ...£2

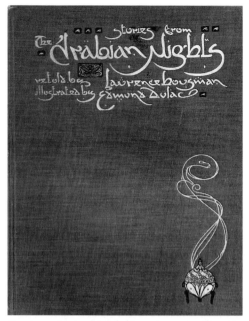

*Edmund Dulac provided eight plates as well as the delightful cover design for Mrs Stawell's **Fairies I Have Met** (1907).*

*The decorative front board of another early Dulac title: his edition of Housman's **Stories from the Arabian Nights**.*

ENCYCLOPEDIA OF THE WORLDS OF DOCTOR WHO: A-D by David Saunders (Piccadilly, 1987) £6
ENCYCLOPEDIA OF THE WORLDS OF DOCTOR WHO: A-D by David Saunders (paperback) (Knight, 1988) £2
THE OFFICIAL DOCTOR WHO AND THE DALEKS BOOK by John Peel and Terry Nation (paperback)
(St Martins Press, U.S., 1989) £3
ENCYCLOPEDIA OF THE WORLDS OF DOCTOR WHO: E-K by David Saunders (Piccadilly, 1989) £6
ENCYCLOPEDIA OF THE WORLDS OF DOCTOR WHO: E-K by David Saunders (paperback) (Knight, 1989) £2
DOCTOR WHO: THE PROGRAMME GUIDE by Jean-Marc Lofficier (paperback) (Target, 1989)...£2
ENCYCLOPEDIA OF THE WORLDS OF DOCTOR WHO: L-R by David Saunders (Piccadilly, 1990) £6
DOCTOR WHO: THE TERRESTRIAL INDEX by Jean-Marc Lofficier (paperback) (Target, 1991)...£2
DOCTOR WHO: THE UNIVERSAL DATA BANK by Jean-Marc Lofficier (paperback) (Doctor Who, 1992) £3
DOCTOR WHO: THE HANDBOOK — THE FOURTH DOCTOR by David J. Howe, Mark Stammers and
Stephen James Walker (paperback) (Doctor Who, 1992) £2
DOCTOR WHO: THE HANDBOOK — THE SIXTH DOCTOR by David J. Howe, Mark Stammers and
Stephen James Walker (paperback) (Doctor Who, 1993) £3

Magazines and Pamphlets
RADIO TIMES — DOCTOR WHO: 10th ANNIVERSARY SPECIAL (November, 1973) £50
DOCTOR WHO: THE DEVELOPING ART by Jeremy Bentham (pamphlet) (British Film Institute, October 1983) £5
RADIO TIMES — DOCTOR WHO: 20th ANNIVERSARY SPECIAL (November 1983) £25
DOCTOR WHO: 30th ANNIVERSARY SPECIAL (based on the '10th Anniversary Special') (Marvel, 1993) £6

DOYLE, Richard
Irish illustrator. Born in 1824, he was one of the main contributors to *Punch* during the 1840s, illustrating a number of children's works following his departure from the title in 1850. Died: 1883.
Prices are for books in Very Good condition.

THE FAIRY RING: A New Collection of Popular Tales by J. and W. Grimm. Translated by J.E. Taylor (John Murray, 1846)....£1,200
FAIRY TALES FROM ALL NATIONS by Anthony R. Montalba (Chapman & Hall, 1849) £120
BOOK OF BALLADS by Sir Theodore Martin (written under the pseudonym 'Bon Gaultier';
illustrated by Richard Doyle and others) (Orr, [1849]) £120
THE ENCHANTED DOLL: A Fairy Tale for Little People by Mark Lemon (Bradbury & Evans, 1849) £85
REBECCA AND ROWENA: A Romance upon Romance by W.M. Thackeray (Chapman & Hall, 1850)................................£300
THE KING OF THE GOLDEN RIVER: A Legend of Stiria by John Ruskin (Smith Elder, 1851) £600
JUVENILE CALENDAR AND ZODIAC FLOWERS by E.L. Hervey (Sampson Low, [1855]) £100
MERRY PICTURES. By the Comic Hands of H.K. Browne, Richard Doyle and Others (Kent, 1857) £60
THE SCOURING OF THE WHITE HORSE by Thomas Hughes (Macmillan, 1859 [1858]) £160
AN OLD FAIRY TALE TOLD ANEW by J.R. Planché (Routledge, [1865]) £55
FAIRY TALES by Mark Lemon (illustrated by Richard Doyle and C.H. Bennett) (Bradbury Evans, 1868) £150
CHRISTMAS BOOKS by Charles Dickens (illustrated by Richard Doyle and others) (Chapman & Hall, 1869) £100

PUCK ON PEGASUS by H.C. Pennell (Routledge, 1869, [1868]) £160
IN FAIRYLAND: A Series of Pictures from the Elf World (with a poem by William Allingham) (Longmans, 1870 [1869])........£650
SNOW-WHITE AND ROSY RED and Other Famous Fairy Tales (Dean, [1871]) £250
THE ENCHANTED CROW and Other Famous Fairy Tales (Dean, [1871]) £170
FEAST OF THE DWARFS and Other Famous Fairy Tales (Dean, [1871]) £170
FORTUNE'S FAVOURITE and Other Famous Fairy Tales (Dean, [1871])...£80
HOMER FOR THE HOLIDAYS by a Boy of Twelve (with extracts from Poe's translation; fifteen plates)
(Pall Mall Gazette Extras, [1883]) £70
THE PRINCESS NOBODY: A Tale of Fairy Land by Andrew Lang (illustrations after drawings by Richard Doyle;
printed in colour by Edmund Evans) (Longmans, [1884]) £500
JACK THE GIANT KILLER (Eyre & Spottiswoode, 1888) £250
THE DOYLE FAIRY BOOK by A.R. Montalba (Dean, 1890)...£180
THE SAD STORY OF A PIG AND LITTLE GIRL by Madeline Wyndham (London, [1901]) £110
THE ENCHANTED DOLL by Mark Lemon (illustrated by Richard Doyle and C.H. Bennett) (Bradbury Evans, 1903) £120

DULAC, Edmund

French illustrator. Born: Toulouse, 1882. Came to London in his early twenties, where he quickly established himself as a rival to Arthur Rackham, illustrating a number of expensive 'gift book' editions of classic children's works, including the *Arabian Nights* (1907). He also worked as a stage designer. Died: 1953.

Prices are for books in Very Good condition without dustjackets.

Books Written and Illustrated by Edmund Dulac

LYRICS PATHETIC AND HUMOROUS FROM A TO Z by Edmund Dulac (24 colour plates by Edmund Dulac) (Warne, 1908) £350
LYRICS PATHETIC AND HUMOROUS FROM A TO Z by Edmund Dulac (portfolio of plates; in cloth-covered box;
limited to 160 copies) (Warne, 1909) £2,500
A FAIRY GARLAND: Being Fairy Tales from the Old French by Edmund Dulac (twelve colour plates by Edmund Dulac)
(Cassell, 1928) £120
A FAIRY GARLAND: Being Fairy Tales from the Old French by Edmund Dulac (twelve colour plates by Edmund Dulac;
De Luxe edition: limited to 1,000 copies, signed by the artist) (Cassell, 1928) £400

Books Illustrated by Edmund Dulac

NOVELS OF THE SISTERS BRONTE (ten volumes; six colour plates by Edmund Dulac in each volume) (Dent, 1905) ....each £40
FAIRIES I HAVE MET by Mrs R. Stawell (eight colour plates by Edmund Dulac) (John Lane, [1907]) £75
FAIRIES I HAVE MET by Mrs R. Stawell (eight colour plates by Edmund Dulac) (Hodder & Stoughton, [1910]) £75
MY DAYS WITH THE FAIRIES by Mrs. R. Stawell (new enlarged edition of above;
eight colour plates by Edmund Dulac) (Hodder & Stoughton, [1913])...£150
STORIES FROM THE ARABIAN NIGHTS. Retold by Laurence Housman (fifty colour plates by Edmund Dulac)
(Hodder & Stoughton, 1907) £200
STORIES FROM THE ARABIAN NIGHTS. Retold by Laurence Housman (fifty colour plates by Edmund Dulac;
De Luxe edition: limited to 350 copies, signed by the artist) (Hodder & Stoughton, 1907) £1,250
THE TEMPEST by William Shakespeare (forty colour plates by Edmund Dulac) (Hodder & Stoughton, [1908]) £200
THE TEMPEST by William Shakespeare (forty colour plates by Edmund Dulac; De Luxe edition:
limited to 500 copies, signed by the artist) (Hodder & Stoughton, [1908])..£1,250
THE RUBAIYAT OF OMAR KHAYYAM (twenty plates by Edmund Dulac) (Hodder & Stoughton, [1909]) £200
THE RUBAIYAT OF OMAR KHAYYAM (twenty plates by Edmund Dulac; De Luxe edition: limited to 750 copies,
signed by the artist) (Hodder & Stoughton, [1909]) £900
THE SLEEPING BEAUTY and Other Fairy Tales by A.T. Quiller Couch (thirty colour plates by Edmund Dulac)
(Hodder & Stoughton, [1910]) £300
THE SLEEPING BEAUTY and Other Fairy Tales (thirty colour plates by Edmund Dulac; De Luxe edition:
limited to 1,000 copies, signed by the artist) (Hodder & Stoughton, [1910]) £850
STORIES FROM HANS ANDERSEN (28 colour plates by Edmund Dulac) (Hodder & Stoughton, [1911]) £300
STORIES FROM HANS ANDERSEN (28 colour plates by Edmund Dulac; De Luxe edition: limited to 750 copies,
signed by the artist) (Hodder & Stoughton, [1911]) £1,300
THE BELLS and Other Poems by Edgar Allan Poe (28 colour plates by Edmund Dulac) (Hodder & Stoughton, [1912]).........£200
THE BELLS and Other Poems by Edgar Allan Poe (28 colour plates by Edmund Dulac; De Luxe edition:
limited to 750 copies, signed by the artist) (Hodder & Stoughton, [1912]) £650
PRINCESS BADOURA: A Tale from The Arabian Nights. Retold by Laurence Housman
(ten colour plates by Edmund Dulac) (Hodder & Stoughton, 1913) £300
PRINCESS BADOURA: A Tale from The Arabian Nights. Retold by Laurence Housman (ten colour plates by
Edmund Dulac; De Luxe edition: limited to 750 copies, signed by the artist) (Hodder & Stoughton, 1913) £1,500
SINBAD THE SAILOR and Other Stories from The Arabian Nights (23 colour plates by Edmund Dulac)
(Hodder & Stoughton, 1914) £500
SINBAD THE SAILOR and Other Stories from the Arabian Nights (23 colour plates by Edmund Dulac;
De Luxe edition: limited to 500 copies, signed by the artist) (Hodder & Stoughton, 1914) £2,250
EDMUND DULAC'S PICTURE-BOOK FOR THE FRENCH RED CROSS (twenty colour plates by Edmund Dulac)
(Hodder & Stoughton, [1915]) £95
THE DREAMER OF DREAMS by Queen Marie of Roumania (six colour plates by Edmund Dulac) (Hodder & Stoughton, [1915]) £50
THE STEALERS OF LIGHT by Queen Marie of Roumania (two colour plates by Edmund Dulac) (Hodder & Stoughton, 1916) £45
EDMUND DULAC'S FAIRY BOOK (fifteen colour plates by Edmund Dulac) (Hodder & Stoughton, 1916) £150
EDMUND DULAC'S FAIRY BOOK (fifteen colour plates by Edmund Dulac; De Luxe edition: limited to 350 copies,
signed by the artist) (Hodder & Stoughton, 1916) £1,000

TANGLEWOOD TALES by Nathaniel Hawthorne (fourteen colour plates by Edmund Dulac)
(Hodder & Stoughton, [1918]) £125

TANGLEWOOD TALES by Nathaniel Hawthorne (fourteen colour plates; De Luxe edition: limited to 500 copies,
signed by the artist) (Hodder & Stoughton, [1918]) £600

THE KINGDOM OF THE PEARL by Leonard Rosenthal (ten colour plates by Edmund Dulac; limited to 675 copies)
(Nisbet, [1920])...£350

THE KINGDOM OF THE PEARL by Leonard Rosenthal (ten colour plates by Edmund Dulac; De Luxe edition:
limited to 100 copies, signed by the author) (Nisbet, [1920]) £1,500

FOUR PLAYS FOR DANCERS by W.B. Yeats (seven illustrations from Dulac's designs) (Macmillan, 1921) £150

THE GREEN LACQUER PAVILION by Helen De V. Beauclerk (nine black-and-white illustrations by
Edmund Dulac and a portrait of author) (Collins, 1926) £25

TREASURE ISLAND by Robert Louis Stevenson (twelve colour plates by Edmund Dulac) (Benn, 1927) £300

TREASURE ISLAND by Robert Louis Stevenson (twelve colour plates by Edmund Dulac; De Luxe edition:
limited to fifty copies, signed by the artist) (Benn, 1927) £4,250

GODS AND MORTALS IN LOVE by Hugh Ross Williamson (nine colour plates by Edmund Dulac)
(Country Life, [1935]) £150

THE DAUGHTERS OF THE STARS by Mary C. Crary (two colour plates by Edmund Dulac) (Hatchard, 1939) £35

THE DAUGHTERS OF THE STARS by Mary C. Crary (two colour plates by Edmund Dulac; De Luxe edition:
limited to 500 copies, signed by the artist) (Hatchard, 1939) £160

THE GOLDEN COCKEREL. Adapted from Alexander Pushkin (limited to 1,500 numbered copies,
signed by the artist) (Limited Editions Club, U.S., 1950) £250

'The Snow Queen', one of 28 colour plates to be found in Dulac's sumptuous edition of **Stories from Hans Andersen** *(1911)*

DUMAS, Alexandre

French author. Born: Villers-Cotterets, 1802. Like Dickens, the great French novelist wrote few works specifically for children, but his best-known adult titles — notably *The Count of Monte-Cristo* and *The Three Musketeers* (both 1846) — have been adapted for young readers. Died: 1870.

Prices are for books in Very Good condition.

GOOD LADY BERTHA'S HONEY BROTH (illustrated by Bertall) (Chapman & Hall: 'Picture Story Books' series, 1846) £130
GOOD LADY BERTHA'S HONEY BROTH (as 'The Honey-Stew of Countess Bertha') (Bohn, 1846) £110
GOOD LADY BERTHA'S HONEY BROTH (as 'The Honey-Stew of Lady Bertha') (Jeremiah How, 1846)................................£110
THE STORY OF A NUTCRACKER (illustrated by Bertall) (Chapman & Hall: 'Picture Story Books' series, 1846) £130
THE STORY OF A NUTCRACKER (as 'Princess Pirlipatine and the Nutcracker'; illustrated by Violet Dale)
  (Philip Allan, 1918)..£25
CAPTAIN PAMPHILE: Episodes (Longmans, 1892) £20
CAPTAIN PAMPHILE (as 'Adventures of Captain Pamphile'; paperback) (Methuen, [1904]) £10
CAPTAIN PAMPHILE (as 'Adventures of Captain Pamphile'; illustrated by Frank Adams; hardback) (Methuen, [1905]) £20
LYDERIC: Count of Flanders (paperback) (Gowans & Gray, 1903) £10
LA JEUNESSE DE PIERROT (Blackie, 1906) £15
THE DUMAS FAIRY TALE BOOK (illustrated by Harry Rountree) (Warne, 1924)..£35
THE PHANTOM WHITE HARE and Other Stories (issued with dustjacket) (Canongate, 1989) £10

'DUMPY' BOOKS

A popular series of numbered, small-format books, selected by E.V. Lucas and published by Grant Richards and later by Chatto & Windus. Helen Bannerman's *Little Black Sambo* was the fourth title in the series.

Prices are for books in Very Good condition.

NO. 1: THE FLAMP AND OTHER STORIES by E.V. Lucas (Grant Richards, 1897) £80
NO. 2: MRS TURNER'S CAUTIONARY STORIES (Grant Richards, 1897) £60
NO. 3: THE BAD FAMILY AND OTHER STORIES by Mrs Fenwick (Grant Richards, 1899) £60
NO. 4: THE STORY OF LITTLE BLACK SAMBO by Helen Bannerman (illustrated by the author)
  (Grant Richards, 1899) £6,000
NO. 5: THE BOUNTIFUL LADY by Thomas Cobb (Grant Richards, 1900) £60
NO. 6: A CAT BOOK by E.V. Lucas (illustrated by H. Officer Smith) (Grant Richards, 1901) £65
NO. 7: A FLOWER BOOK by Eden Coybee (illustrated by Nellie Benson) (Grant Richards, 1901) £60
NO. 8: THE PINK KNIGHT by J. R. Monsell (illustrated by the author) (Grant Richards, 1901) £60
NO. 9: THE LITTLE CLOWN by Thomas Cobb (Grant Richards, 1901) £60
NO. 10: A HORSE BOOK by Mary Tourtel (Grant Richards, 1901) £150
NO. 11: LITTLE PEOPLE: An Alphabet by T.W.H. Crosland (Grant Richards, 1901) £80
NO. 12: A DOG BOOK by Ethel Bicknell (illustrated by C. Moore Park) (Grant Richards, 1902) £70
NO. 13: THE ADVENTURES OF SAMUEL AND SELINA by Jean C. Archer (Grant Richards, 1902) £65
NO. 14: THE LITTLE LOST GIRL by Eleanor Raper (Grant Richards, 1902) £65
NO. 15: DOLLIES by Richard Hunter (illustrated by Ruth Cobb) (Grant Richards, 1902) £90
NO. 16: THE BAD MRS GINGER by Honor C. Appleton (illustrated by the author) (Grant Richards, 1902) £80
NO. 17: PETER PIPER'S PRACTICAL PRINCIPLES (Grant Richards, 1902) £65
NO. 18: LITTLE WHITE BARBARA (Grant Richards, 1902) £70
NO. 19: JAPANESE DUMPY (Grant Richards, 1903)..£80
NO. 20: TOWLOCKS AND HIS WOODEN HORSE by Alice Appleton (illustrated by Honor C. Appleton)
  (Grant Richards, 1903)..£75
NO. 21: THE THREE LITTLE FOXES by Mary Tourtel (Grant Richards, 1903) £150
NO. 22: THE OLD MAN'S BAG by T.W.H. Crosland (illustrated by J.R. Monsell) (Grant Richards, 1903) £65
NO. 23: THE THREE GOBLINS by M.G. Taggart (Grant Richards, 1903) £70
NO. 24: DUMPY PROVERBS by Honor C. Appleton (illustrated by the author) (Grant Richards, 1903) £90
NO. 25: MORE DOLLIES by Richard Hunter (illustrated by Ruth Cobb) (Grant Richards, 1903) £90
NO. 26: LITTLE YELLOW WANG-LO by M.C. Bell (Grant Richards, 1903) £80
NO. 27: PLAIN JANE (Grant Richards, 1903) £70
NO. 28: THE SOOTY MAN (Grant Richards, 1903) £70
NO. 29: FISHY WINKLE by Jean Archer (illustrated by the author) (Grant Richards, 1903) £70
NO. 30: ROSALIND (Grant Richards, 1904) £70
NO. 31: SAMMY AND THE SNARLIWINK (Grant Richards, 1904) £70
NO. 32: THE MOTOR CAR DUMPY BOOK by T.W.H. Crosland (illustrated by J.R. Monsell)
  (Grant Richards, 1904)..£125
NO. 33: IRENE'S CHRISTMAS PARTY by Richard Hunter (illustrated by Ruth Cobb) (Grant Richards, 1904) £65
NO. 34: THE LITTLE SOLDIER BOOK by Jessie Pope (illustrated by Henry Mayor) (Chatto & Windus, 1905) £65
NO. 35: A DUTCH DOLL'S DITTIES (Chatto & Windus, 1905) £75
NO. 36: TEN LITTLE NIGGER BOYS (Chatto & Windus, 1905)...£90
NO. 37: HUMPTY DUMPTY'S LITTLE SON (Chatto & Windus, 1907) £70
NO. 38: SIMPLE SIMON (Chatto & Windus, 1907)..£70
NO. 39: THE LITTLE FRENCHMAN (Chatto & Windus, 1908)..£70
NO. 40: THE POTATO BOOK, or The Story of an Irish Potato by Lily Schofield (Chatto & Windus, 1908) £70

E

'EAGLE' ANNUALS AND BOOKS

Popular British comic annual of the 1950s and '60s. The comic itself was launched on 14th April 1950, the first annual appearing the following year. Among the title's many popular characters were 'Harris Tweed, Extra Special Agent' and Dan Dare.

Prices are for books and annuals in Very Good condition with dustjackets where applicable. See also 'Dan Dare'.

'Eagle' Annuals

NO. 1 (Hulton Press, September 1951) £30
NO. 2 (Hulton Press, September 1952) £20
NO. 3 (Hulton Press, September 1953) £12
NO. 4 (Hulton Press, September 1954) £12
NO. 5 (Hulton Press, September 1955) £12
NO. 6 (Hulton Press, September 1956) £12
NO. 7 (Hulton Press, 1957) £12
NO. 8 (Hulton Press, 1958) £12
NO. 9 (Hulton Press, 1959) £12
NO. 10 (Hulton Press, 1960) £12
NO. 11 (Longacre Press, 1961) £12
NO. 12 (issued without dustjacket) (Longacre Press, 1962) £12
NO. 13 (issued without dustjacket) (Longacre Press, 1963) £12
NO. 14 (issued without dustjacket) (Longacre Press, 1964) £12
NO. 15 (issued without dustjacket) (Longacre Press, 1965) £12
NO. 16 (issued without dustjacket) (Longacre Press, 1966) £12
NO. 17 (issued without dustjacket) (Longacre Press, 1967) £12
NO. 18 (issued without dustjacket) (Longacre Press, 1968) £12
Later Issues (issued without dustjackets) ....each £12

Others

RIDERS OF THE RANGE (Juvenille Productions, 1952-1956) ....each £15
RIDERS OF THE RANGE ANNUALS NOS. 1-6 (Hulton Press/Longacre, 1957-62) ....each £15
JEFF ARNOLD in THE BOZEMAN TRAIL (issued without dustjacket) (Juvenille Productions, [c1962]) £20
EAGLE BOOK OF MAGIC (press-out) (1950s) £150
THE EAGLE BOOK OF ADVENTURE STORIES (includes W.E. Johns' story 'Strange Freight') (1950)...........£25
EAGLE BOOK OF RECORDS AND CHAMPIONS (1951) £15
PC 49 EAGLE STRIP CARTOON BOOK (Preview Publications, 1953) £30
PC 49 EAGLE STRIP CARTOON BOOK NO. 2 (Preview Publications, 1954) £25
EAGLE SPECIAL INVESTIGATOR by Max Hastings (Joseph, 1953) £12
EAGLE BOOK OF TRAINS (1953) £10
EAGLE BOOK OF AIRCRAFT (1953) £10
EAGLE SPORTS ANNUAL NO. 1 (1953) £12
ADVENTURE CALLING by Max Hastings (novel) (1953) £10
EAGLE SPORTS ANNUAL NO. 2 (1954) £12
EAGLE SPORTS ANNUAL NO. 3-Onwards ....each £12
SERGEANT LUCK'S SECRET MISSION (novel) (1956) £15
THE BADEN POWELL STORY (1957) £65
I WANT TO BE...: An Eagle Book of Careers (Hulton Press, 1957) £15
EAGLE BOOK OF TRAINS (Hulton Press, 1957) £10
THE HAPPY WARRIOR (1958) £35
LUCK OF THE LEGION'S FOREIGN ADVENTURE (novel) (1958) £20
EAGLE BOOK OF HOBBIES (Hulton Press, 1958) £15
JACK O'LANTERN AND THE FIGHTING COCK (novel) (1958) £10
EAGLE BOOK OF CARS AND MOTOR SPORTS (Hulton Press, 1958) £15
EAGLE BOOK OF SHIPS AND BOATS (Hulton Press, 1959) £15
EAGLE BOOK OF RECORDS AND CHAMPIONS (Hulton Press, 1959) £25
EAGLE BOOK OF MODEL AIRCRAFT by Ray Malmstrom (Hulton Press, 1959) £20
BEST OF EAGLE ANNUAL 1951-59 ....£10
EAGLE BOOK OF MODEL BOATS by Ray Malmstrom (Longacre Press, 1960) £20
EAGLE BOOK OF TRAINS (Longacre Press, 1960) £15
EAGLE BOOK OF SPACECRAFT MODELS by Ray Malmstrom (Longacre Press, 1960) £20
EAGLE BOOK OF POLICE AND DETECTION by R.M. Harrison (Longacre Press, 1960)............................£20
EAGLE BOOK OF MODEL CARS by Ray Malmstrom (Longacre Press, 1961) £20
EAGLE BOOK OF THE WEST by Charles Chilton (Longacre Press, 1961) £10
EAGLE BOOK OF HOW IT WORKS (Longacre Press, 1962) £10
EAGLE BOOK OF FIGHTING SERVICES (Longacre Press, 1962)..£15
EAGLE FOOTBALL ANNUAL 1962 ....£5

Black Hunting Whip (1950) is one of eleven titles in Monica Edwards' popular 'Punchbowl Farm' series.

No Going Back is part of the 'Romney Marsh' series. It is now valued at £30 in Very Good condition with the dustjacket.

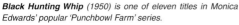

EDWARDS, Monica

British author. Born: Belper, Derbyshire, in 1912. Well-known for her 'Romney Marsh' and 'Punchbowl Farm' series based on real people and places. Died: 1998

Prices are for books in Very Good condition with dustjackets.

'Punchbowl Farm' Books

EDWARDS, Monica

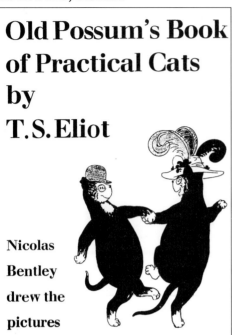

The illustrated edition of T.S. Eliot's only book for children. This appeared in 1940, just one year after the first edition.

One of Nicolas Bentley's superb pictures from the illustrated edition, which is now worth £75 in Very Good condition.

'Romney Marsh' Books

WISH FOR A PONY (Collins, 1947) £30
THE SUMMER OF THE GREAT SECRET (Collins, 1948) £30
THE MIDNIGHT HORSE (Collins, 1949)...£40
THE WHITE RIDERS (Collins, 1950) £40
CARGO OF HORSES (Collins, 1951)..£30
HIDDEN IN A DREAM (Collins, 1952) £30
STORM AHEAD (Collins, 1953) £40
NO ENTRY (Collins, 1954) £35
THE NIGHTBIRD (Collins, 1955) £40
OPERATION SEABIRD (Collins, 1957) £35
STRANGERS TO THE MARSH (Collins, 1957) £30
NO GOING BACK (Collins, 1960)...£30
THE HOODWINKER (Collins, 1962)...£30
DOLPHIN SUMMER (Collins, 1963) £30
A WIND IS BLOWING (Collins, 1969)..£40

Others

JOAN GOES FARMING ('Career books for girls') (The Bodley Head, 1954)..£25
RENNIE GOES RIDING ('Career books for girls') (The Bodley Head, 1956) £25
KILLER DOG (Collins, 1959) £25
UNDER THE ROSE (Collins, 1968)..£25

ELIOT, T.S.

American poet. Born: Thomas Stearns Eliot in Missouri, U.S., in 1888. Eliot's only children's work, *Old Possum's Book of Practical Cats*, takes its title from the nickname given to him by Ezra Pound. A sequence of light verses, it was initially issued in a dustjacket designed by the poet himself, although a new edition with illustrations by Nicolas Bentley followed soon after. The poems provided the inspiration for Andrew Lloyd Webber's hit musical, *Cats* (1981). Died: 1965.

Prices are for books in Very Good condition with dustjackets.

OLD POSSUM'S BOOK OF PRACTICAL CATS (Faber, 1939) £450
OLD POSSUM'S BOOK OF PRACTICAL CATS (illustrated by Nicolas Bentley) (Faber, 1940)................................£75
GROWLTIGER'S LAST STAND and Other Poems (illustrated by Errol Le Cain) (Faber, 1986) £35
MR MISTOFFELEES (illustrated by Errol Le Cain) (Faber, 1990) £35

EMETT, Rowland

British illustrator. Born: London, 1906. Studied at the Birmingham School of Arts and Crafts, subsequently working as a commercial artist before submitting his first illustration to *Punch* in 1939. Best known for his drawings of old-fashioned railway locomotives and other fantastic machines, but has also illustrated two books by Walter de la Mare. Awarded an OBE in 1978. Died: 1990.

Prices are for books in Very Good condition with dustjackets.

PEACOCK PIE by Walter De La Mare (Faber, 1941) £20
BELLS & GRASS: A Book of Rhymes by Walter De La Mare (Faber, 1941)..£20
ANTHONY & ANTIMACASSAR by Mary Emett (Faber, [1943]) £35
THE EMETT FESTIVAL RAILWAY (paperback) (Puffin: 'Cut-Out Book' No. 7, 1951) £35
NELLIE COME HOME (Faber, 1952) £20

ESTES, Eleanor

American author. Born: Connecticut, 1906. Still popular for her 'Moffat' books. Awarded the Newbery Medal for *Ginger Pye* in 1952. Died: 1988.

Prices are for books in Very Good condition with dustjackets where applicable.

THE MOFFATS (illustrated by Louis Slobodkin) (Harcourt Brace, US, 1941)..£50
THE MOFFATS (illustrated by Louis Slobodkin) (The Bodley Head, 1959) £30
THE MIDDLE MOFFAT (illustrated by Louis Slobodkin) (Harcourt Brace, US, 1942) £50
THE MIDDLE MOFFAT (illustrated by Louis Slobodkin) (The Bodley Head, 1960) £25
RUFUS M (illustrated by Louis Slobodkin) (Harcourt Brace, US, 1943) £30
RUFUS M (illustrated by Louis Slobodkin) (The Bodley Head, 1960)..£20
THE SUN AND THE WIND AND MR TODD (illustrated by Louis Slobodkin) (Harcourt Brace, US, 1943) £25
THE SLEEPING GIANT AND OTHER STORIES (illustrated by Eleanor Estes) (Harcourt Brace, US, 1948)...............£20

*The superb Edward Ardizzone jacket from Eleanor Estes' **Pinky Pye**.*

GINGER PYE (illustrated by the author) (Harcourt Brace, US, 1951)...£20
GINGER PYE (illustrated by the author) (The Bodley Head, 1961) £20
A LITTLE OVEN (illustrated by the author) (Harcourt Brace, US, 1955) £20
PINKY PYE (illustrated by Edward Ardizzone) (Harcourt Brace, US, 1958)...£30
PINKY PYE (illustrated by Edward Ardizzone) (Constable, 1959) £30
THE WITCH FAMILY (illustrated by Edward Ardizzone) (Harcourt Brace, US, 1960).................................£35
THE WITCH FAMILY (illustrated by Edward Ardizzone) (Constable, 1962) £35
THE ALLEY (illustrated by Edward Ardizzone) (Harcourt Brace, US, 1964) £25
MIRANDA THE GREAT (illustrated by Edward Ardizzone) (Harcourt Brace, US, 1967) £20
THE TUNNEL OF HUGSY GOODE (illustrated by Edward Ardizzone) (Harcourt Brace, US, 1972) £15
THE COAT-HANGER CHRISTMAS TREE (illustrated by Susanne Suba) (Atheneum, US, 1973) £20
THE COAT-HANGER CHRISTMAS TREE (illustrated by Susanne Suba) (OUP, 1976)................................£20
THE LOST UMBRELLA OF KIM CHU (illustrated by Jacqueline Ayer) (Atheneum, US, 1978) £15
THE MOFFAT MUSEUM (Harcourt Brace, US, 1983) £10
THE CURIOUS ADVENTURES OF JIMMY MCGEE (illustrated by John O'Brien) (Harcourt Brace, US, 1987)...........................£10

Play

THE LOLLIPOP PRINCESS: A PLAY FOR PAPER DOLLS (illustrated by the author) (Harcourt Brace,US, 1969) £15

EWING, Juliana Horatia

British author. Born: Juliana Horatia Gatty in Yorkshire in 1841. Her mother, Margaret Gatty, was a writer of children's stories and, In 1866, founded *Aunt Judy's Magazine*, to which her daughter became a frequent contributor. Her first collection of children's stories had appeared in 1862, and was followed by many more books, notably *The Brownies and Other Tales* (1870) — which gave its name to the junior Girl Guides — *Jan of the Windmill* (1876) and *Jackanapes* (1884). Among the artists who illustrated her works were George Cruikshank and Randolph Caldecott. Kipling and E. Nesbit both admired her writing. Died: 1885.

Prices are for books in Very Good condition.

MELCHIOR'S DREAM and Other Tales by J.H.Gatty (Bell & Daldy, 1862) £40
MRS OVERTHEWAY'S REMEMBRANCES (illustrated by J.A. Pasquier and Joseph Wolf) (Bell & Daldy, 1869).......................£40
THE BROWNIES and Other Tales (illustrated by George Cruikshank) (Bell & Daldy, 1870) £45
THE BROWNIES and Other Stories (illustrated by E.H. Shepard) (Dent: 'Illustrated Children's Classics' series, 1954) £50
A FLAT IRON FOR A FARTHING, or Some Passages in the Life of an Only Son (Bell & Daldy, 1873)................£30
LOB LIE-BY-THE-FIRE, or The Luck of Lingborough and Other Tales (illustrated by George Cruikshank) (Bell, 1874) £35
LOB LIE-BY-THE-FIRE (illustrated by Randolph Caldecott) (SPCK, [1885])...£20
SIX TO SIXTEEN: A Story For Girls (illustrated by Mrs W. Allingham) (Bell, 1876 [1875]).........................£25
JAN OF THE WINDMILL: A Story of the Plains (Bell, 1876) £25
A GREAT EMERGENCY and Other Tales (Bell, 1877) £25
WE AND THE WORLD: A Book for Boys (Bell, 1881 [1880]) £25
BROTHERS OF PITY and Other Tales of Beasts and Men (SPCK, [1882]) £25
OLD-FASHIONED FAIRY TALES (SPCK, [1882]) £50
BLUE AND RED, or The Discontented Lobster (verse; illustrated by R. André) (SPCK, [1883]) £50
MASTER FRITZ (illustrated by R. André) (SPCK, [1883]) £40
OUR GARDEN (verse; illustrated by R. André) (SPCK, [1883]) £40
A SOLDIER'S CHILDREN (illustrated by R. André) (SPCK, 1883) £40
A SWEET LITTLE DEAR (illustrated by R. André) (SPCK, [1883]) £30
THREE LITTLE NEST-BIRDS (illustrated by R. André) (SPCK, [1883])...£30
A WEEK SPENT IN A GLASS POND BY THE GREAT WATER BEETLE (illustrated by R. André and others)
   (Wells Gardner, [1883]) £30
THE DOLLS' WASH (verse; illustrated by R. André) (SPCK, [1883]) £30
A SOLDIER'S CHILDREN and Five Other Tales in Verse (omnibus; illustrated by R. André) (SPCK, [1883]) £40
DOLLS' HOUSEKEEPING (verse; illustrated by R. André) (SPCK, [1884]) £30
DADDY DARWIN'S DOVECOT: A Country Tale (illustrated by Randolph Caldecott) (SPCK, [1884]) £20
JACKANAPES (illustrated by Randolph Caldecott) (SPCK, 1884 [1883]) £20
JACKANAPES (contains 'Daddy Darwin's Dovecot' and 'Lob Lie-By-The-Fire'; illustrated by Randolph Caldecott)
   (SPCK, [1892]) £25
JACKANAPES (illustrated by Tasha Tudor) (OUP, U.S., 1948)...£50
THE BLUE BELLS ON THE LEA (illustrated by R. André) (SPCK, [1884]) £50
LITTLE BOYS AND WOODEN HORSES (illustrated by R. André) (SPCK, [1884]) £30
PAPA POODLE AND OTHER PETS (verse; illustrated by R. André) (SPCK, [1884]) £25
TONGUES IN TREES (illustrated by R. André) (SPCK, [1884]) £25
'TOUCH HIM IF YOU DARE': A Tale of the Hedge (illustrated by R. André) (SPCK, [1884]) £25
THE STORY OF A SHORT LIFE (SPCK, [1885]) £10
POEMS OF CHILD LIFE AND COUNTRY LIFE (six books; illustrated by R. André; wraps) (SPCK, 1885) ....the set £60
MARY'S MEADOW, AND LETTERS FROM A LITTLE GARDEN. Edited by H.K.F. Gatty (SPCK, [1886])..................£15
DANDELION CLOCKS and Other Tales (illustrated by Gordon Browne and others) (SPCK, [1887]) £15
THE PEACE-EGG and A CHRISTMAS MUMMING PLAY (illustrated by Gordon Browne) (SPCK, [1887])........£15
SNAP-DRAGONS. Edited by H.K.F. Gatty (contains 'A Tale of Christmas Eve', 'And Old Father Christmas' and
   'An Old Fashioned Tale of the Young Days of a Grumpy Old God-Father'; illustrated by Gordon Browne) (SPCK, [1888]) £20
MOTHER'S BIRTHDAY REVIEW and Seven Other Tales in Verse (omnibus; illustrated by R. André; boards) (SPCK, 1888) £40

F

FALKNER, John Meade

British author. Born: 1858. A bibliophile and scholar, Falkner wrote two mystery stories — *The Lost Stradivarius* (1895) and *The Nebuly Coat* (1903) — as well as the classic children's novel, *Moonfleet* (1898). Died: 1932.

Price is for books in Very Good condition.

MOONFLEET (Arnold, 1898) £250

FARJEON, Eleanor

British author. Born: 1881. Daughter of the novelist, B.L. Farjeon. Received virtually no formal education, but was encouraged to write from an early age. Produced several volumes of verse for children, notably *Nursery Rhymes of London Town* (1916), as well as fairy tales (*Martin Pippin in the Apple Orchard*, 1921), stories and plays. Her volume of stories, *The Little Bookroom*, won her the Carnegie Medal and the Hans Christian Andersen International Medal. She was a friend of Edward Thomas and Walter de la Mare. Died: 1965.

Prices are for books in Very Good condition (with dustjackets after 1931).

PAN-WORSHIP and Other Poems (Elkin Mathews, 1908) £15
DREAM-SONGS FOR THE BELOVED (Orpheus Press, 1911) £15
TREES (Fellowship Books, 1913) £15
NURSERY RHYMES OF LONDON TOWN (illustrated by Macdonald Gill) (Duckworth, 1916) £80
MORE NURSERY RHYMES OF LONDON TOWN (illustrated by Macdonald Gill) (Duckworth, 1917) £80
ALL THE WAY TO ALFRISTON (verse; illustrated by Robin Guthrie) (Morland Press, 1918) £75
SONNETS AND POEMS (Blackwell, 1918) £15
SINGING GAMES FOR CHILDREN (illustrated by J. Littlejohns) (Dent, [1919]) £60

The Glass Slipper (1946) was Eleanor Farjeon's rewriting of the 'Cinderella' story. It was originally produced as a stage play.

*Like **The Glass Slipper**, the Oxford edition of **The Silver Curlew** (1953) was illustrated by the great E.H. Shepard.*

A FIRST CHAPBOOK OF ROUNDS (verse; illustrated by John Garside; issued without dustjacket)
(Dent, 1919) £40
A SECOND CHAPBOOK OF ROUNDS (verse; illustrated by John Garside; issued without dustjacket)
(Dent, 1919) £30
GYPSY AND GINGER (Dent, 1920) £20
MARTIN PIPPIN IN THE APPLE-ORCHARD (Collins, 1921)..£30
MARTIN PIPPIN IN THE APPLE-ORCHARD (illustrated by C.E. Brock) (Collins, 1925) £45
TUNES OF A PENNY PIPER (illustrated by John Aveten) (Selwyn & Blount, 1922) £20
SONGS FOR MUSIC AND LYRICAL POEMS (illustrated by John Aveten) (Selwyn & Blount, 1922)........£20
THE SOUL OF KOL NIKON (Collins, [1923]) £25
ALL THE YEAR ROUND (verse) (Collins, [1923])..£20
THE COUNTRY CHILD'S ALPHABET (verse; illustrated by William Michael Rothenstein)
(Poetry Bookshop, 1924) £120
THE TOWN CHILD'S ALPHABET (illustrated by David Jones) (Poetry Bookshop, 1924)........£120
MIGHTY MEN: Achilles to Julius Caesar (non-fiction) (Blackwell, 1924) £15
MIGHTY MEN: Beowulf to Harold (non-fiction) (Blackwell, 1925) £15
MIGHTY MEN (omnibus; contains both volumes) (Blackwell, 1928)......................................£20
SONGS FROM 'PUNCH' FOR CHILDREN (verse; card covers) (Saville, 1925) £30
YOUNG FOLK AND OLD (High House Press, 1925) £20
TOM COBBLE (Blackwell, [1925]) £30
FAITHFUL JENNY DOVE and Other Tales (Collins, [1925]) £20
NUTS AND MAY: A Medley for Children (illustrated by Rosalind Thorneycroft) (Collins, [1926])........£80
JOAN'S DOOR (illustrated by Will Townsend) (Collins, [1926]) £25
SINGING GAMES FROM ARCADY (verse) (Blackwell, 1926) £20
THE WONDERFUL KNIGHT (illustrated by Doris Pailthorpe) (Blackwell, [1927]) £20
THE KING'S BARN, or Joan's Tale (Collins, [1927]) £20
THE MILL OF DREAMS, or Jennifer's Tale (Collins, [1927]) £20
YOUNG GERARD, or Joyce's Tale (Collins, [1927]) £20
COME CHRISTMAS (illustrated by Molly McArthur) (Collins, 1927) £20
A BAD DAY FOR MARTHA (illustrated by Eugine Richards) (Blackwell, [1928]) £20
KALEIDOSCOPE (Collins, [1928]) £15
KALEIDOSCOPE (illustrated by Edward Ardizzone) (OUP, 1963) £40
AN ALPHABET OF MAGIC (illustrated by Margaret W. Tarrant) (Medici Society, 1928) £75
OPEN WINKINS, or Jessica's Tale (Collins, 1928) £30
A COLLECTION OF POEMS (Collins, [1929]) £30
THE PERFECT ZOO (Harrap, 1929)..£20
THE KING'S DAUGHTER CRIES FOR THE MOON (illustrated by May Smith) (Blackwell, [1929])........£25
THE TALE OF TOM TIDDLER (illustrated by Norman Tealby) (Collins, 1929) £45
WESTWOODS (illustrated by May Smith) (Blackwell, 1930)..£20
TALES FROM CHAUCER: The Canterbury Tales Done into Prose by Eleanor Farjeon (illustrated by W. Russell Flint)
(Medici Society, 1930) £90
THE OLD NURSE'S STOCKING BASKET (illustrated by E. Herbert Whydale) (University of London, [1931]) £25
THE OLD NURSE'S STOCKING BASKET (illustrated by Edward Ardizzone) (OUP, 1965) £30
LADYBROOK (Collins, 1931) £30
PERKIN THE PEDLAR (illustrated by Clare Leighton) (Faber, 1932)....................................£50
KATY KRUSE AT THE SEASIDE, or The Deserted Islanders (Harrap, 1932) £30
KINGS AND QUEENS. With Herbert Farjeon (illustrated by Rosalind Thorneycroft) (Gollancz, 1932) £75
THE FAIR OF ST. JAMES: A Fantasia (Faber, 1932) £35
AMELIARANNE'S PRIZE PACKET (illustrated by S.B. Pearse) (Harrap, 1933) £75
PANNYCHIS (illustrated by Clare Leighton; limited to 200 copies) (High House Press, 1933) £80
HEROES AND HEROINES (with Herbert Farjeon; illustrated by Rosalind Thorneycroft) (Gollancz, 1933)........£40
OVER THE GARDEN WALL (illustrated by Gwen Raverat) (Faber, 1933) £50
AMELIARANNE'S WASHING DAY (illustrated by S.B. Pearse) (Harrap, 1934) £70
ITALIAN PEEPSHOW and Other Stories (illustrated by Rosalind Thorneycroft) (Blackwell, 1934) £20
ITALIAN PEEPSHOW and Other Stories (illustrated by Edward Ardizzone) (OUP, 1960) £30
JIM AT THE CORNER and Other Stories (illustrated by Irene Mountfort) (Blackwell, 1934) £20
JIM AT THE CORNER and Other Stories (illustrated by Edward Ardizzone) (OUP, 1958)........£40
THE OLD SAILOR'S YARN BOX (illustrated by Irene Mountfort) (Stokes, 1934) £15
THE CLUMBER PUP (illustrated by Irene Mountfort) (Blackwell, [1934]) £35
AND I DANCE MINE OWN CHILD (illustrated by Irene Mountfort) (Blackwell, [1935]) £20
A NURSERY IN THE NINETIES (Gollancz, 1935) £20
JIM AND THE PIRATES (illustrated by Richard Naish) (Blackwell, [1936]) £20
TEN SAINTS (non-fiction; illustrated by Helen Sewell) (OUP, 1936)....................................£20
LECTOR READINGS (illustrated by Ruth Westcott) (Nelson, 1936) £10
HUMMING BIRD (Joseph, 1936) £15
MARTIN PIPPIN IN THE DAISY-FIELD (illustrated by Isobel and John Morton-Sale) (Joseph, 1937) £35
THE WONDERS OF HERODOTUS (illustrated by Edmund Nelson) (Nelson, 1937)..............£12
PALADINS IN SPAIN (illustrated by Katharine Tozer) (Nelson, 1937) £15
SING FOR YOUR SUPPER (illustrated by Isobel and John Morton-Sale) (Joseph, 1938) £20
SONGS OF KINGS AND QUEENS (with Herbert Farjeon) (Arnold, 1938) £15

This irreverent collection of rhymes about the Kings and Queens of England is one of Eleanor Farjeon's best-known works.

Rosalind Thorneycroft provided the spirited illustrations for this book. This is her depiction of Henry VIII, or "Bluff King Hal".

ONE FOOT IN FAIRYLAND: Sixteen Tales (illustrated by Robert Lawson) (Joseph, 1938) £30
GRANNIE GRAY: Children's Plays and Games with Music and Without (illustrated by J. Jefferson Farjeon)
(Dent, 1939) £20
GRANNIE GRAY: Children's Plays and Games with Music and Without (illustrated by Peggy Fortnum)
(OUP, 1956) £20
A SUSSEX ALPHABET (illustrated by Sheila M Thompson) (Pear Tree Press, 1939) £140
THE NEW BOOK OF DAYS (illustrated by Philip Gough and M.W. Hawes) (OUP, 1941) £30
BRAVE OLD WOMAN (Joseph, 1941) £30
MAGIC CASEMENTS (Allen & Unwin, 1941) £20
CHERRYSTONES (illustrated by Isobel and John Morton-Sale) (Joseph, 1942) £25
GOLDEN CONEY (Joseph, [1943])...£20
THE FAIR VENETIAN (Joseph, 1943) £20
AMELIARANNE GIVES A CONCERT (illustrated by S.B. Pearse) (Harrap, 1944) £60
THE MULBERRY BUSH (illustrated by Isobel and John Morton-Sale) (Joseph, 1945)...£20
A PRAYER FOR LITTLE THINGS (Houghton Mifflin, U.S., 1945) £25
DARK WORLD OF ANIMALS (illustrated by T. Stoney) (Sylvan Press, 1945) £20
ARIADNE AND THE BULL (Joseph, 1945) £20
THE GLASS SLIPPER (with Herbert Farjeon; play; illustrated by Hugh Stevens) (Wingate 1946) £15
THE GLASS SLIPPER (illustrated by E.H. Shepard) (OUP, 1955)...£30
FIRST AND SECOND LOVE (verse) (Joseph, 1947) £15
LOVE AFFAIR (Joseph, 1947) £15
THE STARRY FLOOR (illustrated by Isobel and John Morton-Sale) (Joseph, 1949) £25
MRS MALONE (illustrated by David Knight) (Joseph, 1950) £25
MRS MALONE (illustrated by Edward Ardizzone) (OUP, 1962) £40
SILVER SAND AND SNOW (Joseph, 1951)..£25
THE SILVER CURLEW: A Fairy Tale (play; wraps) (Samuel French, [1953]) £15
THE SILVER CURLEW: A Fairy Tale (illustrated by E.H. Shepard) (OUP, 1953) £35
THE LITTLE BOOKROOM (illustrated by Edward Ardizzone) (OUP, 1955)..£45
THE CHILDREN'S BELLS: A Selection of Poems (illustrated by Peggy Fortnum) (OUP, 1957)..............................£25
A PUFFIN QUARTET OF POETS: Eleanor Farjeon, James Reeves, E.V. Rieu and Ian Seraillier
(selected with introductory notes by Eleanor Graham; illustrated by Diana Bloomfield; paperback) (Puffin, 1958) £5
ELEANOR FARJEON'S BOOK: Stories, Verses, Plays (illustrated by Edward Ardizzone; paperback) (Puffin, 1960) £15
MORNING HAS BROKEN (verse; illustrated by Gordon Stowell) (Mowbray, 1981)..£10
INVITATION TO A MOUSE and Other Poems. Chosen by Annabel Farjeon (illustrated by Antony Maitland)
(Pelham, 1981)..£10
THE LITTLE DRESSMAKER (illustrated by Charles Front) (Julia MacRae, 1984) £10

FARRAR, F.W.

British author. Born: Frederick William Farrar in India in 1831. Educated at Kings William's College and London and Cambridge Universities, subsequently becoming a Fellow of Trinity College. Taught at Harrow and was appointed headmaster of Marlborough College, before becoming a Canon of Westminster and finally Dean of Canterbury. Wrote a handful of boys' stories, of which the best known is *Eric, or Little by Little* (1858). Also produced a large number of works on theology, education and other subjects. Died: 1903.

Prices are for books in Very Good condition.

ERIC, or Little By Little: A Tale of Roslyn School (A. & C. Black, 1858) £375
ERIC, or Little By Little: A Tale of Roslyn School (illustrated by Gordon Browne) (A. & C. Black, 1894) £20
ST WINIFRED'S (anonymous) (A. & C. Black, 1862) £175
ST WINIFRED'S, or The World of School (illustrated by Gordon Browne) (A. & C. Black, 1905)...£20

*This first edition of G.E. Farrow's excellent Carroll-inspired children's fantasy, **The Wallypug of Why** (1895).*

FARROW, G.E.

British author. Born: George Edward Farrow in 1862. Wrote a number of nonsense books in the style of Edward Lear, of which the best known is *The Wallypug of Why* (1895). Died: 1920.

Prices are for books in Very Good condition.

THE WALLYPUG OF WHY (illustrated by Harry Furniss; vignettes by Dorothy Furniss) (Hutchinson, [1895]) £120
THE KING'S GARDENS: An Allegory (illustrated by A.L. Bowley) (Hutchinson, 1896) £45
THE MISSING PRINCE (illustrated by Harry Furniss; vignettes by Dorothy Furniss) (Hutchinson, 1896)..........................£45
THE WALLYPUG IN LONDON (illustrated by Alan Wright) (Methuen, 1898 [1897]) £80
ADVENTURES IN WALLYPUG-LAND (illustrated by Alan Wright) (Methuen, 1898)..£80
THE LITTLE PANJANDRUM'S DODO (illustrated by Alan Wright) (Skeffington, 1899) £75
THE MANDARIN'S KITE, or Little Tsu-Foo and Another Boy (illustrated by Alan Wright)
 (Skeffington,1900) £30
BAKER MINOR AND THE DRAGON (illustrated by Alan Wright) (Pearson, 1902 [1901]) £60
THE NEW PANJANDRUM (illustrated by Alan Wright) (Pearson, 1902 [1901])..£50
AN A.B.C. OF EVERY-DAY PEOPLE (illustrated by John Hassall) (Dean, [1902]) £150
IN SEARCH OF THE WALLYPUG (illustrated by Alan Wright) (Pearson, 1903 [1902]) £75
ABSURD DITTIES (illustrated by John Hassall) (Routledge, 1903) £65
PROFESSOR PHILANDERPAN (Pearson, 1904 [1903]) £50
ALL ABOUT THE WALLY-PUG (Raphael Tuck [printed in Germany], [1904]) £65
THE CINEMATOGRAPH TRAIN and Other Stories (illustrated by Alan Wright) (Johnson, 1904) £75
PIXIE PICKLES: The Adventures of Pixene and Pixette in their Woodland Haunts (illustrated by H.B. Neilson)
 (Skeffington, [1904])...£75
WALLYPUG TALES (illustrated) (Raphael Tuck [printed in Germany], [1904])...£65
ROUND THE WORLD A.B.C. (verse; illustrated by John Hassall) (Nister [printed in Germany], [1904])...................£100
THE WALLYPUG BIRTHDAY BOOK (illustrated by Alan Wright) (Routledge, 1904) £55
THE WALLYPUG IN FOGLAND (illustrated by Alan Wright) (Pearson, 1904) £70
LOVELY MAN (Being the Views of Mistress A. Grosspatch) (cover illustration by John Hassall)
 (Skeffington, 1904)..£80
RUFF AND READY: The Fairy Guide by May Byron and G.E. Farrow (illustrated by John Hassall)
 (Cooke, [1905]) £75
THE MYSTERIOUS 'MR PUNCH': A School Story (Christian Knowledge Society, [1905]) £40
THE WALLYPUG BOOK (illustrated by Harry Furniss) (Treherne, [1905])..£50
THE WALLYPUG IN THE MOON, or His Badjesty (illustrated by Alan Wright) (Pearson, 1905) £50
THE ADVENTURES OF JI (illustrated by G.C. Tresidder) (Partridge, [1906]) £45
ESSAYS IN BACON: An Autograph Book (Treherne, [1906]) £45
THE ESCAPE OF THE MULLINGONG: A Zoological Nightmare (illustrated by Gordon Browne)
 (Blackie, 1907 [1906]) £45
THE ADVENTURES OF A DODO (illustrated by Willy Pogány) (Unwin, [1907]) £75
THE DWINDLEBERRY ZOO (illustrated by Gordon Browne) (Blackie, 1909 [1908])..£50
A MYSTERIOUS VOYAGE, or The Adventures of a Dodo (illustrated by K.M. Roberts) (Partridge, [1910]) £50
THE MYSTERIOUS SHIN SHIRA (Hodder & Stoughton, [1915])..£35
ZOO BABIES (illustrated by Cecil Aldin) (Frowde/Hodder & Stoughton, 1913) £135
DON'T TELL (illustrated by John Hassall) (Cooke, no date)..£40
TEN LITTLE JAPPY CHAPS (illustrated by John Hassall) (Treherne: 'Stump Books' series, no date) £40

'FATHER TUCK'S' ANNUALS

Popular series of annuals published by Raphael Tuck between 1898 (dated 1899) and 1935. Those from the 1930s include 'Come to Life Pictures', full-colour panoramas which stand up when the books are opened. The annuals were great favourites of the Royal Family.

Prices are for annuals in Very Good condition.

FATHER TUCK'S ANNUAL (Raphael Tuck, [1899-1931]) ....each £35
TUCK'S ANNUAL (Raphael Tuck, [1932-1935]) ....each £25
FATHER TUCK'S ANNUAL (with 'pop-up' panoramics; several issued during 1930s) ....each £60

'FELIX' ANNUALS

Felix the Cat was the creation of the Pat Sullivan Studio, and was the first animated film character to win a worldwide audience. Launched in America in 1919, he was particularly popular in Britain, appearing in strip form in the *Pearson's Weekly* and the *Illustrated Sunday Herald* and inspiring a series of annuals and other spin-offs.

Prices are for annuals in Very Good condition.

FELIX ANNUAL 1923 ....£120
FELIX ANNUAL 1924-30 ....£100
THE FELIX ANNUAL: Picture Stories of the Famous Film Cat (London, [1926]) £80
FELIX THE CAT ANNUAL 1956 (World Distributors) £60
FELIX THE CAT ANNUAL (London, [1961]) £40
FELIX THE CAT ANNUAL (Purnell, 1962) £40

'FILM FUN' ANNUALS

British comic annual, published by Amalgamated Press and containing stories featuring movie stars such as Harold Lloyd, Buster Keaton and Laurel and Hardy. The comic itself was launched on 17th January 1920, but the first annual didn't appear until 1938. The last edition was dated 1961.

Prices are for annuals in Very Good condition.

FILM FUN ANNUAL 1938	£175
FILM FUN ANNUAL 1939	£120
FILM FUN ANNUAL 1940	£95
FILM FUN ANNUAL 1941	£75
FILM FUN ANNUAL 1942	£75
FILM FUN ANNUAL 1943	£75
FILM FUN ANNUAL 1944	£75
FILM FUN ANNUAL 1945	£45
FILM FUN ANNUAL 1946	£45
FILM FUN ANNUAL 1947	£45
FILM FUN ANNUAL 1948	£45
FILM FUN ANNUAL 1949	£45
FILM FUN ANNUAL 1950	£45
FILM FUN ANNUAL 1951	£25
FILM FUN ANNUAL 1952-60	each £15
FILM FUN ANNUAL 1961	£20

FIRMIN, Peter

British illustrator. Born: Harwich, Essex, 1928. Studied at Colchester School of Art and Central School of Art in London. Worked as a freelance and commercial illustrator before beginning a successful collaboration with the writer, Oliver Postgate, in 1958. Together they have created the children's television programmes, *The Clangers*, *Noggin the Nog*, *Bagpuss* and *Ivor the Engine*, all of which inspired spin-off books. Firmin also made the puppet, Basil Brush, for BBC TV. Two of his daughters, Charlotte and Hannah Firmin, have become successful illustrators.

Prices are for books in Very Good condition with dustjackets where applicable.

IVOR THE ENGINE (with Oliver Postgate) (Abelard-Schuman, [1962])	£30
NOGGIN AND THE WHALE (with Oliver Postgate) (Ward, 1965)	£20
NOGGIN THE KING (with Oliver Postgate) (Ward, 1965)	£20
NOGBAD AND THE ELEPHANTS (with Oliver Postgate) (Kaye & Ward, 1967)	£20
NOGGIN AND THE MOON MOUSE (with Oliver Postgate) (Kaye & Ward, 1967)	£20
TOG SEES THE WORLD: A Pogles' Wood Story (with Oliver Postgate) (Hamlyn, 1967)	£12
THE SAGA OF NOGGIN THE NOG (with Oliver Postgate) (Kaye & Ward, 1968)	£15

FLEMING, Ian

British author. Born: Ian Lancaster Fleming in 1908. Fleming is best known for the 'James Bond' novels, but also enjoyed great success with his three children's books featuring the wonder car, Chitty-Chitty-Bang-Bang. Roald Dahl wrote the script for the successful 1967 film version. Died: 1964.

Prices are for books in Very Good condition.

CHITTY-CHITTY-BANG-BANG, THE MAGICAL CAR: ADVENTURE NUMBER 1 (illustrated by John Burningham)
(Cape, 1964) £100
CHITTY-CHITTY-BANG-BANG, THE MAGICAL CAR: ADVENTURE NUMBER 2 (illustrated by John Burningham)
(Cape, 1964) £100
CHITTY-CHITTY-BANG-BANG, THE MAGICAL CAR: ADVENTURE NUMBER 3 (illustrated by John Burningham)
(Cape, 1965) £100

FOLKARD, Charles

British illustrator. Born: Charles James Folkard in Lewisham in 1878. Studied at the St. John's Wood School of Art and Goldsmith's College School of Art, subsequently illustrating many classic children's works as well as creating the strip cartoon, Teddy Tail, which ran in the *Daily Mail* from 1915 to 1960. He also wrote a number of children's plays. Died: 1963.

Prices are for books in Very Good condition (with dustjackets after 1940).

'Teddy Tail' Books (all written and illustrated by Charles Folkard; boards; issued without dustjackets)

THE ADVENTURES OF TEDDY TAIL OF THE DAILY MAIL (A. & C. Black, 1915)	£30
TEDDY TAIL IN NURSERY RHYME LAND (A. & C. Black, 1915)	£30
TEDDY TAIL IN FAIRYLAND (A. & C. Black, 1916)	£25
TEDDY TAIL IN HISTORYLAND (A. & C. Black, 1917)	£20
TEDDY TAIL'S FAIRY TALE (A. & C. Black, 1919)	£20
TEDDY TAIL IN BABYLAND (A. & C. Black, 1919)	£20
TEDDY TAIL AT THE SEASIDE (A. & C. Black, 1920)	£20

*Although best-known for 'Teddy Tail', Charles Folkard also illustrated a number of children's classics, such as **Pinocchio** (above).*

TEDDY TAIL'S ALPHABET (A. & C. Black, 1921)..£20
TEDDY TAIL IN TOYLAND (A. & C. Black, 1922) £20
TEDDY TAIL'S ADVENTURES IN THE A B SEA (A. & C. Black, 1926) £20

Other Books Illustrated by Charles Folkard

SWISS FAMILY ROBINSON by J.R. Wyss (Dent, 1910) £25
THE FLINT HEART by Eden Phillpotts (sixteen black-and-white illustrations by Charles Folkard) (Smith Elder, 1910) £30
PINOCCHIO by Carlo Collodi (Dent, 1911)..£75
THE CHILDREN'S SHAKESPEARE. Edited by Alice S. Hoffman (Dent, 1911) £60
GRIMMS' FAIRY TALES (A. & C. Black, 1911) £40
AESOP'S FABLES (A. & C. Black, 1912) £35
JOLLY CALLE and Other Swedish Fairy Tales by Helena Nyblom (Dent, [1913]) £40
THE JACKDAW OF RHEIMS by Richard Barham (Gay & Hancock, 1913) £100
THE ARABIAN NIGHTS (A. & C. Black, 1913) £40
BELGIAN PLAYMATES by Nellie Pollock (Gay & Hancock, 1914) £20
OTTOMAN WONDER TALES by Lucy Garnett (A. & C. Black, 1915)..£20
MOTHER GOOSE'S NURSERY RHYMES. Edited by L.E. Walter (A. & C. Black, [1919])..£60
MOTHER GOOSE'S NURSERY TALES. Edited by L.E. Walter (second edition) (A. & C. Black, 1923) £45
BRITISH FAIRY AND FOLK TALES. Edited by William J. Glover (A. & C. Black, 1920) £30
WITCH'S HOLLOW by Arthur Brook (eight colour plates and other illustrations by Charles Folkard) (A. & C. Black, 1920) £40
SONGS FROM ALICE IN WONDERLAND AND THROUGH THE LOOKING-GLASS by Lewis Carroll
    (A. & C. Black, 1921) £75

THE MAGIC EGG by Dorothy Black (A. & C. Black, 1922) £45
GRANNY'S WONDERFUL CHAIR by Frances Browne (A. & C. Black, 1925) £15
TALES FROM SHAKESPEARE by Charles and Mary Lamb (Dent, [1926]) £75
THE TROUBLES OF A GNOME by Zofja Kossak-Szczucka (A. & C. Black, 1928) £30
ALICE'S ADVENTURES IN WONDERLAND by Lewis Carroll (A. & C. Black, 1929) £40
THE LAND OF NURSERY RHYME by Alice Daglish and Ernest Rhys (Dent, 1932) £25
TALES OF THE TAUNUS MOUNTAINS by Olive Dehn (Blackwell, 1937) £25
GRIMMS' FAIRY TALES (Dent, 1949)..£30
THE PRINCESS AND CURDIE by George MacDonald (Dent, 1949) £50
THE PRINCESS AND THE GOBLIN by George MacDonald (Dent, 1949) £50
PINOCCHIO (the original translation by M.A. Murray, revised by G. Tassinari) (Dent, 1951) £35
THE BOOK OF NONSENSE. Edited by Roger Lancelyn Green (Dent, 1956)...........................£30

FOREMAN, Michael

British illustrator. Born: Pakefield, Suffolk, in 1938. Studied at Lowestoft School of Art and at the Royal College of Art, subsequently lecturing at the latter as well as other art schools. Has won several awards for his children's illustrations, notably the Kurt Maschler Award in 1982. He has also written a number of children's books.

Prices are for books in Very Good condition with dustjackets where applicable.

POEMS FOR CHILDREN 1950-1961. Chosen by Michael Baldwin (Routledge, 1962)................£40
THE PERFECT PRESENT (Hamish Hamilton, 1967)..£50
THE TWO GIANTS (Brockhampton Press, 1967) £40
THE GREAT SLEIGH ROBBERY (Hamish Hamilton, 1968) £30
HORATIO (Hamish Hamilton, 1970) £20
MOOSE (Hamish Hamilton, 1971)..£20
DINOSAURS AND ALL THAT RUBBISH (Hamish Hamilton, 1972) £20
MR NOAH AND THE SECOND FLOOD by Sheila Burnford (Gollancz, 1973)......................£15
WAR AND PEAS (Hamish Hamilton, 1974) £15
RAINBOW RIDER by Jane Yolen (Collins, 1975) £15
ALL THE KING'S HORSES (Hamish Hamilton, 1976) £15
HANS ANDERSEN — HIS CLASSIC FAIRYTALES (translated by Eric Haugaard) (Gollancz, 1976) £15
MONKEY AND THE THREE WIZARDS (Collins, 1976)..£20
THE STONE BOOK by Alan Garner (Collins, 1976)..£30
TOM FOBBLE'S DAY by Alan Garner (Collins, 1977) £40
GRANNY REARDUN by Alan Garner (Collins, 1977)..£40
PANDA'S PUZZLE, AND HIS VOYAGE OF DISCOVERY (Hamish Hamilton, 1977) £15
TEENY-TINY AND THE WITCH WOMAN by Barbara Walker (Andersen Press, 1977) £15
THE AIMER GATE by Alan Garner (Collins, 1978) £35
BROTHERS GRIMM: POPULAR FOLK TALES (Gollancz, 1978) £20
MICKEY'S KITCHEN CONTEST (Andersen Press, 1978) £20
THE SELFISH GIANT by Oscar Wilde (Kaye & Ward, 1978) £20
WINTER'S TALES (illustrated by Freire White and Michael Foreman) (Benn, 1979) £15
CITY OF GOLD and Other Stories from the Old Testament by Peter Dickinson (Gollancz, 1980) £20
THE PIG PLANTAGENET by Allen Andrews (Hutchinson, 1980) £15
THE TIGER WHO LOST HIS STRIPES (Andersen Press, 1980) £15
THE FAITHFULL BULL by Ernest Hemingway (Hamish Hamilton, 1980) £30
FAIRY TALES (Pavilion, 1981)...£20
TRICK A TRACKER (Gollancz, 1981)..£15
PANDA AND THE ODD LION (Hamish Hamilton, 1981) £15
SLEEPING BEAUTY AND OTHER FAVOURITE TALES (Gollancz, 1982) £25
THE MAGIC MOUSE AND THE MILLIONAIRE (Hamish Hamilton, 1982) £15
LAND OF DREAMS (Andersen Press, 1982) £15
A CHRISTMAS CAROL (Gollancz, 1983)..£20
THE SAGA OF ERIK THE VIKING (Pavilion, 1983) £20
CAT AND CANARY (Andersen Press, 1984) £30
A CAT AND MOUSE LOVE STORY by Nanette Newman (Heinemann, 1984) £15
PANDA AND THE BUNYIPS (Hamish Hamilton, 1984) £15
LAND OF DREAMS (Andersen Press, 1984) £15
SHAKESPEARE STORIES by Leon Garfield (Gollancz, 1985) £20
SHAKESPEARE STORIES BOOK NUMBER 2 (Gollancz, 1994) £10
BRONTOSAURUS SUPERSTAR (Hamish Hamilton, 1985)...£20
NICOBOBINUS by Terry Jones (Joseph, 1985) £20
SEASONS OF SPLENDOUR by Madhur Jaffrey (Pavilion, 1985) £20
A CHILD'S GARDEN OF VERSES by R.L. Stevenson (Gollancz, 1985) £25
I'LL TAKE YOU TO MRS COLE (Andersen Press, 1985) £15
EARLY IN THE MORNING by Charles Causley (Viking/Kestrel, 1986) £15
TALES FOR THE TELLING: Irish Folk and Fairy Stories (Pavilion, 1986) £20
THE MAGIC OINTMENT and Other Cornish Legends by Eric Quayle (Andersen Press, 1986) £20

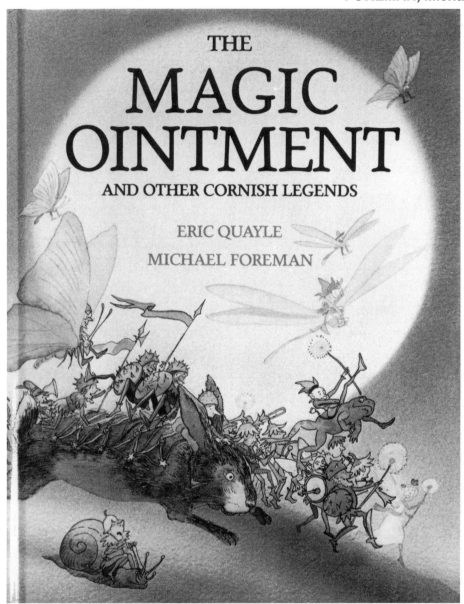

THE

MAGIC OINTMENT

AND OTHER CORNISH LEGENDS

ERIC QUAYLE

MICHAEL FOREMAN

Michael Foreman is amongst the most collectable of contemporary British illustrators. This book from 1986 is worth £20.

Falconer's Lure (1957) is Antonia Forest's most collectable book, and is now valued at £70 in Very Good condition.

Peter's Room (1961) is also a sought-after title, with Very Good copies in the dustjacket selling for £60.

FOREST, Antonia

British author. Born: London. Well-known for her 'Marlowe family' series set in upper-middle-class background with strong characterisation and insight into relationships.

Prices are for books in Very Good condition with dustjackets.

AUTUMN TERM (illustrated by Marjorie Owens) (Faber, 1948) £30
THE MARLOWS AND THE TRAITOR (illustrated by Doritie Kettlewell) (Faber, 1953) £30
FALCONER'S LURE: The Story of a Summer Holiday (illustrated by Tasha Kallin) (Faber, 1957)............................£70
END OF TERM (Faber, 1959) £30
PETER'S ROOM (Faber, 1961)...£60
THE THURSDAY KIDNAPPING (Faber, 1963) £30
THE THUGGERY AFFAIR (Faber, 1965) £25
THE READY-MADE FAMILY (Faber, 1967) £40
THE PLAYER'S BOY (Faber, 1970) £40
THE PLAYERS AND THE REBELS (Faber, 1971)..£40
THE CRICKET TERM (Faber, 1974) £25
THE ATTIC TERM (Faber, 1976)..£25
RUN AWAY HOME (Faber, 1982) £60

GARDAM, Jane

British author. Born: Yorkshire, 1928. Has written several excellent novels of adolescence. After her first five books, she produced a series of readers for younger children, notably *Bridget and William*.

Prices are for books in Very Good condition with dustjacket where applicable.

A FEW FAIR DAYS (illustrated by Peggy Fortnum) (Hamish Hamilton, 1971) £25
A LONG WAY FROM VERONA (Hamish Hamilton, 1971) £25
THE SUMMER AFTER THE FUNERAL (Hamish Hamilton, 1973) £25
BLACK FACES WHITE FACES (Hamish Hamilton, 1975) £15
BILGEWATER (Hamish Hamilton, 1976) £20
THE HOLLOW LAND (illustrated by Janet Rawlins) (Macrae, 1981) £15
BRIDGET AND WILLIAM (illustrated by Janet Rawlins) (Macrae,1981) £15
HORSE (illustrated by Janet Rawlins) (MacRae, 1982) £15
CRUSOE'S DAUGHTER (Hamish Hamilton, 1985) £20
KIT (illustrated by William Geldart) (MacRae, 1986) £15
KIT IN BOOTS (illustrated by William Geldart) (MacRae, 1986)..£15
THROUGH THE DOLL'S HOUSE DOOR (MacRae, 1987)...£15
GOING INTO A DARK HOUSE (short stories) (Sinclair-Stevenson, 1994) £10
FAITH FOX (Sinclair-Stevenson, 1996) £10

GARFIELD, Leon

British author. Born: Brighton, 1921. Served in the Medical Corps during the war, subsequently working as a hospital lab technician before becoming a full-time writer in 1966. His first novel, *Jack Holborn* (1964), was intended for adults but, on his editor's advice, was rewritten for younger readers. This was followed by many more children's novels, often set in the past, the most notable of which are *Smith* (1967) and *The Drummer Boy* (1970). His books are noted for their frank treatment of sexual themes. Died: 1996.

Prices are for books in Very Good condition with dustjackets.

'Apprentices' Books

THE LAMPLIGHTER'S FUNERAL (illustrated by Antony Maitland) (Heinemann, 1976) £20
MIRROR, MIRROR (illustrated by Antony Maitland) (Heinemann, 1976) £15
MOSS AND BLISTER (illustrated by Faith Jaques) (Heinemann, 1976) £15
THE CLOAK (illustrated by Faith Jaques) (Heinemann, 1976)...£15
THE VALENTINE (illustrated by Faith Jaques) (Heinemann, 1977) £15
LABOUR IN VAIN (illustrated by Faith Jaques) (Heinemann, 1977)...£15
THE FOOL (illustrated by Faith Jaques) (Heinemann, 1977) £15
ROSY STARLING (illustrated by Faith Jaques) (Heinemann, 1977) £15
THE DUMB CAKE (illustrated by Faith Jaques) (Heinemann, 1977) £10
TOM TITMARSH'S DEVIL (illustrated by Faith Jaques) (Heinemann, 1977) £10
THE FILTHY BEAST (illustrated by Faith Jaques) (Heinemann, 1978) £10
THE ENEMY (illustrated by Faith Jaques) (Heinemann, 1978)...£10

Others

JACK HOLBORN (illustrated by Antony Maitland) (Constable, 1964) £50
DEVIL-IN-THE-FOG (illustrated by Antony Maitland) (Constable, 1966) £30
SMITH (illustrated by Antony Maitland) (Constable, 1967) £25
BLACK JACK (illustrated by Antony Maitland) (Longman, 1968)...£25
MISTER CORBETT'S GHOST and Other Stories (illustrated by Antony Maitland) (Longman, 1969) £20
THE RESTLESS GHOST: Three Stories (illustrated by Saul Lambert) (Pantheon, U.S., 1969)......................£15
THE BOY AND THE MONKEY (illustrated by Trevor Ridley) (Heinemann, 1969) £15
THE DRUMMER BOY (illustrated by Antony Maitland) (Longman, 1970) £20
THE GOD BENEATH THE SEA (with Edward Blishen; non-fiction; illustrated by Charles Keeping) (Longman, 1970)......£15
THE STRANGE AFFAIR OF ADELAIDE HARRIS (illustrated by Fritz Wegner) (Longman, 1971)..................£15
THE CAPTAIN'S WATCH (illustrated by Trevor Ridley) (Heinemann, 1972)..£15
THE GHOST DOWNSTAIRS (illustrated by Antony Maitland) (Longman, 1972) £15
CHILD O' WAR: The True Story of a Boy Sailor in Nelson's Navy. Recreated by Leon Garfield in consultation with
    David Proctor (non-fiction; illustrated by Antony Maitland) (Collins, 1972) £20
THE GOLDEN SHADOW (with Edward Blishen; non-fiction; illustrated by Charles Keeping) (Longman, 1973) £15
LUCIFER WILKINS (illustrated by Trevor Ridley) (Heinemann, 1973) £20
THE SOUND OF COACHES (illustrated by John Lawrence) (Kestrel, 1974) £25
THE PRISONERS OF SEPTEMBER (paperback) (Puffin, 1975)..£15
THE PLEASURE GARDEN (illustrated by Fritz Wegner) (Kestrel, 1976)...£20
THE HOUSE OF HANOVER: England in the Eighteenth Century (non-fiction) (Deutsch, 1976)......................£15
AN ADELAIDE GHOST (Ward Lock, 1977) £10
THE CONFIDENCE MAN (Kestrel, 1978) £10

*Alan Garner's debut novel, **The Weirdstone of Brisingamen**, is a modern classic. £550 should secure a Very Good copy.*

*His third book, **Elidor** (1965), is illustrated by Charles Keeping, who also provided the striking dustjacket illustration.*

BOSTOCK AND HARRIS, or The Night of the Comet (illustrated by Martin Cottam) (Kestrel, 1979) £10
JOHN DIAMOND (illustrated by Antony Maitland) (Kestrel, 1980) £15
FAIR'S FAIR (illustrated by Margaret Chamberlain) (Macdonald, 1981) £10
KING NIMROD'S TOWER (illustrated by Michael Bragg) (Methuen, 1982) £15
THE WRITING ON THE WALL (illustrated by Michael Bragg) (Methuen, 1983)..£10
THE KING IN THE GARDEN (illustrated by Michael Bragg) (Methuen, 1984) £10
GUILT AND GINGERBREAD (illustrated by Fritz Wegner) (Viking Kestrel, 1984) £10
THE WEDDING GHOST (illustrated by Charles Keeping) (OUP, 1985) £10
SHAKESPEARE STORIES (illustrated by Michael Foreman) (Gollancz, 1985)..£20
THE DECEMBER ROSE (Viking Kestrel, 1986) £10
BLEWCOAT BOY (Gollancz/National Trust, 1988) £10

GARNER, Alan

British author. Born: Congleton, Cheshire, in 1934. Following a long period of illness, he studied at Manchester Grammar School and Magdalen College, Oxford, where he read Classics. Inspired by William Golding's *Lord of the Flies*, he wrote the fantasy novel, *The Weirdstone of Brisingamen* (1960), at the age of 22, and has followed it up with a small number of highly accomplished and sophisticated books for children. He still lives in Cheshire.

Prices are for books in Very Good condition with dustjackets.

THE WEIRDSTONE OF BRISINGAMEN: A Tale of Alderley (Collins, 1960) £550
THE MOON OF GOMRATH (Collins, 1963) £200
ELIDOR (illustrated by Charles Keeping) (Collins, 1965) £180
HOLLY FROM THE BONGS: A Nativity Play (music by William Mayne) (Collins, 1966) £45
THE OLD MAN OF MOW (photographs by Roger Hill) (Collins, 1966 [1967])...£45
THE OWL SERVICE (Collins, 1967) £60
RED SHIFT (Collins, 1973) £40
POTTER THOMPSON (play; music by Gordon Crosse) (OUP, 1975)..£25
THE GUIZER: A Book of Fools (Hamish Hamilton, 1975) £35
THE BREADHORSE (verse; illustrated by Albin Trowski) (Collins, 1975)..£35
THE STONE BOOK (illustrated by Michael Foreman) (Collins: 'Craftsmanship' series No. 1, 1976) £30
TOM FOBBLE'S DAY (illustrated by Michael Foreman) (Collins: 'Craftsmanship' series No. 2, 1977) £40
GRANNY REARDUN (illustrated by Michael Foreman) (Collins: 'Craftsmanship' series No. 3, 1977) £40
THE AIMER GATE (illustrated by Michael Foreman) (Collins: 'Craftsmanship' series No. 4, 1978) £35

FAIRY TALES OF GOLD (four books: 'The Girl of the Golden Gate', 'The Golden Brothers',
'The Princess and the Golden Mane' and 'The Three Golden Heads of the Well') (Collins, 1979) ....each £15
THE LAD OF THE GAD (Collins, 1980) £20
BOOK OF BRITISH FAIRY TALES (Collins, 1984)..£15
A BAG OF MOONSHINE (illustrated by Patrick Lynch) (Collins, 1986) £10
ONCE UPON A TIME... (Dorling Kindersley, 1993) £10
SANDLOPER (Harvil Press, 1996) £15
LITTLE RED HEN (illustrated by Norman Messenger; paper boards) (Dorling Kindersley: 'Nursery Tales' series, 1997) £3
THE VOICE THAT THUNDERS (Harvil Press, 1998) £5
THE WELL OF THE WIND by Alan Garner and Herve Blondon (Dorling Kindersley, 1998) £10

GARNETT, Eve
British author-illustrator. Born: Worcestershire. 1900. Awarded Carnegie Medal, 1938. Best known for her 'One End Street' books, the first successful depiction of a working-class family. Died: 1991.

Prices are for books in Very Good condition with dustjackets where applicable.

Books Written and illustrated by Eve Garnett
THE FAMILY FROM ONE END STREET AND SOME OF THEIR ADVENTURES (Muller, 1937) £80
IS IT WELL WITH THE CHILD? (Muller, 1938)..£30
IN AND OUT AND ROUNDABOUT: STORIES OF A LITTLE TOWN (Muller 1948) £50
A BOOK OF SEASONS (anthology) (OUP, 1952) £30
FURTHER ADVENTURES OF THE FAMILY FROM ONE END STREET (Heinemann,1956)..£60
HOLIDAY AT THE DEW DROP INN : A ONE END STREET STORY (Heinemann, 1962) £50
TO GREENLAND'S ICY MOUNTAINS (non-fiction) (Heinemann, 1968) £20
LOST AND FOUND: Four Stories (Muller, 1974) £20
FIRST AFFECTIONS (Muller, 1982) £20

Books Illustrated by Eve Garnett
THE LONDON CHILD by Evelyn Sharp (John Lane, 1927) £30
THE BAD BARONS OF CRASHBANIA by Norman Hunter (Blackwell, 1932) £50
A CHILD'S GARDEN OF VERSES by Robert Louis Stevenson (paperback) (Penguin: 'Puffin Story Books', 1948) £10
A GOLDEN LAND Edited by James Reeves (illustrated by Eve Garnett and others) (Constable, 1958) £20

GIBBONS, Stella
British author. Born: London, 1902. Best known for her classic comic novel, *Cold Comfort Farm* (1932), but published a solitary children's work in 1935. Died: 1989.

Price is for books in Very Good condition with dustjackets.

THE UNTIDY GNOME (Longmans, 1935)..£40

GIBBS, May
Australian author-illustrator. Born: Cecilia May Gibbs in Surrey in 1877. Emigrated to Australia with her family in 1881. Studied at Church of England Girls' School, Perth, Chelsea Polytechnic and Henry Blackburn School of Black and White Art in London. Drew on the flora and fauna of Western Australia for her highly successful series of books featuring the 'gumnut babies', beginning in 1918 with *Snugglepot and Cuddlepie: Their Adventures Wonderful*. She also drew a long-running newspaper strip featuring two similar characters, Bib and Bub. Died: 1969.

Prices are for books in Very Good condition.

Books Written and Illustrated by May Gibbs
ABOUT US (Nister, 1912) £100
GUM BLOSSOM BABIES (pamphlet) (Angus & Robertson, Sydney, 1916) £150
GUMNUT BABIES (pamphlet) (Angus & Robertson, Sydney, 1916) £130
BORONIA BABIES (pamphlet) (Angus & Robertson, Sydney, 1917) £140
FLANNEL FLOWERS and Other Bush Babies (pamphlet) (Angus & Robertson, Sydney, 1917).............................£100
WATTLE BABIES (pamphlet) (Angus & Robertson, Sydney, 1918)...£100
SNUGGLEPOT AND CUDDLEPIE: Their Adventures Wonderful (Angus & Robertson, Sydney, 1918)..................£350
LITTE RAGGED BLOSSOM and More about Snugglepot and Cuddlepie
(Angus & Robertson, Sydney, 1920) £275
LITTLE OBELIA and Further Adventures of Ragged Blossom, Snugglepot and Cuddlepie
(Angus & Robertson, Sydney, 1921) £225
NUTTYBUB AND NITTERSING (Osboldstone, Melbourne, 1923)..£120
CHUCKLEBUD AND WUNKYDOO (Osboldstone, Melbourne, 1924) £100
CHUCKLEBUD AND WUNKYDOO (as 'Two Little Gumnuts') (Cornstalk, Sydney, 1929) £70
BIB AND BUB: THEIR ADVENTURES (verse; two volumes) (Cornstalk, Sydney, 1925) ....the set £300
THE FURTHER ADVENTURES OF BIB AND BUB (verse) (Cornstalk, Sydney, 1927) £200
MORE FUNNY STORIES ABOUT OLD FRIENDS, BIB AND BUB (verse) (Cornstalk, Sydney, 1928) £150
BIB AND BUB IN GUMNUT TOWN (Halstead, Waterloo, 1929) £200
BIB AND BUB PAINTING BOOK: New Stories (Penfold, Sydney, [c.1930s])..£200

This issue of the **Girl's Own Paper** from November 1906 features an attractive cover painted by Cecil B. Quinnell.

An issue from the paper's heyday in the 1930s. Bound annuals are now much more common than individual numbers.

GUMNUTS (Angus & Robertson, Sydney, 1940) £65
SCOTTY IN GUMNUT LAND (Angus & Robertson, Sydney, 1941) £55
SCOTTY IN GUMNUT LAND (Angus & Robertson, 1956)..£35
MR AND MRS BEAR AND FRIENDS (Angus & Robertson, Sydney, 1943) £50
MR AND MRS BEAR AND FRIENDS (Angus & Robertson, 1957) £30
THE COMPLETE ADVENTURES OF SNUGGLEPOT AND CUDDLEPIE (contains 'Snugglepot and Cuddlepie',
   'Little Ragged Blossom' and 'Little Obelia') (Angus & Robertson, 1946)...£100
PRINCE DANDE LION: A Garden Whim-Wham (Ure Smith, Sydney, 1953) £40
PRINCE DANDE LION: A Garden Whim-Wham (Angus & Robertson, 1954) £20
ALPHABET FRIEZE (Angus & Robertson, Sydney, 1984)..£10
THE MAY GIBBS COLLECTION: GUMNUT CLASSICS. Edited by Maureen Walsh (two volumes)
   (Angus & Robertson, Sydney, 1985) ....the set £200

Book Illustrated by May Gibbs
BARONS AND KINGS (1215-1485) by Estelle Ross (illustrated by May Gibbs and Stephen Reid) (Harrap, 1912) £30

GIRAUD, S.L.
British editor and book designer. Born: Stephen Louis Gerard. Began his career working in the promotions department of the *Daily Express*. Creator, with Theodore Brown, of the modern 'pop-up' annual, with the *Daily Express Children's Annual* and, subsequently, the 'Bookano' series. His ideas were copied by Harold Lentz in America. Died: 1951.

Prices are for books in Very Good condition with all pop-ups in working order.

THE STORY OF JESUS (Strand Publications, 1934) £30
HANS ANDERSEN'S FAIRY STORIES (Strand Publications, 1936) £65
ADVENTURE AND BUILDING BOOK (Strand Publications, 1936) £40
BOOKANO STORIES: With Pictures that Spring Up in Model Form. Edited by S.L. Giraud
   (Strand Publications: 'Bookano Living Pictures' series, [1936-]) £70
BOOKANO ZOO: Animals in Fact, Fancy and Fun. Edited and produced by S.L. Giraud
   (Strand Publications, [1939]) £65
BOOKANO NO. 1: Goblins in a Carpenter's Shop, with Sound Effects of Sawing Wood!
   (Strand Publications, 1934) £90
BOOKANO NO. 2: Cottage, with Semi-Transparent Fairy (Strand Publications, 1935) £80
BOOKANO NO. 3 (Strand Publications, 1936) £70
BOOKANO NO. 4 (Strand Publications, 1937) £70
BOOKANO NO. 5 (Strand Publications, 1938) £60
BOOKANO NO. 6 (Strand Publications, 1939) £60
BOOKANO NO. 7 (Strand Publications, 1940) £60

BOOKANO NO. 8 (Strand Publications, 1941) £60
BOOKANO NO. 9 (Strand Publications, 1942) £60
BOOKANO NO. 10 (Strand Publications, 1943) £55
BOOKANO NO. 11 (Strand Publications, 1944) £55
BOOKANO NO. 12 (Strand Publications, 1945) £55
BOOKANO NO. 13 (Strand Publications, 1946) £55
BOOKANO NO. 14 (Strand Publications, 1947) £55
BOOKANO NO. 15 (Strand Publications, 1948) £55
BOOKANO NO. 16: Tower Bridge (Strand Publications, 1949)..£80
BOOKANO STORIES NO. 17 (Strand Publications, 1950)..£90

'GIRL' ANNUALS

British comic annual published between 1953 and 1965. The title was launched by Hulton as a sister paper to *Eagle*, and was the first post-war British comic aimed specifically at girls.

Prices are for annuals in Very Good condition.

GIRL ANNUAL (Hulton Press, 1953) £20
GIRL ANNUAL (Hulton Press, 1954-57) ....each £10
GIRL ANNUAL (Hulton Press, 1958) £8
GIRL ANNUAL (Hulton Press, 1959-60) ....each £7
GIRL ANNUAL (Longacre Press, 1961-62) ....each £7
GIRL ANNUAL (Longacre Press, 1963) £5
GIRL ANNUAL (Longacre Press, 1964-65) ....each £5

'GIRL'S OWN' ANNUALS

British story annual, published by the Religious Tract Society between 1880 and 1941. The paper itself was launched in January 1880 as a companion to the bestselling *Boy's Own Paper*, and continued, under various titles, until 1965, by which time it was known as *Heiress*. The *Girl's Own Annual* was the first ever annual for girls. Vols. 1-29 edited by Charles Peters, Vols. 30-53 by Flora Klickman.

Prices are for volumes in Very Good condition.

VOLUMES 1-29 (3rd January 1880-26th September 1908) (weekly issues of 'Girl's Own Paper' bound as annual, in 'Girl's Own Annual'; picture boards, or other bindings, with Index. Summer or Christmas Supplements for the current or preceding year are sometimes included in these bound volumes) ....each £30
VOLUMES 30-49 (October 1908-September 1928) (monthly issues of 'Girl's Own Paper & Woman's Magazine' bound in 'Girl's Own Annual' boards or other bindings) ....each £30
VOLUMES 50-51 (October 1928-September 1930) (monthly issue of 'Woman's Magazine & Girl's Own Paper' bound in 'Girl's Own Annual' picture boards or other bindings) ....each £35
VOLUMES 52-53 (October 1930-September 1932) (monthly issues of 'Girl's Own Paper' bound in 'Girl's Own Annual' picture boards)..each £35
VOLUMES 54-56 (October 1932-September 1941) (monthly issues of 'Girl's Own Paper' bound in 'Girl's Own Annual' plain boards) ....each £35
VOLUMES 57-61 (October 1935-September 1940) (monthly issues of 'Girl's Own Paper' bound in 'Girl's Own Annual' plain boards; containing runs of Elsie J. Oxenham stories)..each £50
VOLUME 62 (October 1940-September 1941) (monthly issues of 'Girl's Own Paper' bound in 'Girl's Own Annual' plain boards; contains first ever publication of 'Worrals of the WAAF' by W.E. Johns) £60

'GIRL'S REALM' ANNUALS

British story annual of the early 1900s, published by Hutchinson. Originally intended to be more progressive than established rivals like the *Girl's Own Paper*, but was resolutely conformist by the time it ceased publication in 1915.

Prices are for annuals in Very Good condition in original cloth.

THE GIRL'S REALM: Volumes 1-17 plus late extra volume [November 1915] (November 1908-November 1915)..........each £20

'GIRLS' CRYSTAL' ANNUALS

British story annual published by Amalgamated Press between 1940 and 1976. The paper itself, originally entitled *The Crystal*, was launched on 26th October 1935, becoming *The Girls' Crystal Weekly* from No. 10 onwards. After 908 issues, the title became a comic, and strip stories were introduced into the annuals.

Prices are for annuals in Very Good condition.

GIRLS' CRYSTAL ANNUAL 1940 [1939] £25
GIRLS' CRYSTAL ANNUAL 1941-43 ....each £18
GIRLS' CRYSTAL ANNUAL 1944-49 ....each £15
GIRLS' CRYSTAL ANNUAL 1950-53 ....each £10
GIRLS' CRYSTAL ANNUAL 1954-58 ....each £7
GIRLS' CRYSTAL ANNUAL 1959-68 ....each £5
GIRLS' CRYSTAL ANNUAL 1969-76 ....each £3

GOBLE, Warwick

British illustrator. Born: London, 1862. Studied at the City of London School and Westminster School of Art, subsequently joining the staff of the *Pall Mall Gazette* and *Westminster Gazette* as an artist. Illustrated many colour plate books for A. & C. Black and Macmillan, his style showing the strong influence of Japanese and Chinese art. Travelled extensively, visiting the battlefields of France in 1919. Died: 1943.

Prices are for books in Very Good condition without dustjackets.

THE GRIM HOUSE by Mrs Molesworth (Nisbet, 1899) £30
THE WATER BABIES by Charles Kingsley (32 colour plates by Warwick Goble) (Macmillan, 1909) £350
THE WATER BABIES by Charles Kingsley (32 colour plates by Warwick Goble; limited to 260 copies) (Macmillan, 1909) £1,500
THE WATER BABIES by Charles Kingsley (sixteen colour plates by Warwick Goble) (Macmillan, 1910).....................................£80
THE WATER BABIES by Charles Kingsley (reissue; sixteen colour plates by Warwick Goble) (Macmillan, 1922) £60
GREEN WILLOW and Other Japanese Fairy Tales by Grace James (forty colour plates by Warwick Goble) (Macmillan, 1910)..£600
GREEN WILLOW and Other Japanese Fairy Tales by Grace James (forty colour plates by Warwick Goble;
    De Luxe edition: limited to 500 copies) (Macmillan, 1910) £2,000
GREEN WILLOW and Other Japanese Fairy Tales by Grace James (sixteen colour plates by Warwick Goble) (Macmillan, 1912) £70
GREEN WILLOW and Other Japanese Fairy Tales by Grace James (reissue; sixteen colour plates by Warwick Goble)
    (Macmillan, 1923)..£50
FOLK TALES OF BENGAL by De Lala Vihari (Macmillan, 1912) £200
FOLK TALES OF BENGAL by De Lala Vihari (limited to 150 copies) (Macmillan, 1912)...£1,000
PEEPS AT MANY LANDS — TURKEY by Julius Van Millingen (twelve colour plates by Warwick Goble) (A. & C. Black, 1911) ..£25
STORIES FROM THE PENTAMERONE by Giovanni Battista Basile (Macmillan, 1911) £150

*This plate from **Folk Tales of Bengal** shows why Warwick Goble is one of the most collectable of the 'Golden Age' illustrators.*

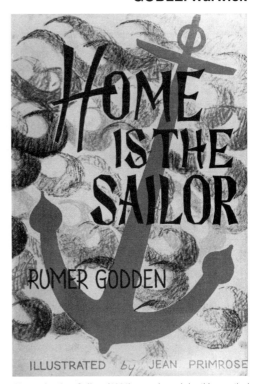

*Rumer Godden is best known for adult novels like **Black Narcissus**, but she also wrote children's titles like this one.*

Home is the Sailor (1964) was issued in this nautical dustjacket. Very Good copies are currently valued at £25.

STORIES FROM THE PENTAMERONE by Giovanni Battista Basile (De Luxe edition: limited to 150 copies) (Macmillan, 1911) **£1,000**
THE FAIRY BOOK by D.M. Craik (32 colour plates by Warwick Goble) (Macmillan, 1913) £250
THE BOOK OF FAIRY POETRY. Edited by Dora Owen (sixteen colour plates by Warwick Goble) (Longmans, 1920) £350

GODDEN, Rumer

British author. Born: Sussex, 1907. Spent most of her life in India, the setting for much of her work. Writer of well-made, traditional children's stories, notably her 'Doll' books. Died: 1998.

Prices are for books in Very Good condition with dustjackets where applicable.

THE DOLL'S HOUSE (illustrated by Dana Saintsbury) (Joseph, 1947) £50
IN NOAH'S ARK (verse) (Joseph, 1949) £25
THE MOUSEWIFE (illustrated by Dana Saintsbury) (Macmillan, 1951) £30
IMPUNITY JANE: The Story of a Pocket Doll (illustrated by Adrienne Adams) (Macmillan, 1955) £30
THE FAIRY DOLL (illustrated by Adrienne Adams) (Macmillan, 1956) £30
MOUSE HOUSE (illustrated by Adrienne Adams) (Macmillan, 1958)...£30
THE GREENGAGE SUMMER (Macmillan, 1958)...£25
THE STORY OF HOLLY AND IVY (illustrated by Adrienne Adams) (Macmillan, 1958)..........................£25
CANDY FLOSS (illustrated by Adrienne Adams) (Macmillan, 1960) £25
ST JEROME AND THE LION (verse) (illustrated by Jean Primrose) (Macmillan, 1961) £25
MISS HAPPINESS AND MISS FLOWER (illustrated by Jean Primrose) (Macmillan, 1961) £25
LITTLE PLUM (illustrated by Jean Primrose) (Macmillan, 1963) £25
HOME IS THE SAILOR (illustrated by Jean Primrose) (Macmillan, 1964) £25
THE KITCHEN MADONNA (illustrated by Carol Barker) (Macmillan, 1967) £20
SWANS AND TURTLES (Macmillan, 1968) £25
OPERATION SIPPACIK (illustrated by Carol Barker) (Macmillan, 1969) £20
THE TALE OF THE TALES: THE BEATRIX POTTER BALLET (Frederick Warne, 1971) £15
THE OLD WOMAN WHO LIVED IN A VINEGAR BOTTLE (illustrated by Mairi Hedderwick) (Macmillan, 1972) £20
THE DIDDAKOI (illustrated by Creina Glegg) (Macmillan, 1972) £20
MR MCFADDEN'S HALLOWE'EN (illustrated by Ann Strugnell) (Macmillan, 1975) £20
THE ROCKING HORSE SECRET (illustrated by Juliet Stanwell Smith) (Macmillan, 1977) £20
A KINDLE OF KITTENS (illustrated by Lynne Byrnes) (Macmillan, 1978)..£20
THE DRAGON OF OG (illustrated by Pauline Baynes) (Macmillan, 1981)..£20
THE VALIANT CHATTI-MAKER (illustrated by Jeroo Roy) (Macmillan, 1983) £25

FOUR DOLLS (illustrated by Pauline Baynes) (Macmillan, 1983) £25
THURSDAY'S CHILDREN (Macmillan, 1984)...£10
FU-DOG (illustrated by Valerie Littlewood) (Julia McRae Books, 1989) £10
GREAT GRANDFATHER'S HOUSE (Macmillan, 1993) £10
LISTEN TO THE NIGHTINGALE (Macmillan, 1993) £10
PREMLATA AND THE FESTIVAL OF LIGHTS (Macmillan, 1993)..£10

GOODALL, John S.

British illustrator. Born: John Strickland Goodall in Heacham, Norfolk, in 1908. He studied at the Royal Academy Schools (1925-29) and began to contribute *to* the *Radio Times* and other magazines. After service in the Second World War and a period of commissioned portrait paintings, he turned to book illustration, often employing Victorian themes and settings. Died: 1996.

Prices are for books in Very Good condition with dustjackets where applicable.

Books Written and Illustrated by John S Goodall

DR OWL'S PARTY: A Tale for Children (Blackie, 1954) £20
FIELD MOUSE HOUSE (Blackie, 1954) £20
SHREWBETTINA'S BIRTHDAY (Macmillan, 1970) £20
THE MIDNIGHT ADVENTURES OF KELLY, DOT, AND ESMERALDA (Macmillan, 1972)......................£20
CREEPY CASTLE (Macmillan, 1975) £20
NAUGHTY NANCY THE BAD BRIDESMAID (Macmillan, 1975) £20
PADDY PORK'S HOLIDAY (Macmillan, 1976) £20
PADDY'S EVENING OUT (Macmillan, 1978) £20
LITTLE RED RIDING HOOD (Deutsch 1980) £20
PADDY'S NEW HAT (Macmillan, 1980) £20
THE ADVENTURES OF PADDY PORK (Macmillan, 1980) £20
THE BALLOONING ADVENTURES OF PADDY PORK (Macmillan, 1980) £20
SHREWBETTINA GOES TO WORK (pop-up book) (Macmillan, 1981) £25
PADDY FINDS A JOB (pop-up book) (Macmillan, 1981) £25
LAVINIA'S COTTAGE (pop-up book) (Macmillan, 1982) £25
PADDY GOES TRAVELLING (Macmillan, 1982) £20

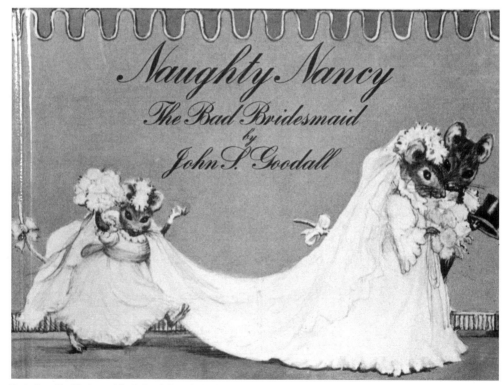

Books by author/illustrator, John S. Goodall, are in the £20-£30 range. This title from 1975 is valued at £25 in Very Good condition.

The very first 'Asterix' book of them all, published in Britain by the Brockhampton Press in 1969 and still as popular as ever.

'Asterix' creators Goscinny and Uderzo also collaborated on a series of books featuring the giant American indian, Ompa-pa.

PADDY UNDER WATER (Macmillan, 1984)	£20
PADDY PORK TO THE RESCUE (Deutsch, 1985)	£20
PUSS IN BOOTS (Deutsch, 1990)	£20

Books Illustrated by John S Goodall

FIVE CHILDREN AND IT by E Nesbit (Random House, 1948)	£30
THE PHOENIX AND THE CARPET by E Nesbit (Random House, 1948)	£30
THE STORY OF THE AMULET by E Nesbit (Random House, 1949)	£30
FIGHT FOR FREEDOM by Ian Serraillier (Heinemann, 1965)	£30

GOSCINNY, René and UDERZO, Albert

French writer/artist team. Born in 1926 and 1927 respectively, the two men have — together or separately — worked on many comic strips, but are best-known for their series of books featuring the 'indomitable Gaul', Asterix. He made his first appearance in the French magazine, *Pilote*, in 1959, and has since featured in well over two dozen books. Goscinny also created the characters Lucky Luke, Ompa-pa, Iznogoud and Nicholas, although in collaboration with other artists. He died in 1977.

Prices are for books in Very Good condition.

'Asterix' Books

ASTERIX THE GAUL (Brockhampton Press, 1969)	£30
ASTERIX AND CLEOPATRA (Brockhampton Press, 1969)	£30
ASTERIX THE GLADIATOR (Brockhampton Press, 1969)	£30
ASTERIX IN BRITAIN (Brockhampton Press, 1970)	£25
ASTERIX THE LEGIONARY (Brockhampton Press, 1970)	£20
ASTERIX IN SPAIN (Brockhampton Press, 1971)	£20
ASTERIX AND THE BIG FIGHT (Brockhampton Press, 1971)	£20
ASTERIX AND THE ROMAN AGENT (Brockhampton Press, 1972)	£20
ASTERIX AT THE OLYMPIC GAMES (Brockhampton Press, 1972)	£20
ASTERIX IN SWITZERLAND (Brockhampton Press, 1973)	£20
THE MANSIONS OF THE GODS (Brockhampton Press, 1973)	£20
ASTERIX AND THE LAUREL WREATH (Brockhampton Press, 1974)	£20
ASTERIX AND THE GOTHS (Brockhampton Press, 1974)	£20
ASTERIX AND THE SOOTHSAYER (Brockhampton Press, 1975)	£20
ASTERIX AND THE GOLDEN SICKLE (Hodder & Stoughton, 1975)	£15
ASTERIX AND THE GREAT CROSSING (Hodder & Stoughton, 1976)	£15
ASTERIX AND THE CAULDRON (Hodder & Stoughton, 1976)	£15

GOSCINNY, René and UDERZO Albert

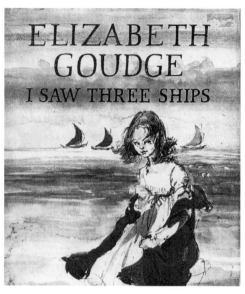

Elizabeth Goudge wrote ten children's books, of which **The Little White Horse** (left) is the best known and the most collectable. It is valued at £60 in Very Good condition, while the later **I Saw Three Ships** (above) is valued at £30.

ASTERIX AND THE CIRCUS OF ROME (push-out book) (GeminiScan Publishing, 1976)......................................£30
ASTERIX AND THE CHIEFTAN'S SHIELD (Hodder & Stoughton, 1977) £15
ASTERIX AND CAESAR'S GIFT (Hodder & Stoughton, 1977)...£15
ASTERIX AND THE NORMANS (Hodder & Stoughton, 1978)...£15
ASTERIX AND THE TWELVE TASKS (push-out book) (GeminiScan Publishing, 1978) £30
ASTRERIX AND THE PIRATES (push-out book) (GeminiScan Publishing, 1978) £30
OBELIX AND CO. (Hodder & Stoughton, 1979) £15
ASTERIX AND THE BANQUET (Hodder & Stoughton, 1979) £15
ASTERIX IN CORSICA (Hodder & Stoughton, 1979 [1980]) £15
THREE ADVENTURES OF ASTERIX (contains 'Asterix in Britain', 'Asterix in Switzerland' and 'Asterix the Gaul')
    (Hodder & Stoughton, [1979]) £10
ASTERIX IN BELGIUM (Hodder & Stoughton, 1980)..£10
ASTERIX AND THE GREAT DIVIDE (Hodder & Stoughton, 1981) £10
ASTERIX AND THE BLACK GOLD (Hodder & Stoughton, 1982) £10
ADVENTURES OF ASTERIX (contains 'Asterix the Gaul', 'Asterix and the Soothsayer', 'Asterix and the Goths' and
    'Asterix and Caesar's Gift') (Hodder & Stoughton, 1982) £10
ASTERIX AND SON (Hodder & Stoughton, 1983) £10
ASTERIX AND THE MAGIC CARPET (Hodder & Stoughton, 1988) £8
HOW OBELIX FELL INTO THE MAGIC POTION WHEN HE WAS A LITTLE BOY (Hodder & Stoughton, 1989) £8
ASTERIX AND THE SECRET WEAPON (Hodder & Stoughton, 1991) £8

'Asterix' Film Books
THE TWELVE TASKS OF ASTERIX (contains 'The Race', 'The Javelin', 'The Judo Match', 'The Isle of Pleasure',
    'The Magician', 'The Chef', 'The Cave of the Beast', 'The Place that Sends You Mad', 'The Crocodiles',
    'The Old Man of the Mountains', 'The Ghostly Legionnaires' and 'The Circus') (Hodder & Stoughton, 1978) £8
ASTERIX VERSUS CAESAR (Hodder & Stoughton, 1986) £5
OPERATION GETAFIX (Hodder & Stoughton, 1990) £5
ASTERIX TASK PACK (contains 'The Race', 'The Javelin', 'The Judo Match', 'The Isle of Pleasure', 'The Magician',
    'The Chef', 'The Cave of the Beast', 'The Place that Sends You Mad', 'The Crocodiles',
    'The Old Man of the Mountains', 'The Legionnaires' and 'The Circus') (Hodder & Stoughton, 1976) ....each £5

'Ompa-Pa' Books
OMPA-PA AND BROTHER TWO SCALP (Methuen, 1977) £15
OMPA-PA SAVES THE DAY (Methuen, 1977) £15
OMPA-PA AND THE PIRATES (Methuen, 1977) £15
OMPA-PA AND THE SECRET MISSION (Methuen, 1978) £12
OMPA-PA AND THE PRUSSIANS (Methuen, 1978) £12

'Lucky Luke' Books (Goscinny and Morris)

JESSE JAMES (Brockhampton Press, 1972)	£15
THE STAGE COACH (Brockhampton Press, 1972)	£12
DALTON CITY (Brockhampton Press, 1973)	£12
THE TENDERFOOT (Brockhampton Press, 1974)	£12
WESTERN CIRCUS (Hodder & Stoughton, 1974)	£12
APACHE CANYON (Hodder & Stoughton, 1974)	£10
MA DALTON (Hodder & Stoughton, 1980)	£10
THE DASHING WHITE COWBOY (Hodder & Stoughton, 1982)	£10
CURING THE DALTONS (Hodder & Stoughton, 1982)	£10

'Iznogoud' Books (Goscinny and Tabary)

IZNOGOUD ON HOLIDAY (Methuen, 1977)	£10
IZNOGOUD THE INFAMOUS (Methuen, 1977)	£10
THE WICKED WILES OF IZNOGOUD (Methuen, 1978)	£8
IZNOGOUD AND THE MAGIC COMPUTER (Methuen, 1978)	£8
A CARROT FOR IZNOGOUD (Egmont, 1979)	£8
IZNOGOUD AND THE DAY OF MISRULE (Egmont, 1979)	£8
IZNOGOUD ROCKETS TO STARDOM (Egmont, 1980)	£10
IZNOGOUD AND THE MAGIC CARPET (Egmont, 1980)	£10

'Nicholas' Books (Goscinny and Sempé)

YOUNG NICOLAS (issued with dustjacket) (Hutchinson, 1961)	£40
NICHOLAS AND THE GANG AT SCHOOL (Abelard-Schuman, 1976)	£10
NICHOLAS AND THE GANG (Abelard-Schuman, 1977)	£10
NICHOLAS AND THE GANG AGAIN (Abelard-Schuman, 1977)	£10
NICHOLAS ON HOLIDAY (Abelard-Schuman, 1978)	£10
NICHOLAS AT LARGE (Abelard-Schuman, 1979)	£10

GOUDGE, Elizabeth

British author. Born: Wells, Somerset, in 1900. Awarded the Carnegie Medal in 1947. Her books are old-fashioned, with an openly religious element. Notable for *The Little White Horse.* Died: 1984.

Prices are for books in Very Good condition with dustjackets where applicable.

THE FAIRIES' BABY and Other Stories (Foyles, 1919)	£30
SISTER OF THE ANGELS: A Christmas Story (illustrated by C. Walter Hodges) (Duckworth, 1939)	£15
SMOKY-HOUSE (illustrated by C. Walter Hodges) (Duckworth, 1940)	£30
HENRIETTA'S HOUSE (illustrated by Lorna R. Steele) (University of London Press/Hodder & Stoughton, 1942)	£30
THE LITTLE WHITE HORSE (illustrated by C. Walter Hodges) (University of London Press, 1946)	£60
MAKE-BELIEVE (illustrated by C. Walter Hodges) (Duckworth, 1949)	£30
THE VALLEY OF SONG (illustrated by Steven Spurrier) (University of London Press, 1951)	£30
LINNETS AND VALERIANS (illustrated by Ian Ribbons) (Brockhampton Press, 1964)	£30
I SAW THREE SHIPS (illustrated by Richard Kennedy) (Brockhampton Press, 1969)	£30
THE LOST ANGEL (illustrated by Shirley Hughes) (Hodder & Stoughton, 1971)	£15

GRAHAME, Kenneth

British author. Born: Edinburgh, 1859. Educated at St. Edward's School, Oxford, he was unable to attend university for financial reasons, instead obtaining a clerkship at the Bank of England, where he remained until 1908. Enjoyed modest success as an essayist before establishing his reputation with the story collections, *The Golden Age* (1895) and *Dream Days* (1898), and finally the classic children's novel, *The Wind in the Willows* (1908). The last was brilliantly illustrated by E.H. Shepard in 1931. Grahame's only son, Alastair, committed suicide while a student at Oxford in 1920. Died: 1932.

Prices are for books in Very Good condition with dustjackets where applicable.

PAGAN PAPERS (frontispiece by Aubrey Beardsley) (John Lane/Elkin Matthews, 1894 [1893])	£130
THE GOLDEN AGE (John Lane, 1895)	£200
THE GOLDEN AGE (illustrated by Maxfield Parrish) (John Lane, 1900)	£50
THE GOLDEN AGE (illustrated by R.J. Enraght-Moony) (John Lane: The Bodley Head, 1915 [1914])	£35
THE GOLDEN AGE (illustrated by Lois Lenski) (The Bodley Head, 1922)	£50
THE GOLDEN AGE (illustrated by E.H. Shepard) (The Bodley Head, 1928)	£100
THE GOLDEN AGE (illustrated by E.H. Shepard; limited to 275 copies, signed by the author and artist; in slipcase) (The Bodley Head, 1928)	£600
DREAM DAYS (John Lane, 1898)	£420
DREAM DAYS (illustrated by Lois Lenski) (The Bodley.Head, 1922)	£60
DREAM DAYS (illustrated by E.H. Shepard) (The Bodley Head, 1930)	£100
DREAM DAYS (illustrated by E.H. Shepard; limited to 275 copies, signed by the author and artist) (The Bodley Head, 1930)	£550
THE GOLDEN AGE and DREAM DAYS (omnibus; illustrated by Charles Keeping) (The Bodley Head, 1962)	£80
THE WIND IN THE WILLOWS (frontispiece by Graham Robertson; issued with dustjacket) (Methuen, 1908)	£45,000
THE WIND IN THE WILLOWS (illustrated by E.H. Shepard) (Methuen, 1931)	£450
THE WIND IN THE WILLOWS (illustrated by E.H. Shepard; limited to 200 copies, signed by the author and artist; issued with dustjacket) (Methuen, 1931)	£3,700

GRAHAME, Kenneth

THE WIND IN THE WILLOWS (illustrated by Arthur Rackham) (Heritage, U.S., 1940) £300
THE WIND IN THE WILLOWS (illustrated by Arthur Rackham; limited to 2,020 numbered copies,
  signed by the designer, Bruce Rogers; in slipcase) (Limited Editions Club, U.S., 1940) £1,350
FIRST WHISPER OF 'THE WIND IN THE WILLOWS'. Edited by Elspeth Grahame (Methuen, 1944) £35
THE WIND IN THE WILLOWS (illustrated by Arthur Rackham; omits several of the colour plates from
  the original American edition) (Methuen, 1950)...£600
THE WIND IN THE WILLOWS (illustrated by Arthur Rackham; limited to 500 copies; in box) (Methuen, 1951)......£1,750
THE WIND IN THE WILLOWS (illustrated by E.H. Shepard; colour plates) (Methuen, 1959)........................£125
THE WIND IN THE WILLOWS (illustrated by E.H. Shepard; first full-colour edition) (Methuen, 1971)............£60
THE WIND IN THE WILLOWS (illustrated by Arthur Rackham; twelve colour plates and fifteen line drawings)
  (Methuen Children's Books, 1975) £75
THE WIND IN THE WILLOWS (illustrated by Michael Hague) (Holt, U.S., 1980) £50
THE WIND IN THE WILLOWS (illustrated by Michael Hague) (Methuen, 1980) £40
THE WIND IN THE WILLOWS (illustrated by John Burningham; in slipcase;) (Viking, 1983) £80
THE CAMBRIDGE BOOK OF POETRY FOR CHILDREN. Edited by Kenneth Grahame (CUP, 1916) £40
THE KENNETH GRAHAME BOOK (contains 'The Golden Age', 'Dream Days' and 'The Wind in the Willows') (Methuen, 1932) £35
SWEET HOME (adapted from 'The Wind in the Willows') (Methuen, 1946) £20
TOAD GOES CARAVANNING (adapted from 'The Wind in the Willows') (Methuen, 1947).................................£20

For most people, E.H. Shepard's illustrations for Kenneth Grahame's **The Wind in the Willows** *(above) remain unsurpassed.*

*The dustjacket and front board of E.H. Shepard's 1928 edition of **The Golden Age**, the first of Kenneth Grahame's classic works.*

BERTIE'S ESCAPADE (reprinted from 'First Whisper of "The Wind in the Willows"') (Methuen, 1949)......................................£60
THE RELUCTANT DRAGON (illustrated by Michael Hague) (Holt, U.S., 1983) £25
MY DEAREST MOUSE: The 'Wind in the Willows' Letters (Methuen, 1988) £25

GRAVES, Robert
British author. Born: Robert von Ranke Graves in 1895. Best known for his poetry and adult novels, notably *I, Claudius* (1934), but also wrote a number of verse and prose works for children. Died: 1985.
Prices are for books in Very Good condition with dustjackets where applicable.

THE PENNY FIDDLE: Poems for Children (illustrated by Edward Ardizzone) (Cassell, 1960) £80
THE BIG GREEN BOOK (illustrated by Maurice Sendak) (Crowell-Crozier, U.S., 1962)..£50
THE BIG GREEN BOOK (illustrated by Maurice Sendak; paperback) (Puffin, 1978) £10
ANN AT HIGHWOOD HALL: Poems for Children (illustrated by Edward Ardizzone) (Cassell, 1964)................................£80
TWO WISE CHILDREN (illustrated by Ralph Pinto) (Quist, U.S., 1967)..£25
THE POOR BOY WHO FOLLOWED HIS STAR (Cassell, 1968) £20
AN ANCIENT CASTLE (Peter Owen, 1980)..£15

GREENAWAY, Kate
British author-illustrator. Born: London, 1846, but spent the formative years of her childhood in Rolleston, a village in Nottinghamshire. Studied at the Female School of Art in South Kensington and the Slade School, subsequently working as a freelance painter/illustrator before Edmund Evans published her first solo 'picture book', the hugely successful *Under the Window*, in 1879. Many more followed, as well as several almanacks. Enjoyed a long friendship with John Ruskin, who was a great admirer of her work. Died: 1901.
Prices are for books in Very Good condition.

Books
AUNT LOUISA'S NURSERY FAVOURITE (Warne, 1870) £300
DIAMONDS AND TOADS (Warne, 1871) £850
PUCK AND BLOSSOM by Rosa Mulholland (Marcus Ward, 1875)..£225
FAIRY GIFTS; or A Wallet of Wonders by Kathleen Knox (Griffith & Farran, 1875) £200
SEVEN BIRTHDAYS by Kathleen Knox (Griffith & Farran, 1876)..£200

GREENAWAY, Kate

*Kate Greenaway's **A Painting Book** (1884) is rarely found in Very Good condition because of the fragility of its paper wraps.*

Two of the charming illustrated Almanacks which Kate Greenaway produced for Routledge in the 1880s and 1890s. The early examples were issued in flimsy envelopes, and you can expect to pay three times as much for copies with these intact.

A DAY IN A CHILD'S LIFE (music by Myles Birket Foster) (Routledge, 1881) £200
LITTLE ANN and Other Poems by J. & A. Taylor (Routledge, 1883)..£125
LANGUAGE OF FLOWERS (Routledge, 1884) £125
A PAINTING BOOK (wrappers) (Routledge, 1884) £225
SONGS FOR THE NURSERY (Routledge, 1884) £125
MARIGOLD GARDEN (Routledge, 1885)...£250
KATE GREENAWAY'S ALBUM (limited to eight copies) (Routledge, 1885)..£6,500
KATE GREENAWAY'S ALPHABET (miniature book; card covers) (Routledge, 1885) £100
ENGLISH SPELLING BOOK (Routledge, 1885)..£100
DAME WIGGINS OF LEE AND HER SEVEN WONDERFUL CATS (George Allen, 1885) £35
A APPLE PIE (Routledge, 1886)..£300
RHYMES FOR THE YOUNG FOLK (Cassell, 1886) £100
QUEEN VICTORIA'S JUBILEE GARLAND (Routledge, 1887) £200
BABY'S BIRTHDAY BOOK (Marcus Ward, 1887) £125
THE PIED PIPER OF HAMELIN by Robert Browning (Routledge, 1888) £150
THE ROYAL PROGRESS OF KING PEPITO by Beatrice Cresswell (SPCK, 1889) £150
KATE GREENAWAY'S BOOK OF GAMES (Routledge, 1889) £300
THE APRIL BABY'S BOOK OF TUNES by the author of 'Elizabeth and Her German Garden' (Macmillan, 1900) £150
LITTLEDOM CASTLE and Other Tales by Mabel H. Spielmann (illustrated by Kate Greenaway and others)
     (Routledge, 1903) £85

Almanacks (prices are for Almanacks without their original envelope. If these are present, prices should be tripled)
1883 (Routledge) £200
1884 (Routledge) £200
1885 (Routledge) £175
1886 (Routledge) £150
1887 (Routledge) £100
1888 (Routledge) £100
1889 (Routledge) £150
1890 (Routledge) £100
1891 (Routledge) £100
1892 (Routledge) £100
1893 (Routledge) £100
1894 (Routledge) £100
1895 (Routledge) £100
1896 ....not published
1897 (leather binding) (Dent)..£600

Calendars

CALENDAR OF THE SEASONS (Marcus Ward, 1876/1877/1881/1882) ....each £75
A CALENDAR OF THE MONTHS (Marcus Ward, 1884) £50
KATE GREENAWAY'S CALENDAR (Routledge, 1884/1897/1899) ....each £100

GREENE, Graham

British author. Born: 1904. The great novelist wrote four 'picture books', the first for Eyre & Spottiswoode while he working as a director of the firm. Originally illustrated by Dorothy Craigie, they were later reissued with pictures by Edward Ardizzone. Died: 1993.

Prices are for books in Very Good condition with dustjackets.

THE LITTLE TRAIN (anonymous; illustrated by Dorothy Craigie) (Eyre & Spottiswoode, [1946]) £450
THE LITTLE TRAIN (illustrated by Edward Ardizzone) (The Bodley Head, 1973) £85
THE LITTLE FIRE ENGINE (illustrated by Dorothy Craigie) (Parrish, [1950]) £350
THE LITTLE FIRE ENGINE (illustrated by Edward Ardizzone) (The Bodley Head, 1973).....................................£85
THE LITTLE HORSE BUS (illustrated by Dorothy Craigie) (Parrish, [1952]) £300
THE LITTLE HORSE BUS (illustrated by Edward Ardizzone) (The Bodley Head, 1974).....................................£85
THE LITTLE STEAM ROLLER (illustrated by Dorothy Craigie) (Parrish, [1953]) £300
THE LITTLE STEAM ROLLER (illustrated by Edward Ardizzone) (The Bodley Head, 1974) £85

'GREYFRIARS HOLIDAY' ANNUALS

British annual almost entirely devoted to the work of 'Frank Richards' (Charles Hamilton), containing stories and features about his most popular schools, Rookwood, St. Jim's and Greyfriars. Published by Amalgamated Press, it was launched in 1919 under the title *The Holiday Annual for Boys and Girls*, but was renamed *The Greyfriars Holiday Annual for Boys and Girls* for the next issue. The title was killed off by the war, the final edition appearing in 1941.

Prices are for books in Very Good condition.

THE HOLIDAY ANNUAL ANNUAL FOR BOYS AND GIRLS 1920 [1919] £50
THE GREYFRIARS HOLIDAY ANNUAL FOR BOYS AND GIRLS 1921 [1920] £35
THE GREYFRIARS HOLIDAY ANNUAL FOR BOYS AND GIRLS 1922 [1921]-1937 [1936] ....each £35
THE GREYFRIARS HOLIDAY ANNUAL FOR BOYS AND GIRLS 1938 [1937]-1939 [1938] ....each £35
THE GREYFRIARS HOLIDAY ANNUAL FOR BOYS AND GIRLS 1940 [1939]-1941 [1940] ....each £30

GRIMM, Jacob and Wilhelm

German philologists and collectors of fairy tales. Jacob Ludwig Carl Grimm and Wilhelm Carl Grimm were born in Hanau, near Frankfurt, in 1785 and 1786 respectively. They both studied at Marburg University, where they developed their interest in German folk literature. The first volume of *Kinder- und Hausmärchen* ('Nursery and Household Tales') was published in 1812, the second appearing two years later. Amongst the tales included in these volumes were versions of 'Little Red Riding-Hood', 'The Sleeping Beauty' and 'Hansel and Gretel'. They were first translated into English by a London lawyer, Edgar Taylor, appearing in two volumes along with illustrations by George Cruikshank. The first comprehensive edition was that of Margaret Hunt (1884), which featured an introduction by Andrew Lang. The brothers died in 1863 and 1859 respectively.

Prices are for books in Very Good condition (with dustjackets after 1971).

GERMAN POPULAR STORIES (first English edition; illustrated by George Cruikshank;
   translated by Edgar Taylor; two volumes) (C. Baldwin, 1824-26)..the set £500
THE FAIRY RING: A New Collection of Popular Tales (illustrated by R. Doyle; translated by Edgar Taylor)
   (John Murray, 1846) £1,200
HOUSEHOLD STORIES (illustrated by E.H. Wehnert; new translation; two volumes) (Addey, 1853) £175
GRIMM'S GOBLINS (illustrated by 'Phiz') ('Fairy Books for Boys and Girls', [1861])................................£175
HOUSEHOLD STORIES (illustrated by Walter Crane; translated by L. Crane) (Macmillan, 1882)....................£80
FAIRY TALES OF THE BROTHERS GRIMM (illustrated by Arthur Rackham; translated by Mrs Edgar Lucas)
   (Freemantle, 1900)..£300
GRIMM'S FAIRY TALES (illustrated by John Hassall) (Sands, 1902) £80
GRIMM'S FAIRY TALES. Selected and edited for little folk (illustrated by Helen Stratton) (Blackie, [1903]) £20
GRIMM'S FAIRY TALES. Edited by J.R. Monsell (illustrated by J.R. Monsell) (Cassell, 1908) £30
GRIMM'S FAIRY TALES. Selected and retold by Githa Sowerby (illustrated by Millicent Sowerby) (Grant Richards, 1909) £100
FAIRY TALES OF THE BROTHERS GRIMM (illustrated by Arthur Rackham; translated by Mrs Edgar Lucas)
   (Constable, 1909)..£750
FAIRY TALES OF THE BROTHERS GRIMM (illustrated by Arthur Rackham; limited to 750 copies, signed by the artist)
   (Constable, 1909) £3,000
FAIRY TALES OF THE BROTHERS GRIMM (illustrated by Arthur Rackham) (Constable, 1920) £300
FAIRY TALES OF THE BROTHERS GRIMM (illustrated by Arthur Rackham) (Heinemann, [1925]) £150
GRIMM'S FAIRY TALES (illustrated by Mabel Lucie Attwell) (Cassell, [1910]) £120
GRIMM'S FAIRY TALES (illustrated by Charles Robinson; translated by L.L. Weedon) (Children's Classics, [1910])...................£50
GRIMM'S FAIRY TALES (illustrated by Charles Folkard; introduction by John Ruskin) (A. & C. Black, 1911).............................£40
GRIMM'S FAIRY STORIES (illustrated by Mabel Lucie Attwell) (Raphael Tuck, 1912) £140

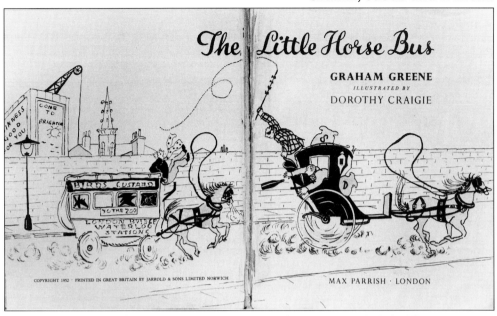

*The opening spread of **The Little Horse Bus** (1952), the third of Graham Greene's four picture books for children.*

HAGUE, Michael

American artist. Born in Los Angeles in 1948, Hague has established an international reputation as an illustrator of children's classics, notably *The Wind in the Willows* (1980).

Prices are for books in Very Good condition with dustjackets where applicable.

EAST OF THE SUN AND WEST OF THE MOON (Harcourt Brace, U.S., 1980) £40
THE WIND IN THE WILLOWS by Kenneth Grahame (Holt, U.S., 1980)...£50
THE WIND IN THE WILLOWS by Kenneth Grahame (Methuen, 1980) £40
MICHAEL HAGUE'S FAVOURITE HANS CHRISTIAN ANDERSEN FAIRY TALES (Holt, U.S., 1981) £30
THE MAN WHO KEPT HOUSE (Harcourt Brace, U.S., 1981) £35
THE NIGHT BEFORE CHRISTMAS by Clement C. Moore (Holt, U.S., 1981) £30
THE WIZARD OF OZ by L. Frank Baum (Holt, U.S., 1982) £40
THE DRAGON KITE (Harcourt Brace, U.S., 1982)...£25
THE RELUCTANT DRAGON by Kenneth Grahame (Holt, U.S., 1983) £25
THE LION, THE WITCH AND THE WARDROBE by C.S. Lewis (Macmillan, U.S., 1983) £60
THE HOBBIT by J.R.R. Tolkien (Houghton Mifflin, U.S., 1984)..£60
THE HOBBIT by J.R.R. Tolkien (as 'The Illustrated Hobbit') (Allen & Unwin, 1984) £60
MOTHER GOOSE: A Collection of Nursery Rhymes. Edited by Michael Hague (Holt, U.S., 1984)...........£25
ALPHABEARS (Holt, U.S., 1984) £25
AESOP'S FABLES. Edited by Michael Hague (Holt, U.S., 1985)..£30
A CHILD'S BOOK OF PRAYERS (Holt, U.S., 1985) £20
ALICE'S ADVENTURES IN WONDERLAND by Lewis Carroll (Holt, U.S., 1985) £30
ALICE'S ADVENTURES IN WONDERLAND by Lewis Carroll (Methuen, 1985)......................................£25
THE LEGEND OF THE VEERY BIRD (Harcourt, U.S., 1985)...£25
OUT OF THE NURSERY, INTO THE NIGHT (Holt, U.S., 1986) £25
NUMBEARS: A Counting Book (Holt, U.S., 1986) £25
MICHAEL HAGUE'S WORLD OF UNICORNS (Holt, U.S., 1986) £20
THE SECRET GARDEN by F.H. Burnett (Holt, U.S., 1987) £30
PETER PAN by J.M. Barrie (Holt, U.S., 1987)...£35
THE LAND OF NOD and Other Poems for Children by R.L. Stevenson. Edited by Michael Hague (Holt, U.S., 1988) £25
THE UNICORN ALPHABET by Marianna Mayer (Mayer, U.S., 1989) £20
CINDERELLA and Other Tales from Perrault (Holt, U.S., 1989) £20
BEAR HUGS (Holt, U.S., 1989)...£12
A UNICORN JOURNAL (Arcade, U.S., 1990) £18
MY SECRET GARDEN DIARY (Arcade, U.S., 1990) £12
OUR BABY: A BOOK OF RECORDS AND MEMORIES (Arcade, U.S., 1990)..£15
MAGIC MOMENTS: A BOOK OF DAYS (Arcade, U.S., 1990)..£15
WE WISH YOU A MERRY CHRISTMAS (Holt, U.S., 1990) £10
BOX OF CHRISTMAS CAROLS (includes 'Jingle Bells', 'Deck the Halls' and 'O Christmas Tree') (Holt, U.S., 1990-)......the set £35
THE BORROWERS by Mary Norton (Harcourt Brace, U.S., 1991) £30
THE FAIRY TALES OF OSCAR WILDE (Holt, U.S., 1993)..£15
TEDDY BEAR TEDDY BEAR (Morrow, U.S., 1993) £5
THE RAINBOW FAIRY BOOK by Andrew Lang (Books of Wonder, U.S., 1993) £10
THE LITTLE MERMAID by Hans Christian Andersen (Holt, U.S., 1994) £10
THE CHILDREN'S BOOK OF VIRTUES by William J. Bennett (Simon &Schuster, U.S., 1995) £10
THE OWL AND THE PUSSY-CAT and Other Nonsense Poems by Edward Lear (North-South, U.S., 1995)............£10
THE PERFECT PRESENT (illustrated by the author) (Morrow, U.S., 1996)..£10
THE CHILDREN'S BOOK OF HEROES by William J. Bennett (Simon &Schuster, U.S., 1997) £10
CALANDARBEARS: A Book of Months by Kathleen Hague (Holt, U.S., 1997) £15

HALE, Kathleen

British author-illustrator. Born: Scotland, 1898. Studied at Manchester and Central Schools of Art. Worked as secretary to the painter, Augustus John, and as a freelance artist before publishing the first of her 'Orlando' books, *Orlando the Marmalade Cat: A Camping Holiday*, in 1938. Her autobiography, *A Slender Reputation*, appeared in 1994. Died: 2000.

Prices are for books in Very Good condition with dustjackets where applicable.

'Orlando' Books (all Written and Illustrated by Kathleen Hale)

ORLANDO THE MARMALADE CAT: A CAMPING HOLIDAY (Country Life, [1938]) £350
ORLANDO THE MARMALADE CAT: A TRIP ABROAD (Country Life, [1938]) £300
ORLANDO'S EVENING OUT (paperback) (Puffin: 'Picture Books' series No. PP14, [1941]) £30
ORLANDO'S HOME LIFE (paperback) (Puffin: 'Picture Books' series No. PP26, [1942]) £30
ORLANDO THE MARMALADE CAT BUYS A FARM (Country Life, 1942) £300
ORLANDO THE MARMALADE CAT: HIS SILVER WEDDING (Country Life, 1944) £300
ORLANDO THE MARMALADE CAT BECOMES A DOCTOR (Country Life, 1944) £200

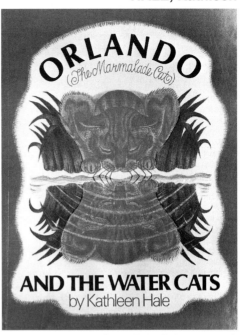

Although best-known for the 'Orlando' series, Kathleen Hale has also produced a single book featuring Manda the calf.

Orlando the Marmalade Cat made his final appearance in **Orlando and the Water Cats**, published by Cape in 1972.

ORLANDO'S INVISIBLE PYJAMAS (Transatlantic Arts, 1947) £95
ORLANDO THE MARMALADE CAT KEEPS A DOG (Country Life, 1949)... £350
ORLANDO THE JUDGE (paperback) (John Murray, 1950) £80
ORLANDO THE MARMALADE CAT: A SEASIDE HOLIDAY (Country Life, 1952)............................ £250
ORLANDO'S ZOO (paperback) (John Murray, 1954) £30
ORLANDO THE MARMALADE CAT: THE FRISKY HOUSEWIFE (Country Life, 1956) £75
ORLANDO'S MAGIC CARPET (John Murray, 1958) £75
ORLANDO THE MARMALADE CAT BUYS A COTTAGE (Country Life, 1963) £75
ORLANDO AND THE THREE GRACES (John Murray, 1965) £75
ORLANDO THE MARMALADE CAT GOES TO THE MOON (John Murray, 1968) £65
ORLANDO THE MARMALADE CAT AND THE WATER CATS (Cape, 1972) £60

'Peep-Show' Books (all Written and Illustrated by Kathleen Hale)
ORLANDO'S COUNTRY LIFE (Chatto & Windus, 1950) £150
PUSS-IN-BOOTS (Chatto & Windus, 1951) £150

Other Books Written and Illustrated by Kathleen Hale
'HENRIETTA' THE FAITHFUL HEN (Transatlantic Arts, 1943)... £100
MANDA THE JERSEY CALF (John Murray, 1952).. £60
HENRIETTA'S MAGIC EGG (Allen & Unwin, 1973) £60

Books Illustrated by Kathleen Hale
I DON'T MIX MUCH WITH FAIRIES by Molly Harrower (Eyre & Spottiswoode, 1928) £90
PLAIN JANE by Molly Harrower (Eyre & Spottiswoode, 1929)... £75
BASIL SEAL RIDES AGAIN by Evelyn Waugh (limited to 750 numbered copies, signed by the author)
    (Chapman & Hall, 1963) £400

HARGREAVES, Roger
British author-illustrator. Born: 1925. Was working as the director of a London advertising agency when, in the early 1970s, he achieved enormous fame with the 'Mr Men' series of picture books. These were followed by the 'Timbuctoo' and 'Little Miss' series. Died: 1988.

Prices are for books in Fine condition.

'Mr Men' Books
MR BUMP (Thurman, 1971) £10	MR SNEEZE (Thurman, 1971) £10
MR GREED (Thurman, 1971) £10	MR SLOW (Thurman, 1971) £10
MR HAPPY (Thurman, 1971) £10	MR NOSEY (Thurman, 1971) £10

HARGREAVES, Roger

MR DAYDREAM (Thurman, 1972) £10
MR SILLY (Thurman, 1972) £10
MR SMALL (Thurman, 1972) £10
MR UPPITY (Thurman, 1972) £10
MR BOUNCE (Thurman, 1976) £10
MR CHATTERBOX (Thurman, 1976) £10
MR DIZZY (Thurman, 1976) £10
MR FORGETFUL (Thurman, 1976) £10
MR FUNNY (Thurman, 1976) £10
MR IMPOSSIBLE (Thurman, 1976) £10
MR JELLY (Thurman, 1976) £10
MR MEAN (Thurman, 1976) £10
MR MEN'S CHRISTMAS (Thurman, 1976) £10
MR MEN ON HOLIDAY (Thurman, 1976) £10
MR MUDDLE (Thurman, 1976) £10
MR NOISY (Thurman, 1976) £10
MR STRONG (Thurman, 1976)..........................£10
MR MEN'S SPORTS DAY (Thurman, 1977).........£8
MR SMALL'S COLOURING BOOK (Thurman, 1977) £8
MR BUSY (Thurman, 1978) £8
MR CLUMSY (Thurman, 1978) £8
MR CLEVER (Thurman, 1978) £8
MR MISCHIEF (Thurman, 1978) £8
MR NONSENSE (Thurman, 1978) £8
MR QUIET (Thurman, 1978) £8
MR RUSH (Thurman, 1978) £8
MR SKINNY (Thurman, 1978)...........................£8

MR WORRY (Thurman, 1978)............................£8
MR TALL (Thurman, 1978) £8
MY OWN MR MEN STORYBOOK (Mirror Books, 1978) £8
THE MR MEN ABC (Thurman, 1978)..................£8
THE MR MEN NO. 1 (Mirror Books, 1978) £8
THE MR MEN [NO. 2] (Mirror Books, 1978) £8
MR GRUMPY (Thurman, 1979) £8
MR TRUMPET (Thurman, 1979) £8
MR TRUMPET'S FRUIT (Thurman, 1979) £8
MR GREEDY GOES SHOPPING (Thurman, [1979]) £8
MR HAPPY AT THE SEASIDE (Thurman, [1979]) £8
MR SILLY ON THE FARM (Thurman, [1979])........£8
MR TICKLE IN THE PARK (Thurman, [1979]) £8
THE SECOND MR MEN STORYBOOK
   (Mirror Books, 1979) £8
MY VERY OWN MR MEN STORYBOOK
   (Thurman, 1979) £5
MR FUNNY AT THE CIRCUS (Thurman, 1980) £5
MR MUDDLE GOES TO SCHOOL (Thurman, 1980)...........£5
MR NOSEY FOLLOWS HIS NOSE (Thurman, 1980) £5
MR STRONG TO THE RESCUE (Thurman, 1980) £5
THE MR MEN RAINY DAY BOOK (Thurman, 1980) £5
THE THIRD MR MEN STORYBOOK (Mirror Books, 1980) ..£5
MR CHRISTMAS (Thurman, 1984).....................£5
MR MEN NUMBER FUN (Thurman, 1984)............£5
MY VERY OWN MR MEN BIRTHDAY BOOK
   (Thurman, 1984) £5

'Little Miss' Books

LITTLE MISS BOSSY (Thurman, 1981) £5
LITTLE MISS HELPFUL (Thurman, 1981) £5
LITTLE MISS LATE (Thurman, 1981) £5
LITTLE MISS NAUGHTY (Thurman, 1981) £5
LITTLE MISS NEAT (Thurman, 1981) £5
LITTLE MISS PLUMP (Thurman, 1981) £5
LITTLE MISS SCATTERBRAIN (Thurman, 1981) £5
LITTLE MISS SHY (Thurman, 1981) £5
LITTLE MISS SPLENDID (Thurman, 1981) £5
LITTLE MISS SUNSHINE (Thurman, 1981) £5
LITTLE MISS TINY (Thurman, 1981) £5

LITTLE MISS TROUBLE (Thurman, 1981) £5
LITTLE MISS MAGIC (Thurman, 1982) £5
LITTLE MISS CHATTERBOX (Thurman, 1984) £5
LITTLE MISS CONTRARY (Thurman, 1984) £5
LITTLE MISS COOK BOOK (Thurman, 1984).......£5
LITTLE MISS DOTTY (Thurman, 1984) £5
LITTLE MISS FICKLE (Thurman, 1984)...............£5
LITTLE MISS LUCKY (Thurman, 1984) £5
LITTLE MISS STAR (Thurman, 1984) £5
LITTLE MISS TWINS (Thurman, 1984) £5

'Hippo, Potto & Mouse' Books

HIPPO, POTTO & MOUSE (Hodder & Stoughton, 1976) £5
HIPPO LEAVES HOME (Hodder & Stoughton, 1976) £5

MOUSE GETS CAUGHT (Hodder & Stoughton, 1976) £5
POTTO FINDS A JOB (Hodder & Stoughton, 1976) £5

'Roar' Books

ROAR (Hodder & Stoughton, 1979) £5
ROAR'S DAY OF MISTAKES (Hodder & Stoughton, 1981) £5

'Timbuctoo' Books

WOOF: A SORT OF DOG FROM TIMBUCTOO! (Hodder & Stoughton, 1978) £5
BUZZ: A SORT OF BEE FROM TIMBUCTOO! (Hodder & Stoughton, 1978) £5
CHIRP: A SORT OF BIRD FROM TIMBUCTOO! (Hodder & Stoughton, 1978)............£5
HISS: A SORT OF SNAKE FROM TIMBUCTOO! (Hodder & Stoughton, 1978) £5
MEOW: A SORT OF CAT FROM TIMBUCTOO! (Hodder & Stoughton, 1978) £5
MOO: A SORT OF COW FROM TIMBUCTOO! (Hodder & Stoughton, 1978) £5
NEIGH: A SORT OF HORSE FROM TIMBUCTOO! (Hodder & Stoughton, 1978) £5
OINK: A SORT OF PIG FROM TIMBUCTOO! (Hodder & Stoughton, 1978) £5
SQUEAK: A SORT OF MOUSE FROM TIMBUCTOO! (Hodder & Stoughton, 1978) £5
TRUMPET: A SORT OF ELEPHANT FROM TIMBUCTOO! (Hodder & Stoughton, 1978) ...£5
SNAP!: A SORT OF CROCODILE FROM TIMBUCTOO! (Hodder & Stoughton, 1978) £5
ROAR: A SORT OF LION FROM TIMBUCTOO! (Hodder & Stoughton, 1978) £5
BAA: A SORT OF SHEEP FROM TIMBUCTOO! (Hodder & Stoughton, 1979) £5
BLEAT: A SORT OF GOAT FROM TIMBUCTOO! (Hodder & Stoughton, 1979) £5
CHATTER : A SORT OF MONKEY FROM TIMBUCTOO! (Hodder & Stoughton, 1979).....£5
CLUCK: A SORT OF HEN FROM TIMBUCTOO! (Hodder & Stoughton, 1979) £5
CROAK: A SORT OF FROG FROM TIMBUCTOO! (Hodder & Stoughton, 1979) £5
GRIZZLE: A SORT OF BEAR FROM TIMBUCTOO! (Hodder & Stoughton, 1979) £5
GROWL: A SORT OF TIGER FROM TIMBUCTOO! (Hodder & Stoughton, 1979) £5
HONK: A SORT OF SEAL FROM TIMBUCTOO! (Hodder & Stoughton, 1979) £5
HOOT: A SORT OF OWL FROM TIMBUCTOO! (Hodder & Stoughton, 1979) £5

Two of Roger Hargreaves' very successful 'Mr Men' books. Even in Fine condition, these are only worth from £5 to £10.

*Ever versatile, Hargreaves turned his attention to ordinary household objects in his witty 1981 picture book, **Things**.*

PUFF: A SORT OF PANDA FROM TIMBUCTOO! (Hodder & Stoughton, 1979) £5
QUACK: A SORT OF DUCK FROM TIMBUCTOO! (Hodder & Stoughton, 1979) £5
SNIFF: A SORT OF RABBIT FROM TIMBUCTOO! (Hodder & Stoughton, 1979)...£5
SQUAWK: A SORT OF PARROT FROM TIMBUCTOO! (Hodder & Stoughton, 1979) £5
TRUMPET (Purnell, 1979)...£5
AN APPLE FOR OINK (Hamlyn, 1981) £5
HISS AND THE STORM (Hamlyn, 1981) £5
MOO'S FANCY HATS (Hamlyn, 1981) £5
NEIGH MOVES HOUSE (Hamlyn, 1981) £5

Others
COUNT WORM (Hodder & Stoughton, 1976) £5
GRANDFATHER CLOCK (Hodder & Stoughton, 1977) £5
ALBERT THE ALPHABETICAL ELEPHANT (Hodder & Stoughton, 1977)...£5
THINGS (Hodder & Stoughton, 1981) £5
ONCE UPON A WORM (Hodder & Stoughton, 1982) £5
I AM A BOOK (Hodder & Stoughton, 1984) £5

HARRIS, Joel Chandler
American author. Born: Georgia, 1848. Worked as a printer's devil and then journalist before writing the 'Uncle Remus' stories, which were based on the folksongs and stories of the blacks of the American South. Originally published in the *Atlanta Constitution*, these were first issued in book form in 1880 under the title *Uncle Remus: His Songs and His Sayings*, and were followed by several sequels. Died: 1908.

Prices are for books in Very Good condition.

UNCLE REMUS: His Songs and his Sayings, The Folk-Lore of the Old Plantation (illustrated by Frederick Church and James Moser) (Appleton, U.S., 1881 [1880]) £3,250
UNCLE REMUS and His Legends of the Old Plantation (animal tales only) (Bogue, 1881) £300
UNCLE REMUS, or Mr Fox, Mr Rabbit and Mr Terrapin (enlarged edition, including 'His Songs and His Sayings' as well as the animal tales) (Routledge, 1881)...£300
UNCLE REMUS: His Songs and his Sayings, The Folk-Lore of the Old Plantation (Ward Lock, [1883]) £300
NIGHTS WITH UNCLE REMUS: Myths and Legends of the Old Plantation (Tribner, U.S., [1883]) £300
DADDY JAKE THE RUNAWAY (Appleton, U.S., 1889) £1,500
UNCLE REMUS AND HIS FRIENDS: Old Plantation Stories, Songs, Ballads, etc. (Osgood McIlvaine, 1892) £200
UNCLE REMUS: His Songs and his Sayings (reprint of the 1881 Routledge edition) (Routledge, 1895) £175
MR RABBIT AT HOME (sequel to 'Little Mr Thimblefinger and his Queer Country'; illustrated by O. Herford) (Osgood McIlvaine, 1895) £150

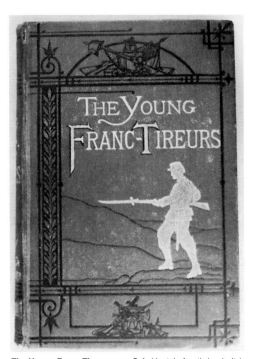

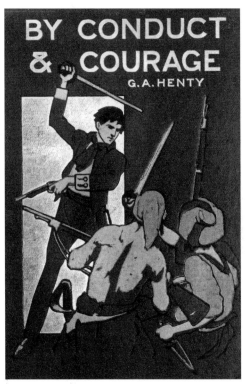

The Young Franc-Tireurs was G.A. Henty's fourth book. It is now valued at £700 for a Very Good copy in the original cloth.

A typically stirring Henty cover. It's worth noting that many of the early titles were issued in more than one type of binding.

THE TAR-BABY and Other Rhymes of Uncle Remus (verse) (Appleton, U.S., 1904) £1,700
UNCLE REMUS (illustrated by Harry Rountree and René Bull) (Nelson, [1906]) £100
LITTLE MR THIMBLEFINGER AND HIS QUEER COUNTRY (illustrated by O. Herford) (Osgood McIlvaine, 1894) £110
WALLY WANDEROON AND HIS STORY-TELLING MACHINE (Grant Richards, U.K./U.S., 1904) £80
A LITTLE UNION SCOUT (Duckworth [printed in the U.S.], 1904) £80
UNCLE REMUS AND BRER RABBIT (Appleton, U.S., 1907)...£220
THE BISHOP AND THE BOOGERMAN (illustrated by Charlotte Harding) (John Murray, 1909)...£60

HASSALL, John

British illustrator. Born: Walmer, Devon, in 1868. Educated at Newton Abbot College and Neuenheim College, Heidelberg, later studying in Antwerp and Paris. From 1895 onwards, he worked as a cartoonist and advertising artist, before turning his attention to children's books. He was one of the first members of the London Sketch Club, becoming President in 1903. Founded the New Art School with Charles van Havermaet. His daughter was the wood engraver, Joan Hassall. Died: 1948.

Prices are for books in Very Good condition.

TWO WELL-WORN SHOE STORIES (illustrated by John Hassall and Cecil Aldin) (Sands, 1899)...£200
THE WOULDBEGOODS by E. Nesbit (illustrated by John Hassall and Arthur Buckland) (Unwin, 1901) £175
AN A.B.C. OF EVERY-DAY PEOPLE by G.E. Farrow (Dean, [1902]) £150
GRIMM'S FAIRY TALES (twelve illustrations by John Hassall) (Sands, 1902)...£80
THE PANTOMIME A.B.C. by R. Carse (Sands, [1902]) £100
SIX AND TWENTY BOYS AND GIRLS by G.C. Bingham (verse) (Blackie, [1902])..£45
ABSURD DITTIES by G.E. Farrow (Routledge, 1903) £65
ROUND THE WORLD A.B.C. by G.E. Farrow (Nister [printed in Germany], [1904]) £100
THE TWINS by Edward Shirley (verse) (Nelson, [1904]) £60
THE OLD NURSERY STORIES AND RHYMES (Blackie, [1904])..£150
ALL THE BEST NURSERY STORIES AND RHYMES (Blackie, [1905]) £150
RUFF AND REDDY: The Fairy Guide by May Byron and G.E. Farrow (Cooke, [1905]) £75
PUG PETER: KING OF MOUSELAND by E. Nesbit (illustrated by John Hassall and Harry Rountree) (Cooke, [1905]) £100
THE MAGIC SHOP by May Byron (Cooke, [1905])..£40
SPORT AND PLAY: A Picture Book by Edward Shirley (Nelson, [1907])..£40
THE HAPPY ANNUAL by Cecil Aldin and John Hassall (Heinemann, 1907) £60

GOOD QUEEN BESS 1533-1603: **A Book for Children** by B. Girvin (David Nutt, [1907])..£40
MOTHER GOOSE'S NURSERY RHYMES. Edited by Walter C. Jerrold (Blackie, 1909 [1908])................................£55
GULLIVER'S TRAVELS by Jonathan Swift (Nelson, [1908]) £50
THE PRINCESS AND THE DRAGON by S.H. Hamer (illustrated by John Hassall and T. Butler-Stoney) (Duckworth, [1908])......£35
MISS MANNERS by Aileen Orr (Andrew Melrose, 1909) £80
TALES AND TALKS FOR NURSERY LAND (illustrated by John Hassall and others) (Blackie, [1909])...............£40
THE DOLL'S DIARY by Rose H. Thomas (24 illustrations by John Hassall) (Grant Richards, 1909) £50
FRIDAY AND SATURDAY: The Adventures of Two Little Pickles by May Byron (verse) (Frowde/Hodder & Stoughton, [1910])..£40
THE SLEEPING BEAUTY and Other Tales from Perrault by C. Perrault (Blackie, [1912]) £50
CHILDREN'S PAINTING BOOK. In Aid of the Belgium Relief Fund by Thomas R. Arkell
   (illustrated by John Hassall, R.I. Jingles and Reginald Arkell) (Odhams Press, 1914) £35
THE HASSALL PAINTING BOOK (Lawrence & Jellicoe, [1915]) £40
THE PETER PAN PAINTING BOOK (Hodder & Stoughton, [1915]) £40
WITH LOVE FROM DADDY: Letters to a Child by R.H. Lindo (Stanley Paul, [1918]) £35
THE HASSALL A.B.C.: A Children's Picture Book (Collins, [1918]) £60
BLACKIE'S POPULAR FAIRY TALES (Blackie, [1921]) £20
OUR DIARY, or Teddy and Me (Nelson, [1928]) £40
ROBINSON CRUSOE, THE SWISS FAMILY ROBINSON AND GULLIVER'S TRAVELS (Blackie, [1930]) £25
BLACKIE'S POPULAR NURSERY STORIES (Blackie, [1931])...£15
DON'T TELL (Cooke, no date) £40
TEN LITTLE JAPPY CHAPS (Treherne: 'Stump Books' series, no date) £40

HENTY, G.A.

British author. Born: George Alfred Henty at Trumpington, Cambridgeshire, in 1832. After a sickly
childhood, he went to Westminster School and Cambridge, where he read Classics. Joined the army on the
outbreak of the Crimean War, leaving five years later to become a roving war correspondent. His hugely successful career as a novelist began in 1867 with the publication of *A Search for a Secret*, his first book for
young readers, *Out on the Pampas, or The Young Settlers* (1871), appearing four years later. Despite his success as a novelist, he continued to report on foreign conflicts until 1876. He edited the story papers, *Union
Jack* and *Boys' Own Magazine*, and collaborated on an annual, *Camps and Quarters*. Died: 1902.

Prices are for books in Very Good condition.

THE MARCH TO MAGDALA (Tinsley Brothers, 1868) £2,000
ALL BUT LOST (three volumes; blue boards) (Tinsley Brothers, 1869) £1,800
OUT ON THE PAMPAS, or The Young Settlers (illustrated by J.B. Zwecker; blue or brown boards)
   (Griffith & Farran, 1871 [1870]) £900
THE YOUNG FRANC-TIREURS (blue, red or green boards) (Griffith & Farran, 1872 [1871]) £700
THE MARCH TO COOMASSIE (second edition; blue boards) (Tinsley Brothers, 1874) £450
SEASIDE MAIDENS (orange boards) (Tinsley Brothers, 1880) £600
THE YOUNG BUGLERS (illustrated by J. Proctor; red or green boards; with adverts dated October 1879)
   (Griffith & Farran, 1880 [1879]) £500
THE CORNET OF HORSE (red boards; with adverts dated January 1881) (Sampson Low & Marston, 1881) £500
IN TIMES OF PERIL (red or blue boards; with adverts dated October 1881) (Griffith & Farran, 1881) £700
FACING DEATH (blue or brown boards) (Blackie, [1882 — though some first edition copies are apparently dated 1883]) £500
WINING HIS SPURS (published in the U.S. as 'Fighting the Saracens' and 'The Boy Knights'; red boards)
   (Sampson Low & Marston, 1882) £550
FRIENDS THOUGH DIVIDED (red, blue brown or green boards; adverts dated September 1883) (Griffith & Farran, 1883) £400
JACK ARCHER (published in the U.S. as 'The Fall of Sebastopol'; red boards) (Sampson Low & Marston, 1883) £400
UNDER DRAKE'S FLAG (green or brown boards) (Blackie, 1883 [1882]) £200
BY SHEER PLUCK (red boards; with adverts headed 'New Series for 1885') (Blackie, 1884 [1883]) £300
WITH CLIVE IN INDIA (red, brown or blue boards) (Blackie, 1884 [1883]) £200
THE YOUNG COLONISTS (blue and gold boards) (Routledge, 1885 [1884]) £200
TRUE TO THE OLD FLAG (blue, grey, red or green boards) (Blackie, 1885 [1884]) £200
IN FREEDOM'S CAUSE (blue, brown or red boards) (Blackie, 1885 [1884])...£100
ST. GEORGE FOR ENGLAND (brown, blue or green boards) (Blackie, 1885 [1884])..£100
THE LION OF THE NORTH (brown or green boards) (Blackie, 1886 [1885])..£140
THE DRAGON AND THE RAVEN (brown or green boards) (Blackie, 1886 [1885])...£200
FOR NAME AND FAME (brown or grey boards) (Blackie, 1886 [1885]) £300
THROUGH THE FRAY (brown or red boards) (Blackie, 1886 [1885]) £150
YARNS ON THE BEACH (brown or red boards) (Blackie, 1886 [1885])...£300
THE YOUNG CARTHAGINIAN (blue or green boards) (Blackie, 1887 [1886])...£200
THE BRAVEST OF THE BRAVE (red or blue boards) (Blackie, 1887 [1886]) £150
A FINAL RECKONING (illustrated by W.B. Wollen; blue or green boards) (Blackie, 1887 [1886])...........................£100
WITH WOLFE IN CANADA (illustrated by Gordon Browne; green, blue or red boards) (Blackie 1887 [1886]) £200
THE SOVEREIGN READER: Scenes from the Life and Reign of Queen Victoria (red or purple boards) (Blackie, [1887])....£150
IN THE REIGN OF TERROR (red, blue, grey or green boards) (Blackie, 1888) £150
STURDY AND STRONG (red, blue or orange boards) (Blackie, 1888 [1887])...£150
ORANGE AND GREEN (red, blue or orange boards) (Blackie 1888 [1887]) £100
BONNIE PRINCE CHARLIE (brown or red boards) (Blackie, 1888 [1887]) £100

HENTY, G.A.

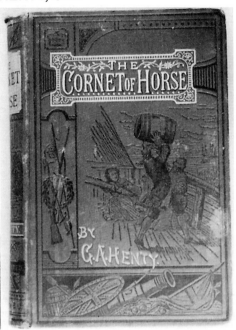

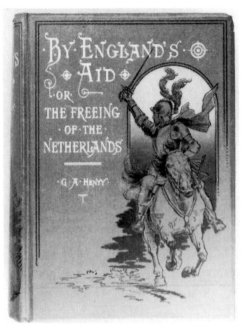

The Cornet of Horse (1881) is another early Henty title. A Very Good copy in the original cloth (above) is valued at £500.

By England's Aid was issued in blue or brown boards. Both issues are now valued at £150 for Very Good copies.

FOR THE TEMPLE (brown, red or blue boards) (Blackie, 1888 [1887]) **£200**
GABRIEL ALLEN MP (red boards) (Spencer & Blackett, [1888]) **£250**
CAPTAIN BAYLEY'S HEIR (red, brown or blue boards) (Blackie, 1889) **£100**
THE CAT OF BUBASTES (blue, brown, grey or green boards) (Blackie, 1889 [1888]) **£200**
THE LION OF ST MARK (red, blue or grey boards) (Blackie, 1889 [1888]) **£80**
THE CURSE OF CARNE'S HOLD (two volumes; blue boards) (Spencer & Blackett, 1889) **£500**
THE PLAGUE SHIP (wraps) (SPCK: 'Penny Library of Fiction' series, 1889) **£600**
BY PIKE AND DYKE (brown or green boards) (Blackie, 1890 [1889]) **£120**
ONE OF THE 28TH (red, brown, green or blue boards) (Blackie, 1890 [1889]) **£200**
TALES OF DARING AND DANGER (blue or green boards) (Blackie, 1889 [1890]) **£300**
WITH LEE IN VIRGINIA (brown or blue boards) (Blackie, 1890 [1889]) **£150**
THOSE OTHER ANIMALS (illustrated by H. Weir; green boards) (Henry & Co, [1891]) **£250**
BY ENGLAND'S AID (blue or brown boards) (Blackie, 1891 [1890]) **£150**
BY RIGHT OF CONQUEST (green or brown boards) (Blackie, 1891 [1890]) **£100**
MAORI AND SETTLER (brown, blue, red or green boards) (Blackie, 1891) **£100**
A CHAPTER OF ADVENTURES (published in the U.S. as 'The Young Midshipman'; blue or grey boards)
 (Blackie, 1891 [1890]) **£1,000**
A HIDDEN FOE (two volumes; grey boards) (Sampson Low & Marston, [1891]) **£2,000**
THE DASH FOR KHARTOUM (brown, red, grey or green boards) (Blackie, 1892 [1891]) **£100**
HELD FAST FOR ENGLAND (red, grey or brown boards) (Blackie, 1892 [1891]) **£100**
REDSKIN AND COWBOY (red, green or brown boards) (Blackie, 1892 [1891]) **£100**
THE RANCH IN THE VALLEY (wraps) (SPCK: 'Penny Library of Fiction' series, 1892) **£500**
BERIC THE BRITON (blue or brown boards) (Blackie, 1893 [1892]) **£150**
CONDEMNED AS A NIHILIST (brown or blue boards) (Blackie, 1893 [1892]) **£150**
IN GREEK WATERS (grey, brown or green boards) (Blackie, 1893 [1892]) **£100**
TALES FROM THE WORKS OF G.A. HENTY (red boards) (Blackie, 1893) **£100**
RUJUB THE JUGGLER (published in the U.S. as 'In the Days of the Mutiny'; three volumes, blue boards)
 (Chatto & Windus, 1893) **£750**
A JACOBITE EXILE (brown, green, grey or blue boards) (Blackie, 1894 [1893]) **£200**
THROUGH THE SIKH WAR (green boards) (Blackie, 1894 [1893]) **£100**
ST BARTHOLOMEW'S EVE (green, blue or red boards) (Blackie, 1894 [1893]) **£100**
DOROTHY'S DOUBLE (three volumes) (Chatto & Windus, 1894) **£750**
WHEN LONDON BURNED (blue boards) (Blackie, 1895 [1894]) **£200**
CUTHBERT HARTINGTON and A WOMAN OF THE COMMUNE (F.V. White, 1895) **£200**
WULF THE SAXON (green boards) (Blackie, 1895 [1894]) **£75**
IN THE HEART OR THE ROCKIES (grey boards) (Blackie, 1895 [1894]) **£100**
A KNIGHT OF THE WHITE CROSS (green boards) (Blackie, 1896 [1895]) **£150**

BEARS AND DACOITS (Blackie, [1896]) £300
SURLY JOE (wraps) (Blackie, [1896]) £200
WHITE-FACED DICK (limp cloth cover) (Blackie, [1896]) £200
THROUGH RUSSIAN SNOWS (grey boards) (Blackie, 1896 [1895]) £100
THE TIGER OF MYSORE (blue boards) (Blackie, 1896 [1895]) £100
ON THE IRRAWADDY (blue boards) (Blackie, 1897 [1896]) £150
AT AGINCOURT (grey boards; with adverts containing no reviews of this title) (Blackie, 1897 [1897]) £150
WITH COCHRANE THE DAUNTLESS (blue boards) (Blackie, 1897) £100
THE QUEEN'S CUP (three volumes; green or blue boards) (Chatto & Windus, 1897) £600
WITH MOORE AT CORUNNA (green or blue boards) (Blackie, 1898 [1897]) £100
COLONEL THORNDYKE'S SECRET (published in the U.S. in an abridged form as
    'The Brahmin's Treasure'; pink boards) (Chatto & Windus, 1898) £150
WITH FREDERICK THE GREAT (red boards; with adverts either headed 'Books for Young People' or
    'Illustrated Story Books') (Blackie, 1898 [1897]) £100
UNDER WELLINGTON'S COMMAND (blue boards) (Blackie, 1899 [1898]) £100
AT ABOUKIR AND ACRE (red boards) (Blackie, 1899 [1898]) £100
BOTH SIDES THE BORDER (blue boards) (Blackie, 1899 [1898]) £75
THE LOST HEIR (green boards; with adverts) (James Bowden, 1899) £150
ON THE SPANISH MAIN (red wraps) (Chambers, [1899]) £100
AT DUTY'S CALL (Chambers, [1899]) £75
A ROVING COMMISSION (illustrated by W. Rainey; red boards) (Blackie, 1900 [1899]) £100
WON BY THE SWORD (illustrated by C.M. Sheldon; blue boards) (Blackie, 1900 [1899]) £75
NO SURRENDER! (red boards) (Blackie, 1900 [1899]) £100
DO YOUR DUTY (blue or green boards) (Blackie, [1900]) £150
THE SOUL SURVIVORS (red wraps) (Chambers, [1901]) £100
IN THE IRISH BRIGADE (green boards; with 32 pages of adverts) (Blackie, 1901 [1900]) £100
OUT WITH GARIBALDI (blue boards) (Blackie, 1901 [1900]) £75
JOHN HAWKE'S FORTUNE (paper cover) (Chapman & Hall: 'Young People's Library' series, 1901) £65
WITH BULLER IN NATAL (blue boards) (Blackie, 1901) £65
QUEEN VICTORIA (purple boards) (Blackie, 1901) £50
TO HERAT AND CABUL (blue boards) (Blackie, 1902 [1901]) £70
WITH ROBERTS TO PRETORIA (red boards) (Blackie, 1902 [1901]) £160
AT THE POINT OF THE BAYONET (green boards) (Blackie, 1902 [1901]) £150
IN THE HANDS OF THE CAVE DWELLERS (Blackie, 1903 [1902]) £150
THE TREASURE OF THE INCAS (green boards) (Blackie, 1903 [1902]) £75
WITH THE BRITISH LEGION (blue or green boards) (Blackie, 1903 [1902]) £75
WITH KITCHENER IN THE SOUDAN (red boards) (Blackie, 1903 [1902]) £65
THROUGH THREE CAMPAIGNS (red boards) (Blackie, 1904 [1903]) £65
WITH THE ALLIES TO PEKIN (green boards) (Blackie, 1904 [1903]) £65
BY CONDUCT AND COURAGE (red boards; with either 381 or 384 numbered pages) (Blackie, 1905 [1904]) £100
GALLANT DEEDS (white or grey boards) (Chambers, 1905) £65
IN THE HANDS OF THE MALAYS (red boards) (Blackie, 1905) £65
AMONG THE BUSHRANGERS (adapted from 'A Final Reckoning') (Blackie, 1906) £40
THE YOUNG CAPTAIN (adapted from 'With Clive in India') (Blackie, 1906) £40
THE TWO PRISONERS (adapted from 'A Soldier's Daughter') (Blackie, 1906 [1905]) £40
CAST ASHORE (adapted from 'Under Drake's Flag') (Blackie, 1906) £35
CHARLIE MARRYAT (adapted from 'With Clive in India') (Blackie, 1906) £35
CORNET WALTER (adapted from 'Orange and Green') (Blackie, 1906) £35
A HIGHLAND CHIEF (adapted from 'In Freedom's Cause') (Blackie, 1906) £35
AN INDIAN RAID (adapted from 'Redskin and Cowboy') (Blackie, 1906) £35
A SOLDIER'S DAUGHTER (red, blue or green boards) (Blackie, 1906 [1905]) £65

HERGÉ

Belgium author-illustrator. Born: George Rémi in Brussels in 1907. In 1925, he joined the Catholic newspaper, Le XX Siècle, for which he created the boy reporter-cum-detective, Tintin. The character first appeared in the children's supplement, Le Petit Vingtième, in 1929, in a story entitled 'Tintin au Pays de Soviets'. This was published in book form in 1930, and was followed by another 22 adventures up to 1976. The first of the books to appear in English were The Crab with the Golden Claws and King Ottokar's Sceptre, which were published simultaneously in 1958. Died: 1983.

Prices are for books in Very Good condition.

'Tintin' Story Books

THE CRAB WITH THE GOLDEN CLAWS (Methuen, 1958) £25
KING OTTOKAR'S SCEPTRE (Methuen, 1958) £25
THE SECRET OF THE UNICORN (Methuen, 1959) £25
RED RACKHAM'S TREASURE (Methuen, 1959) £25
DESTINATION MOON (Methuen, 1959) £25
EXPLORERS ON THE MOON (Methuen, 1959) £25
THE CALCULUS AFFAIR (Methuen, 1960) £25

THE RED SEA SHARKS (Methuen, 1960)..£25
THE SHOOTING STAR (Methuen, 1961) £20
TINTIN IN TIBET (Methuen, 1962) £20
THE SEVEN CRYSTAL BALLS (Methuen, 1962) £15
PRISONERS OF THE SUN (Methuen, 1962) £15
THE CASTAFIORE EMERALD (Methuen, 1963) £20
THE BLACK ISLAND (Methuen, 1966) £25
FLIGHT 714 (Methuen, 1968) £15
CIGARS OF THE PHARAOH (Methuen, 1971) £15
THE LAND OF BLACK GOLD (Methuen, 1972) £15
THE BROKEN EAR (Methuen, 1975) £15
TINTIN AND THE PICAROS (Methuen, 1976) £10
TINTIN IN AMERICA (Methuen, 1978) £10
THE BLUE LOTUS (Methuen, 1983) £10

'Tintin' Film Books
TINTIN AND THE GOLDEN FLEECE (Methuen, 1965) £25
TINTIN AND THE BLUE ORANGES (Methuen, 1967)..£20
TINTIN AND THE LAKE OF SHARKS (Methuen, 1973) £15

Other 'Tintin' Books
THE MAKING OF TINTIN I (Methuen, 1983) £15
THE MAKING OF TINTIN II (Methuen, 1985) £10

'Jo, Zette and Jocko' Books
THE VALLEY OF THE COBRAS (Methuen, 1986)..£15
THE STRATOSHIP H22. PART ONE: MR PUMP'S LEGACY (Methuen, 1987) £15
THE STRATOSHIP H22. PART TWO: DESTINATION NEW YORK (Methuen, 1987) £15

HERRIOT, James

British author. Born: James Alfred Wight in Sunderland in 1916. Studied at Glasgow Veterinary College, subsequently joining a practice in the Yorkshire Dales in 1937. Best known for his enormously successful books of 'rural reminiscences', including *If Only They Could Talk* (1970) and *The Lord God Made Them All* (1981), but also wrote a handful of children's works. Died: 1995.

Prices are for books in Very Good condition with dustjackets where applicable.

IF ONLY THEY COULD TALK (Joseph, 1970) £40
IT SHOULDN'T HAPPEN TO A VET (Joseph, 1972) £20
LET SLEEPING VETS LIE (Joseph, 1973)..£15
VET IN HARNESS (Joseph, 1974) £10
ALL CREATURES GREAT AND SMALL (omnibus) (Joseph, 1975)..£15
VETS MIGHT FLY (Joseph, 1976) £10
ALL THINGS BRIGHT AND BEAUTIFUL (omnibus) (Joseph, 1976) £10
VET IN A SPIN (Joseph, 1977)..£10
ALL THINGS WISE AND WONDERFUL (omnibus) (Joseph, 1978) £10
JAMES HERRIOT'S YORKSHIRE (Joseph, 1979) £10
THE LORD GOD MADE THEM ALL (Joseph, 1981) £10
THE BEST OF JAMES HERRIOT (Joseph, 1982) £10
MOSES THE KITTEN (illustrated by Peter Barrett) (Joseph, 1984) £15
ONLY ONE WOOF (illustrated by Peter Barrett) (Joseph, 1985) £15
JAMES HERRIOT'S DOG STORIES (Joseph, 1986) £10
THE CHRISTMAS DAY KITTEN (illustrated by Ruth Brown) (Joseph, 1986) £20
BONNY'S BIG DAY (Joseph, 1987) £15
THE MARKET SQUARE DOG (Joseph, 1989)..£15
OSCAR, CAT-ABOUT-TOWN (illustrated by Ruth Brown) (Joseph, 1990) £20
SMUDGE'S DAY OUT (illustrated by Ruth Brown) (Joseph, 1991) £15
BLOSSOM COMES HOME (illustrated by Ruth Brown) (Joseph, 1991) £15
EVERY LIVING THING (Joseph, 1992) £10
JAMES HERRIOT'S FAVOURITE DOG STORIES (Joseph, 1992) £10
JAMES HERRIOT'S CAT STORIES (Joseph, 1994) £10

HILL, Eric

British author. Born: London, 1927. Creator of the popular 'Spot' series.

Prices are for books in Very Good condition with dustjackets where applicable.

'Spot' Books
WHERE'S SPOT ? (Heinemann, 1980) £5
SPOT'S FIRST WALK (Heinemann, 1981) £5
SPOT'S BIRTHDAY PARTY (Heinemann, 1982) £5
SPOT'S FIRST CHRISTMAS (Heinemann, 1983) £5

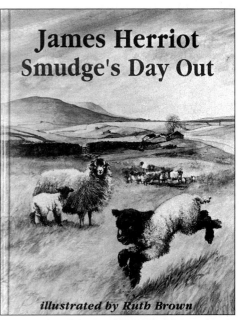

As well as his well-known volumes of memoirs, Yorkshire vet James Herriot wrote a series of children's picture books illustrated by Ruth Brown. Issued in pictorial boards, these charming volumes are now valued at £15-£20 for Very Good copies.

SPOT'S BUSY YEAR (colouring book) (Putnam, 1983) £5
SPOT TELLS THE TIME (colouring book) (Putnam, 1983) £5
SPOT'S ALPHABET (colouring book) (Putnam, 1983) £5
SPOT LEARNS TO COUNT(colouring book) (Putnam, 1983) £5
HERE'S SPOT (Heinemann, 1984) £5
SPOT GOES TO SCHOOL (Heinemann, 1984) £5
PLAY WITH SPOT (Heinemann, 1985) £5
SPOT GOES TO THE BEACH (Heinemann, 1985)..£5

HILL, Eric

SPOT AT THE FAIR (Heinemann, 1985)..£5
SPOT AT THE FARM (Heinemann, 1985)...£5
SPOT GOES ON HOLIDAY (Heinemann, 1985)..£5
SPOT GOES TO THE CIRCUS (Heinemann, 1986) £4
SPOT LOOKS AT COLOURS (Heinemann, 1986) £4
SPOT LOOKS AT SHAPES (Heinemann, 1986) £4
SPOT'S FIRST WORDS (Heinemann, 1986) £4
SPOT GOES TO THE FARM (Heinemann, 1987) £4
SPOT'S FIRST PICNIC (Heinemann, 1987) £4
SPOT'S HOSPITAL VISIT (Heinemann, 1987) £4
SPOT'S FIRST EASTER (Heinemann, 1988) £4
SPOT COUNTS FROM ONE TO TEN (Heinemann, 1989) £4
SPOT LOOKS AT OPPOSITES (Heinemann, 1989) £4
SPOT LOOKS AT THE WEATHER (Heinemann, 1989) £4
SPOT'S BABY SISTER (Heinemann, 1989)..£4
SPOT SLEEPS OVER (Heinemann, 1990) £3
SPOT GOES TO THE PARK (Heinemann, 1991) £3
SPOT IN THE GARDEN (Heinemann, 1991) £3
SPOT'S TOY BOX (Heinemann, 1991) £3
SPOT AT HOME (Heinemann, 1991) £3

'Peek-A-Book' Series for Children; Self-Illustrated :

NURSEY RHYMES (Heinemann, 1982) £4
OPPOSITES (Heinemann, 1982) £4
ANIMALS (Heinemann, 1982)..£4
WHO DOES WHAT ? (Heinemann, 1982) £4
BABY ANIMALS (Heinemann, 1984) £4
MORE OPPOSITES (Heinemann, 1984) £4

'Baby Bear Story-Book' Series For Children; Self-Illustrated :

AT HOME, (Heinemann, 1983) £4
MY PETS (Heinemann, 1983) £4
THE PARK (Heinemann,1983) £4
UP THERE (Heinemann, 1983) £4
BABY BEAR'S BEDTIME (Heinemann, 1984) £4
GOOD MORNING, BABY BEAR (Heinemann, 1984) £4

HILL, Lorna

British author. Born: Durham, 1902. *A Dream of Sadler's Wells* (1950) was the first of a long series of interlocking ballet novels based on her daughter's training at the Sadler Wells Ballet School (now Royal Ballet School). Her realistic picture of family life, *The Vicarage Children*, appeared in 1961. Died: 1991.

Prices are for books in Very Good condition with dustjackets where applicable.

'Marjorie' Books

MARJORIE AND CO (Art and Educational, 1948) £25
MARJORIE AND CO (Nelson, 1958) £10
STOLEN HOLIDAY (Art and Educational, 1948)...£25
STOLEN HOLIDAY (Nelson, 1956) £10
BORDER PEEL (Art and Educational, 1950) £30
BORDER PEEL (Nelson, 1956) £15
CASTLE IN NORTHUMBRIA (Burke, 1953) £20
NO MEDALS FOR GUY (Nelson, 1962) £10
NORTHERN LIGHTS (paperback) (Privately published, 1999)..£15

'Patience' Books

THEY CALLED HER PATIENCE (Burke, 1951) £20
THEY CALLED HER PATIENCE (Burke, 1958) £10
IT WAS ALL THROUGH PATIENCE (Burke, 1952) £20
IT WAS ALL THROUGH PATIENCE (Burke, 1961) £10
SO GUY CAME TOO (Burke, 1954) £15
SO GUY CAME TOO (Burke, 1959) £10
THE FIVE SHILLING HOLIDAY (Burke, 1955) £15
THE FIVE SHILLING HOLIDAY (Burke, 1960) £10

'Sadler's Wells' Books

A DREAM OF SADLER'S WELLS (Evans, 1950) £15
VERONICA AT THE WELLS (Evans, 1951) £15
MASQUERADE AT THE WELLS (Evans, 1952)..£15
NO CASTANETS AT THE WELLS (Evans, 1953)..£15
JANE LEAVES THE WELLS (Evans, 1953) £15

ELLA AT THE WELLS (Evans, 1954) £15
RETURN TO THE WELLS (Evans, 1955) £15
ROSANNA JOINS THE WELLS (Evans, 1956) £15
PRINCIPAL ROLE (Evans, 1957) £15
SWAN FEATHER (Evans, 1958) £15
DRESS-REHEARSAL (Evans, 1959) £15
BACK-STAGE (Evans, 1960) £15
VICKI IN VENICE (Evans, 1962) £20
THE SECRET (Evans, 1964)...£25

'Dancing Peel' Books

DANCING PEEL (Nelson, 1954) £15
DANCER'S PEEL (Nelson, 1955) £15
THE LITTLE DANCER (Nelson, 1956) £15
DANCER IN THE WINGS (Nelson, 1958) £20
DANCER IN DANGER (Nelson, 1960) £20
DANCER ON HOLIDAY (Nelson, 1962) £20

'Vicarage Children' Books

THE VICARAGE CHILDREN (Evans, 1961) £20
MORE ABOUT MANDY (Evans, 1963) £20
THE VICARAGE CHILDREN IN SKYE (Evans, 1966) £20

HOBAN, Russell

American author, resident in Britain since 1969. Born: Russell Conwell Hoban in Lansdale, Pennsylvania, in 1925. Studied at the Philadelphia Museum School of Industrial Art, subsequently working as an illustrator and advertising copywriter. As well as his many children's books — several of them illustrated by his first wife, Lillian — he has written a number of adult novels, notably *The Lion of Boaz-Jachin and Jachin-Boaz* (1973) and *Riddley Walker* (1980).

Prices are for books in Very Good condition with dustjackets where applicable.

WHAT DOES IT DO AND HOW DOES IT WORK? Power Shovel, Dump Truck and Other Heavy Machines (non-fiction)
  (Harper, U.S., 1959) £60
THE ATOMIC SUBMARINE: A Practice Combat Patrol Under the Sea (non-fiction) (Harper, U.S., [1960]) £20
BEDTIME FOR FRANCES (illustrated by Garth Williams) (Harper, U.S., [1960]) £45
HERMAN THE LOSER (illustrated by Lillian Hoban) (Harper, U.S., 1961)......................£25
THE SONG IN MY DRUM (illustrated by Lillian Hoban) (Harper, U.S., 1962) £25
LONDON MEN AND ENGLISH MEN (illustrated by Lillian Hoban) (Harper, U.S., 1962) £25
SOME SNOW SAID HELLO (illustrated by Lillian Hoban) (Harper, U.S., [1963]) £25
THE SORELY TRYING DAY (illustrated by Lillian Hoban) (Harper, U.S., 1964) £25
A BABY SISTER FOR FRANCES (illustrated by Lillian Hoban) (Harper, U.S., 1964) £30
BREAD AND JAM FOR FRANCES (illustrated by Lillian Hoban) (Harper, U.S., 1964) £30
NOTHING TO DO (illustrated by Lillian Hoban) (Harper, U.S., 1964) £20
TOM AND THE TWO HANDLES (illustrated by Lillian Hoban) (Harper, U.S., 1965) £20
WHAT HAPPENED WHEN JACK AND DAISY TRIED TO FOOL THE TOOTH FAIRIES (Four Winds Press, U.S., 1965) £30
GOODNIGHT (verse; illustrated by Lillian Hoban) (Norton, U.S., 1966) £20
HENRY AND THE MONSTROUS DIN (illustrated by Lillian Hoban) (Harper, U.S., 1966)........£20
THE LITTLE BRUTE FAMILY (illustrated by Lillian Hoban) (Macmillan, U.S., 1966) £35
SAVE MY PLACE (illustrated by Lillian Hoban) (Norton, U.S., 1967)......................£15
CHARLIE THE TRAMP (illustrated by Lillian Hoban) (Four Winds Press, U.S., 1967) £25
THE MOUSE AND HIS CHILD (illustrated by Lillian Hoban) (Harper, U.S., 1967) £45
THE PEDALLING MAN and Other Poems (illustrated by Lillian Hoban) (Norton, U.S., 1968)....£20
A BIRTHDAY FOR FRANCES (illustrated by Lillian Hoban) (Harper, U.S., 1968) £30
THE STONE DOLL OF SISTER BRUTE (illustrated by Lillian Hoban) (Macmillan, U.S., 1968) ...£30
HARVEY'S HIDEOUT (illustrated by Lillian Hoban) (Parents' Magazine Press, U.S., 1969) ...£20
BEST FRIENDS FOR FRANCES (illustrated by Lillian Hoban) (Harper, U.S., 1969) £25
THE MOLE FAMILY'S CHRISTMAS (illustrated by Lillian Hoban) (Parents' Magazine Press, U.S., 1969)....£20
UGLY BIRD (illustrated by Lillian Hoban) (Macmillan, U.S., 1969) £20
A BARGAIN FOR FRANCES (illustrated by Lillian Hoban) (Harper, U.S., 1970) £30
EMMET OTTER'S JUG-BAND CHRISTMAS (Parents' Magazine Press, U.S., 1971).................£20
EGG THOUGHTS and Other Frances Songs (Harper, U.S., 1972) £25
THE SEA-THING CHILD (illustrated by Brom Hoban) (Gollancz, 1972) £20
LETITIA RABBIT'S STRING SONG (illustrated by Mary Chalmers) (Coward McCann, U.S., 1973) £20
HOW TOM BEAT CAPTAIN NAJORK AND HIS HIRED SPORTSMEN (illustrated by Quentin Blake) (Cape, 1974)....£25
TEN WHAT? A Mystery Counting Book (illustrated by Sylvie Selig) (Cape, 1974) £20
DINNER AT ALBERTA'S (illustrated by James Marshall) (Crowell, U.S., 1975) £20
CROCODILE AND PIERROT (illustrated by Sylvie Selig) (Cape, 1975) £20
A NEAR THING FOR CAPTAIN NAJORK (illustrated by Quentin Blake) (Cape, 1975) £25
ARTHUR'S NEW POWER (illustrated by Byron Barton) (Crowell, U.S., 1978) £15
THE TWENTY ELEPHANT RESTAURANT (illustrated by Emily Arnold McCully) (Atheneum, U.S., 1978) ...£20

A BIRTHDAY FOR FRANCES

by Russell Hoban
Pictures by Lillian Hoban

*The first edition of Russell Hoban's **A Birthday for Frances**. Like all his early books, this appeared in the United States only.*

JIM FROG (illustrated by Martin Baynton) (Walker, 1983) £10
CHARLIE MEADOWS (illustrated by Martin Baynton) (Walker, 1984) £12
LAVINIA BAT (illustrated by Martin Baynton) (Walker, 1985) £15
THE RAIN DOOR (illustrated by Quentin Blake) (Gollancz, 1986) £20
THE MARZIPAN PIG (illustrated by Quentin Blake) (Cape, 1986) £20
JIM HEDGEHOG'S SUPERNATURAL CHRISTMAS (Clarion Books, U.S., 1992) £10
M.O.L.E. (Much Overworked Little Earthmover) (illustrated by Jan Pienkowski) (Cape, 1993) £15
A BARGAIN FOR FRANCES (illustrated by Lilian Hoban) (HarperCollins, U.S., 1998) £5

HOCKNEY, David

British artist. Born: Bradford, 1937. Studied Bradford Grammar School and the Royal College of Art. Best-known as a painter, he has also produced illustrations to a number of works, both adult and juvenile, often in limited as well as trade editions.

Price is for books in Very Good condition.

SIX FAIRY TALES FROM THE BROTHERS GRIMM (translated by Heiner Bastian) (Petersburg Press/OUP, [1970]) £40
SIX FAIRY TALES FROM THE BROTHERS GRIMM (translated by Heiner Bastian; limited to 575 numbered copies, signed by the artist) (Petersburg Press/Kasmin Gallery, [1970]) £2,750

HODGETTS, Sheila

British author, best known for the 'Toby Twirl' series of books published by Sampson Low Marston in the 1940s and '50s and illustrated by Edward Jeffrey.

Prices are for books in Very Good condition with dustjackets where applicable.

TOBY TWIRL ANNUALS (Sampson Low, 1946-1958) ....each £25
ONE MAGIC NIGHT (illustrated by Edward Jeffrey) (Sampson Low, [1947]) £25
THE SLEEPING CITY (illustrated by Edward Jeffrey) (Sampson Low, [1947]) £25
TOBY TWIRL RESCUES PRINCE APRICOT (illustrated by Edward Jeffrey) (Sampson Low, [1947]) £35
THE TOBY TWIRL STORY BOOK (illustrated by Edward Jeffrey) (Sampson Low, [1947]) £25
TOBY TWIRL AND THE MERMAID PRINCESS (Sampson Low, [1948]) £25
TOBY TWIRL LIBRARY (eight books; illustrated by Edward Jeffrey) (Sampson Low, [1949-1954])........each £20
SLEEPY TIME TALES (Sampson Low, [1951-]) £15
THE TOBY TWIRL COLOUR STRIP ADVENTURE BOOK (illustrated by Edward Jeffrey) (Sampson Low, [1952])..........£25
THE NEW TOBY TWIRL COLOUR STRIP ADVENTURE BOOK (illustrated by Edward Jeffrey) (Sampson Low, [1953]) £25
THE ADVENTURE TWINS COLOUR STRIP BOOK (illustrated by R. MacGillivray) (Sampson Low, [1953]) £15
THRILLS WITH THE ADVENTURE TWINS (illustrated by R. MacGillivray) (Sampson Low, [1954]) £15
TOBY TWIRL ON DAPPLE HEATH (strip book; illustrated by Edward Jeffrey; card covers) (Sampson Low, [1954]).........£25
TOBY TWIRL AND THE TALKING POODLE (illustrated by Edward Jeffrey) (Sampson Low, [1954]).............£25
THE ADVENTURE TWINS COLOUR STRIP BOOK (illustrated by R. MacGillivray) (Sampson Low, [1955]) £15
THE NEW TOBY TWIRL COLOUR STRIP ADVENTURE BOOK (illustrated by Edward Jeffrey) (Sampson Low, [1955]) £15

HOFFMANN, Heinrich

German author-illustrator. Born: Frankfurt, 1809. Studied medicine, and began writing stories for the young patients at a lunatic asylum in which he worked. *Struwwelpeter* ('Shock-headed Peter'), his famous collection of child's fables, was first published under the title *Lustige Gesichten und drollige Bilder* ('Merry Stories and Funny Pictures') in 1845, an English translation published in Leipzig appearingthree years later. The book was a huge success, going through 100 editions in its first thirty years. Hoffmann wrote other picture books, but none enjoyed the same popularity. Died: 1894.

Prices are for books in Very Good condition.

THE ENGLISH STRUWWELPETER, or Pretty Stories and Funny Pictures for Little Children. Translated from the German (first English edition) (Leipzig, 1848) £4,000
DEAN'S SIXPENNY 'ENGLISH STRUWWELPETERS' (thirteen books: Nos. 1-9, 11-14) (Dean, [1859]).........................each £120
THE ENGLISH STRUWWELPETER, or Pretty Stories and Funny Pictures for Little Children (twelfth edition; printed on one side of the leaf only) (Friedrich Volckmar, Leipzig, [1860])............................£250
DER STRUWWELPETER: Oder Lustige Geschichten und Drollige Bilder Für Kinder von 3-6 Jahren (100th German edition; printed on one side of the leaf only; with an additional leaf 'zur hundersten Auflage') (Frankfurt, [1876]) £110
STRUWWELPETER, or Merry Stories and Funny Pictures (printed on one side of the leaf only) (Blackie, 1903) £80
THE ENGLISH STRUWWELPETER, or Pretty Stories and Funny Pictures (Routledge, [1909]) £75
STRUWWELPETER (printed on one side of the leaf only) (Blackie, [1928]) £60
THE LATIN STRUWWELPETER (translated by W.H.D. Rouse) (Blackie, 1934) £80
SLOVENLY PETER (translated by Mark Twain; limited to 1,500 copies) (Limited Editions Club, U.S., 1935) £400
DER STRUWWELPETER (Wiesbaden, [1950]) £60
STRUWWELPETER (illustrated by J. and A.G. Johnstone) (Gifford, 1950) £40
STRUWWELPETER (Blackie, [1960]) £30
PETRUS ERICIUS — STRUWWELPETER: Lepidse Historiolse ab Hugone Henrico Paoli Latinis Versibus Enarratae (Florentiae, [1960])...£30
KING NUT-CRACKER, or The Dream of Poor Reinhold: A Fairy Tale (translated by J.R. Planché) (London [printed in Leipzig], [1853]) £800

KING NUT-CRACKER AND THE POOR BOY, REINHOLD: A Christmas Story with Pictures
(translated by A.H.) (London, 1854)..£700
KING NUT-CRACKER (translated by J.R. Planché) ([1927]) £60
KINDERGARTEN TOYS and How to Use Them: A Practical Explanation of the First Six Gifts of Froebel's Kindergarten
(London, [1874])..£150
KINDERGARTEN TOYS and How to Use Them: A Practical Explanation of the First Six Gifts of Froebel's Kindergarten
(second edition) (London, [1877])..£80

'Struwwelpeter' Pastiches

THE EGYPTIAN STRUWWELPETER: Being the Struwwelpeter Papyrus, with full text and original vignettes from
the Vienna Papyri (H. Grevel, [1899])...£250
SWOLLEN-HEADED WILLIAM: A Satire upon the Emperor William II, founded upon H. Hoffmann's 'Struwwelpeter'.
Adapted by E.V. Lucas (illustrations adapted by G. Morrow) (Methuen, 1914) £60
THE MODERN STRUWWELPETER by Jan Struther (illustrated by E.H. Shepard) (Methuen, 1936) £200

'HOOD'S COMIC' ANNUALS

Popular British annual, edited by Tom Hood (1835-74), son of the poet, Thomas Hood (1799-1845). Tom Hood also wrote and illustrated many children's books, including *Fairy Realm* (1865), a selection of Perrault's fairy tales retold in verse.

Prices are for annuals in Very Good condition.

THE COMIC ANNUAL by Thomas Hood 1830-1842 ([1829-41])..each £50
THE COMIC ANNUAL by Thomas Hood 1843-1867 ([1842-66])..each £40
TOM HOOD'S COMIC ANNUAL 1868-1876 ([1867-1875] — no issue for 1869) ....each £35
HOOD'S COMIC ANNUAL 1877-1895 ([1876-94]) ....each £30
HOOD'S ANNUAL ([1895-1897]) ....each £25

HORWOOD, William

British author. Born: 1944. Began as an English teacher, then worked as a freelance journalist for the *Financial Times*, *Guardian* and *Reader's Digest*. Notable for his 'Duncton Wood' series and for his sequels to *The Wind in the Willows*.

Prices are for books in Very Good condition with dustjackets where applicable.

THE WILLOWS IN WINTER (illustrated by Patrick Benson) (HarperCollins, 1993) £20
TOAD TRIUMPHANT (illustrated by Patrick Benson) (HarperCollins, 1995) £15
THE WILLOWS AND BEYOND (HarperCollins, 1998) £15
WILLOWS AT CHRISTMAS (HarperCollins, 1999) £10

HUGHES, Richard

British author. Born: Richard Arthur Warren Hughes in Caterham, Surrey, in 1900. Best known for his adult novels, including *A High Wind in Jamaica* (1929) and *The Fox in the Attic* (1961), but also produced a handful of children's works. Died: 1976.

Prices are for books in Very Good condition with dustjackets where applicable.

BURIAL, AND THE DARK CHILD (limited to sixty copies) (Privately printed, 1930) £550
THE SPIDER'S PALACE and Other Stories (illustrated by George Charlton) (Chatto & Windus, 1931)...................£50
DON'T BLAME ME! and Other Stories (illustrated by Fritz Eichenberg) (Chatto & Windus, 1940) £25
GERTRUDE'S CHILD (illustrated by Rick Schreiter) (Quist, U.S., 1967) £15
THE WONDER DOG (illustrated by Antony Maitland) (Chatto & Windus: 'Collected Children's Stories' series, 1977) £10

HUGHES, Shirley

British author-illustrator. Born: West Kirby, the Wirral, in 1927. She trained at Liverpool Art School and the Ruskin School of Art, Oxford. Awarded Kate Greenaway Medal in 1977 and the Eleanor Farjeon Award in 1984. Has illustrated numerous young children's books as well as her own, where the emphasis is on the richness and detail of the pictures. Awarded the OBE in 1999.

Prices are for books in Very Good condition with dustjackets where applicable.

Books Written and Illustrated by Shirley Hughes

'Lucy and Tom' Books

LUCY AND TOM'S DAY (boards) (Gollancz, 1960) £45
LUCY AND TOM GO TO SCHOOL (boards) (Gollancz, 1973)...£40
LUCY AND TOM AT THE SEASIDE (boards) (Gollancz, 1976) £40
LUCY AND TOM'S CHRISTMAS (boards) (Gollancz, 1981) £30
LUCY AND TOM'S ABC (boards) (Gollancz, 1984) £20
LUCY AND TOM'S 1,2,3 (boards) (Gollancz, 1987) £20
LUCY AND TOM'S WORLD (boards) (Gollancz, 1993) £20

'Alfie' Books

ALFIE GETS IN FIRST (boards) (The Bodley Head, 1981) £30
ALFIE'S FEET (boards) (The Bodley Head,1982) £20

Alfie and the Birthday Surprise (1997) is the most recent book to feature Shirley Hughes' mischievous little toddler.

ALFIE GIVES A HAND (boards) (The Bodley Head, 1983...£20
AN EVENING AT ALFIE'S (boards) (The Bodley Head, 1984) £20
THE BIG ALFIE AND ANNIE ROSE STORYBOOK (The Bodley Head, 1988) £15
ALFIE'S ALPHABET (boards) (The Bodley Head, 1988)...£15
THE BIG ALFIE OUT OF DOORS STORYBOOK (Walker, 1989) £15
THE ALFIE COLLECTION (The Bodley Head, 1992) £15
THE ALFIE TREASURY (The Bodley Head, 1994)...£15
ALFIE AND THE BIRTHDAY SURPRISE (The Bodley Head, 1997) £10

'Charlie Moon' Books
HERE COMES CHARLIE MOON (The Bodley Head, 1980) £10
CHARLIE MOON AND THE BIG BONANZA BUST UP (The Bodley Head, 1985)...£10

'Chips' Books
CHIPS AND JESSIE (The Bodley Head, 1985) £10
ANOTHER HELPING OF CHIPS (The Bodley Head, 1986)...£10

Others
THE TROUBLE WITH JACK (The Bodley Head, 1970) £15
SALLY'S SECRET (The Bodley Head, 1973) £15
HELPERS (The Bodley Head, 1975)...£15
BEING TOGETHER (boards) (Walker, 1977) £10

HUGHES, Shirley

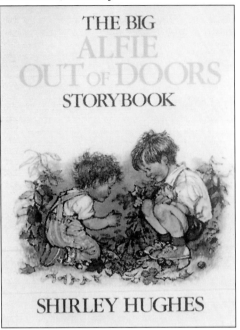

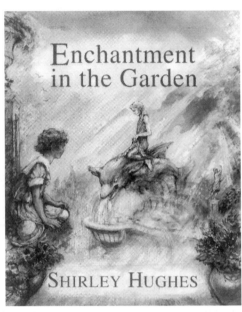

The Big Alfie Out of Doors Storybook (1989) contains some of Hughes' best artwork. Very Good copies are valued at £15.

Enchantment in the Garden (1996) is set in Italy and was inspired by Shirley Hughes' many trips to that country.

DOGGER (boards) (The Bodley Head, 1977) £25
IT'S TOO FRIGHTENING FOR ME ! (Hodder and Stoughton, 1977)........................£10
MOVING MOLLY (boards) (The Bodley Head, 1978) £15
UP AND UP (The Bodley Head, 1979) £15
OVER THE MOON: A BOOK OF SAYINGS (Faber, 1980) £15
NOISY (boards) (Walker, 1985)..£5
WHEN WE WENT TO THE PARK (boards) (Walker, 1985)...................................£5
BATHWATER'S HOT (boards) (Walker, 1985) £5
TWO SHOES, NEW SHOES (boards) (Walker, 1986) £5
COLOURS (boards) (Walker, 1986) £5
ALL SHAPES AND SIZES (boards) (Walker, 1986)..£5
OUT AND ABOUT (boards) (Walker, 1988) £5
THE BIG CONCRETE LORRY (boards) (Walker, 1989)...£5
ANGEL MAE (boards) (Walker, 1989)..£5
MOTYN (boards) (CLC, 1990) £5
THE SNOW LADY (boards) (Walker, 1990) £5
WHEELS (boards) (Walker, 1991)..£5
LLYR MAWR STRAEON ALFIE YN YR AWYR AGORED (boards) (CLC,1992) £5
BOUNCING (boards) (Walker, 1993)..£5
GIVING (boards) (Walker, 1993) £5
STORIES BY FIRELIGHT (Lothrop, 1993) £5
STRAEON YNG NGOLAU'R TAN (boards) (CLC, 1993) £5
CHATTING (boards) (Walker,1994) £5
HIDING (boards) (Walker, 1994) £5
RHYMES FOR ANNIE ROSE (The Bodley Head, 1995) £10
ENCHANTMENT IN THE GARDEN (The Bodley Head, 1996) £10
TALES OF TROTTER STREET (Walker, 1996) £10
THE NURSERY COLLECTION (Walker, 1997) £10
PLAYING (Walker, 1997) £5
THE LION AND THE UNICORN (Cape, 1998) £10
ABEL'S MOON (The Bodley Head, 1999)..£10

Books Illustrated by Shirley Hughes
THE HILL WAR by Olivia Fitzroy (Collins, 1950)..£25
FOURWINDS ISLAND by Vega Stewart (Collins, 1951)..£25
GREAT-UNCLE TOBY by John R. Hale (Faber, 1951) £25
WORLD'S END WAS HOME by Nan Chauncy (OUP, 1952) £25

FOLLOW THE FOOTPRINTS by William Mayne (OUP, 1953) £30
A WEEK OF STORIES by Doris Rust (Faber, 1953)...£20
THE JOURNEY OF JOHNNY REW by Anne Barrett (Collins, 1954) £20
ALL THROUGH THE NIGHT by Rachel Field (Collins, 1954)...£20
THE WORLD UPSIDE DOWN by William Mayne (OUP, 1954)...£30
A STORY A DAY by Doris Rust (Faber, 1954) £15
THE BELL FAMILY by Noel Streatfeild (Collins, 1954)..£20
THE BOYS' COUNTRY BOOK by John Moore (Collins, 1955) £10
 ALL SORTS OF DAYS by Doris Rust (Faber, 1955) £10
LOST LORRENDEN by Mabel Esther Allan (Blackie, 1956) £10
MR PUNCH'S CAP by Kathleen Fidler (Lutterworth, 1956) £10
THE MAN OF THE HOUSE by Allan Campbell Maclean (Collins, 1956) £10
WILLIAM AND THE LORRY by Diana Ross (Faber, 1956) £15
THE ANIMALS AT NUMBER ELEVEN by Doris Rust (Faber, 1956) £10
GUNS IN THE WILD by Ian Serraillier (Heinemann, 1956)...£20
MYSTERY ON RAINBOW ISLAND by Dorothy Clewes (Collins, 1957)...£20
COME TO THE FAIR. Edited by Barbara Ireson (Faber 1957) £10
THE ANIMALS AT ROSE COTTAGE by Doris Rust (Faber, 1957) £10
KATY AT HOME by Ian Serraillier (Heinemann, 1957)...£20
THE MYSTERY OF THE JADE-GREEN CADILLAC by Dorothy Clewes (Collins, 1958) £10
THE BOY AND THE DONKEY by Diana Pullein-Thomson (Collins, 1958) £10
MIXED-MUDDLY ISLAND by Doris Rust (Faber, 1958) £10
KATY AT SCHOOL by Ian Serraillier, based on a story by Susan Coolidge (Heinemann, 1959) £20
NOEL STREATFEILD'S BALLET ANNUAL by Noel Streatfeild (Collins, 1959) £10
THE LOST TOWER TREASURE by Dorothy Clewes (Collins, 1960) £10
ROLLING ON by Mary Cockett (Methuen, 1960) £10
FELL FARM CAMPERS by Marjorie Lloyd (paperback) (Penguin, 1960) £5
NEW TOWN: A Story About the Bell Family by Noel Streatfeild (Collins, 1960) £15
FLOWERING SPRING by Elfrida Vipont (OUP, 1960) £10
THE SINGING STRINGS by Dorothy Clewes (Collins, 1961) £10
MARY ANN GOES TO HOSPITAL by Mary Crockett (Methuen, 1961) £10
FAIRY TALES by Hans Andersen (translated by Caroline Peachey) (Blackie, 1961) £30
THE BRONZE CHRYSANTHEMUM by Sheena Porter (OUP, 1961) £10
PLAIN JANE by Barbara Softly (Macmillan, 1961) £10
THE PAINTED GARDEN by Noel Streatfeild (paperback) (Puffin, 1961) £5
COTTAGE BY THE LOCK by Mary Crockett (Methuen, 1962)...£10
MY NAUGHTY LITTLE SISTER by Dorothy Edwards (Methuen, 1962)...£30
MY NAUGHTY LITTLE SISTER'S FRIENDS by Dorothy Edwards (Methuen, 1962) £25
PLACE MILL by Barbara Softly (Macmillan, 1962) £10
THE SIGN OF THE UNICORN by Mabel Esther Allan (Dent, 1963)..£10
THE SHINTY BOYS by Margaret Macpherson (Collins, 1963) £10
TALES OF TIGGS FARM by Helen Morgan (Faber, 1963) £10
MEET MARY KATE by Helen Morgan (Faber, 1963) £10
WILLY IS MY BROTHER by Peggy Parish (Gollancz, 1963) £10
THE MERRY-GO-ROUND by Diana Ross (Lutterworth, 1963)...£15
FIONA ON THE FOURTEENTH FLOOR by Mabel Esther Allan (Dent, 1964)...£10
OPERATION SMUGGLE by Dorothy Clewes (Collins, 1964) £10
THE CAT AND MRS CARY by Doris Gates (Methuen, 1964) £10
STORIES FROM GRIMM by Roger Lancelyn Green (Blackie, 1964) £20
ROLLER SKATES by Ruth Sawyer (The Bodley Head, 1964) £10
A STONE IN A POOL by Barbara Softly (Macmillan, 1964) £10
JACKO AND OTHER STORIES by Jean Sutcliffe (The Bodley Head 1964) £10
TIM RABBIT'S DOZEN by Alison Uttley (Faber, 1964)...£25
TALES THE MUSES TOLD by Roger Lancelyn Green (The Bodley Head, 1965) £10
A DREAM OF DRAGONS by Helen Morgan (Faber, 1965) £10
LUCINDA'S YEAR OF JUBILEE by Ruth Sawyer (The Bodley Head, 1965)..£10
KATE AND THE FAMILY TREE by Margaret Storey (The Bodley Head, 1965) £10
THE TWELVE DANCING PRINCESSES by Margaret Storey (Nelson, 1965) £10
THE WITCH'S DAUGHTER by Nina Bawden (Gollancz,1966)...£25
LITTLE BEAR'S PONY by Donald Bisset (Benn, 1966)...£10
WAYLAND'S KEEP by Angela Bull (Collins, 1966) £10
FABER BOOK OF NURSERY STORIES by Barbara Ireson (Faber, 1966) £15
SATCHKIN PATCHKIN by Helen Morgan (Faber, 1966)..£10
SOMETHING TO DO by Septima (paperback) (Penguin, 1966) £5
THE SMALLEST DOLL by Margaret Storey (Faber, 1966) £10
THE SMALLEST BRIDESMAID by Margaret Storey (Faber, 1966) £10
WISH ON A PIG by Barbara Ward (Collins, 1966) £10
PORTERHOUSE MAJOR by Margaret J. Baker (Methuen, 1967)..£10
STORIES FOR SIX YEAR OLDS by Sara and Stephen Corrin (Faber, 1967) £10

HUGHES, Shirley

A DAY ON BIG O by Helen Cresswell (Benn, 1967)...£10
MARY KATE AND THE JUMBLE BEAR by Helen Morgan (Faber, 1967)....................................£10
THE WOOD STREET SECRET by Mabel Esther Allan (Methuen, 1968)...................................£10
FLUTES AND CYMBALS. Edited by Leonard Clark (The Bodley Head, 1968) £10
WHEN MY NAUGHTY LITTLE SISTER WAS GOOD by Dorothy Edwards (Methuen, 1968) £15
THE NEW TENANTS by Margaret Macpherson (Collins, 1968)...£10
ROBIN'S REAL ENGINE and Other Stories by William Mayne (Hamish Hamilton, 1968)..........£10
THE TOFFEE JOIN by William Mayne (Hamish Hamilton: 'Gazelle' series, 1968) £20
MRS PINNY AND THE BLOWING DAY by Helen Morgan (Faber, 1968) £10
HOME AND AWAY by Ann Thwaite (Brockhampton Press, 1968) £10
A CROWN FOR A QUEEN by Ursula Moray Williams (Hamish Hamilton, 1968).......................£10
THE TOYMAKER'S DAUGHTER by Ursula Moray Williams (Hamish Hamilton,1968).................£10
THE BICYCLE WHEEL by Ruth Ainsworth (Hamish Hamilton, 1969) £10
GOLDIE by Irma Chilton (Hamish Hamilton, 1969)...£10
ALL ABOUT MY NAUGHTY LITTLE SISTER by Dorothy Edwards (Methuen, 1969)..................£15
MOSHIE CAT: TRUE ADVENTURES OF A MALLORQUIN KITTEN by Helen Griffiths
    (Hutchinson,1969) £15
MRS PINNY AND THE SUDDEN SNOW by Helen Morgan (Faber, 1969) £10
CINDERELLA, OR THE LITTLE GLASS SLIPPER by Charles Perrault (Methuen, 1969) £20
THE RUTH AINSWORTH BOOK by Ruth Ainsworth (Heinemann, 1970) £20
THE WOOD STREET GROUP by Mabel Esther Allan (Methuen, 1970) £10
THE JADE- GREEN CADILLAC by Dorothy Clewes (Howard Baker, 1970) £10
ADVENTURE ON RAINBOW ISLAND by Dorothy Clewes (Howard Baker, 1970) £10
RAINBOW PAVEMENT by Helen Cresswell (Benn, 1970) £10
MORE NAUGHTY LITTLE SISTER STORIES by Dorothy Edwards (Methuen,1970) £10
EIGHT DAYS TO CHRISTMAS by Geraldine Kaye (Macmillan, 1970) £10
MARY KATE AND THE SCHOOL BUS by Helen Morgan (Faber, 1970)...................................£10
MORE FAIRY TALES by Caroline Peachey (Blackie, 1970) £10
THE THREE TOYMAKERS by Ursula Moray Williams (Hamish Hamilton,1970) £10
MALKIN'S MOUNTAIN by Ursula Moray Williams (Hamish Hamilton, 1970)...........................£10
THE WOOD STREET RIVALS by Mabel Esther Allan (Methuen, 1971) £15
SQUIB by Nina Bawden (Gollancz, 1971)..£15
STORIES FOR EIGHT YEAR OLDS by Sara and Stephen Corrin (Faber, 1971) £10
THE LITTLE CAT THAT COULD NOT SLEEP by Frances Margaret Fox (Faber, 1971) £10
THE LOST ANGEL by Elizabeth Goudge (Hodder & Stoughton,1971) £10
FREDERICO by Helen Griffiths (Hutchinson, 1971) £10
MOTHER FARTHING'S LUCK by Helen Morgan (Faber, 1971)..£10
ROBBIE'S MOB by Jo Rice (World's Work, 1971) £10
THE SMELL OF PRIVET by Barbara Sleigh (Hutchinson, 1971) £10
THE LITTLE BROOMSTICK by Mary Stewart (Brockhampton Press, 1971)............................£10
DANCING DAY by Robina Beccles Willson (Benn, 1971) £10
HOSPITAL DAY by Leila Berg (Macmillan, 1972)..£10
L'ARC EN CIEL by Helen Cresswell (Benn, 1972)..£10
LES JEUNES CORSAIRS by Helen Cresswell (Benn, 1972)...£10
MOTHER'S HELP by Sara Dickinson (Collins, 1972) £10
GINGER by Geraldine Kaye (Macmillan, 1972) £10
THE FIRST MARGARET MAHY STORYBOOK by Margaret Mahy (Dent, 1972) £10
MRS PINNY AND THE SALTY SEA DAY by Helen Morgan (Faber, 1972) £10
THE THIRTEEN DAYS OF CHRISTMAS by Jenny Overton (Faber, 1972) £10
THE HOUSE IN THE SQUARE by Joan G. Robinson (Collins, 1972) £10
ANOTHER LUCKY DIP by Ruth Ainsworth (paperback) (Puffin, 1973) £5
THE WOOD STREET HELPERS by Mabel Esther Allan (Methuen, 1973) £10
STORIES FOR FIVE YEAR OLDS by Sara and Stephen Corrin (Faber, 1973) £10
THE HOLLYWELL FAMILY by Margaret Kornitzer (The Bodley Head, 1973) £10
THE SECOND MARGARET MAHY STORYBOOK by Margaret Mahy (Dent, 1973)....................£10
THE PHANTOM FISHERBOY : TALES OF MYSTERY AND MAGIC by Ruth Ainsworth (Deutsch, 1974)........£10
STORIES FOR UNDER FIVES by Sara and Stephen Corrin (Faber, 1974).............................£10
MISS HENDY'S HOUSE by Joan Drake (Brockhampton, Press, 1974) £10
MY NAUGHTY LITTLE SISTER AND BAD HARRY by Dorothy Edwards (Methuen, 1974) £10
THE GAUNTLET FAIR by Alison Farthing (Chatto & Windus, 1974) £10
AWAY FROM WOOD STREET by Mabel Esther Allan (Methuen, 1975) £10
HAZY MOUNTAIN by Donald Bisset (boards) (Kestrel, 1975) £5
THE THIRD MARGARET MAHY STORYBOOK by Magaret Mahy (Dent, 1975) £10
PETER PAN AND WENDY by J.M. Barrie (Hodder & Stoughton, 1976) £15
MY NAUGHTY LITTLE SISTER GOES FISHING by Dorothy Edwards (Methuen, 1976) £15
TATTERCOATS AND OTHER FOLK TALES by Winifred Finlay (Kaye & Ward, 1976) £10
THE SNAKE CROOK by Ruth Tomalin (Faber, 1976) £10
THE NOEL STREATFEILD BIRTHDAY STORY BOOK by Noel Streatfeild, John Pudney and others
    (illustrated by Shirley Hughes and others) (Dent, 1976) £15

MAKE HAY WHILE THE SUN SHINES by Alison M. Abel (Faber, 1977) £15
THE PHANTOM ROUNDABOUT by Ruth Ainsworth (Deutsch,1977) £10
DONKEY DAYS by Helen Cresswell (Benn, 1977) £10
MY NAUGHTY LITTLE SISTER AND BAD HARRY'S RABBIT by Dorothy Edwards (Methuen, 1977) £15
A THRONE FOR SESAME by Helen Young (Deutsch, 1977) £10
MORE STORIES FOR SEVEN YEAR OLDS by Sara and Stephen Corrin (Faber, 1978) £10
POTTLE PIG by Nancy Northcote (Kaye & Ward, 1978) £10
THE TROUBLE WITH DRAGONS by Olive Selfridge (Addison-Wesley, 1978) £10
THE SNAILMAN by Barbara Sivers (Little Brown, 1978) £10
FROM SPRING TO SPRING: STORIES OF THE FOUR SEASONS by Alison Uttley (Faber, 1978)..................£20
STORIES FOR NINE YEAR OLDS by Sara and Stephen Corrins (Faber, 1979) £10
MY NAUGHTY LITTLE SISTER AT THE FAIR by Dorothy Edwards (Methuen, 1979) £15
BOGWOPPIT by Ursula Moray Williams (Hamish Hamilton, 1979) £10
THE PIRATE SHIP and Other Stories by Ruth Ainsworth (Heinemann, 1980) £10
WITCHDUST by Mary Welfare (Murray, 1980) £10
A CAT'S TALE by Rikki Cate (Methuen, 1982) £10
COUSIN PONS by Honore de Balzac (translated and with an introduction by Herbert J Hunt; in slipcase)
   (The Folio Society, 1984) £15
FIVE TO EIGHT by Dorothy Butler (The Bodley Head, 1985) £10
MAHY MAGIC by Margaret Mahy (Dent, 1986) £10
THE HORRIBLE STORY AND OTHERS by Margaret Mahy (Dent, 1987)...£25
THE SECRET GARDEN by Frances Hodgson Burnett (Gollancz, 1988) £15
THE BOY WHO BOUNCED AND OTHER MAGIC TALES by Magaret Mahy (paperback) (Puffin, 1988)...........£5
CHOCOLATE PORRIDGE and Other Stories by Magaret Mahy (paperback) (Puffin, 1989)............................£10
MY NAUGHTY LITTLE SISTER STORYBOOK by Dorothy Edwards (Methuen, 1991).....................................£10
RAINBOW TALES by Alison Uttley (Young Piper, 1991)...£10
THE GIRL WITH THE GREEN EAR by Magaret Mahy (Dent, 1991) £10
LITTLE WOMEN by Louisa May Alcott (paperback) (Puffin, 1994)..£10
THE RAILWAY CHILDREN by Edith Nesbit (Macmillan, 1994) £15
BABIES NEED BOOKS by Dorothy Butler (paperback) (Penguin,1995) £5
THE COMPLETE MY NAUGHTY LITTLE SISTER STORYBOOK by Dorothy Edwards (Methuen, 1997) £10

HUGHES, Ted

British poet. Born: Edward James Hughes in Mytholmroyd, Yorkshire, in 1930. Studied at Pembroke College, Cambridge. Married the poet, Sylvia Plath, in 1963. Appointed Poet Laureate in 1984. Although best known for his adult poetry, collected in volumes such as *The Hawk in the Rain* (1957) and *Lupercal* (1960), he has also written a number of books of children's verse, notably *Meet My Folks!* (1961) and *The Earth-Owl and Other Moon-People* (1963), as well as plays and stories for young readers. Perhaps his best-known children's work is the novel, *The Iron Man* (1968). Died: 1998.

Prices are for books in Very Good condition with dustjackets.

MEET MY FOLKS! (illustrated by George Adamson) (Faber, 1961) £75
HOW THE WHALE BECAME (illustrated by George Adamson) (Faber, 1963) £50
THE EARTH-OWL AND OTHER MOON-PEOPLE (verse; illustrated by R.A. Brandt) (Faber, 1963) £40
NESSIE THE MANNERLESS MONSTER (verse; illustrated by Gerald Rose) (Faber, 1964) £50
POETRY IN THE MAKING: An Anthology of Poems and Programmes from 'Listening and Writing'
   (Faber, 1967) £50
THE IRON MAN: A Story in Five Nights (illustrated by George Adamson) (Faber, 1968)................................£50
FIVE AUTUMN SONGS FOR CHILDREN'S VOICES (illustrated by Nina Carroll; limited to 500 copies: copies 3-11
   — verses in manuscript; with one illustration in watercolour) (Gilberton, 1968 [1970])..............................£250
FIVE AUTUMN SONGS FOR CHILDREN'S VOICES (illustrated by Nina Carroll; limited to 500 copies: copies 12-37
   — verses in manuscript) (Gilberton, 1968 [1970])..£200
FIVE AUTUMN SONGS FOR CHILDREN'S VOICES (illustrated by Nina Carroll; limited to 500 copies: copies 38-188
   — signed by the author) (Gilberton, 1968 [1970])..£75
FIVE AUTUMN SONGS FOR CHILDREN'S VOICES (illustrated by Nina Carroll; limited to 500 copies: copies 189-500
   — numbered) (Gilberton, 1968 [1970]) £40
SPRING, SUMMER, AUTUMN, WINTER (limited to 140 numbered copies, signed by the author)
   (Rainbow Press, 1974)..£175
SPRING, SUMMER, AUTUMN, WINTER (as 'Seasons Songs') (Faber, 1976) £25
EARTH MOON (limited to 200 numbered copies, signed by the author) (Rainbow Press,1976).......................£150
MOON BELLS AND OTHER POEMS (Chatto Windus, 1978) £15
UNDER THE NORTH STAR (verse; illustrated by Leonard Baskin) (Faber, 1981)..£25
WHAT IS THE TRUTH? A Farmyard Fable for the Young (illustrated by R.J. Lloyd) (Faber, 1984)................£20
FFANGS THE VAMPIRE BAT AND THE KISS OF TRUTH (illustrated by Chris Riddell) (Faber, 1986) £15
THE CAT AND THE CUCKOO (Sunstone Press, [1987])...£20
THE MERMAID'S PURSE (Faber, 1991) £15
THE IRON WOMAN (Faber, 1993)..£10
COLLECTED ANIMAL POEMS (four volumes) (Faber, 1994) ....the set £30
DREAM FIGHTER AND OTHER CREATION TALES (Faber, 1995) £10
SHAGGY AND SPOTTY (Faber, 1997)...£10

HUGHES, Thomas

British author. Born: Uffington, Berkshire, in 1822. Studied at Rugby School and Oriel College, Oxford. His experiences at Rugby provided the inspiration for his best-known work, *Tom Brown's Schooldays* (1857). A Christian Socialist, Hughes co-founded the Working Men's College in London and was elected to Parliament in 1865. Became a County Court judge in 1882. Died: 1896.

Prices are for books in Very Good condition.

TOM BROWN'S SCHOOLDAYS: By an Old Boy (blue cloth) (Macmillan, 1857) **£600**
TOM BROWN'S SCHOOLDAYS (early reprints) (Macmillan, 1857-60) **£100**
TOM BROWN'S SCHOOLDAYS (paperback) (Tauchnitz, Germany, 1858) **£50**
TOM BROWN'S SCHOOLDAYS (first illustrated edition; illustrated by Arthur Hughes and Sidney Prior Hall)
(Macmillan, 1869 [1868]) **£80**
TOM BROWN'S SCHOOLDAYS (illustrated by Edmund J. Sullivan) (Macmillan, 1896) **£40**
TOM BROWN'S SCHOOLDAYS (illustrated by E.H. Shepard) (Methuen, [1904]) **£100**
TOM BROWN'S SCHOOLDAYS (illustrated by Hugh Thomson) (Ginn, U.S., [1918]) **£35**
THE SCOURING OF THE WHITE HORSE (illustrated by Richard Doyle) (Macmillan, 1859) **£160**
TOM BROWN AT OXFORD (three volumes) (Macmillan, 1861) ....the set **£300**
NOTES FOR BOYS — AND THEIR FATHERS — ON MORALS, MIND AND MANNERS
(non-fiction) (Elliot Stock, 1885) **£25**
VACATION RAMBLES. Edited by his Daughter (non-fiction) (Macmillan, 1895) **£30**
EARLY MEMORIES FOR THE CHILDREN (non-fiction) (Thomas Burleigh, 1899) **£150**

HUNTER, Norman

British author. Born: Sydenham, Kent, in 1899. Studied at Beckenham School, subsequently becoming an advertising copywriter. Submitted stories to various publications, including *The Merry-Go-Round* and the *Boy's Own Paper*, as well as the BBC's *Children's Hour*, before launching the 'Professor Branestawm' series in 1933 with *The Incredible Adventures of Professor Branestawm*. Also wrote a number of books on conjuring. Died: 1995.

Prices are for books in Very Good condition with dustjackets where applicable.

'Professor Branestawm' Books

THE INCREDIBLE ADVENTURES OF PROFESSOR BRANESTAWM (illustrated by W. Heath Robinson)
(John Lane: The Bodley Head, 1933) **£150**
PROFESSOR BRANESTAWM'S TREASURE HUNT and Other Incredible Adventures (illustrated by James Arnold)
(John Lane: The Bodley Head, 1937) **£100**
STORIES OF PROFESSOR BRANESTAWM (illustrated by W. Heath Robinson; card wraps) (Arnold, [1939]) **£40**
THE PECULIAR TRIUMPH OF PROFESSOR BRANESTAWM (illustrated by George Adamson)
(The Bodley Head, 1970) **£35**
PROFESSOR BRANESTAWM UP THE POLE (illustrated by George Adamson) (The Bodley Head, 1972) **£25**
PROFESSOR BRANESTAWM'S DICTIONARY (illustrated by Derek Cousins) (The Bodley Head, 1973) **£20**
PROFESSOR BRANESTAWM'S GREAT REVOLUTION (The Bodley Head, 1974) **£20**
PROFESSOR BRANESTAWM'S COMPENDIUM OF CONUNDRUMS, RIDDLES, PUZZLES,
BRAIN-TWISTERS AND DOTTY DESCRIPTIONS (The Bodley Head, 1975) **£15**
PROFESSOR BRANESTAWM'S DO-IT-YOURSELF HANDBOOK (The Bodley Head, 1976) **£15**
PROFESSOR BRANESTAWM 'ROUND THE BEND (The Bodley Head, 1977) **£25**
PROFESSOR BRANESTAWM'S PERILOUS PUDDING (The Bodley Head, 1979) **£25**
THE BEST OF BRANESTAWM (The Bodley Head, 1980) **£15**
PROFESSOR BRANESTAWM'S POCKET MOTOR CAR (The Bodley Head, 1981) **£12**
PROFESSOR BRANESTAWM AND THE WILD LETTERS (The Bodley Head, 1981) **£12**
PROFESSOR BRANESTAWM'S MOUSE WAR (The Bodley Head, 1982) **£12**
PROFESSOR BRANESTAWM'S BUILDING BUST-UP (The Bodley Head, 1982) **£12**
PROFESSOR BRANESTAWM'S POCKET MOTOR CAR (contains 'Professor Branestawm's Pocket Motor Car' and
'Professor Branestawm and the Wild Letters'; paperback) (Puffin, 1982) **£5**
PROFESSOR BRANESTAWM'S CRUNCHY CROCKERY (The Bodley Head, 1983) **£10**
PROFESSOR BRANESTAWM'S HAIR-RAISING IDEA (The Bodley Head, 1983) **£10**
PROFESSOR BRANESTAWM'S MOUSE WAR (contains 'Professor Branestawm's Mouse War' and
'Professor Branestawm's Building Bust-Up'; paperback) (Puffin, 1984) **£5**
PROFESSOR BRANESTAWM'S CRUNCHY CROCKERY (contains 'Professor Branestawm's Crunchy Crockery' and
'Professor Branestawm's Hair-Raising Idea'; paperback) (Puffin, 1993) **£5**

Others

THE BAD BARONS OF CRASHBANIA (illustrated by Eve Garnett) (Blackwell, [1932]) **£50**
LARKY LEGENDS (illustrated by James Arnold) (John Lane: The Bodley Head, 1938) **£125**
LARKY LEGENDS (as 'The Dribblesome Teapots and Other Incredible Stories') (The Bodley Head, 1969) **£40**
JINGLE TALES (illustrated by Gordon Robinson) (Warne, [1930]) **£70**
JINGLE TALES (illustrated by Gordon Robinson; paperback) (Warne, [1941]) **£30**
PUFFIN BOOK OF MAGIC (paperback) (Puffin, 1968) **£7**
THE HOME-MADE DRAGON and Other Incredible Stories (The Bodley Head, 1971) **£20**
THE FRANTIC PHANTOM and Other Incredible Stories (illustrated by Geraldine Spence)
(The Bodley Head, 1973) **£20**

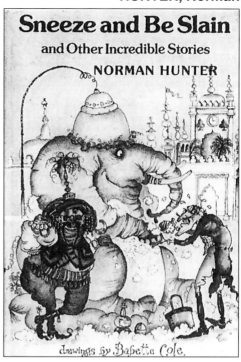

Professor Branestawm's Great Revolution from 1974 is now worth £20 in Very Good condition with the dustjacket.

The crazy kingdom of Incrediblania provides the setting for all the stories in this, Norman Hunter's final collection from 1980.

I

IRVING, Washington

American author. Born in New York City in 1783. Left school at sixteen and worked in a law office. Travelled in Europe during 1804-6. Enjoyed huge success with *The Sketch Book of Geoffrey Crayon, Gent*, which included the story of 'Rip Van Winkle' and 'The Legend of Sleepy Hollow', and his account of an 'Old Christmas' in England. *Bracebridge Hall, or The Humorists* further showed his affinity with English life. Between 1829 and 1832, Irving was secretary to the American legation in London, and received a gold medal from the Royal Society of Literature and an honorary degree from Oxford University. Died: 1859.

Prices are for books in Good condition.

THE SKETCH BOOK OF GEOFFREY CRAYON, GENT (seven numbers: first and second state wrappers)
(C.S. Van Winkle, U.S., May 1819 to September 1820) ....£2,000/£1,500
THE SKETCHBOOK OF GEOFFREY CRAYON, GENT (two volumes) (John Miller, 1820) ....the set £2,000
THE SKETCHBOOK OF GEOFFREY CRAYON, GENT (with 120 engravings on wood) (Bell & Daldy, 1865) £500
BRACEBRIDGE HALL, or THE HUMORISTS: A Medley. By Geoffrey Crayon. Gent (two volumes)
(C.S. Van Winkle, U.S., 1822) £1,500
BRACEBRIDGE HALL, or THE HUMORISTS: A Medley. By Geoffrey Crayon. Gent (two volumes) (John Murray, 1822) ..£1,000
BRACEBRIDGE HALL (illustrated by Randolph Caldecott) (Macmillan, 1877 [1876]) £30
OLD CHRISTMAS (illustrated by Randolph Caldecott) (Macmillan, 1876)..£30
OLD CHRISTMAS (illustrated by Cecil Aldin) (Hodder & Stoughton, 1908)..£125
OLD CHRISTMAS (illustrated by Frank Dadd) (G.P. Putnam's, U.K./U.S., 1916) £30
RIP VAN WINKLE (illustrated by Gordon Browne) (Blackie, 1887 [1886]) £30
RIP VAN WINKLE and THE LEGEND OF SLEEPY HOLLOW (illustrated by G.H. Broughton) (Macmillan, 1893)...................£30
RIP VAN WINKLE (illustrated by Arthur Rackham) (Heinemann, 1905) £800
RIP VAN WINKLE (illustrated by Arthur Rackham; limited to 250 copies, signed by the artist; vellum binding)
(Heinemann, 1905) £3,500
RIP VAN WINKLE (illustrated by Charles Robinson) (T.C. & E.C. Jack, 1913) £30
RIP VAN WINKLE (illustrated by N.C. Wyeth) (David McKay, U.S., 1921) £30
THE LEGEND OF SLEEPY (illustrated by Arthur Keller) (Grant Richards, 1909) £20
THE LEGEND OF SLEEPY HOLLOW (illustrated by Arthur Rackham) (Harrap, 1928) £200
THE LEGEND OF SLEEPY HOLLOW (illustrated by Arthur Rackham; limted to 375 copies,
signed by the artist; vellum binding) (Harrap, 1928) £750

*One of Arthur Rackham's illustrations for Washington Irving's **Rip Van Winkle**. He also illustrated **The Legend of Sleepy Hollow**.*

J

JACOBS, Joseph

Anglo-Australian folklorist. Born: Sydney, Australia, in 1854. Educated at London University and King's College, Cambridge. Edited the British journal, *Folk-Lore*, as well as the *Jewish Encyclopedia*. His two collections, *English Fairy Tales* (1890) and *More English Fairy Tales* (1894), were enormously influential, and were followed by volumes devoted to Celtic and Indian folk tales. Died: 1916.

Prices are for books in Very Good condition.

ENGLISH FAIRY TALES (illustrated by J.D. Batten) (David Nutt, 1890) £45
CELTIC FAIRY TALES (illustrated by J.D. Batten) (David Nutt, 1892 [1891]) £55
INDIAN FAIRY TALES (illustrated by J.D. Batten) (David Nutt, 1892)...£50
INDIAN FAIRY TALES (illustrated by J.D. Batten; limited to 160 copies; printed on Japanese vellum) (David Nutt, 1892) £120
MORE ENGLISH FAIRY TALES (illustrated by J.D. Batten) (David Nutt, 1894 [1893]) £30
MORE ENGLISH FAIRY TALES (limited to 160 copies; printed on Japanese vellum) (David Nutt, 1894 [1893]) £120
MORE CELTIC FAIRY TALES (illustrated by J.D. Batten) (David Nutt, 1894) £40
AESOP'S FABLES (illustrated by Richard Heighway) (Macmillan, 1894) £20
THE BOOK OF WONDER VOYAGES (illustrated by J.D. Batten) (David Nutt, 1896).......................£60
THE BOOK OF WONDER VOYAGES (illustrated by J.D. Batten; limited to 100 copies; printed on Japanese vellum) (David Nutt, 1896) ..£120
ENGLISH FAIRY TALES (revised third edition; illustrated by J.D. Batten) (David Nutt, 1898) £20

JACQUES, Brian

British author. Born: Liverpool, 1939. A playwright and radio presenter for Radio Merseyside, he is best known for the popular 'Redwall' series.

Prices are for books in Very Good condition with dustjackets where applicable.

REDWALL (Hutchinson, 1986) £30
MOSSFLOWER (Hutchinson, 1988) £30
MATTIMEO (Hutchinson, 1989)..£30
MARIEL OF REDWALL (Hutchinson, 1991)..£30
SALAMANDASTRON (Hutchinson, 1992) £30
MARTIN THE WARRIOR : A Tale of Redwall (Hutchinson, 1993)..£20
THE BELLMAKER (Hutchinson, 1994)..£30
OUTCAST OF REDWALL (Hutchinson, 1995) £25
THE PEARLS OF LUTRA (Hutchinson, 1996) £20
THE LONG PATROL : A Tale of Redwall (Hutchinson, 1997) £20
REDWALL MAP AND THE REDWALL RIDER (Hutchinson, 1997).......................................£20
RED FOX (Hutchinson, 1997) £30
MARLFOX (Hutchinson, 1998) £30
REDWALL ABBEY (Hutchinson, 1998) £20
LORD BROCKTREE (Hutchinson, 1999) £10
LEGEND OF LUKE (Hutchinson, 1999) £10
REDWALL FAMILY TREE (Hutchinson, 1999) £10

JAMES, Grace

British author. Born: Tokyo, Japan, in 1885. Her father worked with the Naval Mission in Japan where the family lived until she was twelve years old. Her best-known books feature John and Mary, who are based on her nephew and niece. Died: 1965.

Prices are for books in Very Good condition with dustjackets where applicable.

'John and Mary' Books

JOHN AND MARY (illustrated by Mary Gardiner) (Muller, 1935) £20
MORE ABOUT JOHN AND MARY (illustrated by Mary Gardiner) (Muller, 1936) £20
JOHN AND MARY ABROAD (illustrated by Mary Gardiner) (Muller, 1937)............................£20
JOHN AND MARY, DETECTIVES (illustrated by Mary Gardiner) (Muller, 1938) £20
JOHN AND MARY'S SECRET SOCIETY (illustrated by Mary Gardiner) (Muller, 1939) £20
JOHN AND MARY'S VISITORS (illustrated by Mary Gardiner) (Muller, 1940)........................£20
NEW FRIENDS FOR JOHN AND MARY (illustrated by Mary Gardiner) (Muller, 1941) £20
JOHN AND MARY AND MISS ROSE BROWN (illustrated by Mary Gardiner) (Muller, 1942).....£20
JOHN AND MARY AT SCHOOL (illustrated by Mary Gardiner) (Muller, 1943) £20
JOHN AND MARY'S YOUTH CLUB (illustrated by Mary Gardiner) (Muller, 1945) £20
JOHN AND MARY AT RIVERTON (illustrated by Mary Gardiner) (Muller, 1946) £20
THE ADVENTURES OF JOHN AND MARY (illustrated by Mary Gardiner) (Muller, 1947) £20
JOHN AND MARY'S AUNT (illustrated by Mary Gardiner) (Muller, 1950) £20
JOHN AND MARY IN ROME (illustrated by Mary Gardiner) (Muller, 1954)...........................£20
JOHN AND MARY'S FAIRY TALES (illustrated by Mary Gardiner) (Muller, 1955) £20
JOHN AND MARY BY LAND AND SEA (illustrated by Mary Gardiner) (Muller, 1956).............£20

JAMES, Grace

*An illustration from Tove Jansson's **Moominsummer Madness** (1955), showing a behatted Moominpappa.*

JOHN AND MARY'S JAPANESE FAIRY TALES (illustrated by Mary Gardiner) (Muller, 1957) £20
JOHN AND MARY AND LISETTA (illustrated by Mary Gardiner) (Muller, 1958)..£20
JOHN AND MARY'S TREASURES (illustrated by Mary Gardiner) (Muller, 1960) £20
JOHN AND MARY REVISIT ROME (illustrated by Mary Gardiner) (Muller, 1963)..£20

Others
GREEN WILLOW AND OTHER JAPANESE FAIRY TALES (forty colour plates by Warwick Goble) (Macmillan, 1910).............£600
GREEN WILLOW AND OTHER JAPANESE FAIRY TALES (forty colour plates by Warwick Goble;
De Luxe edition: limited to 500 copies) (Macmillan, 1910) £2,000
GREEN WILLOW AND OTHER JAPANESE FAIRY TALES (sixteen colour plates by Warwick Goble) (Macmillan, 1912) £70
GREEN WILLOW AND OTHER JAPANESE FAIRY TALES (reissue; sixteen colour plates by Warwick Goble) (Macmillan, 1923)..£50
THE BLAKES AND THE BLACKETTS (illustrated by Mary Gardiner) (Muller, 1939) £20
NIBS (illustrated by Mary Gardiner) (Muller, 1951) £20
NIBS AND THE NEW WORLD (illustrated by Mary Gardiner) (Muller, 1953)..£20

Plays
THE DANCING SHOES (wrappers) (French's Plays for Juvenile Performers, 1921) £10
THE PORK PIE HAT A Victorian Play in Two Acts (wrappers) (French's Plays for Schoolgirls, No2, 1922) £10
THE CUCUMBER RING: A Chinese Play (verse; wrappers) (French's Plays for Juvenile Performers, No1, 1924) £10
THE JELLYFISH (wrappers) (French's Plays for Juvenile Performers, No14, 1931) £10
ROBERT AND LOUISA (wrappers) (French's Plays for Boys, 1931) £10
THE THREE DWARF TREES. From an Old Japanese Play (wrappers) (French's Plays for Juvenile performers, No33, 1936) ..£10

JAMES, M.R.
British author. Born: Montague Rhodes James in 1862. Educated at Eton and King's College, Cambridge, becoming Provost of Eton in 1918. Best known for his *Ghost Stories of an Antiquary* (1904), he wrote a single children's work and also translated a volume of Hans Christian Andersen's stories. Awarded the Order of Merit in 1930. Died: 1936.

Prices are for books in Very Good condition with dustjackets.

THE FIVE JARS (illustrated by Gilbert James) (Arnold, 1922)..£250
HANS ANDERSEN, FORTY STORIES (illustrated by Christine Jackson; translated by M.R. James) (Faber, 1930) £40

JANSSON, Tove
Finnish author-illustrator. Born: 1914. Began her famous 'Moomin' series with *Comet in Moominland*, first published in Britain in 1951. Like its sequels, this book was written in Swedish and illustrated by its author. The London *Evening News* ran a 'Moomin' comic strip between 1954 and 1968. Died: 2001.

Prices are for books in Very Good condition with dustjackets where applicable.

FINN FAMILY MOOMINTROLL (illustrated by the author) (Benn, 1950) £100
COMET IN MOOMINLAND (illustrated by the author) (Benn, 1951) £80
THE EXPLOITS OF MOOMINPAPPA: Described by Himself (illustrated by the author) (Benn, 1952)......................................£75

THE BOOK ABOUT MOOMIN, MYMBLE AND LITTLE MY (illustrated by the author) (Benn, 1953) £175
MOOMINSUMMER MADNESS (illustrated by the author) (Benn, 1955) £75
MOOMIN (picture book; quarto; illustrated by the author) (Wingate, 1957) £100
MOOMINLAND MIDWINTER (illustrated by the author) (Benn, 1958) £75
WHO WILL COMFORT TOFFLE? (illustrated by the author) (Benn, 1960) £120
TALES FROM MOOMINVALLEY (illustrated by the author) (Benn, 1963)..£40
MOMMINPAPPA AT SEA (illustrated by the author) (Benn, 1966) £40
MOOMINVALLEY IN NOVEMBER (illustrated by the author) (Benn, 1971) £40
DANGEROUS JOURNEY (illustrated by the author) (Benn, 1978) £80

JARVIS, Robin

British author-illustrator. Born in Liverpool. Worked as model-maker for film and TV. Notable for the 'Deptford Trilogy'.

Prices are for books in Very Good condition with dustjackets where applicable.

'Deptford Mice' Books

THE DARK PORTAL (Macdonald and Co, 1989) £20
THE CRYSTAL PRISON (Macdonald and Co, 1989) £15
THE FINAL RECKONING (Simon and Schuster, 1990) £15

'Deptford Histories' Books

THE ALCHYMIST'S CAT (Simon and Schuster, 1991) £10
THE OAKEN THRONE (Simon and Schuster, 1993) £10

'Whitby' Books

THE WHITBY WITCHES (boards/paperback) (Simon & Schuster, 1991) ....£10/£4
A WARLOCK IN WHITBY (boards/paperback) (Simon & Schuster, 1992) ....£10/£4
THE WHITBY CHILD (boards/paperback) (Simon & Schuster, 1994) ....£10/£4

'Tales From the Wyrd Museum' Books

THE WOVEN PATH (Collins, 1995) £10
THE RAVEN'S KNOT (Collins, 1996) £10
THE FATAL STRAND (Collins, 1998) £10

'Hagwood' Books

THORN OGRES OF HAGWOOD (Puffin Books, 1999) £5

JEFFERIES, Richard

British author. Born: Coate, Wiltshire, in 1848. Worked on the *North Wilts Herald* before moving to London in 1877. Jefferies wrote several volumes of essays — mainly on country matters — and adult novels (including the Wellsian romance, *After London, or Wild England*, 1895), but also published two enduring works for children, *Wood Magic* (1881) and its sequel, *Bevis: The Story of a Boy* (1882). Died: 1887.

Prices are for books in Very Good condition.

WOOD MAGIC (two volumes) (Cassell, Peter & Galpin, 1881) ....the set £200
BEVIS: THE STORY OF A BOY (three volumes) (Sampson Low, 1882) ....the set £750

JOHNS, Captain W.E.

British author. Born: William Earle Johns in Hertford in 1893. Worked as a surveyor after school, serving in the army and, from 1916 onwards, the newly-formed Royal Flying Corps during the First World War. Remained in the Air Force until 1930, when he became a newspaper air correspondent and founded the magazine, *Popular Flying*, in the pages of which his famous character, Biggles (Major James Bigglesworth, DSO, MC), first appeared. A versatile author, Johns also wrote science fiction novels for young readers, and even a book on gardening. The publicity surrounding his centenary in 1993 showed that interest in his work is as great as ever. Died: 1968.

Prices are for books in Very Good condition with dustjackets in similar condition. Hamilton/OUP editions are extremely rare in this state and Fine copies would fetch a premium!

'Biggles' Books

THE CAMELS ARE COMING (written under the pseudonym 'William Earle') (John Hamilton, [1932]) £1,500
THE CRUISE OF THE CONDOR (John Hamilton, [1933]) £1,200
"BIGGLES" OF THE CAMEL SQUADRON (John Hamilton, [1934]) £1,200
BIGGLES FLIES AGAIN (John Hamilton, [1934]) £1,200
BIGGLES LEARNS TO FLY (paperback) ('Boys' Friend Library' No. 469, 1935) £600
BIGGLES LEARNS TO FLY (first hardback edition) (Brockhampton Press, 1955) £50
BIGGLES IN FRANCE (paperback) ('Boys' Friend Library' No. 501, 1935) £600
THE BLACK PERIL: A 'Biggles' Story (John Hamilton, [1935]) £1,200
BIGGLES FLIES EAST (OUP, 1935) £900
BIGGLES HITS THE TRAIL (OUP, 1935) £900
BIGGLES & CO (OUP, 1936) £900

JOHNS, Captain W.E.

BIGGLES IN AFRICA (OUP, 1936)..£900
BIGGLES — AIR COMMODORE (OUP, 1937) £900
BIGGLES FLIES WEST (OUP, 1937) £900
BIGGLES FLIES SOUTH (OUP, 1938) £900
BIGGLES GOES TO WAR (OUP, 1938) £900
THE BIGGLES OMNIBUS (contains 'Biggles Flies East', 'Biggles Hits the Trail' and 'Biggles and Co.') (OUP, 1938) £900
THE RESCUE FLIGHT: A Biggles Story (OUP, 1939) £900
BIGGLES IN SPAIN (OUP, 1939) £900
BIGGLES FLIES NORTH (OUP, 1939) £750
BIGGLES — SECRET AGENT (OUP, 1940) £750
BIGGLES IN THE BALTIC: A Tale of the Second Great War (OUP, 1940) £750
BIGGLES IN THE SOUTH SEAS (OUP, 1940) £600
THE BIGGLES FLYING OMNIBUS (contains 'Biggles Flies North', 'Biggles Flies South' and 'Biggles Flies West') (OUP, 1940) ..£900
BIGGLES DEFIES THE SWASTIKA (OUP, 1941) £600
SPITFIRE PARADE: Stories of Biggles in War-Time (OUP, 1941) £600
BIGGLES SEES IT THROUGH (OUP, 1941) £600
BIGGLES FLIES AGAIN (paperback) (Penguin No. 348, 1941)...£175
THE THIRD BIGGLES OMNIBUS (contains 'Biggles in Spain', 'Biggles Goes to War' and 'Biggles in the Baltic') (OUP, 1941) ..£900
BIGGLES IN THE JUNGLE (OUP, 1942) £300
BIGGLES SWEEPS THE DESERT (Hodder & Stoughton, 1942) £45
BIGGLES — CHARTER PILOT (OUP, 1943) £300
BIGGLES IN BORNEO (OUP, 1943)..£250
BIGGLES 'FAILS TO RETURN' (Hodder & Stoughton, 1943) £45
BIGGLES IN THE ORIENT (Hodder & Stoughton, 1945) £40
BIGGLES DELIVERS THE GOODS (Hodder & Stoughton, 1946) £25
SERGEANT BIGGLESWORTH C.I.D. (Hodder & Stoughton, 1947) £25
BIGGLES' SECOND CASE (Hodder & Stoughton, 1948) £30
BIGGLES HUNTS BIG GAME (Hodder & Stoughton, 1948) £20
BIGGLES TAKES A HOLIDAY (Hodder & Stoughton, 1949) £30
BIGGLES BREAKS THE SILENCE (Hodder & Stoughton, 1949) £20
BIGGLES GETS HIS MEN (Hodder & Stoughton, 1950) £20
BIGGLES — AIR DETECTIVE (Marks & Spencer, 1950) £20
ANOTHER JOB FOR BIGGLES (Hodder & Stoughton, 1951)...£20
BIGGLES GOES TO SCHOOL (Hodder & Stoughton, 1951) £25
BIGGLES WORKS IT OUT (Hodder & Stoughton, 1951) £20
BIGGLES TAKES THE CASE (Hodder & Stoughton, 1952) £25
BIGGLES FOLLOWS ON (Hodder & Stoughton, 1952) £25
BIGGLES AND THE BLACK RAIDER (Hodder & Stoughton, 1953) £30
BIGGLES IN THE BLUE (Brockhampton Press, 1953) £45
BIGGLES IN THE GOBI (Hodder & Stoughton, 1953) £45
BIGGLES OF THE SPECIAL AIR POLICE (Thames, [1953]) £15
THE FIRST BIGGLES OMNIBUS (contains 'Biggles Sweeps the Desert', 'Biggles in the Orient',
   'Biggles Delivers the Goods' and 'Biggles "Fails to Return"') (Hodder & Stoughton, 1953) £45
BIGGLES CUTS IT FINE (Hodder & Stoughton, 1954) £45
BIGGLES AND THE PIRATE TREASURE and Other Biggles Adventures (Brockhampton Press, 1954) £45
BIGGLES, FOREIGN LEGIONNAIRE (Hodder & Stoughton, 1954) £35
BIGGLES, PIONEER AIRFIGHTER (Thames, [1954]) £15
BIGGLES IN AUSTRALIA (Hodder & Stoughton, 1955) £45
BIGGLES' CHINESE PUZZLE and Other Biggles Adventures (Brockhampton Press, 1955) £40
BIGGLES OF 266 (Thames, [1956]) £15
NO REST FOR BIGGLES (Hodder & Stoughton, 1956)..£35
BIGGLES TAKES CHARGE (Brockhampton Press, 1956)..£40
THE BIGGLES AIR DETECTIVE OMNIBUS (contains 'Sergeant Bigglesworth C.I.D.', 'Biggles' Second Case',
   'Another Job for Biggles' and 'Biggles Works it Out') (Hodder & Stoughton, 1956) £45
BIGGLES MAKES ENDS MEET (Hodder & Stoughton, 1957) £40
BIGGLES OF THE INTERPOL (Brockhampton Press, 1957)...£40
BIGGLES ON THE HOME FRONT (Hodder & Stoughton, 1957)..£40
BIGGLES PRESSES ON (Brockhampton Press, 1958) £40
BIGGLES ON MYSTERY ISLAND (Hodder & Stoughton, [1958])..£45
BIGGLES BURIES A HATCHET (Brockhampton Press, 1958) £45
BIGGLES IN MEXICO (Brockhampton Press, 1959) £45
BIGGLES' COMBINED OPERATION (Hodder & Stoughton, [1959])..£45
BIGGLES AT WORLD'S END (Brockhampton Press, 1959) £45
BIGGLES AND THE LEOPARDS OF ZINN (Brockhampton Press, 1960).......................................£45
BIGGLES GOES HOME (Hodder & Stoughton, [1960]) £45
BIGGLES AND THE POOR RICH BOY (Brockhampton Press, 1961)..£30
BIGGLES FORMS A SYNDICATE (Hodder & Stoughton, 1961)...£45
BIGGLES AND THE MISSING MILLIONAIRE (Brockhampton Press, 1961) £45
BIGGLES GOES ALONE (Hodder & Stoughton, [1962]) £50

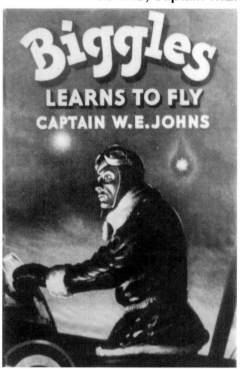

Biggles & Co, the tenth book in W.E. Johns' bestselling series, was published by Oxford University Press in 1936.

*The first hardback edition of **Biggles Learns to Fly** (1955) issued exactly twenty years after the original paperback edition.*

ORCHIDS FOR BIGGLES (Brockhampton Press, 1962) £30
BIGGLES SETS A TRAP (Hodder & Stoughton, 1962) £50
BIGGLES TAKES IT ROUGH (Brockhampton Press, 1963)...£50
BIGGLES FLIES TO WORK (Dean, 1963) £15
BIGGLES TAKES A HAND (Hodder & Stoughton, 1963)..£40
BIGGLES' SPECIAL CASE (Brockhampton Press, 1963) £45
BIGGLES AND THE PLANE THAT DISAPPEARED: A Story of the Air Police (Hodder & Stoughton, 1963) £50
BIGGLES AND THE LOST SOVEREIGNS (Brockhampton Press, 1964) £50
BIGGLES AND THE BLACK MASK (Hodder & Stoughton, 1964) £100
BIGGLES INVESTIGATES and Other Stories of the Air Police (Brockhampton Press, 1964)...........................£60
BIGGLES LOOKS BACK: A Story of Biggles and the Air Police (Hodder & Stoughton, 1965) £75
BIGGLES AND THE PLOT THAT FAILED (Brockhampton Press, 1965)...£100
BIGGLES AND THE BLUE MOON (Brockhampton Press, 1965) £120
BIGGLES SCORES A BULL (Hodder & Stoughton, 1965) £100
THE BIGGLES ADVENTURE OMNIBUS (contains 'Biggles Gets his Men', 'No Rest for Biggles',
   'Another Job for Biggles' and 'Biggles Takes a Holiday') (Hodder & Stoughton, 1965)........................£45
BIGGLES IN THE TERAI (Brockhampton Press, 1966) £120
BIGGLES AND THE GUN RUNNERS (Brockhampton Press, 1966) £120
BIGGLES SORTS IT OUT (Brockhampton Press, 1967) £120
BIGGLES AND THE DARK INTRUDER (paperback) (Knight, 1967) £15
BIGGLES AND THE PENITENT THIEF (Brockhampton Press, 1967) £150
BIGGLES AND THE DEEP BLUE SEA (Brockhampton Press, 1968)..£175
THE BOY BIGGLES (Dean, 1968) £15
BIGGLES IN THE UNDERWORLD (Brockhampton Press, 1968) £175
BIGGLES AND THE LITTLE GREEN GOD (Brockhampton Press, 1969)...£175
BIGGLES AND THE NOBLE LORD (Brockhampton Press, 1969) £175
BIGGLES AND THE DARK INTRUDER (Brockhampton Press, 1970) £165
BIGGLES SEES TOO MUCH (Brockhampton Press, 1970)...£175
BIGGLES OF THE ROYAL FLYING CORPS (Purnell, 1978) £15
THE BUMPER BIGGLES BOOK (Chancellor, 1983) £15
THE BEST OF BIGGLES (Chancellor, 1985) £15
BIGGLES DOES SOME HOMEWORK (paperback) (Wright, 1997) £300
BIGGLES AIR ACE: THE UNCOLLECTED STORIES (paperback) (Wright, 1999)..£75

JOHNS, Captain W.E.

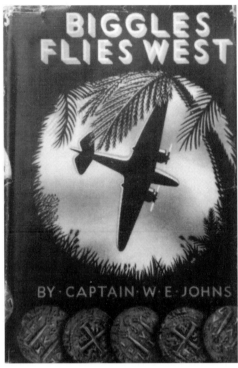

*You can expect to pay £900 for a Very Good copy of the first edition of **Biggles Flies West** in the Howard Leigh dustjacket.*

Although less popular than 'Biggles', W.E. Johns' 'Worrals' books still have a keen following amongst book collectors.

'Worrals' Books

WORRALS OF THE W.A.A.F. (Lutterworth Press, 1941)	£100
WORRALS CARRIES ON (Lutterworth Press, 1942)	£45
WORRALS FLIES AGAIN (Hodder & Stoughton, 1942)	£40
WORRALS ON THE WAR-PATH (Hodder & Stoughton, 1943)	£35
WORRALS GOES EAST (Hodder & Stoughton, 1944)	£35
WORRALS OF THE ISLANDS: A Story of the War in the Pacific (Hodder & Stoughton, 1945)	£35
WORRALS IN THE WILDS (Hodder & Stoughton, 1947)	£20
WORRALS DOWN UNDER (Lutterworth Press, 1948)	£20
WORRALS GOES AFOOT (Lutterworth Press, 1949)	£20
WORRALS IN THE WASTELANDS (Lutterworth Press, 1949)	£20
WORRALS INVESTIGATES (Lutterworth Press, 1950)	£20
THE CHILDREN'S GIFT BOOK (contains a 'Worrals' short story) (Odhams Press, 1946)	£20

'Gimlet' Books

KING OF THE COMMANDOS (University of London Press, 1943)	£35
GIMLET GOES AGAIN (University of London Press, 1944)	£25
GIMLET COMES HOME (University of London Press, 1946)	£20
GIMLET MOPS UP (Brockhampton Press, 1947)	£20
GIMLET'S ORIENTAL QUEST (Brockhampton Press, 1948)	£20
GIMLET LENDS A HAND (Brockhampton Press, 1949)	£20
GIMLET BORES IN (Brockhampton Press, 1950)	£20
GIMLET OFF THE MAP (Brockhampton Press, 1951)	£20
GIMLET GETS THE ANSWER (Brockhampton Press, 1952)	£20
GIMLET TAKES A JOB (Brockhampton Press, 1954)	£20

Science Fiction Books

KINGS OF SPACE: A Story of Interplanetary Explorations (Hodder & Stoughton, 1954)	£20
RETURN TO MARS (Hodder & Stoughton, 1955)	£20
NOW TO THE STARS (Hodder & Stoughton, 1956)	£20
TO OUTER SPACE (Hodder & Stoughton, 1957)	£20
THE EDGE OF BEYOND (Hodder & Stoughton, 1958)	£20
THE DEATH RAYS OF ARDILLA (Hodder & Stoughton, 1959)	£20
TO WORLDS UNKNOWN: A Story of Interplanetary Explorations (Hodder & Stoughton, 1960)	£20

THE QUEST FOR THE PERFECT PLANET (Hodder & Stoughton, 1961) £20
WORLDS OF WONDER: More Adventures in Space (Hodder & Stoughton, 1962) £20
THE MAN WHO VANISHED INTO SPACE (Hodder & Stoughton, 1963) £20

Others Books Written or Edited by W.E. Johns

MOSSYFACE (written under the pseudonym 'William Earle') ('The Weekly Telegraph Novel', 1922) £450
WINGS: A Book of Flying Adventures. Edited by W.E. Johns (Hamilton, [1931]) £275
MODERN BOYS BOOK OF AIRCRAFT (Amalgamated Press, 1931) £50
THE PICTORIAL FLYING COURSE by H.M. Schofield and F/O W.E. Johns (John Hamilton, [1932]) £275
FIGHTING PLANES AND ACES (plates, including portraits) (John Hamilton, [1932]) £250
THE SPY FLYERS (illustrated by Howard Leigh) (John Hamilton, 1933) £400
THE RAID (John Hamilton, [1935]) £350
THE AIR VC's (John Hamilton, [1935]) £300
SOME MILESTONES IN AVIATION (John Hamilton, [1935]) £180
THRILLING FLIGHTS. Edited by W.E. Johns (John Hamilton, [1935]) £275
BLUE BLOOD RUNS RED (written under the pseudonym 'Jon Early') (Newnes, [1936]) £900
MODERN BOY'S BOOK OF ADVENTURE STORIES (Amalgamated Press, 1936) £50
ACE HIGH (Ace, 1936) £75
AIR ADVENTURES (Ace, 1936) £75
SKY HIGH: A 'Steeley' Adventure (Newnes, [1936]) £350
STEELEY FLIES AGAIN (Newnes, [1936]) £350
FLYING STORIES (John Hamilton, 1937) £75
MURDER BY AIR: A 'Steeley' Adventure (Newnes, [1937]) £350
THE PASSING SHOW (My Garden/Newnes, 1937) £75
DESERT NIGHT: A Romance (John Hamilton, [1938]) £225
THE MURDER AT CASTLE DEEPING: A 'Steeley' Adventure (John Hamilton, [1938]) £450
CHAMPION OF THE MAIN (OUP, 1938) £350
WINGS OF ROMANCE: A 'Steeley' Adventure (Newnes, 1939) £275
MODERN BOY'S BOOK OF PIRATES (Amalgamated Press, [1939]) £225
THE UNKNOWN QUANTITY (John Hamilton, [1940]) £225
SINISTER SERVICE: A Tale (OUP, 1942) £100
COMRADES IN ARMS (contains a 'Biggles', 'Worrals' and 'Gimlet' short story) (Hodder & Stoughton, 1947) £30
THE RUSTLERS OF RATTLESNAKE VALLEY (Nelson, 1948) £25
DR VANE ANSWERS THE CALL (Latimer House, 1950) £150
SHORT SORTIES (Latimer House, 1950) £150
SKY FEVER and Other Stories (Latimer House, 1953) £150
ADVENTURE BOUND (illustrated by Douglas Relf) (Nelson, 1955) £12
ADVENTURE UNLIMITED (illustrated by Douglas Relf) (Nelson, 1957) £12
NO MOTIVE FOR MURDER (Hodder & Stoughton, 1958) £150
THE MAN WHO LOST HIS WAY (Macdonald, 1959) £150
THE BIGGLES BOOK OF HEROES (Parrish, 1959) £50
ADVENTURES OF THE JUNIOR DETECTION CLUB (Parrish, 1960) £50
WHERE THE GOLDEN EAGLE SOARS (Hodder & Stoughton, 1960) £30
THE BIGGLES BOOK OF TREASURE HUNTING (Parrish, 1962) £50
THE COCKPIT (contains the W.E. Johns story 'Ace of Spades') (John Hamilton, [1943]) £75
OUT OF THE BLUE (John Hamilton, no date) £75
AIR STORIES BY FLIGHT LIEUTENANT (no date) £75

Books Illustrated by W.E. Johns

DESERT WINGS by Covington Clarke (John Hamilton, [1931]) £75
ACES UP by Covington Clarke (John Hamilton, [1931]) £30
FOR VALOUR by Covington Clarke (John Hamilton, [1931]) £30

JONES, Diana Wynne

British author. Born: 1934. A writer of unconventional fantasy stories with modern settings but featuring witches and mythological figures.

Prices are for books in Very Good condition with dustjackets where applicable.

WILKINS' TOOTH (illustrated by Julia Rodber) (Macmillan, 1973) £40
WILKINS' TOOTH (as 'Witch's Business') (illustrated by Julia Rodber) (Dutton, U.S., 1974) £20
THE OGRE DOWNSTAIRS (Macmillan, 1974) £25
EIGHT DAYS OF LUKE (Macmillan, 1975) £25
CART AND CWIDDER (Macmillan, 1975) £25
DOGSBODY (Macmillan, 1975) £25
POWER OF THREE (Macmillan, 1976) £20
CHARMED LIFE (Macmillan, 1977) £15
DROWNED AMNET (Macmillan, 1977) £15
WHO GOT RID OF ANGUS FLINT (illustrated by John Sewell) (Evans, 1978) £15
THE SPELLCOATS (Macmillan, 1979) £15
THE MAGICIANS OF CAPRONA (Macmillan, 1980) £15

JONES, Diana Wynne

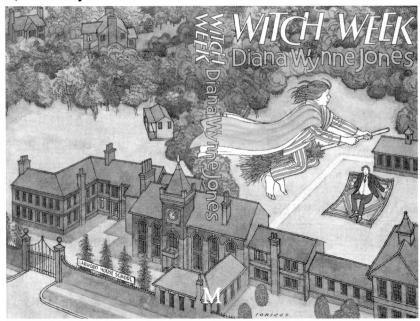

*The wraparound dustjacket for Diana Wynne Jones' 1982 novel, **Witch Week**, was illustrated by Ionicus.*

THE FOUR GRANNIES (illustrated by Thelma Lambert) (Hamish Hamilton, 1980) £15
THE HOMEWARD BOUNDERS (Macmillan, 1981) £10
THE TIME OF THE GHOST (Macmillan, 1981)...£10
WITCH WEEK (Macmillan, 1982) £10
WARLOCK AT THE WHEEL (Macmillan, 1984) £10
ARCHER'S GOON (Methuen, 1984)...£10
FIRE AND HEMLOCK (Methuen, 1985) £10
A TALE OF THE CITY (Methuen, 1987) £10
THE LIVES OF CHRISTOPHER CHANT (Macmillan, 1988) £10
CHAIR PERSON (Macmillan, 1988) £10
CASTLE IN THE AIR (Macmillan, 1990)...£8
BLACK MARIA (Macmillan, 1991) £8
YES, DEAR (Macmillan, 1992) £8
A SUDDEN WILD MAGIC (Macmillan, 1992) £8
STOPPING FOR A SPELL (Macmillan, 1993) £5
A TOUGH GUIDE TO FANTASY LAND (Macmillan, 1996) £5
DEEP SECRET (Macmillan, 1997) £5
LORD OF DERKHOLM (Macmillan, 1998) £5

'JOY STREET' ANNUALS

British annual, published by Blackwell during the 1920s and '30s. Among the contributors were Walter de la Mare, Hilaire Belloc, G.K. Chesterton and A.A. Milne. The monthly magazine, *The Merry-Go-Round*, grew out of the title.

Prices are for annuals in Very Good condition with dustjackets.

NUMBER ONE JOY STREET: A Medley of Prose and Verse for Boys and Girls ([1923]) £40
NUMBER TWO JOY STREET ([1924]) £40
NUMBER THREE JOY STREET ([1925]) £40
NUMBER FOUR JOY STREET ([1926]) £30
NUMBER FIVE JOY STREET ([1927]) £30
NUMBER SIX JOY STREET ([1928]) £30
NUMBER SEVEN JOY STREET ([1929]) £30
NUMBER EIGHT JOY STREET ([1930]) £30
NUMBER NINE JOY STREET ([1931])..£30
NUMBER TEN JOY STREET ([1932])...£30
NUMBER ELEVEN JOY STREET ([1933]) £30
NUMBER TWELVE JOY STREET ([1934]) £30
NUMBER TWELVE 'A' JOY STREET ([1935]) £30
NUMBER FOURTEEN JOY STREET ([1936]) £30

KÄSTNER, Erich

German author. Born: Dresden, 1899. Educated at König Georg Gymnasium and, after service in the First World War, Leipzig University. Moved to Berlin in 1927, where he worked as a freelance journalist. As well as *Emil and the Detectives* (1931) and his other children's books, he also wrote a handful of adult works, notably the novel, *Fabian* (1932), and a volume of verse, *Let's Face It* (1963). Died: 1974.

Prices are for books in Very Good condition with dustjackets.

EMIL AND THE DETECTIVES (illustrated by Walter Trier) (Cape, 1931) £175
ANNALUISE AND ANTON (illustrated by Walter Trier) (Cape, 1932) £100
THE 35TH OF MAY (illustrated by Walter Trier) (Cape, 1933) £50
THE FLYING CLASSROOM (illustrated by Walter Trier) (Cape, 1934)...£65
EMIL AND THE THREE TWINS (illustrated by Walter Trier) (Cape, 1935) £65
EMIL (contains 'Emil and the Detectives', 'Emil and the Three Twins' and 'The 35th of May') (Cape, 1949) £20
LOTTIE AND LISA (illustrated by Walter Trier) (Cape, 1950) £60
THE ANIMALS CONFERENCE (Collins, 1955) £65
WHEN I WAS A LITTLE BOY (autobiography) (Cape, 1959) £5
LET'S FACE IT (verse) (Cape, 1963) £25
THE LITTLE MAN (illustrated by Horst Lemke) (Cape, 1966) £30
TILL EULENSPIEGEL THE CLOWN (illustrated by Walter Trier) (Cape, 1967) £80
PUSS IN BOOTS (illustrated by Walter Trier) (Cape, 1967) £40
THE LITTLE MAN AND THE LITTLE MISS (illustrated by Horst Lemke) (Cape, 1969) £20

KEENE, Carolyn

House name, under which — amongst others — the popular 'Nancy Drew' novels were written. Many of the books were the work of the American author, Harriet S. Adams. Born: 1894. Died: 1982.

Prices are for U.K. editions in Very Good condition with dustjackets where applicable.

'Nancy Drew' Books

THE SECRET OF THE OLD CLOCK (Harold Hill, 1954) £15
THE HIDDEN STAIRCASE (Harold Hill, 1954) £15
THE BUNGALOW MYSTERY (Harold Hill, 1954)...£15

Emil meets his 'detectives' in an illustration from the original edition of Kästner's story.

KEENE, Carolyn

THE MYSTERY OF LILAC INN (Harold Hill, 1954) £15
THE SECRET AT SHADOW RANCH (Harold Hill, 1954) £15
THE SECRET AT RED GATE FARM (Harold Hill, 1954) £15
THE CLUE IN THE DIARY (Harold Hill, 1960) £12
NANCY'S MYSTERIOUS LETTER (Harold Hill, 1960)...£12
THE SIGN OF THE TWISTED CANDLES (Harold Hill, 1960) £12
THE PASSWORD TO LARKSPUR LANE (Harold Hill, 1960) £12
THE CLUE OF THE BROKEN LOCKET (Harold Hill, 1963) £12
THE MESSAGE IN THE HOLLOW OAK (Harold Hill, 1963) £12
THE MYSTERY OF THE FIRE DRAGON (Harold Hill, 1963) £12
THE CLUE OF THE DANCING PUPPET (Harold Hill, 1963) £12
THE SECRET OF THE GOLDEN PAVILION (Harold Hill, 1963) £12
THE HIDDEN WINDOW MYSTERY (Harold Hill, 1964) £12
THE HAUNTED SHOWBOAT (Harold Hill, 1964) £12
THE MOONSTONE CASTLE MYSTERY (Harold Hill, 1964) £12
THE CLUE OF THE WHISTLING BAGPIPES (Harold Hill, 1964) £12
THE CLUE OF THE VELVET MASK (Harold Hill, 1965)...£12
THE WITCHTREE SYMBOL (Harold Hill, 1965) £12
THE RINGMASTER'S SECRET (Harold Hill, 1965) £12
THE SCARLET SLIPPER MYSTERY (Harold Hill, 1965)..£12
THE CLUE OF THE BLACK EYE (Harold Hill, 1966) £12
THE PHANTOM OF PINE HILL (Harold Hill, 1966) £12
THE SECRET OF THE WOODEN LADY (Harold Hill, 1966) £12
THE CLUE OF THE LEANING CHIMNEY (Harold Hill, 1966) £12
MYSTERY OF THE 99 STEPS (Harold Hill, 1967) £12
THE CLUE IN THE OLD ALBUM (Harold Hill, 1967) £12
THE GHOST OF BLACKWOOD HALL (Harold Hill, 1967) £12
THE CLUE IN THE CROSSWORD CIPHER (Harold Hill, 1968) £12
TWIN DILEMMA (Harold Hill, 1968) £12
SWAMI'S RING (Harold Hill, 1968) £12
QUEST OF THE MISSING MAP (Collins, 1971)..£10
THE INVISIBLE INTRUDER (Collins, 1972) £10
THE WHISPERING STATUE (Collins, 1972) £10
THE MYSTERY OF THE MOSS-COVERED MANSION (Collins, 1973).....................£10
THE CLUE IN THE CRUMBLING WALL (paperback) (Armada, 1978) £5
THE FLYING SAUCER MYSTERY (Angus & Robertson, 1980) £10
THE CROOKED BANNISTER (Collins, 1980) £10
THE SKY PHANTOM (Collins, 1980) £10
THE THIRTEENTH PEARL (Collins, 1980)..£10
THE MYSTERIOUS MANNEQUIN (Collins, 1980) £10
THE TRIPLE HOAX (Angus & Robertson, 1980) £10
THE SECRET IN THE OLD ATTIC (paperback) (Armada, 1980) £5
THE SECRET IN THE OLD LACE (Harold Hill, 1981) £10
THE KACHINA DOLL MYSTERY (Harold Hill, 1982)..£10
THE GREEK SYMBOL MYSTERY (Angus & Robertson, 1982) £10
THE SECRET OF THE SWISS CHALET (Sparrow, 1982) £10
RACE AGAINST TIME (Harold Hill, 1983) £10
THE MYSTERY OF THE IVORY CHARM (paperback) (Armada, 1983).....................£5
MYSTERY OF THE WINGED LION (Harold Hill, 1983) £10
THE EMERALD-EYED CAT MYSTERY (Harold Hill, 1985) £10
THE CLUE IN THE OLD STAGE-COACH (paperback) (Armada, 1985) £5
THE BLUEBEARD ROOM (Harold Hill, 1986) £5
THE ESKIMO'S SECRET (Harold Hill, 1986) £5
THE MYSTERIOUS IMAGE (Harold Hill, 1986) £5
THE PHANTOM OF VENICE (Harold Hill, 1986) £7
THE SECRET OF THE FORGOTTEN CITY (paperback) (Armada, 1987)...................£5
THE DOUBLE JINX MYSTERY (paperback) (Armada, 1987) £5
THE STRANGE MESSAGE IN THE PARCHMENT (paperback) (Armada, 1988) £5
THE SPIDER SAPPHIRE MYSTERY (paperback) (Armada, 1992) £5

'Dana Girls' Books
THE MYSTERY OF THE STONE TIGER (Severn House, 1972) £5
THE RIDDLE OF THE FROZEN FOUNTAIN (Sparrow, 1981) £5
THE SECRET OF THE SILVER DOLPHIN (Severn House, 1983)..............................£5

Others
'SUPER SLEUTHS' SERIES (with Franklin Dixon; seven books) (paperback) (Armada, 1983) ....each £5
DANGER ON ICE (with Franklin Dixon; illustrated by Paul Frame; paperback) (Armada: 'Be a Detective' series, 1985) £5
THE SECRET OF THE KNIGHT'S SWORD (with Franklin Dixon; illustrated by Paul Frame; paperback)
    (Armada: 'Be a Detective' series, 1985)..£5

KEEPING, Charles

British author-illustrator. Born: London, 1924. Died: 1988.

Prices are for books in Very Good condition with dustjackets where applicable.

Books Written and Illustrated by Charles Keeping

BLACK DOLLY (Brockhampton Press, 1966)...£35
SHAUN AND THE CART-HORSE (OUP, 1966) £35
CHARLEY, CHARLOTTE AND THE GOLDEN CANARY (OUP, 1967) £35
ALFIE AND THE FERRY BOAT (OUP, 1968) £25
JOSEPH'S YARD (OUP, 1969) £25
THROUGH THE WINDOW (OUP, 1970) £25
THE GARDEN SHED (OUP, 1971) £25
THE SPIDER'S WEB (OUP, 1972) £25
THE NANNY GOAT AND THE FIERCE DOG (Abelard-Schuman, 1973) £25
RICHARD (OUP, 1973) £25
THE RAILWAY PASSAGE (OUP, 1974) £20
WASTEGROUND CIRCUS (OUP,1975) £15
INTER-CITY (OUP, 1977) £15
MISS EMILY AND THE BIRD OF MAKE-BELIEVE (Hutchinson, 1978) £15
WILLIE'S FIRE-ENGINE (OUP, 1980) £15
SAMMY STREETSINGER (OUP, 1984) £15

Books Illustrated by Charles Keeping

THE SILVER BRANCH by Rosemary Sutcliff (OUP, 1957) £25
WARRIOR SCARLET by Rosemary Sutcliff (OUP, 1958)..£25
THE LANTERN BEARERS by Rosemary Sutcliff (OUP, 1959) £25
KNIGHT'S FEE by Rosemary Sutcliff (OUP, 1960) £25
DAWN WIND by Rosemary Sutcliff (OUP, 1961)..£25
BEOWULF. Retold by Rosemary Sutcliff (The Bodley Head, 1961) £25
THE GOLDEN AGE and DREAM DAYS (omnibus) by Kenneth Grahame (The Bodley Head, 1962).............£80
THE HORNED HELMET by Henry Treece (Brockhampton Press, 1963) £20
THE LAST OF THE VIKINGS by Henry Treece (Brockhampton Press, 1964) £25
THE MARK OF THE HORSE LORD by Rosemary Sutcliff (OUP, 1965) £25
HEROES AND HISTORY by Rosemary Sutcliff (Batsford, 1965) £25
ELIDOR by Alan Garner (Collins, 1965) £180
BENT IS THE BOW by Geoffrey Trease (Nelson, 1965) £20
RED TOWERS OF GRANADA by Geoffrey Trease (Macmillan, 1966)..£20
THE COLD FLAME. Based on a Tale from the Collection of the Brothers Grimm (Hamish Hamilton, 1967) £20
THE GOD BENEATH THE SEA by Leon Garfield and Edward Blishen (non-fiction) (Longman, 1970) £15
THE GOLDEN SHADOW by Leon Garfield and Edward Blishen (Longman, 1973).......................................£15
THE CAPRICORN BRACELET by Rosemary Sutcliff (OUP, 1973) £15
ABOUT THE SLEEPING BEAUTY by P.L. Travers (Collins, 1977) £35
BLOOD FEUD by Rosemary Sutcliff (OUP, 1977) £15
THE ROBBERS by Nina Bawden (Gollancz, 1979) £15
THE WEDDING GHOST by Leon Garfield (OUP, 1985) £10
CHARLES KEEPING'S BOOK OF CLASSIC GHOST STORIES (Blackie, 1986) £15
CHARLES KEEPING'S TALES OF THE MACABRE (Blackie, 1987) £15

KING, Clive

British author. Born: 1924. Best known for *Stig of the Dump* (1963), he has written a handful of other children's books, many of them reflecting his work overseas with the British Council.

Prices are for books in Very Good condition with dustjackets where applicable.

THE TOWN THAT WENT SOUTH (illustrated by Maurice Bartlett) (Macmillan, U.S., 1959) £45
STIG OF THE DUMP (illustrated by Edward Ardizzone; paperback) (Puffin Original, 1963) £30
STIG OF THE DUMP (illustrated by Edward Ardizzone) (Hamilton, 1965) £25
THE TWENTY-TWO LETTERS (illustrated by Richard Kennedy) (Hamilton, 1966) £25
THE NIGHT THE WATER CAME (illustrated by Mark Peppé) (Longman, 1973) £20
SNAKES AND SNAKES (illustrated by Richard Kennedy) (Kestrel, 1975) £20
ME AND MY MILLION (Kestrel, 1976) £20
HIGH JACKS, LOW JACKS (illustrated by Jacqueline Atkinson) (Benn, 1976)..£12
FIRST DAY OUT (illustrated by Jacqueline Atkinson) (Benn, 1976)..£12
ACCIDENT (illustrated by Jacqueline Atkinson) (Benn, 1976) £12
THE SECRET (illustrated by Jacqueline Atkinson) (Benn, 1976) £12
THE DEVIL'S CUT (illustrated by Val Biro) (Hodder & Stoughton, 1978) £20
THE BIRDS FROM AFRICA (illustrated by Diana Groves) (Macdonald, 1980) £12
NINNY'S BOAT (illustrated by Ian Newsham) (Kestrel, 1980) £15
THE SOUND OF PROPELLERS (illustrated by David Parkins) (Viking Kestrel, 1986) £15
THE SEASHORE PEOPLE (Viking Kestrel, 1987) £15

KING, Jessie M.

Scottish illustrator. Born: Jessie Marion King in 1875. Studied at the Glasgow School of Art, where she was influenced by the work of Charles Rennie Mackintosh. Subsequently worked as a muralist and costume and jewellery designer, as well as providing illustrations for various books and magazines (notably *The Studio*). Settled in Scotland in 1913 after spending two years in Paris. Died: 1949.

Prices are for books in Very Good condition.

THE HEROES by Charles Kingsley (Routledge, 1907)..£100
A HOUSE OF POMEGRANATES by Oscar Wilde (sixteen illustrations by Jessie M. King) (Methuen, 1915)..........£500
THE LITTLE WHITE TOWN OF NEVER-WEARY (Harrap, [1917]) £250
A CAROL: GOOD KING WENCESLAS (adapted by J.M. Neale) (The Studio, [1919]) £200
GOOD KING WENCESLAS (Harold Hill, [1920]) £100
HOW CINDERELLA WAS ABLE TO GO TO THE BALL by Jessie M. King (brochure; printed on batik) (Foulis, [1924]) £500
THE ENCHANTED CAPITAL OF SCOTLAND: A Tale of Mystery and Adventure by Isobel K.C. Steele
(limited to 500 copies) (1945) £525

KING-SMITH, Dick

British author. Born: Gloucestershire, 1922. His novels are distinguished by their pace and humour.

Prices are for books in Very Good condition with dustjackets where applicable.

THE FOX BUSTERS (illustrated by Jon Miller) (Gollancz, 1978) £45
DAGGIE DOGFOOT (illustrated by Mary Rayner) (Gollancz, 1980) £35
THE MOUSE BUTCHER (illustrated by Wendy Smith) (Gollancz, 1981) £30
MAGNUS POWERMOUSE (illustrated by Mary Rayner) (Gollancz, 1982) £25
THE QUEEN'S NOSE (illustrated by Jill Bennett) (Gollancz, 1983) £25
THE SHEEP-PIG (illustrated by Mary Rayner) (Gollancz, 1983) £25
HARRY'S MAD (illustrated by Jill Bennett) (Gollancz, 1984) £25
LIGHTNING FRED (illustrated by Michael Bragg) (Heinemann, 1985)....................................£15

*The first edition of Dick King-Smith's **Magnus Powermouse**, now valued at £25 in Very Good condition with the dustjacket.*

Having written stories about pigs, mice and other familiar animals, King-Smith turned to dodos with this book from 1989.

SADDLEBOTTOM (illustrated by Alice Englander) (Gollancz, 1985) £15
E.S.P.: ERIC STANLEY PIGEON (illustrated by Peter Wingham) (Deutsch, 1986) £15
H. PRINCE (illustrated by Martin Honeysett) (Walker, 1986) £15
DUMPLING (illustrated by Jo Davies) (Hamish Hamilton, 1986) £15
NOAH'S BROTHER (illustrated by Ian Newsham) (Gollancz, 1986) £15
YOB (illustrated by Abigail Pizer) (Heinemann, 1986)..£15
THE HODGEHEG (illustrated by Linda Birch) (Hamish Hamilton, 1987) £15
TUMBLEWEED (illustrated by Ian Newsham) (Gollancz, 1987)..£15
CUCKOOBUSH FARM (illustrated by Kazuko) (Orchard, 1987)..£10
FRIENDS AND BROTHERS (illustrated by Susan Hellard) (Heinemann, 1987) £12
DODOS ARE FOREVER (illustrated by David Parkins) (Viking Kestrel, 1989) £10
ACE THE VERY IMPORTANT PIG (illustrated by Liz Graham-Yooll) (Gollancz, 1990) £10
TRIFFIC PIG BOOK (pictorial boards) (Gollancz, 1991) £20
SOPHIE'S TOM (illustrated by David Parkins; paperback) (Walker, 1991) £5
THE CUCKOO CHILD (illustrated by David Parkins) (Viking, 1991) £5
THE SWOOSE (illustrated by Judy Brown) (Viking, 1993) £5
I LOVE GUINEA-PIGS (non-fiction; illustrated by Anita Jeram; pictorial boards) (Walker Books: 'Read and Wonder' series, 1994)..£5
ANIMAL FRIENDS (non-fiction) (Walker Books, 1996)...£5

KINGSLEY, Charles

British author. Born: Devon, 1819. Educated at Helston Grammar School and Cambridge University. Ordained shortly before his marriage in 1844, subsequently launching the periodical, *Politics for the People*, with his fellow Christian Socialist, Thomas Hughes. Appointed Regius Professor of Modern History at Cambridge in 1860, and was later Governor of Trinidad. As well as his well-known children book, *The Water Babies* (1863), he wrote a number of works for older readers, including the historical romances, *Westward Ho!* (1855) and *Hereward the Wake* (1866), and the political novels, *Yeast* (1848) and *Alton Locke* (1850). Died: 1875.

Prices are for books in Very Good condition.

GLAUCUS, or The Wonders of the Shore (Cambridge, 1855) £400
WESTWARD HO! (three volumes) (Cambridge, 1855)..the set £275
THE HEROES, or Greek Fairy Tales for My Children (illustrated by the author) (Cambridge, 1856 [1855]) £225
THE HEROES (illustrated by Jessie M. King) (Routledge, 1907) £100
THE HEROES (limited to 500 numbered copies) (Riccardi Press, 1912)..£550
THE WATER BABIES: A Fairy Tale for a Land-Baby (illustrated by J. Noel Paton; 200 copies containing the verse, 'L'Envoi')
    (Macmillan, 1863)..£425
THE WATER BABIES (illustrated by J. Noel Paton; later issues) (Macmillan, 1863) £100
THE WATER BABIES (illustrated by Linley Sambourne) (Macmillan, 1865) £100
THE WATER BABIES (illustrated by J. Noel Paton and Percival Skelton) (Macmillan, 1869) £50
THE WATER BABIES (illustrated by Katherine Cameron) (T.C. & E.C. Jack, [1905]) £50
THE WATER BABIES (illustrated by Margaret Tarrant) (Dent, 1908) £100
THE WATER BABIES (illustrated by Arthur Dixon) (Nister, [1908]) £35
THE WATER BABIES (illustrated by Alice B. Woodward) (Blackie, 1909) £60
THE WATER BABIES (illustrated by Warwick Goble) (Macmillan, 1909) £350
THE WATER BABIES (illustrated by Warwick Goble; limited to 260 numbered copies; in slipcase) (Macmillan, 1909) £1,500
THE WATER BABIES (illustrated by Warwick Goble; reissues) (Macmillan, 1910 & 1922) ....£80/£60
THE WATER BABIES (illustrated by W. Heath Robinson) (Constable, 1915)..£175
THE WATER BABIES (illustrated by Mabel Lucie Attwell; abridged version) (Raphael Tuck, [1915]) £160
THE WATER BABIES (illustrated by Jessie Willcox Smith) (Dodd Mead, U.S., 1916) £100
THE WATER BABIES (illustrated by Jessie Willcox Smith) (Hodder & Stoughton, [1916]) £100
THE WATER BABIES (illustrated by Jessie Willcox Smith) (Hodder & Stoughton/Boots the Chemist, [c.1930])........£75
THE WATER BABIES (illustrated by Jessie Willcox Smith; facsimile of the original 1916 edition;
    limited to 500 numbered copies; in slipcase) (Hodder & Stoughton, 1981) £95
THE WATER BABIES (illustrated by Gordon Robinson) (J.A. Sharp, 1919)..£20
THE WATER BABIES (illustrated by Harry G. Theaker) (Ward Lock, [1922])..£40
THE WATER BABIES (illustrated by Anne Anderson) (T.C. & E.C. Jack, [1924])..£130
THE WATER BABIES (illustrated by Rosalie K. Fry) (Dent, 1957) £25
HEREWARD THE WAKE (Cambridge, 1866) £200
MADAM HOW AND LADY WHY, or First Lessons in Earth Lore for Children (London, 1870).................................£150

KINGSTON, W.H.G.

British author. Born: 1814. Spent much of his youth in Oporto where his father was a merchant. Prolific writer of adventure stories for boys, notably *Peter the Whaler* (1851) and *The Three Midshipmen* (1873) and its sequels. He also edited a number of annuals and periodicals for boys, including the first *Union Jack*. Died: 1880.

Prices are for books in Good condition.

PETER THE WHALER: His Life and Adventures in the Arctic Regions (Grant, 1851) £60
MANCO, THE PERUVIAN CHIEF, or An Englishman's Adventures in the Country of the Incas
    (Grant, 1853 [1852])...£30

SALT WATER (Griffith & Farran, 1857 [1856]) £10
THE EARLY LIFE OF OLD JACK: A Tale for Boys (Nelson, 1858) £25
OLD JACK: A Tale for Boys (Nelson, 1859) £25
ROUND THE WORLD: A Tale for Boys (Nelson, 1859)..£30
WILL WEATHERHELM: Yarns of an Old Sailor (Griffith & Farran, 1859) £30
MY FIRST VOYAGE TO SOUTHERN SEAS (Nelson, 1860) £30
DIGBY HEATHCOTE, or The Early Days of a Country Gentleman's Son and Heir
    (Routledge, Warne & Routledge, 1860) £30
ERNEST BRACEBRIDGE, or School-Boy Days (Sampson Low, 1860 [1859]) £30
TRUE BLUE (Griffith & Farran, 1862 [1861]) £10
MARMADUKE MERRY THE MIDSHIPMAN (Routledge, 1862) £30
PAUL GERRARD, THE CABIN BOY (Routledge, 1866)..£30
THE ROYAL MERCHANT, or Events in the Days of Sir Thomas Gresham (Partridge, 1870)....................£20
IN THE WILDS OF AFRICA: A Tale for Boys (Nelson, 1871 [1870]) £25
ON THE BANKS OF THE AMAZON (Nelson, 1872) £75
THE TRAPPER'S SON (London/Edinburgh, 1873)..£20
THE THREE MIDSHIPMEN (Griffith & Farran, 1873 [1872])..£20
HURRICANE HURRY (illustrated by R. Huttula) (Griffith & Farran, 1874) £20
ELDOL THE DRUID (Partridge, 1874) £20
THE TWO SHIPMATES (SPCK, 1874) £25
STORIES OF ANIMAL SAGACITY (illustrated by Harrison Weir) (Nelson, 1874) £30
THE HEROIC WIFE, or The Wanderers on the Amazon (illustrated by H.W. Petherick) (Griffith & Farran, 1874).......................£15
THE SOUTH SEA WHALER (Nelson, 1875) £25
THE THREE LIEUTENANTS, or Naval Life in the Nineteenth Century (illustrated by D.H. Friston) (Griffith & Farran, 1875) £30
SAVED FROM THE SEA (Nelson, 1876 [1875])..£15
THE THREE COMMANDERS (Griffith & Farran, 1876 [1875])..£40
SNOW-SHOES AND CANOES (Sampson Low, 1876)...£20
THE YOUNG RAJAH: A Story of Indian Life and Adventure (Nelson, 1876) £10
THE WANDERERS: Adventures in Trinidad (Nelson, 1876) £15
TWICE LOST: A Story of Shipwreck and Adventure (Nelson, 1876) £15
THE YOUNG LLANERO (Nelson, 1877) £15
IN THE ROCKY MOUNTAINS (Nelson, 1878 [1877]) £15
WITH AXE AND RIFLE, or The Western Pioneers (Sampson Low, 1878) £10
IN NEW GRANADA, or Heroes and Patriots: A Tale for Boys (Nelson, 1879) £20
IN THE WILDS OF FLORIDA: A Tale of Warfare and Hunting (Nelson, 1880) £95
THE GOLDEN GRASSHOPPER: A Story of the Days of Sir Thomas Gresham (Religious Tract Society, 1880) £15
AMONG THE RED-SKINS, or Over the Rocky Mountains (Cassell, 1880)..£15
THE HEIR OF KILFINNAN (Sampson Low, 1881 [1880]) £10
ROGER WILLOUGHBY: A Story of the Times of Benbow (Nisbet, 1881 [1880]) £20
PADDY FINN: Adventures Afloat and Ashore (Griffith & Farran, 1883) £25
FROM POWDER MONKEY TO ADMIRAL (Hodder, 1883) £20

KIPLING, Rudyard
British author. Born: Bombay, 1865. Brought to England in 1871, later studying at the United Services College, Westward Ho! Returned to India in 1882, spending the next seven years working as a journalist and short story-writer. Lived in the United States from 1892 to 1896, subsequently settling permanently in England. Kipling is a rare example of an author who is equally celebrated for his children's works as his adult ones. Among the former are the two *Jungle Books* (1894/95), *Stalky & Co* (1899), *Just So Stories* (1902) and *Puck of Pook's Hill* (1906). Some of these books contain illustrations either by him or his father, John Lockwood Kipling. Despite the unfashionability of many of Kipling's views, his children's works have remained enduring classics of the genre. Died: 1936.

Prices are for books in Very Good condition.

THE JUNGLE BOOK (illustrated by J. Lockwood Kipling, W.H. Drake and P. Frenzeny) (Macmillan, 1894)............................£1,200
THE SECOND JUNGLE BOOK (illustrated by J. Lockwood Kipling) (Macmillan, 1895) £350
SIXTEEN ILLUSTRATIONS OF SUBJECTS FROM KIPLING'S 'JUNGLE BOOK' (illustrated by M. and E. Detmold)
    (Macmillan, 1903) £1,800
THE JUNGLE BOOK (illustrated by M. and E. Detmold) (Macmillan, 1908) £100
ALL THE MOWGLI STORIES (illustrated by Stuart Tresilian; issued with dustjacket) (Macmillan, 1933) £20
ALL THE MOWGLI STORIES (illustrated by Stuart Tresilian; leather binding; issued with dustjacket) (Macmillan, 1933) £40
CAPTAINS COURAGEOUS: A Story of the Grand Banks (illustrated by I.W. Taber) (Macmillan, 1897) £60
STALKY & CO (Macmillan, 1899) £75
KIM (illustrated by J. Lockwood Kipling) (Macmillan, 1901) £60
JUST SO STORIES FOR LITTLE CHILDREN (illustrated by the author) (Macmillan, 1902) £300
PUCK OF POOK'S HILL (illustrated by H.R. Millar) (Macmillan, 1906) £60
PUCK OF POOK'S HILL (illustrated by Arthur Rackham) (Doubleday, U.S., 1906) £200
A SONG OF THE ENGLISH (verse; illustrated by W. Heath Robinson) (Hodder & Stoughton, 1909) £300
REWARDS AND FAIRIES (illustrated by Frank Craig) (Macmillan, 1910) £50
THE COLLECTED VERSE OF RUDYARD KIPLING (illustrated by W. Heath Robinson) (Doubleday Page, U.S., 1910) £200

A HISTORY OF ENGLAND (with C.R.L. Fletcher; quarto) (OUP/Hodder & Stoughton, 1911) £35
A HISTORY OF ENGLAND (octavo edition for use in schools) (OUP/Hodder & Stoughton, 1911)...£15
LAND AND SEA TALES FOR SCOUTS AND GUIDES (Macmillan, 1923) £30
TOOMAI OF THE ELEPHANTS (tie-in with the film 'Elephant Boy'; issued with dustjacket) (Macmillan, 1937) £8

KNATCHBULL-HUGESSEN, E.H.

British author. Born: Edward Hugessen Knatchbull-Hugessen in 1829. Between 1869 and 1886, he published several volumes of original fairy stories, of which the first was *Stories for my Children* (1869). Modelled on tales of Hans Andersen, these were an important influence on J.R.R. Tolkien. Knatchbull-Hugessen was a great-nephew of Jane Austen, and briefly served as a junior minister in Gladstone's government. Towards the end of his life, Knatchbull-Hugessen received a baronetcy, becoming the first Baron Brabourne. Died: 1893.

Prices are for books in Good condition.

STORIES FOR MY CHILDREN (Macmillan, 1869)..£35
CRACKERS FOR CHRISTMAS: More Stories by E.K.H. (Macmillan, 1870)..£35
CRACKERS FOR CHRISTMAS: More Stories by E.K.H. (new edition) (Routledge, 1883 [1882]) £25
MOONSHINE: Fairy Stories (illustrated by W. Brunton) (Macmillan, 1871)...£35
TALES AT TEA-TIME: Fairy Stories (illustrated by W. Brunton) (Macmillan, 1872) £40
QUEER FOLK: Seven Stories (illustrated by S.E. Waller) (Macmillan, 1873) £40
QUEER FOLK: Seven Stories (new edition) (Routledge, 1883 [1882])..£25
WHISPERS FROM FAIRYLAND (Longmans Green, 1875 [1874]) £30
HIGGLEDY-PIGGLEDY, or Stories for Everybody and Everybody's Children
    (Longmans Green, 1875)...£60
UNCLE JOE'S STORIES (illustrated by E. Griset) (Routledge, 1879 [1878]) £40
OTHER STORIES (illustrated by E. Griset) (Routledge, 1880 [1879]) £40
THE MOUNTAIN-SPRITE'S KINGDOM and Other Stories (illustrated by E. Griset) (Routledge, 1881 [1880]) £40
FERDINAND'S ADVENTURE and Other Stories (illustrated by E. Griset) (Routledge, 1883 [1882]) £40
FRIENDS AND FOES FROM FAIRY LAND (illustrated by L. Sambourne) (Longmans, 1886 [1885])...........................£40
ELLA'S FAULT: Jack Frost's Little Prisoners (with Stella Austin and S. Baring Gould) (Skeffington, 1887) £30
THE MAGIC OAK TREE AND PRINCE FILDERKIN (Unwin, 1894) £30
SOME WHISPERS FROM FAIRYLAND (contains 'The Lost Prince' and 'The Silver Fairies' from 'Whispers from Fairy-Land')
    (Blackie, [1933]) £10

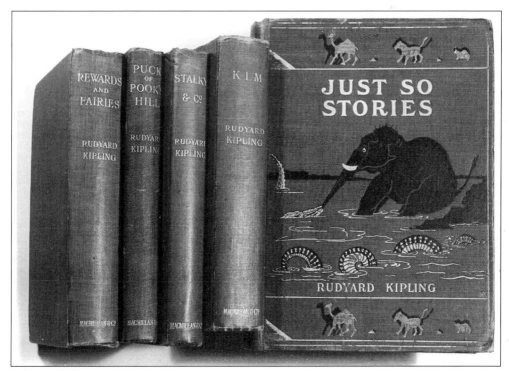

*Five Kipling classics: the two 'Puck' books, **Stalky & Co**, his great novel, **Kim**, and the ever-popular **Just So Stories** (1902).*

L

LADYBIRD BOOKS

Highly successful children's imprint derived from the activities of Loughborough bookseller, Henry Wills (later Wills & Hepworth), who launched the 'Ladybird' logo in 1915. The first book to appear under the imprint was *Little Stories for Little People*, an annual-sized volume published in 1916. The distinctive pocket-sized 'Ladybird' was a result of Second World War paper shortages. The first of these was *Bunnikin's Picnic Party* (1940), issued in boards and a dustjacket. Later editions/issues have no jackets.
Prices are for books in Very Good condition.

Non-Series Books
LITTLE STORIES FOR LITTLE PEOPLE (issued in decorative boards) (1916) £80
ABC PICTURE BOOK (issued in decorative boards) (1916) £50

Series 401
BUNNIKIN'S PICNIC PARTY (1940) £35
BUNNY'S FIRST BIRTHDAY (1940) £35
BOB BUSHTAIL'S ADVENTURE (1941) £35
GINGER'S ADVENTURES (1942) £25
DOWNY DUCKLING (1942) £25
SMOKE AND FLUFF (1942) £25
THE FIRST DAY OF THE HOLIDAYS (1942) £25
PIGGY PLAYS TRUANT (1947) £10
LOST AT THE FAIR (1948) £10
RUNAWAY (1948) £10
THE BUNNY FLUFF'S MOVING DAY (1948) £10
MR BADGER TO THE RESCUE (1949) £10
THE GREEN UMBRELLA (1950) £10
FIVE LITTLE KITTENS (1955) £10

Series 455
IN THE TRAIN WITH UNCLE MAC (1945) £15
IN THE COUNTRY WITH UNCLE MAC (1946) £15
BESIDE THE SEA WITH UNCLE MAC (1959) £15

Series 497
TIPTOES, THE MISCHIEVOUS KITTEN (1949) £10
THE WISE ROBIN (1950) £10

Series 522
THE CHILD OF THE TEMPLE (1953) £10
THE SHEPHERD BOY OF BETHLEHEM (1954) £10
THE LITTLE LORD JESUS (1954) £10
THE STORY OF JESUS (1955) £10
JESUS BY THE SEA OF GALILEE (1958) £10
JESUS CALLS HIS DISCIPLES (1959) £10

Series 536
A BOOK OF BRITISH BIRDS AND THEIR NESTS (1953) £10
A SECOND BOOK OF BRITISH BIRDS AND THEIRS NESTS (1954)..£10
A THIRD BOOK OF BRITISH BIRDS AND THEIR NESTS (1954) £8
BRITISH WILD FLOWERS (1957) £8
BRITISH WILD FLOWERS (1958) £10
WHAT TO LOOK FOR IN WINTER (1959) £8
WHAT TO LOOK FOR IN SUMMER (1960) £8
WHAT TO LOOK FOR IN AUTUMN (1960) £5
WHAT TO LOOK FOR IN SPRING (1961) £5
THE WEATHER (1962) £4
BOOK OF TREES (1963) £4
POND LIFE (1966) £4
YOUR BODY (1967) £4
GARDEN BIRDS (1967) £4
SEA AND ESTUARY BIRDS (1967)..£4

Series 561
KING ALFRED THE GREAT (1956) £10
WILLIAM THE CONQUEROR (1956) £10
SIR WALTER RALEIGH (1957)..£10
THE STORY OF NELSON (1957) £10
THE FIRST QUEEN ELIZABETH (1958) £10

A Second Book of British Birds was issued as part of Series 536, devoted to wildlife and country subjects.

Another title from this series. It was part of a quartet of books devoted to Britain's countryside during the four seasons.

FLORENCE NIGHTINGALE (1959) £8
JULIUS CAESAR AND ROMAN BRITAIN (1959) £8
THE STORY OF CHARLES II (1960) £8
DAVID LIVINGSTONE (1960) £8
STONE AGE MAN IN BRITAIN (1961) £8
THE STORY OF HENRY V (1962) £8
OLIVER CROMWELL (1963) £5
ALEXANDER THE GREAT (1963) £5
RICHARD THE LIONHEART (1965) £5
CLEOPATRA AND ANCIENT EGYPT (1966)...£5
THE KINGS AND QUEENS OF ENGLAND (Book1; 1968) £5
THE KINGS AND QUEENS OF ENGLAND (Book2; 1968) £5
NAPOLEON (1968) £5

Series 563
PUPPIES AND KITTENS (1956)...£10
THE FARM (1958) £10
GOING TO SCHOOL (1959) £10
THE ZOO (1960) £8

Series 587
FLIGHT ONE : AUSTRALIA (1958) £10
FLIGHT TWO : CANADA (1959)...£8
FLIGHT THREE : USA (1959)..£8

Series 601
THE STORY OF FLIGHT (1960) £10
GREAT INVENTIONS (1961) £5,
THE STORY OF RAILWAYS (1961) £5
THE STORY OF SHIPS (1961) £5
THE STORY OF THE MOTOR CAR (1962) £5
THE STORY OF HOUSES AND HOMES (1963) £5
THE STORY OF CLOTHES AND COSTUMES (1964)...£5
CHURCHES AND CATHEDRALS (1964)...£5

LADYBIRD BOOKS

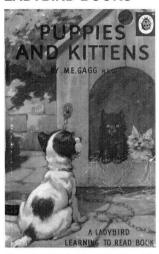

These three books give some idea of the wide range of subjects covered by the various Ladybird series.

THE STORY OF OIL (1968) £5
THE STORY OF NEWSPAPERS (1969)..£5
THE STORY OF PRINTING (1970) £5

Series 606A
JESUS THE HELPER (1960) £5
JESUS THE FRIEND (1961) £5
BABY JESUS (1961)..£5
CHILDREN OF THE BIBLE (1962) £5
A FIRST BOOK OF SAINTS (1963) £5

Series 606B
THE FIREMAN (1960)..£8
THE POLICEMAN (1961) £5
THE NURSE (1963)..£5
THE FISHERMAN (1963) £5
THE BUILDER (1965) £5
THE POSTMAN (1965) £5
THE MINER (1965) £5
THE SOLDIER (1966) £5
THE AIRMAN IN THE ROYAL AIR FORCE (1967) £5

Series 606C
THE STORY OF CRICKET (1964) £5
THE STORY OF FOOTBALL (1964)..£5

Series 606D
THE ELVES AND THE SHOEMAKER (1965)..£5
THREE LITTLE PIGS (1965) £5
SLEEPING BEAUTY (1965) £5
DICK WHITTINGTON AND HIS CAT (1966)..£5
THE PRINCESS AND THE PEA (1967) £5
THE MAGIC PORRIDGE POT (1971) £5
THE BIG PANCAKE (1972) £5
THE OLD WOMAN AND HER PIG (1973) £5
THE MUSICIANS OF BREMEN (1974) £5

Series 606E
ELECTRICITY (1966) £5
GAS (1967) £5
WATER SUPPLY (1969) £5

Series 612
THE LORD'S PRAYER (1961) £8
BOOK OF PRAYERS (1964)..£10

Series 633
THINGS TO MAKE (1963)..£8
TOYS AND GAMES TO MAKE (1966) £5

STAMP COLLECTING (1969)...£5
HOW TO SWIM AND DIVE (1971) £5
LEARNING TO SEW (1972) £5

Series 649
ANIMALS, BIRDS AND PLANTS OF THE BIBLE (1963) £5
WHAT TO LOOK FOR INSIDE A CHURCH (1972) £5
WHAT TO LOOK FOR OUTSIDE A CHURCH (1972) £5

Series 651
ANIMALS AND HOW THEY LIVE (1965) £5
BIRDS AND HOW THEY LIVE (1966) £5

Series 654
HOW IT WORKS – THE MOTOR CAR (1965) £8
HOW IT WORKS – THE COMPUTER (1969) £5
HOW IT WORKS – PRINTING PROCESSES (1971) £5

Series 662
THE STORY OF MUSIC (1968) £5
BALLET (1969) £5
THE LIVES OF GREAT COMPOSERS (Book 1; 1969) £5
THE LIVES OF GREAT COMPOSERS (Book 2; 1969) £5

Series 706
CUB SCOUTS (1970) £5
SCOUTS (1971)...£5
BROWNIE GUIDE (1978) £5
GIRL GUIDE (1980) £5

Series 707
THE STORY OF THE INDIANS (1973) £5
THE BATTLE OF THE LITTLE BIG HORN (1976) £5

Series 727
WILD LIFE IN BRITAIN (1972) £5
DISAPPEARING MAMMALS (1973) £5
WHAT ONEARTH ARE WE DOING (1976) £5
BUTTERFLIES AND MOTHS (1978) £5
HEDGES (1979) £5
UNDERSTANDING THE SEA (1979) £5

Series 737
WATER (1973)..£4
MAN IN THE AIR (1973) £4
MAN AND HIS CAR (1974)..£4
UNDER THE GROUND (1975) £5
THE STREAM (1975) £5

Royalty Series
THE QUEEN (1983)..£5
PRINCE CHARLES (1981) £5
THE QUEEN MOTHER (1982) £10
THE PRINCESS OF WALES (1982) £10
WILLIAM AND HENRY (1982) £10
THE ROYAL WEDDING : PRINCE CHARLES (1981) £10
THE ROYAL WEDDING : PRINCE ANDREW (1986) £5

Miscellaneous
OUR FRIEND (series 6a; 1964) £5
SUNNY DAYS (series 8a; 1964) £5
FUN AT THE FARM (series 4b; 1965)...£5
THE BIG HOUSE (series 8b; 1966) £8
JUMP FROM THE SKY (series 9b; 1966) £5
ADVENTURE ON THE ISLAND (series 10a; 1966) £5
MYSTERY ON THE ISLAND (series 11a; 1966)...£5
THE HOLIDAY CAMP MYSTERY (series 12a; 1966) £8
THE CARNIVAL (series 1b; 1967) £5
ADVENTURE AT THE CASTLE (series 10b; 1967) £5
BOOKS ARE EXCITING (series 11c; 1967) £5
MOUNTAIN ADVENTURE (series 12b; 1967)..£5
YOU MUST BE JOKING (Save the Children Fund, 1986) £5
THE LADYBIRD 50th ANNIVERSARY COMPETITION BOOK (1990) £8

LA FONTAINE, Jean de

French author. Born: Champagne, France, in 1621. Wrote several volumes of adult poetry, but is best known today for his *Fables* — either original, or drawn from Aesop or other classical sources — first published under the title *Fables Choisies Mises en Vers* in 1668. These were first translated into English in 1734, and have been reprinted many times since. Died: 1695.

Prices are for books in Very Good condition with dustjackets where applicable.

FABLES (twelve volumes) (France, 1668-94) ....the set **£10,000**
FABLES (first English edition) (London, 1734) **£1,000**
LA FONTAINE'S FABLES (translated by R. Thomson) (France, 1806) **£450**
FABLES (illustrated by J.J. Grandville; two volumes) (France, 1838) ....the set **£1,250**
FABLES (illustrated by Gustave Doré; two volumes) (Hachette, Paris, 1867) ....the set **£300**
THE FABLES OF LA FONTAINE (illustrated by Gustave Doré; translated into English verse by Walter Thornbury)
    (Cassell, 1868)..**£200**
THE FABLES OF LA FONTAINE (illustrated by Stephen Gooden; translated into English verse by Edward Marsh;
    two volumes; issued with dustjackets) (Heinemann, 1931) ....the set **£100**
LA FONTAINE'S FABLES (translated into English verse by Sir Edward Marsh; issued with dustjacket)
    (Dent: 'Everyman's Library' series, 1953)..**£10**

*The front board of **The Green Fairy Book** (1892), the third in Andrew Lang's famous series.*

THE LION AND THE RAT (illustrated and retold by Brian Wildsmith; issued with dustjacket) (OUP, 1963) **£25**
THE NORTH WIND AND THE SUN (illustrated and retold by Brian Wildsmith; issued with dustjacket) (OUP, 1964) **£25**
THE RICH MAN AND THE SHOE-MAKER (illustrated and retold by Brian Wildsmith; issued with dustjacket)(OUP, 1965).........**£25**
THE HARE AND THE TORTOISE (illustrated and retold by Brian Wildsmith; issued with dustjacket) (OUP, 1966) **£25**
THE FABLES OF LA FONTAINE, including his 'Life of Aesop' (illustrated by J.B. Oudry; translated by Kitty Muggeridge)
(Collins, 1973) **£20**

LAMB, Charles and Mary

British authors. Born: London, in 1775 and 1764 respectively. Charles was educated at Christ's Hospital, subsequently obtaining a clerkship at East India House, where he remained for thirty years. Mary stabbed her mother to death in 1796 and was committed to a lunatic asylum. Following her release in 1799, she lived with her brother until his death in 1834. The two of them collaborated on a number of children's books, most notably their *Tales from Shakespear* of 1807. Charles also achieved great fame with his adult *Essays of Elia* (1823/33). Mary died in 1847.

Prices are for books in Very Good condition.

THE KING AND QUEEN OF HEARTS (verse; wraps) (Godwin: 'Juvenile Library' series, 1805)..**£600**
THE KING AND QUEEN OF HEARTS (facsimile of the first edition; introduction by E.V. Lucas) (Methuen, 1902) **£75**
TALES FROM SHAKESPEARE (two volumes) (Hodgkins, 1807)...the set **£1,500**
TALES FROM SHAKESPEARE (illustrated by Arthur Rackham) (Dent: 'Temple Classics' series, 1899) **£75**
TALES FROM SHAKESPEARE (Nister, [c.1900]) **£50**
TALES FROM SHAKESPEARE (illustrated by Arthur Rackham) (Dent, 1909) **£200**
TALES FROM SHAKESPEARE (illustrated by Arthur Rackham; limited to 750 numbered copies, signed by the artist)
(Dent, 1909) **£1,000**
TALES FROM SHAKESPEARE (illustrated by Charles Folkard) (Dent, [1926]) **£75**
THE ADVENTURES OF ULYSSES (adapted from Chapman's translation of the 'Odyssey';
illustrated by C. Heath after H. Corbould; boards) (Godwin: 'Juvenile Library' series, 1808).....................................**£400**
MRS LEICESTER'S SCHOOL (anonymous) (Godwin: 'Juvenile Library' series, 1809)...**£700**
POETRY FOR CHILDREN (anonymous; wrappers) (Godwin: 'Juvenile Library' series, 1809)...**£600**
A BOOK EXPLAINING THE RANKS AND DIGNITIES OF BRITISH SOCIETY (boards)
(Tabart: 'Juvenile and School Library' series, 1809) **£600**
PRINCE DORUS: A Poetical Version of an Ancient Tale (wraps) (Godwin: 'Juvenile Library' series, 1811)............................**£600**
BEAUTY AND THE BEAST (wraps) (Godwin: 'Juvenile Library' series, [1811])...**£600**
BEAUTY AND THE BEAST (introduction by Andrew Lang; boards) (Field & Tuer/Leadenhall Press, [1887])..............................**£80**
MR H, or Beware a Bad Name (play) (Carey, U.S., 1813)..**£200**
A MASQUE OF DAYS (illustrated by Walter Crane) (Cassell, 1901) **£200**
STORIES FOR CHILDREN (illustrated by Charles Robinson and W. Green) (Dent, 1902) **£60**

LANG, Andrew

Scottish folklorist. Born: Selkirk, Scotland, in 1844. Educated at Edinburgh Academy, St. Andrew's University and Balliol College, Oxford. Subsequently became a Fellow of Merton College, but moved to London in the early 1870s where he worked as a freelance journalist, writing leaders for the *Daily News* and collaborating on translations of the *Odyssey* and the *Iliad*. Wrote/compiled a large number of children's works, but is best known for his 'Fairy Book' series, beginning with *The Blue Fairy Book* in 1889 and ending with *The Lilac Fairy Book* in 1910. Also collaborated with H. Rider Haggard on a novel, *The World's Desire* (1890). As a reviewer/publisher's reader, he forwarded the careers of Haggard, Rudyard Kipling, Arthur Conan Doyle, Walter de la Mare, F. Anstey and E. Nesbit. Died: 1912.

Prices are for books in Very Good condition.

'Fairy' Books

THE BLUE FAIRY BOOK (illustrated by Henry J. Ford and G.P. Jacomb Hood) (Longmans, 1889)..**£350**
THE RED FAIRY BOOK (illustrated by Henry J. Ford and L. Speed) (Longmans, 1890)..**£300**
THE GREEN FAIRY BOOK (illustrated by Henry J. Ford) (Longmans, 1892) **£300**
THE YELLOW FAIRY BOOK (illustrated by Henry J. Ford) (Longmans, 1894) **£300**
THE PINK FAIRY BOOK (illustrated by Henry J. Ford) (Longmans, 1897) **£275**
THE GREY FAIRY BOOK (illustrated by Henry J. Ford) (Longmans, 1900) **£250**
THE VIOLET FAIRY BOOK (illustrated by Henry J. Ford) (Longmans, 1901) **£250**
THE CRIMSON FAIRY BOOK (illustrated by Henry J. Ford) (Longmans, 1903) **£250**
THE BROWN FAIRY BOOK (illustrated by Henry J. Ford) (Longmans, 1904)..**£250**
THE ORANGE FAIRY BOOK (illustrated by Henry J. Ford) (Longmans, 1906)..**£200**
THE OLIVE FAIRY BOOK (illustrated by Henry J. Ford) (Longmans, 1907) **£200**
THE LILAC FAIRY BOOK (illustrated by Henry J. Ford) (Longmans, 1910) **£200**

Others

THE PRINCESS NOBODY: A Tale of Fairy Land (illustrated by Richard Doyle) (Longmans, [1884]) **£500**
JOHNNY NUT AND THE GOLDEN GOOSE (Longmans, 1888) **£100**
THE GOLD OF FAIRNILEE (illustrated by T. Scott and E.A. Lemann) (Arrowsmith, [1888]) **£120**
PRINCE PRIGIO (illustrated by Gordon Browne) (Arrowsmith, 1889) **£100**
THE WORLD'S DESIRE (with H. Rider Haggard) (Longmans, 1890) **£60**

THE BLUE POETRY BOOK (illustrated by Henry J. Ford and Lancelot Speed) (Longmans, 1891) £100
THE TRUE STORY BOOK (illustrated by L. Bogle, Lucien Davis, Henry J Ford, C.H.M. Kerr and Lancelot Speed)
(Longmans, 1893) £75
PRINCE RICARDO OF PANTOUFLIA: Being the Adventures of Prince Prigo's Son (illustrated by Gordon Browne)
(Arrowsmith, [1893]) £80
THE RED TRUE STORY BOOK (illustrated by Henry J. Ford) (Longmans, 1895) £70
THE ANIMAL STORY BOOK (illustrated by Henry J. Ford) (Longmans, 1896) £70
THE ARABIAN NIGHTS ENTERTAINMENTS. Edited by Andrew Lang (illustrated by Henry J. Ford) (Longmans, 1898) £200
THE RED BOOK OF ANIMAL STORIES (illustrated by Henry J. Ford) (Longmans, 1899) £70
THE BOOK OF ROMANCE (illustrated by Henry J. Ford) (Longmans, 1902) £100
THE RED ROMANCE BOOK (illustrated by Henry J. Ford) (Longmans, 1905) £120
TALES OF A FAIRY COURT (contains 'Prince Prigo' and 'Prince Ricardo of Pantouflia'; illustrated by A.A. Dixon)
(Arrowsmith, [1907]) £80
TALES OF TROY AND GREECE (illustrated by Henry J. Ford) (Longmans, 1907) £75
THE BOOK OF PRINCES AND PRINCESSES (illustrated by Henry J. Ford) (Longmans, 1908) £80
THE RED BOOK OF HEROES (illustrated by Henry J. Ford) (Longmans, 1909) £80
THE ALL SORTS OF STORIES BOOK (illustrated by Henry J. Ford) (Longmans, 1911) £70
THE BOOK OF SAINTS AND HEROES (illustrated by Henry J. Ford) (Longmans, 1912) £70
THE STRANGE STORY BOOK (illustrated by Henry J. Ford) (Longmans, 1913) £75
THE ROSE FAIRY BOOK (illustrated by Vera Bock) (Longmans, [1948]) £80

LAWSON, Robert
American author-illustrator. Born: 1892. The creator of 'Uncle Analdas', an irascible old rabbit, who appeared In several stories. Won the Newbery Medal for *Rabbit Hill* (1944). Died: 1957.

Prices are for books in Very Good condition with dustjackets where applicable.

Books Written and Illustrated by Robert Lawson
BEN AND ME (Little Brown, U.S., 1939)..£120
THEY WERE STRONG AND GOOD (Little Brown, U.S., 1940) £40
I DISCOVER COLUMBUS (Little Brown, U.S., 1941) £75
COUNTRY COLIC (Little Brown, U.S., 1944) £30
RABBIT HILL (Viking, U.S., 1944) £50
AT THAT TIME (Viking, U.S., 1947) £35
THE FABULOUS FLIGHT (Little Brown, U.S., 1949) £35
ROBBUT, A TALE OF TAILS (Heinemann, 1949)...£30
MR REVERE AND I (Little Brown, U.S., 1953) £45
THE TOUGH OF WINTER (Little Brown U.S., 1954) £30
CAPT KIDD'S CAT (Muller, 1956)...£45
THE GREAT WHEEL (Viking, U.S., 1964) £50

Books Illustrated by Robert Lawson
THE WEE MEN OF BALLYWOODEN by Arthur Mason (Heinemann, 1931)..£50
THE STORY OF FERDINAND by Munro Leaf (Hamish Hamilton, 1937)...£50
ONE FOOT IN FAIRYLAND : Sixteen Tales by Eleanor Farjeon (Joseph, 1938) £30
WEE GILLIS by Munro Leaf (Viking, U.S., 1938) £50
MR POPPER'S PENGUINS by Richard and Florence Atwater (Harrap, 1939) £30
POO-POO AND THE DRAGONS by CS Forester (Joseph, 1942) £75
ADAM OF THE ROAD by Janet Gray (A. & C. Black, 1943) £25
SIMPSON AND SAMPSON by Munro Leaf (Warne, 1944) £25

LE CAIN, Errol
British author-illustrator. Born: Singapore, 1941. Worked in advertising and animation for TV and films. He wrote and illustrated several books for children, but most of his work was for other writers. He won the Kate Greenaway Medal *with Hiawatha's Childhood* in 1985. Died: 1989.

Prices are for books in Very Good condition with dustjackets where applicable.

Books Illustrated by Errol Le Cain
SIR ORFEO by Anthea Davis (Faber, 1970) £20
THE CHILD IN THE BAMBOO GROVE by Rosemary Harris (Faber, 1971) £15
THE BEACHCOMBERS by Helen Cresswell (Faber, 1972) £15
THE KING'S WHITE ELEPHANT by Rosemary Harris (Faber, 1973) £15
THE LOTUS AND THE GRAIL by Rosemary Harris (Faber, 1974) £15
THE FLYING SHIP by Rosemary Harris (Faber, 1975)..£15
THORN ROSE. Taken from the Brothers Grimm by Errol Le Cain (Faber, 1975)..£35
THE LITTLE DOG OF FO by Rosemary Harris (Faber, 1976) £15
THE SLY CORMORANT AND THE FISHES by Brian Patten (verse) (Kestrel, 1977) £25
THE TWELVE DANCING PRINCESSES. Taken from the Brothers Grimm by Erroll Le Cain (Faber, 1978) £25
BEAUTY AND THE BEAST by Rosemary Harris (Faber, 1979)..£15
THE SNOW QUEEN. New Adapted Version from Hans Christian Andersen by Naomi Lewis (Kestrel, 1979) £25

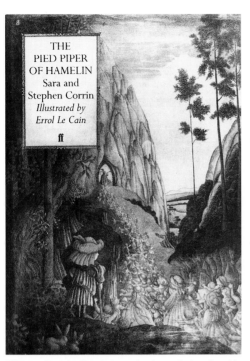

Illustrator Errol Le Cain is becoming increasingly collectable. His edition of **The Pied Piper of Hamelin** is now valued at £20.

The first U.K. hardback edition of **A Wizard of Earthsea**. The book was originally published as a Puffin paperback in 1971.

MRS FOX'S WEDDING by Sara and Stephen Corrin (Faber, 1980) £20
THE THREE MAGIC GIFTS by Riordan James (Kaye & Ward, 1980) £20
ALADDIN AND THE WONDERFUL LAMP. Retold by Andrew Lang (pictorial boards) (Faber, 1981)..£25
MOLLY WHUPPIE. Retold by Walter de la Mare (pictorial boards) (Faber, 1983) £20
HIAWATHA'S CHILDHOOD by Henry Wadsworth Longfellow (Faber, 1984)....................................£30
GROWLTIGER'S LAST STAND and Other Poems by T.S. Eliot (Faber, 1986) £35
THE ENCHANTER'S DAUGHTER by Antonia Barber (Cape, 1987) £20
CHRISTMAS 1993 or SANTA'S LAST RIDE by Leslie Bricasse (Faber, 1987) £20
THE PIED PIPER OF HAMELIN. Retold by Sara and Stephen Corrin (Faber, 1988) £20
TAIL FEATHERS FROM MOTHER GOOSE by Iona Opie (illustrated by Nicola Bayley, Babette Cole and Erroll Le Cain)
  (Walker, 1988) £25
THE CHRISTMAS STOCKINGS by Mathew Price (Angus and Robertson, 1989) £20
MR MISTOFFELEES by T.S. Eliot (Faber, 1990)....................................£35

LE GUIN, Ursula

American author. Born: Ursula Kroeber in Berkeley, California, in 1929. Educated at Radcliffe College, Massachusetts, and Columbia University. Married the historian, Charles A. Le Guin, in 1953. Best known for her 'Earthsea' trilogy of children's novels, she has also written a number of science fiction/fantasy works for adults.

Prices are for books in Very Good condition with dustjackets.

A WIZARD OF EARTHSEA (Parnassus Press, U.S., 1968)....................................£125
A WIZARD OF EARTHSEA (illustrated by Ruth Robbins; paperback) (Puffin, 1971) £10
A WIZARD OF EARTHSEA (Gollancz, 1971)....................................£150
THE TOMBS OF ATUAN (Atheneum, U.S., 1971) £125
THE TOMBS OF ATUAN (Gollancz, 1972) £100
THE FARTHEST SHORE (Atheneum, U.S., 1972) £100
THE FARTHEST SHORE (Gollancz, 1973) £85
A VERY LONG WAY FROM ANYWHERE ELSE (Gollancz, 1976) £20
A VERY LONG WAY FROM ANYWHERE ELSE (as 'Very Far Away from Anywhere Else') (Atheneum, U.S., 1976)..................£25
EARTHSEA (omnibus) (Gollancz, 1977)....................................£25
LEESE WEBSTER (Atheneum, U.S., 1979) £20

THE BEGINNING PLACE (Harper, U.S., 1980) £20
THRESHOLD, or The Beginning Place (Gollancz, 1980) £20
LEESE WEBSTER (Gollancz, 1981)...£20
VISIT FROM DR KATZ (picture book; boards) (Collins, 1988) £10
VISIT FROM DR KATZ (picture book) (Atheneum, U.S., 1988) £10
CATWINGS (Orchard, U.S., 1988) £10
CATWINGS RETURN (Orchard, U.S., 1989) £10
FIRE AND STONE (Atheneum, U.S., 1989) £10
TEHANU (Gollancz, 1990) £15
TEHANU (Atheneum, U.S., 1990)..£15

LE MAIR, H. Willebeek

Dutch illustrator. Born: Henriette Willebeek Le Mair in Rotterdam in 1889. Her first book, *Premières Rondes Enfantines*, was published when she was only fifteen, but she is best known in Britain for her later nursery rhyme illustrations. She ran a primary school for several years. Died: 1966.

Prices are for books in Very Good condition.

OUR OLD NURSERY RHYMES (Augener, 1911) £200
OUR OLD NURSERY RHYMES (De Luxe edition; signed by the artist; vellum binding) (Augener, 1911) £2,000
LITTLE SONGS OF LONG AGO (Augener, 1912) £200
LITTLE SONGS OF LONG AGO (De Luxe edition; signed by the artist; vellum binding) (Augener, 1912) £2,000
AUNTIE'S LITTLE RHYME BOOK (Augener, 1913) £120
NURSIE'S LITTLE RHYME BOOK (Augener, 1913) £120
GRANNY'S LITTLE RHYME BOOK (Augener, 1913) £120
SCHUMANN'S PIANO ALBUM OF CHILDREN'S PIECES (Augener, [1913]) £150
MOTHER'S LITTLE RHYME BOOK (Augener, [1913]) £120
THE CHILDREN'S CORNER by Rosie Helen Elkin (Augener, [1914])...............................£200
THE CHILDREN'S CORNER by Rosie Helen Elkin (De Luxe edition; signed by the artist; vellum binding) (Augener, 1914) ..£2,000
OLD NURSERY RHYMES (Augener, [1914]) £200
LITTLE PEOPLE by Rosie Helen Elkin (Augener, [1915]) £200
OLD DUTCH NURSERY RHYMES (Augener, 1917) £200
DADDY'S LITTLE RHYME BOOK (Augener, [c.1920]) £120
BABY'S LITTLE RHYME BOOK (Augener, [c.1920])..£120
A GALLERY OF CHILDREN by A.A. Milne (Stanley Paul, 1925)..£500
A GALLERY OF CHILDREN by A.A. Milne (limited to 500 numbered copies, signed by the author) (Stanley Paul, 1925)......£1,000
A CHILD'S GARDEN OF VERSE by R.L. Stevenson (Harrap, 1931)....................................£200
TWENTY JAKATA TALES. Retold by Noor Inayat Khan (Harrap, 1939) £100
CHRISTMAS CAROLS FOR YOUNG PEOPLE by Dawn and Peter Cope (Fine Books, 1976) £40

LEAR, Edward

British author-illustrator. Born: London, 1812. An accomplished artist, Lear published a book of *Illustrations of the Family of Psittacidae, or Parrots* when he was only twenty. Inspired by the limerick collection, *Anecdotes and Adventures of Fifteen Gentlemen*, he began to write humorous verses, the best of which were included in his *Book of Nonsense* (1846). Lear spent long periods in Italy and the Greek Islands during the 1840s and 1850s, recording his experiences in a number of books. Died: 1888.

Prices are for books in Very Good condition with dustjackets where applicable.

A BOOK OF NONSENSE (written under the pseudonym 'Derry Down Derry';
  illustrated by the author; two volumes; wraps) (Thomas Maclean, 1846)....................the set £65,000
A BOOK OF NONSENSE by Edward Lear (enlarged edition; illustrated by the author) (Routledge, [1861]) £700
NONSENSE SONGS, STORIES, BOTANY AND ALPHABETS (illustrated by the author) (Robert John Bush, 1871)...............£800
MORE NONSENSE, PICTURES, RHYMES, BOTANY, ETC. (illustrated by the author) (Robert John Bush, 1872 [1874]) £700
LAUGHABLE LYRICS: A Fourth Book of Nonsense Poems, Songs, Botany, Music, etc.
  (illustrated by the author) (Robert John Bush, 1877 [1876])..£500
THE JUMBLIES and Other Nonsense Poems, Songs, Botany, Music (illustrated by the author) (Warne, 1877 [1876]) £200
NONSENSE DROLLERIES (contains 'The Owl and the Pussy Cat' and 'The Duck and the Kangaroo';
  illustrated by W. Foster) (Warne, 1889) £125
A NONSENSE BIRTHDAY BOOK (illustrated by the author) (Warne, [1894]) £150
NONSENSE SONGS AND STORIES (introduction by Edward Strachey) (Warne, 1895) £100
NONSENSE SONGS AND STORIES (illustrated by L. Leslie Brooke) (Warne, 1900).........£60
THE PELICAN CHORUS and Other Nonsense Verses (illustrated by L. Leslie Brooke) (Warne, 1900)...............£100
QUEERY LEARY NONSENSE. Edited by Lady Strachey (illustrated by the author; introduction by the Earl of Cromer)
  (Mills & Boon, 1911)..£65
THE LEAR COLOURED BIRD BOOK FOR CHILDREN (illustrated by the author; foreword by J. St. Loe Strachey)
  (Mills & Boon, [1912])..£60
CALICO PIE (illustrated by the author) (Warne, [1924]) £75
THE OWL AND THE PUSSY CAT (illustrated by the author) (Warne, [1924]) £75
A BOOK OF NONSENSE. Edited by Ernest Rhys (contains works by Edward Lear and various other authors;
  illustrated by the authors; issued with dustjacket) (Dent: 'Everyman's Library' series, [1917]) £40
THE POBBLE (illustrated by the author; limited to fifty copies) (Hugh Sharp, 1934) £300

*The first edition of Edward Lear's **Nonsense Songs and Stories** is now worth £100 in Very Good condition.*

THE QUANGLE WANGLE'S HAT (illustrated by the author; limited to fifty copies) (Hugh Sharp, 1933) £300
NONSENSE SONGS AND LAUGHABLE LYRICS (illustrated by the author; limited to 950 copies)
(Peter Pauper Press, U.S., 1935)...£75
EDWARD LEAR'S NONSENSE SONGS (illustrated by the author; issued with dustjacket) (Chatto & Windus, 1938).................£50
A BOOK OF LEAR. Edited by R.L. Megroz (illustrated by the author; paperback; issued with dustjacket) (Penguin, 1939) £15
EDWARD LEAR'S NONSENSE OMNIBUS (illustrated by the author; issued with dustjacket) (Warne, 1943) £25
THE COMPLETE NONSENSE OF EDWARD LEAR. Edited and with an introduction by Holbrook Jackson
(illustrated by the author; issued with dustjacket) (Faber, 1947) £25
THE COMPLETE NONSENSE SONGS OF EDWARD LEAR (illustrated by the author;
introduction by Leonard Russell; issued with dustjacket) (Grey Walls Press, 1947) £15
EDWARD LEAR'S NONSENSE ALPHABET (illustrated by G.S. Sherwood; issued with dustjacket)
(Collins, [1949]) £50
A NONSENSE ALPHABET (illustrated by the author; issued with dustjacket) (HMSO, 1952) £30
TEAPOTS AND QUAILS and Other Nonsense. Edited and introduced by Angus Davidson and Philip Hofer
(illustrated by the author; issued with dustjacket) (John Murray, 1953) £40
ABC (illustrated by the author; issued with dustjacket) (Constable: 'Young Books' series, 1965)...£20

LEWIS, C. Day

Anglo-Irish author. Born: Cecil Day Lewis in Ireland in 1904. Best known for his adult poetry — he was appointed Poet Laureate in 1968 — his children's story, *The Otterbury Incident*, has been a firm favourite since it was first published in 1948. He has also written a number of detective novels under the pseudonym, 'Nicholas Blake'. Died: 1972.

Prices are for books in Very Good condition with dustjackets.

DICK WILLOUGHBY (Blackwell, [1933]) £40
POETRY FOR YOU: A Book for Boys and Girls on the Enjoyment of Poetry (Blackwell, 1944) £30
THE OTTERBURY INCIDENT: A Tale (illustrated by Edward Ardizzone) (Putnam, 1948) £40

LEWIS, C.S.

British author. Born: Clive Staples Lewis in Belfast in 1898. Educated at Malvern College and University College, Oxford. In 1925, he was made a Fellow of Magdalen College, remaining there until 1954, when he received a Cambridge professorship. At Oxford, he was a member of the informal group known as the 'Inklings', along with Charles Williams and J.R.R. Tolkien. His Christian faith is evident in his bestselling 'Narnia' series of children's books (1950-56), as well as several non-fiction works for adults (notably *The Screwtape Letters*, 1942). He also wrote a handful of accomplished science fiction novels. His short-lived marriage to the American, Joy Davidman, was the subject of the 1994 film, *Shadowlands*. Died: 1963.

Prices are for books in Very Good condition with dustjackets,

THE LION, THE WITCH AND THE WARDROBE (illustrated by Pauline Baynes) (Bles, 1950).....................£2,250
THE LION, THE WITCH AND THE WARDROBE (illustrated by Michael Hague) (Macmillan, U.S., 1983) £60
PRINCE CASPIAN: THE RETURN TO NARNIA (illustrated by Pauline Baynes) (Bles, 1951) £1,500
THE VOYAGE OF THE DAWN TREADER (illustrated by Pauline Baynes) (Bles, 1952) £1,500
THE SILVER CHAIR (illustrated by Pauline Baynes) (Bles, 1953)...£1,500
THE HORSE AND HIS BOY (illustrated by Pauline Baynes) (Bles, 1954) £1,500
THE MAGICIAN'S NEPHEW (illustrated by Pauline Baynes) (The Bodley Head, 1955) £1,500
THE LAST BATTLE (illustrated by Pauline Baynes) (The Bodley Head, 1956) £1,500

LINDGREN, Astrid

Swedish author. Born: Vimmerby, Sweden, in 1907. Has written over fifty children's books, including adventure and detective stories, but is best known for *Pippi Longstocking* (1954) and its many sequels. In the mid-Forties, she became a children's books editor with the Stockholm publishers, Raban & Sjören.

Prices are for books in Very Good condition with dustjackets where applicable.

PIPPI LONGSTOCKING (illustrated by Richard Kennedy; translated by Edna Harup) (OUP, 1954) £125
PIPPI GOES ABROAD (illustrated by Richard Kennedy; translated by Marianne Turner) (OUP, 1956)...........................£100
PIPPI IN THE SOUTH SEAS (illustrated by Richard Kennedy; translated by Marianne Turner) (OUP, 1957) £85
NORIKO-SAN GIRL OF JAPAN (illustrated by Anna Riwkin-Brick; translated by Leila Bery) (Methuen, 1958) £60
ERIC AND KARLSSON-ON-THE-ROOF (illustrated by Richard Kennedy; translated by Marianne Turner)
    (OUP, 1958) £55
SIA LIVES ON KILIMANJARO (photographs by Anna Riwkin-Brick) (Methuen, 1959)...........................£55
CIRCUS CHILD (photographs by Anna Riwkin-Brick) (Methuen, 1960) £40
MY SWEDISH COUSINS (photographs by Anna Riwkin-Brick) (Macmillan, [1960]) £40
MY SWEDISH COUSINS (photographs by Anna Riwkin-Brick) (Methuen: 'Children Everywhere' series, 1961)...........................£40
RASMUS AND THE TRAMP (illustrated by Eric Palmquist; translated by Gerry Bothmer) (Methuen, 1961) £40
RASMUS AND THE VAGABOND, RASMUS AND THE TRAMP (Methuen, 1961) £40
THE TOMTEN (adapted by Astrid Lindgren from a poem by Victor Rydberg; illustrated by Harald Wiberg)
    (Constable, 1962)...£40
KATI IN ITALY (illustrated by Daniel Dupuy) (Brockhampton Press, 1962) £40
DIRK LIVES IN HOLLAND (with Anna Riwken-Brick) (Methuen: 'Children Everywhere' series, 1963) £20
MARKO LIVES IN YUGOSLAVIA (with Anna Riwken-Brick) (Methuen: 'Children Everywhere' series, 1963) £20
MADICKEN (illustrated by Ilon Wikland; translated by Marianne Turner) (OUP, 1963)...........................£25
THE SIX BULLERBY CHILDREN (illustrated by Ilon Wikland; translated by Evelyn Ramsden) (Methuen, 1963) £20
CHRISTMAS IN THE STABLE (illustrated by Harald Wiberg; translated by Anthea Bell) (Brockhampton Press, 1963) £20
CHERRY TIME AT BULLERBY (illustrated by Ilon Wikland; translated by Florence Lamborn) (Methuen, 1964) £20
HAPPY DAYS AT BULLERBY (Methuen, 1964) £20
CHRISTMAS AT BULLERBY (illustrated by Ilon Wikland) (Methuen, 1964) £20
KATI IN AMERICA (illustrated by Daniel Dupuy; translated by Marianne Turner) (Brockhampton Press, 1964) £12
SIMON SMALL MOVES IN (illustrated by Ilon Wikland; translated by Marianne Turner)
    (Burke: 'Read for Fun' series, 1965)...£12
GERDA LIVES IN NORWAY (with Anna Riwken-Brick) (Methuen, 1965) £12
THE FOX AND THE TOMTEN (after a poem by Karl-Erik Forsslund; illustrated by Harald Wiberg) (Constable, [1966])...........................£25
KATI IN PARIS (illustrated by Daniel Dupuy) (Brockhampton Press, 1966) £12
BRENDA HELPS GRANDMOTHER (illustrated by Ilon Wikland; translated by Marianne Helweg)
    (Burke: 'Read for Fun' series, 1966)...£30
A DAY AT BULLERBY (Methuen, 1967)...£20
NOY LIVES IN THAILAND (photographs by Anna Riwkin-Brick) (Methuen: 'Children Everywhere' series, 1967)...........................£12

SCARECROW ISLAND (Oliver & Boyd, 1968) £12
SCRAN AND THE PIRATES (Oliver & Boyd, 1968) £12
THE MISCHIEVOUS MARTENS (Methuen, 1968) £12
MATTI LIVES IN FINLAND (photographs by Anna Riwkin-Brick) (Methuen: 'Children Everywhere' series, 1969) £12
LOTTA LEAVES HOME (Methuen, 1969)..£12
LOTTA'S BIKE (Methuen, 1973)..£12
THAT EMIL (Brockhampton Press, 1973) £12
EMIL AND HIS CLEVER PIG (Brockhampton Press, 1974)...£12
MY VERY OWN SISTER (Methuen, 1974) £12
THE BROTHERS LIONHEART (illustrated by Ilon Wikland; translated by John Tate) (Brockhampton Press, 1975) £12
KARLSSON FLIES AGAIN (Methuen, 1977) £12
EMIL AND LINA'S BAD TOOTH (Brockhampton Press, 1977) £12
LOTTA'S CHRISTMAS SURPRISE (Methuen, 1978)..£12
MARDIE (Methuen, 1979) £12
I WANT TO GO TO SCHOOL TOO (Methuen, 1980) £12
THE WORLD'S BEST KARLSON (Methuen, 1980) £12
THAT'S MY BABY (Methuen, 1980) £12
SPRINGTIME AT BULLERBY (Methuen, 1981)..£12
MARDIE TO THE RESCUE (Methuen, 1981) £12
THE RUNAWAY SLEIGH RIDE (illustrated by Ilon Wikland; laminated boards) (Methuen, 1984) £8
THE ROBBER'S DAUGHTER (illustrated by Ilon Wikland; translated by Patricia Crampton) (Methuen, 1984) £10
MY NIGHTINGALE IS SINGING (Methuen, 1985) £10
EMIL'S LITTLE SISTER (Hodder & Stoughton, 1985) £10
EMIL'S STICKY PROBLEM (Hodder & Stoughton, 1986) £10
THE DRAGON WITH RED EYES (Methuen, 1986) £10
THE GHOST OF SKINNY JACK (Methuen, 1988)..£10
LOTTA'S EASTER SURPRISE (illustrated by Ilon Wikland; translated by Patricia Crampton; laminated boards)
(Raben Strogren, 1991) £6

LINDSAY, Norman

Australian author-illustrator. Born: 1879. Worked as chief cartoonist of the Sydney *Bulletin*, and wrote and illustrated several novels, including the works of Dickens and Balzac. He wrote his classic children's novel, *The Magic Pudding* (1918), as a distraction from the horrors of the First World War, later dismissing it as a "little bundle of piffle". A follow-up, *The Flyaway Highway* (1936), was less successful. Died: 1969.

Prices are for books in Very Good condition with dustjackets.

THE MAGIC PUDDING: The Adventures of Bunyip Bluegum (illustrated by the author) (Sydney, 1918)............................£1,750
THE MAGIC PUDDING (Angus & Robertson, Sydney, 1930) £100
THE MAGIC PUDDING (Hamish Hamilton, 1936) £40
THE FLYAWAY HIGHWAY (Angus & Robertson, Sydney, 1936) £40

LINGARD, Joan

Scottish author. Born: Edinburgh. She spent her formative years in Belfast, which provided the background for her first book *The Twelfth of July* (1970). Awarded the West German Buxtehuder Bulle in 1986 for *Across the Barricades*, and the Scottish Arts Council Children's Book Award 1999 for *Tom and the Tree House*. She was awarded the MBE in 1998.

Prices are for books in Very Good condition with dustjackets where applicable.

THE TWELFTH DAY OF CHRISTMAS (Hamish Hamilton, 1970) £40
FRYING AS USUAL (illustrated by Pricilla Clive) (Hamish Hamilton, 1971)...£35
ACROSS THE BARRICADES (Hamish Hamilton, 1972) £30
INTO EXILE (Hamish Hamilton, 1973) £30
THE CLEARANCE (Hamish Hamilton, 1974)..£25
THE RESETTLING (Hamish Hamilton, 1975) £25
A PROPER PLACE (Hamish Hamilton, 1975) £25
THE PILGRIMAGE (Hamish Hamilton, 1976) £20
HOSTAGES TO FORTUNE (Hamish Hamilton, 1976) £20
THE REUNION (Hamish Hamilton, 1977) £20
SNAKE AMONG THE SUNFLOWERS (Hamish Hamilton, 1977) £20
THE GOOSEBERRY (Hamish Hamilton, 1978) £20
THE FILE ON FRAULIEN BERG (Macrae, 1980) £20
STRANGERS IN THE HOUSE (Hamish Hamilton, 1981)...£20
THE WINTER VISITOR (Hamish Hamilton, 1983)...£15
THE FREEDOM MACHINE (Hamish Hamilton, 1986) £15
THE GUILTY PARTY (Hamish Hamilton, 1987) £15
RAGS AND RICHES (Hamish Hamilton, 1988) £10
THE WOMEN'S HOUSE (Hamish Hamilton, 1989)...£10
TUG OF WAR (Hamish Hamilton, 1989) £10
GLAD RAGS (Hamish Hamilton, 1990) £10

LINGARD, Joan

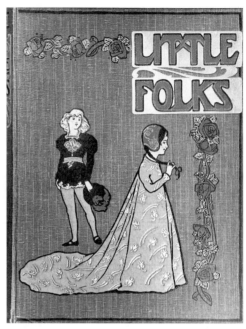

SECRETS AND SURPRISES (illustrated by Jacqui Thomas) (Macmillan, 1991) £10
BETWEEN TWO WORLDS (Hamish Hamilton, 1991) £10
HANDS OFF OUR SCHOOL (Hamish Hamilton, 1992) £10
NIGHT FIRES (Hamish Hamilton, 1993) £10
CLEVER CLIVE AND LOOPY LUCY (illustrated by Jacqui Thomas) (Macmillan, 1993) £10
SLOW FLO AND BOOMERANG BILL (illustrated by Jacqui Thomas) (Macmillan, 1994) £10
LIZZIE'S LEAVING (Hamish Hamilton, 1995)...£10
SULKY SUZY, JITTERY JACK (Hamish Hamilton) £10
A SECRET PLACE (Hodder, 1998) £10
DARK SHADOWS (Hamish Hamilton, 1998) £10
TOM AND THE TREE HOUSE (illustrated by Paul Howard) (Hodder, 1998) £10
THE EGG THIEVES (illustrated by Paul Howard) (Hodder, 1999) £10
NATASHA'S WILL (Hamish Hamilton, 2000) £10
RIVER EYES (Hodder, 2000) £10

Picture Books
CAN YOU FIND SAMMY THE HAMSTER? (illustrated by Jan Lewis) (Walker Books, 1990) £5
MORAG AND THE LAMB (illustrated by Patricia Casey) (Walker, 1991)...£5

'LITTLE FOLKS' MAGAZINE
British illustrated magazine published by Cassell. Harry Rountree was among the artists who contributed to the series. Bound into half-yearly volumes.

Prices are for bound copies in Very Good condition. Volumes bound in publisher's special pictorial boards sell for more than double these prices.

LITTLE FOLKS 1875-1895 (Vols. 1-42) ....each £40
LITTLE FOLKS 1896-1897 (Vols. 43-46) ....each £50
LITTLE FOLKS 1898 (Vol. 47) £35
LITTLE FOLKS 1898-1903 (Vols. 48-58) ....each £60
LITTLE FOLKS 1904 (Vol. 59) £35
LITTLE FOLKS 1904-1906 (Vols. 60-63) ....each £60
LITTLE FOLKS 1906-1907 (Vols. 64-65) ....each £35
LITTLE FOLKS 1907 (Vol. 66) £50
LITTLE FOLKS 1908 (Vols. 67-68) ....each £35
LITTLE FOLKS 1909 (Vol. 69) £50
LITTLE FOLKS 1909-1915 (Vols. 70-82) ....each £50
LITTLE FOLKS 1916-1933 (Vols. 83-118) ....each £30

LIVELY, Penelope

British author. Born: Penelope Margaret Lively in Cairo in 1933. Educated at St. Anne's College, Oxford. Although best known as an adult novelist — she won the Booker Prize for *Moon Tiger* in 1986 — Penelope Lively began her career writing for children. Her most famous work for young readers is probably *The Ghost of Thomas Kempe* (1973), for which she was awarded the Carnegie Medal.

Prices are for books in Very Good condition with dustjackets.

ASTERCOTE (illustrated by Antony Maitland) (Heinemann, 1970) £40
THE WHISPERING KNIGHTS (illustrated by Gareth Floyd) (Heinemann, 1971)..£35
THE WILD HUNT OF HAGWORTHY (illustrated by Juliet Mozley) (Heinemann, 1971) £35
THE DRIFTWAY (Heinemann, 1972) £35
THE GHOST OF THOMAS KEMPE (illustrated by Anthony Maitland) (Heinemann, 1973).............................£30
THE HOUSE IN NORHAM GARDENS (Heinemann, 1974)...£30
GOING BACK (Heinemann, 1975) £25
BOY WITHOUT A NAME (Heinemann, 1975)..£25
A STITCH IN TIME (Heinemann, 1976) £25
THE STAINED GLASS WINDOW (illustrated by Michael Pollard) (Abelard-Schuman, 1976) £20
FANNY'S SISTER (illustrated by John Lawrence) (Heinemann, 1976) £20
THE VOYAGE OF QV 66 (illustrated by Harold Jones) (Heinemann, 1978)...£20
FANNY AND THE MONSTERS (illustrated by John Lawrence) (Heinemann, 1979) £20
FANNY AND THE BATTLE OF POTTER'S PIECE (illustrated by John Lawrence) (Heinemann, 1981)...............£20
THE REVENGE OF SAMUEL STOKES (Heinemann, 1981)...£15
UNINVITED GHOSTS and Other Stories (illustrated by John Lawrence) (Heinemann, 1984).........................£15
A HOUSE INSIDE OUT (illustrated by David Parkins) (Deutsch, 1987) £12

LOFTING, Hugh

British author-illustrator. Born: Hugh John Lofting in Maidenhead, Berkshire, in 1889. Educated at Massachusetts Institute of Technology and London Polytechnic. Moved to the United States in 1912, where he supported himself by writing for humorous magazines. Joined the Irish Guards in 1916, being invalided out in 1917. His humour and deep compassion — particularly for animals — are evident in *The Story of Doctor Dolittle* (1920) and its many sequels. Died: 1947.

Prices are for books in Very Good condition with dustjackets.

THE STORY OF DOCTOR DOLITTLE (Stokes, U.S., 1920) £1,000
THE STORY OF DOCTOR DOLITTLE (illustrated by the author) (Cape, 1922) £300
THE VOYAGES OF DOCTOR DOLITTLE (illustrated by the author) (Stokes, U.S., 1922) £500
THE VOYAGES OF DOCTOR DOLITTLE (illustrated by the author) (Cape, 1923) £250
DOCTOR DOLITTLE'S POST OFFICE (illustrated by the author) (Stokes, U.S., [1923]) £350
DOCTOR DOLITTLE'S POST OFFICE (illustrated by the author) (Cape, 1924) £175

*All of the 'Doctor Dolittle' books were illustrated by the author, Hugh Lofting. This drawing is from **The Story of Doctor Dolittle**.*

LOFTING, Hugh

THE STORY OF MRS TUBBS (illustrated by the author) (Stokes, U.S., [1923]) £200
THE STORY OF MRS TUBBS (illustrated by the author) (Cape, 1924) £150
PORRIDGE POETRY (illustrated by the author) (Cape, 1925) £100
DOCTOR DOLITTLE'S CIRCUS (illustrated by the author) (Cape, [1925]) £120
DOCTOR DOLITTLE'S ZOO (illustrated by the author) (Cape, 1926) £100
DOCTOR DOLITTLE'S CARAVAN (illustrated by the author) (Stokes, U.S., 1926)................................£120
DOCTOR DOLITTLE'S CARAVAN (illustrated by the author) (Cape, 1927) £100
DOCTOR DOLITTLE'S GARDEN (illustrated by the author) (Cape, 1928) £90
DOCTOR DOLITTLE IN THE MOON (illustrated by the author) (Cape, 1929)..£100
NOISY NORA (illustrated by the author) (Cape, 1929) £50
THE TWILIGHT OF MAGIC (illustrated by Lois Lenski) (Cape, 1930) £50
DOCTOR DOLITTLE'S RETURN (illustrated by the author) (Stokes, U.S., 1930) £100
GUB GUB'S BOOK (illustrated by the author) (Cape, 1932) £50
DOCTOR DOLITTLE'S RETURN (illustrated by the author) (Cape, 1933) £70
DOCTOR DOLITTLE'S BIRTHDAY BOOK (Stokes, U.S., 1935) £80
TOMMY, TILLY AND MRS TUBBS (illustrated by the author) (Cape, 1937)..£30
VICTORY FOR THE SLAIN (Cape, 1942)..£30
DOCTOR DOLITTLE AND THE SECRET LAKE (illustrated by the author) (Cape, 1949) £100
DOCTOR DOLITTLE AND THE GREEN CANARY (illustrated by the author) (Cape, 1951)........................£85
DOCTOR DOLITTLE'S PUDDLEBY ADVENTURES (illustrated by the author) (Cape, 1953) £75
DOCTOR DOLITTLE: A TREASURY. Compiled by Olga Fricker (illustrated by the author) (Cape, 1968) £25
DOCTOR DOLITTLE AND HIS FRIENDS (illustrated by Leon Jason) (Collins, 1968) £10

LONDON, Jack

American author. Born: John Griffith Chaney in San Francisco in 1876. Educated at various schools in Oakland, subsequently entering Berkeley University as a Special Student. Travelled to the Yukon in 1897, his experiences there providing the basis for a number of bestselling stories and novels, two of which — *The Call of the Wild* (1903) and *White Fang* (1905) — have become established children's classics. Died: 1916.

Prices are for books in Very Good condition.

THE CALL OF THE WILD (illustrated by Philip R. Goodwin and Charles Livingston Bull) (Macmillan, U.S., 1903) £1,300
THE CALL OF THE WILD (illustrated by Philip R. Goodwin and Charles Livingston Bull) (Heinemann, 1903)............£150
TALES OF THE FISH PATROL (Macmillan, U.S., 1905) £100
TALES OF THE FISH PATROL (Heinemann, 1906)..£60
WHITE FANG (Macmillan, U.S., 1905) £120
WHITE FANG (Methuen, 1907)..£75

LUCAS, E.V.

British author. Born: Edward Verral Lucas in Eltham, Kent, in 1868. He acquired much of his education working in a Brighton bookshop. Thereafter he wrote prolifically on a great variety of subjects, including art, literature and travel. He edited the works of Charles and Mary Lamb (1903-35) and a number of books for children, including *Old Fashion Tales* (1905). Died: 1938.

Prices are for books in Good condition.

THE SCHOOLBOY'S APPRENTICE (Methuen, 1897)..£30
A BOOK OF VERSES FOR CHILDREN. Edited by E.V. Lucas (Grant Richards, 1897) £30
THE FRAMP, THE AMELIORATOR AND THE SCHOOLBOY'S APPRENTICE (Grant Richards: 'Dumpy Book' No.1, 1897) £80
A CAT BOOK (illustrated by H Officer Smith) (Grant Richards: 'Dumpy Book' No.6, 1897) £65
THE BOOK OF SHOPS (illustrated by F.D. Bedford) (Grant Richards, 1899) £350
FOUR AND TWENTY TOILERS (illustrated by F.D. Bedford) (Grant Richards, 1900) £200
THREE HUNDRED GAMES AND PASTIMES (Grant Richards, 1903) £45
OLD FASHIONED TALES (Wells Gardner, 1905)..£30
FORGOTTEN TALES OF LONG AGO (Wells Gardner, 1906) £30
RUNAWAYS AND CASTAWAYS (illustrated by F.D. Bedford) (Wells Gardner, 1908) £50
THE SLOWCOACH: A Story of Roadside Adventure (illustrated by M.V. Wheelhouse) (Wells Gardner, 1910)........................£75
SWOLLEN-HEADED WILLIAM. Adapted by E.V. Lucas (illustrated by G. Morrow) (Methuen, 1914) £60
PLAYTIME & COMPANY: A Book for Children (illustrated by E.H. Shepard) (Methuen, 1925) £100

LYNCH, Patricia

Irish author. Born: Cork, 1898. Her work amalgamates the traditional folktale with the present-day children's story. One of her best-known books is *The Turf-Cutter's Donkey* (1934). Died: 1972.

Prices are for books in Very Good condition with dustjackets where applicable.

THE GREEN DRAGON (illustrated by Dorothy Hardy) (Harrap, 1925)..£50
THE COBBLER'S APPRENTICE (illustrated by Mildred R. Lamb) (Shaylor, 1930)....................................£45
KING OF THE TINKERS (illustrated by Katherine C. Lloyd) (Dent, 1938) £35
THE GREY GOOSE OF KILNEVEN (illustrated by John Keating) (Dent, 1939) £35
FIDDLER'S QUEST (illustrated by Isobel Morton-Sale) (Dent, 1941) £30

*The pictorial front board (left) and title-page (right) of E.V. Lucas's 'story of roadside adventure', **The Slowcoach** (1910).*

LISHEEN AT THE VALLEY FARM and Other Stories (illustrated by Beatrice Salkeld)
(Gayfield Press, Dublin, 1945) £25
KNIGHTS OF GOD: Stories of the Irish Saints (illustrated by Alfred E. Kerr) (Hollis & Carter, 1945) £30
THE MAD O'HARA'S (illustrated by Elizabeth Rivers) (Dent, 1948) £25
STRANGERS AT THE FAIR and Other Stories (illustrated by Eileen Coghlan; paperback) (Penguin, 1949) £10
THE SEVENTH PIG and Other Irish Fairy Tales (illustrated by Jerome Sullivan) (Dent, 1950)............................£25
THE DARK SAILOR OF YOUGHAL (illustrated by Jerome Sullivan) (Dent, 1951) £25
THE BOY AT THE SWINGING LANTERN (illustrated by Joan Kiddell-Monroe) (Dent, 1952)..............................£25
TALES OF IRISH ENCHANTMENT (legends; illustrated by Fergus O'Ryan) (Burn Oates, 1952)..........................£25
TALES OF IRISH ENCHANTMENT (legends; illustrated by Fergus O'Ryan) (Clonmore & Reynolds, Dublin, 1952) £20
DELIA DALY OF GALLOPING GREEN (illustrated by Joan Kiddell-Monroe) (Dent, 1953) £25
ORLA OF BURREN (illustrated by Joan Kiddell-Monroe) (Dent, 1954) £25
TINKER BOY (illustrated by Harry Kernoff) (Dent, 1955) £25
THE BOOKSHOP ON THE QUAY (illustrated by Peggy Fortnum) (Dent, 1956) £25
FIONA LEAPS THE BONFIRE (illustrated by Peggy Fortnum) (Dent, 1957)..£25
COBBLER'S LUCK (illustrated by Christopher Brooker) (Burke, 1957)..£25
THE OLD BLACK SEA CHEST : A Story of Bantry Bay (illustrated by Peggy Fortnum) (Dent, 1958)....................£25
THE STONE HOUSE AT KILGOBBIN (illustrated by Christopher Brooker) (Burke, 1959) £25
THE RUNAWAYS (Blackwell, 1959) £20
JINNY THE CHANGELING (illustrated by Peggy Fortnum) (Dent, 1959)...£25
THE BLACK GOAT OF SLIEVEMORE and Other Irish Tales (revised edition of 'The Seventh Pig and
Other Irish Fairy Tales') (Dent, 1959)..£20
SALLY FROM CORK (illustrated by Elizabeth Grant) (Dent, 1960) £15
THE LOST FISHERMAN OF CARRIGMOR (illustrated by Christopher Brooker) (Burke, 1960)............................£15
RYAN'S FORT (illustrated by Elizabeth Grant) (Dent, 1961) £15
THE LONGEST WAY ROUND (illustrated by D.G. Valentine) (Burke, 1961) £15
THE GOLDEN CADDY (illustrated by Juliette Palmer) (Dent, 1962) £15
THE HOUSE BY LOUGH NEAGH (illustrated by Nina Ross) (Dent, 1963) £15
HOLIDAY AT ROSQUIN (illustrated by Mary Shillabeer) (Dent, 1964)..£15
THE TWISTED KEY and Other Stories (illustrated by Joan Kiddell-Monroe) (Harrap, 1964)...............................£15
MONA OF THE ISLE (illustrated by Mary Shillabeer) (Dent, 1965) £15
BACK OF BEYOND (illustrated by Susannah Holden) (Dent, 1966) £15
THE KERRY CARAVAN (illustrated by James Hunt) (Dent, 1967)...£15

LYNCH, Patricia

*One of Jack B. Yeats' illustrations for Patricia Lynch's most famous book, **The Turf-Cutter's Donkey**, published by Dent in 1934.*

'Turf-Cutter's Donkey' Books
THE TURF-CUTTER'S DONKEY: An Irish Story of Mystery and Adventure (illustrated by Jack B. Yeats) (Dent, 1934) £100
THE TURF-CUTTER'S DONKEY GOES VISITING: The Story of an Island Holiday
   (illustrated by George Altendorf) (Dent, 1935)..£40
LONG EARS: The Story of a Little Grey Donkey (illustrated by Joan Kiddell-Monroe) (Dent, 1943) £20
THE TURF-CUTTER'S DONKEY KICKS UP HIS HEELS (illustrated by Eileen Coghlan) (Dutton, U.S., 1939)...........£35
THE TURF-CUTTER'S DONKEY KICKS UP HIS HEELS (illustrated by Eileen Coghlan) (Browne & Nolan, Dublin, 1946) £30

'Brogeen' Books
BROGEEN OF THE STEPPING STONES (illustrated by Alfred Kerr) (Kerr-Cross Publishing, 1947) £30
BROGEEN FOLLOWS THE MAGIC TUNE (illustrated by Peggy Fortnum) (Burke, 1952) £25
BROGEEN AND THE GREEN SHOES (illustrated by Peggy Fortnum) (Burke, 1953) £25
BROGEEN AND THE BRONZE LIZARD (illustrated by Grace Golden) (Burke, 1954) £25
BROGEEN AND THE PRINCESS OF SHEEN (illustrated by Christopher Brooker) (Burke, 1955)............................£25
BROGEEN AND THE LOST CASTLE (illustrated by Christopher Brooker) (Burke, 1956) £25
BROGEEN AND THE BLACK ENCHANTER (illustrated by Christopher Brooker) (Burke, 1958)................................£25
BROGEEN AND THE LITTLE WIND (illustrated by Beryl Sanders) (Burke, 1962) £25
BROGEEN AND THE RED FEZ (illustrated by Beryl Sanders) (Burke, 1963)..£25
GUESTS AT THE BEECH TREE: A Brogeen Story (illustrated by Beryl Sanders) (Burke, 1964) £25

M

MACDONALD, George

Scottish author. Born: Huntly, Aberdeenshire, in 1824. Won a bursary to King's College, Aberdeen. Moved to London in 1845, subsequently serving as a Congregationalist minister before becoming Professor of English Literature at Bedford College. Began his literary career with the dramatic poem, *Within and Without* (1855), and the adult fairy tale, *Phantastes* (1858), his earliest children's stories being collected as *Dealings with the Fairies* in 1867. His best-known works, *At the Back of the North Wind* (1871) and *The Princess and the Goblin* (1872), were both initially serialised in Alexander Strahan's *Good Words for the Young*. These were followed by many more children's works, notably *The Princess and Curdie* (1883). Mark Twain, John Ruskin, Lewis Carroll and William Morris (who bought Kelmscott House in Hammersmith from MacDonald) were amongst his friends. Died: 1905.

Prices are for books in Very Good condition with dustjackets where applicable.

DEALINGS WITH THE FAIRIES (illustrated by Arthur Hughes) (Strahan, 1867) £2,500
AT THE BACK OF THE NORTH WIND (illustrated by Arthur Hughes) (Strahan, 1871) £2,500
AT THE BACK OF THE NORTH WIND (illustrated by Jessie Willcox Smith) (David McKay, U.S., 1920) £250
AT THE BACK OF THE NORTH WIND (illustrated by E.H. Shepard; issued with dustjacket) (Dent, 1956)................£60
AT THE BACK OF THE NORTH WIND (illustrated by Charles Mozley; issued with dustjacket) (Nonesuch Press, 1963) £45
RANALD BANNERMAN'S BOYHOOD (illustrated by Arthur Hughes) (Strahan, 1871) £700
RANALD BANNERMAN'S BOYHOOD (illustrated by Arthur Hughes) (Blackie, [1890]) £50
RANALD BANNERMAN'S BOYHOOD (illustrated by M.V. Wheelhouse) (Blackie, no date).................................£40
THE PRINCESS AND THE GOBLIN (illustrated by Arthur Hughes) (Strahan, 1872) £1,500
THE PRINCESS AND THE GOBLIN (illustrated by Arthur Hughes and Helen Stratton) (Blackie, 1911) £60
THE PRINCESS AND THE GOBLIN (illustrated by Jessie Willcox Smith) (David McKay, U.S., 1921) £200
THE PRINCESS AND THE GOBLIN (illustrated by Charles Folkard; issued with dustjacket) (Dent, 1949) £50
GUTTA PERCHA WILLIE: THE WORKING GENIUS (illustrated by Arthur Hughes) (Henry S. King, 1873) £500
GUTTA PERCHA WILLIE: THE WORKING GENIUS (as 'The History of Gutta Percha Willie') (Blackie, 1887) £50
THE WISE WOMAN: A PARABLE (Strahan, 1875) £200
THE WISE WOMAN (as 'The Lost Princess, or The Wise Woman'; illustrated by A.G. Walker) (Wells Gardner, 1895)..............£100
THE LOST PRINCESS (as 'The Lost Princess'; illustrated by 'BB'; issued with dustjacket) (Dent, 1967) £50

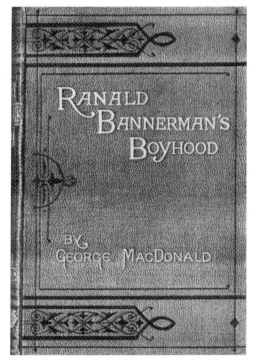

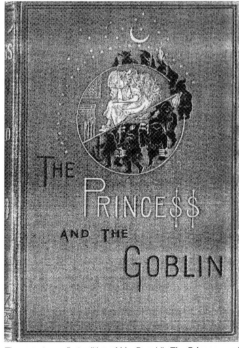

George MacDonald's **Ranald Bannerman's Boyhood** *(1871) is a largely autobiographical account of a Highland childhood.*

*The sumptuous first edition of MacDonald's **The Princess and the Goblin**, which is now worth £1,500 in Very Good condition.*

THE PRINCESS AND CURDIE (illustrated by James Allen) (Chatto & Windus, 1883 [1882]) £400
THE PRINCESS AND CURDIE (illustrated by Helen Stratton) (Blackie, 1911) £35
THE PRINCESS AND CURDIE (illustrated by Charles Folkard; issued with dustjacket) (Dent, 1949) £40
THE PRINCESS AND CURDIE (illustrated by Peter Warne; issued with dustjacket) (Ark Publishing, 1979) £25
CROSS PURPOSE and THE SHADOWS (illustrated by H.M. Brock) (Blackie, [1886]) £30
THE LIGHT PRINCESS and Other Fairy Stories (illustrated by L. Leslie Brooke) (Blackie, [1890]) £125
THE LIGHT PRINCESS (illustated by F.D. Bedford) (Blackie, [c.1926]) £40
THE LIGHT PRINCESS and Other Tales of Fantasy (contains all eight of George MacDonald's short fairy stories;
   introduction by Roger Lancelyn Green; illustrated by Arthur Hughes; issued with dustjacket) (Gollancz, 1961) £40
THE LIGHT PRINCESS (illustrated by Maurice Sendak; issued with dustjacket) (The Bodley Head, 1969) £50
THE GOLDEN KEY (illustrated by Maurice Sendak; afterword by W.H. Auden; issued with dustjacket)
   (The Bodley Head, 1972) £40

MARCHANT, Bessie

British author. Born: Elizabeth Marchant in Petham, Kent, in 1862. Educated at Petham County Primary School. Moved to London while in her early twenties, where she taught at a Baptist school. Hugely prolific author of stories for both girls and boys, many of them set overseas, despite the fact that Marchant herself never left Britain. Died: 1941.

Prices are for books in Very Good condition.

BROKEN BARRIERS (Toulson, 1889) £45
UNDER CLEARER SKIES (James Knapp, 1892) £45
THE OLD HOUSE BY THE WATER (Religious Tract Society, [1894]) £25
IN THE CRADLE OF THE NORTH WIND: A Tale (W.P. Nimmo, 1896) £30
WEASEL TIM: A Tale (Robert Culley, [1896]) £40
YUPPIE: The Land Beyond the Flood (Robert Culley, [1898]) £25
THE BONDED THREE: A Tale (illustrated by William Rainey) (Blackie, [1898]) £30
AMONG THE TORCHES OF THE ANDES: A Tale (W.P. Nimmo, 1898) £20
THE HUMBLING OF MARK LESTER (Simpkin Marshall, [1899]) £35
THE RAJAH'S DAUGHTER, or The Half-Moon Girl (Partridge, 1899) £25
TELL-TALE-TIT (Robert Culley, [1899]) £35
WINNING HIS WAY: A Story for Boys (Gall & Inglis, [1899]) £20
CECILY FROME, THE CAPTAIN'S DAUGHTER (W.P. Nimmo, [1900]) £15
THE GHOST OF ROCK GRANGE (SPCK, [1900]) £40
THE GIRL CAPTIVES: A Story of the Indian Frontier (illustrated by William Rainey) (Blackie, 1900 [1899]) £15
IN THE TOILS OF THE TRIBESMEN: A Story of the Indian Frontier (Gall & Inglis, [1900]) £25
AMONG HOSTILE HORDES: A Story of the Tai-Ping Rebellion (Gall & Inglis, [1901]) £15
FROM THE SCOURGE OF THE TONGUE: A Tale (Andrew Melrose, 1901) £30
THE FUN OF THE FAIR (Robert Culley, [1901]) £30
HELD AT RANSOM: A Story of Colonial Life (Blackie, 1901 [1900]) £15
IN PERILOUS TIMES: A Tale of Old Canterbury (Gall & Inglis, [1901]) £15
THAT DREADFUL BOY! (Robert Culley, [1901]) £25
THREE GIRLS ON A RANCH: A Story of New Mexico (illustrated by William Rainey) (Blackie, [1901]) £15
TOMMY'S TREK: A Transvaal Story (Blackie, [1901]) £20
A BRAVE LITTLE COUSIN (SPCK, [1902]) £12
BETRAMS OF LADYWELL (illustrated by John Jellicoe) (Wells Gardner, 1902) £12
FLECKIE: A Story of the Desert (Blackie, [1902]) £20
THE HOUSE AT BRAMBLING MINSTER (SPCK, [1902]) £15
LEONARD'S TEMPTATION: A Story of Gambling (Robert Culley, 1902) £15
THE SECRET OF THE EVERGLADES: A Story of Adventure in Florida (Blackie, [1902]) £25
LOST ON THE SANGUENAY (Collins, [1903]) £20
THE OWNER OF RUSHCOTE (Robert Culley, 1903) £20
THE CAPTIVES OF KAID (Collins, [1904]) £12
CHUPSIE: The Story of a Baby (Robert Culley, 1904) £12
THE GIRLS OF WAKENSIDE: A Story for Girls (Collins, [1904]) £20
HEROINE OF THE SEA (Blackie, 1904) £20
YEW TREE FARM (SPCK, [1904]) £12
CASPAR'S FIND (Robert Culley, 1905) £15
THE DEBT OF THE DAMERALS (Clarke, 1905) £15
HOPE'S TRYST: A Story of the Siberian Frontier (Blackie, 1905) £20
THE MYSTERIOUS CITY (illustrated by W.S. Stacey) (SPCK, [1905]) £30
QUEEN OF SHINDY FLAT (illustrated by Charles Sheldon) (Wells Gardner, 1905) £30
ATHABASCA BILLI: A Tale of the Far West (illustrated by H. Piffard) (SPCK, [1906]) £20
A DAUGHTER OF THE RANGES: A Story of Western Canada (illustrated by A.A. Dixon) (Blackie, 1906 [1905]) £20
KENEALY'S RIDE: A Tale of the Pampas (Gall & Inglis, [1906]) £20
MAISIE'S DISCOVERY (illustrated by R. Tod) (Collins, [1906]) £30
UNCLE GREG'S MANHUNT: A Story of Texan Horse Thieves (Robert Culley, [1906]) £30
DARLING OF SANDY POINT (illustrated by Harold Piffard) (SPCK, [1907]) £15
A GIRL OF THE FORTUNATE ISLES (illustrated by Paul Hardy) (Blackie, 1907 [1906]) £15

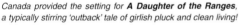

*Canada provided the setting for **A Daughter of the Ranges**, a typically stirring 'outback' tale of girlish pluck and clean living!*

With one or two exceptions, later Bessie Marchant titles like this one are worth between £10 and £15 in Very Good condition.

MARCHANT, Bessie

*Like so many of Marchant's novels, **A Girl of Distinction** was set overseas, even though she herself never left Britain!*

LOIS IN CHARGE, or A Girl of Grit: The Story of a Plantation in Brazil (illustrated by Cyrus Cuneo) (Blackie, [1918]) £20
NORAH TO THE RESCUE: A Story of the Philippines (Blackie, [1919])...£15
A TRANSPORT GIRL IN FRANCE (Blackie, [1919]) £15
SALLY MAKES GOOD: A Story of Tasmania (illustrated by Leo Bates) (Blackie, [1920])...£25
THE GIRL OF THE PAMPAS (Blackie, [1921]) £15
ISLAND BORN: A Tale of Hawaii (illustrated by Leo Bates) (Blackie, [1921]) £30
THE MISTRESS OF PURITY GAP (Cassell, [1921]) £15
HARRIET GOES A-ROAMING (Blackie, [1922]) £10
THE FORTUNES OF PRUE (Ward Lock, 1923) £10
RACHEL OUT WEST (illustrated by Henry Coller) (Blackie, [1923]) £10
A BID FOR SAFETY (Ward Lock, 1924)...£10
DIANA CARRIES ON (Nelson, [1924]) £10
THE MOST POPULAR GIRL IN THE SCHOOL (Partridge, [1924])..£10
SYLVIA'S SECRET (illustrated by W.E. Wightman) (Blackie, [1924]) £10
HER OWN KIN (Blackie, [1925]) £10
TO SAVE HER SCHOOL (illustrated by H.L. Bacon) (Partridge, 1925) £15
BY HONOUR BOUND (Nelson, [1925]) £15
DELMAYNE'S ADVENTURES (Collins, 1925) £15
COUSIN PETER'S MONEY (Sheldon, 1926) £15
DI THE DAUNTLESS (illustrated by W.E. Wightman) (Blackie, [1926]) £10
MILLICENT GWENT, SCHOOLGIRL (Warne, [1926]) £15
MOLLY IN THE WEST (illustrated by F.E. Hiley) (Blackie, [1927]) £10
THE TWO NEW GIRLS (Warne, [1927]) £12
GLENALLAN'S DAUGHTERS (Nelson, [1928]) £15
LUCIE'S LUCK (illustrated by F.E. Hiley) (Blackie, [1928]) £10
THE BANNISTER TWINS (illustrated by E. Brier) (Nelson, [1929]) £10
HILDA HOLDS ON (illustrated by F.E. Hiley) (Blackie, [1929]) £12
HOW NELL SCORED (Nelson, [1929]) £10
LAUREL THE LEADER (Blackie, [1930]) £12
CUCKOO OF THE LOG RAFT (Newnes, [1931]) £10
TWO ON THEIR OWN (illustrated by F.E. Hiley) (Blackie, [1931]) £10
THE HOMESTEADER GIRL (illustrated by V. Cooley) (Nelson, [1932])..£15
JANE FILLS THE BREACH (illustrated by F.E. Hiley) (Blackie, [1932]) £10
SILLA THE SEVENTH (Newnes, 1932) £10
DEBORAH'S FIND (illustrated by Henry Coller) (Blackie, [1933]) £10
THE COURAGE OF KATRINE (Warne, 1934) £10
HOSEA'S GIRL (Hutchinson, 1934) £15
LESBIA'S LITTLE BLUNDER (Warne, [1934]) £10
ERICA'S RANCH (Blackie, [1934]) £10
ANNA OF THE TENTERFORD (illustrated by F.E. Hiley) (Blackie, [1935])..£10
FELICITY'S FORTUNE (Blackie, [1936]) £10
NANCY AFLOAT (Nelson, [1936]) £12
A DAUGHTER OF THE DESERT (Blackie, 1937)...£10
TOMMY'S TREK (with 'Peter's Sparrow' by Mary Burns) (Blackie, [1937])..£10
MISS WILMER'S GANG (illustrated by J.A. May) (Blackie, 1938) £10
WAIFS OF WOLLAMOO: A Story for Girls (Warne, [1938])..£25
A GIRL UNDAUNTED, or The Honey Queen (illustrated by J.A. May) (Blackie, 1939)..£10
MARTA THE MAINSTAY (Blackie, [1940]) £12
TWO OF A KIND (Blackie, 1941) £10
THE TRIUMPHS OF THREE (Blackie, [1942]) £10

MARRYAT, Captain

British author. Born: Frederick Marryat in London in 1792. Entered the Royal Navy in 1806, seeing action on board Lord Cochrane's frigate, 'H.M.S. Impérieuse', and subsequently serving in the American war of 1812 and on St. Helena, where he made a death-bed sketch of Napoleon. His first book, a *Code of Signals* for merchant ships, was published in 1817, and was followed by a *Suggestion for the Abolition of Impressment* (1822) and many adventure novels. These included several for children, notably *Masterman Ready* (1841-42) and *The Children of the New Forest* (1847). Settled in Langham, Norfolk, where he pursued a number of disastrous and expensive experiments in agriculture. Died: 1848.

Prices are for books in Very Good condition.

THE NAVAL OFFICER, or Scenes and Adventures in the Life of Frank Mildmay
(anonymous; three volumes) (Colburn, 1829) ....the set £300
THE KING'S OWN (anonymous; three volumes) (Colburn & Bentley, 1830) ....the set £200
NEWTON FORSTER, or The Merchant Service (anonymous; three volumes) (James Cochrane, 1832) ......the set £175
PETER SIMPLE (anonymous; three volumes) (Saunders & Otley, 1834) ....the set £350
PETER SIMPLE (second edition; three volumes; reset text) (Saunders & Otley, 1834 ....the set £250
JACOB FAITHFUL (anonymous; three volumes) (Saunders & Otley, 1834) ....the set £350
JACOB FAITHFUL (illustrated by R.W. Buss; three volumes) (Saunders & Otley, 1837)...........................the set £350

JACOB FAITHFUL (illustrated by R.W. Buss; introduction by George Saintsbury; limited to 750 copies; two volumes) (Constable, 1928)..the set £150
THE PACHA OF MANY TALES (short stories; anonymous; three volumes) (Saunders & Otley, 1835)...........................the set £160
THE PIRATE and THE THREE CUTTERS (novellas; one volume) (Longmans Green, 1836)..£125
JAPHET IN SEARCH OF A FATHER (anonymous; three volumes) (Saunders & Otley, 1836).............................the set £200
MR MIDSHIPMAN EASY (anonymous; three volumes) (Saunders & Otley, 1836) ....the set £300
SNARLEYYOW, or The Dog Fiend (anonymous; three volumes) (Colburn, 1837) ....the set £200
THE PHANTOM SHIP (three volumes) (Colburn, 1839)...the set £425
POOR JACK (twelve monthly parts; octavo) (Longmans Green, January-December 1840) ....the set £300
POOR JACK (first edition in book form; illustrated by Clarkson Stanfield) (Longmans Green, 1840)...........................£200
MASTERMAN READY, or The Wreck of the Pacific. Written for Young People (illustrated by the author; three volumes) (Longmans Green, 1841-1842) ....the set £300
JOSEPH RUSHBROOK, or The Poacher (anonymous; three volumes) (Longmans Green, 1841) ....the set £150
PERCIVAL KEENE (three volumes) (Colburn, 1842) ....the set £150
NARRATIVE OF THE TRAVELS AND ADVENTURES OF MONSIEUR VIOLET IN CALIFORNIA, SONORA,
   AND WESTERN TEXAS (three volumes) (Longmans Green, 1843) ....the set £500
NARRATIVE OF THE TRAVELS AND ADVENTURES OF MONSIEUR VIOLET... (as 'The Travels and Romantic Adventures of Monsieur Violet, among the Snake Indians and Wild Tribes of the Great Western Prairies') (Longmans Green, 1843) ..£300
THE SETTLERS IN CANADA. Written for Young People (two volumes) (Longmans Green, 1844) ....the set £150
THE MISSION, or Scenes in Africa. Written for Young People (two volumes) (Longmans Green, 1845) ....the set £175
THE PRIVATEERSMAN, or One Hundred Years Ago (two volumes) (Longmans Green, 1846) ....the set £150
THE CHILDREN OF THE NEW FOREST (illustrated by Frank Marryat; two volumes) (Hurst, [1847]) ....the set £850
THE LITTLE SAVAGE (two volumes) (Hurst, 1848-49) ....the set £175

MARTIN, J.P.

British author. Born: Scarborough, Yorkshire, 1880. Became a Methodist minister in 1902. His stories belong to the distinctive English tradition of high-spirited fantasy, his six 'Uncle' books developing a struggle for supremacy between virtue and villainy. Died: 1966.

Prices are for books in Very Good condition with dustjackets.

UNCLE (illustrated by Quentin Blake) (Cape, 1964) £45
UNCLE CLEANS UP (illustrated by Quentin Blake) (Cape, 1965) £45
UNCLE AND HIS DETECTIVE (illustrated by Quentin Blake) (Cape, 1966) £45
UNCLE AND HIS TREACLE TROUBLE (illustrated by Quentin Blake) (Cape, 1967) £45
UNCLE AND CLAUDIUS THE CAMEL (illustrated by Quentin Blake) (Cape, 1969)..£45
UNCLE AND THE BATTLE FOR BADGERTOWN (illustrated by Quentin Blake) (Cape, 1973) £45

MASEFIELD, John

British author. Born: 1878. Poet Laureate from 1930 to 1967, and — like his three successors (C. Day Lewis, John Betjeman and Ted Hughes) — a very popular writer for children. His most collectable fantasies are *The Midnight Folk* (1927) and *The Box of Delights* (1935), both of which have been dramatised on radio and TV. Died: 1967.

Prices are for books in Very Good condition (with dustjackets after 1920).

LOST ENDEAVOUR (Wells Gardner, 1910) £50
MARTIN HYDE (Wells Gardner, 1910) £50
A BOOK OF DISCOVERIES (Wells Gardner, 1910)...£35
JIM DAVIS (Wells Gardner, 1911) £85
THE MIDNIGHT FOLK (issued in dustjacket) (Heinemann, 1927) £50
THE MIDNIGHT FOLK (illustrated by Rowland Hilder; issued with dustjacket) (Heinemann, 1931) £100
THE BIRD OF DAWNING (issued with dustjacket) (Heinemann, 1933) £45
THE BOX OF DELIGHTS (issued with dustjacket) (Heinemann, 1935) £150
DEAD NED (issued with dustjacket) (Heinemann, 1938) £40
LIVE AND KICKING NED (issued with dustjacket) (Heinemann, 1939)...£40

MAYNE, William

British author. Born: William Cyril Mayne in Hull in 1928. Educated at Canterbury Cathedral Choir School, subsequently working for the BBC and as a teacher. His first novel was published in 1953, since when he has written over 100 more. Lectured at Deakin University, Geelong, in 1976/77, and in 1979 was granted a one-year Fellowship in Creative Writing at Rolle College in Exmouth. He lives in Yorkshire.

Prices are for books in Very Good condition with dustjackets where applicable.

FOLLOW THE FOOTPRINTS (illustrated by Shirley Hughes) (OUP, 1953) £30
THE WORLD UPSIDE DOWN (illustrated by Shirley Hughes) (OUP, 1954)...£30
A SWARM IN MAY (illustrated by C. Walter Hodges) (OUP, 1955)..£45
THE MEMBER FOR THE MARSH (illustrated by Lynton Lamb) (OUP, 1956) £45
CHORISTERS' CAKE (illustrated by C. Walter Hodges) (OUP, 1956) £45
THE BLUE BOAT (illustrated by Geraldine Spence) (OUP, 1957) £35
A GRASS ROPE (illustrated by Lynton Lamb) (OUP, 1957)...£40

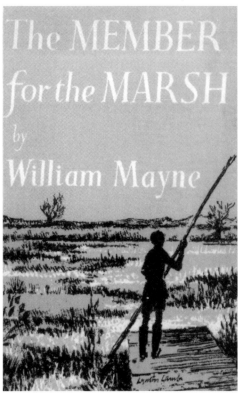

The first of J.P. Martin's six 'Uncle' books is now worth £45 in Very Good condition with the Quentin Blake dustjacket.

*The same amount should secure a Very Good first of William Mayne's fourth book, **The Member for the Marsh**.*

THE LONG NIGHT (illustrated by 'BB') (Blackwell, 1957 [1958]) £45
UNDERGROUND ALLEY (illustrated by Marcia Lane Foster) (OUP, 1958)..£30
THE GOBBLING BILLY (written under the pseudonym 'Dynely James'; with Dick Caesar) (Gollancz, 1959) £45
THE GOBBLING BILLY (Brockhampton Press, 1969) £15
THIRTEEN O'CLOCK (illustrated by 'BB') (Blackwell, 1959) £35
THE THUMBSTICK (illustrated by Tessa Theobald) (OUP, 1959)...£25
THE ROLLING SEASON (illustrated by Christopher Brooker) (OUP, 1960)..£25
CATHEDRAL WEDNESDAY (illustrated by C. Walter Hodges) (OUP, 1960) £25
THE FISHING PARTY (illustrated by Christopher Brooker) (Hamish Hamilton, 1960) £25
SUMMER VISITORS (illustrated by William Stobbs) (OUP, 1961) £25
THE CHANGELING (illustrated by Victor G. Ambrus) (OUP, 1961) £25
THE GLASS BALL (illustrated by Janet Duchesne) (Hamish Hamilton, 1961) £25
THE LAST BUS (illustrated by Margery Gill) (Hamish Hamilton, 1962) £25
THE TWELVE DANCERS (illustrated by Lynton Lamb) (Hamish Hamilton, 1962) £25
THE MAN FROM THE NORTH POLE (illustrated by Prudence Seward) (Hamish Hamilton, 1963) £25
ON THE STEPPING STONES (illustrated by Prudence Seward) (Hamish Hamilton, 1963) £25
WORDS AND MUSIC (illustrated by Lynton Lamb) (Hamish Hamilton, 1963) ..:...£25
PLOT NIGHT (illustrated by Janet Duchesne) (Hamish Hamilton, 1963) £25
A PARCEL OF TREES (illustrated by Margery Gill; paperback) (Puffin, 1963) £10
WATER BOATMAN (illustrated by Anne Linton) (Hamish Hamilton, 1964) £20
WHISTLING RUFUS (illustrated by Raymond Briggs) (Hamish Hamilton, 1964)..£25
SAND (illustrated by Margery Gill) (Hamish Hamilton, 1964) £20
A DAY WITHOUT WIND (illustrated by Margery Gill) (Hamish Hamilton, 1964)..£20
THE BIG WHEEL AND THE LITTLE WHEEL (illustrated by Janet Duchesne) (Hamish Hamilton, 1965)...................£20
PIG IN THE MIDDLE (illustrated by Mary Russon) (Hamish Hamilton, 1965) £20
NO MORE SCHOOL (illustrated by Peter Warner) (Hamish Hamilton, 1965) £20
DORMOUSE TALES (five books: 'The Lost Thimble', 'The Steam Roller', 'The Picnic', 'The Football' and
   'The Tea Party'; written under the pseudonym 'Charles Molin'; illustrated by Leslie Wood) (Hamish Hamilton, 1966) ..each £10
EARTHFASTS (Hamish Hamilton, 1966) £20
ROOFTOPS (illustrated by Mary Russon) (Hamish Hamilton, 1966) £20
THE OLD ZION (illustrated by Margery Gill) (Hamish Hamilton, 1966) £20

MAYNE, William

THE BATTLEFIELD (illustrated by Mary Russon) (Hamish Hamilton, 1967) £20
THE BIG EGG (illustrated by Margery Gill) (Hamish Hamilton, 1967) £20
THE TOFFEE JOIN (illustrated by Shirley Hughes) (Hamish Hamilton, 1968) £20
OVER THE HILLS AND FAR AWAY (Hamish Hamilton, 1968) £20
THE YELLOW AEROPLANE (illustrated by Trevor Stubley) (Hamish Hamilton, 1968) £20
THE HOUSE ON FAIRMOUNT (illustrated by Fritz Wegner) (Hamish Hamilton, 1968) £20
THE HILL ROAD (Dutton, 1969) £10
RAVENSGILL (Hamish Hamilton, 1970) £20
ROYAL HARRY (Hamish Hamilton, 1971) £20
A GAME OF DARK (Hamish Hamilton, 1971) £20
THE INCLINE (illustrated by Trevor Stubley) (Hamish Hamilton, 1972) £20
THE SWALLOWS (written under the pseudonym 'Martin Cobalt') (Heinemann, 1972) £20
ROBIN'S REAL ENGINE (illustrated by Mary Dinsdale) (Hamish Hamilton, 1972) £20
SKIFFY (illustrated by Nicholas Fisk) (Hamish Hamilton, 1972) £20
THE JERSEY SHORE (Hamish Hamilton, 1973) £20
A YEAR AND A DAY (illustrated by Krystyna Turska) (Hamish Hamilton, 1976) £15
PARTY PANTS (illustrated by Joanna Stubs) (Knight, 1977) £10
MAX'S DREAM (illustrated by Laszio Acs) (Hamish Hamilton, 1977) £15
IT (Hamish Hamilton, 1977) £15
WHILE THE BELLS RING (illustrated by Janet Rawlins) (Hamish Hamilton, 1979) £20
SALT RIVER TIMES (illustrated by Elizabeth Honey) (Hamish Hamilton, 1980) £15
THE MOUSE AND THE EGG (illustrated by Krystyna Turska) (Julia MacRae, 1980) £20
THE PATCHWORK CAT (illustrated by Nicola Bayley) (Cape, 1981) £30
ALL THE KING'S MEN (Cape, 1982) £15
WINTER QUARTERS (Cape, 1982) £15
SKIFFY AND THE TWIN PLANETS (Hamish Hamilton, 1982) £15
A SMALL PUDDING FOR WEE GOWRIE and Other Stories of Underground Creatures (Macmillan, 1983) £15
THE MOULDY (illustrated by Nicola Bayley) (Cape, 1983) £25
THE RED BOOK OF HOB STORIES (illustrated by Patrick Benson) (Walker, 1984) £15
THE GREEN BOOK OF HOB STORIES (illustrated by Patrick Benson) (Walker, 1984) £15
THE YELLOW BOOK OF HOB STORIES (illustrated by Patrick Benson) (Walker, 1984) £15
THE BLUE BOOK OF HOB STORIES (illustrated by Patrick Benson) (Walker, 1984) £15
DRIFT (Cape, 1985) £10
BARNABAS WALKS (illustrated by B. Firth) (Walker: 'Animal Library' series, 1986) £10
COME, COME TO MY CORNER (illustrated by Kenneth Lilly) (Walker: 'Animal Library' series, 1986) £10
TIBBER (illustrated by Jonathan Heale) (Walker: 'Animal Library' series, 1986) £10
CORBIE (illustrated by Peter Visscher) (Walker: 'Animal Library' series, 1986) £10
GIDEON AHOY! (Viking Kestrel, 1987) £12
KELPIE (Cape, 1987) £12
THE BLEMYAH STORIES (illustrated by Juan Wijguard) (Walker, 1987) £12
ANTAR AND THE EAGLES (Walker, 1989) £12
HOUSE IN TOWN (Walker, 1989) £12
NETTA NEXT (Hamish Hamilton, 1990) £10
THURSDAY CREATURE (Heinemann, 1990) £10
COMPLETE BOOK OF HOB STORIES (Walker, 1991) £20
TIGER'S RAILWAY (Walker, 1991) £8
LOW TIDE (Cape, 1992) £8
AND NETTA AGAIN (Hamish Hamilton, 1992) £8
EGG TIMER (Heinemann, 1993) £8
OH GRANDMA (Hamish Hamilton, 1993) £8
CUDDY (Cape, 1994) £8
BELLS ON HER TOES (Hamish Hamilton, 1994) £8
MIDNIGHT FAIR (Hodder Children's Books, 1997) £4

MEADE, L.T.

Irish author. Born: Elizabeth Thomasina Meade in Brandon, County Cork, in 1844. Prolific writer for the middle-class child, especially school stories for girls in which she stressed adolescent passion. Her most famous story is *Beyond the Blue Mountains* (1893). Died: 1914.

Prices are for books in Good condition.

LOTTIE'S LAST HOME (Shaw, 1875) £25
KNIGHT OF TODAY (Shaw, 1877) £15
SCAMP AND I (Shaw, 1877) £20
BEL AND MARJORY (Shaw, 1878) £20
THE CHILDREN'S KINGDOM (Shaw, 1878) £15
YOUR BROTHER AND MINE (Shaw, 1878) £15
WATER LILLIES and Other Tales (Shaw, 1878) £15
DOT AND HER TREASURES (Shaw, 1879) £15
WATER GIPSIES (Shaw, 1879) £15

*A rare jacketed copy of L.T. Meade's novel, **Jill the Irresistible**, published by Chambers in 1915.*

A DWELLER IN TENTS (Isbister, 1880) £15
MOU-SETSE by L.T. Meade with THE ORPHAN'S PILGRIMAGE by T. Von Gumbert (Isbister, 1880) £15
THE FLOATING LIGHT OF RING-FINNAN, AND THE GUARDIAN ANGELS (MacNiven, 1880) £15
MOTHER HERRING'S CHICKEN (Isbister, 1881) £10
A LONDON BABY (Nisbet, 1882)..£10
THE CHILDREN'S PILGRIMAGE (Nisbet, 1883) £10
HERMIE'S ROSE-BUDS and Other Stories (Hodder & Stoughton, 1883) £10
THE AUTOCRAT OF THE NURSERY (Hodder & Stoughton, 1884) £10
A BAND OF THREE (Isbister, 1884) £10
SCARLET ANEMONES (Hodder & Stoughton, 1884) £10
THE TWO SISTERS (Hodder & Stoughton, 1884) £10
THE ANGEL OF LOVE (Hodder & Stoughton, 1885) £10
A LITTLE SILVER TRUMPET (Hodder & Stoughton, 1885) £10

A WORLD OF GIRLS (Cassell, 1886)......£10
DADDY'S BOY (Hatchards, 1887)......£10
THE O'DONNELLS OF INCHFAWN (Hatchards, 1887)......£10
THE PALACE BEAUTIFUL (Cassell, 1887)......£10
SWEET NANCY (Partridge, 1887)......£10
DEB AND THE DUCHESS (Hatchard, 1888)......£10
NOBODY'S NEIGHBOURS (Isbister, 1888)......£10
A FARTHINGFUL (Chambers, 1889)......£10
THE GOLDEN LADY (Chambers, 1889)......£10
THE LADY OF THE FOREST (Partridge, 1889)......£10
THE LITTLE PRINCESS OF TOWER HILL (Partridge, 1889)......£10
POOR MISS CAROLINA (Chambers, 1889)......£10
A NEW-FASHIONED GIRL (Cassell, 1889)......£10
THE BERESFORD PRIZE (Longman, 1890)......£10
DICKORY DOCK (Chambers, 1890)......£10
ENGAGED TO BE MARRIED (Simpkin Marshall, 1890)......£10
HEART OF GOLD (Warne, 1890)......£10
JUST A LOVE STORY (Blackett, 1890)......£10
MARIGOLD (Partridge, 1890)......£10
HEPSY GIPSY (Methuen, 1891)......£10
THE CHILDREN OF WILTON CHASE (Chambers, 1891)......£15
A SWEET GIRL-GRADUATE (Cassell, 1891)......£15
LITTLE MARY and Other Stories (Chambers, 1891)......£10
BASHFUL FIFTEEN (Cassell, 1892)......£15
FOUR ON AN ISLAND (Chambers, 1892)......£15
OUT OF THE FASHION (Methuen, 1892)......£10
A RING OF RUBIES (Cassell, 1892)......£10
BEYOND THE BLUE MOUNTAINS (Cassell, 1893)......£75
A YOUNG MUTINEER (Wells Gardner, 1893)......£10
BETTY (Chambers, 1894)......£10
IN AN IRON GRIP (two volumes) (Chatto & Windus, 1894)......the set £20
RED ROSE AND TIGER LILY (Cassell, 1894)......£10
GIRLS, NEW AND OLD (Chambers, 1895)......£15
THE LEAST OF THESE and Other Stories (Chambers, 1895)......£10
CATALINA, ART STUDENT (Chambers, 1896)......£15
A GIRL IN TEN THOUSAND (Oliphant, 1896)......£10
GOOD LUCK (Nisbet, 1896)......£10
A LITTLE MOTHER TO THE OTHERS (White, 1896)......£10
MERRY GIRLS OF ENGLAND (Cassell, 1896)......£10
PLAYMATES (Chambers, 1896)......£10
THE WHITE TZAR (Russell, 1896)......£10
THE HOUSE OF SURPRISES (Longman, 1896)......£10
BAD LITTLE HANNAH (White, 1897)......£10
A HANDFUL OF SILVER (Oliphant, 1897)......£10
WILD KITTY (Chambers, 1897)......£10
CAVE PERILOUS (RTS, 1898)......£10
A BUNCH OF CHERRIES (Isbister, 1898)......£10
THE CLEVEREST WOMAN IN ENGLAND (Nisbet, 1898)......£10
MARY GIFFORD, MB (Wells Gardner, 1898)......£10
THE GIRLS OF ST WODE'S (Chambers 1898)......£15
THE REBELLION OF LIL CARRINGTON (Cassell, 1898)......£15
THE SIREN (White, 1898)......£10
ADVENTURESS (Chatto & Windus, 1899)......£10
ALL SORTS (Nisbet, 1899)......£10
LIGHT O' THE MORNING (Chambers, 1899)......£10
THE ODDS AND EVENS (Chambers,1899)......£10
WAGES (Nisbet, 1900)......£10
A PLUCKY GIRL (Chambers, 1900)......£10
THE BEAUFORTS (Griffith & Farran, 1900)......£10
A BRAVE POOR THING (Isbister, 1900)......£10
DADDY'S GIRL (Newnes, 1900)......£10
MISS NONENTITY (Chambers, 1900)......£15
SEVEN MAIDS (Chambers, 1900)......£10
A SISTER OF THE RED CROSS (Nelson, 1900)......£10
IN TIME OF ROSES (Nelson, 1900)......£10
IN TIME OF ROSES (Nister, 1900)......£30
WHEELS OF IRON (Nisbet, 1901)......£10
THE BLUE DIAMOND (Chatto & Windus, 1901)......£10
COSEY CORNER (Chambers, 1901)......£10

GIRLS OF THE TRUE BLUE (Chambers, 1901)..£15
THE NEW MRS LASCELLES (Clarke, 1901)..£10
A STUMBLE BY THE WAY (Chatto & Windus, 1901)...£10
A VERY NAUGHTY GIRL (Chambers, 1901)..£15
DRIFT (Methuen, 1902)..£10
MARGARET (White, 1902)..£10
THE PURSUIT OF PENELOPE (Digby Long, 1902)..£10
THE PRINCESS WHO GAVE ALL AWAY AND THE NAUGHTY ONE OF THE FAMILY
    (Nister, 1902)...£10
GIRLS OF THE FOREST (Chambers, 1902)..£15
QUEEN ROSE (Chambers, 1902)...£10
THE REBEL OF THE SCHOOL (Chambers, 1902)..£15
THE SQUIRE'S LITTLE GIRL (Chambers, 1902)..£10
THROUGH PERIL FOR A WIFE (Digby Long, 1902)...£10
RESURGAM (Methuen, 1903)..£10
ROSEBURY (Chatto & Windus, 1903)...£10
PETER THE PILGRIM (Chambers, 1903)..£10
THE WITCH MAID (Nisbet, 1903)...£10
THE BURDEN OF HER YOUTH (Long, 1903)..£10
BY MUTUAL CONSENT (Long, 1903)..£10
A GAY CHARMER (Chambers, 1903)...£10
THE MANOR SCHOOL (Chambers,1903)..£15
THAT BRILLIANT PEGGY (Hodder & Stoughton, 1903)...£15
A MAID OF MYSTERY (White, 1904)..£15
THE ADVENTURES OF MIRANDA (John Long, 1904)...£15
AT THE BACK OF THE WORLD (Hurst & Blackett, 1904)...£10
THE LADY CAKE-MAKER (Hodder & Stoughton, 1904)...£10
CASTLE POVERTY (Nisbet, 1904)...£10
LOVE TRIUMPHANT (T. Fisher Unwin, 1904)..£10
A MADCAP (Cassell, 1904)...£15
NURSE CHARLOTTE (John Long, 1904)...£10
THE GIRLS OF MRS PRITCHARD'S SCHOOL (Chambers, 1904)...£15
A MODERN TOMBOY (Chambers, 1904)..£15
PETRONELLA AND THE COMING OF POLLY (Chambers, 1904)..£10
WILFUL COUSIN KATE (Chambers, 1905)..£10
BESS OF DELANEY'S (Digby Long, 1905)...£10
HIS MASCOT (John Long, 1905)..£10
LITTLE WIFE HESTER (John Long, 1905)..£10
LOVEDAY (Hodder & Stoughton, 1905)...£10
OLD READMONEY'S DAUGHTER (Partridge, 1905)...£10
VIRGINIA (Digby Long, 1905)...£10
DUMPS (Chambers, 1905)..£10
A BEVY OF GIRLS (Chambers, 1905)..£15
THE COLONEL AND THE BOY (Hodder & Stoughton, 1906)..£10
THE FACE OF JULIET (John Long, 1906)...£10
THE GIRL AND HER FORTUNE (Hodder & Stoughton, 1906)...£10
THE HEART OF HELEN (John Long, 1906)...£10
THE HOME OF SWEET CONTENT (White, 1906)..£10
IN THE FLOWER OF HER YOUTH (Nisbet, 1906)...£10
THE MAID WITH THE GOGGLES (Digby Long, 1906)...£10
SUE (Chambers, 1906)..£10
VICTORY (Methuen, 1906)...£10
THE HILL-TOP GIRL (Chambers, 1906)...£15
TURQUOISE AND RUBY (illustrated by Mabel Lucie Attwell) (Chambers, 1906)............................£50
THE COLONEL'S CONQUEST (Jacobs, U.S., 1907)...£10
THE CURSE OF THE FEVERALS (John Long, 1907)..£10
A GIRL FROM AMERICA (Chambers, 1907)..£10
THE HOME OF SILENCE (Sisley, 1907)...£10
KINDRED SPIRITS (John Long, 1907)..£10
THE LADY OF DELIGHT (Hodder & Stoughton, 1907)..£10
LITTLE JOSEPHINE (John Long, 1907)..£10
THE LITTLE SCHOOL-MOTHERS (Cassell, 1907)..£15
THE LOVE OF SUSAN CARDIGAN (Digby Long, 1907)..£10
THE RED CAP OF LIBERTY (Nisbet, 1907)..£10
THE RED RUTH (Laurie, 1907)...£10
THE SCAMP FAMILY (Chambers, 1907)..£15
THREE GIRLS FROM SCHOOL (Chambers, 1907)...£15
THE SCHOOL FAVOURITE (Chambers, 1908)..£15
THE AIM OF HER LIFE (John Long, 1908)..£10

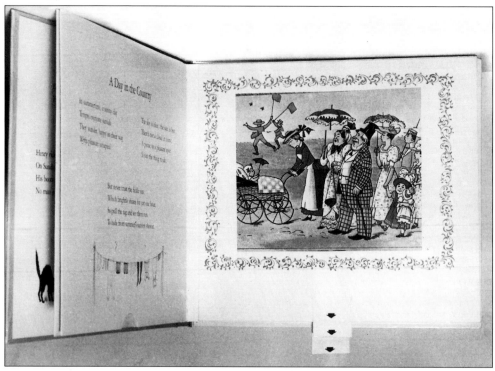

A good example of a movable 'slat' picture, perfected by the brilliant German illustrator, Lothar Meggendorfer (1847-1925).

A GIRL OF THE PEOPLE (Everett, 1912) £10
KITTY O'DONOVAN (Chambers, 1912) £10
LORD AND LADY KITTY (White, 1912) £10
LOVE'S CROSS ROADS (Stanley Paul, 1912).....£10
PEGGY FROM KERRY (Chambers, 1912) £10
THE CHESTERTON GIRL GRADUATES (Chambers, 1913).....£10
THE GIRLS OF ABINGER CLOSE (Chambers, 1913) £10
THE GIRLS OF KING'S ROYAL (Chambers, 1913) £10
THE PASSION OF KATHLEEN DUVEEN (Stanley Paul, 1913).....£10
A BAND OF MIRTH (illustrated by Mabel Lucie Attwell) (Chambers, 1914) £50
COL TRACEY'S WIFE (Aldine, 1914) £10
ELIZABETH'S PRISON (Stanley Paul, 1914).....£10
A GIRL OF HIGH ADVENTURE (Chambers, 1914) £10
HER HAPPY FACE (Ward Lock, 1914).....£10
THE QUEEN OF JOY (Chambers, 1914) £10
THE WOOING OF MONICA (John Long, 1914) £10
THE DARLING OF THE SCHOOL (Chambers, 1915) £10
GREATER THAN GOLD (Ward Lock, 1915).....£10
JILL THE IRRESISTIBLE (Chambers, 1915) £10
HOLLYHOCK (Chambers, 1916).....£10
MADGE MOSTYN'S NIECES (Chambers, 1916) £10
THE MAID INDOMITABLE (Ward Lock, 1916) £10
MOTHER MARY (Chambers, 1916) £10
DAUGHTERS OF TODAY (Hodder & Stoughton, 1916) £10
BETTER THAN RICHES (Chambers, 1917) £10
THE FAIRY GODMOTHER (Chambers, 1917) £10
MISS PATRICIA (John Long, 1925) £15
ROSES AND THORNS (John Long, 1928) £15

MEGGENDORFER, Lothar

German illustrator and creator of movable picture books. Born: 1847. Worked for many years on the German equivalent of *Punch*. Created movable books for a variety of publishers, including Braun & Schneider of Munich and the British firm, Dean & Son. Best known for books like *Always Jolly!* and *Travels of Little Lord Thumb and his Man Damien* (both 1891), in which puppet figures are made to move by pulling on a tab. Died: 1925.

Prices are for books in Very Good condition in full working order. Note that prices vary considerably according to condition. Many titles have been reissued over the last twenty years, and these reprints are worth between £20 and £40.

NEU LEBENDE BILDER (Braun & Schneider, Munich, [c.1880]) £1,000
AUS DER KINDRERSTUBE (Esslingen, [c.1885]) £1,000
BEWEGLICHE SCHATTENBILDER (H. Vorstellung, Munich, [1886]).....£1,000
NAH UND FERN. Ein Tierbilderbuch zum Ziehen (Munich, [1887]) £1,000
INTERNATIONALER ZIRKUS (H. Grevel, 1887) £1,000
ARTISTIC PUSSY AND HER STUDIO: Moving Pictures and Other Tales (L.W. Walter, U.S., [c.1890]).....£1,000
THE CITY PARK: A Panoramic Stand-Up Book (H. Grevel, [c.1890]) £1,000
MILITARITCHES ZIEBITDERBUCH (Munich, [c.1890]) £1,000
AFFENTHEATER (Munich, [c.1890]) £1,000
FROM FAR AND NEAR (H. Grevel, [c.1890]) £1,000
HUTOMATEN THEATER (Stuttgart, [c.1890]) £1,000
LEBENDE TIERBILDER (Braun & Schneider, Munich, [c.1890]) £1,000
TRANSFORMATION SCENES (H. Grevel, [c.1890]) £1,000
ZWOLF SCHONE GESCHICHTEN (Munich, [c.1890]) £1,000
COMIC ACTORS: A New Movable Toybook (H. Grevel, [1891]) £1,000
ALWAYS JOLLY! A Movable Toybook (H. Grevel, [1891]) £1,000
CURIOUS CREATURES: A New Movable Toybook of All Kinds of Animals (H. Grevel, [1891]) £1,000
MERRY COMPANY: A Funny Movable Toybook (H. Grevel, [1891]).....£1,000
TRAVELS OF LITTLE LORD THUMB AND HIS MAN DAMIEN: A Movable Toybook (H. Grevel, [1891]).....£1,000
ALL ALIVE (H. Grevel, [c.1892]) £1,000
HUMOROUS PICTURE BOOK (H. Grevel, [1894]) £1,000
LOOK AT ME! A New Movable Toybook (H. Grevel, [1894]) £1,000
COMICS FACE: A Movable Toybook (H. Grevel, [1895]) £1,000
SCENES OF ANIMAL LIFE: A Movable Toybook (H. Grevel, [1895]) £1,000
WHAT'S O'CLOCK? A Toy Book to Teach Children the Time (H. Grevel, [1897]).....£1,000
NUR FUR BRAVE KINDER (J.F. Schreiber, 1899) £1,000
CLOWN PUTTY FACE: The Quick Change Artist (H. Grevel, [1900]).....£1,000
THE DOLL'S HOUSE: A Present for Good Little Children (H. Grevel, [c.1900]) £1,000
OUR AUNTS: A Humorous Album of 400 Transformations (H. Grevel, [1900]) £1,000
THE TRICKS OF NAUGHTY BOYS: A Series of Amusing Transformation Scenes (H. Grevel, [1900]) £1,000
COMIC ZOOLOGY (H. Grevel, 1902]) £1,000

MILLIGAN, Spike

British author. Born: India, 1918. Off-beat, witty and anarchic humour in stories and verse with great appeal to children.

Prices are for books in Very Good condition with dustjackets where applicable.

SILLY VERSE FOR KIDS (Dobson, 1959) £150
A BOOK OF MILLIGANIMALS (Dobson, 1968)..£20
THE BALD TWIT LION (Dobson, 1968) £25
MILLIGAN'S ARK (illustrated by Giles, Ronald Searle, Ralph Steadman and Terry Gilliam) (Hobbs, 1971) £15
BAD JELLY THE WITCH: A Fairy Story (Hobbs/Joseph, 1973) £25
DIP THE PUPPY: A Fairy Story; with The Terrible Monster Jelly (Hobbs/Joseph, 1974) £25
GOBLINS (illustrated by W Heath Robinson) (Hutchinson, 1978) £12
UNSPUN SOCKS FROM A CHICKEN'S LAUNDRY (Hobbs/Joseph, 1981)...£15
SIR NOBONK AND THE TERRIBLE, AWFUL, DREADFUL, NAUGHTY, NASTY DRAGON (Hobbs/Joseph, 1982) £20
FLEAS, KNEES & HIDDEN ELEPHANTS (Boxtree, 1994) £6

MILLS, Annette

British author. Born: 1894. Mills was best known for her series of stories featuring Muffin the Mule. She was the sister of the actor, John Mills. Died: 1955.

Prices are for books in Very Good condition with dustjackets where applicable.

MUFFIN THE MULE (illustrated by Molly Blake) (University of London Press, 1949) £45
MORE ABOUT MUFFIN (illustrated by Molly Blake) (University of London Press, 1950) £40
MUFFIN AND THE MAGIC HAT (illustrated by Molly Blake) (University of London Press, [1951]) £35
HERE COMES MUFFIN (illustrated by Molly Blake) (University of London Press, [1952]) £35
JENNIFER AND THE FLOWER FAIRIES (illustrated by Molly Blake) (News of the World, [1952]).........£25
PRUDENCE KITTEN (illustrated by Molly Blake) (University of London Press, [1952])........................£25
MUFFIN AT THE SEASIDE (illustrated by Molly Blake) (University of London Press, [1953]) £35
COLONEL CROCK (illustrated by Edward Andrewes) (Harrap, 1953)..£15
MUFFIN'S SPLENDID ADVENTURE (illustrated by Molly Blake) (University of London Press, [1954]) £35
MERRY MUFFIN BOOKS (three books; illustrated by Neville Main) (Brockhampton Press, 1954) ....each £20
PRUDENCE KITTEN AND PUFFER OF CHILDREN'S TELEVISION (illustrated by George Fry) (Publicity Productions, [1955]) ..£12

MILNE, A.A.

British author. Born: Alan Alexander Milne in London in 1882. Educated at Westminster School and Trinity College, Cambridge, where he read mathematics. Became assistant editor of *Punch* at the age of 24, remaining with the magazine until the outbreak of the First World War, when he joined the army. He had his first literary success as a playwright, but was encouraged to write children's verse by Rose Fyleman, who published his poem, 'The Dormouse and the Doctor', in *The Merry-Go-Round*. His first collection, *When We Were Very Young* (1924), sold half a million copies in its first ten years, and was followed by another volume of verse, *Now We Are Six* (1927), and the story-books, *Winnie-the-Pooh* (1926) and *The House at Pooh Corner* (1928). Thereafter, he concentrated on the theatre, producing only two more children's works, notably *Toad of Toad Hall* (1929), a stage version of Kenneth Grahame's *The Wind in the Willows*. Died: 1956.

Prices are for books in Very Good condition with dustjackets where applicable.

ONCE ON A TIME: A Fairy Story (illustrated by H.M. Brock) (Hodder & Stoughton, 1917) £150
ONCE ON A TIME (illustrated by Charles Robinson) (Hodder & Stoughton, [1925]) £120
WHEN WE WERE VERY YOUNG (verse; illustrated by E.H. Shepard) (Methuen, 1924) £5,000
WHEN WE WERE VERY YOUNG (verse; illustrated by E.H. Shepard; limited to 100 numbered copies,
  signed by the author and artist) (Methuen, 1924) £6,000
WHEN WE WERE VERY YOUNG (verse; illustrated by E.H. Shepard; limited to 300 numbered copies,
  signed by Christopher Milne) (Methuen, 1974) £500
VESPERS: A Poem (illustrated by E.H. Shepard; music by H. Fraser-Simson) (Methuen, [1924]) £150
MAKE-BELIEVE: A Children's Play in a Prologue and Three Acts (lyrics by C.E. Burton) (Methuen, 1925) £100
A GALLERY OF CHILDREN (illustrated by H. Willebeek le Mair under the pseudonym 'Saida') (Stanley Paul, 1925) £500
A GALLERY OF CHILDREN (illustrated by H. Willebeek le Mair under the pseudonym 'Saida';
  limited to 500 numbered copies, signed by the author) (Stanley Paul, 1925) £1,000
THE KING'S BREAKFAST (illustrated by E.H. Shepard; music by H. Fraser-Simson) (Methuen, 1925) £200
WINNIE-THE-POOH (stories; illustrated by E.H. Shepard) (Methuen, 1926) £2,500
WINNIE-THE-POOH (stories; illustrated by E.H. Shepard; De Luxe edition: red, green or blue leather binding; in slipcase)
  (Methuen, 1926) £3,000
WINNIE-THE-POOH (stories; illustrated by E.H. Shepard; limited to 350 copies, signed by the author and artist) (Methuen, 1926) ..£5,000
WINNIE-THE-POOH (stories; illustrated in colour by E.H. Shepard) (Methuen, 1973)............................£80
WINNIE-THE-POOH (stories; illustrated by E.H. Shepard; limited to 300 numbered copies,
  signed by the artist) (Methuen, 1973) £600
WINNIE-THE-POOH AND EEYORE'S TAIL: A Pop-Up Picture Book (adapted by A. Schenk from the
  original illustrations by E.H. Shepard) (Methuen, [1953]) £75
WINNIE-THE-POOH AND THE BEES: A Pop-Up Picture Book (adapted by A. Schenk from
  the original illustrations by E.H. Shepard) (Methuen, [1953]) £75
TEDDY BEAR and Other Songs From 'When We Were Very Young' (illustrated by A.A. Milne; music by H. Fraser-Simson)
  (Methuen, 1926)..£200

Three of A.A. Milne's best-known works in their rare dustjackets. All these works were also issued in signed, limited editions.

NOW WE ARE SIX (verse; illustrated by E.H. Shepard) (Methuen, 1927) £800
NOW WE ARE SIX (verse; illustrated by E.H. Shepard; De Luxe edition: red,
blue or green leather binding; in slipcase) (Methuen, 1927)..£1,500
NOW WE ARE SIX (verse; illustrated by E.H. Shepard; limited to 200 numbered copies,
signed by the author and artist) (Methuen, 1927) £2,000
NOW WE ARE SIX (verse; illustrated by E.H. Shepard; limited to 300 numbered copies,
signed by Christopher Milne) (Methuen, 1927) £400
SONGS FROM 'NOW WE ARE SIX' (music by H. Fraser-Simson) (Methuen, 1927)..................................£200
MORE VERY YOUNG SONGS (Methuen, 1928)..£175
THE HOUSE AT POOH CORNER (stories; illustrated by E.H. Shepard) (Methuen, 1928).....................£1,000
THE HOUSE AT POOH CORNER (stories; illustrated by E.H. Shepard; De Luxe edition: red,
green or blue leather binding; in slipcase) (Methuen, 1928)...£2,500
THE HOUSE AT POOH CORNER (stories; illustrated by E.H. Shepard; limited to 350 numbered copies,
signed by the author and artist) (Methuen, 1928) £4,000
THE HOUSE AT POOH CORNER (illustrated by E.H. Shepard) (Methuen, 1974) £60
THE CHRISTOPHER ROBIN CALENDAR (verse; illustrated by E.H. Shepard) (Methuen: 'Ephemerides' series, [1928]) £75
THE CHRISTOPHER ROBIN STORY BOOK (selections from 'When We Were Very Young', 'Now We Are Six',
'Winnie-the-Pooh' and 'The House at Pooh Corner'; new preface by the author) (Methuen, 1929) £400
THE HUMS OF POOH (illustrated by E.H. Shepard; music by H. Fraser-Simson) (Methuen, 1929) £200
TOAD OF TOAD HALL: A Play Taken from Kenneth Grahame's 'The Wind in the Willows' (Methuen, 1929).......................£100
TOAD OF TOAD HALL (limited to 200 numbered copies, signed by Kenneth Grahame and A.A. Milne) (Methuen, 1929)......£1,000
TALES OF POOH (selections from 'Winnie-the-Pooh' and 'The House at Pooh Corner';
illustrated by E.H. Shepard) (Methuen: 'Modern Classics' series, [1930]) £200
THE CHRISTOPHER ROBIN BIRTHDAY BOOK (selections from 'When We Were Very Young', 'Now We Are Six',
'Winnie-the-Pooh' and 'The House at Pooh Corner'; illustrated by E.H. Shepard) (Methuen, 1930)....................£150
THE CHRISTOPHER ROBIN VERSES (contains 'When We Were Very Young' and 'Now We Are Six';
illustrated by E.H. Shepard) (Methuen, 1932) £250
INTRODUCING WINNIE-THE-POOH (Methuen, 1947) £75
THE WORLD OF POOH (eight new colour plates by E.H. Shepard) (Methuen, 1958) £100
THE WORLD OF CHRISTOPHER ROBIN (eight new colour plates by E.H. Shepard) (Methuen, 1959) £100
PRINCE RABBIT and THE PRINCESS WHO COULD NOT LAUGH (illustrated by Mary Shepard) (Ward Lock, 1966) £30
THE POOH STORY BOOK (new illustrations and colour plates by E.H. Shepard) (Methuen, 1967) £60
THE CHRISTOPHER ROBIN VERSE BOOK (illustrated in colour by E.H. Shepard) (Methuen, 1969)....................£60

MOLESWORTH, Mrs

British author. Born: Mary Louisa Stewart in Manchester in 1839. An enormously prolific author, she began by writing adult novels, but turned to children's fiction on the advice of the illustrator, Sir Noel Paton. Amongst her best-known titles are *The Cuckoo Clock* (1877), *The Tapestry Room* (1879) and *The Carved Lions* (1895). Although rather dated now, her books have been admired by Swinburne, Gillian Avery and Roger Lancelyn Green. Died: 1921.

Prices are for books in Very Good condition.

TELL ME A STORY (written under the pseudonym 'Ennis Graham'; illustrated by Walter Crane) (Macmillan, 1875) £65
CARROTS: Just a Little Boy (written under the pseudonym 'Ennis Graham'; illustrated by Walter Crane) (Macmillan, 1876) £65
THE CUCKOO CLOCK (written under the pseudonym 'Ennis Graham'; illustrated by Walter Crane) (Macmillan, 1877) £65
GRANDMOTHER DEAR (illustrated by Walter Crane) (Macmillan, 1878) £45
THE TAPESTRY ROOM (illustrated by Walter Crane) (Macmillan, 1879)...£45
A CHRISTMAS CHILD (illustrated by Walter Crane) (Macmillan, 1880) £45
HERMY: The Story of a Little Girl (illustrated by Mary Ellen Edwards) (Routledge, 1881 [1880]) £40
THE ADVENTURES OF HERR BABY (illustrated by Walter Crane) (Macmillan, 1881) £30
HOODIE (illustrated by Mary Ellen Edwards) (Routledge, 1882) £30
SUMMER STORIES FOR BOYS AND GIRLS (illustrated by Mary Ellen Edwards) (Macmillan, 1882) £30
ROSY (illustrated by Walter Crane) (Macmillan, 1882) £35
THE BOYS AND I (illustrated by Mary Ellen Edwards) (Routledge, 1883)...£25
TWO LITTLE WAIFS (illustrated by Walter Crane) (Macmillan, 1883) £35
CHRISTMAS-TREE LAND (illustrated by Walter Crane) (Macmillan, 1884) £35
THE LITTLE OLD PORTRAIT (illustrated by W. Gunston) (SPCK, [1884]) £20
LETTICE (illustrated by Frank Dadd) (SPCK, [1884]) £25
US: An Old-Fashioned Story (illustrated by Walter Crane) (Macmillan, 1885) £35
A CHARGE FULFILLED (illustrated by R. Caton Woodville) (SPCK, [1886]) £25
SILVERTHORNS (illustrated by J. Noel Paton) (Hatchards, [1887]) £30
FOUR WIND'S FARM (illustrated by Walter Crane) (Macmillan, 1887) £35
LITTLE MISS PEGGY (illustrated by Walter Crane) (Macmillan, 1887) £35
THE PALACE IN THE GARDEN (illustrated by Harriet M. Bennett) (Hatchards, 1887) £25
THE ABBEY BY THE SEA and FELIX, AN OUTCAST (illustrated by Frank Dadd) (SPCK, [1887]) £25
THE THIRD MISS ST. QUENTIN (Hatchards, 1888) £20
FIVE MINUTES STORIES (illustrated by Gordon Browne and others) (SPCK, [1888]) £20
A CHRISTMAS POSY (illustrated by Walter Crane) (Macmillan, 1888) £40
THE RECTORY CHILDREN (illustrated by Walter Crane) (Macmillan, 1889) £35
A HOUSE TO LET (illustrated by W.J. Morgan) (SPCK, [1889]) £25
GREAT UNCLE HOOT-TOOT (illustrated by Gordon Browne and others) (SPCK, [1889]) £25
THE OLD PINCUSHION, or Aunt Clotilda's Guests (illustrated by Mrs A. Hope) (Griffith & Farran, [1889]) £25
THE OLD PINCUSHION (illustrated by Mabel Lucie Attwell) (Chambers, 1910) £60
NEIGHBOURS (illustrated by Mary Ellen Edwards) (Hatchards, 1889) £20
NESTA, or Fragments of a Little Life (Chambers, 1889) £20
THE GREEN CASKET and Other Stories (illustrated by R. Barnes and W.J. Morgan) (Chambers, 1890) £20
TWELVE TINY TALES (illustrated by W.J. Morgan) (SPCK, [1890]) £20
FAMILY TROUBLES (MR NOBODY) (illustrated by W.J. Morgan) (SPCK, [1890]) £20
THE CHILDREN OF THE CASTLE (illustrated by Walter Crane) (Macmillan, 1890) £35
LITTLE MOTHER BUNCH (illustrated by Mary Ellen Edwards) (Cassell, 1890) £20
THE STORY OF A SPRING MORNING (illustrated by Mary Ellen Edwards) (Longman, 1890) £20
THE RED GRANGE (illustrated by Gordon Browne) (Methuen, 1891)..£20
THE BEWITCHED LAMP (illustrated by Robert Barnes) (Chambers, 1891) £20
THE LUCKY DUCKS and Other Stories (illustrated by W.J. Morgan) (SPCK, [1891]) £20
SWEET CONTENT (illustrated by William Rainey) (Griffith & Farran, 1891) £30
NURSE HEATHERDALE'S STORY (illustrated by L. Leslie Brooke) (Macmillan, 1891) £35
THE GIRLS AND I: A Veracious History (illustrated by L. Leslie Brooke) (Macmillan, 1892) £30
IMOGEN, or Only Eighteen (illustrated by H.A. Bone) (Chambers, 1892) £20
AN ENCHANTED GARDEN — FAIRY STORIES (illustrated by W.J. Hennessy) (Unwin, 1892)....................................£30
FARTHINGS: The Story of a Stray and a Waif (illustrated by G.M. Broadley) (Wells Gardner, 1892) £20
THE MAN WITH THE PAN-PIPES and Other Stories (illustrated by W.J. Morgan) (SPCK, [1892])..............................£25
ROBIN REDBREAST: A Story for Girls (illustrated by Robert Barnes) (Chamber, 1892) £20
THE NEXT-DOOR HOUSE (illustrated by W. Hatherell) (Chambers, 1893) £20
STUDIES AND STORIES (illustrated by Walter Crane) (A.D. Innes, 1893) £35
THE THIRTEEN LITTLE BLACK PIGS and Other Stories (illustrated by W.J. Morgan) (SPCK, [1893]) £20
MARY: A Nursery Story for Very Little Children (illustrated by L. Leslie Brooke) (Macmillan, 1893) £30
OLIVIA: A Story for Girls (illustrated by Robert Barnes) (Chambers, 1893 [1894]) £30
BLANCHE: A Story for Girls (illustrated by Robert Barnes) (Chambers, 1894 [1893]) £20
MY NEW HOME (illustrated by L. Leslie Brooke) (Macmillan, 1894) £30
THE CARVED LIONS (illustrated by L. Leslie Brooke) (Macmillan, 1895) £30
SHEILA'S MYSTERY (illustrated by L. Leslie Brooke) (Macmillan, 1895)...£30
OPPOSITE NEIGHBOURS and Other Stories (illustrated by W.J. Morgan) (SPCK, [1895]) £15
WHITE TURRETS (illustrated by William Rainey) (Chambers, 1896 [1895]) £15

FRIENDLY JOEY and Other Stories (illustrated by W.J. Morgan) (SPCK, [1896]) £15
THE ORIEL WINDOW (illustrated by L. Leslie Brooke) (Macmillan, 1896) £30
MISS MOUSE AND HER BOYS (illustrated by L. Leslie Brooke) (Macmillan, 1897) £30
PHILIPPA (illustrated by J. Finnemore) (Chambers, 1897 [1896]) £15
MEG LANGHOLME, or The Day After Tomorrow (illustrated by William Rainey) (Chambers, 1897) £15
STORIES FOR CHILDREN IN ILLUSTRATION OF THE LORD'S PRAYER (illustrated by Gordon Browne and others)
  (Gardner & Darton, 1897) £25
GREYLING TOWERS: A Story for the Young (illustrated by Percy Tarrant) (Chambers, 1898) £20
THE MAGIC NUTS (illustrated by Rosie Pitman) (Macmillan, 1898) £25
THE GRIM HOUSE (illustrated by Warwick Goble) (Nisbet, 1899) £30
THIS AND THAT: A Tale of Two Tinies (illustrated by Hugh Thomson) (Macmillan, 1899) £35
THE CHILDREN'S HOUR (Nelson, [1899]) £20
THE THREE WITCHES (illustrated by Lewis Baumer) (Chambers, [1900]) £20
THE HOUSE THAT GREW (illustrated by Alice B. Woodward) (Macmillan, 1900) £20
THE WOOD-PIGEONS AND MARY (illustrated by H.R. Millar) (Macmillan, 1901) £20
'MY PRETTY' AND HER LITTLE BROTHER 'TOO' and Other Stories (illustrated by Lewis Baumer)
  (Chambers, [1901]) £20
THE BLUE BABY and Other Stories (illustrated by Maud C. Foster) (Unwin, [1901]) £20
PETERKIN (illustrated by H.R. Millar) (Macmillan, 1902) £20
THE MYSTERY OF THE PINEWOOD AND HOLLOW TREE HOUSE (illustrated by A.A. Dixon) (Nister, 1903) £20
THE RUBY RING (illustrated by Rosie Pitman) (Macmillan, 1904) £20
THE BOLTED DOOR and Other Stories (illustrated by L. Baumer) (Chambers, [1906]) £20
JASPER: A Story for Children (illustrated by Gertrude D. Holland) (Macmillan, 1906) £20
THE LITTLE GUEST: A Story for Children (illustrated by Gertrude D. Holland) (Macmillan, 1907) £20
FAIRIES — OF SORTS (illustrated by Gertrude D. Holland) (Macmillan, 1908) £20
THE FEBRUARY BOYS (illustrated by Mabel Lucie Attwell) (Chambers, 1909) £60
THE STORY OF A YEAR (illustrated by Gertrude D. Holland) (Macmillan, 1910) £20
FAIRIES AFIELD (illustrated by Gertrude D. Holland) (Macmillan, 1911) £20
THE CUCKOO CLOCK (illustrated by E.H. Shepard) (Dent: 'Children's Illustrated Classics' series, 1954)............£30
FAIRY STORIES. Edited by Roger Lancelyn Green (issued with dustjacket) (Harvill, 1957) £8

MONTGOMERY, L.M.

Canadian author. Born: Lucy Maud Montgomery in Clifton, Prince Edward Island, in 1874. Studied to be a teacher, but joined the *Halifax Chronicle* in 1901, having already contributed poems and stories to various papers. Her bestselling novel, *Anne of Green Gables* (1908), was followed by a number of sequels. Died: 1942.

Prices are for books in Very Good condition with dustjackets.

'Anne Shirley' Books

ANNE OF GREEN GABLES (illustrated by M.A. and W.A. Claus) (Pitman, 1908) £200
ANNE OF AVONLEA (Pitman, 1909) £150
CHRONICLES OF AVONLEA (Sampson Low, 1912)...£100
ANNE OF THE ISLAND (Pitman, 1915) £120
ANNE'S HOUSE OF DREAMS (Constable, 1917) £80
RAINBOW VALLEY (Constable, 1920) £100
RILLA OF INGLESIDE (Hodder & Stoughton, [1921]) £75
FURTHER CHRONICLES OF AVONLEA (Harrap, 1925) £100
ANNE OF WINDY WILLOWS (Harrap, 1936) £30
ANNE OF INGLESIDE (Harrap, 1939) £30

'Emily Starr' Books

EMILY OF NEW MOON (Hodder & Stoughton, [1923]) £130
EMILY CLIMBS (Hodder & Stoughton, [1925]) £100
EMILY'S QUEST (Hodder & Stoughton, [1927]) £65

'Pat Gardiner' Books

PAT OF SILVER BUSH (Hodder & Stoughton, [1933]) £40
MISTRESS PAT (Harrap, 1935)..£45

Others

KILMENY OF THE ORCHARD (illustrated by George Gibbs) (Pitman, 1910) £175
THE STORY GIRL (Pitman, 1911) £200
THE GOLDEN ROAD (Cassell, 1914)..£200
THE WATCHMAN and Other Poems (Constable, 1920) £55
THE BLUE CASTLE (Hodder & Stoughton, [1926]) £60
MAGIC FOR MARIGOLD (Hodder & Stoughton, [1929]) £60
AUNT BECKY BEGAN IT (Hodder & Stoughton, [1931])...£60
JANE OF LANTERN HILL (Harrap, 1937) £40
THE ROAD TO YESTERDAY (Angus & Robertson, 1975) £20
THE DOCTOR'S SWEETHEART and Other Stories (Harrap, 1979) £20

'MOTHER GOOSE'

The figure of 'Mother Goose' as a teller of folk tales and rhymes has its roots in both German and French folklore. Its English origins can be traced back to the first translation of Charles Perrault's *Histories, or Tales of Past Times* (1729; *Histories, ou Contes du temps passé*), where the expression 'Contes de Ma Mère L'Oye' was translated as 'Mother Goose's Tales'. Subsequent edition of the stories were published under the title, *Mother Goose's Tales*, and the phrase became commonplace to describe any book of 'traditional' rhymes or fables, especially in America.

Prices are for books in Very Good condition.

THE ENTERTAINING TALES OF MOTHER GOOSE (Lumsden, [c.1815]) £1,300
MOTHER GOOSE'S MELODY. Containing the Most Celebrated Songs of the Old British Nurses (Marshall, 1817) £800
MOTHER GOOSE, or Harlequin and the Golden Egg: An Original Shadow Pantomime (London, 1864) £550
MOTHER GOOSE'S MELODIES (illustrated by J. Ralson Chase) (Philadelphia, U.S., [1870]) £450
MOTHER GOOSE'S MELODIES FOR CHILDREN, or Songs for the Nursery. Edited by G.A.R.
    (illustrated by H.L. Stephens and G. Fay) (London, 1872 [1871]) £450
MOTHER GOOSE'S NURSERY RHYMES (illustrated by Sir John Gilbert, John Tenniel and others)
    (Routledge, 1877 [1876]) £100
MOTHER GOOSE'S JINGLES (illustrated by H. Weir, Walter Crane and others) (London, 1878 [1877]) £75
MOTHER GOOSE'S NURSERY RHYMES AND FAIRY TALES (two volumes) (Routledge, 1878 [1877]) ....the set £50
MOTHER GOOSE, or The Old Nursery Rhymes (illustrated by Kate Greenaway) (Routledge, [1881]) £150
OLD MOTHER GOOSE and Other Rhymes (illustrated by H. Weir) (Routledge, [1886]) £60
MOTHER GOOSE'S NURSERY RHYMES, TALES AND JINGLES (Warne, [1890]) £50
OLD MOTHER GOOSE'S RHYMES AND TALES (illustrated by Constance Haslewood) (Warne, 1890)................................£50
LITTLE MOTHER GOOSE (illustrated by Jessie Watkins) (Ward, [1892]) £125
MOTHER GOOSE IN PROSE: Nursery Rhymes with Stories Founded on Them by L. Frank Baum
    (illustrated by M. Parrish) (Chicago, U.S., [1897]) £2,750
DENSLOW'S MOTHER GOOSE: Being the Old Familiar Rhymes and Jingles of Mother Goose.
    Edited by W.W. Denslow (illustrated by W.W. Denslow) (New York, U.S., 1901)...................................£1,200
MOTHER GOOSE'S NURSERY RHYMES (illustrated by Mabel Chadburn) (Dent, 1903) £50
MOTHER GOOSE'S NURSERY RHYMES. Edited by Walter C. Jerrold (illustrated by John Hassall) (Blackie, 1909 [1908]) £55
MOTHER GOOSE'S BOOK OF NURSERY RHYMES AND SONGS. Edited by Ernest and Grace Rhys (Dent, [1910]).............£30
MOTHER GOOSE (illustrated by Mabel Lucie Attwell) (Raphael Tuck, 1910) £150
MOTHER GOOSE JINGLES (Nister, [c.1910]) £75
MOTHER GOOSE: The Old Nursery Rhymes (illustrated by Arthur Rackham) (Heinemann, [1913]) £350
MOTHER GOOSE: The Old Nursery Rhymes (illustrated by Arthur Rackham; limited to 1,130 copies,
    signed by the artist) (Heinemann, [1913]) £1,500
THE LITTLE MOTHER GOOSE (illustrated by Jessie Willcox Smith; selected and adapted by Samuel McChord Crothers)
    (Dodd Mead, U.S., [1915]) £70
MOTHER GOOSE'S NURSERY RHYMES. Edited by L.E. Walter (illustrated by Charles Folkard)
    (A. & C. Black, [1919]) £60
MOTHER GOOSE'S NURSERY RHYMES. Edited by L.E. Walter (illustrated by Charles Folkard; second edition)
    (A. & C. Black, 1923) £45
THE BOYD SMITH MOTHER GOOSE (illustrated by E. Boyd Smith; text collated by Lawrence Elmendorf)
    (Putnam, 1920) £50
THE OLD MOTHER GOOSE NURSERY RHYME BOOK (illustrated by Anne Anderson) (Nelson, [1926]) £85
MOTHER GOOSE NURSERY RHYMES (illustrated by Charles Robinson) (Collins, [1928]) £75
MOTHER GOOSE: Nursery Rhymes (illustrated by Margaret W. Tarrant) (Ward Lock, [1929]) £60
WILLY POGÁNY'S MOTHER GOOSE (illustrated by Willy Pogány) (Nelson, U.K./U.S., [1929])...............................£150
MOTHER GOOSE (illustrated by Sybil Tawse) (Harrap, 1932) £40
THE POP-UP MOTHER GOOSE (New York, U.S., [1933])...£400
MOTHER GOOSE RHYMES (illustrated by S.B. Pearse and Winifred M. Ackroyd) (Coker, [1935]) £50
MOTHER GOOSE: The Old Nursery Rhymes (illustrated by Arthur Rackham; two volumes) (Heinemann, [1952]) ......the set £150
THE MOTHER GOOSE TREASURY (illustrated by Raymond Briggs) (Hamish Hamilton, 1966) £60
MOTHER GOOSE: A Collection of Nursery Rhymes. Edited by Michael Hague (Holt, U.S., 1984) £25
TAIL FEATHERS FROM MOTHER GOOSE: The Opie Rhyme Book by Iona and Peter Opie (Pavilion, 1988) £25

MURPHY, Jill

British author-illustrator. Born: London, 1949. Author of the 'Worst Witch' series.

Prices are for books in Very Good condition with dustjackets where applicable.

THE WORST WITCH (Alison & Busby, 1974) £25
THE WORST WITCH STRIKES AGAIN (Alison & Busby, 1980) £20
A BAD SPELL FOR THE WORST WITCH (Kestrel, 1982)..£15
WHATEVER NEXT? (Walker, 1983) £10
GEOFFREY STRANGEWAYS (Walker, 1990) £10
WORLDS APART (Walker, 1991) £10
THE WORST WITCH ALL AT SEA (Viking, 1993) £10

Picture Books : 1-5

ON THE WAY HOME (Walker, 1982)..£10

*'The Crooked Man' from Arthur Rackham's 1913 edition of **Mother Goose**, issued by Heinemann in both trade and limited editions.*

NEEDHAM, Violet

British author. Born: 1876. She was 63 when her first novel, *The Black Riders* (1939), was published, although she had submitted it unsuccessfully to several firms twenty years earlier. This was followed by seventeen more children's books, most of them illustrated by her friend and neighbour, Joyce Bruce. Eight of her novels are set in a series of imaginary Central European countries, reflecting her childhood travels on the Continent. Died: 1967.

Prices are for books in Very Good condition with dustjackets.

THE BLACK RIDERS (illustrated by Anne Bullen) (Collins, 1939) £75
THE EMERALD CROWN (illustrated by Anne Bullen) (Collins, 1940) £75
THE STORMY PETREL (illustrated by Joyce Bruce) (Collins, 1942) £70
THE HORN OF MERLYNS (illustrated by Joyce Bruce) (Collins, 1943)...£45
THE WOODS OF WINDRI (illustrated by Joyce Bruce) (Collins, 1944) £35
THE HOUSE OF THE PALADIN (illustrated by Joyce Bruce) (Collins, 1945) £35
THE CHANGELING OF MONTE LUCIO (illustrated by Joyce Bruce) (Collins, 1946) £30
THE BELL OF THE FOUR EVANGELISTS (illustrated by Joyce Bruce) (Collins, 1947).....................................£90
THE BOY IN RED (illustrated by Joyce Bruce) (Collins, 1948)...£45
THE BETRAYER (illustrated by Joyce Bruce) (Collins, 1950) £45
PANDORA OF PARRHAM ROYAL (illustrated by Joyce Bruce) (Collins, 1951) £100
THE AVENUE (illustrated by Joyce Bruce) (Collins, 1952) £45
HOW MANY MILES TO BABYLON? (illustrated by Joyce Bruce) (Collins, 1953) £100
ADVENTURES AT HAMPTON COURT (illustrated by Will Nickless) (Lutterworth Press, 1954) £90
RICHARD AND THE GOLDEN HORSE SHOE (illustrated by Joyce Bruce) (Collins, 1954) £120
THE GREAT HOUSE OF ESTRAVILLE (illustrated by Joyce Bruce) (Collins, 1955) £120
THE SECRET OF THE WHITE PEACOCK (illustrated by Joyce Bruce) (Collins, 1956) £90
ADVENTURES AT WINDSOR CASTLE (illustrated by David Walsh) (Lutterworth Press, 1957) £90
THE RED ROSE OF RUVINA (illustrated by Richard Kennedy) (Collins, 1957) £75

Violet Needham's **Pandora of Parrham Royal** has never been reprinted, which explains why the first edition is now worth £100.

Like many of Needham's books, **How Many Miles to Babylon?** is illustrated by her friend and neighbour, Joyce Bruce.

NESBIT, E.

British author. Born: Edith Nesbit in Kennington, London, in 1858. Following the death of her father when she was four, she spent the next nine years travelling with her family in France and Germany, during which time she had little formal schooling. She had her first poem accepted for publication when she was fifteen, and continued to write for various magazines after her marriage to Hubert Bland, one of the founder members of the Fabian Society, in 1880. She thought of herself primarily as a poet, but following the success of *The Story of the Treasure Seekers* (1899), parts of which had originally appeared in *Pall Mall* and *Windsor* magazines, she concentrated on writing for children. Among her best-known works in the field are *Five Children and It* (1902), *The Phoenix and the Carpet* (1904) and *The Railway Children* (1906), the first two of which were illustrated by H.R. Millar. Died: 1924.

Prices are for books in Very Good condition (with dustjackets after 1940).

CORALS, SEA SONGS (Nister, [1889]) £300
SONGS OF TWO SEASONS (verse; illustrated by J. MacIntyre) (Raphael Tuck, [1890]) £250
THE VOYAGE OF COLUMBUS, 1492: The Discovery of America (verse; illustrated by Will and Frances Brundage)
   (Raphael Tuck, 1892) £175
OUR FRIENDS AND ALL ABOUT THEM (verse) (Raphael Tuck, [1893])...£130
LISTEN LONG AND LISTEN WELL (with others) (Raphael Tuck, 1893)...£100
SUNNY TAILS FOR SNOWY DAYS (with others) (Raphael Tuck, 1893) £100
TOLD BY SUNBEAMS AND ME (with others) (Raphael Tuck, 1893) £100
FLOWERS I BRING AND SONGS I SING (verse; contains poems by E. Nesbit written under the name 'E. Bland')
   (Raphael Tuck, [1893]) £100
FUR AND FEATHERS: Tales for All Weathers (with others) (Raphael Tuck, 1894) £100
LADS AND LASSIES (with others) (Raphael Tuck, 1894) £100
TALES THAT ARE TRUE, FOR BROWN EYES AND BLUE (with others; illustrated by M. Goodman) (Raphael Tuck, 1894) £100
TALES TO DELIGHT, FROM MORNING TILL NIGHT (with others; illustrated by M. Goodman) (Raphael Tuck, 1894) £100
HOURS IN MANY LANDS: Stories and Poems (with others; illustrated by Frances Brundage) (Raphael Tuck, 1894).............£100
THE GIRL'S OWN BIRTHDAY BOOK (Drane, [1894]) £25
DOGGY TALES (illustrated by Lucie Kemp-Welch) (Marcus Ward, [1895]) £65
PUSSY TALES (illustrated by Lucie Kemp-Welch) (Marcus Ward, [1895])...£65
TALES OF THE CLOCK (illustrated by Helen Jackson) (Raphael Tuck, 1895) £35
DULCIE'S LANTERN and Other Stories (with others) (Griffith Farran, 1895) £70
TREASURES FROM STORYLAND (with others) (Raphael Tuck, 1895) £70
HOLLY AND MISTLETOE: A Book of Christmas Verse (with others) (Wood, [1895])..£50
AS HAPPY AS A KING (illustrated by S.R. Praeger) (Marcus Ward, [1896])..£65
THE CHILDREN'S SHAKESPEARE. Edited by Edric Veredenburg (Raphael Tuck, [1897]) £65
TALES TOLD IN THE TWILIGHT (with others) (Raphael Tuck, [1897]) £65
DINNA FORGET (with G.C. Bingham; verse) (Nister, 1897)..£75
ROYAL CHILDREN OF ENGLISH HISTORY (Raphael Tuck, 1897) £50
A BOOK OF DOGS (illustrated by Winifred Austin) (Dent, 1898)..£50
PUSSY AND DOGGY TALES (illustrated by Lucy Kemp-Welch) (Dent, 1899) £65
THE STORY OF THE TREASURE SEEKERS: Being the Adventures of the Bastable Children in Search of a Fortune
   (illustrated by Gordon Browne and Lewis Baumer) (Unwin, 1899) £125
THE BOOK OF DRAGONS (illustrated by H.R. Millar and H. Granville Fell) (Harper, 1901 [1900]) £120
NINE UNLIKELY TALES FOR CHILDREN (illustrated by H.R. Millar and C. Shepperson) (Unwin, 1901) £75
THE WOULDBEGOODS: Being the Further Adventures of the Treasure Seekers
   (illustrated by Arthur Buckland and John Hassall) (Unwin, 1901) £175
TO WISH YOU JOY (verse) (Raphael Tuck, 1901) £55
FIVE CHILDREN AND IT (illustrated by H.R. Millar) (Unwin, 1902) £175
THE REVOLT OF THE TOYS and WHAT COMES OF QUARRELLING (stories; illustrated by Ambrose Dudley)
   (Nister [printed in Germany], [1902]) £150
THE RAINBOW QUEEN and Other Stories (Raphael Tuck, [1903])..£50
PLAYTIME STORIES (Raphael Tuck, 1903) £50
THE PHOENIX AND THE CARPET (illustrated by H.R. Millar) (Newnes, [1904]) £175
THE STORY OF THE FIVE REBELLIOUS DOLLS (Nister, 1904) £150
NEW TREASURE SEEKERS (illustrated by Gordon Baumer and Lewis Baumer) (Unwin, 1904) £100
CAT TALES (with Rosamund Bland; illustrated by Isabel Watkin) (Nister, 1904) £75
OSWALD BASTABLE AND OTHERS (illustrated by C.E. Brock and H.R. Millar) (Wells Gardner, 1905) £160
PUG PETER: KING OF MOUSELAND (illustrated by Harry Rountree and John Hassall) (Cooke, [1905]) £100
THE STORY OF THE AMULET (illustrated by H.R. Millar) (Unwin, 1906) £125
THE RAILWAY CHILDREN (illustrated by C.E. Brock) (Wells Gardner, 1906) £300
THE ENCHANTED CASTLE (illustated by H.R. Millar) (Unwin, 1907) £100
THE HOUSE OF ARDEN (illustrated by H.R. Millar) (Unwin, 1908)...£100
THE OLD NURSEY STORIES (illustrated by W.H. Margetson) (Hodder & Stoughton/Frowde, 1908)......................£40
DAPHNE IN FITZROY STREET (George Allen, 1909) £35
THESE LITTLE ONES (illustrated by Spencer Pryse) (George Allen, 1909) £60
HARDING'S LUCK (illustrated by H.R. Millar) (Hodder & Stoughton, 1909) £80
HIDE AND SEEK STORIES (with others) (Nister, [c.1909]) £65
THE MAGIC CITY (illustrated by H.R. Millar) (Macmillan, 1910) £125

*Beverley Nichols' **The Tree that Sat Down** (1945) was the first of four children's books about an enchanted wood.*

The Mountain of Magic (1950) was the third book in the series. All the books are currently valued at £25 for Very Good copies.

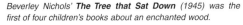

MY SEASIDE STORY BOOK (with George Manville Fenn) (Nister, 1911) £45
THE WONDERFUL GARDEN, or The Three C's (illustrated by H.R. Millar) (Macmillan, 1911) £100
THE MAGIC WORLD (illustrated by H.R. Millar and Spencer Pryse) (Macmillan, 1912) £100
WET MAGIC (illustrated by H.R. Millar) (Werner Laurie, [1913]) £100
OUR NEW STORY BOOK (with others) (Nister/Dutton, U.S., 1913) £65
FIVE OF US — AND MADELINE (illustrated by Norah Unwin) (Unwin, 1925) £45
COMPLETE HISTORY OF THE BASTABLE FAMILY (illustrated by H.R. Millar and others) (Benn, 1928)................£60
THE HOUSE WITH NO ADDRESS (Newnes, [1947]) £25
LONG AGO WHEN I WAS YOUNG (illustrated by Edward Ardizzone) (Whiting & Wheaton, 1966)............................£35
FAIRY STORIES (illustrated by Brian Robb) (Benn, 1977) £15

NICHOLS, Beverley
British author. Born: 1898. He wrote four children's books about a magic wood, beginning with *The Tree That Sat Down* (1945). Died: 1983.

Prices are for books in Very Good condition in dustjackets where applicable.

THE TREE THAT SAT DOWN (illustrated by Isobel and John Morton-Sale) (Cape, 1945) £25
THE STREAM THAT STOOD STILL (illustrated by Richard Kennedy) (Cape, 1948) £25
THE MOUNTAIN OF MAGIC (illustrated by Peggy Fortnum) (Cape, 1950) £25
THE WICKEDEST WITCH IN THE WORLD (W.H. Allen, 1971) £25

NIELSEN, Kay
Danish illustrator. Born in Copenhagen in 1886. Studied art at Colarossi's and the Academie Julien in Paris. Moved to London in 1911, where he was commissioned to illustrate Sir Arthur Quiller-Couch's *In Powder and Crinoline* (1913) by Hodder & Stoughton. This was followed by handsome 'Gift Book' editions of the fairy tales of Hans Andersen (1924) and the Brothers Grimm (*Hansel and Gretel*, 1925). Moved to California in 1938 hoping to find work as a set designer in Hollywood, but met with little success. Died: 1957.

Prices are for books in Very Good condition.

IN POWDER AND CRINOLINE. Old Fairy Tales retold by Sir Arthur Quiller-Couch
(24 colour plates by Kay Nielsen; cloth binding) (Hodder & Stoughton, [1913]) £700
IN POWDER AND CRINOLINE. Old Fairy Tales retold by Sir Arthur Quiller-Couch
(26 colour plates by Kay Nielsen; Large Paper edition) (Hodder & Stoughton, [1913]) £1,200

IN POWDER AND CRINOLINE. Old Fairy Tales retold by Sir Arthur Quiller-Couch (26 colour plates by Kay Nielsen; De Luxe edition: limited to 500 copies, signed by the artist; green vellum binding) (Hodder & Stoughton, [1913])...........**£2,000**

EAST OF THE SUN AND WEST OF THE MOON: Old Tales from the North retold by Peter C. Asbjörnsen and Jorgen Moe (25 colour plates by Kay Nielsen; blue cloth binding) (Hodder & Stoughton, [1914]) **£1,750**

EAST OF THE SUN AND WEST OF THE MOON. Old Tales from the North retold by Peter C. Asbjörnsen and Jorgen Moe (25 colour plates by Kay Nielsen; De Luxe edition: limited to 500 copies; 25 colour plates; white vellum binding) (Hodder & Stoughton, [1914])..**£3,725**

HANS ANDERSEN'S FAIRY TALES (twelve colour plates by Kay Nielsen; blue cloth binding) (Hodder & Stoughton, [1924]) ..**£600**

HANS ANDERSEN'S FAIRY TALES (twelve colour plates by Kay Nielsen; De Luxe edition: limited to 500 copies, signed by the artist; blue cloth binding, issued with dustjacket — or white vellum binding) (Hodder & Stoughton, [1924])....**£1,000/£2,000**

HANSEL AND GRETEL and Other Stories (twelve colour plates by Kay Nielsen) (Hodder & Stoughton, [1925]) **£800**

HANSEL AND GRETEL and Other Stories (twelve colour plates by Kay Nielsen; limited to 600 copies, signed by the artist; cream buckram binding) (Hodder & Stoughton, [1925])..**£2,000**

RED MAGIC. A Collection of the World's Best Fairy Tales from all Countries. Edited and arranged by Romer Wilson (red cloth binding) (Cape, 1930) **£350**

NISTER, Ernest

German publisher of movable picture books. Although based in Nuremburg, Nister set up a London office in 1888 which, under the direction of the writer Robert Ellice Mack, provided many of the designs for the firm's books. These contained a variety of novelties, including 'pop-up' panoramas, revolving pictures, and 'slat' mechanisms that replace one picture with another at the pull of a tab.

Prices are for books in Very Good condition.

Pop-Up Books

LITTLE PETS, PANORAMA PICTURES ON VIEW WITHIN (Nister, [c.1893])...**£500**

PEEPS INTO FAIRYLAND by F.E. Weatherly (Nister, [c.1895]) **£500**

THE MODEL MENAGERIE by L.L. Weedon and Evelyn Fletcher (Nister, [c.1895]) **£550**

*One of Kay Nielsen's plates from **In Powder and Crinoline**, the book that launched his career as a book illustrator. The first edition came in three formats.*

NISTER, Ernest

THE LAND OF LONG AGO (illustrated by E. Stuart Hardy) (Nister, [c.1898]) £700

Movables and Panorama Books

LITTLE FOLK'S SURPRISES by Hope Myrtoun (verse; illustrations by Percy Hickling) (Nister, [c.1890]) £500
WONDERLAND PICTURES (Nister, [c.1890]) £500
MAGIC MOMENTS (Nister, [c.1892]) £500
TWINKLING PICTURES by L.L. Weedon (verse) (Nister, [c.1892]) £500
PLEASANT PASTIME PICTURES (Nister, [c.1895]) £500
MORE PLEASANT SURPRISES by F.E. Weatherly (movable book) (Nister, [1895]) £500
CHANGING PETS (Nister, [c.1905]) £250
COME AND GO!: A Novel Book for Children by Clifton Bingham (verse) (Nister, [c.1905]) £1,200

'Nister's Holiday' Annuals

NISTER'S HOLIDAY ANNUAL: Pictures and Stories for Little Folk. Edited by R.E. Mack (Nister, [1888-1916]) ....each £200

Others

WINTER SONGS AND SKETCHES. Edited by E. Nesbit and R. Ellice Mack (Nister/Griffith Farran, [c.1880]).............................£50
SCENES FROM THE BIBLE (picture puzzle book; contains four jigsaws; in box) (Nister, [c.1880]) £100
WHEN ALL IS YOUNG by Robert E. Mack (verse; illustrated by Harriet M. Bennet) (Nister/Dutton, U.S., 1888) £200
DICK AND HIS DOG (shaped picture book) (Nister, [c.1890]) £100
PLAY HOUR STORY BOOK (Nister, [c.1890]) £75
GULLIVER'S TRAVELS (illustrated by A. Jackson) (Nister, [c.1890]) £75
AS THY DAYS, SO SHALL THY STRENGTH BE (Nister, [c.1890])...£75
HOLLOW TREE HOUSE by E. Nesbit, Mrs Molesworth and others (Nister, [1892]) £90
PICTURE HOUSE (Nister, 1893)..£300
PICTURES AND PLUMS FOR FINGERS AND THUMBS (Nister, [c.1893]) £300
SHORT AND SWEET STORIES (Nister, [c.1893]) £60
NISTER'S NONSENSE (verse and prose by various authors) (Nister, [1894]) £75
MORE NISTER'S NONSENSE (verse and prose by various authors) (Nister, [1894]) £75
PICTURE BOOK GARDEN AND STORY LAND (short stories and verse) (Nister, 1894) £300
MORE JINGLES, JOKES AND FUNNY FOLKS by Louis Wain and Clifton Bingham (Nister, 1898) £250
PATHWAY OF FLOWERS — A CALENDAR FOR 1898 (with silk ties) (Nister, [c.1898]) £75
THREE LITTLE PETS (Nister, [c.1898]) £100
PICTURE COMPANIONS (Nister, [c.1899]) £300

Above: A fine example of a Nister picture book from the late 1890s. Like all the others, it was printed in Bavaria.

*Right: The first British edition of **The Magic Bedknob** by 'Borrowers' author, Mary Norton. It is now worth £80.*

WHEN MOTHER WAS A LITTLE GIRL by Blanchard (verse) (Nister, [c.1900]) £400
PIG TALES by Lilian Gask (Nister, [c.1900]) £75
AS WITH GLADNESS (pamphlet) (Nister, [c.1900]) £50
MY LITTLE CIRCUS BOOK by Lavine Helmer (Nister, [c.1900]) £40
THE GAMES BOOK FOR BOYS AND GIRLS (Nister, [c.1900]) £80
KING ROBERT'S PAGE (Nister, 1900) £50
LET'S PRETEND (Nister, [c.1900]) £200
MERRY CHILDREN'S NURSERY RHYMES (Nister, [c.1900]) £80
LAMBS' TALES FROM SHAKESPEARE (Nister, [c.1900]) £60
NURSERY TALES (illustrated by E. Stuart Hardy) (Nister, [c.1900]) £40
MY DOLLY'S TOY BOOK (untearable book) (Nister, [c.1900]) £150
COSY CORNER STORIES (Nister, [c.1900]) £60
GRANDMA'S MEMORIES by Mary D. Brine (illustrated by Ambrose Dudley) (Nister/Dutton, U.S., [c.1900]) £50
WARRIORS BRAVE: A Story of Little Lead Soldiers (illustrated by M.M. Jamieson)
   (Nister: 'Little Mother' series, [c.1900]) £175
A BOOK OF GNOMES by E. Weatherly (Nister, [c.1900]) £300
THE DANDY LION by Louis Wain and Clifton Bingham (Nister, [c.1900]) £300
FUN ALL THE WAY (Nister, 1900) £100
FUN AND FROLIC by Louis Wain and Clifton Bingham (Nister, [1902]) £650
FUN FOR EVERYONE (Nister, 1902) £100
THE REVOLT OF THE TOYS AND WHAT BECAME OF QUARRELLING: Two Stories by E. Nesbit (Nister, 1902) £150
THE DOINGS OF A DEAR LITTLE COUPLE BY MARY BRINE (Nister, [c.1902]) £50
MARCUS THE YOUNG CENTURION by George Manville Fenn (Nister, 1904) £60
SHAKESPEARE'S HEROINES by Anna Jameson (Nister, [c.1904]) £50
THE STORY OF THE FIVE REBELLIOUS DOLLS (Nister, 1904) £200
FUNNY FAVOURITES by Clifton Bingham (Nister, 1904) £300
PAUL CRESWICK IN ALFRED'S DAY (Nister, [c.1905]) £30
DICK OF TEMPLE BAR by M.C. Roswell (illustrated by I. Thackeray) (Nister/Dutton, U.S., [c.1905]) £35
OH! SUCH FUN (Nister, [c.1905]) £60
STORIES AND RHYMES FOR HOLIDAY TIMES (Nister, [c.1907]) £60
FAIRY TALES (illustrated by Arthur A. Dixon) (Nister, 1908) £60
FULL OF FUN by Clifton Bingham (Nister, [c.1908]) £300
HIDE AND SEEK STORIES (Nister, [c.1909]) £75
PLAYTIME STORIES (Nister, [c.1909]) £50
THE POET AND OTHER ANIMALS (illustrated by H.G.H. Thompson) (Nister, [1909]) £175
FAVOURITE FAIRY TALES (Nister, [c.1910]) £60
HAPPY HEARTS AND MERRY EYES (Nister, [c.1910]) £60
MOTHER GOOSE JINGLES (Nister, [c.1910]) £80
MY SEASIDE STORY BOOK by E. Nesbit and George Manville Fenn (Nister, 1911) £60
OUR NEW STORY BOOK by E. Nesbit and others (Nister/Dutton, U.S., 1913) £75
ROSY CHEEKS FUNNY BOOK (Nister, [c.1917]) £100
WILD ANIMAL TALES (Nister, [c.1917]) £50

NORTON, Mary

British author. Born: Mary Pearson in London in 1903. Educated at St. Margaret's Convent, East Grinstead, and Lilian Baylis's Old Vic Theatre School, subsequently working as an actress. Her first children's work, *The Magic Bed-Knob* (1945), was the inspiration for the Disney film, *Bedknobs and Broomsticks* (1971), but she is best known for her 'Borrowers' books, featuring the diminutive Clock family. She moved to Ireland in 1972. Died: 1992.

Prices are for books in Very Good condition with dustjackets.

'Bedknobs' Books

THE MAGIC BED-KNOB (illustrated by Joan Kiddell-Monroe) (Dent, 1945) £80
BONFIRES AND BROOMSTICKS (illustrated by Mary Adshead) (Dent, 1947) £60
BEDKNOB AND BROOMSTICK (adapted from 'The Magic Bed-Knob' and 'Bonfires and Broomsticks';
   illustrated by Erik Blegvad) (Dent, 1957) £25

'Borrowers' Books

THE BORROWERS (illustrated by Diana Stanley) (Dent, 1952) £100
THE BORROWERS (illustrated by Michael Hague) (Harcourt Brace, U.S., 1991) £30
THE BORROWERS AFIELD (illustrated by Diana Stanley) (Dent, 1955) £80
THE BORROWERS AFLOAT (illustrated by Diana Stanley) (Dent, 1959) £75
THE BORROWERS ALOFT (illustrated by Diana Stanley) (Dent, 1961) £40
THE BORROWERS OMNIBUS (contains 'The Borrowers', 'The Borrowers Afield', 'The Borrowers Afloat' and
   'The Borrowers Aloft'; illustrated by Diana Stanley) (Dent, 1966) £30
POOR STAINLESS (Dent, 1971) £15
THE BORROWERS AVENGED (illustrated by Pauline Baynes) (Kestrel, 1982) £15

Others

ARE ALL THE GIANTS DEAD? (illustrated by Brian Froud) (Dent, 1975) £25

'OOR WULLIE' ANNUALS

Spin-offs from Dudley Watkins' popular strip, 'The Broons', published biennially by D.C. Thomson. The annuals were undated before 1967, and there were no editions for 1945 and 1947 due to paper shortages.

Prices are for annuals in Very Good condition (with cover description for undated annuals).

OOR WULLIE 1941 (Oor Wullie sitting on bucket)..£2,000
OOR WULLIE 1943 (Oor Wullie standing next to a bucket with frog) £1,000
OOR WULLIE 1949 (sixteen caption portraits of Oor Wullie)..£700
OOR WULLIE 1951 (large head-and-shoulders portrait of Oor Wullie) £500
OOR WULLIE 1953 (Oor Wullie's year month-by-month)..£300
OOR WULLIE 1955 (Oor Wullie reading a copy of 'Oor Wullie')..£175
OOR WULLIE 1957 (Oor Wullie snowman sitting on a bucket, with a cabin in the background) £125
OOR WULLIE 1959 (Oor Wullie looking over fence with his body painted on the front) £80
OOR WULLIE 1961 (Oor Wullie sitting at table holding a knife and fork) £60
OOR WULLIE 1963 (Oor Wullie walking beside a brick wall, his shadow in the shape of a policeman) £45
OOR WULLIE 1965 (Oor Wullie polishing a bucket) £40
OOR WULLIE 1967 ....£20
OOR WULLIE 1969 ....£20
OOR WULLIE 1971 ....£15
OOR WULLIE 1973 ....£15
OOR WULLIE 1974 ....£10
OOR WULLIE 1975-79 ....each £6
OOR WULLIE 1981-Present ....each £5

OPIE, Iona and Peter

British folklorists. Born: Peter Mason Opie and Iona Margaret Balfour Archibald in 1918 and 1923 respectively. Educated at Eton, Peter published an autobiography, *I Want to Be a Success*, at the age of only 21. Following wartime service with the Royal Sussex Regiment, he joined the BBC and wrote two more volumes of reminiscences. He married Iona in 1943 and, following the birth of their first child in 1944, the two of them set about studying the folklore of childhood, subsequently co-compiling several volumes of nursery rhymes and children's verses. Both of them were awarded honorary Masterships of Arts from Oxford University in 1962. Peter died in 1982.

Prices are for books in Very Good condition with dustjackets.

I SAW ESAU: Traditional Rhymes of Youth (Williams & Norgate, 1947) £80
I SAW ESAU: Traditional Rhymes of Youth (illustrated by Maurice Sendak) (Walker, 1992)................£25
THE OXFORD DICTIONARY OF NURSERY RHYMES (Clarendon Press, 1951)...............................£70
THE OXFORD NURSERY RHYME BOOK (illustrated by Joan Hassall) (Clarendon Press, 1955) £60
CHRISTMAS PARTY GAMES (OUP, U.S., 1957)...£60
THE LORE AND LANGUAGE OF SCHOOLCHILDREN (Clarendon Press, 1959)............................£60
THE PUFFIN BOOK OF NURSERY RHYMES (illustrated by Pauline Baynes; paperback)
  (Puffin, 1963) £10
A FAMILY BOOK OF NURSERY RHYMES (Clarendon Press, 1964) £40
CHILDREN'S GAMES IN STREET AND PLAYGROUND (Clarendon Press, 1969) £40
THE OXFORD BOOK OF CHILDREN'S VERSE (Clarendon Press, 1973)..£25
THREE CENTURIES OF NURSERY RHYMES AND POETRY FOR CHILDREN (exhibition catalogue)
  (National Book League, [1973]) £40
THREE CENTURIES OF NURSERY RHYMES AND POETRY FOR CHILDREN
  (exhibition catalogue; enlarged edition) (National Book League, 1977) £40
THE CLASSIC FAIRY TALES (1974) £30
A NURSERY COMPANION (Clarendon Press, 1980) £30
THE SINGING GAME (Pavilion, 1985) £30
THE TREASURES OF CHILDHOOD (with Brian Alderson) (Pavilion, 1988).....................................£30
TAIL FEATHERS FROM MOTHER GOOSE: The Opie Rhyme Book (Pavilion, 1988) £25

OUTCAULT, Richard Felton

American illustrator, best known for the 'Buster Brown' books. Born: 1863. Died: 1928.

Prices are for books in Very Good condition.

BUSTER BROWN BUSY BODY (Chambers, 1903)..£100
BUSTER BROWN (Chambers, [1904]) £90
BUSTER BROWN (Stokes, U.S., 1904) £80
BUSTER BROWN ABROAD (illustrated by the author) (Chambers, [1905]) £75
TIGE — HIS STORY (illustrated by the author) (Stokes, U.S., [1905]) £135

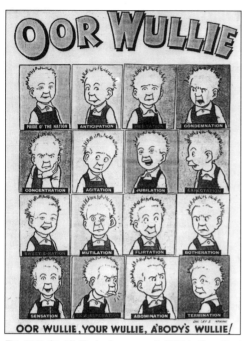

*The 1949 **Oor Wullie** book, now worth £800 in Very Good condition. This was previously mistaken for the 1951 edition.*

A Nursery Companion (1980) is one of several volumes about children's literature compiled by folklorists, Iona and Peter Opie.

MY RESOLUTIONS: BUSTER BROWN (Stokes, U.S., 1906) £75
BUSTER BROWN (Dean, [1906]) £60
BUSTER BROWN'S MAXIMS FOR MEN (Chambers, [1907])...£45
BUSTER BROWN NUGGETS (Dean, [1908]) £40
BUSTER BROWN'S AUTOBIOGRAPHY (Chambers, [1909]) £40
BUSTER AND TIGE HERE AGAIN (Stokes, U.S., 1914) £40

OUTHWAITE, Ida Rentoul

Australian author-illustrator. Born: Ida Rentoul in 1888. Illustrated a number of picture books in the first four decades of this century, including several written by her sister, Annie R. Rentoul. Died: 1960.

Prices are for books in Very Good condition.

ELVES AND FAIRIES (Lothian, Melbourne/Sydney, 1916)..£400
ELVES AND FAIRIES (limited to 1500 copies, signed by the artist)
   (Lothian, Melbourne/Sydney, 1916) £2,000
THE ENCHANTED FOREST (with Grenbry Outhwaite; sixteen colour plates and fifteen black-and-white plates
   by Ida Rentoul Outhwaite) (A. & C. Black, 1921) £600
THE ENCHANTED FOREST (with Grenbry Outhwaite; sixteen colour plates and fifteen black-and-white plates
   by Ida Rentoul Outhwaite; limited to 500 copies, signed by the artist) (A. & C. Black, 1921) £2,000
THE LITTLE GREEN ROAD TO FAIRYLAND (with Annie R. Rentoul; eight colour plates and eight black-and-white plates
   by Ida Rentoul Outhwaite; limited to 300 copies, signed by the artist) (A. & C. Black, 1922) £2,000
THE LITTLE GREEN ROAD TO FAIRYLAND (A. & C. Black, 1922) £600
THE LITTLE GREEN ROAD TO FAIRYLAND (second edition) (A. & C. Black, 1925)......................£200
THE LITTLE FAIRY SISTER (A. & C. Black, 1923)..£400
THE LITTLE FAIRY SISTER (second edition) (A. & C. Black, 1929) £300
FAIRYLAND OF IDA RENTOUL OUTHWAITE by Annie R. Rentoul, Grenbry Outhwaite and Ida Rentoul Outhwaite
   (verse and stories; limited to 1,000 copies, signed by the artist) (Ramsay, Melbourne, 1926) £2,000
FAIRYLAND OF IDA RENTOUL OUTHWAITE (Stokes, U.S., 1929) £1,000
FAIRYLAND OF IDA RENTOUL OUTHWAITE (A. & C. Black, 1931) £600
BLOSSOM: A Fairy Story (A. & C. Black, 1928) £300
BUNNY AND BROWNIE: The Adventures of George and Wiggle by Ida Rentoul Outhwaite
   (A. & C. Black, 1930) £425
A BUNCH OF WILD FLOWERS by Ida Rentoul Outhwaite (Angus & Robertson, Sydney, 1933).....£200
THE OTHER SIDE OF NOWHERE by Tarella Quin (Lothian, Melbourne/Sydney, 1934)................£300
CHIMNEY TOWN by Tarell Quin Daskein (stories) (A. & C. Black, 1934) £150
SIXPENCE TO SPEND (Australia, 1935) £300

Girls of the Hamlet Club (1914), the first of Elsie J. Oxenham's famous 'Abbey' books, is worth £600 in Very Good condition.

The 'Abbey' series eventually ran to some 44 individual titles. Jandy Mac Comes Back was published by Collins in 1941.

OXENBURY, Helen

British author-illustrator. Born: Suffolk, 1938. Married John Burningham in 1964. Awarded Kate Greenaway Medal in 1969. A very successful series of board books for Walker in the 1980s established her as a household name. These were followed later by fourteen 'Tom and Pippo' books.

Prices are for books in Very Good condition with dustjackets where applicable.

Books Written and Illustrated by Helen Oxenbury

HELEN OXENBURY'S ABC OF THINGS (Heinemann, 1971) £15
PIG TALE (Heinemann, 1973) £15
THE QUEEN AND ROSIE RANDALL (Heinemann, 1978)..£15
729 ANIMAL ALLSORTS (Methuen, 1980) £10
BILL AND STANLEY (Benn, 1981)..£10
BEDTIME (Walker, 1982) £10
MOTHER'S HELPER (Walker, 1982)...£10
SHOPPING TRIP (Walker, 1982)...£10
GOOD NIGHT, GOOD MORNING (Walker, 1982) £10
BEACH DAY (Walker, 1982)...£10
NUMBERS OF THINGS (London, Delacorte, 1983) £15
THE BIRTHDAY PARTY (Walker, 1983) £10
THE DRIVE (Walker, 1983) £10
THE FIRST CHECK-UP (Walker,1983)...£10
THE DANCING CLASS (Walker, 1983)...£10
EATING OUT (Walker, 1983)..£10
PLAYSCHOOL (Walker, 1983) £10
GRAN AND GRANPA (Walker, 1984)..£10
THE VISITOR (Walker, 1984)..£10
OUR DOG (Walker, 1984) £10
THE HELEN OXENBURY NURSERY STORY BOOK (Walker, 1985) £15
I CAN (Walker, 1986)..£10
I HEAR (Walker, 1986) £10
I SEE (Walker, 1986) £10
I TOUCH (Walker, 1986) £10

BABY'S FIRST BOOK AND DOLL (Walker, 1986) £10
ALL FALL DOWN (Walker, 1987) £10
SAY GOODNIGHT (Walker, 1987) £10
TICKLE TICKLE (Walker, 1987) £10
CLAP HANDS (Walker, 1987)..£10
MONKEY SEE, MONKEY DO (Walker, 1991) £10
THE HELEN OXENBURY NURSERY TREASURY (Heinemann, 1992)..£15
THE THREE LITTLE WOLVES AND THE BIG, BAD PIG (Heinemann, 1993) £10

'Tom and Pippo' Books

TOM AND PIPPO GO FOR A WALK (Walker, 1988) £15
TOM AND PIPPO MAKE A MESS (Walker, 1988) £15
TOM AND PIPPO READ A STORY (Walker, 1988) £15
TOM AND PIPPO AND THE WASHING MACHINE (Walker, 1988) £15
TOM AND PIPPO'S DAY (Walker, 1988) £15
TOM AND PIPPO GO SHOPPING (Walker, 1989) £15
TOM AND PIPPO SEE THE MOON (Walker, 1989) £15
TOM AND PIPPO IN THE GARDEN (Walker, 1989)..£15
TOM AND PIPPO IN THE SNOW (Walker, 1989) £15
TOM AND PIPPO MAKE A FRIEND (Walker, 1989) £15
PIPPO GETS LOST (Walker, 1989) £15

Others

GREAT BIG ENORMOUS TURNIP by Alexei Tolstoy (Watts, 1968)..£10
THE HUNTING OF THE SNARK by Lewis Carroll (Heinemann, 1970) £15
CAKES AND CUSTARD by Brian Alderson (Heinemann, 1974) £30
A CHILD'S BOOK OF MANNERS by Fay Maschler (Cape, 1978) £15
ALL FALL DOWN (Walker, 1987) £10
FARMER DUCK (Walker, 1991) £10
SO MUCH by Trish Cooke (Walker, 1994)..£10
IT'S MY BIRTHDAY (Walker, 1994) £5
ALICE'S ADVENTURES IN WONDERLAND by Lewis Carroll (Walker,1999) £20

OXENHAM, Elsie J.

British author. Born: Elsie Jeanette Dunkerley in Southport in 1880. She took her pseudonym from that of her father, the novelist John Oxenham ('J.O.'). Under this name, she wrote many school novels, the best-known set in the imaginary Abbey School, Wycombe, based on Cleeve Abbey in Somerset. She was an enthusiastic supporter of the English Folk Dance Society and the American Camp Fire Movement. Died: 1960.

Prices are for books in Very Good condition (with dustjackets after 1937 — after 1931 for 'Abbey' books).

'Abbey' Books

GIRLS OF THE HAMLET CLUB (illustrated by H.C. Earnshaw) (Chambers, 1914) £600
THE ABBEY GIRLS (illustrated by Arthur A. Dixon) (Collins, [1920]) £250
THE GIRLS OF THE ABBEY SCHOOL (illustrated by Elsie Anna Wood) (Collins, [1921])................£150
THE ABBEY GIRLS GO BACK TO SCHOOL (illustrated by Elsie Anna Wood) (Collins, [1922]) £150
THE NEW ABBEY GIRLS (illustrated by Elsie Anna Wood) (Collins, [1923]) £150
THE ABBEY GIRLS AGAIN (illustrated by Elsie Anna Wood) (Collins, [1924])..................................£150
THE ABBEY GIRLS IN TOWN (illustrated by Rosa C. Petherick) (Collins, [1925]) £150
QUEEN OF THE ABBEY GIRLS (illustrated by E.J. Kealey) (Collins, [1926]) £150
JEN OF THE ABBEY SCHOOL (Collins, [1927]) £150
THE ABBEY GIRLS WIN THROUGH (Collins, [1928]) £150
THE ABBEY SCHOOL (omnibus; illustrated by Elsie Anna Wood) (Collins, [1928]) £150
THE ABBEY GIRLS AT HOME (illustrated by Inder Burns) (Collins, [1929])......................................£60
THE GIRLS OF ROCKLANDS SCHOOL (adapted from 'Jen of the Abbey School') (Collins, 1929) £35
THE SECOND TERM AT ROCKLANDS (adapted from 'Jen of the Abbey School') (Collins, [1930]) £35
THE ABBEY GIRLS PLAY UP (Collins, [1930]) £125
THE THIRD TERM AT ROCKLANDS (adapted from 'Jen of the Abbey School') (Collins, [1931])........£30
THE ABBEY GIRLS ON TRIAL (Collins, [1931]) £125
THE GIRLS OF SQUIRREL HOUSE (adapted from 'Rosamund's Victory') (Collins, [1932])...............£30
BIDDY'S SECRET: A Romance of the Abbey Girls (Chambers, 1932)..£750
THE E.J. OXENHAM OMNIBUS (contains 'The Abbey Girls Win Through', 'The Abbey Girls at Home' and
   'The Abbey Girls Play Up'; issued without dustjacket) (Collins, [1932]) £75
ROSAMUND'S VICTORY: A Romance of the Abbey Girls (Harrap, 1933) £250
MAIDLIN TO THE RESCUE: A Story of the Abbey Girls (illustrated by Rene Cloke) (Chambers, 1934) £750
THE CALL OF THE ABBEY SCHOOL (adapted from 'Queen of the Abbey Girls') (Collins, [1934])....£20
JOY'S NEW ADVENTURE: A Romance of the Abbey Girls (illustrated by Rene Cloke) (Chambers, 1935) £750
MAIDLIN BEARS THE TORCH: An Abbey Story (Religious Tract Societ/Girl's Own Paper, [1937]) £750
ROSAMUND'S TUCK-SHOP: A School Story (Religious Tract Society/Girl's Own Paper, [1937]) £225

ROSAMUND'S CASTLE (Religious Tract Society/Girl's Own Paper, [1938]) £750
SCHOOLDAYS AT THE ABBEY (Collins, 1938)..£60
SECRETS OF THE ABBEY (illustrated by Heade) (Collins, 1939)..£60
STOWAWAYS IN THE ABBEY (illustrated by Heade) (Collins, 1940) £60
JANDY MAC COMES BACK (illustrated by Heade) (Collins, 1941)...£50
MAID OF THE ABBEY (illustrated by Heade) (Collins, 1943) £30
TWO JOANS AT THE ABBEY (illustrated by Margaret Horder) (Collins, 1945)............................£45
AN ABBEY CHAMPION (illustrated by Margaret Horder) (Muller, 1946) £130
ROBINS IN THE ABBEY (illustrated by Margaret Horder) (Collins, 1947) £30
A FIDDLER FOR THE ABBEY (illustrated by Margaret Horder) (Muller, 1948) £130
GUARDIANS OF THE ABBEY (illustrated by Margaret Horder) (Muller, 1950) £130
SCHOOLGIRL JEN AT THE ABBEY (Collins, [1950]) £30
STRANGERS AT THE ABBEY (Collins, 1951)...£30
RACHEL IN THE ABBEY (illustrated by M.D. Neilson) (Muller, 1951) £130
SELMA AT THE ABBEY (Collins, 1952)...£25
A DANCER FROM THE ABBEY (Collins, 1953)...£25
THE SONG OF THE ABBEY (Collins, 1954) £25
TOMBOYS AT THE ABBEY (illustrated by Frank Varty) (Collins, 1957)......................................£25
TWO QUEENS AT THE ABBEY (Collins, 1959) £30

Others

GOBLIN ISLAND (illustrated by Thomas Heath Robinson) (Collins, [1907]) £120
A PRINCESS IN TATTERS (illustrated by Frank Adams) (Collins, [1908]) £100
THE CONQUEST OF CHRISTINA (illustrated by G.B. Foyster) (Collins, [1909])........................£120
THE GIRL WHO WOULDN'T MAKE FRIENDS (illustrated by P.B. Hickling) (Nelson, [1909])........£65
MISTRESS NANCIEBEL (illustrated by James Durden) (Hodder & Stoughton, 1910 [1909])........£90
A HOLIDAY QUEEN (illustrated by E.A. Overnell) (Collins, [1910]) £100
ROSALY'S NEW SCHOOL (illustrated by T.J. Overnell) (Chambers, 1913).................................£90
SCHOOLGIRLS AND SCOUTS (illustrated by Arthur H. Dixon) (Collins, [1914]) £80
AT SCHOOL WITH THE ROUNDHEADS (illustrated by H.C. Earnshaw) (Chambers, 1915) £120
FINDING HER FAMILY (illustrated by W.S. Stacey) (SPCK, [1916])...£130
THE TUCK-SHOP GIRL: A School Story of Girl Guides (illustrated by H.C. Earnshaw) (Chambers, 1916) £160
A SCHOOL CAMP FIRE (illustrated by Percy Tarrant) (Chambers, 1917) £150
THE SCHOOL OF UPS AND DOWNS: The Story of a Summer Camp (illustrated by H.C. Earnshaw) (Chambers, 1918) £200
EXPELLED FROM SCHOOL (illustrated by Victor Prout) (Collins, [1919]) £50
A GO-AHEAD SCHOOLGIRL (illustrated by H.C. Earnshaw) (Chambers, 1919) £150
THE SCHOOL TORMENT (illustrated by H.C. Earnshaw) (Chambers, 1920) £150
THE TWINS OF CASTLE CHARMING (Swarthmore Press, [1920]) £275
THE TWO FORM CAPTAINS (illustrated by Percy Tarrant) (Chambers, 1921) £160
THE CAPTAIN OF THE FIFTH (illustrated by Percy Tarrant) (Chambers, 1922) £130
PATIENCE JOAN, OUTSIDER (Cassell, [1922])...£110
THE JUNIOR CAPTAIN (illustrated by Percy Tarrant) (Chambers, [1923]) £130
THE SCHOOL WITHOUT A NAME (illustrated by Nina K. Brisley) (Chambers, [1924]) £275
THE GIRLS OF GWYNFA (Warne, 1924)...£75
'TICKLES', or The School that was Different (Partridge, [1924]) £50
THE TESTING OF THE TORMENT (illustrated by P.B. Hickling) (Cassell, 1925) £95
VEN AT GREGORY'S (illustrated by Nina K. Brisley) (Chambers, [1925]).................................£200
THE CAMP FIRE TORMENT (illustrated by Enid W. Browne) (Chambers, 1926) £135
THE TROUBLES OF TAZY (illustrated by Percy Tarrant) (Chambers, [1926]) £175
PATIENCE AND HER PROBLEMS (illustrated by Molly Benatar) (Chambers, [1927]) £130
PEGGY MAKES GOOD (Partridge, [1927]) £50
THE CRISIS IN CAMP KEEMA (illustrated by Percy Tarrant) (Chambers, [1928]) £175
DEB AT SCHOOL (illustrated by Nina K. Brisley) (Chambers, 1929)..£175
DOROTHY'S DILEMMA (illustrated by Nina K. Brisley) (Chambers, 1930) £175
DEB OF SEA HOUSE (Chambers, 1931)...£175
THE CAMP MYSTERY (Collins, [1932]) £60
THE REFORMATION OF JINTY (Chambers, 1933)..£175
JINTY'S PATROL (Newnes, [1934]) £80
PEGGY AND THE BROTHERHOOD (Religious Tract Society/Girl's Own Paper, [1936]) £135
DAMARIS AT DOROTHY'S (Sheldon Press, [1937]) £130
SYLVIA OF SARN (Warne, 1937) £60
DAMARIS DANCES (illustrated by Margaret Horder) (OUP, 1940) £40
PATCH AND A PAWN (Warne, 1940) £55
ADVENTURE FOR TWO (illustrated by Margaret Horder) (OUP, 1941) £45
PERNEL WINS (illustrated by Margaret Horder) (Muller, 1942) £100
ELSA PUTS THINGS RIGHT (Muller, 1944) £100
DARING DORANNE (Muller, 1945)..£100
THE SECRETS OF VAIRY (illustrated by Margaret Horder) (Muller, 1947) £100
MARGERY MEETS THE ROSES (Lutterworth Press, 1947) £110
NEW GIRLS AT WOOD END (Blackie, 1957)..£130

P

PARDOE, Margot

British author. Born: Margot Mary Pardoe in London in 1902. Studied at Abbotts Hill School, Hertfordshire, and trained to be an opera singer. Made her debut as a children's writer with *The Far Island* (1936), but is best known for the 'Bunkle' series, which began with *Four Plus Bunkle* (1939). She has also written romance-thrillers and 'time-travel' historical novels for young readers. Died: 1996.

Prices are for books in Very Good condition in dustjackets.

THE FAR ISLAND: A Story for Girls and Boys (illustrated by R.M. Turvey) (Routledge, 1936) £60
FOUR PLUS BUNKLE (illustrated by J.D. Evans) (Routledge, 1939)...£60
BUNKLE BEGAN IT (illustrated by Julie Neild) (Routledge, 1942) £35
BUNKLE BUTTS IN (illustrated by Julie Neild) (Routledge, 1943)..£35
BUNKLE BOUGHT IT (illustrated by Julie Neild) (Routledge, 1945) £30
BUNKLE BREAKS AWAY (illustrated by Julie Neild) (Routledge, 1947)..£30
BUNKLE AND BELINDA (illustrated by Julie Neild) (Routledge, 1947)...£25
BUNKLE BAFFLES THEM (illustrated by Julie Neild) (Routledge, 1949) £25
BUNKLE WENT FOR SIX (illustrated by Julie Neild) (Routledge, 1950) £25
BUNKLE GETS BUSY (illustrated by Julie Neild) (Routledge, 1951)..£30
THE GHOST BOAT (with Howard Biggs; illustrated by Webster Murray) (Hodder & Stoughton, 1951)..........................£35
BUNKLE'S BRAINWAVE (illustrated by Mary Smith) (Routledge, 1952)...£30
BUNKLE SCENTS A CLUE (illustrated by Pamela Kemp) (Routledge, 1953)..£30
THE BOAT SEEKERS (illustrated by B. Kay) (Hodder & Stoughton, 1953) £30
CHARLES ARRIVING (illustrated by Leslie Atkinson) (Routledge, 1954) £30
THE DUTCH BOAT (illustrated by Leslie Atkinson) (Hodder & Stoughton, 1955) £30
MAY MADRIGAL (illustrated by Leslie Atkinson) (Routledge, 1955) £25
ARGLE'S MIST (illustrated by Leslie Atkinson) (Routledge, 1956) £25
THE NAMELESS BOAT (illustrated by Leslie Atkinson) (Hodder & Stoughton, 1957)...£30
ARGLE'S CAUSEWAY (illustrated by Leslie Atkinson) (Routledge, 1958) £25
ARGLE'S ORACLE (illustrated by Audrey Fawley) (Routledge, 1959)..£25
THE GREEK BOAT MYSTERY (Hodder & Stoughton, [1960]) £25
BUNKLE BRINGS IT OFF (illustrated by Audrey Fawley) (Routledge, 1961) £35

The second and third books in Margot Pardoe's popular 'Bunkle' series. They are now worth £60 and £35 in Very Good condition.

PEAKE, Mervyn

British author-illustrator. Born: Mervyn Laurence Peake in China in 1911. Studied painting at the Royal Academy Schools in London. Wrote a number of children's books, of which the best known are the three 'Gormenghast' novels, and also illustrated several children's classics, including *Treasure Island* (1949) and the two 'Alice' books (1954). Never recovered from a breakdown brought on by his war service. Died: 1968.

Prices are for books in Very Good condition with dustjackets.

Books Written and Illustrated by Mervyn Peake

CAPTAIN SLAUGHTERBOARD DROPS ANCHOR (Country Life, 1939) £2,000
CAPTAIN SLAUGHTERBOARD DROPS ANCHOR (Eyre & Spottiswoode, 1945) £80
TITUS GROAN (Eyre & Spottiswode, 1946) £200
LETTERS FROM A LOST UNCLE from Polar Regions (Eyre & Spottiswoode, 1948) £100
GORMENGHAST (Eyre & Spottiswoode, 1950) £150
TITUS ALONE (Eyre & Spotiswoode, 1959) £80
A BOOK OF NONSENSE (Peter Owen, 1972)...£30

Books Illustrated by Mervyn Peake

RIDE A COCK-HORSE and Other Nursery Rhymes (Chatto & Windus, 1940)................................£200
THE HUNTING OF THE SNARK by Lewis Carroll (Chatto & Windus, 1941) £60
THE HUNTING OF THE SNARK by Lewis Carroll (Chatto & Windus: 'Zodiac Books' series, 1941) £30
RIME OF THE ANCIENT MARINER by Samuel Coleridge (Chatto & Windus, 1943) £30
HOUSEHOLD TALES by the Brothers Grimm (Eyre & Spottiswoode, 1946) £60
ALICE'S ADVENTURES IN WONDERLAND and THROUGH THE LOOKING GLASS by Lewis Carroll
    (Zephyr Books, Sweden, 1946) £150
ALICE'S ADVENTURES IN WONDERLAND and THROUGH THE LOOKING GLASS (Wingate, 1954)............£60
TREASURE ISLAND by Robert Louis Stevenson (Eyre & Spottiswoode, 1949) £30
THE SWISS FAMILY ROBINSON by J. Wyss (Heirloom Library, [1950])..£15
THE BOOK OF LYONNE by Burgess Drake (The Falcon Press, 1952)..£30
THE YOUNG BLACKBIRD by E. Clepham Palmer (Wingate, 1954) £30
THE WONDERFUL LIFE & ADVENTURES OF TOM THUMB by Paul Britten Austin
    (two volumes; card covers; issued without dustjackets) (Radiotjänst, Sweden, 1954 & 1955) ....the set £60
A POT OF GOLD and Two Other Tales by Aaron Judah (Faber, 1959) £30
SKETCHES FROM BLEAK HOUSE (Methuen, 1983)...£15

PEARCE, Philippa

British author. Born: Ann Philippa Pearce in Great Shelford, Cambridgeshire, in 1920. Studied at Girton College, Cambridge, subsequently working as a civil servant, a BBC radio producer and a children's book editor. Won the Carnegie Medal for her second book, *Tom's Midnight Garden* (1958), subsequently producing a steady stream of novels, story collections and picture books.

Prices are for books in Very Good condition with dustjackets.

MINNOW ON THE SAY (illustrated by Edward Ardizzone) (OUP, 1955).......................................£50
TOM'S MIDNIGHT GARDEN (illustrated by Susan Einzig) (OUP, 1958) £60
STILL JIM AND SILENT JIM (Blackwell, 1959 [1960])...£25
MRS COCKLE'S CAT (illustrated by Antony Maitland) (Constable, 1961)....................................£25
A DOG SO SMALL (illustrated by Antony Maitland) (Constable, 1962) £25
THE STRANGE SUNFLOWER (illustrated by Kathleen Williams; issued without dustjacket) (Nelson, 1966) £10
THE CHILDREN OF THE HOUSE. Written with Brian Fairfax-Lucy (illustrated by John Sergeant) (Longman, 1968) £20
THE ELM STREET LOT (illustrated by Maina Martinez; paperback) (BBC, 1969)..............................£6
THE SQUIRREL WIFE (illustrated by Derek Collard) (Longman, 1971) £12
WHAT THE NEIGHBOURS DID and Other Stories (illustrated by Faith Jaques) (Longman, 1972)............£12
THE SHADOW-CAGE and Other Tales of the Supernatural (illustrated by Janet Archer) (Kestrel, 1977) £12
THE BATTLE OF BUBBLE AND SQUEAK (illustrated by Alan Barker) (Deutsch, 1978) £12
WINGS OF COURAGE (illustrated by Hilary Abrahams) (Kestrel, 1982) £12
THE WAY TO SATTIN SHORE (illustrated by Charlotte Voake) (Kestrel, 1983) £12
LION AT SCHOOL and Other Stories (illustrated by Caroline Sharpe) (Viking, 1985).......................£12
WHO'S AFRAID? and Other Strange Stories (illustrated by Peter Melnyczuk) (Viking Kestrel, 1986) £12
EMILY'S OWN ELEPHANT (illustrated by John Lawrence) (MacRae, 1987)..................................£12
THE TOOTHBALL (illustrated by Helen Ganly) (Deutsch, 1987) £10

PEARSE, S.B.

British illustrator. Born: Susan Beatrice Pearse in Fair Oak, Hampshire, in 1878. Studied at the Royal College of Art. Best-known for her 'Ameliaranne' books, but also contributed illustrations to *Little Folks* and *Playbox Annual*. Designed the 'two-children' poster for Start-Rite shoes. Died: 1980.

Prices are for books in Very Good condition with dustjackets where applicable.

THE PENDLETON TWINS by E.M. Jameson (Hodder & Stoughton, 1908) £75
THE MAGIC FISHBONE by Charles Dickens (Saint Catherine Press/Nisbet, [1912]) £30
AMELIARANNE AND THE GREEN UMBRELLA by Constance Heward (Harrap, 1920) £150

THE TWINS AND TABIFFA by Constance Heward (Harrap, 1923) £100
AMELIARANNE CINEMA STAR (Harrap, 1924) £100
AMELIARANNE IN TOWN by Natalie Joan (Harrap, 1930) £90
THE PARTY BOOK by Madeline Barnes (Blackie, [c.1930]) £60
AMELIARANNE AT THE CIRCUS by Margaret Gilmour (Harrap, 1931) £90
AMELIARANNE AND THE BIG TREASURE by Natalie Joan (Harrap, 1932) £75
AMELIARANNE'S PRIZE PACKET by Eleanor Farjeon (Harrap, 1933) £75
AMELIARANNE'S WASHING DAY by Eleanor Farjeon (Harrap, 1934) £70
AMELIARANNE AT THE SEASIDE by Margaret Gilmour (Harrap, 1935) £65
MOTHER GOOSE RHYMES (illustrated by S.B. Pearse and Winifred M. Ackroyd) (Coker, [1935]) £50
AMELIARANNE AT THE ZOO by K.L. Thompson (Harrap, 1936) £65
AMELIARANNE AT THE FARM by Constance Heward (Harrap, 1937)...£65
AMELIARANNE GIVES A CHRISTMAS PARTY by Constance Heward (Harrap, 1938) £65
AMELIARANNE KEEPS SCHOOL by Constance Heward (Harrap, 1940) £60
AMELIARANNE GOES TOURING by Constance Heward (Harrap, 1941) £60
AMELIARANNE AND THE JUMBLE SALE by Eileen M. Osborne (Harrap, 1943)..........................£60
AMELIARANNE GIVES A CONCERT by Eleanor Farjeon (Harrap, 1944) £60
AMELIARANNE BRIDESMAID by Ethelberta Morris (Harrap, 1946)..£60
AMELIARANNE GOES DIGGING by Lorna Wood (Harrap, 1948) £60
NURSERY VERSERY by Patience Strong (Muller, 1948) £20
ADVENTURES OF CHRISTABEL, JANE AND CHIRPY by Constance Heward (Harrap, 1955) £15

PERRAULT, Charles

French author-folklorist. Born: Paris, 1628. Studied law, subsequently working in Louis XIV's civil service. His first collection of traditional fairy stories, *Histoires ou contes du temps passé* (1697), contained versions of 'Little Red Riding Hood', 'Bluebeard', 'Cinderella', 'Hop o' my Thumb' and 'Puss in Boots'. Elected to the Académie Française in 1671. Died: 1703.

Prices are for books in Very Good condition.

HISTOIRES, OU CONTES DU TEMPS PASSE, AVEC DES MORALITEZ (Paris, 1697) £8,000
LES CONTES DE PERRAULT (illustrated by Gustav Doré) (Paris, 1862) £250
PERRAULT'S POPULAR TALES. Edited by Andrew Lang (Clarendon Press, 1888) £40
TALES OF PASSED TIMES (illustrated by Charles Robinson) (Dent: 'Temple Classics for Young People' series, [1899]) £50
CONTES DE PERRAULT. Adapted by Kathleen Fitzgerald (illustrated by Margaret Tarrant) (Siegle & Hill, 1910) £65
PERRAULT'S FAIRY TALES (illustrated by Honor C. Appleton; translated by S.R. Littlewood) (Herbert Daniel, [1911]) £65
THE SLEEPING BEAUTY and Other Tales (illustrated by John Hassall) (Blackie, [1912]) £50
FAIRY TALES (illustrated by Charles Robinson) (Dent, [1913]) £50
CINDERELLA. Adapted by E.L. Elias (illustrated by Willy Pogány) (Harrap, [1915]) £40
CINDERELLA. Adapted by Githa Sowerby (illustrated by Millicent Sowerby) (Hodder & Stoughton, [1915]) £70
CINDERELLA. Adapted by Charles S. Evans (illustrated by Arthur Rackham) (Heinemann, 1919) £200
CINDERELLA. Adapted by Charles S. Evans (illustrated by Arthur Rackham; De Luxe edition: limited to 525 copies,
  signed by the artist; on handmade paper) (Heinemann, 1919) £750
CINDERELLA. Adapted by Charles S. Evans (illustrated by Arthur Rackham; De Luxe vellum edition:
  limited to 325 copies, signed by the artist; on Japanese vellum) (Heinemann, 1919) £1,000
THE SLEEPING BEAUTY. Adapted by Charles S. Evans (illustrated by Arthur Rackham) (Heinemann, 1920) £200
THE SLEEPING BEAUTY. Adapted by Charles S. Evans (illustrated by Arthur Rackham; with extra plate;
  limited to 625 copies, signed by the artist) (Heinemann, 1920) £650
OLD TIME STORIES (illustrated by W. Heath Robinson; translated by A.E. Johnson) (Constable, 1921) £300
THE FAIRY TALES OF CHARLES PERRAULT (illustrated by Harry Clarke; cloth or buckram binding) (Harrap, [1922])...........£300
THE FAIRY TALES OF CHARLES PERRAULT (illustrated by Harry Clarke; De Luxe edition: Persian Levant leather binding)
  (Harrap, [1922]) £500
TALES OF PAST TIMES (illustrated by John Austen) (Selwyn & Blount, 1922).................................£100
TALES OF PAST TIMES (illustrated by John Austen; limited to 200 copies, signed by the artist) (Selwyn & Blount, 1922) £175
CINDERELLA and Other Tales from Perrault (illustrated by Michael Hague) (Holt, U.S., 1989)...........£20

PETO, Gladys

British illustrator. Born: Gladys Emma Peto in Maidenhead, Berkshire, in 1890. Studied at the Maidenhead School of Art, subsequently working as a fabric and pottery designer as well as illustrator. Contributed an illustrated diary to the *Sketch* between 1915 annd 1926, subsequently publishing a number of lighthearted travel books. Produced a series of children's annuals in the 1930s. Died: 1977.

Prices are for books in Very Good condition.

GLADYS PETO'S CHILDREN ANNUAL 1923 (Sampson Low, 1923) £75
GLADYS PETO'S CHILDREN ANNUAL 1924 (Sampson Low, 1924) £70
DAPHNE AND THE FAIRY and Other Stories (Sampson Low, 1924) £100
JOAN'S VISIT TO TOYLAND and Other Tales (Sampson Low, 1924) £100
SNOWMAN and Other Tales (Sampson Low, 1924) £90
GLADYS PETO'S CHILDREN'S BOOK (Sampson Low, 1925)...£70
THE CHINA COW and Other Stories by Sewell Stokes and others (Sampson Low, [1929]) £70

GLADYS PETO'S BEDTIME STORIES (Shaw, [1931]) £70
TWILIGHT STORIES (Shaw, [1932])..£65
GLADYS PETO'S GIRLS' OWN STORIES (Shaw, [1933])...£65
SUNSHINE TALES (Shaw, [1935]) £55
THE FOUR-LEAVED CLOVER and Other Stories (Juvenile Productions, [1937]) £50

PEYTON, K.M.

British author. Born: Kathleen Wendy Herald in Birmingham in 1929. Studied at Wimbledon High School and Manchester Art School. Published her first book, *Sabre: The Horse from the Sea* (1948), when she was only nineteen, and has since written many more, notably the 'Flambards' series. She won the Carnegie Medal for the second book in the sequence, *The Edge of the Cloud* (1969). Collaborated with her husband, Michael Peyton, on several early stories, subsequently retaining his initial on her books.

Prices are for books in Very Good condition with dustjackets.

SABRE: The Horse from the Sea (written under the name 'Kathleen Herald'; illustrated by Lionel Edwards)
(A. & C. Black, 1948) £20
THE MANDRAKE: A Pony (written under the name 'Kathleen Herald'; illustrated by Lionel Edwards) (A. & C. Black, 1949) £20
CRAB THE ROAN (written under the name 'Kathleen Herald'; illustrated by Peter Biegel) (A. & C. Black, 1953) £20
NORTH TO ADVENTURE (Collins, 1958)..£15
STORMCOCK MEETS TROUBLE (Collins, 1961) £10
THE HARD WAY HOME (illustrated by R.A. Branton) (Collins, 1962) £10
WINDFALL (illustrated by Victor G. Ambrus) (OUP, 1962) £15
BROWNSEA SILVER (illustrated by Victor G. Ambrus) (Collins, 1964) £10
THE MAPLIN BIRD (illustrated by Victor G. Ambrus) (OUP, 1964) £10
THE PLAN FOR BIRDSMARSH (illustrated by Victor G. Ambrus) (OUP, 1965) £20
THUNDER IN THE SKY (illustrated by Victor G. Ambrus) (OUP, 1966) £10
FLAMBARDS (illustrated by Victor G. Ambrus) (OUP, 1967) £25
FLY-BY-NIGHT (illustrated by the author) (OUP, 1968) £15
THE EDGE OF THE CLOUD (illustrated by Victor G. Ambrus) (OUP, 1969) £20
FLAMBARDS IN THE SUMMER (OUP, 1969) £20
PENNINGTON'S SEVENTEENTH SUMMER (illustrated by the author) (OUP, 1970) £10
THE BEETHOVEN MEDAL (illustrated by the author) (OUP, 1971)..£10
A PATTERN OF ROSES (illustrated by the author) (OUP, 1972) £10
PENNINGTON'S HEIR (illustrated by the author) (OUP, 1973) £10
THE TEAM (illustrated by the author) (OUP, 1975) £20
THE RIGHT-HAND MAN (illustrated by Victor G. Ambrus) (OUP, 1977) £15
PROVE YOURSELF A HERO (OUP, 1977)..£10
A MIDSUMMER NIGHT'S DEATH (OUP, 1978) £10

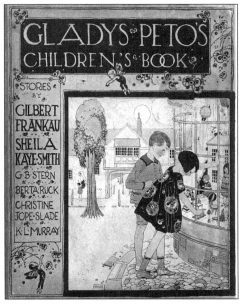

*The works of the British Illustrator, Gladys Peto, are becoming very collectable. Her **Children's Book** (1925) is now worth £70.*

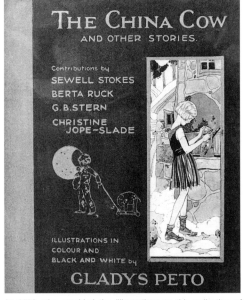

In 1929, she provided the illiustrations to this collection of stories by, amongst others, Sewell Stokes and G.B. Stern.

MARION'S ANGELS (OUP, 1979) £10
MARION'S ANGELS (as 'Falling Angel') (Methuen, 1983)...£10
FLAMBARDS DIVIDED (OUP, 1981) £15
DEAR FRED (illustrated by the author) (The Bodley Head, 1981) £10
GOING HOME (illustrated by the author) (OUP, 1982) £10
WHO, SIR? ME, SIR? (OUP, 1983)...£10
THE LAST DITCH (OUP, 1984)..£10
FROGGETT'S REVENGE (OUP, 1985) £10
PLAIN JACK (illustrated by the author) (OUP, 1988) £10
DOWNHILL ALL THE WAY (OUP, 1988) £10
SKYLARK (OUP, 1989)..£10
DARKLING (paperback) (Corgi, 1989) £3

PIENKOWSKI, Jan

Polish illustrator. Born: Jan Michel Pienkowski in Warsaw in 1936. Studied in London and at King's College, Cambridge. Began his artistic career by designing posters and greetings cards, but later turned to children's book illustration, winning the Kate Greenaway Medal for his drawings for Joan Aiken's *The Kingdom Under the Sea* (1971). Perhaps his finest works are the pop-up books, *Haunted House* (1979) and *Robot* (1981), the first of which has sold over one million copies.

Prices are for books in Very Good condition with dustjackets where applicable.

'Pop-Up' Books

HAUNTED HOUSE (Heinemann, 1979) £50
DINNERTIME (Minipop; with Anne Carter) (Gallery Five, 1981)...£10
ROBOT (Heinemann, 1981) £35
LITTLE MONSTERS (Minipop) (Orchard, 1986)..£20
SMALL TALK (Minipop) (Orchard, 1987) £10
FANCY THAT (Minipop) (Orchard, 1991) £10
DOORBELL (Orchard, 1992) £8
ABC DINOSAUR (Heinemann, 1993) £20

Other Books Written and Illustrated by Jan Pienkowski

NUMBERS (Heinemann, 1973)..£10
COLOURS (Heinemann, 1973) £10
SHAPES (Heinemann, 1973) £10
SIZES (Heinemann, 1973)...£10
HOMES (Heinemann, 1979) £10
WEATHER (Heinemann, 1979) £10
ABC (Heinemann, 1980) £10
TIME (Heinemann, 1980) £10
QUEST FOR THE GLOOP (with Helen Nicoll) (Heinemann, 1980) £12
GOSSIP (Heinemann/Gallery Five, 1983) £10
ABC COLOURING BOOK (paperback) (Puffin, 1984) £8
123 COLOURING BOOK (paperback) (Puffin, 1984) £8
CHRISTMAS: The King James Version (Heinemann, 1984) £20
FARM: Colouring Book (paperback) (Puffin, 1985)...£8
FARM: Nursery Book (Heinemann, 1985) £10
ZOO: Colouring Book (paperback) (Puffin, 1985)...£8
ZOO: Nursery Book (Heinemann, 1985) £10
I'M CAT (Walker, 1985) £10
I'M FROG (Walker, 1985) £10
I'M MOUSE (Walker, 1985) £10
I'M PANDA (Walker, 1985) £10
FOOD (Heinemann, 1986)...£10
FACES (Heinemann, 1986) £10
EASTER: The King James Version (Heinemann, 1989) £20
OH MY! A FLY! (Orchard, 1989) £10
EGGS FOR TEA (Orchard, 1989) £10
PET FOOD (Orchard, 1989) £10

'Meg and Mog' Books (all Written by Helen Nicoll and Illustrated by Jan Pienkowski)

MEG AND MOG (Heinemann, 1972) £20
MEG'S CAR (Heinemann, 1975)...£20
MEG'S CASTLE (Heinemann, 1975) £20
MEG'S VEG (Heinemann, 1976) £15
MOG'S MUMPS (Heinemann, 1976)...£15
MEG AND MOG BIRTHDAY BOOK (Heinemann, 1979) £15
MOG AT THE ZOO (Heinemann, 1982) £15
MOG IN THE FOG (Heinemann, 1984)..£15
OWL AT SCHOOL (Heinemann, 1984)..£10

PIENKOWSKI, Jan

*A nice example of an early 'Pip & Squeak' annual, derived from the **Daily Mirror** comic strip.*

Other Books Illustrated by Jan Pienkowski

ANNIE, BRIDGET AND CHARLIE: An ABC for Children of Rhymes by Jessie Gertrude Townsend (1967)............................£25

A NECKLACE OF RAINDROPS and Other Stories by Joan Aiken (Cape, 1968) £30

THE KINGDOM UNDER THE SEA and Other Stories by Joan Aiken (Cape, 1971) £25

GHOSTS AND BOGLES by Dinah Starkey (Hutchinson, 1976)..£25

THE AMBER MOUNTAIN and Other Folk Stories by Agnes Szudek (Hutchinson, 1976)..£20

JACK AND THE BEANSTALK by Jacob and Wilhelm Grimm (translated by Joseph Jacobs; issued without dustjacket)
(Heinemann/Gallery Five: 'Jan Pienkowski's Fairy Tale Library' series, 1977) £15

SNOW WHITE by Jacob and Wilhelm Grimm (issued without dustjacket) (Heinemann/Gallery Five:
'Jan Pienkowski's Fairy Tale Library' series, 1977) £15

SLEEPING BEAUTY by Jacob and Wilhelm Grimm (translated by David Walser; issued without dustjacket)
(Heinemann/Gallery Five: 'Jan Pienkowski's Fairy Tale Library' series, 1977) £15
HANSEL AND GRETEL by Jacob and Wilhelm Grimm (issued without dustjacket) (Heinemann/Gallery Five:
'Jan Pienkowski's Fairy Tale Library' series, 1977) £15
PUSS IN BOOTS by Charles Perrault (translated by David Walser; issued without dustjacket)
(Heinemann/Gallery Five: 'Jan Pienkowski Fairy Tale Library' series, 1977)...£15
CINDERELLA by Charles Perrault (translated by David Walser; issued without dustjacket)
(Heinemann/Gallery Five: 'Jan Pienkowski's Fairy Tale Library' series, 1977) £15
JAN PIENKOWSKI'S FAIRY TALE LIBRARY (six books: 'Jack and the Beanstalk', 'Snow White',
'Sleeping Beauty', 'Hansel and Gretel', 'Puss in Boots' and 'Cinderella'; in box; issued without dustjackets)
(Heinemann/Gallery Five, 1977) ....the set £100
TALE OF A ONE-WAY STREET and Other Stories by Joan Aiken (Cape, 1978) £25
PAST EIGHT O'CLOCK by Joan Aiken (Cape, 1986) £15
A FOOT IN THE GRAVE by Joan Aiken (Cape, 1989) £20
HOME SWEET HOME (Orchard, 1989) £10
M.O.L.E. (Much Overworked Little Earthmover) by Russell Hoban (Cape, 1993) £15
GOODNIGHT MOO (Orion, 1994)..£5
BRONTO'S BRUNCH (Orion, 1994) £5

'PIP & SQUEAK (& WILFRED)' ANNUALS

British comic annuals featuring — respectively — a dog, a penguin and a baby rabbit. The original strip ran
in the *Daily Mirror* from 1919 to 1953.

Prices are for annuals in Very Good condition.

'Pip & Squeak' Annuals

PIP & SQUEAK ANNUAL (Daily Mirror, 1923 [1922]-35) ....each £25
PIP & SQUEAK ANNUAL (Daily Mirror, 1936-40) ....each £20

'Wilfred's' Annuals

WILFRED'S ANNUAL (Daily Mirror, 1924-35) ....each £25
WILFRED'S ANNUAL (Daily Mirror, 1936-39) ....each £20

'Pip, Squeak & Wilfred' Annuals

PIP, SQUEAK & WILFRED ANNUAL (Daily Mirror, [1953-55]) ....each £12

'PLAYBOX' ANNUALS

Highly influential British comic annuals, published by Amalgamated Press between 1909 and 1956. Its
best-known character was Tiger Tim, who first appeared in the *Daily Mirror* in 1904, subsequently featuring
in the magazine supplements, *The Playbox* and *The Playhour*, before being chosen for the *Playbox Annual*.
Also included were several of W. Heath Robinson's eccentric 'inventions' from the *Strand*.

Prices are for annuals in Very Good condition.

PLAYBOX ANNUAL 1909 ....£60
PLAYBOX ANNUAL 1910 ....£40
PLAYBOX ANNUAL 1911 ....£35
PLAYBOX ANNUAL 1912-15 ....each £30
PLAYBOX ANNUAL 1916-20 ....each £25
PLAYBOX ANNUAL 1921-42 ....each £20
PLAYBOX ANNUAL 1943-46 ....each £18
PLAYBOX ANNUAL 1947-48 ....each £15
PLAYBOX ANNUAL 1949 ....£12
PLAYBOX ANNUAL 1950-51 ....each £10
PLAYBOX ANNUAL 1952 ....£8
PLAYBOX ANNUAL 1953-56 ....each £7

POGÁNY, Willy

Hungarian illustrator. Born: Vilmos Andreas Pogány in Szeged, Hungary, in 1882. Studied at the Technical
University of Budapest and the Budapest Art School. Lived in London between 1906 and 1914, during
which time he illustrated a number of children's books for Harrap and other publishers, notably *A Treasury
of Verse for Little Children* (1908), *Folk Tales from Many Lands* (1910) and *The Hungarian Fairy Book* (1913).
The quality of his work declined following his move to America in 1914, although he continued to be a
prolific illustrator and also worked as a set designer on several classic films, notably Boris Karloff's
The Mummy. Died: 1955.

Prices are for books in Very Good condition.

THE WELSH FAIRY BOOK by W. Jenkyn Thomas (100 illustrations by Willy Pogány) (Unwin, [1907]) £100
THE ADVENTURES OF A DODO by G.E. Farrow (seventy illustrations by Willy Pogány) (Unwin, [1907])..................£75
MILLY AND OLLY by Mrs Mary Augusta Ward (48 illustrations by Willy Pogány) (Unwin, 1907) £40
A TREASURY OF VERSE FOR LITTLE CHILDREN by Madalen G. Edgar (Harrap, [1908]) £100
THE RUBAIYAT OF OMAR KHAYYAM (24 colour illustrations by Willy Pogány) (Harrap, 1909) £150

THE RUBAIYAT OF OMAR KHAYYAM (24 colour illustrations by Willy Pogány; De Luxe edition: limited to 500 copies, signed by the artist) (Harrap, 1909) £1,000

TANGLEWOOD TALES by Nathaniel Hawthorne (Unwin, [1909]) £50

NORSE WONDER TALES by Sir George Dasent (Collins, [1909]) £20

GISLI THE OUTLAW by Sir George Dasent (Harrap, [1909]) £20

THE RIME OF THE ANCIENT MARINER by S.T. Coleridge (twenty colour illustrations by Willy Pogány) (Harrap, 1910) £450

THE RIME OF THE ANCIENT MARINER by S.T. Coleridge (twenty colour illustrations by Willy Pogány; limited to 525 copies, signed by the artist) (Harrap, 1910) £2,500

THE BLUE LAGOON by H. de Vere Stacpoole (Unwin, 1910) £175

FOLK TALES FROM MANY LANDS by Lilian Gask (Harrap, 1910) £100

THE WITCH'S KITCHEN, or The India Rubber Doctor by Gerald Young (Harrap, [1910]) £40

TANNHAUSER by Richard Wagner (eight colour plates by Willy Pogány) (Harrap, 1911) £150

TANNHAUSER by Richard Wagner (eight colour plates by Willy Pogány; limited to 525 copies, signed by the artist) (Harrap, 1911) £500

PARSIFAL by Richard Wagner (eight colour plates by Willy Pogány) (Harrap, 1912) £150

PARSIFAL by Richard Wagner (eight colour plates by Willy Pogány; limited to 525 copies, signed by the artist) (Harrap, 1912) £500

THE FAIRIES AND THE CHRISTMAS CHILD by Lilian Gask (Harrap, [1912]) £40

THE TALE OF LOHENGRIN by Richard Wagner (eight colour plates by Willy Pogány) (Harrap, 1913) ...£150

THE TALE OF LOHENGRIN by Richard Wagner (eight colour plates by Willy Pogány; limited to 525 copies, signed by the artist) (Harrap, 1913) £500

ATTA TROLL by Heinrich Heine (Sidgwick & Jackson, 1913) £60

THE HUNGARIAN FAIRY BOOK by Nandor Pogány (Unwin, 1913) £120

FORTY-FOUR TURKISH FAIRY TALES by Ignacz Kunos (Harrap, [1913]) £50

FORTY-FOUR TURKISH FAIRY TALES by Ignacz Kunos (De Luxe edition: leather binding) (Harrap, [1913]) £70

WILLY POGÁNY CHILDREN (five books: 'Children at the Pole', 'Hiawatha', 'Red Riding Hood', 'Robinson Crusoe' and 'The Three Bears') (Harrap, [1914]) ....each £20

THE CHILDREN IN JAPAN by Grace Bartruse (Harrap, [1915]) £20

CINDERELLA. Adapted by E.L. Elias (Harrap, [1915]) £40

THE GINGERBREAD MAN by Lionel Fable (Harrap, [1915]) £60

MORE TALES FROM THE ARABIAN NIGHTS by Frances J. Olcott (Holt, U.S., 1915) £45

HOME BOOK OF VERSE FOR YOUNG CHILDREN. Edited by B.E. Stevenson (Holt, U.S., 1915) £20

STORIES TO TELL THE LITTLEST ONES by Sara Cone Bryant (Houghton Mifflin, U.S., 1916) £20

STORIES TO TELL THE LITTLEST ONES by Sara Cone Bryant (Harrap, 1918) £20

THE KING OF IRELAND'S SON by Padraic Colum (Macmillan, U.S., 1916) £20

THE KING OF IRELAND'S SON by Padraic Colum (Harrap, 1920) £50

BIBLE STORIES TO READ AND TELL by Frances J. Olcott (Houghton Mifflin, U.S., 1916)....................£15

TALES OF THE PERSIAN GENII by Frances J. Olcott (Houghton Mifflin, U.S., 1917) £30

TALES OF THE PERSIAN GENII by Frances J. Olcott (Harrap, 1919) £30

GULLIVER'S TRAVELS by Jonathan Swift. Adapted by Padraic Colum (Macmillan, U.S., 1917) £50

GULLIVER'S TRAVELS by Jonathan Swift. Adapted by Padraic Colum (Harrap, 1919) £50

LITTLE TAILOR OF THE WINDING WAY by Gertrude Crownfield (Macmillan, U.S., 1917)......................£30

POLLY'S GARDEN by Helen Ward Banks (Macmillan, U.S., 1918) £30

THE ADVENTURES OF ODYSSEUS AND THE TALE OF TROY by Padraic Colum (Macmillan, U.S., 1918) ...£50

THE ADVENTURES OF ODYSSEUS AND THE TALE OF TROY by Padraic Colum (Harrap, [1920]) £50

CHILDREN'S PLAYS by Eleanor and Ada Skinner (Appleton, U.S., 1919) £20

UNCLE DAVIE'S CHILDREN by Agnes McClelland Daulton (Macmillan, U.S., 1920)..............................£20

THE CHILDREN OF ODIN: A Book of Northern Myths by Padraic Colum (Macmillan, U.S., 1920) £20

THE CHILDREN OF ODIN: A Book of Northern Myths by Padraic Colum (Harrap, 1922)......................£30

THE GOLDEN FLEECE and the Heroes Who Lived Before Achilles by Padraic Colum (Macmillan, U.S., 1921) £30

THE ADVENTURES OF HAROUN EL RASCHID by Frances J. Olcott (Holt, U.S., 1923) £30

FAIRY FLOWERS: Nature Legends of Fact and Fantasy by Isidora Newman (Holt, U.S., 1926).........£200

FAIRY FLOWERS: Nature Legends of Fact and Fantasy by Isidora Newman (Humphrey Milford, [1926]) ...£200

GEORGE WASHINGTON GOES AROUND THE WORLD by Margaret L. Thomas (Nelson, 1927) £20

LOOKING OUT FOR JIMMIE by Helen H. Flanders (Dent [printed in the U.S.], [1928]) £25

TISZA TALES by Rosika Schwimmer (Doubleday Doran, U.S., [1928]) £40

ALICE'S ADVENTURES IN WONDERLAND by Lewis Carroll (Dutton, U.S., 1929) £50

ALICE'S ADVENTURES IN WONDERLAND by Lewis Carroll (signed, limited edition) (Dutton, U.S., 1929) ...£250

WILLY POGÁNY'S MOTHER GOOSE (Nelson, U.K./U.S., [1929]) £150

MAGYAR FAIRY TALES by Nandor Pogány (Dutton, U.S., 1930) £60

THE WIMP AND THE WOODLE by Helen von Kolnitz Hyer (Suttonhouse, U.S., 1935) £30

THE CHILDREN'S GULLIVER (adapted by F.H. Lee) (Harrap, 1935) £30

THE GOOSE GIRL OF NURNBERG by H.S. Hawley (Suttonhouse, U.S., 1936) £30

COPPA HAMBA by Blanche Ambrose (Suttonhouse, U.S., 1936) £30

HOW SANTA FOUND THE COBBLER'S SHOP by Margaretta Harmon (Suttonhouse, U.S., 1936) £30

THE GOLDEN COCKEREL by Alexander Pushkin (adapted by Elaine Pogány) (Nelson, U.S., 1938).....£90

PETERKIN by Elaine and Willy Pogány (McKay, U.S., 1940) £80

THE FRENZIED PRINCE: Being Heroic Stories of Ancient Ireland by Padraic Colum (McKay, U.S., 1943) ...£45

RUNNING AWAY WITH NEBBY by Philis Garrard (McKay, U.S., 1944) £60

*A plate from **The Tale of Lohengrin** (1913), one of three Willy Pogány gift books based on the operas of Richard Wagner.*

Two of Beatrix Potter's ever-popular picture books. **The Tailor of Gloucester** *(right) was originally printed at Potter's expense.*

PORTER, Eleanor H.

American author. Born: Eleanor Hodgman Porter in 1868. Wrote a number of popular children's novels, but is best known for *Pollyanna* (1913), about a good-natured girl whose sunny temperament overcomes all adversity. Sequels were written by a number of other authors. Died: 1920.

Prices are for books in Very Good condition.

CROSS CURRENTS (illustrated by William Stecher) (Wilde, 1907) £60
CROSS CURRENTS (illustrated by William Stecher) (Harrap, 1928) £20
THE TURN OF THE TIDE (illustrated by Frank Merrill) (Wilde, 1908) £55
THE TURN OF THE TIDE (illustrated by Frank Merrill) (Harrap, 1928) £20
THE SUNBRIDGE GIRLS AT SIX STAR RANCH (written under the pseudonym 'Eleanor Stuart'; illustrated by Frank Murch)
 (Page, U.S., 1913) £65
THE SUNBRIDGE GIRLS AT SIX STAR RANCH (as 'Six Star Ranch') (Stanley Paul, 1916) £45
POLLYANNA (illustrated by Stockton Mulford) (Page, U.S., 1913) £300
POLLYANNA (illustrated by Stockton Mulford) (Pitman, 1913) £150
POLLYANNA GROWS UP (illustrated by H. Weston Taylor) (Page, U.S., 1915) £100
POLLYANNA (illustrated by H. Weston Taylor) (Pitman, 1915) £75
MISS BILLY (Stanley Paul, 1914) £35
MISS BILLY — MARRIED (Page, U.S., 1914) £35
MISS BILLY — MARRIED (Stanley Paul, 1915)..£35
MISS BILLY'S DECISION (Stanley Paul, [1915]) £35
JUST DAVID (Constable, 1916) £35
THE ROAD TO UNDERSTANDING (Constable, [1917])...£25
OH, MONEY! MONEY! (Constable, 1918) £30
KEITH'S DARK TOWER (Constable, 1919) £30
MARY MARIE (Constable, U.K./U.S., [1920]) £20
THE STORY OF MARCO (Stanley Paul, [1920]) £20
SISTER SUE (Constable, U.K./U.S., [1921]) £20
MONEY, LOVE AND KATE, together with 'The Story of a Nickel' (Hodder & Stoughton, [1924]) £25
LITTLE PARDNER and Other Stories (Hodder & Stoughton, 1926) £20
THE 'MISS BILLY' STORIES (contains 'Miss Billy', 'Miss Billy's Decision' and 'Miss Billy Married') (Harrap, 1927) £20

PORTER, Gene Stratton

American author. Born: Geneva Grace Stratton Porter in Wabash County, Indiana, in 1863. As well as her children's books, she wrote extensively on natural history. Died: 1924.

Prices are for books in Very Good condition.

FRECKLES (illustrated by E. Stetson Crawford) (Doubleday, U.S., 1904) £100
FRECKLES (illustrated by E. Stetson Crawford) (John Murray, 1905) £50
A GIRL OF THE LIMBERLOST (illustrated by Wladyslaw T. Benda) (Doubleday, U.S., 1909) £150

A GIRL OF THE LIMBERLOST (illustrated by Wladyslaw T. Benda) (Hodder & Stoughton, 1911) £100
MORNING FACE (illustrated by the author) (Doubleday, U.S., 1916) £10
MORNING FACE (illustrated by the author) (John Murray, 1916) £60
THE MAGIC GARDEN (illustrated by Lee Thayer) (Doubleday, U.S., 1917) £40
THE MAGIC GARDEN (illustrated by Lee Thayer) (Hutchinson, [1927]) £25
THE WHITE FLAG (John Murray, 1923) £75

POTTER, Beatrix

British author-illustrator. Born: Helen Beatrix Potter in London in 1866. Educated at home by governesses, and showed an early love of art and of nature. In 1893, she sketched out her 'Tale of Peter Rabbit' in a letter to the son of one of her governesses, and eight years later she had the work privately printed in an edition of 250 copies. A trade edition was later issued by Frederick Warne, who published all her subsequent picture books. Died: 1943.

Prices are for books in Very Good condition.

THE TALE OF PETER RABBIT (limited to 250 copies; flat spine) (Privately printed, [1901])................................£40,000
THE TALE OF PETER RABBIT (limited to 200 copies; round spine) (Privately printed, 1902) £15,000
THE TALE OF PETER RABBIT (first trade edition) (Warne, [1902])..£3,000
THE TALE OF PETER RABBIT (cloth binding) (Warne, 1902) £3,000
THE TAILOR OF GLOUCESTER (limited to 500 copies) (Privately printed, 1902)..£4,000
THE TAILOR OF GLOUCESTER (first trade edition) (Warne, 1903)..£1,000
THE TAILOR OF GLOUCESTER (decorated cloth binding) (Warne, 1903) £3,000
THE TALE OF SQUIRREL NUTKIN (Warne, 1903)...£1,000
THE TALE OF SQUIRREL NUTKIN (decorated cloth binding) (Warne, 1903) £2,500
THE TALE OF BENJAMIN BUNNY (Warne, 1904) £1,000
THE TALE OF BENJAMIN BUNNY (decorated cloth binding) (Warne, 1904) £2,500
THE TALE OF TWO BAD MICE (Warne, 1904) £600
THE TALE OF TWO BAD MICE (decorated cloth binding) (Warne, 1904) £2,000
THE TALE OF MRS TIGGY-WINKLE (Warne, 1905)..£500
THE TALE OF MRS TIGGY-WINKLE (decorated cloth binding) (Warne, 1905) £2,000
THE PIE AND THE PATTY-PAN (large format) (Warne, 1905)..£400
THE TALE OF MR JEREMY FISHER (Warne, 1906) £400
THE STORY OF A FIERCE BAD RABBIT (panorama) (Warne, 1906) £600
THE STORY OF MISS MOPPET (panorama) (Warne, 1906)...£600
THE TALE OF TOM KITTEN (Warne, 1907) £400

*This picture clearly shows the unusually large format of Beatrix Potter's 1909 picture book, **Ginger & Pickles** (left).*

POTTER, Beatrix

THE TALE OF JEMIMA PUDDLE-DUCK (Warne, 1908) £600
THE ROLY-POLY PUDDING (large format) (Warne, 1908) £300
THE ROLY-POLY PUDDING (as 'The Tale of Samuel Whiskers') (Warne, [1926]) £600
THE TALE OF THE FLOPSY BUNNIES (Warne, 1909) £600
THE TALE OF THE FLOPSY BUNNIES (decorated cloth binding) (Warne, 1909) £2,000
GINGER & PICKLES (large format) (Warne, 1909) £500
THE TALE OF MRS TITTLEMOUSE (Warne, 1910)..£400
PETER RABBIT'S PAINTING BOOK (Warne, [1911])...£600
THE TALE OF TIMMY TIPTOES (Warne, 1911) £500
THE TALE OF MR TOD (Warne, 1912) £500
THE TALE OF PIGLING BLAND (Warne, 1913) £500
APPLEY DAPPLY'S NURSERY RHYMES (Warne, 1917) £600
TOM KITTEN'S PAINTING BOOK (Warne, 1917) £500
THE TALE OF JOHNNY TOWN-MOUSE (Warne, [1918]) £400
CECILY PARSLEY'S NURSERY RHYMES (small format) (Warne, 1922) £1,000
JEMIMA PUDDLE-DUCK'S PAINTING BOOK (Warne, [1925]) £500
PETER RABBIT'S ALMANAC FOR 1929 (Warne, [1928]) £500
THE FAIRY CARAVAN (McKay, U.S., 1929) £200
THE FAIRY CARAVAN (issued with dustjacket) (Warne, 1952) £80
THE TALE OF LITTLE PIG ROBINSON (large format) (Warne, [1930]) £300
SISTER ANNE (McKay, U.S., 1932) £300
WAG-BY-WALL (limited to 100 copies) (Warne, [1944]) £600
JEMIMA PUDDLE-DUCK'S PAINTING BOOK. From the Original Designs by B. Potter (Warne, [1954])............£80
JEREMY FISHER'S PAINTING BOOK. From the Original Designs by B. Potter (Warne, [1954]) £80
PETER RABBIT'S PAINTING BOOK. From the Original Designs by B. Potter (Warne, [1954]) £80
TOM KITTEN'S PAINTING BOOK. From the Original Designs by B. Potter (Warne, [1954]) £80
THE TALE OF THE FAITHFUL DOVE (illustrated by Marie Angel; limited to 100 copies) (Warne, [1955]) ...£400
THE TAILOR OF GLOUCESTER (facsimile; limited to 1,500 numbered copies; in box) (Warne, 1968) £100
THE TAILOR OF GLOUCESTER (facsimile of the original manuscript) (Warne, 1969)...............£60
THE SLY OLD CAT (issued with dustjacket) (Warne, 1971) £50
THE TALE OF TUPENNY (illustrated by Marie Angel; issued with dustjacket) (Warne, 1973).....................£40
THE TALE OF PETER RABBIT (boxed set; contains facsimiles of the 1901 first edition,
    the first Warne cloth-bound edition of 1902, and the original 'Peter Rabbit' letter from Beatrix Potter;
    limited to 750 numbered sets) (Warne, 1993) ....the set £200

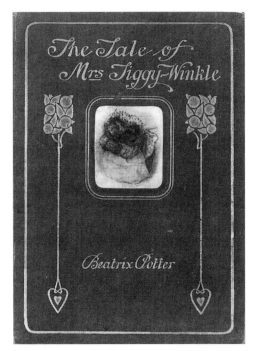

*Like many Beatrix Potter titles, **The Tale of Mrs Tiggy-Winkle** was issued in both trade and De Luxe (above) editions..*

*The De Luxe edition of **The Tale of the Flopsy Bunnies**, issued in 1909 by Potter's regular publisher, Frederick Warne.*

PRATCHETT, Terry

British author. Born: Beaconsfield, 1948. Best known for his hugely successful series of humorous science fantasy novels set in the imaginary 'Discworld', but began his career with a children's novel, *The Carpet People* (1971), subsequently producing the 'Nomes' trilogy (*Truckers*, *Diggers* and *Wings*) and a pair of books featuring the youngster, Johnny Maxwell.

Prices are for books in Very Good condition with dustjackets.

THE CARPET PEOPLE (illustrated by the author) (Colin Smythe, 1971) £575
THE CARPET PEOPLE (revised Edition; unillustrated) (Doubleday, 1992) £30
TRUCKERS (Doubleday, 1989)..£20
DIGGERS (Doubleday, 1990) £25
WINGS (Doubleday, 1990)..£25
ONLY YOU CAN SAVE MANKIND (Doubleday, 1992) £20
JOHNNY AND THE DEAD (Doubleday, 1993) £20

PRESTON, Chloe

British author-illustrator. Born: 1887. She illustrated stories by May Byron and Tom Preston, notably those featuring the 'Peek-a-Boos' and the little wooden 'Chunkies'. She also designed numerous postcards for Valentines and Raphael Tuck, soft toys for Farnells and nursery designs for Paragon China Co. Died: 1969.

Prices are for books in Good condition.

'Peek-a-Boo' Books

THE PEEK-A-BOOS (Henry Frowde/Hodder & Stoughton, 1911) £100
THE PEEK-A-BOOS IN WINTER (verses and illustrations) (Henry Frowde/Hodder & Stoughton, 1911) £100
THE PEEK-A-BOO BUNNIES by Z.H. [G.H. Vyse] (Henry Frowde/Hodder & Stoughton, 1912)...........................£100
THE PEEK-A-BOO AMONG THE BUNNIES by Z.H. [G.H. Vyse] (Henry Frowde/Hodder & Stoughton, 1912) £100
THE PEEK-A-BOO JAPS by Tom Preston (Henry Frowde/Hodder & Stoughton, 1912) £100
THE PEEK-A-BOOS' HOLIDAY by Tom Preston (Henry Frowde/Hodder & Stoughton, 1912) £100
THE PEEK-A-BOO TWINS by Tom Preston (Henry Frowde/Hodder & Stoughton, 1913) £100
THE PEEK-A-BOOS IN TOWN by May Byron (Henry Frowde/Hodder & Stoughton, 1913) £100
THE PEEK-A-BOOS' DESERT ISLAND by Max Byron (Henry Frowde/Hodder & Stoughton, 1914) £150
THE PEEK-A-BOOS AT THE ZOO by May Bryon (Henry Frowde/Hodder & Stoughton, 1914) £100
THE PEEK-A-BOOS AT SCHOOL by May Byron (Henry Frowde/Hodder & Stoughton, 1915) £100
THE PEEK-A-BOOS IN CAMP by May Byron (Henry Frowde/Hodder & Stoughton, 1915) £100
THE PEEK-A-BOOS IN WAR TIME by May Byron (Henry Frowde/Hodder & Stoughton, 1916) £100
THE PEEK-A-BOO FARMERS by May Byron (Henry Frowde/Hodder & Stoughton, 1917) £100
THE PEEK-A-BOO CIRCUS by May Byron (Humphrey Milford, 1919) £100
THE PEEK-A-BOO CHRISTMAS by May Byron (Humphrey Milford, 1920) £100
THE PEEK-A-BOO GARDENERS (Humphrey Milford, 1921) £100
THE PEEK-A-BOO BOOKLETS by May Byron (Humphrey Milford, 1916-) ....each £20
THE PEEK-A-BOOS GO SHOPPING (Humphrey Milford, 1922)..£100
THE PEEK-A-BOO GIPSIES by May Byron (OUP, 1923) £100
THE PEEK-A-BOO PLAY BOOKS (Humphrey Milford, 1927-) ....each £20

'Chunkies' Books

THE CHUNKIES by May Byron (Humphrey Milford, 1916)...£75
FIVE BAD CHUNKIES by May Byron (Humphrey Milford, 1921) £75
THE CHUNKIES' ADVENTURES (Humphrey Milford, 1921) £75
THE CHUNKY BOOKLETS (Humphrey Milford, 1921-) ....each £20
THE CHUNKIES' PLAY BOOK (OUP, 1930) £75

Others

ZH (illustrated by Chloe Preston and George Howard-Vyse) (Hodder & Stoughton, [c1913]) £50
WILLIAM AND WOGGS by May Byron (Hodder & Stoughton, 1915) £50
BOB THE BOLD by Ella Maclennan (Hodder & Stoughton, [c1920])..£50
LITTLE TOMMY TUCKER and Other Stories (Samuel Lowe Kenosha, 1940) £50
NURSERY RHYMES FOR CHILDREN (Samuel Lowe Kenosha, 1942) £50

PRICE, Evadne

British author. Born: Helen Zenna Smith in 1896. Best known for her children's novels featuring 'Jane' Turpin, a female William Brown. Also wrote adult novels under her own name. Died: 1985.

Prices are for books in Very Good condition with dustjackets.

JUST JANE (John Hamilton, [1928])..£150
JUST JANE (illustrated by Frank R. Grey) (Robert Hale, 1937) £50
MEET JANE (Marriott, 1930)...£100
MEET JANE (illustrated by Frank R. Grey) (Robert Hale, 1937) £50
ENTER — JANE (Newnes, [1932])..£100
ENTER — JANE (illustrated by Frank R. Grey) (Robert Hale, 1937) £50
JANE THE FOURTH (illustrated by Frank R. Grey) (Robert Hale, 1937) £70

JANE THE SLEUTH (illustrated by Frank R. Grey) (Robert Hale, 1939) £60
JANE THE UNLUCKY (illustrated by Frank R. Grey) (Robert Hale, 1939) £45
JANE THE POPULAR (illustrated by Frank R. Grey) (Robert Hale, 1939) £45
JANE THE PATIENT (illustrated by Frank R. Grey) (Robert Hale, 1940) £40
JANE GETS BUSY (illustrated by Frank R. Grey) (Robert Hale, 1940) £40
JANE AT WAR (illustrated by Frank R. Grey) (Robert Hale, 1947).....................................£40
JANE AND CO (selections from various books; illustrated by Frank R. Grey) (Macmillan, 1985) £15

PRICE, Willard

American author. Born: Peterborough, Ontario, Canada, in 1887. Best known for the highly improbable adventures of Hal and Roger Hunt in realistic settings. Died: 1983.

Prices are for books in Very Good condition with dustjackets

AMAZON ADVENTURE (illustrated by George Hartmann) (Cape, 1951) £25
SOUTH SEA ADVENTURE (Cape, 1952) £25
UNDERWATER ADVENTURE (Cape, 1955) £20
VOLCANO ADVENTURE (Cape, 1956) £20
WHALE ADVENTURE (Cape, 1960) £20
AFRICAN ADVENTURE (Cape, 1963) £20
ELEPHANT ADVENTURE (Cape, 1964) £20
SAFARI ADVENTURE (Cape, 1966) £20
LION ADVENTURE (Cape, 1967) £15
GORILLA ADVENTURE (Cape, 1969) £15
DIVING ADVENTURE (Cape, 1970) £15
CANNIBAL ADVENTURE (illustrated by Pat Marriott) (Cape, 1972) £15
TIGER ADVENTURE (illustrated by Pat Marriott) (Cape, 1979) £15
ARCTIC ADVENTURE (illustrated by Pat Marriott) (Cape, 1980).....................................£15

'PRIZE' ANNUALS

Early British annuals published by Dean. Edited by J.E. Clarke up to 1875.

Prices are for annuals in Very Good condition.

THE CHILDREN'S PRIZE 1863-75 ....each £40
THE PRIZE FOR GIRLS AND BOYS 1876-23 ....each £30

PRØYSEN, Alf

Norwegian author. Born: 1914. Creator of 'Mrs Pepperpot' series, all illustrated by Bjorn Berg. Died: 1970.

Prices are for books in Very Good condition with dustjackets where applicable.

LITTLE OLD MRS PEPPERPOT and Other Stories (illustrated by Bjorn Berg) (Hutchinson, 1959) £40
MRS PEPPERPOT AGAIN and Other Stories (illustrated by Bjorn Berg) (Hutchinson, 1960)................£30
MRS PEPPERPOT TO THE RESCUE and Other Stories (illustrated by Bjorn Berg) (Hutchinson, 1963) £25
MRS PEPPERPOT IN THE MAGIC WOOD and Other Stories (illustrated by Bjorn Berg) (Hutchinson, 1968) ...£20
MRS PEPPERPOT'S BUSY DAY (illustrated by Bjorn Berg) (Hutchinson, 1970) £20
MRS PEPPERPOT'S OUTING (illustrated by Bjorn Berg) (Hutchinson, 1971) £20
MRS PEPPERPOT'S CHRISTMAS (illustrated by Bjorn Berg) (Hutchinson, 1972)...........................£20
MRS PEPPERPOT'S YEAR (illustrated by Bjorn Berg) (Hutchinson, 1973) £20

PUDNEY, John

British author. Born: Langley, Buckinghamshire, in 1909. Notable for the 'Fred and I' adventure stories and the 'Hartwarp' series for the younger age group. Died: 1977.

Prices are for books in Very Good condition with dustjackets where applicable.

SATURDAY ADVENTURE (Evans, 1950) £15
SUNDAY ADVENTURE (Evans, 1951) £15
MONDAY ADVENTURE (Evans, 1952)...£15
TUESDAY ADVENTURE: The Affray in the Sardanger Fjord (Evans, 1953) £15
WEDNESDAY ADVENTURE (Evans, 1954) £15
THURSDAY ADVENTURE: The Stolen Airliner (Evans, 1955)..£15
FRIDAY ADVENTURE (Evans, 1956) £15
SPRING ADVENTURE (illustrated by Douglas Relf) (Evans, 1961)...................................£15
SUMMER ADVENTURE (illustrated by Douglas Relf) (Evans, 1962)...................................£15
AUTUMN ADVENTURE (illustrated by Douglas Relf) (Evans, 1963)...................................£15
WINTER ADVENTURE (illustrated by Douglas Relf) (Evans, 1964)...................................£15
THE GRANDFATHER CLOCK (illustrated by Peggy Beetles) (Hamish Hamilton, 1957)....................£10
CROSSING THE ROAD (illustrated by Janet and Anne Grahame Johnstone) (Hamish Hamilton, 1958) £10
THE HARTWARP LIGHT RAILWAY (illustrated by Ferelith Eccles Williams) (Hamish Hamilton, 1962) £10
THE HARTWARP DUMP (illustrated by Ferelith Eccles Williams) (Hamish Hamilton, 1962)..............£10
THE HARTWARP BALLOON (illustrated by Ferelith Eccles Williams) (Hamish Hamilton, 1962) £10
THE HARTWARP CIRCUS (illustrated by Ferelith Eccles Williams) (Hamish Hamilton, 1963) £10
THE HARTWARP BAKEHOUSE (illustrated by Ferelith Eccles Williams) (Hamish Hamilton, 1964) £10

The splendid cover of **Howard Pyle's Book of Pirates** (1921).

THE HARTWARP EXPLOSION (illustrated by Ferelith Eccles Williams) (Hanish Hamilton, 1965) £10
THE HARTWARP JETS (illustrated by Ferelith Eccles Williams) (Hamish Hamilton, 1967) £10
TUNNEL TO THE SKY (illustrated by Christine Marsh) (Hamish Hamilton, 1965) £10
THE NOEL STREATFEILD BIRTHDAY STORY BOOK by Noel Streatfeild, John Pudney and others
(illustrated by Shirley Hughes and others) (Dent, 1976) £15

PYLE, Howard

American author-illustrator. Born: Wilmington, Delaware, in 1853. Began contributing illustrated fables to *St. Nicholas* magazine at the age of 21, subsequently achieving fame with *The Merry Adventures of Robin Hood* (1883), which he both wrote and illustrated. This was followed by several historical and adventure novels, three collections of fairy tales and a four-volume retelling of the legends of King Arthur. N.C. Wyeth, Maxfield Parrish and Jessie Willcox Smith were amongst his pupils. Died: 1911.

Prices are for books in Very Good condition.

THE MERRY ADVENTURES OF ROBIN HOOD of Great Renown in Nottinghamshire (Scribner, U.S., 1883) £300
THE MERRY ADVENTURES OF ROBIN HOOD of Great Renown in Nottinghamshire (Sampson Low, 1883) £50
PEPPER AND SALT, or Seasoning for Young Folk (stories) (Sampson Low, U.S., 1886) £200
PEPPER AND SALT, or Seasoning for Young Folk (stories) (Sampson Low, 1888)...£100
THE WONDER CLOCK, or Four and Twenty Marvellous Tales (stories; with Katherine Pyle) (Harper, U.S., 1888) £250
OTTO OF THE SILVER HAND (novel) (Sampson Low, 1888) £200
THE ROSE OF PARADISE (Harper, U.S., 1888) £200
MEN OF IRON (novel) (Osgood McIlvaine, 1892 [1891]) £200
TWILIGHT LAND (Osgood McIlvaine, 1895 [1894]) £200
THE STORY OF JACK BALLISTER'S FORTUNES (novel) (Century, U.S., 1895) £200
THE STORY OF JACK BALLISTER'S FORTUNES (novel) (Osgood McIlvaine, 1897 [1896]).......................................£200
THE GARDEN BEHIND THE MOON: A Real Story of the Moon Angel (novel) (Lawrence & Bullen, 1896) £200
THE STORY OF KING ARTHUR AND HIS KNIGHTS (Newnes, 1903)...£200
THE STORY OF THE CHAMPIONS OF THE ROUND TABLE (Newnes, 1905) £200
THE STORY OF LAUNCELOT AND HIS COMPANIONS (Chapman & Hall, 1907) £200
THE RUBY OF KISHMOOR (Harper, U.S., 1908) £200
HOWARD PYLE'S BOOK OF PIRATES. Compiled by Merle Johnson (Harper, U.S., 1921) £100

R

RACKHAM, Arthur

British illustrator. Born: London, 1867. Studied at the City of London School and the Lambeth School of Art. Began by contributing illustrations to the *Westminster Budget*, *Little Folks* and other magazines, launching his career as a highly successful illustrator of children's books with editions of the *Ingoldsby Legends* (1898), Lambs *Tales from Shakespeare* (1899) and the Grimms' *Fairy Tales* (1900). Most of his pre-First World War 'Gift Books' were issued in sumptuous limited editions as well as standard trade editions. Married the Irish portrait painter, Edyth Starkie, in 1903. Died: 1939.

Prices are for books in Very Good condition.

THE ZANKIWANK AND THE BLETHERWITCH by S.J.A. Fitzgerald (seventeen full-page drawings and
    24 smaller drawings by Arthur Rackham; issued without dustjacket) (Dent, 1896) £1,000
TWO OLD LADIES by Maggie Browne (four colour plates and nineteen black-and-white illustrations by
    Arthur Rackham; issued without dustjacket) (Cassell, 1897) £250
TWO OLD LADIES by Maggie Browne (as 'The Surprising Adventures of Tuppy and Tue') (Cassell, 1904) £150
THE INGOLDSBY LEGENDS by Richard H. Barham (Dent, 1898) £120
THE INGOLDSBY LEGENDS by Richard H. Barham (Dent, 1907) £400
THE INGOLDSBY LEGENDS by Richard H. Barham (limited to 560 copies, signed by the artist) (Dent, 1907) £1,500
TALES FROM SHAKESPEARE by Charles and Mary Lamb (twelve illustrations by Arthur Rackham)
    (Dent: 'Temple Classics' series, 1899) £75
TALES FROM SHAKESPEARE by Charles and Mary Lamb (Dent, 1909) £200
TALES FROM SHAKESPEARE by Charles and Mary Lamb (limited to 750 copies, signed by the artist) (Dent, 1909) £1,000
GULLIVER'S TRAVELS by Jonathan Swift (issued without dustjacket) (Dent: 'Temple Classics' series, 1900) £75
GULLIVER'S TRAVELS by Jonathan Swift (Dent, 1909) £250
GULLIVER'S TRAVELS by Jonathan Swift (with extra plate; limited to 750 copies, signed by the artist) (Dent, 1909) £1,000
GULLIVER'S TRAVELS by Jonathan Swift (adapted by F.C. Tilney)
    (Dent: 'Tales for Children from Many Lands' series, [1913]) £50
GULLIVER'S TRAVELS by Jonathan Swift (Dent: 'Children's Illustrated Classics' series, 1952)..£20
FAIRY TALES OF THE BROTHERS GRIMM (Freemantle, 1900) £300
FAIRY TALES OF THE BROTHERS GRIMM (translated by Mrs Edgar Lucas) (Constable, 1909) £750
FAIRY TALES OF THE BROTHERS GRIMM (limited to 750 copies, signed by the artist) (Constable, 1909) £3,000

*Shakespeare's **A Midsummer Night's Dream** is one of several classic works illustrated by the prolific Arthur Rackham.*

*This **Fairy Book** (1933) was one of Rackham's very last works for children. It was published in both trade and De Luxe editions.*

*An unusually spare illustration by Rackham from his second edition of Barham's **Ingoldsby Legends**, published by Dent in 1907.*

*Arthur Rackham's illustrations for J.M. Barrie's **Peter Pan in Kensington Gardens** (above) are amongst his very finest works.*

FAIRY TALES OF THE BROTHERS GRIMM (Constable, 1920) £300
FAIRY TALES OF THE BROTHERS GRIMM (Heinemann, [1925]) £150
THE GREEK HEROES (four colour plates and eight black-and-white illustrations by Arthur Rackham) (Cassell, 1903) £80
THE GREEK HEROES (reissue of 1903 edition; four colour plates and eight black-and-white illustrations by Arthur Rackham) (Cassell, 1910)..£75
KINGDOMS CURIOUS by Myra Hamilton (illustrated by Arthur Rackham, H.R. Millar and others) (Heinemann, 1905) £100
RIP VAN WINKLE by Washington Irving (Heinemann, 1905) £800
RIP VAN WINKLE by Washington Irving (limited to 250 copies, signed by the artist) (Heinemann, 1905) £3,500
PUCK OF POOK'S HILL by Rudyard Kipling (four colour plates by Arthur Rackham) (Doubleday Page, U.S., 1906) £200
PETER PAN IN KENSINGTON GARDENS by J.M. Barrie (Hodder & Stoughton, [1906]) £1,000
PETER PAN IN KENSINGTON GARDENS by J.M. Barrie (limited to 500 copies, signed by the artist) (Hodder & Stoughton, [1906])...£3,750
PETER PAN IN KENSINGTON GARDENS by J.M. Barrie (new edition) (Hodder & Stoughton, 1912) £1,500
PETER PAN IN KENSINGTON GARDENS (facsimile of the 1912 edition; limited to 500 numbered copies) (Hodder & Stoughton, 1983) £150
J.M. BARRIE'S PETER PAN IN KENSINGTON GARDENS by M.C. Byron (Hodder & Stoughton, [1929]) £50
THE PETER PAN PORTFOLIO (limited to 500 copies, numbered 101-600) (Hodder & Stoughton, [1912]) £1,750
THE PETER PAN PORTFOLIO (limited to twenty copies, each plate signed by the artist) (Hodder & Stoughton, 1912) £6,000
PETER AND WENDY by J.M. Barrie (enlarged edition; issued with dustjacket) (Hodder & Stoughton, [1912]) £1,250
PETER AND WENDY by J.M. Barrie (limited to 500 copies, numbered 101-600, signed by the publisher, engravers and printers) (Hodder & Stoughton, [1912]) £1,750
ALICE'S ADVENTURES IN WONDERLAND by Lewis Carroll (with poem by Austin Dobson; green cloth binding) (Heinemann, [1907]) £300
ALICE'S ADVENTURES IN WONDERLAND by Lewis Carroll (with poem by Austin Dobson; De Luxe edition: limited to 1,130 copies [unsigned]; white vellum binding) (Heinemann, [1907]) £1,750
THE LAND OF ENCHANTMENT (Cassell, 1907) £200
A MIDSUMMER NIGHT'S DREAM by William Shakespeare (Heinemann, 1908) £450
A MIDSUMMER NIGHT'S DREAM by William Shakespeare (limited to 1,000 copies, signed by the artist) (Heinemann, 1908) £1,750
UNDINE by Friedrich de la Motte Fouqué (translated by W.L. Courtney) (Heinemann, 1909) £300
UNDINE by Friedrich de la Motte Fouqué (translated by W.L. Courtney; limited to 1,000 copies, signed by the artist) (Heinemann, 1909) £1,250
THE RAINBOW BOOK by Mabel H. Spielmann (illustrated by Arthur Rackham and others) (Chatto & Windus, 1909) £100
THE BOOK OF BETTY BARBER by Maggie Browne (Duckworth, [1910]) £200
STORIES OF KING ARTHUR by A.L. Haydon (four colour plates and other illustrations by Arthur Rackham) (Cassell, 1910) £75

*The dustjacket of Rackham's edition of **A Christmas Carol**, featuring a sketch of Marley posing as Scrooge's doorknocker!*

Even Rackham's later works sell for large sums today. This 1921 title is worth £150 in Very Good condition without the jacket.

*The artwork on the jacket of Rackham's edition of **Cinderella** reflects the 'silhouette-style' illustrations found in the book.*

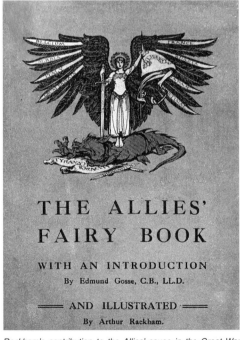

THE ALLIES' FAIRY BOOK

WITH AN INTRODUCTION
By Edmund Gosse, C.B., LL.D.

=== AND ILLUSTRATED ===
By Arthur Rackham.

Rackham's contribution to the Allies' cause in the Great War was to provide the illustrations for this fund-raising volume.

THE SLEEPING BEAUTY. Adapted by Charles S. Evans (with extra plate; limited to 625 copies, signed by the artist) (Heinemann, 1920) £650

IRISH FAIRY TALES by James Stephens (Macmillan, 1920) £400

IRISH FAIRY TALES by James Stephens (limited to 520 copies, signed by the artist) (Macmillan, 1920) £1,000

A DISH OF APPLES by Eden Phillpotts (Hodder & Stoughton, [1921]) £150

A DISH OF APPLES by Eden Phillpotts (limited to 500 copies, signed by the artist) (Hodder & Stoughton, [1921]) £700

A WONDER BOOK by Nathaniel Hawthorne (Hodder & Stoughton, 1922) £550

A WONDER BOOK by Nathaniel Hawthorne (limited to 600 copies, signed by the artist) (Hodder & Stoughton, [1922]) £1,000

WHERE THE BLUE BEGINS by Christopher Morley (Heinemann, [1925]) £300

WHERE THE BLUE BEGINS by Christopher Morley (limited to 175 copies, signed by the artist) (Heinemann, [1925]) £1,000

POOR CECCO by M. Bianco (Chatto & Windus, 1925) £350

POOR CECCO by M. Bianco (limited to 105 copies, signed by the author) (Doran, U.S., [1925]) £5,000

THE LEGEND OF SLEEPY HOLLOW by Washington Irving (Harrap, 1928) £200

THE LEGEND OF SLEEPY HOLLOW by Washington Irving (limited to 375 copies, signed by the artist; vellum binding) (Harrap, 1928) £750

THE NIGHT BEFORE CHRISTMAS: A Visit from St. Nicholas by Clement C. Moore (Harrap, 1931) £150

THE NIGHT BEFORE CHRISTMAS: A Visit from St. Nicholas by Clement C. Moore (limited to 550 copies, signed by the artist) (Harrap, 1931) £1,200

THE CHIMES by Charles Dickens (limited to 1,500 copies, signed by the artist; in slipcase) (Limited Editions Club, U.S., 1931) £600

THE KING OF THE GOLDEN RIVER by John Ruskin (Harrap, 1932) £125

THE KING OF THE GOLDEN RIVER by John Ruskin (limited to 750 copies, signed by the artist) (Harrap, 1932) £550

FAIRY TALES by Hans C. Andersen (selected and illustrated by Arthur Rackham) (Harrap, 1932) £400

FAIRY TALES by Hans C. Andersen (selected and illustrated by Arthur Rackham; limited to 525 copies, signed by the artist) (Harrap, 1932) £2,000

GOBLIN MARKET by Christina G. Rossetti (Harrap, 1933) £125

GOBLIN MARKET by Christina G. Rossetti (limited to 410 copies, signed by the artist) (Harrap, 1933) £600

THE ARTHUR RACKHAM FAIRY BOOK (Harrap, 1933) £350

THE ARTHUR RACKHAM FAIRY BOOK (limited to 460 copies, signed by the artist) (Harrap, 1933) £1,625

THE PIED PIPER OF HAMELIN by Robert Browning (Harrap 1934) £125

THE PIED PIPER OF HAMELIN by Robert Browning (limited to 410 copies, signed by the artist) (Harrap, 1934) £600

THE WIND IN THE WILLOWS by Kenneth Grahame (Heritage, U.S., 1940) £300

THE WIND IN THE WILLOWS by Kenneth Grahame (limited to 2,020 numbered copies, signed by the designer, Bruce Rogers; in slipcase) (Limited Editions Club, U.S., 1940) £1,350

THE WIND IN THE WILLOWS by Kenneth Grahame (omits several of the colour plates from the original American edition) (Methuen, 1950) £600

THE WIND IN THE WILLOWS by Kenneth Grahame (limited to 500 copies; in box) (Methuen, 1951) £1,750

THE WIND IN THE WILLOWS by Kenneth Grahame (twelve colour plates and fifteen line drawings by Arthur Rackham) (Methuen, 1975) £75

'RADIO FUN' ANNUALS

British comic annual published by Amalgamated Press and featuring the stars of British radio, notably Arthur Askey, Tommy Trinder and Duggie Wakefield.

Prices are for annuals in Very Good condition.

RADIO FUN ANNUAL 1940 ......£100
RADIO FUN ANNUAL 1941 ......£70
RADIO FUN ANNUAL 1942 ......£65
RADIO FUN ANNUAL 1943 ......£55
RADIO FUN ANNUAL 1944 ......£50
RADIO FUN ANNUAL 1945 ......£45
RADIO FUN ANNUAL 1946 ......£40
RADIO FUN ANNUAL 1947-48 ......each £35
RADIO FUN ANNUAL 1949 ......£30
RADIO FUN ANNUAL 1950-55 ......each £25
RADIO FUN ANNUAL 1956-58 ......each £20
RADIO FUN ANNUAL 1959-60 ......each £15

RAE, Gwynedd

British author. Born: 1892. The creator of 'Mary Plain', the bear from Berne, Switzerland, who featured in a series of droll and endearing stories with a discreet touch of fantasy. Died: 1977.

Prices are for books in Very Good condition with dustjackets where applicable.

MOSTLY MARY (Routledge, 1930) £75
ALL MARY (Routledge, 1931) £45
MARY PLAIN ON HOLIDAY (illustrated by Irene Williamson) (Routledge, 1937) £40
MARY PLAIN IN TROUBLE (Routledge, 1940) £40
MARY PLAIN IN WAR-TIME (Routledge, 1942) £40

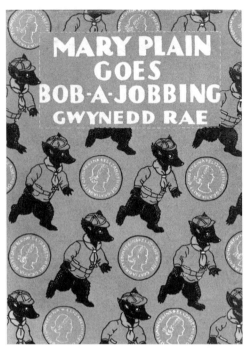

Mary Plain in Trouble (1940) was the fourth book by Gwynedd Rae featuring the endearing 'bear from Berne'.

Like most of the later books in the series, this 'Mary Jane' title from 1954 is worth £40 in Very Good condition with the jacket.

MARY PLAIN'S BIG ADVENTURE (Routledge, 1944)..£40
MARY PLAIN IN TOWN (Routledge, 1947)..£40
MARY PLAIN TO THE RESCUE (Routledge, 1950) £40
MARY PLAIN AND THE TWINS (illustrated by Irene Williamson) (Routledge, 1952) £40
MARY PLAIN GOES BOB-A-JOBBING (illustrated by Irene Williamson) (Routledge, 1954) £40
MARY PLAIN GOES TO AMERICA (illustrated by Irene Williamson) (Routledge, 1957)....................................£40
MARY PLAIN VIP (illustrated by Irene Williamson) (Routledge, 1961)..£40
MARY PLAIN'S "WHODUNIT" (Routledge, 1965) £40

RANSOME, Arthur

British author. Born: Arthur Michell Ransome in Leeds in 1884. Studied at Rugby School and Leeds University, leaving the latter at the age of seventeen to become an office boy at the publishers, Grant Richards. Gave up his job in 1903 to become a freelance writer, contributing essays and articles to a variety of publications and subsequently becoming overseas correspondent for the *Manchester Guardian*. Left the paper in 1929 to write *Swallows and Amazons* (1930), the first in a series of books describing the Walker family's adventures in the Lake District. Amongst his many other books were critical studies of Edgar Allan Poe (1910) and Oscar Wilde (1912). Died: 1967.

Prices are for books in Very Good condition (with dustjackets after 1920).

'Swallows and Amazons' Books

SWALLOWS AND AMAZONS (vignette and endpaper & frontispiece maps illustrated by Stephen [Steven] Spurrier)
    (Cape, 1930) £1,200
SWALLOWS AND AMAZONS (illustrated by Clifford Webb) (Cape, 1931) £220
SWALLOWS AND AMAZONS (illustrated by Arthur Ransome) (Cape, 1938)..£125
THE SWALLOWS & AMAZONS (original draft of 'Swallows and Amazons'; issued in pictorial boards with dustjacket
    (50 copies) or pictorial wrappers [500 copies]) (Amazon Publications/The Arthur Ransome Society, 1997) ....£50/£20
SWALLOWDALE (illustrated by Clifford Webb) (Cape, 1931) £750
SWALLOWDALE (illustrated by Arthur Ransome) (Cape, 1936) £75
PETER DUCK (illustrated by the author) (Cape, 1932) £250
WINTER HOLIDAY (illustrated by the author) (Cape, 1933)..£300
COOT CLUB (illustrated by the author and Helene Carter) (Cape, 1934) £300
PIGEON POST (illustrated by the author) (Cape, 1936)..£200
WE DIDN'T MEAN TO GO TO SEA (illustrated by the author) (Cape, 1937)..£150
SECRET WATER (illustrated by the author) (Cape, 1939) £120

THE BIG SIX (illustrated by the author) (Cape, 1940) £120
MISSEE LEE (illustrated by the author) (Cape, 1941) £100
THE PICTS AND THE MARTYRS, or Not Welcome At All (illustrated by the author) (Cape, 1943) £100
GREAT NORTHERN? (Cape, 1947) £100
COOTS IN THE NORTH and Other Stories (Cape, 1988) £12

Others

THE CHILD'S BOOK OF THE SEASONS (non-fiction) (Treherne, 1906) £75
POND AND STREAM (non-fiction) (Treherne, 1906) £75
THE THINGS IN OUR GARDEN (non-fiction) (Treherne, 1906) £75
HIGHWAYS AND BYWAYS IN FAIRYLAND (Alston Rivers: 'Pinafore Library' series, [1906])....................£100
THE IMP AND THE ELF AND THE OGRE (contains 'The Child's Book of the Seasons', 'Pond and Stream' and
'The Things in Our Garden') (Nisbet, 1910)..£100
OLD PETER'S RUSSIAN TALES (illustrated by Dmitri Mitrokhin) (T.C. & E.C. Jack, 1916) £150
AL ADDIN AND HIS WONDERFUL LAMP (illustrated by Mackenzie) (Nisbet, [1919])............................£150
AL ADDIN AND HIS WONDERFUL LAMP (limited to 250 numbered copies, signed by the artist; illustrated by Mackenzie)
(Nisbet, [1919]) £1,500
THE SOLDIER AND DEATH: A Russian Folk Tale (Privately printed, 1920) £50
THE WAR OF THE BIRDS AND THE BEASTS AND OTHER RUSSIAN TALES (Cape, 1984) £12
THE BLUE TREACLE: The Story of an Escape (issued in paper boards [25 copies] or wrappers [375 copies])
(The Arthur Ransome Society, 1993)...£40/£20
ALADDIN AND HIS LAMP in Five Scenes of Ten Minutes Each (wrappers [80 copies]) (The Arthur Ransome Society, 1997) ..£10

REEVES, James

British author. Born: London, 1909. Prolific wrtiter of prose and verse for both children and adults, and edited many other books. His *Complete Poems for Children*, illustrated by Edward Ardizzone, was published in 1973. Died: 1978.

Prices are for books in Very Good condition with dustjackets where applicable.

THE WANDERING MOON (illustrated by Evadne Rowan) (Heinemann, 1950) £20
MULCASTER MARKET Three Plays for Young People (illustrated by Dudley Cutler) (Heinemann, 1951) £20
THE BLACKBIRD IN THE LILAC (verse; illustrated by Edward Ardizzone) (OUP, 1952) £45
THE KING WHO TOOK SUNSHINE (Heinemann, 1954) £15
ENGLISH FABLES AND FAIRY STORIES, RETOLD (illustrated by Joan Kiddell-Monroe) (Blackie, 1954) £15
PIGEONS AND PRINCESSES (illustrated by Edward Ardizzone) (Heinemann, 1956) £40
A HEALTH TO JOHN PATCH A Ballad Operetta (Boosey, 1957) £15
PREFABULOUS ANIMILES (illustrated by Edward Ardizzone) (Heinemann, 1957) £35
WANDERING MOON (illustrated by Edward Ardizzone) (Heinemann, 1957) £35
A GOLDEN LAND. Edited by James Reeves (illustrated by Gillian Conway, Eve Garnett and others) (Constable 1958) £20
MULBRIDGE MANOR (illustrated by Geraldine Spence) (Heinemann, 1958) £15
TITUS IN TROUBLE (illustrated by Edward Ardizzone) (The Bodley Head, 1959) £40
EXPLOITS OF DON QUIXOTE, RETOLD (illustrated by Edward Ardizzone) (Blackie, 1959) £40
RAGGED ROBIN (illustrated by Jane Paton) (Heinemann, 1961) £15
FABLES FROM AESOP, RETOLD (illustrated by Maurice Wilson) (Blackie, 1961) £15
HURDY-GURDY: Selected Poems for Children (illustrated by Edward Ardizzone) (Heinemann, 1961) £40
SAILOR RUMBELOW AND BRITTANIA (illustrated by Edward Ardizzone) (Dutton, 1962) £40
THE STRANGE LIGHT (illustrated by Lynton Lamb) (Heinemann, 1964) £25
THREE TALL TALES: Chosen from Traditional Sources (illustrated by Edward Ardizzone) (Abelard-Schuman, 1964) £30
THE STORY OF JACKIE THIMBLE (illustrated by Edward Ardizzone) (Chatto & Windus, 1965) £30
THE ROAD TO A KINGDOM: Stories from the Old and New Testaments (illustrated by Richard Kennedy)
(Heinemann, 1965) £15
THE PILLAR-BOX THIEVES (illustrated by Dick Hart) (Nelson, 1965) £20
THE SECRET SHOEMAKERS and Other Stories (illustrated by Edward Ardizzone) (Abelard-Schuman, 1966) £40
THE COLD FLAME: Based on a Tale from the Collection of the Brothers Grimm (illustrated by Charles Keeping)
(Hamish Hamilton, 1967) £20
RHYMING WILL (illustrated by Edward Ardizzone) (Hamish Hamilton, 1967) £25
THE CHRISTMAS BOOKS (illustrated by Raymond Briggs) (Heinemann, 1968) £30
MR HORROX AND THE GRATCH (illustrated by Quentin Blake) (Abelard-Schuman, 1969) £25
HEROES AND MONSTERS: Legends of Ancient Greece Retold — Gods and Voyagers
(illustrated by Sarah Nechamkin) (Blackie, 1969) £15
THE ANGEL AND THE DONKEY (illustrated by Edward Ardizzone) (Hamish Hamilton, 1969) £20
MAILDON THE VOYAGER (illustrated by John Lawrence) (Hamish Hamilton, 1971) £15
HOW THE MOON BEGAN (illustrated by Edward Ardizzone) (Abelard-Schuman, 1971) £20
THE PATH OF GOLD (illustrated by Krystyna Turska) (Hamish Hamilton, 1972) £20
COMPLETE POEMS FOR CHILDREN (illustrated by Edward Ardizzone) (Heinemann, 1973)........................£25
THE FORBIDDEN FOREST and Other Stories (illustrated by Raymond Briggs) (Heinemann, 1973)...............£25
THE VOYAGE OF ODYSSEUS: Homer's Odyssey Retold (Blackie, 1973) £15
TWO GREEDY BEARS (illustrated by Gareth Floyd) (Hamish Hamilton, 1974) £15
THE LION THAT FLEW (illustrated by Edward Ardizzone) (Chatto & Windus, 1974) £25
MORE PREFABULOUS ANIMILES (illustrated by Edward Ardizzone) (Heinemann, 1975) £25

THE CLEVER MOUSE (illustrated by Barbara Swiderska) (Chatto & Windus, 1976) £20
QUEST AND CONQUEST: Pilgrim's Progress Retold (illustrated by Joanna Troughton) (Blackie, 1976) £10
ARCADIAN BALLADS (illustrated by Edward Ardizzone) (Heinemann, 1977) £20
EGGTIME STORIES (illustrated by Colin McNaughton) (Blackie, 1978) £10
THE JAMES REEVES STORYBOOK (illustrated by Edward Ardizzone) (Heinemann, 1978) £25
A PRINCE IN DANGER (illustrated by Gareth Floyd) (Kaye & Ward, 1979) £10
SNOW-WHITE AND ROSE-RED (illustrated by Jenny Rodwell) (Andersen Press, 1979) £10

RICHARDS, Frank

British author. Born: Charles Harold St. John Hamilton in Ealing, London, in 1876. Studied at various day schools in West London, including Thorne House, but never attended a boarding school. Began to write in his teens, contributing boys' stories to, amongst other titles, Pearson's *Big Budget* and, from 1895 onwards, the Harmsworth magazines *Pluck*, *Gem* and *Magnet*. His first 'Greyfriars' story, featuring the immortal Billy Bunter, appeared in the opening issue of *Magnet* under the pseudonym, 'Frank Richards', derived from a character in Scott's *Rob Roy* and his brother, Richard Hamilton. After *Gem* and *Magnet* folded during the war, Richards wrote a series of successful 'Greyfriars' novels for Skilton and, later, Cassell. Died: 1961.

Prices are for books in Very Good condition with dustjackets.

'Billy Bunter' Books

BILLY BUNTER OF GREYFRIARS SCHOOL (illustrated by R.J. Macdonald) (Charles Skilton, 1947) £70
BILLY BUNTER'S BANKNOTE (Charles Skilton, 1948) £45
BILLY BUNTER'S BARRING-OUT (illustrated by R.J. Macdonald) (Charles Skilton, 1948) £45
BILLY BUNTER IN BRAZIL (Charles Skilton, 1949) £45
BILLY BUNTER'S CHRISTMAS PARTY (illustrated by R.J. Macdonald) (Charles Skilton, 1949) £45
BILLY BUNTER'S BENEFIT (illustrated by H.J. Macdonald) (Charles Skilton, 1950) £30
BILLY BUNTER AMONG THE CANNIBALS (illustrated by R.J. Macdonald) (Charles Skilton, 1950) £30
BILLY BUNTER'S POSTAL ORDER (illustrated by R.J. Macdonald) (Charles Skilton, 1951) £30
BILLY BUNTER BUTTS IN (illustrated by R.J. Macdonald) (Charles Skilton, 1951) £30
BILLY BUNTER AND THE BLUE MAURITIUS (illustrated by R.J. Macdonald) (Charles Skilton, 1952) £40
BILLY BUNTER'S BEANFEAST (illustrated by R.J. Macdonald) (Cassell, 1952) £30
BILLY BUNTER'S BRAINWAVE (illustrated by R.J. Macdonald) (Cassell, 1953) £30
BILLY BUNTER'S FIRST CASE (illustrated by R.J. Macdonald) (Cassell, 1953) £30
BILLY BUNTER'S OWN (annual) (Mandeville/Oxenhoath Press, [1953-61]) ....each £8
BILLY BUNTER THE BOLD (illustrated by R.J. Macdonald) (Cassell, 1954) £25
BUNTER DOES HIS BEST (illustrated by R.J. Macdonald) (Cassell, 1954) £25
BILLY BUNTER'S DOUBLE (illustrated by R.J. Macdonald) (Cassell, 1955) £25
BACKING UP BILLY BUNTER (illustrated by C.H. Chapman) (Cassell, 1955) £25
LORD BILLY BUNTER (illustrated by C.H. Chapman) (Cassell, 1956) £25
THE BANISHING OF BILLY BUNTER (illustrated by C.H. Chapman) (Cassell, 1956) £25
BILLY BUNTER'S BOLT (illustrated by C.H. Chapman) (Cassell, 1957) £25
BILLY BUNTER AFLOAT (illustrated by C.H. Chapman) (Cassell, 1957) £25
BILLY BUNTER'S BARGAIN (illustrated by C.H. Chapman) (Cassell, 1958) £25
BILLY BUNTER THE HIKER (illustrated by C.H. Chapman) (Cassell, 1958) £25
BUNTER OUT OF BOUNDS (illustrated by C.H. Chapman) (Cassell, 1959) £25
BUNTER COMES FOR CHRISTMAS (illustrated by C.H. Chapman) (Cassell, 1959) £25
BUNTER THE BAD LAD (illustrated by C.H. Chapman) (Cassell, 1960) £25
BUNTER KEEPS IT DARK (illustrated by C.H. Chapman) (Cassell, 1960) £25
BILLY BUNTER'S TREASURE-HUNT (illustrated by C.H. Chapman) (Cassell, 1961) £22
BILLY BUNTER AT BUTLINS (illustrated by C.H. Chapman) (Cassell, 1961) £18
BILLY BUNTER AT BUTLINS (Butlin's 'Beaver Club' edition; issued with TV tie-in dustjacket) (Cassell, 1961) £3
BUNTER THE VENTRILOQUIST (illustrated by C.H. Chapman) (Cassell, 1961) £20
BUNTER THE CARAVANNER (illustrated by C.H. Chapman) (Cassell, 1962) £20
BILLY BUNTER'S BODYGUARD (illustrated by C.H. Chapman) (Cassell, 1962) £20
BIG CHIEF BUNTER (illustrated by C.H. Chapman) (Cassell, 1963) £20
JUST LIKE BUNTER (illustrated by C.H. Chapman) (Cassell, 1963) £20
BUNTER THE STOWAWAY (illustrated by C.H. Chapman) (Cassell, 1964) £20
THANKS TO BUNTER (illustrated by C.H. Chapman) (Cassell, 1964) £20
BUNTER THE SPORTSMAN (illustrated by C.H. Chapman) (Cassell, 1965) £20
BUNTER'S LAST FLING (illustrated by C.H. Chapman) (Cassell, 1965) £20

'Jack' Books

JACK OF ALL TRADES (Mandeville, 1950) £25
JACK'S THE LAD (Spring Books, 1957) £8
JACK OF THE CIRCUS (Spring Books, 1957) £8

'Tom Merry' Books

THE SECRET OF THE STUDY (written under the pseudonym 'Martin Clifford') (Mandeville, 1949) £8
TALBOT'S SECRET (Mandeville, 1949) £8

The sixth of Frank Richards' 'Billy Bunter' novels, which revived the Fat Owl's flagging fortunes in the years following the war.

*You can expect to pay £25 for a Very Good copy of Richards' 1954 novel, **Billy Bunter the Bold**, in its colourful dustjacket.*

TOM MERRY AND CO OF ST JIM'S (written under the pseudonym 'Martin Clifford') (Mandeville, 1949) £8
RALLYING ROUND GUSSY (written under the pseudonym 'Martin Clifford') (Mandeville, 1950) £8
THE SCAPEGRACE OF ST JIM'S (written under the pseudonym 'Martin Clifford') (Mandeville, 1951) £8
THE RIVALS OF ROOKWOOD (written under the pseudonym 'Owen Conquest') (Mandeville, 1951) £5
TOM MERRY'S SECRET (written under the pseudonym 'Martin Clifford') (Hamilton, 1952) £8
TOM MERRY'S RIVAL (written under the pseudonym 'Martin Clifford') (Hamilton, 1952) £10
TROUBLE FOR TOM MERRY (Spring Books, 1953) £6
DOWN AND OUT (Spring Books, 1953) £8
CARDEW'S CATCH (Spring Books, 1954) £8
THE DISAPPEARANCE OF TOM MERRY (Spring Books, 1954) £8
THROUGH THICK AND THIN (Spring Books, 1955) £8
TOM MERRY'S TRIUMPH (Spring Books, 1956) £8
TOM MERRY & CO, CARAVANNERS (Spring Books, 1956) £5

Other Books Written as 'Martin Clifford'
THE MAN FROM THE PAST (Hamilton, 1952) £5
WHO RAGGED RAILTON? (Hamilton, 1952) £5
SKIMPOLE'S SNAPSHOT (Hamilton, 1952) £5
TROUBLE FOR TRIMBLE (Hamilton, 1952) £5
D'ARCY IN DANGER (Hamilton, 1952) £5
D'ARCY ON THE WARPATH (Hamilton, 1952) £5
D'ARCY'S DISAPPEARANCE (Hamilton, 1952) £5
D'ARCY THE REFORMER (Hamilton, 1952) £5
D'ARCY'S DAY OFF (Hamilton, 1952) £5

Books Written as 'Hilda Richards'
BESSIE BUNTER OF CLIFF HOUSE SCHOOL (illustrated by R.J. Macdonald) (Charles Skilton, 1949) £60

Others
THE SECRET OF THE SCHOOL (Merrett, 1946) £8
THE BLACK SHEEP OF SPARSHOTT (Merrett, 1946) £8
FIRST MAN IN (Merrett, 1946) £8
LOOKING AFTER LAMB (Merrett, 1946) £8

RICHARDS, Frank

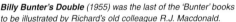

Billy Bunter's Double (1955) was the last of the 'Bunter' books to be illustrated by Richard's old colleague R.J. Macdonald.

*His place was taken by C.H. Chapman for the next novel, **Backing Up Billy Bunter**, published by Cassell that same year.*

THE HERO OF SPARSHOTT (Merrett, 1946)..£8
PLUCK WILL TELL (Merrett, 1946) £8
TOP STUDY AT TOPHAM (Matthew, 1947) £8
BUNNY BINKS ON THE WARPATH (Matthew, 1947) £8
THE DANDY OF TOPHAM (Matthew, 1947) £8
SENT TO COVENTRY (Matthew, 1947) £8
THE LONE TEXAN (Atlantic, 1954)..£8

'ROBIN HOOD' BOOKS AND ANNUALS

Legendary English outlaw who, despite continuing controversy over his origins and/or identity, has inspired countless books and ephemera from the early seventeenth century onwards.

Prices are for books in Very Good condition with dustjackets where applicable.

'Robin Hood' Books

LIFE AND BALLADS OF ROBIN HOOD (Milner & Sowerby, 1865) £350
THE MERRY ADVENTURES OF ROBIN HOOD of Great Renown in Nottinghamshire by Howard Pyle
(Scribner, U.S., 1883)..£300
THE MERRY ADVENTURES OF ROBIN HOOD of Great Renown in Nottinghamshire by Howard Pyle
(Sampson Low, 1883) £50
STORIES OF ROBIN HOOD by H.E. Marshall (illustrated by A.S. Forrest) ('Told to the Children' series, [1905])........................£12
ROBIN HOOD by H. Gilbert (illustrated by Walter Crane) (T.C. & E.C. Jack, 1912) £50
ROBIN HOOD, HIS DEEDS AND ADVENTURES AS RECOUNTED IN OLD ENGLISH BALLADS
(selected and illustrated by Lucy Fitch Perkins) (T.C. & E.C. Jack, [1913]) £100
ROBIN HOOD AND HIS MERRY MEN by E. Charles Vivian (illustrated by Harry G. Theaker) (Ward Lock, [1927]) £30
TALES OF ROBIN HOOD by Enid Blyton (Newnes: 'John O'London's Children's Library' series, [1930]) £30
BOWS AGAINST THE BARONS by Geoffrey Trease (Martin Lawrence, 1934)..£40
THE CHILDREN'S ROBIN HOOD. Retold by Frank H. Lee (Harrap, 1934) £15
THE ADVENTURES OF ROBIN HOOD (tie-in with the film 'The Adventures of Robin Hood', starring Errol Flynn;
eight colour plates) (Ward Lock, [1939]) £25
THE ADVENTURES OF ROBIN HOOD (reissue of the 1939 tie-in edition; eight colour plates) (Ward Lock, [1954] £20
THE CHRONICLES OF ROBIN HOOD by Rosemary Sutcliff (illustrated by C. Walter Hodges) (OUP, 1950)..............................£30
ROBIN HOOD by Antonia Fraser (illustrated by Victor Ambrus) (Weidenfeld & Nicolson: 'Heirloom Library' series, 1955)...........£15

THE ADVENTURES OF ROBIN HOOD. Collected and retold by Roger Lancelyn Green (paperback)
(Penguin, 1956) £10
ROBIN AND HIS MERRY MEN by Ian Serraillier (illustrated by Victor Ambrus) (OUP, 1969) £20
ROBIN OF SHERWOOD by Richard Carpenter (paperback) (Puffin, 1985) £5

'Robin Hood' Comics and Annuals

ROBIN HOOD LIBRARY Nos. 1-88 (First Series) (Aldine, 1901-06) ....each £10
THRILLER COMICS/THRILLER PICTURE LIBRARY
(issues containing comic strip 'Robin Hood Told in Pictures'; 56 in all) (Fleetway, 1951-63) ....each £8
THE ADVENTURES OF ROBIN HOOD NO. 1 (Adprint/Rand McNally, 1956)...£8
THE ADVENTURES OF ROBIN HOOD NO. 2 (Adprint/Rand McNally, 1957)..£8
THE ADVENTURES OF ROBIN HOOD NO. 3 (Adprint, 1958) £8
THE ADVENTURES OF ROBIN HOOD NO. 4 (Adprint, 1959) £8
ROBIN HOOD ANNUAL 1957 (Amalgamated Press, 1956) £10
ROBIN HOOD ANNUAL 1958 (Amalgamated Press, 1957) £10
ROBIN HOOD ANNUAL 1959 (Amalgamated Press, 1958) £10
ROBIN HOOD ANNUAL 1960 (Fleetway, 1959) £10
ROBIN OF SHERWOOD ANNUAL 1986 (World International, 1985) £5

ROBINSON, Charles

British illustrator. Born: London, 1870, son of the wood engraver, Thomas Robinson, and the elder brother of the illustrator, W. Heath Robinson. Studied at Islington High School and Highbury School of Art. Established his reputation with his 1896 edition of Stevenson's *A Child's Garden of Verses*, and went on to illustrate more than 100 further titles. Died: 1937.

Prices are for books in Very Good condition.

Books Written and Illustrated by Charles Robinson

CHRISTMAS DREAMS (written under the pseudonym 'Awfly Weirdly') (Marcus Ward, 1896) £150
THE TEN LITTLE BABIES (SPCK, [1905])..£150
FANCIFUL FOWLS (Dent, 1906) £100
PECULIAR PIGGIES (Dent, 1906) £100
BLACK BUNNIES (Blackie, [1907]) £100
BLACK DOGGIES (Blackie, [1907]) £100
BLACK SAMBOS (Blackie, [1907])..£150

'Picture Books for Children' by Walter Copeland
Illustrated by Charles Robinson

THE BOOK OF THE ZOO (Dent, 1902) £100
THE BLACK CAT BOOK (Blackie, [1905]) £125
THE BOOK OF DUCKS AND DUTCHIES (Blackie, 1905)..£100
THE BOOK OF THE DUTCH DOLLS (Blackie, 1905) £125
THE BOOK OF THE FAN (Blackie, 1905)..£125
THE BOOK OF THE LITTLE JDs (Blackie, 1905) £100
THE BOOK OF THE MANDARINFANTS (Blackie, 1905)..£125
THE BOOK OF THE LITTLE DUTCH DOTS (Blackie, 1905) £125
THE SILLY SUBMARINE (Blackie, 1906)..£100
THE BOOK OF DOLLY'S DOINGS (Blackie, 1906) £125
BOUNCING BABIES (Blackie, 1906) £100
THE BOOK OF DOLLY'S HOUSE (Blackie, 1906)..£125
THE BOOK OF DOLLY-LAND (Blackie, 1906)...£125
AWFUL AIRSHIP (Blackie, 1906) £150
MAD MOTOR (Blackie, 1906) £125
THE SWEET SHOP (Blackie, 1907) £100
THE TOY SHOP (Blackie, 1907) £100
THE CAKE SHOP (Blackie, 1907) £100
BABES AND BLOSSOMS (Blackie, [1908])..£150
THE BOOK OF OTHER PEOPLE (Blackie, 1908) £100
THE BOOK OF SAILORS (Blackie, 1908) £100
THE BOOK OF SOLDIERS (Blackie, 1908) £125

Other Books Illustrated by Charles Robinson

AESOP'S FABLES (Dent: 'Banbury Cross' series, 1895) £100
THE INFANT READER (Macmillan, 1895) £50
THE FIRST PRIMER (Macmillan, 1895) £50
THE SECOND PRIMER (Macmillan, 1895)...£50
A CHILD'S GARDEN OF VERSES by R.L. Stevenson (John Lane: The Bodley Head, 1896 [1895]) £350
A CHILD'S GARDEN OF VERSES by R.L. Stevenson (reissue) (John Lane: The Bodley Head, 1921) £150
ANIMALS IN THE WRONG PLACES by E. Carrington (Bell, 1896) £50
MINSTREL DICK by C.R. Coleridge (Gardner Darton, 1896) £50
MAKE BELIEVE by H.D. Lowry (John Lane, 1896) £50

ROBINSON, Charles

THE CHILD WORLD by G. Setoun (John Lane, 1896) £20
DOBBIES' LITTLE MASTER by Mrs A. Bell (Bell, 1897) £50
LULLABY LAND: Songs of Childhood by E. Field (selected by K. Grahame) (John Lane, 1898 [1897]) £100
KING LONGBEARD by B. MacGregor (John Lane, 1898 [1897]) £50
LILLIPUT LYRICS by W.B. Rands. Edited R. Brimley Johnson (John Lane, 1899 [1898]) £50
THE NEW NOAH'S ARK by J.J. Bell (verse) (John Lane, 1899 [1898]) £50
TALES OF PASSED TIMES by Charles Perrault (Dent: 'Temple Classic for Young People' series, [1899]) £50
THE MASTER MOSAIC-WORKERS by George Sand (twelve illustrations by Charles Robinson; translated by C.C. Johnson)
   (Dent: 'Temple Classics for Young People' series, 1899) £50
FAIRY TALES FROM HANS CHRISTIAN ANDERSEN (illustrated by Charles, Thomas and
   William Heath Robinson; translated by Mrs E. Lucas) (Dent, 1899) £125
CHILD VOICES by William Edward Cule (Andrew Melrose, [1899]) £50
JACK OF ALL TRADES by John Joy Bell (verse) (John Lane, 1900 [1899]) £50
THE SUITORS OF APRILLE by N. Garstin (John Lane, 1900 [1899]) £50
PIERRETTE by H. de Vere Stacpoole (John Lane, 1900 [1899]) £60
THE LITTLE LIVES OF THE SAINTS by Rev Percy Dearmer (Wells Gardner, 1900) £50
SINTRAM AND HIS COMPANIONS by F.H.C. de la Motte Fouque (Dent, 1900) £50
THE TRUE ANNALS OF FAIRYLAND: The Reign of King Herla. Edited by W. Canton (Dent, 1900) £50
THE ADVENTURES OF ODYSSEUS by Homer. Retold by F.S. Marvin, R.J.G. Mayor and F.M. Stawell
   (Dent, [1900]) £50
THE TRUE ANNALS OF FAIRYLAND: The Reign of Old King Cole. Edited by J.M. Gibbon (three volumes)
   (Dent, 1901) ....the set £100
THE BOOK OF DAYS FOR LITTLE ONES by Clare Bridgman (Dent, 1901) £200
THE FARM BOOK FOR LITTLE ONES by Walter Copeland (Dent, [1901]) £175
THE TRUE ANNALS OF FAIRY-LAND: The Reign of King Oberon. Edited by Walter Jerrold (three volumes)
   (Dent, 1902) ....the set £100
STORIES FOR CHILDREN by Charles and Mary Lamb (illustrated by Charles Robinson and W. Green)
   (Dent, 1902) £60
THE BAIRNS CORONATION BOOK by Clare Bridgman (Dent, [1902]) £85
NONSENSE! NONSENSE! by Walter Jerrold (Blackie, 1902) £65
THE SHOPPING DAY by C. Bridgman (Dent, 1902) £55
THE MOTHERS' BOOK OF SONG. Compiled by John Henry Burn (Wells Gardner, [1902]) £30
THE BIG BOOK OF NURSERY RHYMES. Edited by J. Jerrold (Blackie, [1903]) £150
FIRESIDE SAINTS by Douglas W. Jerrold (Blackie, 1903) £20
THE CLOUD KINGDOM by I.H. Wallis (John Lane, [1905]) £35
A BOOKFUL OF FUN (Sealey Clark, [1905]) £45
ROAD, RAIL AND SEA by Clare Jerrold (Blackie, [1906]) £100
BABY TOWN BALLADS by 'Netta' (Sealey Clark, 1906) £50
THE CHILD'S CHRISTMAS by E. Sharp (Blackie, [1906]) £50
THE STORY OF THE WEATHERCOCK by E. Sharp (Blackie, [1907]) £75
PRINCE BABILLON by 'Netta' (Sealey Clark, 1907) £50
ALICE'S ADVENTURES IN WONDERLAND by Lewis Carroll (eight colour plates and 112 other illustrations by
   Charles Robinson) (Cassell, 1907) £150
SONGS OF LOVE AND PRAISE by A. Matheson (Dent, 1907) £40
THE FAIRIES' FOUNTAIN by Countess E. Martinengo-Cesaresco (Fairbairns, 1908) £70
SONGS OF HAPPY CHILDHOOD by I. Maunder (Sealey Clark, 1908) £55
IN THE BEGINNING by S.B. Macy (Sealey Clark, 1910) £50
THE VANISHING PRINCES by N. Syrett (David Nutt, [1910]) £50
BROWNIKINS AND OTHER FANCIES by Ruth Arkwright (music by J.W. Wilson) (Wells Gardner, [1910]) £50
GRIMM'S FAIRY TALES (translated by L.L. Weedon) (Nister: 'Children's Classics' series, [1910]) £50
BABES AND BIRDS by Jessie Pope (Blackie, [1910]) £50
THE SECRET GARDEN by F. Hodgson Burnett (Heinemann, 1911) £350
THE BIG BOOK OF FAIRY TALES. Edited by Walter Jerrold (Blackie, 1911) £200
THE SENSITIVE PLANT by Percy Bysshe Shelley (Heinemann, [1911]) £350
THE BABY SCOUTS by Jessie Pope (Blackie, [1911]) £65
BABES AND BEASTS by Jessie Pope (Blackie, [1912]) £65
THE FOUR GARDENS by 'Handasyde' (Heinemann, 1912) £60
THE BIG BOOK OF FABLES. Edited by Walter Jerrold (Blackie, 1912) £175
BEE, THE PRINCESS OF THE DWARFS by Anatole France (translated by Peter Wright) (Dent, 1912) £50
FAIRY TALES by Charles Perrault (Dent: 'Tales for Children from Many Lands' series, [1913]) £50
MARGARET'S BOOK by H. Fielding-Hall (Hutchinson, [1913]) £150
TOPSY TURVY by W.J. Minnion (The Connoisseur, 1913) £50
THE HAPPY PRINCE and Other Tales by Oscar Wilde (Duckworth, 1913) £250
THE HAPPY PRINCE and Other Tales by Oscar Wilde (limited to 250 copies, signed by the artist; vellum binding)
   (Duckworth, 1913) £1,000
THE OPEN WINDOW by E. Temple Thurston (Chambers, 1913) £35
A CHILD'S BOOK OF EMPIRE by A.T. Morris (Blackie, [1914]) £35
OUR SENTIMENTAL GARDEN by A. and E. Castle (Heinemann, 1914) £75
FROM THE ARABIAN NIGHTS ENTERTAINMENTS: The Story of Prince Ahmed and the Fairy Perie Banou
   (Gay & Hancock, [1915]) £50

SONGS AND SONNETS OF SHAKESPEARE (Duckworth, 1915) £125
WHAT HAPPENED AT CHRISTMAS by Evelyn Sharp (Blackie, [1915])...£55
THE LITTLE HUNCHBACK ZIA by F. Hodgson Burnett (Heinemann, 1916)......................................£60
BRIDGET'S FAIRIES by Mrs M. Stevenson (Religious Tract Society, [1919]) £50
SONGS OF HAPPY CHILDHOOD by I. Maunder (Sealey Clark, 1920)...£50
TEDDY'S YEAR WITH THE FAIRIES by M. Elsie Gullick (Religious Tract Society, [1920]) £60
THE CHILDREN'S GARLAND OF VERSES by G. Rhys (Dent, 1921) £60
FATHER TIME STORIES by John G. Stevenson (Religious Tract Society, [1921]) £25
DORIS AND DAVID ALL ALONE by Elizabeth Marc (Hutchinson, [1922]) £35
ONCE ON A TIME by A.A. Milne (Hodder & Stoughton, [1925])..£120
FATHER TIME STORIES by John G. Stevenson (Religious Tract Society, [1925]) £50
THE SAINT'S GARDEN by W. Radcliffe (Religious Tract Society, 1927) £15
MOTHER GOOSE NURSERY RHYMES (Collins, [1928]) £75
THE RUBAIYAT OF OMAR KHAYYAM (introduction by Laurence Housman; translated by Edward Fitzgerald)
      (Collins, [1928]) £100
GRANNY'S BOOK OF FAIRY STORIES (Blackie, 1930)...£50
YOUNG HOPEFUL by Jennie Dunbar (Herbert Jenkins, 1932) £50

ROBINSON, W. Heath

British author-illustrator. Born: William Heath Robinson in London in 1872, the son of the wood engraver, Thomas Robinson, and the younger brother of the illustrator, Charles Robinson. Studied at the Islington School of Art and the Royal Academy Schools. His first important works were editions of *Don Quixote* and Hans Andersen's *Fairy Tales* (both 1897), but his distinctive style was first evident in the illustrations for his own comic tale, *The Adventures of Uncle Lubin* (1902). Wrote and illustrated several more children's books, but is perhaps best known for the weird and wonderful 'inventions' he drew for the *Strand* magazine. Died: 1944.

Prices are for books in Very Good condition.

DANISH FAIRY TALES AND LEGENDS by H.C. Andersen (sixteen illustrations by W. Heath Robinson)
      (Sands, 1897)..£100
THE LIFE AND EXPLOITS OF DON QUIXOTE by Cervantes (sixteen illustrations by W. Heath Robinson)
      (Sands, 1897)..£100
THE PILGRIM'S PROGRESS by John Bunyan (24 illustrations by W. Heath Robinson) (Sands, 1897) £75
THE GIANT CRAB and Other Tales from Old India by W.H.D. Rouse (David Nutt, 1897) £350
THE QUEEN'S STORY BOOK. Edited by L. Gomme (Constable, 1898) £60
THE ARABIAN NIGHTS ENTERTAINMENTS (Newnes/Constable, 1899) £100
FAIRY TALES FROM HANS CHRISTIAN ANDERSEN (illustrated by W. Heath Robinson,
      Charles Robinson and Thomas Heath Robinson) (Dent, 1899)...£125
THE TALKING THRUSH by William Crooke (Dent, 1899)..£300
TALES FOR TOBY by A.R. Hope (Dent, 1900)..£50
THE ADVENTURES OF DON QUIXOTE OF LA MANCHA by Cervantes (Dent, 1902) £80
MEDIAEVAL STORIES by J.H.E. Schuck (Sands, 1902)..£70
THE ADVENTURES OF UNCLE LUBIN (Grant Richards, 1902) £350
THE ADVENTURES OF UNCLE LUBIN (new edition) (Grant Richards, 1925) £100
THE SURPRISING TRAVELS AND ADVENTURES OF BARON MUNCHAUSEN by R.E. Raspe
      (Grant Richards, 1902)..£100
RAMA AND THE MONKEYS. Edited by G. Hodgson (Dent, 1903) £70
THE CHILD'S ARABIAN NIGHTS (Grant Richards, 1903) £250
STORIES FROM THE ILIAD. Edited by Jeanie Lang (T.C. & E.C. Jack, [1906]) £40
STORIES FROM THE ODYSSEY. Edited by Jeanie Lang (T.C. & E.C. Jack, [1906]).......................£40
THE MONARCHS OF MERRY ENGLAND by Roland Carse (Cooke, [1908])...................................£175
MORE MONARCHS OF MERRY ENGLAND by Roland Carse (Unwin, [1908]) £175
THE MONARCHS OF MERRY ENGLAND and MORE MONARCHS OF MERRY ENGLAND by Roland Carse
      (four parts; ten plates by W. Heath Robinson in each) (Unwin, [1908])..................the set £225
A SONG OF THE ENGLISH by Rudyard Kipling (thirty colour plates by W. Heath Robinson)
      (Hodder & Stoughton, 1909) £300
THE COLLECTED VERSE OF RUDYARD KIPLING (Doubleday Page, U.S., 1910)...........................£200
BILL THE MINDER (Constable, 1912) £450
BILL THE MINDER (De Luxe edition: limited to 380 copies, signed by the author; vellum binding)
      (Constable, 1912) £1,500
HANS ANDERSEN'S FAIRY TALES (Constable, 1913) £600
HANS ANDERSEN'S FAIRY TALES (De Luxe edition: limited to 100 copies; vellum binding)
      (Constable, 1913) £3,000
THE WATER BABIES by Charles Kingsley (Constable, 1915) £175
PEACOCK PIE by Walter de la Mare (Constable, [1916]) £75
GET ON WITH IT (cartoons) (Robinson & Birch, [1920]) £130
OLD TIME STORIES by Charles Perrault (Constable, 1921) £300
FLY PAPERS (cartoons) (Duckworth, [1921]) £80
THE HOME-MADE CAR (Duckworth, [1921])...£125
PETER QUIP IN SEARCH OF A FRIEND (Partridge, [1922]) £750

ROBINSON, W. Heath

HANS ANDERSEN'S FAIRY TALES (new edition) (Hodder & Stoughton, [1923]) **£100**
TOPSY TURVY TALES by E.S. Munro (John Lane: The Bodley Head, 1923) **£100**
BILL THE MINDER (Hodder & Stoughton, [1924]) **£10**
HANS ANDERSEN'S FAIRY TALES (Boots edition; reissue of 1923 edition) (Hodder & Stoughton, [1927]) **£80**

*One of the plates from the hugely successful **Bill the Minder** (1912), which was both written and illustrated by W. Heath Robinson.*

THE INCREDIBLE ADVENTURES OF PROFESSOR BRANESTAWM by Norman Hunter
(24 illustrations by W. Heath Robinson) (John Lane: The Bodley Head, 1933) £160
HEATH ROBINSON'S BOOK OF GOBLINS (contains stories from F.T. Vernaleken's 'In the Land of Marvels')
(Hutchinson, [1934]) £150
MY LINE OF LIFE (autobiography) (Blackie, 1938) £150
LET'S LAUGH: A Book of Humorous Inventions (Hutchinson, [1939]) £40
STORIES OF PROFESSOR BRANESTAWM by Norman Hunter (card wraps) (Arnold, [1939]) £40
ONCE UPON A TIME by L.M.C. Clopet (Muller, 1944) £175

'ROSEBUD' ANNUALS

Early British annual published by James Clark. It was the first annual to contain the work of the celebrated cat artist, Louis Wain.

Prices are for annuals in Very Good condition. Annuals containing illustrations by Louis Wain sell for up to four times this price.

THE ROSEBUD ANNUAL 1889 [1890] — Onwards [c.1915] .... each £40

ROSS, Diana

British author. Born: Malta, 1910. Well known for her 'Little Red Engine' series, illustrated by herself and signed 'Gri'. Died: 2000.

Prices are for books in Very Good condition with dustjackets where applicable.

'Little Red Engine' Books

THE LITTLE RED ENGINE GETS A NAME (illustrated by George Lewitt-Him) (Faber, 1942) £30
THE STORY OF THE LITTLE RED ENGINE (illustrated by Leslie Wood) (Faber, 1945).............................. £30
THE LITTLE RED ENGINE GOES TO MARKET (illustrated by Leslie Wood) (Faber, 1946) £20
THE LITTLE RED ENGINE GOES TO TOWN (illustrated by Leslie Wood) (Faber, 1952) £20
THE LITTLE RED ENGINE GOES TRAVELLING (illustrated by Leslie Wood) (Faber, 1955)...................... £20
THE LITTLE RED ENGINE AND THE ROCKET (illustrated by Leslie Wood) (Faber, 1956)....................... £20
THE LITTLE RED ENGINE GOES HOME (illustrated by Leslie Wood) (Faber, 1958).............................. £20
THE LITTLE RED ENGINE GOES TO BE MENDED (illustrated by Leslie Wood) (Faber, 1966) £20
THE LITTLE RED ENGINE AND THE TADDLECOMBE OUTING (illustrated by Leslie Wood) (Faber, 1968) £20
THE LITTLE RED ENGINE GOES CAROLLING (illustrated by Leslie Wood) (Faber, 1971) £20

Others

THE WORLD AT WORK: Getting You Things (Country Life, 1939) £35
THE WORLD AT WORK: Making You Things (Country Life, 1939).. £35
THE STORY OF THE BEETLE WHO LIVED ALONE (illustrated by Margaret Kaye) (Faber, 1941) £25
UNCLE ANTY'S ALBUM (illustrated by Antony Denny) (Faber, 1941) £25
THE GOLDEN HEN and Other Stories (illustrated by Gri) (Faber, 1942) £25
THE WILD CHERRY (illustrated by Gri) (Faber, 1943) £25
NURSERY TALES (illustrated by Nancy Innes) (Faber, 1944) £25
THE STORY OF LOUISA (illustrated by Margaret Kaye) (Penguin, 1945).. £25
WHOO, WHOO, THE WIND BLEW (illustrated by Leslie Wood) (Faber, 1946)... £15
THE TOOTER and Other Nursery Tales (illustrated by Irene Hawkins) (Faber, 1951) £15
THE ENORMOUS APPLE PIE AND OTHER MISS PUSSY TALES (illustrated by Peggy Fortnum) (Lutterworth Press, 1951) ..£25
EBENEZER THE BIG BALLOON (illlustrated by Leslie Wood) (Faber, 1952) £20
THE BRIDAL GOWN and Other Stories (illustrated by Gri) (Faber, 1952) £15
THE BRAN TUB (illustrated by Gri) (Lutterworth Press, 1954)... £15
WILLIAM AND THE LORRY (illustrated by Shiley Hughes) (Faber, 1956).. £15
CHILD OF AIR (illustrated by Gri) (Lutterworth Press, 1957)... £15
THE DREADFUL BOY (illustrated by Prudence Seward) (Hamish Hamilton, 1959) £15
THE MERRY-GO-ROUND (illustrated by Shirley Hughes) (Lutterworth Press, 1963) £15
OLD PERISHER (illustrated by Edward Ardizzone) (Faber, 1965) £30
NOTHING TO DO (illustrated by Constance Marshall) (Hamish Hamilton, 1966)...................................... £15
I LOVE MY LIFE WITH AN A: WHERE IS HE? (illustrated by Leslie Wood) (Faber, 1972)......................... £15

ROSSETTI, Christina

British poet. Born: Christina Georgina Rossetti in London in 1830, the younger sister of the poet and painter, D.G. Rossetti. She contributed some verses to the Pre-Raphaelite journal, *The Germ*, and published her first collection, *Goblin Market and Other Poems*, in 1862. The title-poem has become something of a children's classic, and has been illustrated by Arthur Rackham (1933) amongst others. She also wrote the well-known hymn, 'In the bleak mid winter'. Died: 1894.

Prices are for books in Very Good condition.

GOBLIN MARKET and Other Poems (illustrated by D.G. Rossetti) (Macmillan, 1862) £1,000
THE PRINCE'S PROGRESS and Other Poems (illustrated by D.G. Rossetti) (Macmillan, 1866) £500
SING-SONG: A Nursery Rhyme Book (illustrated by Arthur Hughes) (Macmillan, 1872) £400
SPEAKING LIKENESSES (illustrated by Arthur Hughes) (Macmillan, 1874) £100
MAUDE: A Story for Girls (introduction by W.M. Rossetti) (Bowden, 1897) £40

ROWLING, J.K.

British author. Born: Chepstow, Kent, in 1965. After Exeter University she worked for Amnesty International and later taught English in Portugal. She now lives in Edinburgh. Her numerous British and foreign awards for each of her first three 'Harry Potter' books include the British Book Awards' Children's Book of the Year, 1997, 1998 and 1999, and the Nestle Smarties Book Prize 9-11 years, 1997, 1998 and 1999. She was the bestselling author of 1999 in the U.K. Awarded the OBE in 2000.

Prices are for books in Very Good condition with dustjackets where applicable.

HARRY POTTER AND THE PHILOSOPHER'S STONE (print-run of 500 copies; laminated boards;
issued without dustjacket) (Bloomsbury, 1997)...£8,000
HARRY POTTER AND THE PHILOSOPHER'S STONE (paperback: standard cover)
(Bloomsbury, 1997) £75
HARRY POTTER AND THE PHILOSOPHER'S STONE (paperback: 'adult' cover)
(Bloomsbury, 1997) £75
HARRY POTTER AND THE PHILOSOPHER'S STONE (collectors' edition: limited to 4,000 copies)
(Bloomsbury, 1999) £60
HARRY POTTER AND THE PHILOSOPHER'S STONE (uncorrected proof: limited to 200 copies)
(Bloomsbury, 1997)...£2,000
HARRY POTTER AND THE CHAMBER OF SECRETS (Bloomsbury, 1998) £1,000
HARRY POTTER AND THE CHAMBER OF SECRETS (paperback: standard cover) (Bloomsbury, 1998) £20
HARRY POTTER AND THE CHAMBER OF SECRETS (paperback: 'adult' cover) (Bloomsbury, 1998) £20
HARRY POTTER AND THE CHAMBER OF SECRETS (collectors' edition: limited to 4,000 copies)
(Bloomsbury, 1999) £60
HARRY POTTER AND THE CHAMBER OF SECRETS (uncorrected proof: limited to approximately 300 copies)
(Bloomsbury, 1998)...£1,500
HARRY POTTER AND THE PRISONER OF AZKABAN (first printing, first state: 'Joanne Rowling'
on verso of title-page, text misalignment p7) (Bloomsbury, 1999)...£75
HARRY POTTER AND THE PRISONER OF AZKABAN (first printing, second state: 'J.K. Rowling'
on verso of title-page) (Bloomsbury, 1999) £25
HARRY POTTER AND THE PRISONER OF AZKABAN (trade hardback: first printing, third state: 'J.K. Rowling'
on verso of title-page, printer's name omitted, adverts at rear) (Bloomsbury, 1999).......................................£25

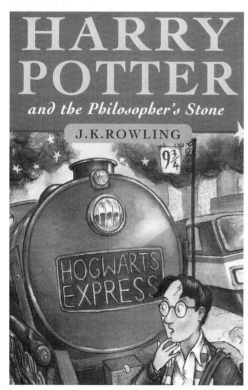

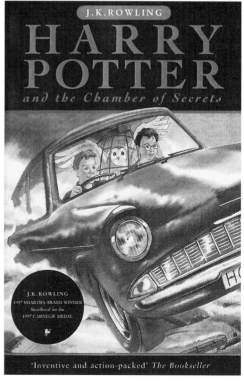

*There were only 500 copies of the first edition of **Harry Potter and the Philosopher's Stone**, issued in laminated boards.*

*The dustjacket from the first edition of **Harry Potter and the Chamber of Secrets**, the second book in the popular series.*

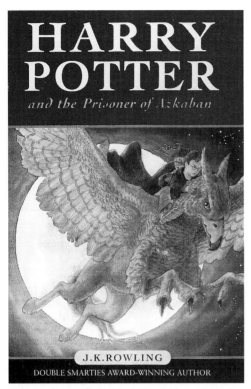

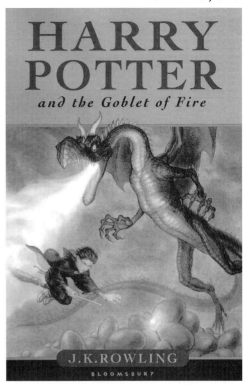

*The first edition of the third book, **The Prisoner of Azkaban**, is now valued at £75 in Very Good condition with the jacket.*

*The fourth book, **The Goblet of Fire**, had an initial print-run of one million copies, and these are now worth only £5.*

HARRY POTTER AND THE PRISONER OF AZKABAN (paperback: standard cover)
(Bloomsbury, 2000) £6
HARRY POTTER AND THE PRISONER OF AZKABAN (paperback: 'adult' cover) (Bloomsbury, 2000) £7
HARRY POTTER AND THE PRISONER OF AZKABAN (collectors' edition: limited to 1,000 copies)
(Bloomsbury, 1999) £300
HARRY POTTER AND THE PRISONER OF AZKABAN (uncorrected proof: first state, limited to approximately 50 copies)
(Bloomsbury, 1999) £1,500
HARRY POTTER AND THE PRISONER OF AZKABAN (uncorrected proof: second state, limited to approximately 250 copies)
(Bloomsbury, 1999) £1,000
HARRY POTTER AND THE GOBLET OF FIRE (Bloomsbury, 2000) £5

'RUPERT' ANNUALS

Popular series of annuals published by the *Daily Express* and featuring the adventures of Rupert Bear. The character was the creation of Mary Tourtel and first appeared in the paper on 8th November 1920. The 'Rupert' annuals were launched in 1936, one year after the strip had been taken over by Alfred Bestall (1892-1986). Since 1976, it has been drawn by John Harrold.

Prices are for books and annuals in Very Good condition.

'Rupert' Annuals

1936 (with dustjacket) (Daily Express) **£2,800**	**1960-66** ('Magic Painting' pages coloured in)	
1936 (without dustjacket) (Daily Express) **£400**	(Daily Express)..each **£40**	
1937 & 1938 (Daily Express) ....each **£400**	**1967-68** ('Magic Painting' pages coloured in)	
1939-41 (Daily Express) ....each **£500**	(Daily Express)..each **£30**	
1942 (wraps) (Daily Express) **£600**	**1960-66** ('Magic Painting' pages not coloured in)	
1943 (wraps) (Daily Express) **£400**	(Daily Express)..each **£100**	
1944 (wraps) (Daily Express) **£250**	**1967-68** ('Magic Painting' pages not coloured in)	
1945 (wraps) (Daily Express) **£200**	(Daily Express)..each **£100**	
1946 & 1947 (wraps) (Daily Express).....................each **£200**	**1969** (Daily Express)..**£20**	
1948 & 1949 (wraps) (Daily Express)........................each **£150**	**1970-89** (Daily Express)...each **£10**	
1950-54 (boards) (Daily Express)........................each **£125**	**1990-98** (Daily Express)..each **£10**	
1955-59 (boards) (Daily Express)...............................each **£75**	**1999** (Daily Express)..**£5**	

Facsimiles (prices are for annuals in Mint condition with dustjackets/slipcases where applicable)

1936 (issued with dustjacket) (Daily Express, 1985).........£120
1937 (Daily Express, 1986) £80
1938 (Daily Express, 1989) £100
1939 (Daily Express, 1991) £30
1940 & 1941 (Pedigree, 1992 & 1993).......................each £30

1942 (in slipcase) (Pedigree, 1994) £80
1943 (in slipcase) (Pedigree, 1995) £40
1944 (in slipcase) (Pedigree, 1996) £35
1945 (in slipcase) (Pedigree, 1997) £40
1948-50 (in slipcase)(Pedigree, 1998-2000) ....each £20

'Monster Rupert' Books (with cover description)

1931 (Rupert watching wolf leap from bed) (Sampson Low, no date) £900
1932 (Rupert sitting on a log) (Sampson Low, no date) £800
1933 (Rupert being hidden by female bird) (Sampson Low, no date)..£800
1934 (Rupert and small boy in storeroom) (Sampson Low, no date) £800

'The Monster Rupert' Books (with cover description)

1948 (Rupert sitting on a log; with dustjacket) (Sampson Low, no date) £80
1949 (Rupert watching fox leap from bed; with dustjacket) (Sampson Low, no date)..£100
1950 (Rupert helping small boy out of hole; issued with dustjacket) (Sampson Low, no date) £60

'Adventure' Series

NO. 1 (Daily Express) £40
NOS. 2-9 (Daily Express) ....each £20
NO. 10 (Daily Express) £25
NOS. 11-20 (Daily Express) ....each £20
NOS. 21-30 (Daily Express) ....each £25
NOS. 31-35 (Daily Express) ....each £30

NOS. 36-40 (Daily Express).........................each £35
NOS. 41-46 (Daily Express).........................each £50
NOS. 47-48 (Daily Express).........................each £70
NO. 49 (Daily Express) £100
NO. 50 (Daily Express) £120

RUSKIN, John

British author. Born: Surrey, 1819. Studied at Christ Church, Oxford. The celebrated critic and philosopher wrote only two children's books, the first, *The King of the Golden River* (1851), was one of the earliest English fantasies for children. He was a friend of, and influence on, the children's artist, Kate Greenaway. Died: 1900.

Prices are for books in Very Good condition.

THE KING OF THE GOLDEN RIVER, or The Black Brothers: A Legend of Stiria (illustrated by Richard Doyle)
(Smith Elder, 1851) £600
THE KING OF THE GOLDEN RIVER (illustrated by Arthur Rackham) (Harrap, 1932) £125
THE KING OF THE GOLDEN RIVER (illustrated by Arthur Rackham; limited to 750 copies, signed by the artist)
(Harrap, 1932) £550
THE ETHICS OF THE DUST (Smith Elder, 1866)..£625
DAME WIGGINS OF LEE AND HER SEVEN WONDERFUL CATS. Edited from the original 1823 version by John Ruskin
(illustrated by Kate Greenaway and others; with original verses by John Ruskin) (George Allen, 1885) £150

RYAN, John

British author. Born: Edinburgh, 1921. Began as art master at Harrow and later became a cartoonist for the *Catholic Herald*. Created the popular children's animated TV series, *Captain Pugwash*.

Prices are for books in Very Good condition with dustjackets where applicable.

Books Written and Illustrated by John Ryan

CAPTAIN PUGWASH (The Bodley Head, 1957) £40
PUGWASH ALOFT (The Bodley Head, 1958) £35
PUGWASH AND THE GHOST SHIP (The Bodley Head, 1962)...£30
PUGWASH IN THE PACIFIC (The Bodley Head, 1973) £25
CAPTAIN PUGWASH ANNUAL 1976 (World Distributors, 1975) £20
DODO'S DELIGHT or Doodle and the State Secret (Deutsch, 1977) £10
DOODLE'S HOMEWORK (Deutsch, 1978) £5
CROCKLE AND THE KITE (Hamlyn, 1980) £10
ALL ABOARD (Hamlyn, 1980) £10
PUGWASH AND THE FANCY-DRESS PARTY (The Bodley Head, 1982) £20
CAPTAIN PUGWASH: THE QUEST OF THE GOLDEN HANDSHAKE (The Bodley Head, 1983) £20
CAPTAIN PUGWASH: THE BATTLE OF BUNKUM BAY (pictorial boards; illustrated by the author)
(The Bodley Head, 1984)..£15
PUGWASH AND THE MIDNIGHT FEAST and PUGWASH AND THE WRECKERS (paperback)
(Puffin, 1986) £10
EAGLE CLASSICS – HARRIS TWEED, EXTRA SPECIAL AGENT (Hawk Books, 1990) £6
CAPTAIN PUGWASH AND THE HUGE REWARD (Gungarden Books, 1991) £10
THE CAPTAIN PUGWASH COLLECTION (Ted Smart, 1992)...£10
FATSO THE FATHEAD (The Bodley Head, 1993) £10
MUDGE THE SMUGGLER (Macmillan, 1995) £10
GIANT-KILLER: The Story of David and Goliath and the Man who Carried the Shield (Lion Picture Story, 1995)....................£5

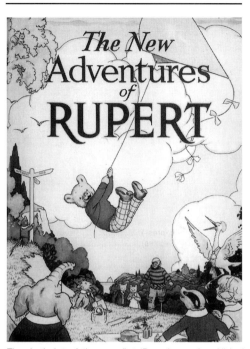

The dustjacket of the very first 'Rupert' annual, published in 1936 under the title, **The New Adventures of Rupert**.

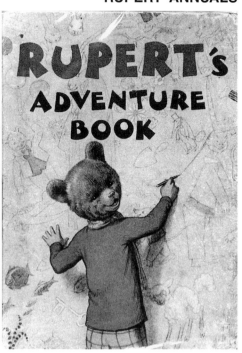

There were a total of fifty Rupert 'Adventure Books', with values now ranging from £20 to £120 for Very Good copies.

Unusually, it's the later 'Rupert Adventure Books' that now sell for most. This one is worth £50 in Very Good condition.

On the cover of the 1973 annual, Rupert was given a white face, much to the chagrin of author-artist, Alfred Bestall.

SAINT-EXUPÉRY, Antoine de

French author. Born: Lyons, France, in 1900. Was a commercial pilot during the 1930s and '40s, drawing on his experiences for several adult novels about aviation. His only children's book, *The Little Prince* (1943), was first published in America, in both French and English. Saint-Exupéry died whilst on a reconnaissance flight in 1944.

Prices are for books in Very Good condition with dustjackets..

THE LITTLE PRINCE (illustrated by the author; translated by Katherine Woods) (Reynel & Hitchcock, U.S., 1943) **£350**
THE LITTLE PRINCE (illustrated by the author; translated by Katherine Woods; limited to 500 copies)
(Reynel & Hitchcock, U.S., 1943) **£1,400**
THE LITTLE PRINCE (illustrated by the author; translated by Katherine Woods) (Heinemann, 1945) **£300**

SAVILLE, Malcolm

British author. Born: Leonard Malcolm Saville in Hastings, Sussex, in 1901. Educated privately, subsequently working for Amalgamated Press and the publishers, Cassell and George Newnes. Wrote a large number of children's books, but is best-known for the series featuring a group of children known as the 'Lone Piners' who were introduced in his first novel, *Mystery at Witchend* (1943). Died: 1982.

Prices are for books in Very Good condition with dustjackets.

'Lone Pine' Books

MYSTERY AT WITCHEND (illustrated by G.E. Breary) (Newnes, 1943) **£125**
SEVEN WHITE GATES (illustrated by Bertram Prance) (Newnes, 1944)..**£90**
THE GAY DOLPHIN ADVENTURE (illustrated by Bertram Prance) (Newnes, 1945) **£90**
THE SECRET OF GREY WALLS (illustrated by Bertram Prance) (Newnes, 1947)..**£75**
LONE PINE FIVE (illustrated by Bertram Prance) (Newnes, 1949) **£70**
THE ELUSIVE GRASSHOPPER (illustrated by Bertram Prance) (Newnes, 1951) **£75**
THE NEGLECTED MOUNTAIN (illustrated by Bertram Prance) (Newnes, 1953) **£75**
SAUCERS OVER THE MOOR (illustrated by Bertram Prance) (Newnes, 1955) **£75**
WINGS OVER WITCHEND (Newnes, 1956) **£50**
LONE PINE LONDON (Newnes, 1957) **£50**
THE SECRET OF THE GORGE (Newnes, 1958) **£50**
MYSTERY MINE (Newnes, 1959) **£50**
SEA WITCH COMES HOME (Newnes, 1960) **£50**
NOT SCARLET BUT GOLD (illustrated by A.R. Whitear) (Newnes, 1962) **£50**
TREASURE AT AMORYS (illustrated by T.R. Freeman) (Newnes, 1964) **£55**
MAN WITH THREE FINGERS (illustrated by Michael Whittlesea) (Newnes, 1966) **£75**
RYE ROYAL (Collins, 1969)..**£70**
STRANGERS AT WITCHEND (Collins, 1970) **£50**
WHERE'S MY GIRL (Collins, 1972) **£75**
HOME TO WITCHEND (paperback) (Armada, 1978) **£20**
HOME TO WITCHEND (Severn House, 1979) **£80**

'Jilly Family' Books

REDSHANK'S WARNING (illustrated by Lunt Roberts) (Lutterworth Press, 1948) **£40**
TWO FAIR PLAITS (illustrated by Lunt Roberts) (Lutterworth Press, 1948) **£40**
STRANGERS AT SNOWFELL (illustrated by Wynne) (Lutterworth Press, 1949) **£40**
THE SIGN OF THE ALPINE ROSE (illustrated by Wynne) (Lutterworth Press, 1950)..**£30**
THE LUCK OF SALLOWBY (illustrated by Tidden Reeves) (Lutterworth Press, 1952)..**£30**
THE AMBERMERE TREASURE (illustrated by Marcia Lane Foster) (Lutterworth Press, 1953)..................................**£35**

'Buckingham Family' Books

THE MASTER OF MARYKNOLL (illustrated by Alice Bush) (Evans, 1950) **£40**
THE BUCKINGHAMS AT RAVENSWYKE (illustrated by Alice Bush) (Evans, 1952) **£40**
THE LONG PASSAGE (illustrated by Alice Bush) (Evans, [1954])...**£40**
A PALACE FOR THE BUCKINGHAMS (illustrated by Alice Bush) (Evans, 1963)..**£50**
THE SECRET OF VILLA ROSA (Collins, 1971) **£35**
DIAMONDS IN THE SKY (Collins, 1974) **£40**

'Marston Baines' Books

THREE TOWERS IN TUSCANY (Heinemann, 1963) **£30**
THE PURPLE VALLEY (Heinemann, 1964) **£30**
DARK DANGER (Heinemann, 1965) **£30**
WHITE FIRE (Heinemann, 1966) **£50**
POWER OF THREE (Heinemann, 1968)..**£35**
THE DAGGER AND THE FLAME (Heinemann, 1970) **£35**
MARSTON MASTER SPY (Heinemann, 1978) **£55**

The Gay Dolphin Adventure (1945) was the third novel in Malcolm Saville's enduringly popular 'Lone Pine' series.

The first edition of The Neglected Mountain (1953) features this atmospheric dustjacket designed by Bertram Prance.

'Mike and Mary' Books

TROUBLE AT TOWNSEND (illustrated by Lunt Roberts) (Transatlantic Arts, 1945) £30
THE RIDDLE OF THE PAINTED BOX (illustrated by Lunt Roberts) (Carrington, 1947) £30
THE FLYING FISH ADVENTURE (illustrated by Lunt Roberts) (John Murray, 1950)..............................£30
WHERE THE BUS STOPPED (Blackwell, 1955 [1956]) £80
THE FOURTH KEY (illustrated by Lunt Roberts) (John Murray, 1957)...£30

'Susan and Bill' Books

SUSAN, BILL AND THE WOLF-DOG (illustrated by E.H. Shepard) (Nelson, 1954) £35
SUSAN, BILL AND THE IVY-CLAD OAK (illustrated by E.H. Shepard) (Nelson, 1954) £35
SUSAN, BILL AND THE VANISHING BOY (illustrated by E.H. Shepard) (Nelson, 1955) £35
SUSAN, BILL AND THE GOLDEN CLOCK (illustrated by E.H. Shepard) (Nelson, 1955) £35
SUSAN, BILL AND THE DARK STRANGER (illustrated by E.H. Shepard) (Nelson, 1956) £35
SUSAN, BILL AND THE 'SAUCY KATE' (illustrated by E.H. Shepard) (Nelson, [1956])........................£35
SUSAN, BILL AND THE BRIGHT STAR CIRCUS (illustrated by T.R. Freeman) (Nelson, [1960]) £35
SUSAN, BILL AND THE PIRATES BOLD (illustrated by T.R. Freeman) (Nelson, [1961]) £35

'Nettleford' Books

ALL SUMMER THROUGH (illustrated by Joan Kiddell-Monroe) (Hodder & Stoughton, 1951) £30
CHRISTMAS AT NETTLEFORD (illustrated by Joan Kiddell-Monroe) (Hodder & Stoughton, 1953).....£30
SPRING COMES TO NETTLEFORD (illustrated by Joan Kiddell-Monroe) (Hodder & Stoughton, 1954) ...£30
THE SECRET OF BUZZARD SCAR (illustrated by Joan Kiddell-Monroe) (Hodder & Stoughton, 1955) ...£30

'Lucy and Humf' Books

FOUR-AND-TWENTY BLACKBIRDS (illustrated by Lilian Buchanan) (Newnes, 1959) £45
THE SECRET GALLEYBIRD PIT (adapted from 'Four-and-Twenty Blackbirds'; paperback) (Armada, 1968) £8
GOOD DOG DANDY (paperback) (Armada, 1971)...£10
GOOD DOG DANDY (hardback) (White Lion, 1977) £25
THE ROMAN TREASURE MYSTERY (paperback) (Armada, 1973) £20

Others

COUNTRY SCRAPBOOK FOR BOYS AND GIRLS (non-fiction) (National Magazine Co, [1944]).............£20
COUNTRY SCRAPBOOK FOR BOYS AND GIRLS (non-fiction; revised and enlarged edition) (Gramol, 1945) £20
OPEN AIR SCRAPBOOK FOR BOYS AND GIRLS (non-fiction) (Gramol, [1945])..................................£20
SEASIDE SCRAPBOOK FOR BOYS AND GIRLS (non-fiction) (Gramol, 1946)......................................£20

SAVILLE, Malcolm

JANE'S COUNTRY YEAR (non-fiction; illustrated by Bernard Bowerman) (Newnes, 1946) £35
THE ADVENTURE OF THE LIFEBOAT SERVICE (non-fiction) (Macdonald, 1950) £30
CORONATION GIFT BOOK FOR BOYS AND GIRLS (non-fiction) (Daily Graphic/Pitkin, 1952) £25
THE SECRET OF THE HIDDEN POOL (illustrated by Lunt Roberts) (John Murray, 1953) £30
YOUNG JOHNNIE BIMBO (illustrated by Lunt Roberts) (John Murray, 1956) £30
READ ALOUD TALES FOR SUNNY STORIES. Edited by Malcom Saville (Newnes, 1956) £10
TREASURE AT THE MILL (illustrated by Harry Pettit) (Newnes, 1957) £40
KING OF KINGS (non-fiction) (Nelson, [1958]) £25
KING OF KINGS (non-fiction; revised edition) (Lion, 1975) £20
SMALL CREATURES (non-fiction; illustrated by John T. Kenney) (Edmund Ward, 1959) £35
MALCOLM SAVILLE'S COUNTRY BOOK (non-fiction) (Cassell, 1961) £20
MALCOLM SAVILLE'S SEASIDE BOOK (non-fiction) (Cassell, 1962) £20
THE THIN GREY MAN (illustrated by Desmond Knight) (Macmillan, 1966) £35
STRANGE STORY (Mowbray, 1967) £25
COME TO LONDON: A Personal Introduction to the World's Greatest City (non-fiction) (Heinemann 1967) £25
COME TO DEVON (non-fiction) (Benn 1969) £25
COME TO CORNWALL (non-fiction) (Benn, 1969) £25
COME TO SOMERSET (non-fiction) (Benn, 1970) £25
SEE HOW IT GROWS (non-fiction; illustrated by Robert Micklewright) (OUP, 1971) £25
EAT WHAT YOU GROW (non-fiction; illustrated by Robert Micklewright; paperback) (Carousel, 1975).....£15
PORTRAIT OF RYE (non-fiction; illustrated by Michael Renton; paperback) (Goulden, 1976) £25
DISCOVERING THE WOODLAND (non-fiction; illustrated by Elsie Wrigley; paperback) (Carousel, 1978) £10
COUNTRYSIDE QUIZ (non-fiction; illustrated by Robert Micklewright; paperback) (Carousel, 1978) £8
THE WONDER WHY BOOK OF EXPLORING A WOOD (non-fiction; paperback) (Transworld, 1979) £8
THE WONDER WHY BOOK OF EXPLORING THE SEASIDE (non-fiction; paperback) (Transworld, 1979).......£8
WORD OF ALL SEASONS (non-fiction; illustrated by E. and P. Wrigley) (Lutterworth Press, 1979).........£30

SCARRY, Richard

American author-illustrator. Born: Richard McClure Scarry in Boston, Massachusetts, in 1919. Has produced many large format 'picture books', distinguished by their vast range of animal characters and well-filled pages. Died: 1994.

Prices are for books in Very Good to Fine condition with dustjackets where applicable.

THE ANIMALS' MERRY CHRISTMAS by Kathryn Jackson (Simon & Schuster, U.S., 1950) £40
THE ANIMALS' MERRY CHRISTMAS by Kathryn Jackson (Collins, 1977) £5
THE GREAT BIG CAR AND TRUCK BOOK (Simon & Schuster, U.S., 1951)...£25
RABBIT AND HIS FRIENDS (Simon & Schuster, U.S., 1953) £30
RABBIT AND HIS FRIENDS (Muller, 1954) £25
NURSERY TALES (Simon & Schuster, U.S., 1958) £18
NAUGHTY BUNNY (Golden Press, U.S., 1959) £22
NAUGHTY BUNNY (Muller, 1959) £18
TINKER AND TANKER (Doubleday, U.S., 1960) £18
TINKER AND TANKER (Hamlyn, 1969) £12
TINKER AND TANKER OUT WEST (Doubleday, U.S., 1961) £18
TINKER AND TANKER OUT WEST (Hamlyn, 1969) £12
TINKER AND TANKER AND THE PIRATES (Doubleday, U.S., 1961) £18
TINKER AND TANKER AND THEIR SPACE SHIP (Doubleday, U.S., 1961) £18
MANNERS (Golden Press, U.S., 1962)...£18
TINKER AND TANKER, KNIGHTS OF THE ROUND TABLE (Doubleday, U.S., 1963) £18
TINKER AND TANKER, KNIGHTS OF THE ROUND TABLE (Hamlyn, 1969)..£12
TINKER AND TANKER IN AFRICA (Doubleday, U.S., 1963) £18
TINKER AND TANKER IN AFRICA (Hamlyn, 1969) £12
A TINKER AND TANKER COLOURING BOOK (Doubleday, U.S., 1963) £12
BEST WORD BOOK EVER (Golden Press, U.S., 1963) £18
BEST WORD BOOK EVER (Hamlyn, 1964) £12
WHAT ANIMALS DO (Golden Press, U.S., 1963) £18
THE ROOSTER STRUTS (Golden Press, U.S., 1963) £18
THE ROOSTER STRUTS (as 'The Golden Happy Book of Animals') (Golden Press, U.S., 1964) £12
THE ROOSTER STRUTS (as 'Animals') (Hamlyn, 1964) £10
POLITE ELEPHANT (Golden Press, U.S., 1964) £18
IS THIS THE HOUSE OF MISTRESS MOUSE? (Golden Press, U.S., 1964) £18
ANIMAL MOTHER GOOSE (Golden Press, U.S., 1964) £18
ANIMAL MOTHER GOOSE (Hamlyn, 1965) £12
BEST NURSERY RHYMES EVER (Golden Press, U.S., 1964) £18
BEST NURSERY RHYMES EVER (Hamlyn, 1971) £12
TEENY TINY TALES (Golden Press, U.S., 1965) £18
TEENY TINY TALES (Hamlyn, 1970) £12
THE SANTA CLAUS BOOK (Golden Press, U.S., 1965) £18
THE BUNNY BOOK (Golden Press, U.S., 1965) £18

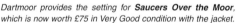

*Dartmoor provides the setting for **Saucers Over the Moor**, which is now worth £75 in Very Good condition with the jacket.*

Saville has also produced a number of non-fiction works, including this sensitively written life of Christ from 1958.

THE BUNNY BOOK (Hamlyn, 1966) £12
BUSY BUSY WORLD (Golden Press, U.S., 1965) £18
BUSY BUSY WORLD (Hamlyn, 1966) £12
STORYBOOK DICTIONARY (Random House, U.S., 1966) £12
THE EGG IN THE HOLE BOOK (Golden Press, U.S., 1967)..£18
PLANES (Golden Press, U.S., 1967) £12
TRAINS (Golden Press, U.S., 1967) £12
BOATS (Golden Press, U.S., 1967)...£12
CARS (Golden Press, U.S., 1967)...£12
THE EARLY BIRD (Random House, U.S., 1968) £12
THE EARLY BIRD (Collins, 1970)..£6
WHAT DO PEOPLE DO ALL DAY? (Random House, U.S., 1968) £12
WHAT DO PEOPLE DO ALL DAY? (Collins, 1969) £6
THE GREAT PIE ROBBERY (Random House, U.S., 1969) £12
THE GREAT PIE ROBBERY (Collins, 1969) £6
THE SUPERMARKET MYSTERY (Random House, U.S., 1969) £12
THE SUPERMARKET MYSTERY (Collins, 1969) £6
GREAT BIG SCHOOLHOUSE (Random House, U.S., 1969) £12
GREAT BIG SCHOOLHOUSE (Collins, 1969) £6
THINGS TO KNOW (Random House, U.S., 1970) £6
THINGS TO KNOW (Collins, 1976) £6
GREAT BIG AIR BOOK (Random House, U.S., 1971)..£12
GREAT BIG AIR BOOK (Collins, 1971) £6
ABC WORD BOOK (Random House, U.S., 1971) £12
ABC WORD BOOK (Collins, 1972)...£6
LOOK AND LEARN LIBRARY (four books: 'Best Stories Ever', 'Fun with Words', 'Going Places' and
   'Things to Know') (Golden Press, U.S., 1971) ....each £6
FUNNIEST STORYBOOK EVER (Random House, U.S., 1972)..£12
FUNNIEST STORYBOOK EVER (Collins, 1972) £6
NICKY GOES TO THE DOCTOR (Golden Press, U.S., 1972) £12
NICKY GOES TO THE DOCTOR (Hamlyn, 1972)..£6
HOP ABOARD, HERE WE GO! (Random House, U.S., 1972)...£12
HOP ABOARD, HERE WE GO! (Hamlyn, 1972) £6

SCARRY, Richard

GREAT BIG MYSTERY BOOK (Collins, 1973) £6
SILLY STORIES (Golden Press, U.S., 1973) £12
SILLY STORIES (Hamlyn, 1974) £6
BABYKINS AND HIS FAMILY (Golden Press, U.S., 1973) £12
BABYKINS AND HIS FAMILY (Hamlyn, 1974) £6
FIND YOUR ABCs (Random House, U.S., 1973) £10
PLEASE AND THANK YOU BOOK (Random House, U.S., 1973) £10
CARS AND TRUCKS AND THINGS THAT GO (Golden Press, U.S., 1974) £6
CARS AND TRUCKS AND THINGS THAT GO (Collins, 1974) £6
EUROPEAN WORD BOOK (Hamlyn, 1974) £10
BEST RAINY DAY BOOK EVER (Random House, U.S., 1974) £10
BEST RAINY DAY BOOK EVER (Hamlyn, 1975) £6
GREAT STEAMBOAT MYSTERY (Random House, U.S., 1975) £10
GREAT STEAMBOAT MYSTERY (Collins, 1976) £6
ALL DAY LONG by J.D. Bevington (Hamlyn, 1975) £6
WITH THE ANIMALS by J.D. Bevington (Hamlyn, 1975) £6
WORK AND PLAY BOOK (Collins, 1975) £6
ANIMAL NURSERY TALES (Golden Press, U.S., 1975) £10
ANIMAL NURSERY TALES (Collins, 1975) £6
FAVOURITE STORYBOOK (Random House, U.S., 1976) £10
FAVOURITE STORYBOOK (Collins, 1976) £6
BUSY TOWN, BUSY PEOPLE (Random House, U.S., 1976) £10
BUSY TOWN, BUSY PEOPLE (Collins, 1976) £6
STORYTIME (Collins, 1976) £6
ALL DAY LONG (Golden Press: 'Look-Look' series, U.S., 1976) £6
ALL DAY LONG (Hamlyn: 'Look-Look' series, 1977) £6
ALL YEAR LONG (Golden Press: 'Look-Look' series, U.S., 1976) £6
ALL YEAR LONG (Hamlyn: 'Look-Look' series, 1977) £6
IN MY TOWN (Golden Press: 'Look-Look' series, U.S., 1976) £6
IN MY TOWN (Hamlyn: 'Look-Look' series, 1977) £6
LEARN TO COUNT (Golden Press: 'Look-Look' series, U.S., 1976) £6
LEARN TO COUNT (Hamlyn: 'Look-Look' series, 1977) £6
ABOUT ANIMALS (Golden Press: 'Look-Look' series, U.S., 1976) £6
ABOUT ANIMALS (Hamlyn: 'Look-Look' series, 1977) £6
AT WORK (Golden Press: 'Look-Look' series, U.S., 1976) £6
AT WORK (Hamlyn: 'Look-Look' series, 1977) £6
MY HOUSE (Golden Press: 'Look-Look' series, U.S., 1976) £6
MY HOUSE (Hamlyn: 'Look-Look' series, 1977) £6
ON THE FARM (Golden Press: 'Look-Look' series, U.S., 1976) £6
ON THE FARM (Hamlyn: 'Look-Look' series, 1977) £6
ON VACATION (Golden Press: 'Look-Look' series, U.S., 1976) £6
ON VACATION (Hamlyn: 'Look-Look' series, 1977) £6
SHORT AND TALL (Golden Press: 'Look-Look' series, U.S., 1976) £6
SHORT AND TALL (Hamlyn: 'Look-Look' series, 1977) £6
TEENY TINY ABC (Golden Press, U.S., 1976) £6
TEENY TINY ABC (Hamlyn, 1975) £6
EARLY WORDS (Random House, U.S., 1976) £6
EARLY WORDS (Collins, 1977) £6
COLOUR BOOK (Random House, U.S., 1976) £6
COLOUR BOOK (Collins, 1977) £6
LAUGH AND LEARN LIBRARY (Collins, 1976) £6
PICTURE DICTIONARY (Collins, 1976) £6
LITTLE ABC (Random House, U.S., 1976) £6
LITTLE ABC (Collins, 1976) £6
BUSIEST PEOPLE EVER (Random House, U.S., 1976) £6
BUSIEST PEOPLE EVER (Collins, 1976) £6
BEST COUNTING BOOK EVER (Random House, U.S., 1976) £6
BEST COUNTING BOOK EVER (Collins, 1977) £6
LOWLY WORM STORY BOOK (contains 'The Talking Bread', 'Please Move to the Back of the Bus'
'Lowly Worm's Birthday' and 'Rudolf's Aeroplane') (Random House, U.S., 1977) £6
LOWLY WORM STORY BOOK (Collins, 1979) £6
BUSY, BUSY WORD BOOK (Collins, 1977) £6
MR FIXIT and Other Stories (Collins, 1977) £6
LITTLE BEDTIME BOOK (Collins, 1977) £6
BEST MAKE-IT BOOK EVER (Random House, U.S., 1977) £6
BEST MAKE-IT BOOK EVER (Collins, 1978) £6
LITTLE COUNTING BOOK (Random House, U.S., 1978) £6
LITTLE COUNTING BOOK (as 'Busy-Busy Counting Book') (Collins, 1977) £6
LOWLY WORM SNIFFY BOOK (Random House, U.S., 1978) £6

POSTMAN PIG AND HIS BUSY NEIGHBOURS (Random House, U.S., 1978) £6
POSTMAN PIG AND HIS BUSY NEIGHBOURS (Collins, 1978) £6
TOY BOOK (Random House, U.S., 1978)..£6
TOY BOOK (Collins, 1979) £6
STORIES TO COLOUR (Random House, U.S., 1978) £6
STORIES TO COLOUR (Collins, 1979)..£6
HOLIDAY BOOK (Collins, 1979) £6
FIRST RICHARD SCARRY OMNIBUS (contains 'Cars and Trucks and Things That Go', 'Busiest People Ever'
    and 'Best Counting Book Ever') (Collins, [1979])...£10
MIX OR MATCH STORYBOOK (Random House, U.S., 1979)..£6
MIX OR MATCH BOOK (Collins, 1980) £6
BEST FIRST BOOK EVER (Random House, U.S., 1979) £6
BEST FIRST BOOK EVER (Collins, 1980) £6
HUCKLE'S BOOK (Random House, U.S., 1979) £6
HUCKLE'S BOOK (Collins, 1979) £6
BUSYTOWN POP-UP BOOK (Random House, U.S., 1979) £6
BUSYTOWN POP-UP BOOK (Collins, 1980) £6
CAN YOU COUNT? (Collins, 1979)..£6
LOWLY WORM THINGS ON WHEELS (Random House, U.S., 1980) £6
LOWLY WORM THINGS ON WHEELS (Collins, 1979)..£6
LOWLY WORM WHERE DOES IT COME FROM BOOK (Random House, U.S., 1980) £6
LOWLY WORM WHERE DOES IT COME FROM BOOK (Collins, 1979)...£6
LOWLY WORM TELL-TIME BOOK (Random House, U.S., 1980) £6
LOWLY WORM TELL-TIME BOOK (Collins, 1979) £6
PEASANT PIG AND THE TERRIBLE DRAGON (Random House, U.S., 1980)...£6
PEASANT PIG AND THE TERRIBLE DRAGON (Collins, 1981) £6
THE THREE LITTLE PIGS (Collins, 1981) £6
LOWLY WORM WORD BOOK (Random House, U.S., 1981)..£6
LOWLY WORM WORD BOOK (Collins, 1982) £6
CHRISTMAS MICE (Golden Press, U.S., 1981) £6
BEST CHRISTMAS BOOK EVER (Random House, U.S., 1981)...£6
BEST CHRISTMAS BOOK EVER (Collins, 1981) £6
THE WOLF AND THE SEVEN KIDS (Collins, 1981) £6
LITTLE RED RIDING HOOD (Collins, 1981) £6
GOLDILOCKS AND THE THREE BEARS (Collins, 1981) £6
BUSY HOUSES (Random House, U.S., 1981) £6
BUSY HOUSES (Collins, 1982) £6
FOUR BUSY WORD BOOKS (Random House, U.S., 1982) £6
BUSYTOWN SHAPE BOOKS (Collins, 1982) £6
STICKER BOOKS (three books: 'On Holiday', 'At School' and 'I Can Count to Eleven') (Collins, 1982)............each £6
BOARD BOOKS (four books: 'Colours', 'Words', 'My House' and 'Things I Do') (Collins, 1982) ....each £6
OLD MOTHER HUBBARD AND OTHER RHYMES (Hamlyn, 1983) £6
THIS LITTLE PIG WENT TO MARKET AND OTHER RHYMES (Hamlyn, 1983) £6
ONE, TWO, BUCKLE MY SHOE AND OTHER RHYMES (Hamlyn, 1983) £6
LITTLE MISS MUFFET AND OTHER RHYMES (Hamlyn, 1983)...£6
MEET THE ANIMALS text by J.D. Bevington (Hamlyn, 1984) £6
PIG WILL AND PIG WON'T: A Book of Manners (Collins, 1984) £6
BEST BUMPER BOOK EVER (contains 'What Do People Do All Day', 'ABC Work Book' and
    'Funniest Storybook Ever') (Collins, 1984) £6
THE BEST MISTAKES EVER! and Other Stories (Random House, U.S., 1984)..£6
THE BEST MISTAKES EVER! and Other Stories (Collins, 1985) £6
THE BIGGEST WORD BOOK EVER (Hamlyn, 1986) £6
BIG AND LITTLE (Western, U.S., 1987)...£6
THE BUSY FUN AND LEARN BOOK (Hamlyn, 1987) £6
THE BEST EVER MUSIC BOOK (Random House, U.S., 1987) £6
THE BEST EVER MUSIC BOOK (Hamlyn, 1987) £6
BOARD BOOKS (four books: 'Going Places on the Water', 'Going Places in the Air',
    'Going Places in the Car' and 'Going Places with Goldbug') (Collins, 1987) ....each £5
SPLISH SPLASH SOUNDS (Western, U.S. 1987) £4
BUSY WORKERS (Western, U.S., 1988) £4
COUNTING COLOUR (Western, U.S., 1992) £4
COPY COLOUR (Western, U.S., 1992) £4
MAGIC PAINTING (World International, 1992) £4
BIGGEST POP-UP EVER (World International, 1992) £12
ABC's (Western: 'Golden Little-Look Books' series, U.S., 1992) £4
MR FUMBLE'S STICKER FUN (World International, 1992)..£4
BEST FRIEND EVER (Western: 'Golden Little-Look Books' series, 1992) £4
NURSERY RHYMES (Western, U.S., 1993) £4
STORY BOOK (Dean, 1993)..£4
GETTING READY FOR SCHOOL (Dean, 1993) £4

SCARRY, Richard

The innocent joys of school life, as depicted by the incomparable Ronald Searle in **Hurrah for St Trinian's!** *(1948)*

SNOWSTORM SURPRISE (Western, U.S., 1994) £4
WORDS AND COUNTING 4-5 YEARS (Dean, 1994)...£4
BIGGEST CATCH EVER (Western, U.S., 1994) £4
BUSIEST FIREFIGHTERS EVER (Western, U.S., 1994) £4
DINGO, THE WORST DRIVER EVER (Western, U.S., 1994) £4
FLOATING BANANAS (Western, U.S., 1994) £4
LETTERS AND NUMBERS 3-4 YEARS (Dean, 1994)..£4
MR FUMBLE'S COFFEE SHOP DISASTER (Western, U.S., 1994) £4
READING AND SUMS 5-6 YEARS (Dean, 1994)...£4

SEARLE, Ronald

British illustrator. Born: St. Andrews, Cambridge, in 1920. Studied at Cambridge School of Art. Drew his first 'St. Trinian's' cartoon in 1941 whilst stationed in Scotland with the army, enjoying huge success with the subsequent series of books and with his illustrations for Geoffrey Willans' four 'Molesworth' titles. Moved to France in 1961 following a breakdown. Provided the animated sequences for the films *Those Magnificent Men in their Flying Machines* (1965) and *Monte Carlo or Bust* (1969).

Prices are for books in Very Good condition with dustjackets where applicable.

'Molesworth' Books (all Written by Geoffrey Willans and Illustrated by Ronald Searle)

DOWN WITH SKOOL (Parrish, 1953) £15
HOW TO BE TOPP (Parrish, 1954) £15
WHIZZ FOR ATOMS (Parrish, 1956) £15
THE COMPLEET MOLESWORTH (contains 'Down with Skool', 'How to Be Topp' and 'Whizz for Atoms') (Parrish, 1958) £15
BACK IN THE JUG AGANE (Parrish, 1959) £15

'St Trinian's' Books

HURRAH FOR ST. TRINIAN'S! (foreword by D.B. Wyndham Lewis) (Macdonald, 1948) £30
THE FEMALE APPROACH (includes some 'St Trinian's' cartoons; preface by Sir Max Beerbohm) (Macdonald, 1949)...............£15
BACK TO THE SLAUGHTERHOUSE (includes some 'St Trinian's' cartoons) (Macdonald, 1951)........................£20
THE TERROR OF ST. TRINIAN'S (with D.B. Wyndham Lewis) (Parrish, 1952) £20
SOULS IN TORMENT (includes some 'St Trinian's' cartoons) (Perpetua, 1953) £20
THE ST. TRINIAN'S STORY (with Kaye Webb) (Perpetua, 1959) £20

Others

JOHN GILPIN by William Cowper (Chiswick Press, 1952) £30
JOHN GILPIN by William Cowper (King Penguin, 1953) £15
A CHRISTMAS CAROL by Charles Dickens (Perpetua, 1961) £20
OLIVER TWIST by Charles Dickens (Joseph, 1962) £15
GREAT EXPECTATIONS by Charles Dickens (Joseph, 1962) £15
THE HUNCHBACK OF NOTRE-DAME by Victor Hugo (Readers Digest, 1966) £12
THE ADVENTURES OF BARON MUNCHAUSEN by R.E. Raspe (Pantheon, U.S., 1969) £20

SENDAK, Maurice

American illustrator. Born: Maurice Bernard Sendak in New York in 1928. Studied at Lafayette High School, subsequently working as a window-dresser and enjoying his first major success as an illustrator with Ruth Krauss's *A Hole is to Dig* (1952). Best known for his 1963 picture book, *Where the Wild Things Are*.

Prices are for books in Very Good condition with dustjackets where applicable.

WONDERFUL FARM by Marcel Aymé (Harper, U.S., 1951) £160
MAGGIE ROSE — HER BIRTHDAY CHRISTMAS by R. Sawyer (Harper, U.S., 1952)....................................£130
A HOLE IS TO DIG: A First Book of First Definitions by Ruth Krauss (Harper, U.S., 1952) £100
A HOLE IS TO DIG: A First Book of First Definitions by Ruth Krauss (Hamish Hamilton, 1963) £65
SHADRACH by Meindart de Jong (Harper, U.S., 1953) £70
A VERY SPECIAL HOUSE by Ruth Krauss (Harper, U.S., 1953) £100
I'LL BE YOU AND YOU BE ME by Ruth Krauss (Harper, U.S., 1954) £200
MAGIC PICTURES by Marcel Aymé (Harper, U.S., 1954) £85
THE WHEEL ON THE SCHOOL by Meindart de Jong (Harper, U.S., 1954) £70
THE WHEEL ON THE SCHOOL by Meindart de Jong (Lutterworth Press, 1956) £50
I WANT TO PAINT MY BATHROOM BLUE by Ruth Krauss (Harper, U.S., 1954) £70
TIN FIDDLE by E. Tripp (OUP, 1954)...£70
THE LITTLE COW AND THE TURTLE by Meindart de Jong (Harper, U.S., 1955) £60
THE LITTLE COW AND THE TURTLE by Meindart de Jong (Lutterworth Press, 1961) £50
WHAT CAN YOU DO WITH A SHOE? by B.S. de Regniers (Harper, U.S., 1955) £70
CHARLOTTE AND THE WHITE HORSE by Ruth Krauss (Harper, U.S., 1955) £90
CHARLOTTE AND THE WHITE HORSE by Ruth Krauss (The Bodley Head, 1977)...£50
KENNY'S WINDOW: A Tale for Children (Harper, U.S., [1956]) £130
THE HOUSE OF SIXTY FATHERS by Meindart de Jong (Harper, U.S., 1956) £50
HAPPY RAIN by Maurice Sendak (Harper, U.S., 1956) £70

SENDAK, Maurice

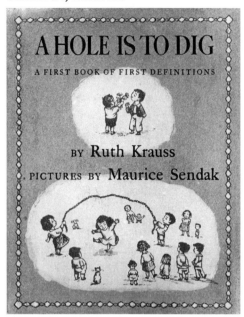

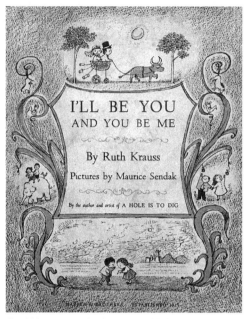

A Hole is to Dig was only the third book to be illustrated by Maurice Sendak. This is the first American edition, from 1952.

Sendak's most sought-after work, published in the U.S. only in 1954 and now worth £200 in Very Good condition.

ANIMAL PEOPLE by Randall Jarrell (Random House, U.S., 1965) £50
THE ANIMAL FAMILY by Randall Jarrell (Pantheon, U.S., 1965) £85
THE ANIMAL FAMILY by Randall Jarrell (Hart-Davis, 1967) £50
HIGGLETY PIGGLETY POP! or There Must be More to Life by Maurice Sendak (Harper, U.S., 1967) £50
HIGGLETY PIGGLETY POP! or There Must be More to Life by Maurice Sendak (The Bodley Head, 1969) £40
A KISS FOR LITTLE BEAR by Else Holmelund Minarik (Harper, U.S., 1968) £50
A KISS FOR LITTLE BEAR by Else Holmelund Minarik (World's Work, 1969) £40
MR RABBIT AND THE LOVELY PRESENT by Charlotte Zolotow (The Bodley Head, 1968) £40
LULLABIES AND NIGHT SONGS (The Bodley Head, 1969) £55
THE LIGHT PRINCESS by George MacDonald (The Bodley Head, 1969) £50
IN THE NIGHT KITCHEN (Harper, U.S., 1970)..£125
IN THE NIGHT KITCHEN (The Bodley Head, 1971)...£60
ZLATEH THE GOAT and Other Stories by Isaac Bashevis Singer (Longmans, 1970)................................£25
THE MAGICIAN: A Counting Book (Rosenbach, U.S., 1971) £45
PICTURES (Harper, U.S., 1971) £55
PICTURES (The Bodley Head, 1972) £35
IN SARAH'S ROOM (The Bodley Head, 1972) £30
FANTASY SKETCHES (Rosenbach, U.S., 1972)...£25
THE GOLDEN KEY by George MacDonald (afterword by W.H. Auden; issued with dustjacket) (The Bodley Head, 1972) £40
THE JUNIPER TREE and Other Tales from Grimm (selected by Lore Segal and Maurice Sendak; translated by Lore Segal
    and Randall Jarrell; two volumes; issued with dustjackets; in slipcase) (Farrar, Straus & Giroux, U.S., 1973)...........the set £85
THE JUNIPER TREE and Other Tales from Grimm (selected by Lore Segal and Maurice Sendak; translated by
    Lore Segal and Randall Jarrell; two volumes; issued with dustjackets; in slipcase) (The Bodley Head, 1974) ....the set £75
KING GRISLY-BEARD by Wilhelm and Jacob Grimm (The Bodley Head, 1974) £30
REALLY ROSIE (play; adapted from 'The Sign on Rosie's Door' and 'The Nutshell Library') (Harper, 1975) £35
SEVEN LITTLE MONSTERS by Maurice Sendak (Harper, U.S., 1976)..£45
SEVEN LITTLE MONSTERS by Maurice Sendak (The Bodley Head, 1977) £35
FLY BY NIGHT by Randall Jarrell (Farrar, Straus & Giroux, U.S., 1976) £45
FLY BY NIGHT by Randall Jarrell (The Bodley Head, 1977) £35
SOME SWELL PUP, or Are You Sure You Want a Dog? by Maurice Sendak and Matthew Margolis
    (Farrar, Straus & Giroux, 1976) £50
SOME SWELL PUP, or Are You Sure You Want a Dog? by Maurice Sendak and Matthew Margolis (The Bodley Head, 1976) ..£20
CINDERELLA (Heinemann/Gallery Five, 1977) £20
THE ART OF MAURICE SENDAK by G. Selma Lanes (The Bodley Head, 1980) £90
OUTSIDE OVER THERE by Maurice Sendak (Harper, U.S., 1984) £30
OUTSIDE OVER THERE by Maurice Sendak (The Bodley Head, 1981) £25
THE NUTCRACKER by E.T.A. Hoffmann (translated by Ralph Manheim) (Harper, U.S., 1984) £70
THE NUTCRACKER by E.T.A. Hoffman (The Bodley Head, 1984) £65

The U.K. edition of Sendak's 'Nutshell Library': four little books of poetry, issued in a decorative cardboard slipcase (far left).

LOVE FOR THREE ORANGES (Farrar, Strauss & Giroux, U.S., 1984) £60
LOVE FOR THREE ORANGES (The Bodley Head, 1984) £45
THE CUNNING LITTLE VIXEN by Rudolf Tesnohlidek (Farrar, Straus & Giroux, U.S., 1985) £75
IN GRANDPA'S HOUSE by P. Sendak (The Bodley Head, 1986) £30
THE POSTERS (Harmony, 1987) £60
THE POSTERS (The Bodley Head, 1987) £30
DEAR MILI by Wilhelm Grimm (Michael di Capua/Farrar, Strauss & Giroux, U.S., 1988) £35
DEAR MILI by Wilhelm Grimm (Viking Kestrel, 1988)..£30
I SAW ESAU by Iona Opie (Walker, 1992) £25

SEREDY, Kate

American (originally Hungarian) author-illustrator. Born: Budapest, 1899. She drew upon her Hungarian background for several stories, notably *The Good Master* (1935). Won the Newbery Medal for *The White Stag* (1937). Died: 1975.

Prices are for books in Very Good condition with dustjackets where applicable.

Books Written and Illustrated by Kate Seredy

THE GOOD MASTER (Viking Press, U.S., 1935) £45
THE GOOD MASTER (Harrap, 1937) £40
LISTENING (Viking Press, U.S. 1936)..£40
THE WHITE STAG (Viking Press, U.S., 1937) £30
THE WHITE STAG (Harrap, 1938) £25
THE SINGING TREE (Viking Press, U.S., 1939) £30
THE SINGING TREE (Harrap, 1940)..£30
A TREE FOR PETER (Viking Press, U.S., 1941) £30
THE OPEN GATE (Viking Press, U.S., 1943) £30
THE OPEN GATE (Harrap, 1947) £25
THE CHESTRY OAK (Viking Press, U.S., 1948) £45
THE CHESTRY OAK (Harrap, 1957) £30
GYPSY (Viking Press, U.S., 1951) £20
GYPSY (Harrap, 1952) £15
PHILOMENA (Viking Press, U.S., 1955)..£30

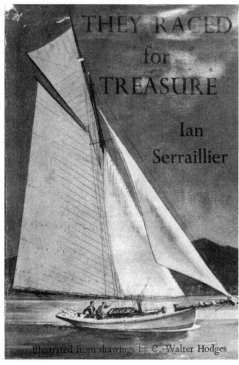

They Raced for Treasure was Ian Serraillier's second children's book. It was published by Jonathan Cape in 1946.

His 1956 book, *The Silver Sword*, is now valued at £50 in Very Good condition with the C. Walter Hodges dustjacket.

PHILOMENA (Harrap, 1957) £20
THE TENEMENT TREE (Viking Press, U.S., 1959) £20
THE TENEMENT TREE (Harrap, 1960)...£15
A BRAND-NEW UNCLE (Viking Press, U.S., 1961)...£15
LAZY TINKS (Viking Press, U.S., 1962) £10
LAZY TINKS (Harrap, 1964) £10

SERRAILLIER, Ian

British author. Born: 1912. Best known for *The Silver Sword* (1956), also several adventure stories and a verse retelling of *Beowulf* in *The Windmill Book of Ballads* (1962). Died: 1994.

Prices are for books in Very Good condition with dustjackets where applicable.

THE WEAVER BIRDS (verse; illustrated) (Macmillan, 1944) £35
THEY RACED FOR TREASURE (illustrated by C. Walter Hodges) (Cape, 1946) £30
FLIGHT TO ADVENTURE (illustrated by C. Walter Hodges) (Cape, 1946) £30
CAPTAIN BOUNDSABOARD AND THE PIRATE (illustrated by Michael Bartlett and Arline Braybrooke) (Cape, 1949) £30
THERE'S NO ESCAPE (illustrated by C. Walter Hodges) (Cape, 1950) £30
JUNGLE ADVENTURE. Based on a Story by R.M. Ballantyne (illustrated by Vera Jarman) (Heinemann, 1953)......................£20
THE ADVENTURES OF DICK VARLEY. Based on a Story by R.M. Ballantyne (illustrated by Vera Jarman) (Heinemann, 1955)..£20
BEOWULF THE WARRIOR (verse; illustrated by Mark Severidon) (OUP, 1954) £20
MAKING GOOD (illustrated by Vera Jarman) (Heinemann, 1955) £25
THE SILVER SWORD (illustrated by C. Walter Hodges) (Cape, 1956) £50
GUNS IN THE WILD. Based on a Story by R.M. Ballantyne (illustrated by Shirley Hughes) (Heinemann, 1956) £20
KATY AT HOME. Based on a Story by Susan Coolidge (illustrated by Shirley Hughes) (Heinemann, 1957) £20
KATY AT SCHOOL. Based on a Story by Susan Coolidge (illustrated by Shirley Hughes) (Heinemann, 1959).....................£20
THE IVORY HORN. Retold from the Song of Roland (illustrated by William Stobbs) (Oxford University Press, 1960) £15
THE GORGON'S HEAD: The Song of Perseus (illustrated by William Stobbs) (Oxford University Press, 1961) £15
THE WINDMILL BOOK OF BALLADS (illustrated by Mark Severin and Leonard Rosoman) (Heinemann, 1962) £20
THE WAY OF DANGER: The Story of Theseus (illustrated by William Stobbs) (Oxford University Press, 1962) £15
THE CLASHING ROCKS: The Story of Jason (illustrated by William Stobbs) (Oxford University Press, 1962) £15
THE ENCHANTED ISLAND: Stories from Shakespeare (illustrated by Peter Farmer) (Oxford University Press, 1964) £15
THE CAVE OF DEATH (illustrated by Stuart Tresilian) (Heinemann, 1965) £20
FIGHT FOR FREEDOM (illustrated by John S. Goodall) (Heinemann, 1965) £20
A FALL FROM THE SKY: The Story of Daedalus (illustrated by William Stobbs) (Nelson, 1966) £15
CHAUCER AND HIS WORLD (Lutterworth Press, 1967) £15
HAVELOK THE WARRIOR (illustrated by Elaine Raphael) (Hamish Hamilton, 1968) £15
ROBIN HOOD AND HIS MERRY MEN (illustrated by Victor Ambrus) (OUP, 1969)..................£20
THE TALE OF THREE LANDLUBBERS (illustrated by Raymond Briggs) (Hamish Hamilton, 1970) £20
HERACLES THE STRONG (illustrated by Rocco Negri) (Hamish Hamilton, 1971) £15

SEUSS, Dr

American author-illustrator. Born: Theodor Seuss Geisel in Springfield, Massachusetts, in 1904. Studied at Dartmouth College and Lincoln College, Oxford, subsequently working as a freelance cartoonist and film animator. Produced many popular picture books, of which the best known is *The Cat in the Hat* (1956). Received a doctorate from Dartmouth College in 1955. Died: 1991.

Prices are for books in Very Good condition with dustjackets where applicable.

AND TO THINK THAT I SAW IT ON MULBERRY STREET (Vanguard Press, U.S., 1937) £90
AND TO THINK THAT I SAW IT ON MULBERRY STREET (Country Life, 1939) £75
THE 500 HATS OF BARTHOLOMEW CUBBINS (Vanguard Press, U.S., 1938) £75
THE 500 HATS OF BARTHOLOMEW CUBBINS (OUP, [1940]) £60
THE KING'S STILTS (Random House, U.S., 1939) £75
THE KING'S STILTS (Hamish Hamilton, 1942) £60
HORTON HATCHES THE EGG (Random House, U.S., 1940) £75
HORTON HATCHES THE EGG (Hamish Hamilton, 1942) £60
HORTON HATCHES THE EGG (reissue) (Collins, 1962) £40
McELLIGOT'S POOL (Random House, U.S., 1947) £80
McELLIGOT'S POOL (Collins, 1975) £40
THIDWICK THE BIG-HEARTED MOOSE (Random House, U.S., 1948) £60
THIDWICK THE BIG-HEARTED MOOSE (Collins, 1968) £40
BARTHOLOMEW AND THE OOBLECK (Random House, U.S., 1949)......................................£60
IF I RAN THE ZOO (Random House, U.S., 1950)...£60
SCRAMBLED EGGS SUPER! (Random House, U.S., 1953) £60
HORTON HEARS A WHO! (Random House, U.S., 1954) £60
HORTON HEARS A WHO! (Collins, 1976) £30
ON BEYOND ZEBRA (Random House, U.S., 1955) £60
IF I RAN THE CIRCUS (Random House, U.S., 1956)..£60
IF I RAN THE CIRCUS (Collins, 1969) £60
THE CAT IN THE HAT (Random House, U.S., 1956)..£500

An early work by 'Cat in the Hat' creator, Dr Seuss. The original U.S. edition is now worth £75 in Very Good condition.

This 'Beginner Book' from 1980 was one of his very last titles. As you can see, his style of illustration hadn't changed much!

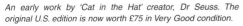

THE CAT IN THE HAT (Hutchinson, 1958)	£100
THE CAT IN THE HAT (Collins, 1961)	£50
HOW THE GRINCH STOLE CHRISTMAS (Random House, U.S., 1957)	£75
HOW THE GRINCH STOLE CHRISTMAS (Collins, 1973)	£75
THE CAT IN THE HAT COMES BACK (Random House, U.S., 1958)	£100
THE CAT IN THE HAT COMES BACK (Collins, 1961)	£50
YERTLE THE TURTLE (Random House, U.S., 1958)	£75
YERTLE THE TURTLE (Collins, 1963)	£30
HAPPY BIRTHDAY TO YOU! (Random House, U.S., 1959)	£40
ONE FISH, TWO FISH, RED FISH, BLUE FISH (Random House, U.S., 1960)	£40
ONE FISH, TWO FISH, RED FISH, BLUE FISH (Collins, 1960)	£30
GREEN EGGS AND HAM (Random House, U.S., 1960)	£75
GREEN EGGS AND HAM (Collins, 1962)	£40
THE SNEETCHES and WHAT WAS I SCARED OF? (Random House, U.S., 1961)	£60
THE SNEETCHES and WHAT WAS I SCARED OF? (Collins, 1965)	£40
SLEEP BOOK (Random House, U.S., 1962)	£60
SLEEP BOOK (Collins, 1964)	£30
HOP ON POP (Random House, U.S., 1963)	£60
HOP ON POP (Collins, 1964)	£30
DR SEUSS ABC (Random House, U.S., 1963)	£40
DR SEUSS ABC (Collins, 1964)	£30
THE CAT IN THE HAT DICTIONARY, BY THE CAT HIMSELF (with Philip D. Eastman) (Random House, U.S., 1964)	£40
FOX IN SOCKS (Random House, U.S., 1965)	£40
FOX IN SOCKS (Collins, 1966)	£30
I HAD TROUBLE IN GETTING TO SOLLA SOLLEW (Random House, U.S., 1965)	£75
I HAD TROUBLE IN GETTING TO SOLLA SOLLEW (Collins, 1967)	£75
THE CAT IN THE HAT SONGBOOK (Random House, U.S., 1967)	£60
THE CAT IN THE HAT STORYBOOK (Collins, 1968)	£30
THE FOOT BOOK (Random House, U.S., 1968)	£25
THE FOOT BOOK (Collins, 1969)	£15
MY BOOK ABOUT ME (with Roy McKie) (Random House, U.S., 1969)	£30
MY BOOK ABOUT ME (with Roy McKie) (Collins, 1973)	£20
I CAN LICK 30 TIGERS TODAY (Random House, U.S., 1969)	£40
I CAN LICK 30 TIGERS TODAY (Collins, 1970)	£30
I CAN DRAW IT MYSELF (Random House, U.S., 1970)	£30

MR BROWN CAN MOO, CAN YOU? (Random House, U.S., 1970)..£30
MR BROWN CAN MOO, CAN YOU? (Collins, 1971) £20
THE LORAX (Random House, U.S., 1971)...£75
THE LORAX (Collins, 1972) £40
MARVIN K. MOONEY WILL YOU PLEASE GO NOW? (Random House, U.S., 1972) £30
MARVIN K. MOONEY WILL YOU PLEASE GO NOW? (Collins, 1973) £20
DID I EVER TELL YOU HOW LUCKY YOU ARE? (Random House, U.S., 1973) £40
DID I EVER TELL YOU HOW LUCKY YOU ARE? (Collins, 1974) £30
THE SHAPE OF ME AND OTHER STUFF (Random House, U.S., 1973) £25
THE SHAPE OF ME AND OTHER STUFF (Collins, 1974) £15
THERE'S A WOCKET IN MY POCKET! (Random House, U.S., 1974)...£25
THERE'S A WOCKET IN MY POCKET! (Collins, 1975) £20
DR SEUSS STORYTIME (four volumes) (Random House, U.S., 1974) ....the set £60
DR SEUSS STORYTIME (four volumes) (Collins, 1979) ....the set £30
A GREAT DAY FOR UP! (illustrated by Quentin Blake) (Random House, U.S., 1974) £25
A GREAT DAY FOR UP! (illustrated by Quentin Blake) (Collins, 1975) £15
OH, THE THINKS YOU CAN THINK (Random House, U.S., 1975) £30
OH, THE THINKS YOU CAN THINK (Collins, 1976) £25
THE CAT'S QUIZZER (Random House, U.S., 1976) £40
THE CAT'S QUIZZER (Collins, 1977) £40
I CAN READ WITH MY EYES SHUT! (Random House, U.S., 1978) £30
I CAN READ WITH MY EYES SHUT! (Collins, 1979) £30
OH SAY CAN YOU SAY? (Random House, U.S., 1979)...£30
OH SAY CAN YOU SAY? (Collins, 1980) £20
HUNCHES IN BUNCHES (Random House, U.S., 1982) £40
HUNCHES IN BUNCHES (Collins, 1982) £40
BEGINNER BOOK DICTIONARY (Random House, U.S., 1986) £30
BEGINNER BOOK DICTIONARY (Collins, 1987)..£20
I'M NOT GOING TO GET UP TODAY (Collins, 1988) £20
OH, THE PLACES YOU'LL GO (Collins, 1990) £20

Books Written as 'Theo Le Sieg'

TEN APPLES UP ON TOP (illustrated by Roy McKie) (Random House, U.S., 1961) £25
TEN APPLES UP ON TOP (illustrated by Roy McKie) (Collins, 1963) £15
I WISH THAT I HAD DUCK FEET (illustrated by B. Tobey) (Random House, U.S., 1965) £25
I WISH THAT I HAD DUCK FEET (illustrated by B. Tobey) (Collins, 1967) £15
COME OVER TO MY HOUSE (illustrated by Richard Erdoes) (Random House, U.S., 1966) £25
COME OVER TO MY HOUSE (illustrated by Richard Erdoes) (Collins, 1967) £15
THE EYE BOOK (illustrated by Roy McKie) (Random House, U.S., 1968) £25
THE EYE BOOK (illustrated by Roy McKie) (Collins, 1969) £15
IN A PEOPLE HOUSE (illustrated by Roy McKie) (Random House, U.S., 1972) £20
IN A PEOPLE HOUSE (illustrated by Roy McKie) (Collins, 1973) £10
THE MANY MICE OF MR BRICE (illustrated by Roy McKie) (Random House, U.S., 1973) £20
THE MANY MICE OF MR BRICE (illustrated by Roy McKie) (Collins, 1974) £10
WACKY WEDNESDAY (illustrated by George Booth) (Random House, U.S., 1974) £15
WACKY WEDNESDAY (illustrated by George Booth) (Collins, 1975)...£10
WOULD YOU RATHER BE A BULLFROG? (illustrated by Roy McKie) (Random House, U.S., 1975)...........£15
WOULD YOU RATHER BE A BULLFROG? (illustrated by Roy McKie) (Collins, 1976) £10
HOOPER HUMPERDINK — ? NOT HIM! (illustrated by Charles E. Martin) (Random House, U.S. 1976) £15
HOOPER HUMPERDINK — ? NOT HIM! (illustrated by Charles E. Martin) (Collins, 1977) £10
PLEASE TRY TO REMEMBER THE FIRST OF OCTEMBER (illustrated by Art Cunnings) (Random House, U.S., 1977)...........£20
PLEASE TRY TO REMEMBER THE FIRST OF OCTEMBER (illustrated by Art Cunnings) (Collins, 1978) £10
MAYBE YOU SHOULD FLY A JET! MAYBE YOU SHOULD BE A VET! (illustrated by Michael J. Smollin)
    (Random House, U.S., 1980)..£20
MAYBE YOU SHOULD BE A VET! (Collins, 1981)...£10
THE TOOTH BOOK (illustrated by Roy McKie) (Random House, U.S., 1981) £20
THE TOOTH BOOK (illustrated by Roy McKie) (Collins, 1982) £10

SEWELL, Anna

British author. Born: Great Yarmouth, Norfolk, in 1820, the daughter of the writer, Mary Sewell. Studied at a Quaker school until the age of fifteen, when she became a semi-invalid following a fall. Her only novel, *Black Beauty* (1877), was written to encourage the better treatment of horses and was published only five months before her death in 1878.

Prices are for books in Very Good condition.

BLACK BEAUTY: His Grooms and Companions. The Autobiography of a Horse. Translated from the original equine by Anna
    Sewell (Jarrold, 1877) £12,000
BLACK BEAUTY (illustrated by John Beer) (Jarrold, 1894) £100
BLACK BEAUTY (illustrated by Maude Scrivener and others) (Jarrold, [1909]) £60
BLACK BEAUTY (illustrated by Cecil Aldin) (Jarrold, [1912])..£125

SEWELL, Anna

*Scottish girls' author, Jane Shaw, has commanded a following in recent years. **Susan Pulls the Strings** is now valued at £10.*

Looking after Thomas (1957) features a dustjacket design by the best of Jane Shaw's illustrators, Gilbert Dunlop.

BLACK BEAUTY (illustrated by Lucy Kemp-Welch) (Dent, 1915) £100
BLACK BEAUTY (illustrated by Lucy Kemp-Welch; limited to 600 copies, signed by the artist) (Dent, 1915) £550
BLACK BEAUTY (illustrated by Alice B. Woodward) (Bell, 1931)..£60
BLACK BEAUTY (illustrated by Rowland Wheelwright) (Harrap, 1932)..£50
BLACK BEAUTY (illustrated by Lionel Edwards) (Lunn, 1946) £50

SHAW, Jane
Scottish author. Born: Jean Bell Shaw Patrick in Glasgow in 1910. Studied at Park School, Glasgow, Glasgow University and the Maria Grey Training College, London. Worked for the Times Book Club and the publishers, Collins, before publishing her first two children's works, *My Own Book of Baby Beasts* and *My Own Book of Other Lands*, in 1938 under the name 'Jean Patrick'. *Breton Holiday*, her first book to appear under the pseudonym 'Jane Shaw', followed a year later. Her best-known works are the eleven novels featuring the schoolgirl, Susan Lyle, beginning with *Susan Pulls the Strings* (1952). She also contributed short stories to several Collins annuals during the 1940s. Lived in South Africa for many years, working in the Children's Bookshop in Johannesburg.

Prices are for books in Very Good condition with dustjackets.

MY OWN BOOK OF BABY BEASTS (written under the name 'Jean Patrick') (Collins, 1938) £8
MY OWN BOOK OF OTHER LANDS (written under the name 'Jean Patrick') (Collins, 1938) £8
BRETON HOLIDAY (reissued as 'Breton Adventure') (Collins, 1939) £15
BERMESE HOLIDAY (reissued as 'Bermese Adventure') (Collins, 1940) £15
HIGHLAND HOLIDAY (Collins, 1942)..£15
MAGIC SHIPS (Collins, 1943)..£15
THE HOUSE OF THE GLIMMERING LIGHT (Collins, 1943) £15
THE CREW OF THE BELINDA (Collins, 1945) £15
THE MOOCHERS (Lutterworth Press, 1950) £15
THE MOOCHERS ABROAD (Lutterworth Press, 1951) £15
MOOCHERS AND PREFECTS (Lutterworth Press, 1951)..£15
SUSAN PULLS THE STRINGS (Collins, 1952) £10
FARM FRIENDS (Collins, 1953) £8
PUPPY TALES (Collins, 1953) £8
PENNY FOOLISH (Nelson, 1953)...£10
TWOPENCE COLOURED (Nelson, 1954) £10

SUSAN'S HELPING HAND (Collins, 1955) £10
THREEPENNY BIT (Nelson, 1955)...£10
FOURPENNY FAIR (Nelson, 1956) £12
SUSAN RUSHES IN (Collins, 1956) £10
LOOKING AFTER THOMAS (Nelson, 1957) £5
SUSAN INTERFERES (Collins, 1957) £10
FIVEPENNY MYSTERY (Nelson, 1958) £12
CROOKED SIXPENCE (Nelson, 1958)..£12
SUSAN AT SCHOOL (Collins, 1958) £10
WILLOW GREEN MYSTERY (Nelson, 1958) £6
UNCLE REMUS STORIES (Retold) (Collins, 1960) £10
SUSAN MUDDLES THROUGH (Collins, 1960) £12
THE TALL MAN (Nelson, 1960) £6
VENTURE TO SOUTH AFRICA (Nelson, 1960) £15
HEIDI GROWS UP (Retold) (Collins, 1961) £10
NEW HOUSE AT NORTHMEAD (Nelson, 1961) £15
SUSAN'S TRYING TERM (Collins, 1961) £12
NO TROUBLE FOR SUSAN (Collins, 1962)..£15
LEFT-HANDED TUMFY (Lutterworth Press, 1962)..£7
CROOKS TOUR (Collins, 1962) £7
NORTHMEAD NUISANCE (Nelson, 1963) £15
ANYTHING CAN HAPPEN (Nelson, 1964)..£15
NOTHING HAPPENED AFTER ALL (Nelson, 1965) £15
SUSAN'S KIND HEART (Collins, 1965) £15
PADDY TURNS DETECTIVE (written under the pseudonym 'Jean Bell'; paperback) (Collins: 'Spitfire' series, 1967) £3
THE PENHALLOW MYSTERY (written under the pseudonym 'Jean Bell'; paperback) (Collins: 'Spitfire' series, 1967) £3
WHERE IS SUSAN? (Collins, 1968) £15
A JOB FOR SUSAN (Collins, 1969) £15
BRER RABBIT AND BRER FOX (Collins, 1969) £10

SHEPARD, E.H.

British illustrator. Born: Ernest Howard Shepard in London in 1879. Studied at St. Paul's School, Heatherley's and the Royal Academy Schools. By 1914, he was a regular contributor to *Punch*, which led to a commission to illustrate A.A. Milne's *When We Were Very Young* (1924), and later his 'Winnie-the-Pooh' books. Subsequently illustrated such children's classics as *Bevis* (1932) and Hans Andersen's fairy tales (1961), but his masterpiece is undoubtedly his edition of Kenneth Grahame's *The Wind in the Willows* (1931). Died: 1976.

Prices are for books in Very Good condition with dustjackets where applicable.

Books by A.A. Milne Illustrated by E.H. Shepard

WHEN WE WERE VERY YOUNG (verse) (Methuen, 1924) £5,000
WHEN WE WERE VERY YOUNG (limited to 100 numbered copies, signed by the author and artist) (Methuen, 1924) £6,000
WHEN WE WERE VERY YOUNG (limited to 300 numbered copies, signed by Christopher Milne) (Methuen, 1974) £500
VESPERS: A Poem (verse; music by H. Fraser-Simson) (Methuen, [1924]) £150
THE KING'S BREAKFAST (music by H. Fraser-Simson) (Methuen, 1925) £200
WINNIE-THE-POOH (stories) (Methuen, 1926) £2,500
WINNIE-THE-POOH (limited to 350 copies, signed by the author and artist) (Methuen, 1926) £5,000
WINNIE-THE-POOH (De Luxe edition: red, green or blue leather binding; in slipcase) (Methuen, 1926)............£3,000
WINNIE-THE-POOH (illustrated in colour by E.H. Shepard) (Methuen, 1973) £80
WINNIE-THE-POOH (limited to 300 numbered copies, signed by Christopher Milne) (Methuen, 1976) £600
NOW WE ARE SIX (verse) (Methuen, 1927) £800
NOW WE ARE SIX (limited to 200 numbered copies, signed by the author and artist) (Methuen, 1927)............£2,000
NOW WE ARE SIX (De Luxe edition: red, blue or green leather binding; in slipcase) (Methuen, 1927)............£1,500
NOW WE ARE SIX (limited to 300 numbered copies, signed by Christopher Milne) (Methuen, 1976) £400
THE HOUSE AT POOH CORNER (stories) (Methuen, 1928) £1,000
THE HOUSE AT POOH CORNER (limited to 350 numbered copies, signed by the author and artist)
(Methuen, 1928) £4,000
THE HOUSE AT POOH CORNER (De Luxe edition: red, green or blue leather binding; in slipcase) (Methuen, 1928)............£2,500
THE HOUSE AT POOH CORNER (illustrated in colour by E.H. Shepard) (Methuen, 1974) £60
THE CHRISTOPHER ROBIN CALENDAR (verses) (Methuen, [1928]) £75
THE HUMS OF POOH (music by H. Fraser-Simson) (Methuen, 1929) £200
THE CHRISTOPHER ROBIN STORY BOOK (selections from 'When We Were Very Young',
'Now We Are Six', 'Winnie-the-Pooh' and 'The House at Pooh Corner'; new preface by the author) (Methuen, 1929) £400
THE CHRISTOPHER ROBIN BIRTHDAY BOOK (selections from 'When We Were Very Young',
'Now We Are Six', 'Winnie-the-Pooh' and 'The House at Pooh Corner') (Methuen, 1930) £150
TALES OF POOH (selections from 'Winnie-the-Pooh' and 'The House at Pooh Corner'; 87 illustrations by E.H. Shepard)
(Methuen, [1930])...£200
THE CHRISTOPHER ROBIN VERSES (contains 'When We Were Very Young' and 'Now We Are Six';
twelve plates and text decorations by E.H. Shepard) (Methuen, 1932).......................£250

WHEN WE WERE VERY YOUNG

A. A. MILNE

Decorations by

E. H. SHEPARD

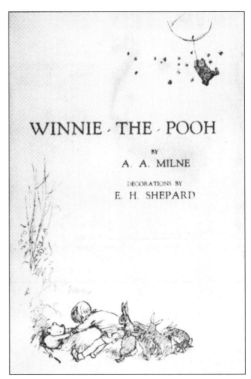

WINNIE · THE · POOH

BY

A. A. MILNE

DECORATIONS BY

E. H. SHEPARD

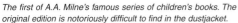

The first of A.A. Milne's famous series of children's books. The original edition is notoriously difficult to find in the dustjacket.

*The dustjacket from the first edition of **Winnie-the-Pooh**, featuring one of E.H. Shepard's incomparable drawings.*

WINNIE-THE-POOH AND EEYORE'S TAIL: A Pop-Up Picture Book (adapted by A. Schenk from the original illustrations by E.H. Shepard) (Methuen, [1953]) £75
WINNIE-THE-POOH AND THE BEES: A Pop-Up Picture Book (adapted by A. Schenk from the original illustrations by E.H. Shepard) (Methuen, [1953]) £75
THE WORLD OF POOH (contains 'Winnie-the-Pooh' and 'The House at Pooh Corner'; eight new colour plates by E.H. Shepard) (Methuen, 1958) £100
THE WORLD OF CHRISTOPHER ROBIN (contains 'When We Were Very Young' and 'Now We Are Six'; eight new colour plates by E.H. Shepard) (Methuen, 1959) £100
THE POOH STORY BOOK (new illustrations and colour plates by E.H. Shepard) (Methuen, 1967) £60
THE CHRISTOPHER ROBIN VERSE BOOK (illustrated in colour by E.H. Shepard) (Methuen, 1969)..............£60
THE POOH COOK BOOK by Katie Stewart (Methuen, 1971) £25
THE HUMS OF POOH: Lyrics by Pooh, Additional Lyrics by Eeyore (Methuen, [1972]) £40
THE POOH SKETCH BOOK (Methuen, 1982)..£20

Books by Kenneth Grahame Illustrated by E.H. Shepard
THE GOLDEN AGE (The Bodley Head, 1928) £100
THE GOLDEN AGE (limited to 275 copies, signed by the author and artist; in slipcase) (The Bodley Head, 1928)..................£600
THE GOLDEN AGE (The Bodley Head, 1973) £25
DREAM DAYS (The Bodley Head, 1930) £100
DREAM DAYS (The Bodley Head, 1973) £25
DREAM DAYS (limited to 275 copies, signed by the author and artist; in slipcase) (The Bodley Head, 1930) £550
THE WIND IN THE WILLOWS (first Shepard edition [38th edition]) (Methuen, 1931) £450
THE WIND IN THE WILLOWS (illustrated by E.H. Shepard; limited to 200 copies, signed by the author and artist) (Methuen, 1931) £4,000
THE WIND IN THE WILLOWS (colour plates by E.H. Shepard) (Methuen, 1959) £125
THE WIND IN THE WILLOWS (first full-colour Shepard edition [105th]) (Methuen, 1971)................................£60
BERTIE'S ESCAPADE (reprinted from 'First Whisper of "The Wind in the Willows"') (Methuen, 1949)................£60

Books by Malcolm Saville Illustrated by E.H. Shepard
SUSAN, BILL AND THE WOLF-DOG (Nelson, 1954) £35
SUSAN, BILL AND THE IVY-CLAD OAK (Nelson, 1954) £35
SUSAN, BILL AND THE VANISHING BOY (Nelson, 1955) £35
SUSAN, BILL AND THE GOLDEN CLOCK (Nelson, 1955)..£35
SUSAN, BILL AND THE DARK STRANGER (Nelson, 1956) £35
SUSAN, BILL AND THE 'SAUCY KATE' (Nelson, [1956]) £35

Other Books Illustrated by E.H. Shepard

TOM BROWN'S SCHOOLDAYS by Thomas Hughes (Methuen, [1904]) £100
PLAYTIME AND COMPANY by E.V. Lucas (Methuen, 1925)..£100
THE HOLLY TREE and Other Christmas Stories by Charles Dickens (Partridge, [1926]) £50
LET'S PRETEND by Georgette Agnew (Saville, 1927)..£50
THE LITTLE ONE'S LOG by Eva Violet Isaacs, Marchioness of Reading (Partridge, 1927)...................£40
CHRISTMAS POEMS by John Drinkwater (Sidgwick & Jackson, 1931) £25
BEVIS by Richard Jefferies (Cape, 1932)...£60
THE SEVENTH DAUGHTER by Barbara Euphan Todd (Burns Oates, 1935) £50
THE MODERN STRUWWELPETER by Jan Struther (Methuen, 1936) £200
THE ISLANDERS by Roland Pertwee (Methuen, 1950)..£40
THE SILVER CURLEW: A Fairy Tale by Eleanor Farjeon (OUP, 1953) £35
THE BROWNIES and Other Stories by J.H. Ewing (Dent: 'Children's Illustrated Classics' series, 1954)........£50
THE CUCKOO CLOCK by Mrs Molesworth (Dent: 'Children's Illustrated Classics' series, 1954) £30
THE GLASS SLIPPER by Eleanor Farjeon (OUP, 1955) £30
FROGMORTON by Susan Colling (Collins, 1955) £30
MODERN FAIRY STORIES. Chosen and Introduced by Roger Lancelyn Green
    (Dent: 'Children's Illustrated Classics' series, 1955)..£25
AT THE BACK OF THE NORTH WIND by George MacDonald (Dent: 'Children's Illustrated Classics' series, 1956) £60
THE SECRET GARDEN by Frances Hodgson Burnett (1956)..£40
THE PANCAKE. Edited by J.H. Fassett (Ginn, 1957) £30
BRIAR ROSE. Edited by J.H. Fassett (Ginn, 1958) £30
OLD GREEK FAIRY TALES by Roger Lancelyn Green (Bell, [1958]) £25
HANS ANDERSEN'S FAIRY TALES by Hans Christian Andersen (translated by L.W. Kingland) (OUP, 1961) £30
A NOBLE COMPANY. Edited by J. Compton (1961) £25
THE FLATTERED FLYING FISH and Other Poems by E.V. Rieu (Methuen, 1962) £25

Books Written and Illustrated by E.H. Shepard

FUN AND FANTASY: A Book of Drawings (Methuen, 1927) £65
DRAWN FROM MEMORY: On the Author's Childhood (Methuen, 1957) £65
DRAWN FROM LIFE: On the Author's Childhood (sequel to the above) (Methuen, 1961) £45
BEN AND BROCK (Methuen, 1965)..£30
BETSY AND JOE (Methuen, 1966) £25

*Shepard's finest work is probably to be found in his definitive edition of Kenneth Grahame's **The Wind in the Willows** (above).*

SMITH, Dodie

British author. Born: Dorothy Gladys Smith in Lancashire in 1896. Best known for her 1956 children's classic, *The One Hundred and One Dalmatians*, brilliantly filmed by Disney in 1960. She also wrote a number of adult plays and the novel, *I Capture the Castle* (1952). Died: 1990.

Prices are for books in Very Good condition with dustjackets.

I CAPTURE THE CASTLE (Heinemann, 1949)	£60
THE ONE HUNDRED AND ONE DALMATIANS (Heinemann, 1956)	£75
THE STARLIGHT BARKING: More About the Hundred and One Dalmatians (illustrated by Janet and Anne Grahame-Johnstone) (Heinemann, 1967)	£45
THE MIDNIGHT KITTENS (W.H. Allen, 1978)	£30

SMITH, Jessie Willcox

American illustrator. Born: Philadelphia, 1863. Studied with Howard Pyle at the Philadelphia Fine Art Institute, subsequently specialising in children's books. Died: 1935.

Prices are for books in Very Good condition.

Books Written and Illustrated by Jessie Willcox Smith

BOTH SIDES (Nisbet, 1887)	£100
STEPHEN GILMORE'S DREAM, or Coals of Fire (Nisbet, 1887)	£75
DICKENS' CHILDREN: A Calendar of 1912 (Scribners, U.S., [1911])	£100

Books Illustrated by Jessie Willcox Smith

EVANGELINE by H.W. Longfellow (illustrated by Jessie Willcox Smith and V. Oakley) (Houghton Mifflin, U.S., 1897)	£100
AN OLD FASHIONED GIRL by Louisa May Alcott (Little Brown, U.S., 1902)	£40
THE BOOK OF THE CHILD by Mabel Humphrey (Stokes, U.S., 1903)	£400
RHYMES OF REAL CHILDREN by Elizabeth Sage Goodwin (Duffield, U.S., 1903)	£150
IN THE CLOSED ROOM by Frances Hodgson Burnett (McClure Philips, U.S., 1904)	£75
A CHILD'S GARDEN OF VERSES by R.L. Stevenson (Scribners, U.S., 1905)	£150
DREAM BLOCKS by Aileen C. Higgins (Duffield, U.S., 1908)	£85
THE SEVEN AGES OF CHILDHOOD by Carolyn Wells (Moffat Yard, U.S., 1909)	£100
A CHILD'S BOOK OF OLD VERSES (Duffield, U.S., 1910)	£150
A CHILD'S BOOK OF STORIES. Complied by Penrhyn Wingfield Coussens (Duffield, U.S., 1911)	£100
THE NOW-A-DAYS FAIRY BOOK by Anna A. Chapin (Dodd Mead, U.S., 1911)	£75
'TWAS THE NIGHT BEFORE CHRISTMAS by Clement Moore (Houghton Mifflin, U.S., 1912)	£100
LITTLE WOMEN by Louisa M. Alcott (Little Brown, U.S., 1915)	£50
A CHILD'S STAMP BOOK OF OLD VERSES (Duffield, U.S., 1915)	£100
WHEN CHRISTMAS COMES AROUND by Priscilla Underwood (Duffield, U.S., 1915)	£100
THE EVERYDAY FAIRY BOOK by Anna A. Chapin (Dodd Mead, U.S., 1915)	£75
THE LITTLE MOTHER GOOSE (selected and adapted by Samuel McChord Crothers) (Dodd Mead, U.S., [1915])	£70
THE WATER BABIES by Charles Kingsley (Dodd Mead, U.S., 1916)	£150
THE WATER BABIES by Charles Kingsley (Hodder & Stoughton, [1916])	£150
THE WATER BABIES by Charles Kingsley (Hodder & Stoughton/Boots the Chemist, [c.1930])	£75
THE WATER BABIES by Charles Kingsley (facsimile of the original 1916 edition; limited to 500 numbered copies; in slipcase) (Hodder & Stoughton, 1981)	£95
THE WAY TO WONDERLAND by Mary Stewart Sheldon (Dodd Mead, U.S., 1917)	£100
AT THE BACK OF THE NORTH WIND by George MacDonald (David McKay, U.S., 1920)	£250
A CHILD'S BOOK OF MODERN STORIES. Edited by Ada and Eleanor Skinner (anthology) (Duffield, U.S., 1920)	£60
THE PRINCESS AND THE GOBLIN by George MacDonald (David McKay, U.S., 1921)	£200
A LITTLE CHILD'S BOOK OF STORIES. Edited by Ada and Eleanor Skinner (anthology) (Duffield, U.S., 1922)	£55
HEIDI by Johanna Spyri (David McKay, U.S., 1922)	£250
A VERY LITTLE CHILD'S BOOK OF STORIES. Edited by Ada and Eleanor Skinner (anthology) (Duffield, U.S., 1923)	£55
A CHILD'S PRAYER by Cora Cassard Toogood (David McKay, U.S., 1925)	£55
THE CHILDREN OF DICKENS. Compiled by S. McChord Crothers (Scribners, U.S., 1925)	£55
A CHILD'S BOOK OF COUNTRY STORIES. Edited by Ada and Eleanor Skinner (anthology) (Duffield, U.S., 1925)	£55

SOPER, Eileen

British illustrator. Born: 1905. She was encouraged by her father, the artist George Soper (1870-1942) and was elected to The Print Makers Society of California in 1921 after her first exhibition of etchings. She illustrated the entire series of Enid Blyton's 'Famous Five' adventures and a vast range of other books. She was a founder member of the Society of Wildlife Artists (1964) and a member of the Royal Society of Miniature Painters (1972). Died:1990.

Prices are for books in Very Good condition with dustjackets.

Books Written and Illustrated by Eileen Soper

HAPPY RABBIT (Macmillan, 1947)	£40
DORMOUSE AWAKE (Macmillan, 1948)	£40
SAIL AWAY SHREW (Macmillan, 1949)	£40

'Famous Five' Books Illustrated by Eileen Soper

FIVE ON A TREASURE ISLAND: An Adventure Story (Hodder & Stoughton, 1942) £500
FIVE GO ADVENTURING AGAIN (Hodder & Stoughton, 1943) £250
FIVE RUN AWAY TOGETHER (Hodder & Stoughton, 1944) £200
FIVE GO TO SMUGGLERS' TOP (Hodder & Stoughton, 1945) £300
FIVE GO OFF IN A CARAVAN (Hodder & Stoughton, 1946)..£200
FIVE ON KIRRIN ISLAND AGAIN (Hodder & Stoughton, 1947) £150
FIVE GO OFF TO CAMP (Hodder & Stoughton, 1948) £120

One of Jessie Willcox Smith's illustrations for **The Water Babies**. *Hers is amongst the most collected editions of this classic work.*

SOPER, Eileen

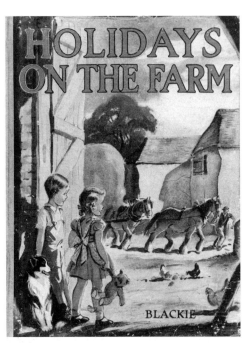

This 1944 Blackie volume is illustrated by Eileen Soper, best known for her illustrations for the 'Famous Five' series.

*Soper's 1947 edition of **Alice in Wonderland** is now valued at £40 in Very Good condition with the dustjacket (above).*

FIVE GET INTO TROUBLE (Hodder & Stoughton, 1949)..£100
FIVE FALL INTO ADVENTURE (Hodder & Stoughton, 1950) £75
FIVE ON A HIKE TOGETHER (Hodder & Stoughton, 1951) £55
FIVE HAVE A WONDERFUL TIME (Hodder & Stoughton, 1952)...£55
FIVE GO DOWN TO THE SEA (Hodder & Stoughton, 1953) £45
FIVE GO TO MYSTERY MOOR (Hodder & Stoughton, 1954) £45
FIVE HAVE PLENTY OF FUN (Hodder & Stoughton, 1955) £40
FIVE ON A SECRET TRAIL (Hodder & Stoughton, 1956) £40
FIVE GO TO BILLYCOCK HILL (Hodder & Stoughton, 1957) £40
FIVE GET INTO A FIX (Hodder & Stoughton, 1958) £35
FIVE ON FINNISTON FARM (Hodder & Stoughton, 1960)...£35
FIVE GO TO DEMON'S ROCK (Hodder & Stoughton, 1961)..£35
FIVE HAVE A MYSTERY TO SOLVE (Hodder & Stoughton, 1962) £35
FIVE ARE TOGETHER AGAIN (Hodder & Stoughton, 1963)..£35
THE FAMOUS FIVE SPECIAL (contains 'Five go off to Camp', 'Five go off in a Caravan' and 'Five Have a Wonderful Time')
(Hodder & Stoughton, 1959) £35
THE FAMOUS FIVE BIG BOOK (contains 'Five on a Treasure Island', 'Five Go Adventuring Again' and
'Five Run Away Together') (Hodder & Stoughton, 1964)..£35

Other Enid Blyton Books Illustrated by Eileen Soper

I'LL TELL YOU A STORY (Macmillan, 1942) £30
ENID BLYTON'S MERRY STORY BOOK (Hodder & Stoughton, 1943) £30
THE TOYS COME TO LIFE (Brockhampton Press, [1944]) £30
COME TO THE CIRCUS (Brockhampton Press, [1944])..£30
ENID BLYTON'S JOLLY STORY BOOK (Hodder & Stoughton, 1944) £30
POLLY PIGLET (Brockhampton Press, [1944]) £30
TALES FROM THE BIBLE (Methuen, 1944)..£30
THE BLUE STORY BOOK (Methuen, 1945) £30
THE CONJURING WIZARD and Other Stories (Macmillan, 1945)...£30
THE RUNAWAY KITTEN (Brockhampton Press, [1945]) £30
THE TWINS GO TO NURSERY-RHYME LAND (Brockhampton Press, [1945]) £30
THE TEDDY BEAR'S PARTY (Brockhampton Press, [1945])..£30
THE BAD LITTLE MONKEY (Brockhampton Press, [1946]) £30

ENID BLYTON'S GAY STORY BOOK (Hodder & Stoughton, 1946) £35
THE LITTLE WHITE DUCK and Other Stories (Macmillan, 1946) £30
THE SURPRISING CARAVAN (Brockhampton Press, 1946)..£30
THE TRAIN THAT LOST ITS WAY (Brockhampton Press, [1946])..£30
AT SEASIDE COTTAGE (Brockhampton Press, [1947])..£25
THE GREEN STORY BOOK (Methuen, 1947) £25
ENID BLYTON'S LUCKY STORY BOOK (Hodder & Stoughton, 1947)..£30
SECRET OF THE OLD MILL (Brockhampton Press, [1948]) £30
TALES OF THE TWINS (Brockhampton Press, [1948]) £20
THE ASTONISHING LADDER and Other Stories (Macmillan, 1950)..£30
THE THREE NAUGHTY CHILDREN and Other Stories (Macmillan, 1950) £30
TRICKY THE GOBLIN and Other Stories (Macmillan, 1950) £25
ENID BLYTON'S BOOK OF THE YEAR (music by Alec Rowley) (Evans, 1950) £25
ENID BLYTON'S BRIGHT STORY BOOK (Brockhampton Press, 1952)...£25
MY FIRST NATURE BOOK (Macmillan, 1952) £10
ENID BLYTON'S FRIENDLY STORY BOOK (Brockhampton Press, 1954)..£25

Other Books Illustrated by Eileen Soper

A CASTLE FOR JOHN-PETER by Ursula Moray Williams (Harrap, 1941) £15
MALTA: A KITTEN by Mary Moore (Macmillan, 1943) £15
RABBIT TALES by Mary Moore (Macmillan 1944) £15
COUNTRY DAYS by E. Gould (Blackie, 1944) £15
HOLIDAYS ON THE FARM by E. Gould (Blackie, 1944) £15
HAPPY DAYS ON THE FARM by E. Gould (Blackie, 1944) £15
ALICE IN WONDERLAND by Lewis Carroll (Harrap, 1947) £40
THE SONG OF LAMBERT by Mazo de la Roch (Macmillan, 1955)...£25
HOW TO OBSERVE WILD ANIMALS by Maxwell Knight (Routledge, 1957) £15
BULLY AND THE BADGER by Charles Malins (Robert Yeatman, 1974) £15
NO BADGERS IN MY WOOD by Phil Drabble (Michael Joseph, 1979)...£15

SOWERBY, Millicent

British illustrator. Born: Amy Millicent Sowerby in 1878, the daughter of the illustrator, J.G. Sowerby. Largely self-taught, she collaborated with her sister, Githa Sowerby, on a series of children's books, as well as illustrating such classics as *Alice in Wonderland* (1907) and Stevenson's *A Child's Garden of Verses* (1908). Died: 1967.

Prices are for books in Very Good condition.

THE WISE BOOK by Githa Sowerby (Dent, 1906) £80
ALICE'S ADVENTURES IN WONDERLAND by Lewis Carroll (Chatto & Windus, 1907) £120
THE BUMBLETOES by Githa Sowerby (verse) (Chatto & Windus, 1907) £80
CHILDHOOD by Githa Sowerby (verse) (Chatto & Windus, 1907) £90
YESTERDAY'S CHILDREN by Githa Sowerby (verse) (Chatto & Windus, 1908) £55
A CHILD'S GARDEN OF VERSES by R.L. Stevenson (Chatto & Windus, 1908) £100
GRIMM'S FAIRY TALES. Selected and retold by Githa Sowerby (twelve colour illustrations by Millicent Sowerby)
    (Grant Richards, 1909)..£100
THE HAPPY BOOK by Githa Sowerby (Hodder & Stoughton, [1909])..£60
LITTLE PLAYS FOR LITTLE PEOPLE by Githa Sowerby (Hodder & Stoughton, [1910])..........................£60
THE MERRY BOOK by Githa Sowerby (Hodder & Stoughton, [1911]) £60
MY BIRTHDAY by Githa Sowerby (Hodder & Stoughton, [1911]) £55
POEMS OF CHILDHOOD by Githa Sowerby (Hodder & Stoughton, [1912]) £55
THE PRETTY BOOK by Githa Sowerby (verse) (Frowde, [1915]) £60
CINDERELLA. Adapted by Githa Sowerby (Hodder & Stoughton, [1915])...£70
THE DAINTY BOOK by Githa Sowerby (verse) (Hodder & Stoughton, [1915]) £60
THE GAY BOOK by Githa Sowerby (verse) (Hodder & Stoughton, [1915]) £60
THE BRIGHT BOOK by Githa Sowerby (verse) (Hodder & Stoughton, [1916]) £60
THE BONNIE BOOK by Githa Sowerby (verse) (Humphrey Milford, [1918]) £60
THE WISE BOOK by Githa Sowerby (verse) (Milford & Warner, [1921]) £60

SPYRI, Johanna

Swiss author. Born: Johanna Heusser in Zurich in 1827. Wrote a number of children's books, but is best known for *Heidi*, about a Swiss orphan girl. Died: 1901.

Prices are for books in Very Good condition (with dustjackets after 1930).

HEIDI'S EARLY EXPERIENCES: A Story for Children (Sampson Low, 1884)..£1,500
HEIDI'S FURTHER EXPERIENCES: A Story for Children (Sampson Low, 1884) £1,500
HEIDI: Her Years of Wandering and Learning (translated by Louise Brooks) (Boston, U.S., 1885 [1884]) £1,000
HEIDI (illustrated by Lizzie Lawson) (Dent, [1909]) £100
HEIDI (illustrated by Maria L. Kirk; translated by Elisabeth P. Stork) (Lippincott, U.S., [1919]) £50
HEIDI (illustrated by Jessie Willcox Smith) (David McKay, U.S., 1922)...£250
HEIDI (illustrated by Anne Anderson; translated by Helene S. White) (Harrap, 1924) £75

SPYRI, Johanna

SHIRLEY TEMPLE IN 'HEIDI' (tie-in with the film 'Heidi', starring Shirley Temple) (Saalfield, U.S., 1937) £50
HEIDI (illustrated by Vincent O. Cohen; issued with dustjacket) (Dent, 1950) £10
HEIDI (illustrated by Raymond Sheppard; translated by Marian Edwardes; issued with dustjacket) (Blackie, 1955)....................£10
HEIDI (illustrated by Cecil Leslie; translated by Eileen Hall; paperback) (Puffin, 1956) £3
SWISS STORIES FOR CHILDREN (translated by L. Wheelock) (Blackie, 1889 [1888]) £250
IN SAFE KEEPING (translated by L. Wheelock) (Blackie, [1896]) £100
HEIMATLOS: Two Stories for Children, and Those Who Love Children (illustrated by Frederick Richardson;
    translated by Emma Stelter Hopkins) (Ginn, U.S., 1912) £75
CORNELLI (illustrated by Maria L. Kirk; translated by Elisabeth P. Stork) (Lippincott, U.S./U.K., 1920) £50
MÄZLI: A Story of the Swiss Valleys (translated by Elisabeth P. Stork) (Lippincott, U.S./U.K., 1921)..................£50
FRANCESCA AT HINTERWALD (Lippincott, U.S./U.K., [1923]) £50
VINZI: A Story of the Swiss Alps (translated by Elisabeth P. Stork) (Lippincott, U.S./U.K., 1923)....................£30
DORA (translated by Elisabeth P. Stork) (Lippincott, U.S./U.K., [1924]) £30
GRITLI'S CHILDREN (translated by Elisabeth P. Stork) (Lippincott, U.S./U.K., [1924]) £30
CHILDREN OF THE ALPS (translated by Elisabeth P. Stork) (Lippincott, U.S./U.K., [1925])......................£30
EVELI, THE LITTLE SINGER (translated by Elisabeth P. Stork) (Lippincott, U.S./U.K., [1926]).................£30
PEPPINO (translated by Elisabeth P. Stork) (Lippincott, U.S./U.K., [1926]) £30
JÖRLI, or The Stauffer Mill (translated by Elisabeth P. Stork) (Lippincott, U.S./U.K., 1928) £30
SWISS STORIES FROM MADAME JOHANNA SPYRI and Two Stories from Madame Kabalinsky (Gresham, [1930]) £15
ALL ALONE IN THE WORLD (illustrated by Michael Ross; translated by M.E. Calthrop; issued with dustjacket) (Dent, 1958) £10

STEADMAN, Ralph

British illustrator. Born: Liverpool, 1936. Studied at Abergele Grammar School and the London College of Printing. Best known for his grotesque illustrations for magazines such as *Private Eye* and the *New Statesman*, but has illustrated a handful of children's books, winning the Francis Williams Award for his edition of *Alice in Wonderland* (1967).

Prices are for books in Very Good condition with dustjackets.

FLY AWAY PETER by Frank Dickens (Dobson, 1964) £40
THE BIG SQUIRREL AND THE LITTLE RHINOCEROS by Mischa Damjan (Dobson, 1965) £35
ALICE IN WONDERLAND by Lewis Carroll (Dobson, 1967) £70
RALPH STEADMAN'S JELLY BOOK (Dobson, 1967)...£45
THE LITTLE RED COMPUTER (McGraw, U.S., 1969)..£40
TWO CATS IN AMERICA by Mischa Damjan (Longman, 1970) £35
THROUGH THE LOOKING GLASS AND WHAT ALICE FOUND THERE by Lewis Carroll (MacGibbon & Kee, 1972) £60
RALPH STEADMAN'S BUMPER TO BUMPER BOOK FOR CHILDREN (Pan, 1973)......................................£30
THE BRIDGE (Collins, 1974) £25
THE HUNTING OF THE SNARK (Dempsey, 1975) £45
CHERRYWOOD CANNON. Based on a story by Dimitri Sidjanski (Paddington Press, 1978)....................£30
EMERGENCY MOUSE by Bernard Stone (Anderson Press, 1978) £25
INSPECTOR MOUSE by Bernard Stone (Anderson Press, 1980) £25
QUASIMODO MOUSE by Bernard Stone (Anderson Press, 1984) £25
TREASURE ISLAND (Harrap, 1985) £35
THE COMPLETE ALICE and THE HUNTING OF THE SNARK (Cape, 1986) £30

STEVENSON, Robert Louis

Scottish author. Born: Robert Lewis Balfour Stevenson in Edinburgh in 1850. Studied at Edinburgh Academy and Edinburgh University. Enjoyed his first success with *Travels with a Donkey* (1879), but is now best known for his adventure stories, *Treasure Island* (1883) and *Kidnapped* (1886), and the macabre tale, *The Strange Case of Dr Jekyll and Mr Hyde* (1886). Other children's works include *The Black Arrow* (1888) and *A Child's Garden of Verses* (1885). Settled in the Pacific island of Samoa in 1891. Died: 1894.

Prices are for books in Very Good condition.

TREASURE ISLAND (Cassell, 1883) £5,000
TREASURE ISLAND (illustrated by Mervyn Peake) (Eyre & Spottiswoode, 1949) £15
TREASURE ISLAND (illustrated by Ralph Steadman; issued with dustjacket) (Harrap, 1985) £35
A CHILD'S GARDEN OF VERSES (Longmans Green, 1885) £3,000
A CHILD'S GARDEN OF VERSES (illustrated by Charles Robinson) (John Lane: The Bodley Head, 1896 [1895]) £350
A CHILD'S GARDEN OF VERSES (illustrated by Charles Robinson; reissue) (John Lane: The Bodley Head, 1921) £150
A CHILD'S GARDEN OF VERSES (illustrated by Jessie Willcox Smith) (Scribners, U.S., 1905) £150
A CHILD'S GARDEN OF VERSES (illustrated by Millicent Sowerby) (Chatto & Windus, 1908) £100
A CHILD'S GARDEN OF VERSES (illustrated by H. Willebeek Le Mair) (Harrap, 1931) £200
SONGS WITH MUSIC FROM 'A CHILD'S GARDEN OF VERSES' (illustrated by Margaret Tarrant) (T.C. & E.C. Jack, [1918]) ..£50
KIDNAPPED (Cassell, 1886) £2,500
THE MERRY MEN and Other Tales (Chatto & Windus, 1887) £100
THE BLACK ARROW (Cassell, 1888) £80
THE MASTER OF BALLANTRAE (Cassell, 1889)...£350
THE LAND OF NOD and Other Poems for Children. Edited by Michael Hague (Holt, U.S., 1988) £25

STOKER, Bram

Irish author. Born: Abraham Stoker in Dublin in 1847. The author of *Dracula* wrote a single children's work, a collection of weird, allegorical fables for young readers. Died: 1912.

Prices are for books in Very Good condition.

UNDER THE SUNSET (illustrated by W. Fitzgerald and W.V. Cockburn; full parchment vellum binding)
(Sampson Low, 1882 [1881]) £300
UNDER THE SUNSET (second edition; green cloth binding) (Sampson Low, 1882) £75

STRANG, Herbert

Pseudonym of George Herbert Ely (1866-1958) and C. James l'Estrange (1867-1947). Unique collaboration between two men as 'Herbert Strang' produced a huge number of patriotic adventure stories in addition to editing Herbert Strang annuals.

Prices are for books in Good condition.

'Herbert Strang's Historical Series'

WITH MARLBOROUGH TO MALPLAQUET (with Richard Stead) (Hodder & Stoughton, 1908) £10
WITH THE BLACK PRINCE (with Richard Stead) (Hodder & Stoughton, 1908) £10
A MARINER OF ENGLAND (with Richard Stead) (Hodder & Stoughton, 1908) £10
ONE OF RUPERT'S HORSE (with Richard Stead) (Hodder & Stoughton, 1908) £10
LION-HEART (with Richard Stead) (Hodder & Stoughton, 1908)...£10
CLAUD THE ARCHER (with John Aston) (Hodder & Stoughton, 1908)..£10
IN THE FOREST (with John Aston) (Hodder & Stoughton, 1908) £10
ROGER THE SCOUT (with George Lawrence) (Hodder & Stoughton, 1908) £10
FOR THE WHITE ROSE (with George Lawrence) (Hodder & Stoughton, 1908) £10

'Strang's Penny Books'

THREE BOYS AT THE FAIR (Humphrey Milford, 1926-27) £10
KITTY'S KITTEN (Humphrey Milford, 1926-27) £10
THE CINEMA DOG (Humphrey Milford, 1926-27) £10
BILL SAWYER'S VC (Humphrey Milford, 1926-27) £10
THE GAME OF BROWNIES (Humphrey Milford, 1926-27) £10
JENNY'S ARK (Humphrey Milford, 1926-27) £10
BAA-BAA AND THE WIDE WORLD (Humphrey Milford, 1926-27) £10
TOM LEAVES SCHOOL (Humphrey Milford, 1926-27) £10
THE MISCHIEF-MAKING MAGPIE (Humphrey Milford, 1926-27) £10
A RIDE WITH ROBIN HOOD (Humphrey Milford, 1926-27) £10
PETE'S ELEPHANT (Humphrey Milford, 1926-27) £10
TEN POUNDS REWARD (Humphrey Milford, 1926-27) £10
ADOLF'S DOG (Humphrey Milford, 1926-27)...£10
THE ADVENTURES OF A PENNY STAMP (Humphrey Milford, 1926-27) £10
DON'T BE TOO SURE (Humphrey Milford, 1926-27) £10
JACK AND JOCKO (Humphrey Milford, 1926-27) £10
THE PRINCESS AND THE ROBBERS (Humphrey Milford, 1926-27) £10
THE CHRISTMAS FAIRY (Humphrey Milford, 1926-27)..£10
THE SEVEN SONS (Humphrey Milford, 1926-27) £10
THE RED CANDLE (Humphrey Milford, 1926-27) £10
THE MILLER'S DAUGHTER (Humphrey Milford, 1926-27) £10
THE GREY GOOSE FEATHERS (Humphrey Milford, 1926-27) £10
THE BIRTHDAY PRESENT (Humphrey Milford, 1926-27) £10
THERE WAS A LITTLE PIG (Humphrey Milford, 1926-27) £10
THE MAGIC SMOKE (Humphrey Milford, 1926-27) £10
THE CHILDREN OF THE FERRY (Humphrey Milford, 1926-27) £10
SUGAR CANDY TOWN (Humphrey Milford, 1926-27) £10
LITTLE MR PIXIE (Humphrey Milford, 1926-27)...£10
THE LITTLE SEA HORSE (Humphrey Milford, 1926-27) £10
THE LITTLE BLUE-GREY HARE (Humphrey Milford, 1926-27) £10

Others

TOM BURNABY (Blackie, 1904) £60
BOYS OF THE LIGHT BRIGADE (Blackie, 1904) £50
KOBO (illustrated by William Rainey) (Blackie, 1904) £40
BROWN OF MOUKDEN (Blackie, 1905) £40
BROWN OF MOUKDEN (reissued as 'Jack Brown in China') (OUP, 1923) £20
THE ADVENTURES OF HARRY ROCHESTER (illustrated by William Rainey) (Blackie, 1905) £25
JACK HARDY (illustrated by William Rainey) (Hodder & Stoughton, 1905) £25
ONE OF CLIVE'S HEROES (illustrated by William Rainey) (Hodder & Stoughton, 1906) £25
SAMBA (illustrated by William Rainey) (Hodder & Stoughton, 1906) £25
ROB THE RANGER (illustrated by W.H. Margetson) (Hodder & Stoughton, 1907) £25
WITH DRAKE ON THE SPANISH MAIN (illustrated by Archibald Webb) (Hodder & Stoughton, 1907) £25

KING OF THE AIR (illustrated by W.E. Webster) (Hodder & Stoughton, 1907) £25
HUMPHREY BOLD (Hodder & Stoughton, 1908)...£25
BARCLAY OF THE GUIDES (illustrated by H.W. Koekkoek) (Hodder & Stoughton, 1908) £25
LORD OF THE SEAS (illustrated by C. Fleming Williams) (Hodder & Stoughton, 1908) £25
PALM TREE ISLAND (illustrated by Archibald Webb and Alan Wright) (Hodder & Stoughton, 1909) £25
SETTLERS AND SCOUTS (illustrated by T.C. Dugdale) (Hodder & Stoughton, 1909) £25
SWIFT AND SURE (Hodder & Stoughton, 1909) £25
THE CRUISE OF THE GYRO-CAR (illustrated by A.C. Michael) (Hodder & Stoughton, 1910) £25
THE ADVENTURES OF DICK TREVANION (illustrated by William Rainey) (Hodder & Stoughton, 1910) £25
ROUND THE WORLD IN SEVEN DAYS (illustrated by A.C. Michael) (Hodder & Stoughton, 1910) £25
THE FLYING BOAT (illustrated by T.C. Dugdale) (Hodder & Stoughton, 1911) £25
THE AIR SCOUT (illustrated by W.R.S. Stott) (Hodder & Stoughton, 1911)..£25
THE MOTOR SCOUT (illustrated by Cyril Cuneo) (Hodder & Stoughton, 1912) £25
THE AIR PATROL (illustrated by Cyril Cuneo) (Hodder & Stoughton, 1912) £25
CERDIC THE SAXON (illustrated by L.L. Weedon) (Hodder & Stoughton, 1913) £25
A LITTLE NORMAN MAID (Hodder & Stoughton, 1913) £25
SULTAN JIM, EMPIRE-BUILDER (Hodder & Stoughton, 1913)...£25
A GENTLEMAN-AT-ARMS (Hodder & Stoughton, 1914) £25
A HERO OF LIEGE (Hodder & Stoughton, 1914)..£25
FIGHTING WITH FRENCH (Hodder & Stoughton, 1915) £25
THE BOY WHO WOULD NOT LEARN (OUP, 1915)...£25
THE SILVER SHOT (OUP, 1915) £25
IN TRAFALGAR'S BAY (OUP, 1915) £25
BURTON OF THE FLYING CORPS (Hodder & Stoughton, 1916) £25
FRANK FORESTER (Hodder & Stoughton, 1916)..£25
THE OLD MAN OF THE MOUNTAIN (illustrated by Rene Bull) (Hodder & Stoughton, 1916).............£25
THROUGH THE ENEMY'S LINES (illustrated by H.E. Elcock) (Hodder & Stoughton, 1916) £25
CARRY ON ! (illustrated by H.E. Elcock and H. Evison) (Hodder & Stoughton, 1917)........................£25
WITH HAIG ON THE SOMME (OUP, 1917) £25
STEADY, BOYS, STEADY (Hodder & Stoughton, 1917) £25
THE LONG TRAIL (OUP, 1918) £25
TOM WILLOUGHBY'S SCOUTS (OUP, 1919) £25
THE BLUE RAIDER (OUP, 1919) £25
BRIGHT IDEAS (illustrated by C.E. Brock) (OUP, 1920) £25
NO MAN'S ISLAND (illustrated by C.E. Brock) (OUP, 1921) £25
THE CAVE IN THE HILLS (OUP, 1922) £25
BASTABLE COVE (OUP, 1922) £25
WINNING HIS NAME (illustrated by C.E. Brock) (OUP, 1922) £25
HONOUR FIRST (illustrated by W.E. Wightman) (OUP, 1923) £25
TRUE AS STEEL (illustrated by C.E. Brock) (OUP, 1923) £25
A THOUSAND MILES AN HOUR (OUP, 1924)..£25
THE HEIR OF A HUNDRED KINGS (OUP, 1924) £25
YOUNG JACK (OUP, 1924)..£25
MARTIN OF OLD LONDON (OUP, 1925) £25
OLWYN'S SECRET (OUP, 1925) £25
DAN BOLTON'S DISCOVERY (OUP, 1926) £25
LOST IN LONDON (OUP, 1927) £15
THE RIVER PIRATES (OUP, 1927)...£15
THE RIDERS (OUP, 1928) £10
ON LONDON RIVER (OUP, 1929) £10
SHIPS AND THEIR STORY: Scouting stories (OUP, 1931) £10
DICKON OF THE CHASE (OUP, 1931)..£10
A SERVANT OF JOHN COMPANY (OUP, 1932) £10

STREATFEILD, Noel

British author. Born: Sussex, 1895. Studied at the Academy of Dramatic Art, London, subsequently working as an actress until she turned to writing in 1929. Produced a handful of adult novels until the success of *Ballet Shoes* (1936) launched her as a children's author. Awarded the Carnegie Medal for *The Circus is Coming* (1938), and an OBE in 1983. Died: 1986.

Prices are for books in Very Good condition with dustjackets where applicable.

THE WHICHARTS (Heinemann, 1931) £50
TOP AND BOTTOMS (Heinemann, 1933) £45
SHEPHERDESS OF SHEEP (Heinemann, 1934) £45
THE CHILDREN'S MATINEE (plays) (Heinemann, 1934) £30
BALLET SHOES: A Story of Three Children on the Stage (illustrated by Ruth Gervis) (Dent, 1936) £50
IT PAYS TO BE GOOD (Heinemann, 1936) £25
WISDOM TEETH (play) (Samuel French: 'Acting Edition', [1936]) £15
TENNIS SHOES (illustrated by D.L. Mays) (Dent, 1937) £250

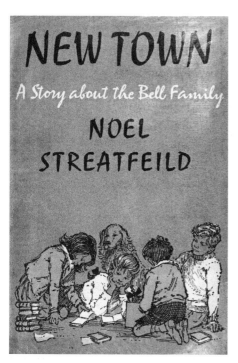

Left: Noel Streatfeild's **New Town** *(1960) is valued at £20 in Very Good condition with the Shirley Hughes dustjacket.*

Above: One of Ruth Gervis's illustrations for Streatfeild's most famous work, **Ballet Shoes** *(1936), now valued at £50.*

CAROLINE ENGLAND (Heinemann, 1937) £25
THE CIRCUS IS COMING (illustrated by Steven Spurrier) (Dent, 1938) £40
DENNIS THE DRAGON (verse; illustrated by Ruth Gervis) (Dent, 1939)..£20
LUKE (Heinemann, 1939) £20
THE HOUSE IN CORNWALL (illustrated by D.L. Mays) (Dent, 1940) £20
THE WINTER IS PAST (Collins, [1940]) £20
THE CHILDREN OF PRIMROSE LANE (illustrated by Marcia Lane Foster) (Dent, 1941) £20
HARLEQUINADE (illustrated by Clarke Hutton) (Chatto & Windus, 1943)......................................£20
CURTAIN UP (illustrated by D.L. Mays) (Dent, 1944) £20
MYRA CARROL (Collins, 1944) £20
SAPLINGS (Collins, 1945) £25
PARTY FROCK (illustrated by Anna Zinkeisen) (Collins, 1946) £30
THE PAINTED GARDEN (illustrated by Ley Kenyon) (Collins, 1949)..£20
OSBERT (Rand McNally, U.S., 1950) £15
MOTHERING SUNDAY (Collins, 1950) £20
THE YEARS OF GRACE. Edited by Noel Streatfeild (essays by various authors) (Evans, 1950) £15
THE THEATER CAT (illustrated by Susanne Shuba) (Rand McNally, U.S., 1951) £15
WHITE BOOTS (illustrated by Milein Cosman) (Collins, 1951)..£20
THE PICTURE STORY OF BRITAIN (non-fiction) (Watts, U.S., 1951)...£10
AUNT CLARA (Collins, 1952) £20
THE FEARLESS TREASURE: A Story of England from Then to Now (illustrated by Dorothea Braby)
   (Joseph, 1953) £15
THE FIRST BOOK OF BALLET (non-fiction) (Watts, U.S., 1953) £15
BY SPECIAL REQUEST. Edited by Noel Streatfeild (stories by various authors) (Collins, 1953) £15
THE BELL FAMILY (illustrated by Shirley Hughes) (Collins, 1954) £20
GROWING UP GRACEFULLY: Etiquette. Edited by Noel Streatfeild (illustrated by John Dugan) (Arthur Barker, 1955)...............£7
THE DAY BEFORE YESTERDAY: Firsthand Stories of Fifty Years Ago.
   Edited by Noel Streatfeild (stories by various authors; illustrated by Dick Hart) (Collins, 1956) £10
THE GREY FAMILY (illustrated by Pat Marriott) (Hamish Hamilton, 1956) £15
JUDITH (Collins, 1956) £15
THE FIRST BOOK OF BALLET (non-fiction) (Bailey & Swinfen, 1956) £15
WINTLE'S WONDERS (illustrated by Richard Kennedy) (Collins, 1957) £15
THE FIRST BOOK OF ENGLAND (non-fiction; illustrated by Gioia Fiammenghi) (Watts, U.S., [1958]) £10
THE FIRST BOOK OF ENGLAND (non-fiction; illustrated by Gioia Fiammenghi) (Bailey & Swinfen, 1958) £10
QUEEN VICTORIA (non-fiction; illustrated by Robert Frankenburg) (Random House, U.S., 1958) £10
QUEEN VICTORIA (non-fiction; illustrated by Robert Frankenburg) (W.H. Allen, 1961)........................£10
THE ROYAL BALLET SCHOOL (non-fiction; photographs by Gabor Denes) (Collins, 1959) £15
NOEL STREATFEILD'S BALLET ANNUAL (non-fiction) (Collins, 1959) £12

BABY BOOK SERIES (twelve parts) (Arthur Barker, 1959) ....each £10
BERTRAM (illustrated by Margery Gill) (Hamish Hamilton, 1959) £10
CHRISTMAS WITH THE CHRYSTALS (Blackwell, 1959 [1960]) £12
LOOK AT THE CIRCUS (non-fiction) (Hamish Hamilton, 1960) £8
NEW TOWN: A Story about the Bell Family (illustrated by Shirley Hughes) (Collins, 1960) £15
THE PAINTED GARDEN: A Story of a Holiday in Hollywood (illustrated by Shirley Hughes; paperback) (Puffin, 1961) £5
THE SILENT SPEAKER (Collins, 1961) £8
APPLE BOUGH (illustrated by Margery Gill) (Collins, 1962) £15
LISA GOES TO RUSSIA (illustrated by Geraldine Spence) (Collins, 1963) £8
A VICARAGE FAMILY (illustrated by Charles Mozley) (Collins, 1963) £12
CONFIRMATION AND AFTER. Edited by Noel Streatfeild (Heinemann, 1963)..£5
PRISKA by Merja Otava. Edited by Noel Streatfeild (Benn, 1964) £6
THE CHILDREN ON THE TOP FLOOR (illustrated by Jillian Willet) (Collins, 1964) £12
THE THAMES: LONDON'S RIVER (non-fiction; illustrated by Kurt Wiese) (Champaign Garrard, U.S., 1964)
THE THAMES: LONDON'S RIVER (non-fiction; illustrated by Kurt Wiese) (Muller, 1966)...........................£6
LET'S GO COACHING (illustrated by Peter Warner) (Hamish Hamilton, 1965)...£8
AWAY FROM THE VICARAGE (Collins, 1965) £20
THE GROWING SUMMER (illustrated by Edward Ardizzone) (Collins, 1966) £35
OLD CHAIRS TO MEND (illustrated by Barry Wilkinson) (Hamish Hamilton, 1966) £15
ENJOYING OPERA (non-fiction; illustrated by Hilary Abrahams) (Dobson, 1966).....................................£5
BEFORE CONFIRMATION (non-fiction) (Heinemann, 1967) £5
THE FIRST BOOK OF SHOES (non-fiction) (Watts, U.S., 1967) £5
THE FIRST BOOKS OF SHOES (non-fiction) (Watts, 1971) £5
CALDICOTT PLACE (illustrated by Betty Maxey) (Collins, 1967) £20
THE BARROW LANE GANG (BBC, 1968) £5
GEMMA (illustrated by Betty Maxey) (May Fair, 1968) £4
GEMMA AND SISTERS (illustrated by Betty Maxey) (May Fair, 1968) £4
NICHOLAS by Marlie Brande. Edited by Noel Streatfeild (Benn, 1968) £6
GEMMA ALONE (May Fair, 1969) £4
GOODBYE GEMMA (May Fair, 1969) £4
THURSDAY'S CHILD (illustrated by Peggy Fortnum) (Collins, 1970) £20
RED RIDING HOOD (non-fiction) (Benn, 1970) £8
SLEEPY NICHOLAS by Marle Brande. Edited by Noel Streatfeild (Benn, 1970).....................................£8
BEYOND THE VICARAGE (Collins, 1971) £15
BALLET SHOES FOR ANNA (illustrated by Mary Dinsdale) (Collins, 1972) £15
THE BOY PHAROAH, TUTANKHAMEN (non-fiction) (Joseph, 1972) £10
THE NOEL STREATFEILD SUMMER HOLIDAY BOOK (illustrated by Sara Silcock) (Dent, 1973) £7
THE NOEL STREATFEILD CHRISTMAS HOLIDAY BOOK (illustrated by Sara Silcock) (Dent, 1973) £7
THE NOEL STREATFEILD EASTER HOLIDAY BOOK (illustrated by Sara Silcock) (Dent, 1974)............£7
WHEN THE SIREN WAILED (illustrated by Margery Gill) (Collins, 1974)..£10
GRAN-NANNIE (Joseph, 1975) £15
A YOUNG PERSON'S GUIDE TO BALLET (non-fiction) (Warne, 1975) £6
FAR TO GO (illustrated by Charles Mozley) (Collins, 1976) £15
THE NOEL STREATFEILD BIRTHDAY STORY BOOK (Dent, 1976) £7
THE NOEL STREATFEILD WEEKEND STORY BOOK (Dent, 1977) £7
MEET THE MAITLANDS (illustrated by Antony Maitland) (W.H. Allen, 1978) £12
THE MAITLANDS: ALL CHANGE AT CUCKLY PLACE (illustrated by Antony Maitland) (W.H. Allen, 1979)..............£10

STUDDY, G.E.

British artist. Born: 1878. Best known as the creator of Bonzo the dog. Died: 1948.

Prices are for books and annuals in Very Good condition.

'Bonzo' Annuals

BONZO LAUGHTER ANNUAL [1935] £140
BONZO'S ANNUAL [1936] (Bonzo sitting on throne)...£125
BONZO'S ANNUAL [1937] (Bonzo dressed as clown with balloon)..£120
BONZO'S ANNUAL [1938] (Bonzo skipping) £120
BONZO'S ANNUAL [1947] (Bonzo and jack-in-the-box) £50
BONZO'S ANNUAL [1948] (Bonzo with a donkey and cart) £50
BONZO'S ANNUAL [1949] (Bonzo wearing a fez and firing a peashooter) £50
BONZO'S ANNUAL [1950] (Bonzo with parrot) £50
BONZO'S ANNUAL [1951] (Bonzo as a cowboy)..£45
BONZO'S ANNUAL [1952] (Bonzo on a moon rocket)..£40
THE BONZO PORTFOLIO (1-10) ....each £250

'Bonzo' Books

BONZO'S HAPPY DAY (Dunlop Press, no date) £150
BONZO'S LEAP YEAR (Dunlop Press, no date) £150
BONZO'S HAPPY FAMILY (Dunlop Press, no date) £150

*Above: Five little dancers from Noel Streatfeild's **Ballet Shoes**. Streatfeild went on to write several more books about the ballet.*

*Right: Charles Keeping provided the dustjacket illustration for Rosemary Sutcliff's 1965 novel, **The Mark of the Horse Lord**.*

BONZO'S LITTLE HOLIDAY (Dunlop Press, no date) £150
BACHELOR BONZO (Dunlop Press, no date) £150
BONZO'S BRAN PIE (Dunlop Press, no date) £150
MR BONZO COMES TO TOWN (Thomas Allen, Toronto, 1923-1927) £150
BAD BOY BONZO (Thomas Allen, Toronto, 1923-1927) £150
BONZO'S SEASIDE HOLIDAY (Thomas Allen, Toronto, 1923-1927) £150
BONZO'S COUNTRY HOLIDAY (Thomas Allen, Toronto, 1923-1927) £150
THE GOOD DEEDS OF BONZO (Thomas Allen, Toronto, 1923-1927) £150
THE ADVENTURES OF BONZO (Thomas Allen, Toronto, 1923-1927) £150
BONZO PAINTING BOOK (Swain, [1924]) £150
THE BONZO BOOK (Partridge, [1925]) £200
THE NEW BONZO BOOK (Partridge, [1927]) £200
THE BONZOOLOO BOOK (Partridge, [1929]) £200
BONZO AND US (Partridge, 1931) £160
BONZO: The Great Big Holiday Book (cover shows Bonzo on rocking horse) (Dean, 1934) £75
BONZO: The Great Big Holiday Book (cover shows Bonzo's head) (Dean, 1934) £75
BONZO COLOURING BOOK (Dean, [1934]) £70

Others
A BOX OF TRICKS (Swain, no date) £100
A LUCKY DIP (Swain, [c.1920s]) £100
PUPPY TAILS (Swain, [c.1920s]) £100
THE STUDDY DOGS PORTFOLIOS (six portfolios; colour plates) (The Sketch, [1922-]) ....each £250
UNCLE'S ANIMAL BOOK by G.E. Studdy (verse) (Warne, [1923]) £200
JEEK by G.E. Studdy (Hamish Hamilton, 1940) £175

SUTCLIFF, Rosemary
British author. Born: Surrey, 1920. Regarded as one of the leading writers of historical novels, enjoyed by adults and children. Particularly notable are *The Eagle of the Ninth* (1954) and *Warrior Scarlet* (1958). Died: 1992.

Prices are for books in Very Good condition with dustjackets where applicable.

THE CHRONICLES OF ROBIN HOOD (illustrated by C. Walter Hodges) (OUP, 1950) £30
THE QUEEN ELIZABETH STORY (illustrated by C. Walter Hodges) (OUP, 1950) £30
THE ARMOURER'S HOUSE (illustrated by C. Walter Hodges) (OUP, 1951) £30
BROTHER DUSTY-FEET (illustrated by C. Walter Hodges) (OUP, 1952) £30
SIMON (illustrated by Richard Kennedy) (OUP, 1953) £30
THE EAGLE OF THE NINTH (illustrated by C. Walter Hodges) (OUP, 1954) £35
OUTCAST (illustrated by Richard Kennedy) (OUP, 1955) £25

THE SHIELD RING (illustrated by C. Walter Hodges) (OUP, 1956) £25
THE SILVER BRANCH (illustrated by Charles Keeping) (OUP, 1957) £25
WARRIOR SCARLET (illustrated by Charles Keeping) (OUP, 1958) £25
THE LANTERN BEARERS (illustrated by Charles Keeping) (OUP, 1959)..£25
THE RIDER ON THE WHITE HORSE (Hodder & Stoughton, 1959) £35
THE BRIDGE BUILDERS (Blackwell, 1959)..£20
KNIGHT'S FEE (illustrated by Charles Keeping) (OUP, 1960) £25
HOUSES AND HISTORY (illustrated by William Stobbs) (Batsford, 1960)...£20
DAWN WIND (illustrated by Charles Keeping) (OUP, 1961) £25
BEOWULF (illustrated by Charles Keeping) (The Bodley Head, 1961) £25
THE HOUND OF ULSTER (illustrated by Victor Ambrus) (The Bodley Head, 1963) £20
SWORD AT SUNSET (Hodder & Stoughton, 1963) £20
THE MARK OF THE HORSE LORD (illustrated by Charles Keeping) (OUP, 1965)...................................£25
A SAXON SETTLER (illustrated by John Lawrence) (OUP, 1965) £20
HEROES AND HISTORY (illustrated by Charles Keeping) (Batsford, 1965) £25
THE CHIEF'S DAUGHTER (illustrated by Victor Ambrus) (Hamish Hamilton, 1967) £20
THE HIGH DEEDS OF FINN MACCOOL (illustrated by Michael Charlton) (The Bodley Head, 1967) £15
A CIRCLET OF OAK LEAVES (illustrated by Victor Ambrus) (Hamish Hamilton, 1968) £15
THE FLOWERS OF ADONIS (Hodder & Stoughton, 1969) £30
THE WITCH'S BRAT (illustrated by Robert Micklewright) (OUP,1970)...£15
THE TRUCE OF THE GAMES (illustrated by Victor Ambrus) (Hamish Hamilton, 1971) £15
TRISTAN AND ISEULT (illustrated by Victor Ambrus) (TheBodley Head, 1971) £12
HEATHER, OAK, AND OLIVE: Three Stories (illustrated by Victor Ambrus) (Dutton, 1972) £15
THE CAPRICORN BRACELET (illustrated by Charles Keeping) (OUP,1973)...£15
THE CHANGELING (illustrated by Victor Ambrus) (Hamish Hamilton, 1974) £15
WE LIVED IN DRUMFYVIE (illustrated by Margaret Lyford-Pike) (Blackie, 1975) £15
BLOOD FEUD (illustrated by Charles Keeping) (OUP, 1977)..£15
SHIFTING SANDS (illustrated by Laszlo Acs) (Hamish Hamilton, 1977) £15
SUN HORSE, MOON HORSE (illustrated by Shirley Felts) (The Bodley Head, 1977) £15
SONG FOR A DARK QUEEN (Pelham, 1978) £20
THE LIGHT BEYOND THE FOREST: The Quest for the Holy Grail (illustrated by Shirley Felts) (The Bodley Head, 1979) £12
FRONTIER WOLF (OUP, 1980)...£15
THE SWORD AND THE CIRCLE: King Arthur and the Knights of the Round Table (illustrated by Shirley Felts)
(The Bodley Head, 1981)..£12
EAGLE'S EGG (illustrated by Victor Ambrus) (Hamish Hamilton, 1981) £15
THE ROAD TO CAMLANN: The Death of King Arthur (illustrated by Shirley Felts) (The Bodley Head, 1981) £12
BONNY DUNDEE (The Bodley Head, 1982) £15
THE ROUNDABOUT HORSE (illustrated by Alan Marks) (Hamish Hamilton, 1986) £10
FLAME-COLOURED TAFFETA (OUP, 1986) £10
A LITTLE DOG LIKE YOU (illustrated by Jane Johnson) (Orchard, 1987)..£10

SWIFT, Jonathan

Anglo-Irish author. Born: Dublin, 1667. Studied at Kilkenny Grammar School and Trinity College, Dublin. His novel, *Gulliver's Travels*, has become a children's classic, although invariably in a revised form. Died: 1745.

Prices are for books in Very Good condition (with dustjackets after 1940).

TRAVELS INTO SEVERAL REMOTE NATIONS OF THE WORLD by Lemuel Gulliver (two volumes)
(London, 1726) ....the set £20,000
GULLIVER'S TRAVELS (illustrated by H.K. Browne) (Warne, [1879])...£60
GULLIVER'S TRAVELS (illustrated by Gordon Browne) (Routledge, [1880]) £60
GULLIVER'S TRAVELS (illustrated by A.E. Jackson) (Nister, [c.1890])..£60
GULLIVER'S TRAVELS (illustrated by C.E. Brock; preface by H. Craik) (London, 1894) £40
GULLIVER'S TRAVELS (illustrated by Arthur Rackham) (Dent, 1900) £75
GULLIVER'S TRAVELS (illustrated by Arthur Rackham) (Dent, 1909) £250
GULLIVER'S TRAVELS (illustrated by Arthur Rackham; with extra plate; limited to 750 copies, signed by the artist)
(Dent, 1909) £1,000
GULLIVER'S TRAVELS (illustrated by Arthur Rackham; adapted by F.C. Tilney)
(Dent: 'Tales for Children from Many Lands' series, [1913]) £50
GULLIVER'S TRAVELS (illustrated by John Hassall) (Nelson, [1908]) £50
GULLIVER'S TRAVELS. Adapted by Padraic Colum (illustrated by Willy Pogány) (Macmillan, U.S., 1917) £50
GULLIVER'S TRAVELS. Adapted by Padraic Colum (illustrated by Willy Pogány) (Harrap, 1919) £50
GULLIVER'S TRAVELS (illustrated by Jean de Bosschere) (Heinemann, 1920) £75
GULLIVER'S TRAVELS (illustrated by Louis Rhead) (Harper, U.S., [1923]) £40
TRAVELS INTO REMOTE NATIONS OF THE WORLD by Lemuel Gulliver (illustrated by David Jones;
limited to 480 copies; two volumes) (Golden Cockerel Press, 1925) ....the set £2,000
GULLIVER'S TRAVELS (illustrated by Rex Whistler; De Luxe edition: twelve hand-coloured engraved plates;
limited to 205 copies; two volumes; in slipcase) (Cresset Press, 1930)...£6,000
THE CHILDREN'S GULLIVER. Adapted by F.H. Lee (illustrated by Willy Pogány) (Harrap, 1935) £30
GULLIVER'S TRAVELS (illustrated by Jack Matthews) (Routledge, 1947) £20
GULLIVER'S TRAVELS (illustrated by Edward Bawden) (Folio Society, 1948) £35

TARRANT, Margaret W.

British illustrator. Born in 1888, the daughter of the artist, Percy Tarrant. Studied at Clapham School of Art and Heatherley's. Began her career designing cards and calendars for the Medici Society, subsequently illustrating a number of children's classics. She was a close friend of Cicely Mary Barker. Died: 1959.

Prices are for books in Very Good condition (with dustjackets after 1920).

Books Written and Illustrated by Margaret W. Tarrant

OUR DAY: A Book of Nursery Times and Playtime Rhymes (48 colour plates by Margaret W. Tarrant) (Ward Lock, [1923])....**£60**
THE MARGARET TARRANT BIRTHDAY BOOK. Compiled by Frank S. Cole (Medici Society, [1932]) **£60**
JOAN IN FLOWERLAND by Margaret W. Tarrant and Lewis Dutton (Warne, [1935]) **£60**
THE MARGARET TARRANT NURSERY RHYME BOOK (Collins, [1944]) **£60**

Books Illustrated by Margaret W. Tarrant

THE WATER-BABIES by Charles Kingsley (Dent, 1908) **£100**
CONTES DE PERRAULT. Adapted by Kathleen Fitzgerald (Siegle & Hill, 1910) **£65**
THE BOOK OF SPRING (George Allen, 1910) **£75**
THE BOOK OF SUMMER (George Allen, 1910) **£75**
THE BOOK OF AUTUMN (George Allen, 1910)..**£75**
THE BOOK OF WINTER (George Allen, 1910) **£75**
THE BOOK OF THE SEASONS (verse; selected by George A.B. Dewar) (George Allen, 1910) **£200**
THE PIED PIPER OF HAMELIN by Robert Browning (Dent, 1912) **£75**
GOBLIN MARKET by Christina Rossetti (Routledge/Dutton, U.S., [1912]) **£70**
MERRY ANIMAL TALES by Madge A. Bigham (Harrap, 1913) **£65**
NURSERY RHYMES (48 colour plates by Margaret W. Tarrant) (Ward Lock: 'Rainbow' series, 1914) **£50**
THE LITTLEST ONE by Marion St. John Webb (verse) (Harrap, 1914) **£50**
GAMES FOR PLAYTIME AND PARTIES: With and Without Music, for Children of All Ages by S.V. Wilman
(T.C. & E.C. Jack, [1914]) **£90**
A PICTURE BIRTHDAY-BOOK FOR BOYS AND GIRLS by Frank Cole (Harrap, [1915]) **£75**
FAIRY TALES. Edited by Harry Golding (48 colour plates by Margaret W. Tarrant) (Ward Lock, 1915)......................................**£60**
THE GIRLHOOD OF FAMOUS WOMEN by F.J. Snell (Harrap, 1915) **£20**

'Hare's Foot Clover', one of the plates from Margaret Tarrant's **Joan in Flowerland***, which she co-wrote with Lewis Dutton.*

'The Goblin Market' from Christina Rossetti's classic poem, as depicted by Margaret Tarrant in her 1912 edition of the work.

TARRANT, Margaret W.

The first of Kay Thompson's four 'Eloise' books, now worth £75 in Very Good condition with the Hilary Knight dustjacket.

The title-page of **The Ship that Sailed to Mars**, decorated — like the rest of the book — by author, William M. Timlin.

ALICE'S ADVENTURES IN WONDERLAND by Lewis Carroll (48 colour plates by Margaret W. Tarrant) (Ward Lock, 1916) **£110**
FAIRY STORIES FROM HANS CHRISTIAN ANDERSEN (48 colour plates by Margaret W. Tarrant) (Ward Lock, 1917) **£60**
KNOCK THREE TIMES: A Tale for Children by Marion St.John Webb (Harrap, 1917) **£70**
SONGS WITH MUSIC FROM 'A CHILD'S GARDEN OF VERSES' by R.L. Stevenson (T.C. & E.C. Jack, [1918]) **£50**
VERSES FOR CHILDREN. Edited by H. Golding (48 colour plates by Margaret W. Tarrant) (Ward Lock, 1918) **£60**
IN WHEELABOUT AND COCKALONE by Grace Rhys (illustrated by Margaret W. Tarrant and Megan Rhys)
  (G.G. Harrap & Co., 1918) **£20**
THE TOOKEY AND ALICE MARY TALES by Robert de M. Rudolf (Harrap, 1919) **£35**
ELIZ'BETH, PHIL AND ME by Marion St. John Webb (Harrap, 1919) **£50**
ZOO DAYS by Harry Golding (48 colour plates by Margaret W. Tarrant) (Ward Lock, 1919) **£50**
THE ANIMAL ABC by Harry Golding (Ward Lock, 1920)..**£150**
THE LITTLEST ONE AGAIN by Marion St. John Webb (Harrap, 1923)..**£40**
THE FOREST FAIRIES by Marion St, John Webb (verse) (Modern Art Society, [1925]) **£100**
THE HOUSE FAIRIES by Marion St. John Webb (verse) (Modern Art Society, [1925]) **£100**
THE HEATH FAIRIES by Marion St. John Webb (verse) (Modern Art Society, [1925]) **£100**
THE SEED FAIRIES by Marion St. John Webb (verse) (Modern Art Society, [1925]) **£100**
THE INSECT FAIRIES by Marion St. John Webb (verse) (Modern Art Society, [1925])..**£100**
THE POND FAIRIES by Marion St. John Webb (verse) (Modern Art Society, 1925) **£100**
THE SEA-SHORE FAIRIES by Marion St. John Webb (verse) (Modern Art Society, [1925])...**£100**
THE WILD-FRUIT FAIRIES by Marion St. John Webb (verse) (Modern Art Society, [1925]) **£100**
RHYMES OF OLD TIMES (Medici Society, 1925)..**£40**
THE TALES THE LETTERS TELL (five books; illustrated by M.W. Tarrant and others) (Grant Educational, 1925) ....each **£20**
THE MAGIC LAMPLIGHTER by Marion St. John Webb (verse) (Medici Society, 1926) **£45**
THE WEATHER FAIRIES by Marion St. John Webb (verse) (Modern Art Society, [1927])..**£100**
THE TWILIGHT FAIRIES by Marion St. John Webb (Modern Art Society, [1928]) **£100**
AN ALPHABET OF MAGIC by Eleanor Farjeon (Medici Society, 1928) **£75**
THE ORCHARD FAIRIES by Marion St.John Webb (verse) (Modern Art Society, [1928]) **£100**
MOTHER GOOSE: Nursery Rhymes (24 colour plates by Margaret W. Tarrant) (Ward Lock, [1929]) **£60**
OUR ANIMAL FRIENDS by Harry Golding (Ward Lock: 'Sunshine' series, [1930]) **£40**
SIMPLE COMPOSITION STEPS by Rose Meeres (written under the pseudonym 'S.N.D.') (Grant Educational, [1930]) **£20**
THE SONGS THE LETTERS SING by Rose Meeres (written under the pseudonym 'S.N.D.') (Grant Educational, [1930]) ..each **£20**
THE HIDDEN YEARS by John Oxenham (fourteen illustrations by Margaret W. Tarrant) (Longmans, 1931) **£20**
MAGIC HOUSES by Barbara Todd (verse) (Medici Society, [1932])...**£120**

MAGIC FLOWERS by Barbara Todd (verse) (Medici Society, [1933]) £120
DREAMLAND FAIRIES by Mary Gann (Duckworth, 1936) £150
FLOWERS OF THE COUNTRYSIDE (illustrated by Margaret W. Tarrant, M. Forestier and Eileen & Eva Soper)
(Medici Society, 1943) £60
JOHANN THE WOOD CARVER by Gilmore Wood (Warne, 1949)..£30
THE STORY OF CHRISTMAS (Medici Society, 1952) £12

THACKERAY, W.M.
British author. Born: William Makepeace Thackeray in Calcutta in 1811. Studied at Charterhouse and Trinity College, Cambridge. The author of *Vanity Fair* (1847) wrote a series of 'Christmas Books' between 1846 and 1855, of which the last, *The Rose and the Ring*, has been the most enduring. Died: 1863.

Prices are for books in Very Good condition.

'Christmas' Books
MRS PERKINS' BALL (illustrated by the author) (Chapman & Hall, [1847]...£300
OUR STREET (illustrated by the author) (Chapman & Hall, 1848)...£300
DR BIRCH AND HIS YOUNG FRIENDS (illustrated by the author) (Chapman & Hall, 1849) £300
REBECCA AND ROWENA: A Romance upon Romance (illustrated by Richard Doyle) (Chapman & Hall, 1850)...................£300
THE KICKLEBURYS ON THE RHINE (Smith Elder, 1850) £300
THE ROSE AND THE RING, or The History of Prince Giglio and Prince Bulbo:
A Far-Side Pantomime for Great and Small Children (illustrated by the author) (Smith Elder, 1855) £400

THOMPSON, Kay
American author. Born: 1912. Best known for the 'Eloise' books. Died: 1998.

Prices are for books in Very Good condition with dustjackets.

ELOISE: A Book for Precocious Grown-ups (illustrated by Hilary Knight) (Max Reinhardt, 1957) £75
ELOISE IN PARIS (illustrated by Hilary Knight) (Max Reinhardt, 1958)...£60
KAY THOMPSON'S ELOISE AT CHRISTMASTIME (illustrated by Hilary Knight) (Max Reinhardt, 1959) £60
ELOISE IN MOSCOW (illustrated by Hilary Knight) (Max Reinhardt, 1960)..£60

THOMSON, Hugh
British artist-illustrator. Born: Coleraine, Co. Londonderry, in 1860. Had little formal training, serving his apprenticeship at the card manufacturers, Marcus Ward. Made his first contributions to the *English Illustrated Magazine*, subsequently illustrating a number of classic works, specialising in those written or set in the eighteenth century. An important influence on C.E. and H.M. Brock. Died: 1920.

Prices are for books in Very Good condition.

THE PIPER OF HAMELIN by R.W. Buchanan (Heinemann, 1893) £50
JACK THE GIANT KILLER (Macmillan, 1898) £225
THIS AND THAT: A Tale of Two Tinies by Mrs Molesworth (Macmillan, 1899) £35
THE CHIMES by Charles Dickens (Hodder & Stoughton, [1913]) £35
TOM BROWN'S SCHOOLDAYS by Thomas Hughes. Edited by H.C. Bradby (Ginn, U.S., [1918]) £35
THE CRICKET ON THE HEARTH by Charles Dickens (introduction by Walter de la Mare) (Golden Cockerel Press, 1933) £60

THURBER, James
American author-illustrator. Born: James Grover Thurber in 1894. Best known for his humorous contributions to the *New Yorker* magazine, Thurber also wrote a handful of children's books, of which *The 13 Clocks* (1950) and *The Wonderful O* (1955) are the best known. Died: 1961.

Prices are for books in Very Good condition with dustjackets.

MANY MOONS (illustrated by Louis Slobodkin) (Harcourt Brace, U.S., 1943)..£75
MANY MOONS (illustrated by Louis Slobodkin) (Hamish Hamilton, 1944) £60
THE GREAT QUILLOW (illustrated by Doris Lee) (Harcourt Brace, U.S., 1944) £60
THE WHITE DEER (illustrated by James Thurber and Don Freeman) (Harcourt Brace, U.S., 1945)...............£50
THE WHITE DEER (illustrated by James Thurber and Don Freeman) (Hamish Hamilton, 1946) £40
THE 13 CLOCKS (illustrated by Mark [Marc] Simont) (Simon & Schuster, U.S., 1950)................................£50
THE 13 CLOCKS (illustrated by Marc Simont) (Hamish Hamilton, 1951) £40
THE WONDERFUL O (illustrated by Marc Simont) (Simon & Schuster, U.S., 1957) £40
THE WONDERFUL O (illustrated by Marc Simont) (Hamish Hamilton, 1958) £30

TIMLIN, William M.
British author-illustrator. Born: William Mitcheson Timlin in Ashington, Northumberland, in 1892. Studied at Morpeth Grammar School and the Armstrong School of Art in Newcastle. Moved to South Africa in 1912. His solitary children's book, *The Ship that Sailed to Mars* (1923), is one of the classic works of fantasy. Died: 1943.

Price is for books in Very Good condition with dustjackets.

THE SHIP THAT SAILED TO MARS: A Fantasy (illustrated by the author) (Harrap, [1923])................................£1,250

Worzel Gummidge and Saucy Nancy (1947) was the fourth book in the popular series. It is now valued at £50.

*Barbara Euphan Todd also wrote several non-'Gummidge' children's books, including **The Box in the Attic** (1970).*

TODD, Barbara Euphan

British author. Born: Yorkshire, 1897. Prolific children's author, best known for her series of novels featuring the walking, talking scarecrow, Worzel Gummidge. Under the pseudonym 'Euphan', Todd contributed a number of humorous verses to *Punch* in the 1920s. Died: 1976.

Prices are for books in Very Good condition with dustjackets where applicable.

THE 'NORMOUS SATURDAY FAIRY BOOK (with Marjory Royce and Moira Meighn) (Stanley Paul, 1924) £45
THE 'NORMOUS SUNDAY STORY BOOK (with Marjory Royce and Moira Meighn) (Stanley Paul, 1925) £40
THE VERY GOOD WALKERS (with Marjory Royce; illustrated by H.R. Millar) (Methuen, 1925)......................................£40
MR BLOSSOM'S SHOP (Nelson, [1929])...£50
HAPPY COTTAGE (with Marjory Royce) (Collins, [1930]) £50
MAGIC HOUSES (verse) (Medici Society, [1932]) £120
MAGIC FLOWERS (verse) (Medici Society, [1933]) £120
SOUTH COUNTRY SECRETS: A Description of Southern England Written in the Form of a Tale
    (written with John Graham Bower under the pseudonyms 'Euphan' and 'Klaxon') (Burns Oates, 1935) £50
THE SEVENTH DAUGHTER (illustrated by E.H. Shepard) (Burns Oates, 1935)...£50
THE TOUCHSTONE: Tales (with 'Klaxon' [John Graham Bower]) (Burns Oates, 1936)...£50
WORZEL GUMMIDGE, or The Scarecrow of Scatterbrook (illustrated by Elizabeth Alldridge) (Burns Oates, 1936) £150
WORZEL GUMMIDGE AGAIN (illustrated by Elizabeth Alldridge) (Burns Oates, 1937) £120
THE MYSTERY TRAIN (University of London, 1937) £50
THE SPLENDID PICNIC (University of London, 1937)...£50
MORE ABOUT WORZEL GUMMIDGE (Burns Oates, 1938)...£90
MR DOCK'S GARDEN (illustrated by Ruth Westcott) (Arnold, [1939]) £50
GERTRUDE THE GREEDY GOOSE (illustrated by Benjamin Rabier) (Muller, [1939]) £50
THE HOUSE THAT RAN BEHIND (with Esther Boumphrey) (Muller, 1943) £40
MISS RANSKILL COMES HOME (Chapman & Hall, 1946)..£30
WORZEL GUMMIDGE AND SAUCY NANCY (illustrated by Will Nickless) (Hollis & Carter, 1947) £50
WORZEL GUMMIDGE TAKES A HOLIDAY (illustrated by Will Nickless) (Hollis & Carter, 1949) £50
ALOYSIUS LET LOOSE by John Graham Bower (written under the pseudonym 'Klaxon',
    with Barbara Euphan Todd; illustrated by A.E. Batchelor) (Collins, 1950) £40
EARTHY MANGOLD AND WORZEL GUMMIDGE (illustrated by J.J. Crockford) (Hollis & Carter, 1954)......................£50

WORZEL GUMMIDGE AND THE RAILWAY SCARECROWS (illustrated by Jill Crockford) (Evans, 1955) £50
WORZEL GUMMIDGE AT THE CIRCUS (illustrated by Jill Crockford) (Evans, 1956)..£50
THE BOY WITH THE GREEN THUMB (illustrated by Charlotte Hough) (Hamish Hamilton, 1956) £15
THE WIZARD AND THE UNICORN (illustrated by Prudence Seward) (Hamish Hamilton, 1957) £15
WORZEL GUMMIDGE AND THE TREASURE SHIP (illustrated by Jill Crockford) (Evans, 1958) £35
THE SHOP AROUND THE CORNER (illustrated by Olive Coughlan) (Hamish Hamilton, 1959)................................£15
DETECTIVE WORZEL GUMMIDGE (illustrated by Jill Crockford) (Evans, 1963) £50
THE SHOP BY THE SEA (illustrated by Sarah Garland) (Hamish Hamilton, 1966)..£15
THE CLOCK SHOP (illustrated by Jill Crockford) (World's Work, 1967)..£15
THE SHOP ON WHEELS (illustrated by Jill Crockford) (World's Work, 1968) £15
THE BOX IN THE ATTIC (illustrated by Lynette Hemmant) (World's Work, 1970) £10
THE WAND FROM FRANCE (illustrated by Lynette Hemmant) (World's Work, [1972])..£10

TOLKIEN, J.R.R.

British author. Born: John Ronald Reuel Tolkien in Bloemfontein, South Africa, in 1892. Studied at King Edward's School, Birmingham, and Exeter College, Oxford. Appointed Professor of Anglo-Saxon at Oxford in 1925. Published a number of scholarly works on philology and English literature, but is best-known for his three books about the mythical land of 'Middle Earth', *The Hobbit* (1937), *The Lord of the Rings* (1954-55) and *The Silmarillion* (1977), the last begun while he was a soldier in the First World War. Drew tremendous strength and inspiration from his friendship with C.S. Lewis, the two of them forming an informal literary society known as 'The Inklings'. Died: 1973.

Prices are for books in Very Good condition with dustjackets where applicable.
The U.S. edition is listed only where it precedes the U.K. edition.

'The Hobbit, or There and Back Again'

FIRST EDITION (illustrated by the author) (Allen & Unwin, 1937)..£18,000
SECOND IMPRESSION (four new colour plates by the author) (Allen & Unwin, 1938) £2,500
SECOND EDITION (contains revised version of 'Riddle in the Dark') (Allen & Unwin, 1951) £200
FIRST PAPERBACK EDITION (Puffin, 1961)..£20
THIRD (REVISED) EDITION (Allen & Unwin, 1966)..£50
SCHOOLS EDITION (introduction by R.S. Fowler; paperback) (Allen & Unwin, 1972) £10
DE LUXE EDITION (some of Tolkien's original illustrations coloured by H.E. Riddett; in slipcase) (Allen & Unwin, 1976) £100
FIRST FOLIO SOCIETY EDITION (Society's own binding of Allen & Unwin's 1976 De Luxe edition; in slipcase)
    (Folio Society, 1976)..£100
SECOND FOLIO SOCIETY EDITION (illustrated by Eric Fraser; in slipcase) (Folio Society, 1979) £40
MICHAEL HAGUE EDITION (Houghton Mifflin, U.S., 1984)..£60

*The dustjacket of the first edition of **The Hobbit** (1937) features this superb 'wraparound' drawing by J.R.R. Tolkien himself.*

TOLKIEN, J.R.R.

MICHAEL HAGUE EDITION (as 'The Illustrated Hobbit') (Allen & Unwin, 1984)..£60
FIFTIETH ANNIVERSARY EDITION (new introduction by Christopher Tolkien) (Allen & Unwin, 1987) £30
DE LUXE FIFTIETH ANNIVERSARY EDITION (limited to 500 copies; leather binding) (Allen & Unwin, 1987) £200
THE ANNOTATED HOBBIT (annotated by Douglas A. Anderson) (Unwin Hyman, 1988)..£30
CENTENARY EDITION (Harper Collins, 1991)...£25
THE HOBBIT: THE GRAPHIC NOVEL (illustrated by David Wenzel; adapted by Charles Dixon with Sean Demming)
   (Grafton, 1991)..£20

'The Lord of the Rings'
'The Fellowship of the Ring, being the First Part of "The Lord of the Rings"'
FIRST EDITION (Allen & Unwin, 1954) £4,000
REVISED EDITION (new foreword and prologue by author) (Allen & Unwin, 1966) £400
CENTENARY EDITION (Harper Collins, 1991)...£30

'The Two Towers, being the Second Part of "The Lord of the Rings"'
FIRST EDITION (Allen & Unwin, 1954) £3,500
REVISED EDITION (Allen & Unwin, 1966) £400
CENTENARY EDITION (Harper Collins, 1991)...£30

'The Return of the King, being the Third Part of "The Lord of the Rings"'
FIRST EDITION (Allen & Unwin, 1955) £3,000
REVISED EDITION (Allen & Unwin, 1966) £400
CENTENARY EDITION (Harper Collins, 1991)...£30

'The Lord of the Rings'
COMPLETE SET OF FIRST EDITIONS (three volumes) (Allen & Unwin, 1954-55).....................................the set £15,000
FIRST COMBINED EDITION (three volumes; in grey box) (Allen & Unwin, 1962) ....the set £100
DE LUXE COMBINED EDITION (three volumes; black buckram bindings; gilt edges;
   in box decorated by Pauline Baynes) (Allen & Unwin, 1964) ....the set £125
FIRST PAPERBACK EDITION (one volume) (Allen & Unwin, 1968) £20
INDIA PAPER EDITION (one volume; in slipcase) (Allen & Unwin, 1969) £100
THREE-VOLUME PAPERBACK EDITION (Allen & Unwin, 1974) ....the set £25
FOLIO SOCIETY EDITION (illustrated by Ingahild Grathmer; illustrations drawn by Eric Fraser;
   three volumes; in box) (Folio Society, 1977)..the set £150
25TH ANNIVERSARY EDITION (three volumes plus sixteen-page booklet; paperbacks; in box) (Unwin, [1980]) ....the set £50
THREE-VOLUME BOXED EDITION (Unwin Hyman, 1985)...the set £100
CENTENARY EDITION (three volumes; in box) (Harper Collins, 1991)...the set £100
ILLUSTRATED CENTENARY EDITION (illustrated by Alan Lee) (Harper Collins, 1991) £50
DE LUXE ILLUSTRATED CENTENARY EDITION (limited to 250 numbered copies, signed by the artist;
   quarter leather binding; in slipcase) (Harper Collins, 1991) £400
ONE-VOLUME CENTENARY EDITION (Harper Collins, 1992) £25

'The Silmarillion'
FIRST EDITION: Billing & Sons issue (printed by Billing & Sons; cloth binding) (Allen & Unwin, 1977)................£45
FIRST EDITION: Clowes issue (printed by William Clowes; cloth or paper binding) (Allen & Unwin, 1977) £30
DE LUXE EDITION (limited to 900 numbered [101-1,000] copies; leather binding; printed by William Clowes)
   (Allen & Unwin, 1982) £150
SIGNED DE LUXE EDITION (limited to 100 numbered [1-100] copies, signed by Christopher Tolkien;
   leather binding; printed by William Clowes) (Allen & Unwin, 1982)..£200
CENTENARY EDITION (Harper Collins, 1992)...£20

'The History of Middle-Earth' (all Books Edited by Christopher Tolkien)
THE BOOK OF LOST TALES Part 1 (Volume I of 'The History of Middle-Earth') (Allen & Unwin, 1983) £25
THE BOOK OF LOST TALES Part 2 (Volume II of 'The History of Middle-Earth') (Allen & Unwin, 1984) £25
THE LAYS OF BELERIAND (Volume III of 'The History of Middle-Earth') (Allen & Unwin, 1985).........................£25
THE SHAPING OF MIDDLE-EARTH (Volume IV of 'The History of Middle-Earth') (Allen & Unwin, 1986)..............£25
THE LOST ROAD (Volume V of 'The History of Middle-Earth') (Unwin Hyman, 1987) £25
THE RETURN OF THE SHADOW: The History of 'The Lord of the Rings' Part 1
   (Volume VI of 'The History of Middle-Earth') (Unwin Hyman, 1988) £25
THE TREASON OF ISENGARD: The History of 'The Lord of the Rings' Part 2
   (Volume VII of 'The History of Middle-Earth') (Unwin Hyman, 1989)...£25
THE WAR OF THE RING: The History of 'The Lord of the Rings' Part 3
   (Volume VIII of 'The History of Middle-Earth') (Unwin Hyman, 1990) £25
SAURON DEFEATED: The History of 'The Lord of the Rings' Part 4
   (Volume IX of 'The History of Middle-Earth') (Harper Collins, 1992) £25

Other 'Middle-Earth' Books
THE ADVENTURES OF TOM BOMBADIL and Other Verses from 'The Red Book'
   (illustrated by Pauline Baynes) (Allen & Unwin, 1962)..£85
THE ADVENTURES OF TOM BOMBADIL and Other Verses from 'The Red Book'
   (with 'Farmer Giles of Ham') (Unwin, 1975)...£20
THE ADVENTURES OF TOM BOMBADIL and Other Verses from 'The Red Book'
   (illustrated by Roger Garland) (Unwin Hyman, 1990) £15
THE ROAD GOES EVER ON: A Song Cycle (music by Donald Swann) (Houghton Mifflin, U.S., 1967) £45

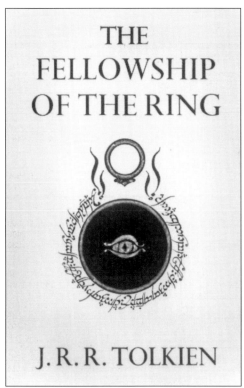

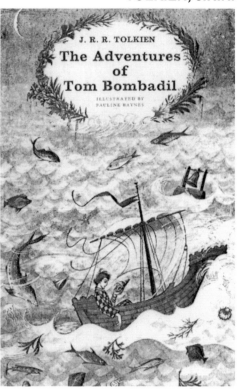

The first of the three books that together make up Tolkien's great masterpiece, **The Lord of the Rings** (1954-55).

This book from 1962 focuses on one of the most memorable characters from the trilogy. It is illustrated by Pauline Baynes.

THE ROAD GOES EVER ON: A Song Cycle (music by Donald Swann) (Allen & Unwin, 1968) £35
BILBO'S LAST SONG (illustrated by Pauline Baynes; poster) (Allen & Unwin, 1974)...£30
BILBO'S LAST SONG (illustrated by Pauline Baynes; hardback) (Unwin Hyman, 1990) £25
BILBO'S LAST SONG (illustrated by Pauline Baynes; paperback) (Arrow, 1992) £6
THE FILM BOOK OF J.R.R. TOLKIEN'S 'THE LORD OF THE RINGS' (130 stills from the film; paperback)
    (Methuen, Toronto, 1978) £10
THE FILM BOOK OF J.R.R. TOLKIEN'S 'THE LORD OF THE RINGS' (130 stills from the film; paperback)
    (Fantasy Film Books, 1979) £20
UNFINISHED TALES OF NUMENOR AND MIDDLE-EARTH. Edited by Christopher Tolkien (Allen & Unwin, 1980)...................£45
STORIES FROM THE THIRD AGE (contains 'The Hobbit', 'The Lord of the Rings' and 'The Silmarillion';
    four volumes; paperbacks; in box) (Unwin, [1980]) ....the set £12
THE MIDDLE-EARTH COLLECTION (contains 'The Hobbit', 'The Lord of the Rings' and 'The Silmarillion';
    five volumes; paperbacks; in box]) (Unwin, [1980])..the set £15

Books About 'Middle-Earth'

A GUIDE TO MIDDLE-EARTH by Robert Foster (Mirage Press, U.S., 1971) £10
A GUIDE TO MIDDLE-EARTH by Robert Foster (revised edition; as 'The Complete Guide to Middle-Earth,
    from "The Hobbit" to "The Silmarillion"') (Allen & Unwin, 1978)..£6
A TOLKIEN COMPASS. Edited by Jared Lobdell (includes Tolkien's 'Guide to the Names in "The Lord of the Rings"')
    (Open Court, U.S., 1975) £10
THE TOLKIEN COMPANION by J.E.A. Tyler (illustrated by Kevin Reilly) (Macmillan, 1976) £8
THE TOLKIEN COMPANION by J.E.A. Tyler (revised edition; as 'The New Tolkien Companion') (Macmillan, 1979) £12
J.R.R. TOLKIEN: THE COMPLETE GUIDE (includes Foster's 'The Complete Guide to Middle-Earth' and
    Humphrey Carpenter's 'J.R.R. Tolkien: A Biography'; paperback; in slipcase) (Unwin, 1978) £8
AN INTRODUCTION TO ELVISH: and to Other Tongues and Proper Names . . . of Middle-Earth. Edited by Jim Allan
    (Bran's Head, 1978) £8
A MIDDLE-EARTH ALBUM by Joan Wyatt (Thames & Hudson, 1979)..£12
A TOLKIEN BESTIARY by David Day (llustrated by Ian Miller) (Mitchell Beazley, 1979)...£20
THE TOLKIEN QUIZ-BOOK by Bart Andrews and Bernice Zuber (paperback) (Sphere, 1979) £3
THE MIDDLE-EARTH QUIZ BOOK by Suzanne Buchholz (paperback) (Thames & Hudson, 1980) £3
JOURNEYS OF FRODO by Barbara Strachey (Allen & Unwin, 1981) £20
AN ATLAS OF MIDDLE-EARTH by Karen Fenstad (Houghton Mifflin, U.S., 1981)...£15

This lighthearted picture book wasn't published until 1982, nine years after its author's death. Very Good copies are now worth £18.

THE TOLKIEN QUIZ BOOK by Nigel Robinson and Linda Wilson (paperback) (Star, 1981)..£3
THE ROAD TO MIDDLE-EARTH by Tom Shippey (Allen & Unwin, 1982) £12
A DICTIONARY OF QUENYA AND OF PROTO-ELDARIN. Compiled by J.C. Bradfield ([J.C. Bradfield], 1982) £12
THE SONG OF MIDDLE-EARTH: J.R.R. Tolkien's Themes, Symbols and Myths by David Harvey (Allen & Unwin, 1985) £12
A TOLKIEN THESAURUS by Richard A. Blackwelder (Garland, U.S., 1990)..£45
TOLKIEN: THE ILLUSTRATED ENCYCLOPEDIA by David Day (Mitchell Beazley, 1991) £20

Others
OXFORD POETRY 1915. Edited by G.D.H. Cole and T.W. Earp (includes Tolkien's poem 'Goblin Feet') (Blackwell, 1915) £25
OXFORD POETRY 1914-1916 (includes Tolkien's poem 'Goblin Feet') (Blackwell, 1917) £20
THE BOOK OF FAIRY POETRY. Edited by Dora Owen (includes Tolkien's poem 'Goblin Feet') (Longmans, 1920) £90
FIFTY NEW POEMS FOR CHILDREN (includes Tolkien's poem 'Goblin Feet') (Blackwell, 1922) £15
FARMER GILES OF HAM (illustrated by Pauline Baynes) (Allen & Unwin, 1949)...£200
FARMER GILES OF HAM (illustrated by Roger Garland) (Unwin Hyman, 1990) £15
TREE AND LEAF (includes Tolkien's essay 'On Fairy-Stories' and his story 'Leaf by Niggle') (Allen & Unwin, 1964) £100
TREE AND LEAF (paperback; simultaneous with the above) (Allen & Unwin, 1964) £10
TREE AND LEAF (revised edition; contains first printing of the full version of the poem 'Mythopoeia') (Unwin Hyman, 1988) £8
WINTER'S TALES FOR CHILDREN 1. Edited by Caroline Hillier (includes Tolkien's poems 'Once Upon a Time' and
'The Dragon's Visit') (Macmillan, 1965) £10
THE TOLKIEN READER (contains 'The Homecoming of Beorhtnoth', 'On Fairy-Stories', 'Leaf by Niggle',
'Farmer Giles of Ham' and 'The Adventures of Tom Bombadil') (Ballantine, U.S., 1966) £20
SMITH OF WOOTTON MAJOR (boards; issued without dustjacket) (Allen & Unwin, 1967) £40
SMITH OF WOOTTON MAJOR (illustrated by Roger Garland) (Unwin Hyman, 1990) £12
SMITH OF WOOTTON MAJOR and FARMER GILES OF HAM (paperback) (Ballantine, U.S., [1969]) £5
THE HAMISH HAMILTON BOOK OF DRAGONS. Edited by Roger Lancelyn Green (includes Tolkien's poem 'The Hoard')
(Hamish Hamilton, 1970) £10
THE HOMECOMING OF BEORHTNOTH (Allen & Unwin, 1975)..£15
TREE AND LEAF, SMITH OF WOOTTON MAJOR and THE HOMECOMING OF BEORHTNOTH (paperback) (Unwin, 1975) £5
FARMER GILES OF HAM and THE ADVENTURES OF TOM BOMBADIL (paperback) (Unwin, 1975).........................£5
THE FATHER CHRISTMAS LETTERS. Edited by Baillie Tolkien (Allen & Unwin, 1976)..£30
DRAWINGS BY TOLKIEN (exhibition catalogue; introduction by Baillie Tolkien and Humphrey Carpenter)
(Ashmolean Museum, Oxford/National Book League, 1976)...£20
PICTURES BY J.R.R. TOLKIEN (in slipcase) (Allen & Unwin, 1979)..£40
POEMS AND STORIES (contains 'The Adventures of Tom Bombadil', 'The Homecoming of Beorhtnoth Beorthelm's Son',
'On Fairy-Stories', 'Leaf by Niggle', 'Farmer Giles of Ham' and 'Smith of Wootton Major';
illustrated by Pauline Baynes; in box) (Allen & Unwin, 1980) £50

THE LETTERS OF J.R.R. TOLKIEN. Edited by Humphrey Carpenter and Christopher Tolkien (Allen & Unwin, 1981) £15
MR BLISS (Allen & Unwin, 1982) £18
SMITH OF WOOTTON MAJOR and LEAF BY NIGGLE (illustrated by Pauline Baynes; paperback) (Unwin, 1983) £5
THE HOMECOMING OF BEORHTNOTH (pamphlet; limited to 300 copies) (Anglo Saxon Books, 1991) £8

'TOPPER' ANNUALS

Popular British comic annual, published by D.C. Thomson. The comic itself was launched on 7th February 1953, the first *Topper Book* appearing later that year. All the annuals published up until 1959 were oblong in format. All were issued in boards except the first, which had card covers.

Prices are for annuals in Very Good condition.

THE TOPPER PICTURE BOOK £100
THE TOPPER BOOK 1955 ....£50
THE TOPPER BOOK 1956-57 ....each £30
THE TOPPER BOOK 1958-59 ....each £25
THE TOPPER BOOK 1960 ....£20
THE TOPPER BOOK 1961 ....£15
THE TOPPER BOOK 1962-65 ....each £15
THE TOPPER BOOK 1966-69 ....each £10
THE TOPPER BOOK 1970 ....£8
THE TOPPER BOOK 1971-72 ....each £6
THE TOPPER BOOK 1973-79 ....each £4
THE TOPPER BOOK 1980-Present ....each £3

TOURTEL, Mary

British author-illustrator. Born: Mary Caldwell in Canterbury, Kent, in 1873. Contributed two titles to Grant Richards' famous 'Dumpy Books' series, but is best-known as the creator of Rupert Bear, launched in the *Daily Express* in November 1920 as a rival to the *Daily Mail*'s 'Teddy Tail'. She was forced to abandon the strip in 1935 due to failing eyesight. Died: 1948.

Prices are for books in Very Good condition.

Early 'Rupert' Books

THE ADVENTURES OF RUPERT THE LITTLE LOST BEAR. Reprinted from the 'Daily Express' (Nelson, [1921]) £850
THE LITTLE BEAR AND THE FAIRY CHILD. Reprinted from the 'Daily Express' (Nelson, [1922]) £950
MARGOT THE MIDGET AND LITTLE BEAR'S CHRISTMAS. Reprinted from the 'Daily Express' (Nelson, [1922]) £850
THE LITTLE BEAR AND THE OGRES (Nelson, 1922) £950
'RUPERT LITTLE BEAR'S ADVENTURES' (three books) (Sampson Low, 1924-25) ....each £800
'RUPERT — LITTLE BEAR SERIES' (six books) (Sampson Low, 1925-27) ....each £350

'Little Bear Library' Books

NO. 1: RUPERT AND THE ENCHANTED PRINCESS (Sampson Low, [1928])...£50
NO. 2: RUPERT AND THE BLACK DWARF (Sampson Low, [1928]) £50
NO. 3: RUPERT AND HIS PET MONKEY (Sampson Low, [1928]) £50
NO. 4: RUPERT AND HIS FRIEND MARGOT and RUPERT, MARGOT AND THE FAIRIES (Sampson Low, [1928]).................£50
NO. 5: RUPERT IN THE WOOD OF MYSTERY (Sampson Low, [1929]) £50
NO. 6: FURTHER ADVENTURES OF RUPERT AND HIS PET MONKEY and RUPERT AND THE STOLEN APPLES
(Sampson Low, [1929]) £50
NO. 7: RUPERT AND THE THREE ROBBERS (Sampson Low, [1929]) £50
NO. 8: RUPERT, THE KNIGHT AND THE LADY and RUPERT AND THE WISE GOAT'S BIRTHDAY CAKE
(Sampson Low, [1929]) £50
NO. 9: RUPERT AND THE CIRCUS CLOWN (Sampson Low, [1929])..£50
NO. 10: RUPERT AND THE MAGIC HAT (Sampson Low, [1929]) £50
NO. 11: RUPERT AND THE LITTLE PRINCE (Sampson Low, [1930]) £50
NO. 12 : RUPERT AND KING PIPPIN (Sampson Low, [1930]) £50
NO. 13: RUPERT AND THE WILFUL PRINCESS (Sampson Low, [1930]) £50
NO. 14: RUPERT'S MYSTERIOUS FLIGHT (Sampson Low, [1930]) £50
NO. 15: RUPERT IN TROUBLE AGAIN and RUPERT AND THE FANCY DRESS PARTY (Sampson Low, [1930]) £50
NO. 16: RUPERT AND THE WOODEN SOLDIERS and RUPERT'S CHRISTMAS ADVENTURE
(Sampson Low, [1930]) £50
NO. 17: RUPERT AND THE OLD MAN OF THE SEA (Sampson Low, [1931]) £50
NO. 18: RUPERT AND ALGY AT HAWTHORNE FARM (Sampson Low, [1931]) £50
NO. 19: RUPERT AND THE MAGIC WHISTLE (Sampson Low, [1931]) £50
NO. 20: RUPERT GETS STOLEN (Sampson Low, [1931]) £50
NO. 21: RUPERT AND THE WONDERFUL BOOTS (Sampson Low, [1931]) £50
NO. 22: RUPERT AND THE CHRISTMAS TREE FAIRIES and RUPERT AND BILL BADGER'S PICNIC PARTY
(Sampson Low, [1931]) £50
NO. 23: RUPERT AND HIS PET MONKEY AGAIN and BEPPO BACK WITH RUPERT (Sampson Low, [1932]) £50
NO. 24: RUPERT AND THE ROBBER WOLF (Sampson Low, [1932]) £50
NO. 25: RUPERT'S LATEST ADVENTURE (Sampson Low, [1932]) £50

NO. 26: RUPERT AND PRINCE HUMPTY DUMPTY (Sampson Low, [1932])..£50
NO. 27: RUPERT'S HOLIDAY ADVENTURE and RUPERT'S MESSAGE TO FATHER CHRISTMAS and
RUPERT'S NEW YEAR'S EVE PARTY (Sampson Low, [1932]) £50
NO. 28 : RUPERT'S CHRISTMAS TREE and RUPERT'S PICNIC PARTY (Sampson Low, [1932])...........................£50
NO. 29 : RUPERT, THE WITCH AND TABITHA (Sampson Low, [1933]) £50
NO. 30: RUPERT GOES HIKING (Sampson Low, [1933]) £50
NO. 31: RUPERT AND WILLY WISPE (Sampson Low, [1933]) £50
NO. 32: RUPERT MARGOT AND THE BANDITS and RUPERT AT SCHOOL (Sampson Low, [1933])....................£50
NO. 33: RUPERT AND THE MAGIC TOWYMAN (Sampson Low, [1933]) £50
NO. 34: RUPERT AND BILL KEEP SHOP and RUPERT'S CHRISTMAS THRILLS (Sampson Low, [1933]) £50
NO. 35: RUPERT AND ALGERNON and RUPERT AND THE WHITE DOVE (Sampson Low, [1934])....................£50
NO. 36: RUPERT AND BEPPO AGAIN (Sampson Low, [1934]) £50
NO. 37 : RUPERT AND DAPPLE (Sampson Low, [1934]) £50
NO. 38: RUPERT AND BILL'S AEROPLANE ADVENTURE (Sampson Low, [1934]) £50
NO. 39: RUPERT AND THE MAGICIAN'S UMBRELLA (Sampson Low, [1934]) £50
NO. 40: RUPERT AND BILL AND THE PIRATES (Sampson Low, [1935]) £50
NO. 41: RUPERT AT THE SEASIDE and RUPERT AND BINGO (Sampson Low, [1935]) £50
NO. 42 : RUPERT GETS CAPTURED and RUPERT AND THE SNOW BABE'S CHRISTMAS ADVENTURES
(Sampson Low, [1935])...£50
NO. 43: RUPERT, THE MANIKIN AND THE BLACK KNIGHT (Sampson Low, [1935])...£50
NO. 44: RUPERT AND THE GREEDY PRINCESS (Sampson Low, [1935]) £50
NO. 45 : RUPERT AND BILL'S SEASIDE HOLIDAY and RUPERT AND THE TWINS' BIRTHDAY CAKE
(Sampson Low, [1936]) £50
NO. 46: RUPERT AND EDWARD AND THE CIRCUS and RUPERT AND THE SNOWMAN (Sampson Low, [1936]).................£50

Other 'Rupert' Books
DAILY EXPRESS CHILDREN'S ANNUAL 1930-31 (Lane, 1930-31) ....each £100
DAILY EXPRESS CHILDREN'S ANNUAL 1932-34 (Lane, 1932-34) ....each £75
MONSTER RUPERT (four volumes) (Sampson Low, 1931-34)..each £800
MONSTER RUPERT (three volumes) (Sampson Low, 1948-50)..each £40
MONSTER RUPERT (with all cut-outs intact [200 in total]) (Sampson Low, 1950) £50
MONSTER RUPERT (with all cut-outs intact [120 in total]) (Sampson Low, 1953) £40
THE RUPERT STORY BOOK (Sampson Low, [1938])...£450
RUPERT LITTLE BEAR, MORE STORIES (Sampson Low, [1939]) £450
RUPERT AGAIN (Sampson Low, [1940]) £450

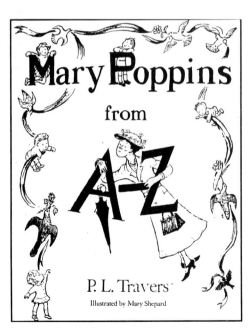

This delightful 'Mary Poppins' alphabet appeared in 1963, nearly thirty years after the original novel. It is valued at £40.

*P.L. Travers was fascinated by fairy tales, and she compiled this collection **About the Sleeping Beauty** in the mid-1970s.*

Others

A HORSE BOOK by Mary Tourtel (Grant Richards: 'Dumpy Books for Children' series No. 10, 1901) £150
THE HUMPTY DUMPTY BOOK: Nursery Rhymes Told in Pictures (Treherne, [1902]) £150
THE THREE LITTLE FOXES by Mary Tourtel (Grant Richards: 'Dumpy Books for Children's series No. 21, 1903) £150

TOWNSEND, John Rowe

British author. Born: Yorkshire, 1922. He has a considerable reputation, especially for *The Intruder* (1969) and his history of children's literature, *Written for Children* (1965; revised: 1974 & 1983).

Prices are for books in Very Good condition with dustjackets where applicable.

GUMBLE'S YARD (illustrated by Dick Hart) (Hutchinson, 1961) £55
HELL'S EDGE (Hutchinson, 1963) £50
WIDDERSHINS CRESCENT (Hutchinson, 1965) £50
WIDDERSHINS CRESCENT (as 'Goodbye to Gumble's Yard'; paperback) (Puffin, 1981)..£10
THE HALLERSAGE SOUND (Hutchinson, 1966) £30
PIRATE'S ISLAND (illustrated by Douglas Hall) (OUP, 1968) £30
THE INTRUDER (illustrated by Graham Humphrey) (OUP, 1969) £30
GOODNIGHT, PROF, LOVE (illustrated by Peter Farmer) (OUP, 1970) £25
THE SUMMER PEOPLE (illustrated by Robert Micklewright) (OUP, 1972) £25
A WISH FOR WINGS (illustrated by Philip Gough) (Heinemann, 1972) £25
FOREST OF THE NIGHT (OUP, 1974) £25
NOAH'S CASTLE (OUP, 1975) £25
TOP OF THE WORLD (illustrated by Nikki Jones) (OUP, 1976) £20
THE XANADU MANUSCRIPT (illustrated by Paul Ritchie) (OUP, 1977) £20
KING CREATURE, COME (OUP, 1980) £15
THE ISLANDERS (OUP, 1981) £15
CLEVER DICK (OUP, 1982) £15
A FOREIGN AFFAIR (Kestrel, 1982) £15
DAN ALONE (Kestrel, 1983) £15
CLOUDY-BRIGHT (Kestrel, 1984)...£15
TOM TIDDLER'S GROUND (illustrated by Marke Peppe) (Viking Kestrel, 1986)...£15
THE PERSUADING STICK (Viking Kestrel, 1986) £15
ROB'S PLACE (Viking Kestrel, 1987) £15

TOZER, Katharine

British author-illustrator. Born: 1905. Best known for her series of books featuring the toy elephant, Mumfie. Died: 1943.

Prices are for books in Very Good condition.

Books Written and Illustrated by Katharine Tozer

THE WANDERINGS OF MUMFIE (John Murray, 1935) £65
HERE COMES MUMFIE (John Murray, 1936) £60
MUMFIE THE ADMIRAL (John Murray, 1937) £60
MUMFIE'S PICTURE BOOK (selected by Eiluned Lewis) (John Murray, 1937) £60
MUMFIE'S MAGIC BOX (John Murray, 1938)..£60
MUMFIE'S UNCLE SAMUEL (John Murray, 1939)..£60
NOAH: The Story of Another Ark (John Murray, 1940) £20
THE ADVENTURES OF ALFIE (John Murray, 1941) £20
MUMFIE MARCHES ON (John Murray, 1942) £40

Books Illustrated by Katharine Tozer

PALADINS IN SPAIN by Eleanor Farjeon (Nelson, 1937) £15
THE CHINESE CHILDREN NEXT DOOR by Pearl S. Buck (Methuen, 1943) £15

TRAVERS, P.L.

Australian author. Born: Pamela Lyndon Travers in Queensland, Australia, in 1899. Moved to Britain in 1923, working as an actress and dancer until 1936. She wrote a number of children's books, but is best known for her 'Mary Poppins' stories, which inspired Walt Disney's memorable 1964 film starring Julie Andrews. Died: 1996.

Prices are for books in Very Good condition with dustjackets.

MARY POPPINS (illustrated by Mary Shepard) (Howe, 1934) £350
MARY POPPINS COMES BACK (illustrated by Mary Shepard) (Dickson & Thompson, 1935)......................................£125
HAPPY EVER AFTER (illustrated by Mary Shepard) (Privately printed, 1940) £150
I GO BY SEA, I GO BY LAND (illustrated by Gertrude Hermes) (Davies, 1941)..£55
MARY POPPINS OPENS THE DOOR (illustrated by Mary Shepard and Agnes Sims) (Davies, 1944) £75
MARY POPPINS IN THE PARK (illustrated by Mary Shepard) (Davies, 1952) £60
THE FOX AT THE MANGER (illustrated by Thomas Bewick) (Collins, 1963)...£25

MARY POPPINS FROM A TO Z (illustrated by Mary Shepard) (Collins, 1963) £40
FRIEND MONKEY (Collins, 1972) £10
ABOUT THE SLEEPING BEAUTY (illustrated by Charles Keeping) (Collins, 1977) £25
MARY POPPINS IN THE KITCHEN (with Maurice Moore-Betty; illustrated by Mary Shepard) (Collins, 1977)............£15
MARY POPPINS IN CHERRY TREE LANE (illustrated by Mary Shepard) (Collins, 1982) £15

TREASE, Geoffrey

British author. Born: Robert Geoffrey Trease in Nottingham in 1909. Studied at Nottingham High School and Queen's College, Oxford. Worked as a teacher and journalist before publishing his first novel, *Bows against the Barons*, in 1934. Like many of his works, this book reflects the author's strong left-wing convictions. Has also written a study of children's writing, *Tales Out of School* (1948). Died: 1998.

Prices are for books in Very Good condition with dustjackets.

BOWS AGAINST THE BARONS (illustrated by Michael Boland) (Martin Lawrence, 1934)..............................£40
COMRADES FOR THE CHARTER (illustrated by Michael Boland) (Martin Lawrence, 1934) £40
UNSLEEPING SWORD (Martin Lawrence, 1934)..£35
THE CALL TO ARMS (Martin Lawrence, 1935) £35
MISSING FROM HOME (illustrated by Scott) (Lawrence & Wishart, [1936]) £30
RED COMET: A Tale of Travel in the USSR (illustrated by Fred Ellis) (Lawrence & Wishart, 1937) £30
THE CHRISTMAS HOLIDAY MYSTERY (illustrated by Alfred Sindall) (A. & C. Black, 1937) £30
MYSTERY ON THE MOORS (illustrated by Alfred Sindall) (A. & C. Black, 1937) £30
DETECTIVES OF THE DALES (illustrated by J.C.B. Knight) (A. & C. Black, 1938) £30
IN THE LAND OF THE MOGUL: A Story of the East India Company's First Adventure in India
   (illustrated by J.C.B. Knight) (Blackwell, 1938) £30
THE DRAGON WHO WAS DIFFERENT and Other Plays for Children (Muller, 1938) £30
NORTH SEA SPY (Fore, [1939])..£30
CLEM VOROSHILVO: The Red Marshal (Pilot Press, [1940]) £25
CUE FOR TREASON (illustrated by Beatrice Goldsmith) (Blackwell, 1940)..£25
THE RUNNING OF THE DEER (illustrated by W. Lindsay Cable) (Harrap, [1941]) £20
THE GREY ADVENTURER (illustrated by Beatrice Goldsmith) (Blackwell, 1942)................................£25
BLACK NIGHT, RED MORNING (illustrated by Donia Nachsen) (Shakespeare Head Press, 1944) £25
ARMY WITHOUT BANNERS (Fore, 1945) £25
TRUMPETS IN THE WEST (illustrated by Alan Blyth) (Blackwell, 1947) £25
SILVER GUARD (illustrated by Alan Blyth) (Blackwell, 1948) £25
THE HILLS OF VARNA (illustrated by Treyer Evans) (Macmillan, 1948) £25
TALES OUT OF SCHOOL (Heinemann, 1948) £15
THE MYSTERY OF MOORSIDE FARM (illustrated by Alan Blyth) (Blackwell, 1949) £25
NO BOATS ON BANNERMERE (illustrated by Richard Kennedy) (Heinemann, 1949) £30
THE SECRET FIORD (illustrated by H.M. Brock) (Macmillan, 1949) £25
FORTUNE, MY FOE: The Story of Sir Walter Raleigh (Methuen 1949)..£25
THE YOUNG TRAVELLER IN INDIA AND PAKISTAN (Phoenix House, 1949) £15
UNDER BLACK BANNER (illustrated by Richard Kennedy) (Heinemann, 1951) £25
ENJOYING BOOKS (Phoenix House: 'Excursions Series for Young People', 1951) £10
THE CROWN OF VIOLET (illustrated by C. Walter Hodges) (Macmillan, 1952)..................................£25
THE BARONS' HOSTAGE: A Story of Simon de Montfort (illustrated by Alan Jessett) (Phoenix House, 1952) £25
BLACK BANNER PLAYERS (illustrated by Richard Kennedy) (Heinemann, 1952) £25
THE PAGEANT BOOKS. Edited by Geoffrey Trease (Phoenix House, 1952) £10
THE NEW HOUSE AT HARDALE (Lutterworth Press, 1953) £15
THE SILKEN SECRET (illustrated by Alan Jessett) (Blackwell, 1953)..£25
THE SEVEN QUEENS OF ENGLAND (Heinemann, 1953) £15
THE SHADOW OF SPAIN and Other Plays (Blackwell, [1953]) £10
THE YOUNG TRAVELLER IN ENGLAND AND WALES (Phoenix House, 1953) £10
BLACK BANNER ABROAD (Heinemann, 1954) £25
THE YOUNG TRAVELLER IN GREECE (Phoenix House, 1955 [1956]) £10
THE FAIR FLOWER OF DANGER (Blackwell, 1955 [1956])..£20
WORD TO CAESAR (illustrated by Geoffrey Whittam) (Macmillan, 1955 [1956]) £20
SIX OF THE BEST by Kitty Barne and others. Edited by G. Trease (stories) (Blackwell, 1955)..............£15
THE SEVEN KINGS OF ENGLAND (illustrated by Leslie Atkinson) (Heinemann, 1955) £12
IN THE BLOOD (Blackwell, [1956])..£20
THE GATES OF BANNERDALE (Heinemann, 1956)..£20
SECRET OF SHAM (Blackwell, [1956]) £20
SNARED NIGHTINGALE (Macmillan, 1957) £20
MIST OVER ATHELNEY (illustrated by R.S. Sherriffs and J.L. Stokle) (Macmillan, 1958)....................£20
EDWARD ELGAR: MAKER OF MUSIC (adapted from the play 'Elgar of England') (Macmillan, 1959) £15
SO WILD THE HEART (Macmillan, 1959)..£20
THE MAYTHORN STORY (illustrated by Robert Hodgson) (Heinemann, 1960) £20
THUNDER OF VALMY (illustrated by John S. Goodall) (Macmillan, 1960) £15
THE YOUNG WRITER (illustrated by Carl Hollander) (Nelson, [1961])..£10
WOLFGANG MOZART: The Young Composer (Macmillan 1961) £10

CHANGE AT MAYTHORN (illustrated by Robert Hodgson) (Heinemann, 1962) £15
FOLLOW MY BLACK PLUME (illustrated by Brian Wildsmith) (Macmillan, 1963) £30
THE ITALIAN STORY: From the Earliest Times to 1946 (Macmillan, 1963) £10
A THOUSAND FOR SICILY (illustrated by Brian Wildsmith) (Macmillan, 1964)..£30
SEVEN STAGES (Heinemann, 1964) £15
THE DUTCH ARE COMING (illustrated by Lynette Hemmant) (Hamish Hamilton, 1965) £15
BENT IS THE BOW (illustrated by Charles Keeping) (Nelson, 1965)..£20
THE RED TOWERS OF GRANADA (illustrated by Charles Keeping) (Macmillan, 1966) £20
COMPANIONS OF FORTUNE by René Guiullot (translated by G. Trease) (Childrens Library, 1967) £10
THE WHITE NIGHTS OF ST. PETERSBURG (illustrated by William Stobbs) (Macmillan, 1967) £15
THE RUNAWAY SERF (illustrated by Mary Russon) (Hamilton, 1968) £15
SEVEN SOVEREIGN QUEENS (Heinemann, [1968]) £10
BYRON: A Poet Dangerous to Know (Macmillan, 1969) £15
A MASQUE FOR THE QUEEN (illustrated by Krystyna Turska) (Hamish Hamilton, 1970) £15
THE CONDOTIERRI: Soldiers of Fortune (Thames & Hudson, [1970])...£15
A WHIFF OF BURNT BOATS (Macmillan, 1971) £15
HORSEMEN ON THE HILLS (Macmillan, 1971)...£15
A SHIP TO ROME (illustrated by Leslie Atkinson) (Heinemann, 1972) £15
SAMUEL PEPYS AND HIS WORLD (Thames & Hudson, [1972])...£10
A VOICE IN THE NIGHT (illustrated by Sara Silcock) (Heinemann, 1973) £15
POPINJAY STAIRS (Macmillan, 1973) £15
D.H. LAWRENCE: The Phoenix and the Flame (Macmillan, 1973) £20
DAYS TO REMEMBER: A Garland of Historic Anniversaries (illustrated by Joanna Troughton) (Heinemann, 1973) £15
THE CHOCOLATE BOY (illustrated by David Walker) (Heinemann, 1975) £15
THE IRON TSAR (Macmillan, 1975) £15
WHEN THE DRUMS BEAT (illustrated by Janet Marsh) (Heinemann, 1976)...£15
VIOLET FOR BONAPARTE (Macmillan, 1976) £15
THE SEAS OF MORNING (illustrated by David Smee; paperback) (Puffin, 1976)..£5
THE SPY CATCHERS (illustrated by Geoffrey Bargery) (Hamish Hamilton, 1976) £15
THE FIELD OF THE FORTY FOOTSTEPS (Macmillan, 1977)..£15
THE CLAWS OF THE EAGLE (illustrated by Ionicus) (Heinemann, 1977) £15
MANDEVILLE (Macmillan, 1980) £10
A WOOD BY MOONLIGHT and Other Stories (Chatto & Windus, 1981)...£10
SARABAND FOR SHADOWS (Macmillan, 1982) £10
THE CORMORANT VENTURE (Macmillan, 1984) £10
TOMORROW IS A STRANGER (Heinemann, 1987) £10

TREECE, Henry

British author. Born: Wednesbury, Staffordshire, in 1911. Studied at Wednesbury High School and Birmingham University. Taught English at Barton on Humber Grammar School in Lincolnshire between 1946 and 1959. Began his literary career as a poet and was co-founder of the New Apocalypse movement, but turned to novel writing in the early 1950s, producing a series of historical novels for adults and children. Died: 1966.

Prices are for books in Very Good condition with dustjackets.

LEGIONS OF THE EAGLE (illustrated by Christine Price) (The Bodley Head, 1954) £40
THE EAGLES HAVE FLOWN (illustrated by Christine Price) (The Bodley Head, 1954) £35
DESPERATE JOURNEY: A Tale (illustrated by Richard Kennedy) (Faber, 1954) £30
ASK FOR KING BILLY (illustrated by Richard Kennedy) (Faber, 1955)...£30
VIKING'S DAWN (illustrated by Christine Price) (The Bodley Head, 1955) £30
HOUNDS OF THE KING (illustrated by Christine Price) (The Bodley Head, 1955) £30
MEN OF THE HILLS (illustrated by Christine Price) (The Bodley Head, 1957) £30
THE ROAD TO MIKLAGARD (illustrated by Christine Price) (The Bodley Head, 1957) £20
HUNTER HUNTED (illustrated by Richard Kennedy) (Faber, 1957)...£20
DON'T EXPECT ANY MERCY! (Faber, 1958) £20
THE CHILDREN'S CRUSADE (illustrated by Christine Price) (The Bodley Head, 1958) £20
THE RETURN OF ROBINSON CRUSOE (illustrated by Will Nickless) (Hulton Press, [1958]) £30
THE BOMBARD (illustrated by Christine Price) (The Bodley Head, 1959) £20
WICKHAM AND THE ARMADA (illustrated by Hookway Cowles) (Hulton Press, 1959) £20
CASTLES AND KINGS (non-fiction; illustrated by C. Walter Hodges) (Batsford, 1959)...................................£20
VIKING'S SUNSET (illustrated by Christine Price) (The Bodley Head, 1960) £20
RED SETTLEMENT (The Bodley Head, 1960)..£20
THE TRUE BOOK ABOUT CASTLES (non-fiction; illustrated by G.H. Channing) (Muller, 1960) £10
THE JET BEADS (illustrated by W.A. Sillince) (Brockhampton Press, 1961) £20
THE GOLDEN ONE (illustrated by William Stobbs) (The Bodley Head, 1961) £20
MAN WITH A SWORD (illustrated by William Stobbs) (The Bodley Head, 1962) £20
WAR DOG (illustrated by Roger Payne) (Brockhampton Press, 1962)..£20
HORNED HELMET (illustrated by Charles Keeping) (Brockhampton Press, 1963) £20
KNOW ABOUT THE CRUSADES (non-fiction) (Blackie, [1963]) £15

FIGHTING MEN: How Men have Fought Through the Ages (with Ronald Ewart Oakeshott) (Brockhampton Press, 1963) **£15**
THE BURNING OF NJAL (illustrated by Bernard Blatch) (The Bodley Head, 1963) **£15**
THE LAST OF THE VIKINGS (illustrated by Charles Keeping) (Brockhampton Press, 1964) **£25**
HOUNDS OF THE KING, with Two Radio Plays (contains 'Hounds of the King', 'Harold Godwinson' and 'William,
  Duke of Normandy'; illustrated by Stuart Tresilian) (Longman, 1965) **£15**
THE BRONZE SWORD (illustrated by Mary Russon) (Hamish Hamilton: 'Antelope Books' series, 1965)................**£10**
SPLINTERED SWORD (illustrated by Charles Keeping) (Brockhampton Press, 1965) **£25**
KILLER IN DARK GLASSES (Faber, 1965) **£20**
BANG, YOU'RE DEAD! (Faber, 1966) **£20**
THE QUEEN'S BROOCH (Hamish Hamilton, 1966)...**£15**
SWORDS FROM THE NORTH (illustrated by Charles Keeping) (Faber, 1967) **£15**
THE WINDSWEPT CITY (illustrated by Faith Jaques) (Hamish Hamilton, 1967) **£10**
VINLAND THE GOOD (illustrated by William Stobbs) (The Bodley Head, 1967) **£15**
THE DREAM-TIME (illustrated by Charles Keeping) (Brockhampton Press, 1967) **£30**
THE INVADERS (illustrated by Charles Keeping) (Brockhampton Press, 1972) **£20**
LEGIONS OF THE EAGLE (The Bodley Head, 1972) **£15**

TREVOR, Elleston

British author. Born: 1920. Also wrote as Mansell Black, Roger Fitzalan, Adam Hall, Simon Rattray, Warwick Scott, Caesar Smith, Lesley Stone. Writer of adult mystery and crime, and lively action and animal stories for children. Died: 1995.

Prices are for books in Very Good condition with dustjackets.

DEEP WOOD (illustrated by David Williams) (Gerald G. Swan, 1945) **£30**
WUMPUS (illustrated by J. McCail) (Gerald G. Swan, 1945) **£45**
WUMPUS AGAIN (illustrated by J. McCail) (Gerald G. Swan, 1946) **£40**
HEATHER HILL (Gerald G. Swan, 1946) **£20**
MORE ABOUT WUMPUS (illustrated by J. McCail) (Gerald G. Swan, 1947) **£40**
THE WIZARD OF THE WOOD (illustrated by Leslie Atkinson) (Falcon Press, 1948)..**£40**
THE SECRET TRAVELLERS (illustrated by David Williams) (Gerald G. Swan, 1948) **£20**
BADGER'S MOON (illustrated by Leslie Atkinson) (Falcon Press, 1949) **£20**
ANT'S CASTLE (illustrated by David Williams) (Falcon Press, 1949) **£20**
MOLE'S CASTLE (illustrated by Leslie Atkinson) (Falcon Press, 1950) **£20**
SWEETHALLOW VALLEY (illustrated by Leslie Atkinson) (Falcon Press, 1950) **£20**

TUDOR, Tasha

American author-illustrator. Born Starling Burgess in 1915. Wrote poetry, fairy tales and a series of 'Becky' books. Best known for her first book, *Pumpkin Moonshine* (1938).

Prices are for books in Very Good condition with dustjackets where applicable.

Books Written and Illustrated by Tasha Tudor

A TALE FOR EASTER (OUP, 1943) **£65**
LINSEY WOOLSEY (OUP, 1946) **£180**
THISTLY B (OUP, 1949) **£230**
A IS FOR ANNABELLE (OUP, 1954) **£170**
1 IS ONE (Rand McNally, U.S., [1956]) **£15**
AROUND THE YEAR (OUP, 1957) **£80**
AND SO IT WAS (Westminster Press, 1958) **£85**
AND SO IT WAS (paperback) (Westminster Press, 1988) **£15**
THE TASHA TUDOR BOOK OF FAIRY TALES (Platt & Munk, U.S., 1961)..**£45**
WINGS FROM THE WIND (Lippincott, U.S., 1964) **£75**
TASHA TUDOR'S FAVOURITE STORIES (Lippincott, U.S., 1965) **£45**
TAKE JOY! THE TASHA TUDOR CHRISTMAS BOOK (World, U.S., 1966) **£40**
FIRST DELIGHTS: A Book About the Five Senses (Platt & Munk, U.S., 1966) **£50**
FIRST POEMS OF CHILDHOOD (Platt & Munk, U.S., 1967)...**£25**
CORGIVILLE FAIR (Crowell, U.S., 1971) **£140**
TASHA TUDOR'S FIVE SENSES (Platt & Munk, U.S., 1978) **£40**
THE SPRINGS OF JOY (Rand McNally, U.S., 1979) **£40**
TASHA TUDOR'S SEASON'S OF DELIGHT: A Year on an Old-Fashioned Farm (a three-dimensional pop-up book)
  (Philomel, U.S., 1986) **£40**
THE PRIVATE WORLD OF TASHA TUDOR (Little Brown, U.S., 1992) **£35**
THE TASHA TUDOR COOKBOOK RECIPES AND REMINISCENCES (Little Brown, U.S., 1993)........................**£35**
THE DOLL'S CHRISTMAS (Simon & Schuster, U.S., 1999) **£30**
ALL FOR LOVE (Simon & Schuster, U.S., 2000) **£30**

Books Illustrated by Tasha Tudor

THE DOLL'S HOUSE by Rumer Godden (Viking, U.S., 1947) **£50**
THE DOLL'S HOUSE by Rumer Godden (Macmillan, 1963) **£50**
JACKANAPES by Juliana H. Ewing (OUP, U.S., 1948) **£100**

FIRST PRAYERS (OUP, U.S., 1952) £100
FIRST GRACES (Henry Z. Walck, U.S., 1955) £90
FIRST GRACES (Lutterworth Press, 1964) £10
THE TWENTY THIRD PSALM-MINIATURE (St Onge Press, 1965) £65
REAL DIARY OF A REAL BOY by Henry Shute (The Noone House, U.S., 1967) £45
MORE PRAYERS (Lutterworth Press, 1968) £10
THE LORD IS MY SHEPHERD (Philomel, U.S., 1980) £30
A CHILD'S GARDEN OF VERSES by R.L. Stevenson (Rand McNally, U.S., 1981) £35
THE NEW ENGLAND BUTT'RY SHELF ALMANAC by Mary Mason Campbell (Stephen Greene, U.S., 1982) £35
A BASKET OF HERBS : A Book of American Sentiments Edited by Mary Campbell (Stephen Greene, U.S., 1983) £150
GIVE US THIS DAY THE LORD'S PRAYER (paperback) (Paper Star, U.S., 1987) £10

TWAIN, Mark

American author. Born: Samuel Langhorne Clemens in Missouri in 1835. Left school at twelve, subsequently working as a printer and river-boatman. Became a reporter during the Civil War, adopting the pseudonym, Mark Twain (a boatmen's call meaning 'two fathoms deep'). As well as such classic children's works as *The Adventures of Tom Sawyer* (1876), *Huckleberry Finn* (1884) and *The Prince and the Pauper* (1881), he wrote a number of satirical novels and volumes of reminiscences. Died: 1910.

Prices are for books in Very Good condition.

THE CELEBRATED JUMPING FROG OF CALAVERAS COUNTY AND OTHER SKETCHES (Routledge, 1867) £1,400
THE INNOCENTS ABROAD (Hotten, [1870]) £1,000
THE NEW PILGRIM'S PROGRESS (Hotten, [1870]) £600
ROUGHING IT (two volumes) (Routledge, 1872) .... the set £300
THE INNOCENTS AT HOME (Routledge, 1872) £450
A CURIOUS DREAM AND OTHER SKETCHES (Routledge, [1872]) £275
MARK TWAIN'S SKETCHES (Routledge, 1872) £225
THE CHOICE HUMOROUS WORKS (Hotten, [1873]) £225
THE GILDED AGE (with C.D. Warner; three volumes) (Routledge, 1874) .... the set £450
INFORMATION WANTED AND OTHER SKETCHES (Routledge, [1876]) £225
THE ADVENTURES OF TOM SAWYER (Chatto & Windus, 1876) £1,800
THE ADVENTURES OF TOM SAWYER (illustrated by Edward Ardizzone) (Heinemann, 1961) £35

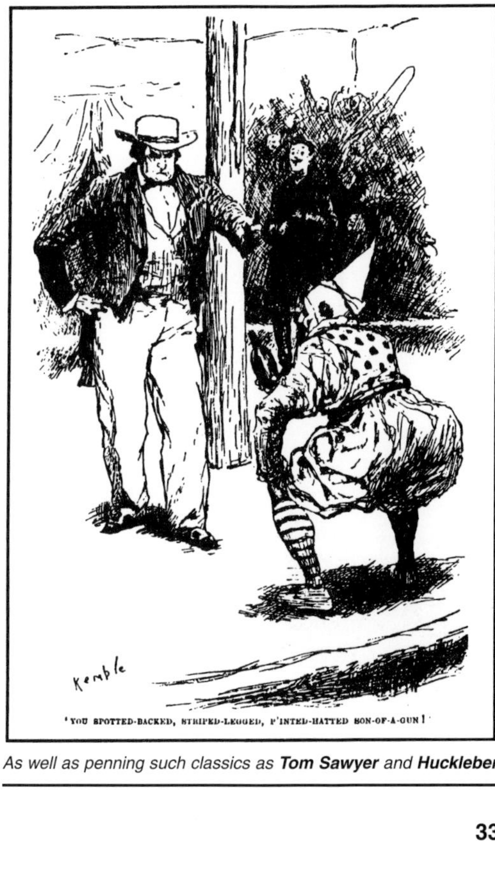

'YOU SPOTTED-BACKED, STRIPED-LEGGED, P'INTED-HATTED SON-OF-A-GUN!'

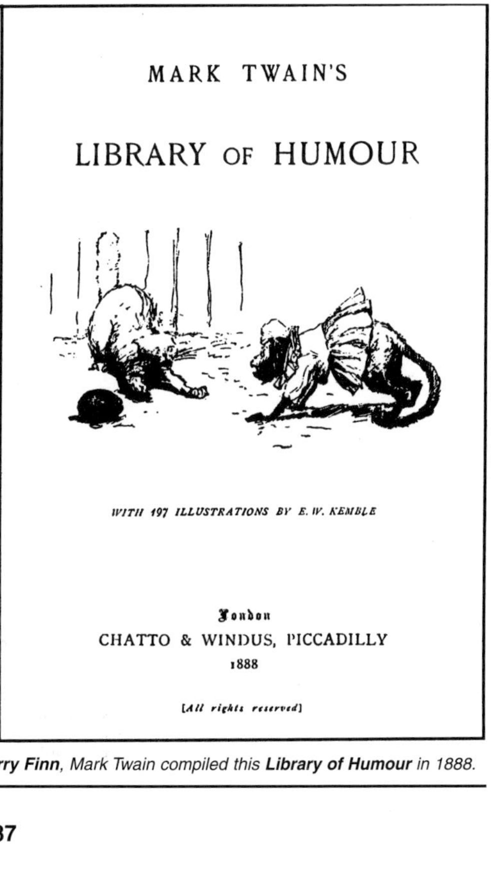

MARK TWAIN'S

LIBRARY OF HUMOUR

WITH 197 ILLUSTRATIONS BY E. W. KEMBLE

London
CHATTO & WINDUS, PICCADILLY
1888

[All rights reserved]

*As well as penning such classics as **Tom Sawyer** and **Huckleberry Finn**, Mark Twain compiled this **Library of Humour** in 1888.*

TWAIN, Mark

A YANKEE AT THE COURT

OF KING ARTHUR

BY

MARK TWAIN

(SAMUEL L. CLEMENS)

WITH 220 ILLUSTRATIONS BY DAN. BEARD

London
CHATTO & WINDUS, PICCADILLY
1889

[All rights reserved]

'GREAT SCOTT, CAN'T YOU UNDERSTAND A LITTLE THING LIKE THAT?'

*The opening spread from the first British edition of Mark Twain's **A Yankee at the Court of King Arthur**, published in 1889.*

A TRAMP ABROAD (Chatto & Windus, 1880) **£800**
THE PRINCE AND THE PAUPER: A Tale for Young People of All Ages (Chatto & Windus, 1881) **£225**
THE STOLEN WHITE ELEPHANT (Chatto & Windus, 1882) **£175**
LIFE ON THE MISSISSIPPI (Chatto & Windus, 1883) **£1,000**
THE ADVENTURES OF HUCKLEBERRY FINN, Tom Sawyer's Comrade (Chatto & Windus, 1884) **£1,800**
THE ADVENTURES OF HUCKLEBERRY FINN, Tom Sawyer's Comrade (illustrated by Edward Ardizzone)
  (Heinemann, 1961) **£35**
MARK TWAIN'S LIBRARY OF HUMOUR (Chatto & Windus, 1888) **£175**
A YANKEE AT THE COURT OF KING ARTHUR (Chatto & Windus, 1889) **£750**
THE AMERICAN CLAIMANT (Chatto & Windus, 1892) **£100**
THE $1,000,000 BANK NOTE (Chatto & Windus, 1893) **£100**
TOM SAWYER ABROAD (illustrated by Dan Beard) (Chatto & Windus, 1894) **£1,000**
PUDD'NHEAD WILSON (Chatto & Windus, 1894) **£200**
TOM SAWYER, DETECTIVE: As Told by Huck Finn, and Other Tales (Chatto & Windus, 1897 [1896]) **£850**
MORE TRAMPS ABROAD (Chatto & Windus, 1897) **£100**
THE MAN THAT CORRUPTED HADLEYBURG (Chatto & Windus, 1900) **£150**
A DOUBLE BARRELLED DETECTIVE STORY (Chatto & Windus, 1902) **£100**
EXTRACTS FROM ADAM'S DIARY (Harper, U.K./U.S., 1904) **£75**
A DOG'S TALE (Harper, U.K./U.S., 1904)..**£75**
EVE'S DIARY (Harper, U.K./U.S., 1906) **£75**
THE $30,000 BEQUEST (Harper, U.K./U.S., 1906) **£75**
A HORSE'S TALE (Harper, U.K./U.S., 1907) **£60**

U

UPTON, Florence K.

Anglo-American illustrator. Born: Florence Kate Upton in New York in 1873, but moved permanently to England in 1893. Created the 'Golliwogg' in a series of picture books which were written by her mother, Bertha Upton (1849-1912), beginning with *The Adventures of Two Dutch Dolls and a 'Golliwogg'* (1895). The books started a 'Golliwogg' craze and spawned a whole range of ephemera and novelty items. Died: 1922.

Prices are for books in Very Good condition.

THE ADVENTURES OF TWO DUTCH DOLLS AND A GOLLIWOGG by Bertha Upton (verse) (Longmans, [1895]) £400
THE GOLLIWOGG'S BICYCLE CLUB by Bertha Upton (verse) (Longmans, [1896])..£350
LITTLE HEARTS by Bertha Upton (Routledge, 1897) £350
THE VEGE-MEN'S REVENGE by Bertha Upton (verse) (Longmans, [1897]) £350
THE GOLLIWOGG AT THE SEA-SIDE by Bertha Upton (verse) (Longmans, 1898)...£350
THE GOLLIWOGG IN WAR! by Bertha Upton (verse) (Longmans, 1899)..£350
THE GOLLIWOGG'S POLAR ADVENTURES by Bertha Upton (verse) (Longmans, [1900]) £350
THE GOLLIWOGG'S "AUTO-GO-CART" by Bertha Upton (verse) (Longmans, [1901])..£350
THE GOLLIWOGG'S AIR-SHIP by Bertha Upton (verse) (Longmans, [1902]) £350
THE GOLLIWOGG'S CIRCUS by Bertha Upton (verse) (Longmans, [1903]) £350
THE GOLLIWOGG IN HOLLAND by Bertha Upton (verse) (Longmans, [1904])...£350
THE GOLLIWOGG'S FOX-HUNT by Bertha Upton (verse) (Longmans, [1905]) £350
THE GOLLIWOGG'S DESERT ISLAND by Bertha Upton (verse) (Longmans, [1906]) £350
THE GOLLIWOGG'S CHRISTMAS by Bertha Upton (verse) (Longmans, 1907) £450
THE ADVENTURES OF BORBEE AND THE WISP: The Story of a Sophisticated Little Girl and
    an Unsophisticated Little Boy by Florence K. Upton (Longmans, 1908) £350
GOLLIWOGG IN THE AFRICAN JUNGLE by Bertha Upton (verse) (Longmans, 1909)..£400

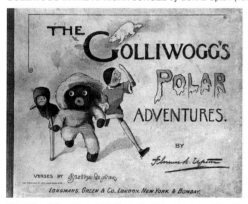

The fifth of the famous 'Golliwogg' picture books, written by Bertha Upton and illustrated by her daughter, Florence.

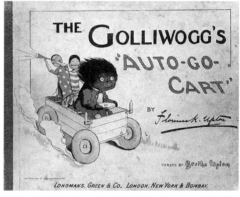

All the books in the series fetch three-figure sums in Very Good condition. This example from 1901 is now worth £350.

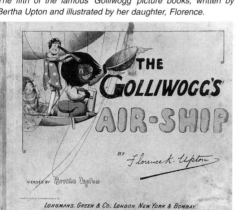

The Golliwoggs certainly weren't averse to new technology! In 1902, they reached for the sky in **The Golliwogg's Air-Ship**.

Perhaps the most politically incorrect book of all time: **The Golliwogg's Fox-Hunt**, published by Longmans in 1905.

UTTLEY, Alison

British author. Born: Cromford, Derbyshire, in 1884. Studied at Manchester and Cambridge Universities, subsequently working as a schoolteacher. Wrote a number of children's books, but is best known for her 'Little Grey Rabbit' series, and for those featuring Sam Pig. Also wrote a play about the life and works of Hans Andersen. Died: 1976.

Prices are for books in Very Good condition with dustjackets.

'Grey Rabbit' Books

THE SQUIRREL, THE HARE AND THE LITTLE GREY RABBIT (illustrated by Margaret Tempest) (Heinemann, 1929) £80
HOW LITTLE GREY RABBIT GOT BACK HER TAIL (illustrated by Margaret Tempest) (Heinemann, 1930) £70
THE GREAT ADVENTURE OF HARE (illustrated by Margaret Tempest) (Heinemann, 1931) £65
THE STORY OF FUZZYPEG THE HEDGEHOG (illustrated by Margaret Tempest) (Heinemann, 1932).....................£65
SQUIRREL GOES SKATING (illustrated by Margaret Tempest) (Collins, 1934) £60
WISE OWL'S STORY (illustrated by Margaret Tempest) (Collins, 1935) £60
LITTLE GREY RABBIT'S PARTY (illustrated by Margaret Tempest) (Collins, 1936)..£60
THE KNOT SQUIRREL TIED (illustrated by Margaret Tempest) (Collins, 1937) £55
FUZZYPEG GOES TO SCHOOL (illustrated by Margaret Tempest) (Collins, 1938) £50
LITTLE GREY RABBIT'S CHRISTMAS (illustrated by Margaret Tempest) (Collins, 1939).....................................£45
MY LITTLE GREY RABBIT PAINTING BOOK (illustrated by Margaret Tempest) (Collins, 1940).............................£40
MOLDY WARP THE MOLE (illustrated by Margaret Tempest) (Collins, 1940) £40
HARE JOINS THE HOME GUARD (illustrated by Margaret Tempest) (Collins, 1942)..£45
LITTLE GREY RABBIT'S WASHING DAY (illustrated by Margaret Tempest) (Collins, 1942) £40
WATER RAT'S PICNIC (illustrated by Margaret Tempest) (Collins, 1943) £40
LITTLE GREY RABBIT'S BIRTHDAY (illustrated by Margaret Tempest) (Collins, 1944) £40
THE SPECKLEDY HEN (illustrated by Margaret Tempest) (Collins, 1945) £40
LITTLE GREY RABBIT TO THE RESCUE (play; illustrated by Margaret Tempest) (Collins, 1945).........................£40
LITTLE GREY RABBIT AND THE WEASELS (illustrated by Margaret Tempest) (Collins, 1947) £40
GREY RABBIT AND THE WANDERING HEDGEHOG (illustrated by Margaret Tempest) (Collins, 1948) £40
LITTLE GREY RABBIT MAKES LACE (illustrated by Margaret Tempest) (Collins, 1950) £40
HARE AND THE EASTER EGGS (illustrated by Margaret Tempest) (Collins, 1952)...£40
LITTLE GREY RABBIT'S VALENTINE (illustrated by Margaret Tempest) (Collins, 1953).....................................£40
LITTLE GREY RABBIT GOES TO THE SEA (illustrated by Margaret Tempest) (Collins, 1954) £40
HARE AND GUY FAWKES (illustrated by Margaret Tempest) (Collins, 1956)...£40
LITTLE GREY RABBIT'S PAINT-BOX (illustrated by Margaret Tempest) (Collins, [1958]) £40

The second of Alison Uttley's 'Grey Rabbit' books, now worth £70 in Very Good condition with the Margaret Tempest jacket.

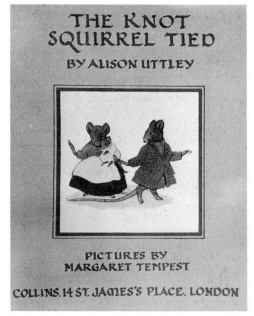

All the books were issued in dustjackets, but even without them they have a great deal of charm, as this example shows.

*The front board of **Little Grey Rabbit's Christmas** (1939) features a very appropriate 'snowflake' background design.*

*Post-war titles like **Grey Rabbit and the Wandering Hedgehog** are worth £30-£40 in their original dustjackets.*

GREY RABBIT FINDS A SHOE (illustrated by Margaret Tempest) (Collins, 1960) £40
GREY RABBIT AND THE CIRCUS (illustrated by Margaret Tempest) (Collins, 1961) £40
THREE LITTLE GREY RABBIT PLAYS (contains 'The Grey Rabbit's Hospital', 'The Robber' and 'A Christmas Story')
(Heinemann, 1961) £30
GREY RABBIT'S MAY DAY (illustrated by Margaret Tempest) (Collins, 1963) £40
HARE GOES SHOPPING (illustrated by Margaret Tempest) (Collins, 1965) £40
LITTLE GREY RABBIT'S PANCAKE DAY (illustrated by Margaret Tempest) (Collins, 1967).................£40
LITTLE GREY RABBIT GOES TO THE NORTH POLE (illustrated by Katherine Wigglesworth) (Collins, 1970) £40
FUZZYPEG'S BROTHER (illustrated by Katherine Wigglesworth) (Heinemann, 1971) £40
LITTLE GREY RABBIT'S SPRING CLEANING PARTY (illustrated by Katherine Wigglesworth) (Collins, 1972)..........£40
LITTLE GREY RABBIT AND THE SNOW-BABY (illustrated by Katherine Wigglesworth) (Collins, 1973) £40
HARE AND THE RAINBOW (illustrated by Katherine Wigglesworth) (Collins, 1975) £40

'Sam Pig' Books
TALES OF THE FOUR PIGS AND BROCK THE BADGER (illustrated by Alec Buckels) (Faber, 1939).................£40
THE ADVENTURES OF SAM PIG (illustrated by Francis Gower) (Faber, 1940) £40
SAM PIG GOES TO MARKET (illustrated by A.E. Kennedy) (Faber, 1941) £40
SIX TALES OF BROCK THE BADGER (illustrated by Alec Buckels and Francis Gower) (Faber, 1941)................£40
SIX TALES OF SAM PIG (illustrated by Francis Gower) (Faber, 1941) £40
SIX TALES OF THE FOUR PIGS (illustrated by Alec Buckels) (Faber, 1941) £40
SAM PIG AND SALLY (illustrated by A.E. Kennedy) (Faber, 1942) £40
SAM PIG AT THE CIRCUS (illustrated by A.E. Kennedy) (Faber, 1943) £40
SAM PIG IN TROUBLE (illustrated by A.E. Kennedy) (Faber, 1948) £40
YOURS EVER, SAM PIG (illustrated by A.E. Kennedy) (Faber, 1951) £35
SAM PIG AND THE SINGING GATE (illustrated by A.E. Kennedy) (Faber, 1955).................................£30
SAM PIG GOES TO THE SEASIDE (illustrated by A.E. Kennedy) (Faber, 1960) £30
THE SAM PIG STORYBOOK (illustrated by Cecil Leslie) (Faber, 1965) £30

'Tim Rabbit' Books
THE ADVENTURES OF NO ORDINARY RABBIT (illustrated by Alec Buckels) (Faber, [1937])..................£60
TEN TALES OF TIM RABBIT (illustrated by Alec Buckels) (Faber, 1941) £50
ADVENTURES OF TIM RABBIT (illustrated by A.E. Kennedy) (Faber, 1945) £40
TIM RABBIT AND COMPANY (illustrated by A.E. Kennedy) (Faber, 1959) £30
TIM RABBIT'S DOZEN (illustrated by Shirley Hughes) (Faber, 1964) £25

'Little Brown Mouse' Books
SNUG AND SERENA MEET A QUEEN (illustrated by Katherine Wigglesworth) (Heinemann, 1950) £45
SNUG AND SERENA PICK COWSLIPS (illustrated by Katherine Wigglesworth) (Heinemann, 1950) £50
GOING TO THE FAIR (illustrated by Katherine Wigglesworth) (Heinemann, 1951) £35

TOAD'S CASTLE (illustrated by Katherine Wigglesworth) (Heinemann, 1951) £35
MRS MOUSE SPRING-CLEANS (illustrated by Katherine Wigglesworth) (Heinemann, 1952) £35
CHRISTMAS AT THE ROSE AND CROWN (illustrated by Katherine Wigglesworth) (Heinemann, 1952) £35
THE GYPSY HEDGEHOGS (illustrated by Katherine Wigglesworth) (Heinemann, 1953) £35
SNUG AND THE CHIMNEY-SWEEPER (illustrated by Katherine Wigglesworth) (Heinemann, 1953) £35
THE MOUSE TELEGRAMS (illustrated by Katherine Wigglesworth) (Heinemann, 1955) £35
THE FLOWER SHOW (illustrated by Katherine Wigglesworth) (Heinemann, 1955) £35
SNUG AND THE SILVER SPOON (illustrated by Katherine Wigglesworth) (Heinemann, 1957) £30
MR STOAT WALKS IN (illustrated by Katherine Wigglesworth) (Heinemann, 1957) £30
SNUG AND SERENA COUNT TWELVE (illustrated by Katherine Wigglesworth) (Heinemann, 1959) £25
SNUG AND SERENA GO TO TOWN (illustrated by Katherine Wigglesworth) (Heinemann, 1961) £25
THE BROWN MOUSE BOOK: Magical Tales of Two Little Mice (illustrated by Katherine Wigglesworth) (Heinemann, 1971) ..£30

'Little Red Fox' Books

LITTLE RED FOX AND THE WICKED UNCLE (illustrated by Katherine Wigglesworth) (Heinemann, 1954) £70
LITTLE RED FOX AND CINDERELLA (illustrated by Katherine Wigglesworth) (Heinemann, 1956) £60
LITTLE RED FOX AND THE MAGIC MOON (illustrated by Katherine Wigglesworth) (Heinemann, 1958) £60
LITTLE RED FOX AND THE UNICORN (illustrated by Katherine Wigglesworth) (Heinemann, 1962) £50
THE LITTLE RED FOX AND THE BIG TREE (illustrated by Jennie Corbett) (Heinemann, 1968)..........................£45

Others

THE COUNTRY CHILD (illustrated by C.F. Tunnicliffe) (Faber, 1931) £100
MOONSHINE AND MAGIC (illustrated by William Townsend) (Faber, 1932) £90
THE ADVENTURES OF PETER AND JUDY IN BUNNYLAND (illustrated by L. Young) (Collins, 1935) £75
CANDLELIGHT TALES (illustrated by Elinor Bellingham-Smith) (Faber, 1936) £55
AMBUSH OF YOUNG DAYS (Faber, 1937) £50
MUSTARD, PEPPER AND SALT (illustrated by Gwen Raverat) (Faber, 1938) £75
HIGH MEADOWS (Faber, 1938) £40
A TRAVELLER IN TIME (illustrated by Phyllis Bray) (Faber, 1939) £35
THE FARM ON THE HILL (Faber, 1941) £30
NINE STARLIGHT TALES (illustrated by Irene Hawkins) (Faber, 1942)...£30
TEN CANDLELIGHT TALES (selections from 'Candlelight Tales') (Faber, 1942)......................................£30
CUCKOO CHERRY-TREE (illustrated by Irene Hawkins) (Faber, 1943) £30
COUNTRY HOARD (illustrated by C.F. Tunnicliffe) (Faber, 1943) £35
THE SPICE WOMAN'S BASKET and Other Tales (illustrated by Irene Hawkins) (Faber, 1944) £35
MRS NIMBLE AND MR BUMBLE (illustrated by Horace Knowles) (James, 1944) £45
SOME MOONSHINE TALES (illustrated by Sarah Nechamkin) (Faber, 1945)...£25
THE WEATHER COCK and Other Stories (illustrated by Nancy Innes) (Faber, 1945) £30
WHEN ALL IS DONE (Faber, 1945) £30
COUNTRY THINGS (illustrated by C.F. Tunnicliffe) (Faber, 1946) £40
THE WASHERWOMAN'S CHILD: A Play on the Life and Stories of Hans Christian Andersen
   (illustrated by Irene Hawkins) (Faber, 1946) £35
JOHN BARLEYCORN: Twelve Tales of Fairy and Magic (illustrated by Philip Hepworth) (Faber, 1948) £40

A selection of titles featuring three of the other characters in the 'Grey Rabbit' series: Hare, Squirrel and Moldy Warp the Mole.

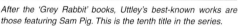

After the 'Grey Rabbit' books, Uttley's best-known works are those featuring Sam Pig. This is the tenth title in the series.

Uttley also wrote a number of 'miscellaneous' titles, like this story about a young boy's holiday on his grandfather's farm.

CARTS AND CANDLESTICKS (essays; illustrated by C.F. Tunnicliffe) (Faber, 1948) £40
IN PRAISE OF COUNTRY LIFE: An Anthology. Edited by Alison Uttley (Muller, 1949) £35
THE COBBLER'S SHOP and Other Tales (illustrated by Irene Hawkins) (Faber, 1950) £35
MACDUFF (illustrated by A.E. Kennedy) (Faber, 1950) £25
AMBUSH OF YOUNG DAYS (illustrated by C.F. Tunnicliffe) (Faber, 1951 [1952]) £40
PLOWMEN'S CLOCKS (essays; illustrated by C.F. Tunnicliffe) (Faber, 1952) £40
THE STUFF OF DREAMS (Faber, 1953) £25
MAGIC IN MY POCKET: A Selection of Tales (illustrated by Judith Brook; paperback) (Puffin, 1957) £10
THE SWANS FLY OVER (illustrated by C.F. Tunnicliffe) (Faber, 1959)..£40
SOMETHING FOR NOTHING (illustrated by C.F. Tunnicliffe) (Faber, 1960)..£40
JOHN AT THE OLD FARM (illustrated by Jennifer Miles) (Heinemann, 1960)..£45
THE LITTLE KNIFE WHO DID ALL THE WORK: Twelve Tales of Magic (illustrated by Pauline Baynes) (Faber, 1962) £25
WILD HONEY (illustrated by C.F. Tunnicliffe) (Faber, 1962) £40
CUCKOO IN JUNE (illustrated by C.F. Tunnicliffe) (Faber, 1964) £40
THE MOUSE, THE RABBIT AND THE LITTLE WHITE HEN (illustrated by Jennie Corbett; boards)
      (Heinemann: 'Cowslip' series, 1966) £20
ENCHANTMENT (illustrated by Jennie Corbett; boards) (Heinemann: 'Cowslip' series, 1966) £20
A PECK OF GOLD (illustrated by C.F. Tunnicliffe) (Faber, 1966) £40
THE BUTTON-BOX and Other Essays (illustrated by C.F. Tunnicliffe) (Faber, 1968) £40
LAVENDER SHOES: Eight Tales of Enchantment (illustrated by Janina Ede) (Faber, 1970) £20
A TEN O'CLOCK SCHOLAR and Other Essays (illustrated by C.F. Tunnicliffe) (Faber, 1970) £40
SECRET PLACES and Other Essays (illustrated by C.F. Tunnicliffe) (Faber, 1972) £50
FAIRY TALES. Edited by Kathleen Lines (illustrated by Ann Strugwell) (Faber, 1975)..£20
FROM SPRING TO SPRING: Stories of the Four Seasons. Edited by Kathleen Lines
      (anthology; illustrated by Shirley Hughes) (Faber, 1978) £20
STORIES FOR CHRISTMAS. Chosen by Kathleen Lines (illustrated by Gavin Rowe) (Faber, 1977) £20

VERNE, Jules

French author. Born: Nantes, 1828. Famous for his escapist adventure novels and short stories. Died: 1905.

Prices are for books in Good condition (with dustjackets after 1940).

FIVE WEEKS IN A BALLOON (Chapman & Hall, 1870) £250
A JOURNEY TO THE CENTRE OF THE EARTH (Griffith & Farran, 1872 [1871])...............................£400
TWENTY THOUSAND LEAGUES UNDER THE SEA (Sampson Low, 1873 [1872])......................£400
FROM THE EARTH TO THE MOON DIRECT IN 97 HOURS, 20 MINUTES, AND A TRIP ROUND IT (Sampson Low, 1873)....£500
MERIDIANA: The Adventures of Three Englishmen and Three Russians in South Africa (Sampson Low, 1873)...............£100
THE FAR COUNTRY (Sampson Low, 1874 [1873]) £100
AROUND THE WORLD IN EIGHTY DAYS (Sampson Low, 1874 [1873]) £300
A FLOATING CITY, AND THE BLOCKADE RUNNERS (Sampson Low, 1874) £100
DR OX'S EXPERIMENT and Other Stories (Sampson Low, 1875) £60
THE MYSTERIOUS ISLAND (three volumes : 'Dropped from the Clouds', 'Abandoned' and 'The Secret of the Island')
  (Sampson Low, 1875) ....the set £400
THE ENGLISH AT THE NORTH POLE — I: THE ADVENTURES OF CAPTAIN HATTERAS (Routledge, 1875 [1874])..............£60
THE ENGLISH AT THE NORTH POLE — II: THE FIELD OF ICE (Routledge, 1876) £60
THE SURVIVORS OF THE 'CHANCELLOR' (Sampson Low, 1875) £60
MARTIN PAZ (Sampson Low, 1876)...£60
A WINTER AMID THE ICE and Other Stories (Sampson Low, 1876) £75
A VOYAGE ROUND THE WORLD (three volumes : 'South America', 'Australia' & 'New Zealand') (Routledge, 1876-77) ..the set £150
MICHAEL STROGOFF (Sampson Low, 1877 [1876]) £75
THE CHILD OF THE CAVERN (Sampson Low, 1877) £75
HECTOR SERVADAC (Sampson Low, 1878) £75
DICK SANDS, THE BOY CAPTAIN (Sampson Low, 1879 [1878]) £75
THE BEGUM'S FORTUNE (Sampson Low, 1880 [1879]) £60
THE TRIBULATIONS OF A CHINAMAN (Sampson Low, 1880) £60
THE STEAM HOUSE (two volumes: ' Demon of Cawnpore' and 'Tigers and Traitors') (Sampson Low, 1881)....the set £150
THE GIANT RAFT (two volumes: 'Down the Amazon' and 'The Cryptogram') (Sampson Low, 1881) ....the set £150
GODFREY MORGAN, A CALIFORNIAN MYSTERY (Sampson Low, 1883)..£60
THE GREEN RAY (Sampson Low, 1883) £75
KERABAN THE INFLEXIBLE (two vols: 'The Captain of the Guidara' & 'Scarpante the Spy') (Sampson Low, 1884-85) the set £125
THE VANISHED DIAMOND (Sampson Low, 1885) £60
THE ARCHIPELAGO ON FIRE (Sampson Low, 1886) £75
MATHIAS SANDORF (Sampson Low, 1886) £75
THE CLIPPER OF THE CLOUDS (Sampson Low, 1887)..£60
THE LOTTERY TICKET (Sampson Low, 1887) £60
THE FLIGHT TO FRANCE (Sampson Low, 1888) £60
NORTH AGAINST SOUTH (Sampson Low, 1888) £60
ADRIFT IN THE PACIFIC (Sampson Low, 1889) £60
A FAMILY WITHOUT A NAME (Sampson Low, 1891 [1890]) £60
THE PURCHASE OF THE NORTH POLE (Sampson Low, 1891 [1890])...£60
CAESAR CASCABEL (Sampson Low, 1891)...£60
MISTRESS BRANICAN (Sampson Low, 1892) £60
THE CASTLE OF THE CARPATHIANS (Sampson Low, 1893) £60
CLAUDIUS BOMBARNAC (Sampson Low, 1894) £60
FOUNDLING MICK (Sampson Low, 1895) £60
CAPTAIN ANTIFER (Sampson Low, 1895) £60
THE FLOATING ISLAND (Sampson Low, 1896) £60
CLOVIS DARDENTOR (Sampson Low, 1897) £60
FOR THE FLAG (Sampson Low, 1897)..£60
AN ANTARTIC MYSTERY (Sampson Low, 1898) £75
THE WILL OF AN ECCENTRIC (Sampson Low, 1900) £50
THE CHASE OF THE GOLDEN METEOR (Grant Richards, 1909) £30
MASTER OF THE WORLD (Sampson Low, [1914]) £30
THE LIGHTHOUSE AT THE END OF THE WORLD (Sampson Low, [1923]) £30
THEIR ISLAND HOME (Sampson Low, [1923]) £30
THE CASTAWAYS OF THE FLAG (Sampson Low, [1923]) £30
INTO THE NIGER BEND (Arco, 1960) £10
THE CITY IN THE SAHARA (Arco, 1960)...£10
THE SURVIVORS OF THE JONATHAN: The Masterless Man (Arco, 1962) £10
THE UNWILLING DICTATOR (Arco, 1962) £10
THE GOLDEN VOLCANO: The Claim on Forty Mile Creek (Arco, 1962) £10
FLOOD AND FAME (Arco, 1962) £10
THE SECRET OF THE WILLHELM STORITZ (Arco, 1964) £10

*Jules Vernes' novels are full of weird and wonderful inventions like this one from **Master of the World**.*

W

WAIN, Louis

British illustrator. Born: London, 1860. Studied at the West London School of Art, joining the *Illustrated Sporting and Dramatic News* as a journalist/illustrator in 1882. Began his highly successful career as a cat illustrator in 1886 with *Madame Tabby's Establishment*, producing his first annual in 1901. Worked in America between 1908 and 1910. Committed to a mental hospital in 1924 following an attack on his sister. Died: 1939.

Prices are for books in Very Good condition.

MADAME TABBY'S ESTABLISHMENT by Kari (Macmillan, 1886) £700
OUR FARM: The Trouble and Successes Thereof by F.W. Pattenden (Clarke, 1888) £125
DREAMS BY FRENCH FIRESIDES (written under the pseudonym 'Richard Leander'; stories) (A. & C. Black, 1890)............£125
PETER, A CAT O'ONE TAIL: His Life and Adventures by Charles Morley (Pall Mall Gazette Extras, 1892) £450
OLD RABBIT, THE VOODOO AND OTHER SORCERERS by M.A. Owen (Unwin, 1893) £125
MISS LOVEMOUSE'S LETTERS (Nelson, 1896)..£125
PUPPY DOGS' TALES (Nelson, 1896) £125
THE CHILDREN'S TABLEAUX: The Three Little Kittens (Nister, 1896) £200
MORE JINGLES, JOKES, AND FUNNY FOLKS by Clifton Bingham (Nister, 1898) £260
THE MONKEY THAT WOULD NOT KILL by Henry Drummond (Hodder & Stoughton, 1898) £60
PUSSIES AND PUPPIES. With Verses and Tales by Various Writers (Partridge, [1899]) £200
THE DANDY LION by Louis Wain and Clifton Bingham (Nister, [1900])..£300
FUN ALL THE WAY (Nister, 1900) £100
CATS (written under the pseudonym 'Grimalkin'; verse) (Sands, [1901]) £750
LOUIS WAIN'S ANNUAL (Treherne, 1901) £250
THE LIVING ANIMALS OF THE WORLD by C.J. Cornish ([1901]) £150
FUN FOR EVERYONE (Nister, 1902) £100
FUN AND FROLIC by Louis Wain and Clifton Bingham (Nister, [1902]) £650
PA CATS, MA CATS, AND THEIR KITTENS (written under the pseudonym 'Father Tuck') (Raphael Tuck, [1902]) £850
ALL SORTS OF COMICAL CATS by Clifton Bingham (verse) (Nister, 1902) £750
THE LOUIS WAIN NURSERY BOOK (Clarke, [1902]) £150
LOUIS WAIN'S ANNUAL FOR 1902 (Treherne, 1902)...£250
LOUIS WAIN'S CATS AND DOGS (Raphael Tuck, 1902) £300
PING-PONG CALENDER FOR 1903 by Clifton Bingham (verse) (Raphael Tuck, [1903])................................£250
BIG DOGS, LITTLE DOGS, CATS AND KITTENS (Raphael Tuck, [1903]) £850
KITTENLAND by Clifton Bingham (verse) (Collins, [1903]) £750
COMIC ANNUALS ABC by Louis Wain (Collins, [1903]) £300
LOUIS WAIN'S BABY'S PICTURE BOOK (Clarke, 1903) £200
LOUIS WAIN'S DOG PAINTING BOOK (Raphael Tuck, 1903) £200
LOUIS WAIN'S CAT PAINTING BOOK (Raphael Tuck, 1903) £200
LOUIS WAIN'S SUMMER BOOK (Hutchinson, 1903) £200
LOUIS WAIN'S ANNUAL 1903 (Hutchinson, 1903) £250
THE LOUIS WAIN KITTEN BOOK (printed only on one side of the leaf) (Treherne, [1903])...............................£750
WITH LOUIS WAIN TO FAIRYLAND by Nora Chesson (Raphael Tuck, [1904]) £750
FUNNY ANIMALS AND STORIES ABOUT THEM (Clarke, 1904)...£250
IN ANIMAL LAND WITH LOUIS WAIN (Partridge, [1904]) £650
FUNNY FAVOURITES by Clifton Bingham (verse) (Nister, 1904)..£300
KITS AND CATS (Raphael Tuck, 1904) £300
CLAWS AND PAWS: Stories and Pictures from Kittenland and Puppyland by C. Bingham (Nister, [1904])...........£650
CAT TALES by W.L. Alden (Digby Long, 1905)..£350
LOUIS WAIN'S ANIMAL SHOW. With Stories in Prose and Verse (Clarke, 1905)...£200
LOUIS WAIN'S ANNUAL 1905 (King, 1905) £200
LOUIS WAIN'S SUMMER BOOK FOR 1906 (King, 1906) £200
LOUIS WAIN'S ANNUAL FOR 1906 (Shaw, 1906) £200
THE ADVENTURES OF FRISKERS AND HIS FRIENDS by Marian Hurrell (Culley, 1907) £200
MEPHISTOPHELES: The Autobiography and Adventures of a Tabby Cat by C.Y. Stephenson (Jarrold, 1907)....................£225
LOUIS WAIN'S ANNUAL 1907 (Bemrose, 1907) £200
THE KINGS AND THE CATS: Munster Fairy Tales for Young and Old by John Hannon (Burns & Oates, [1908]) £250
CAT'S CRADLE: A Picture Book for Little Folk by May Clariss Byron (Blackie, [1908]) £250
FULL OF FUN by Clifton Bingham (verse) (Nister, [1908])..£300
ANIMAL PLAYTIME (Clarke, 1908) £225
LOUIS WAIN'S ANNUAL 1908 (Bemrose, 1908) £200
HOLIDAYS IN ANIMAL LAND by A.W. Ridler (Clarke, [1909])..£250
LOUIS WAIN'S ANNUAL 1909-10 (Allen, 1909) £200
TWO CATS AT LARGE: A Book of Surprises by S.C. Woodhouse (verse) (Routledge, [1910]) £300
THE MERRY ANIMAL PICTURE BOOK by A.W. Ridler (Clarke, [1910]) £225
LOUIS WAIN'S ANNUAL 1910-11 (Allen, 1910) £175

Cat books are always popular with collectors, and none more so than those by Louis Wain. This illustration is typical of his work.

WAIN. Louis

Wain's drawings often display a wicked sense of humour, sometimes directed against the forces of law and order (above).

THE HAPPY FAMILY by Edric Vredenburg (Raphael Tuck, 1910) £750
SUCH FUN WITH LOUIS WAIN by Norman Gale (Raphael Tuck, 1910) £300
LOUIS WAIN'S ANNUAL 1911 (Shaw, 1911) £175
CATS AT SCHOOL by S.C. Woodhouse (verse) (Routledge, [1911]) £250
ANIMALS IN FUN-LAND by A.W. Rider (Clarke, 1911) £300
LOUIS WAIN'S ANNUAL 1911-12 (Shaw, 1911) £175
MERRY TIMES IN ANIMAL-LAND by A.W. Rider (Clarke, 1912)..£300
THE CATS SCOUTS: A Picture Book for Little Folk by Jessie Pope (Blackie, [1912])...£450
LOUIS WAIN'S ANNUAL 1912 (Shaw, 1912) £175
IN STORY LAND WITH LOUIS WAIN (Raphael Tuck, 1912) £450
LOUIS WAIN'S HAPPY LAND by A.W. Ridler (Shaw, 1912) £175
LOUIS WAIN'S PAINTING BOOK (Shaw, 1912) £175
LOUIS WAIN'S FATHER CHRISTMAS (Shaw, 1912)...£175
ANIMAL HAPPYLAND (Clarke, 1913) £175
LOUIS WAIN'S ANNUAL 1913 (Shaw, 1913)...£175
HAPPY HOURS WITH LOUIS WAIN (Shaw, 1913) £300
A CAT ALPHABET AND PICTURE BOOK FOR LITTLE FOLK (Blackie, [1914]) £300
TINKER, TAILOR by Eric Vredenburg (Raphael Tuck, 1914) £450
ANIMAL PICTURE-LAND (Clarke, 1914)..£300
LOUIS WAIN'S ANNUAL 1914 (Shaw, 1914)..£175
DADDY CAT (Blackie & Sons, [1915])...£450
ANIMAL FANCY-LAND by A.W. Rider (Clarke, 1915) £300
LITTLE SOLDIERS by May Crommelin (Hutchinson, [1915])..£200
LOUIS WAIN'S ANNUAL 1915 (Shaw, 1915)...£175
MERRY TIMES WITH LOUIS WAIN by Dorothy Black (Raphael Tuck, 1916)..£250
LITTLE RED RIDING HOOD and Other Tales (Gale & Polden, [1917]) £175
CINDERELLA AND OTHER FAIRY TALES (Gale & Polden, 1917) £175
CATS AT PLAY (Blackie, 1917)...£300
ROSY CHEEKS FUNNY BOOK (Nister, [c.1917]) £100
THE STORY OF TABBYKIN TOWN IN SCHOOL AND AT PLAY (written under the pseudonym 'Kittycat') (Faulkner, [1920])....£300
THE TALES OF LITTLE PRISCILLA PURR by Cecily M. Rutley (Valentine, 1920)...£400
THE TALE OF NAUGHTY KITTY CAT by Cecily M. Rutley (Valentine, 1920) £200
THE TALE OF PETER PUSSKIN by Cecily M. Rutley (Valentine, 1920) £200
THE TALE OF THE TABBY TWINS by Cecily M. Rutley (Valentine, 1920)..£200

PUSSY LAND (Geographia, [1920]) £300
LOUIS WAIN'S ANNUAL 1921 (Hutchinson, 1921) £175
THE TEDDY ROCKER: NAUGHTY TEDDY BEAR by Cecily M. Rutley (shape book) (Valentine, 1921) £225
THE PUSSY ROCKER: POLLY PUSS by Cecily M. Rutley (shape book) (Valentine, 1921) £225
THE KITTEN'S HOUSE (Valentine, 1922) £300
CHARLIE'S ADVENTURES (Valentine, 1922) £300
COMICAL KITTENS (painting book; with paints and brush) (Valentine, [1922]) £125
LOUIS WAIN'S CHILDREN'S BOOK (Hutchinson, [1923]) £225
SOUVENIR OF LOUIS WAIN'S WORK (second edition) (Louis Wain Fund, 1925) £175
SOUVENIR OF LOUIS WAIN'S WORK (fourth edition; as 'Animals "Xtra" and Louis Wain's Annual 1925')
    (Louis Wain Fund, [1925]) £175
LOUIS WAIN'S ANIMAL BOOK (Collins: 'Bumper Books' series, [1928]) £150
LOUIS WAIN'S GREAT BIG MIDGET BOOK (Dean, 1934) £150

WALSH, Jill Paton

British author. Born: London, 1937. Her books are aimed at adolescents but are enjoyed by older and younger readers. Notable for *Goldengrove* (1972) and its sequel, *Unleaving* (1976). Won the Whitbread Award for *The Emperor's Winding-Sheet* in 1974.

Prices are for books in Very Good condition with dustjackets where applicable.

HENGEST'S TALE (illustrated by Janet Margrie) (Macmillan, 1966) £40
THE DOLPHIN CROSSING (Macmillan, 1967) £30
WORDHOARD: Anglo-Saxon Stories (with Kevin Crossley-Holland) (Macmillan, 1969) £20
FIREWEED (Macmillan, 1969) £20
GOLDENGROVE (Macmillan, 1972) £20
TOOLMAKER (illustrated by Jeroo Roy) (Macmillan, 1973) £20
THE DAWNSTONE (illustrated by Mary Dinsdale) (Hamish Hamilton, 1973) £20
THE EMPEROR'S WINDING SHEET (Macmillan, 1974) £20
THE BUTTY BOY (illustrated by Juliette Palmer) (Macmillan, 1975) £20
THE BUTTY BOY (as 'The Huffler'; illustrated by Juliette Palmer) (Farrar Straus, U.S., 1975) £20
THE ISLAND SUNRISE: Prehistoric Britain (Deutsch, 1975) £20
UNLEAVING (Macmillan, 1976) £20
CROSSING THE SALAMIS (illustrated by David Smee) (Heinemann, 1977) £10
THE WALLS OF ATHENS (illustrated by David Smee) (Heinemann, 1977) £10
PERSIAN GOLD (illustrated by David Smee) (Heinemann, 1978) £10
CHILDREN OF THE FOX (contains 'Crossing to Salamis', 'The Walls of Athens' and 'Persian Gold') (Farrar Straus, U.S., 1978) £10
A CHANCE CHILD (Macmillan, 1978) £10

Although Wain's cats were usually depicted in human poses, they invariably retained their distinctly feline grace and charm.

THE GREEN BOOK (illustrated by Joanna Stubbs) (Macmillan, 1981) £10
BABYLON (illustrated by Jenny Northway) (Deutsch, 1982) £10
A PARCEL OF PATTERNS (Kestrel, 1983) £10
LOST AND FOUND (illustrated by Mary Rayner) (Deutsch, 1984) £10
GAFFER SAMSON'S LUCK (illustrated by Brock Cole) (Farrar Straus, U.S., 1984) £10
GAFFER SAMSON'S LUCK (illustrated by Brock Cole) (Viking Kestrel, 1985) £10
PEPI AND THE SECRET NAMES (Frances Lincoln, 1994) £10

WEBB, Marion St John

British author. Born: Hampstead, London in the 1890s. Her first book, *The Littlest One*, which appeared in 1914, was enormously successful, as were the 'Mr Papingay' books. Died: 1930.

Prices are for books in Good condition (with dustjackets after 1920).

'Littlest' Books

THE LITTLEST ONE (illustrated by Margaret W. Tarrant) (Harrap, 1914) £50
THE LITTLEST ONE (Harrap, 1918) £35
THE LITTLEST ONE – HIS BOOK (illustrated by Margaret W. Tarrant and Kathleen I. Nixon; music by Ralph Dunstan) (Harrap, 1923) £40
THE LITTLEST ONE AGAIN (illustrated by Margaret W. Tarrant and Kathleen I. Nixon) (Harrap, 1923) £35
THE LITTLEST ONE – HIS BOOK and THE LITTLEST ONE AGAIN (with additional poems) (illustrated by A.H. Watson) (Harrap, 1927) £40
THE LITTLEST ONE'S THIRD BOOK (Harrap, 1928) £35
THE LITTLEST ONE IN BETWEEN (Harrap, 1929) £35

'Fairies' Books

THE FLOWER FAIRIES (Modern Art Society, [1923]) £100
THE SEED FAIRIES (Modern Art Society, [1923]) £100
THE INSECT FAIRIES (illustrated by Margaret W. Tarrant) (Modern Art Society, [1925]) £100
THE FOREST FAIRIES (illustrated by Margaret W. Tarrant) (Modern Art Society, [1925]) £100
THE ORCHARD FAIRIES (illustrated by Margaret W. Tarrant) (Modern Art Society, [1925]) £100
THE HOUSE FAIRIES (illustrated by, Margaret W. Tarrant) (Modern Art Society, [1925]) £100
THE POND FAIRIES (illustrated by Margaret W. Tarrant) (Modern Art Society, [1925]) £100
THE SEA-SHORE FAIRIES (illustrated by Margaret W. Tarrant) (Modern Art Society, [1925]) £100
THE HEATH FAIRIES (Modern Art Society, [1927]) £100
THE WEATHER FAIRIES (illustrated by Margaret W. Tarrant) (Modern Art Society, [1927]) £100
THE TWILIGHT FAIRIES (illustrations by Margaret W. Tarrant) (Modern Art Society, [1928]) £100
THE WILD FRUIT FAIRIES (illustrated by Margaret W. Tarrant) (Modern Art Society, [1932]) £100

'Mr Papingay' Books

THE LITTLE ROUND HOUSE (S. Paul & Co, 1924) £30
THE LITTLE ROUND HOUSE (as 'Mr Papingay and the Little Round House') (Newnes, 1936) £25
MR PAPINGAY'S CARAVAN (illustrated by Frank Rogers) (Collins, [1929]) £25
MR PAPINGAY'S FLYING SHOP (Collins, [1931]) £25
MR PAPINGAY'S SHIP (S. Paul & Co, 1925) £25
MR PAPINGAY'S SHIP (Newnes, [1936]) £25
MR PAPINGAY'S SHIP (illustrated by Jean Walmsley Heap) (Collins, 1957) £25

Others

KNOCK THREE TIMES (illustrated by Margaret W. Tarrant) (Harrap, 1917) £70
THE GIRLS OF CHEQUERTREES (Harrap, 1918) £30
ELIZ'BETH PHIL AND ME (illustrated by Margaret W. Tarrant) (Harrap, 1919) £50
THE HOUSE WITH A TWISTING PASSAGE (illustrated by Doris M. Palmer) (Harrap, 1922) £50
THE MAGIC LAMPLIGHTER (illustrated by Margaret W. Tarrant) (Medici Society, 1926) £45
JOHN AND ME & THE DICKERY DOG (illustrated by A.H. Watson) (Harrap, 1930) £30
TWICE TEN (University of London Press, 1931) £20

WEBSTER, Jean

American author. Born: Alice Jane Chandler Webster in 1876, the daughter of Mark Twain's business partner, Charles L. Webster. Best known for her 1912 novel, *Daddy Long-Legs*, which was later filmed with Mary Pickford in the lead role. Died: 1916.

Prices are for books in Very Good condition without dustjackets.

WHEN PATTY WENT TO COLLEGE (Century, U.S., 1903) £80
THE WHEAT PRINCESS (Century, U.S., 1905) £65
JERRY JUNIOR (illustrated by Orson Lowell) (Century, U.S., 1907) £50
MUCH ADO ABOUT PETER (illustrated by Charlotte Harding and Harry Linnell) (Doubleday Page, U.S., 1909) £50
MUCH ADO ABOUT PETER (Hodder & Stoughton, [1917]) £25
JUST PATTY (illustrated by C.M. Relyea) (Century, U.S., 1911) £45
DADDY LONG-LEGS (illustrated by the author) (Century, U.S., 1912) £125
DADDY LONG-LEGS (illustrated by the author) (Hodder & Stoughton, 1913) £45

DADDY LONG-LEGS: A Comedy in Four Acts (play) (Samuel French: 'Standard Library' edition, U.K./U.S., [1922]) £12
DADDY LONG-LEGS (illustrated by Edward Ardizzone) (Brockhampton Press, 1966) £40
JUST PATTY (Hodder & Stoughton, 1915) £30
PATTY AND PRISCILLA (Hodder & Stoughton, [1915])..£45
DEAR ENEMY (illustrated by the author) (Century, U.S., 1915) £30
DEAR ENEMY (Hodder & Stoughton, [1915])...£15
THE FOUR-POOLS MYSTERY (Hodder & Stoughton, 1916) £35
THE WHEAT PRINCESS (Hodder & Stoughton, 1916) £30
JERRY (Hodder & Stoughton, [1916])...£25

WELCH, Ronald

British author. Born: Glamorganshire, 1909. Ronald Welch was the pseudonym of Ronald Felton, who wrote authentic, exciting historical novels. Awarded the Carnegie Medal for *Knight Crusader* in 1955. Died: 1982.

Prices are for books in Very Good condition with dustjackets where applicable.

THE BLACK CAR MYSTERY (Piman, 1950) £30
THE CLOCK STOOD STILL (Pitman, 1951) £30
THE GAUNTLET (illustrated by T.R. Freeman) (OUP, 1951)...£30
KNIGHT CRUSADER (illustrated by William Stobbs) (OUP, 1954)...£25
SKER HOUSE (written under the pseudonym 'Ronald Felton') (Hutchinson, 1954)..£25
CAPTAIN OF DRAGOONS (illustrated by William Stobbs) (OUP, 1956) £25
THE LONG BOW (Blackwell, 1957) £20
MOHAWK VALLEY (illustrated by William Stobbs) (OUP, 1958) £20
CAPTAIN OF FOOT (illustrated by William Stobbs) (OUP, 1959) £20
ESCAPE FROM FRANCE (illustrated by William Stobbs) (OUP, 1960) £20
FOR THE KING (illustrated by William Stobbs) (OUP, 1961) £20
NICHOLAS CAREY (illustrated by William Stobbs) (OUP, 1963) £20
BOWMAN OF CRECY (illustrated by Ian Ribbons) (OUP, 1966) £20
THE HAWK (illustrated by Gareth Floyd) (OUP, 1967) £20
SUN OF YORK (illustrated by Doreen Roberts) (OUP, 1970) £20
THE GALLEON (illustrated by Victor Ambrus) (OUP, 1971)...£20
TANK COMMANDER (illustrated by Victor Ambrus) (OUP, 1972) £20
ZULU WARRIOR (illustrated by David Harris) (David & Charles, 1974)...£20
ENSIGN CAREY (illustrated by Victor Ambrus) (OUP, 1976) £20

WELLS, H.G.

British author. Born: Herbert George Wells in 1866. The great science fiction novelist wrote three works for children, the best-known of which, *The Adventures of Tommy*, was written in 1898 for the daughter of a friend, but not published until 1929. Died: 1946.

Prices are for books in Very Good condition with dustjackets.

FLOOR GAMES (Palmer, 1911) £125
LITTLE WARS: A Game for Boys (Palmer, 1913) £125
THE ADVENTURES OF TOMMY (illustrated by the author) (Harrap, 1929)...£80

WESTALL, Robert

British author. Born in Newcastle in 1929. Studied at Durham University and the Slade School, subsequently working as an art master at schools in Birmingham and Chester. Won the Carnegie Medal with his first children's book, *The Machine Gunners* (1975), and later with *The Scarecrows* (1981). Died: 1993.

Prices are for books in Very Good condition with dustjackets.

THE MACHINE GUNNERS (Macmillan, 1975) £30
THE WIND EYE (Macmillan, 1976) £20
THE WATCH HOUSE (Macmillan, 1977)..£20
THE DEVIL ON THE ROAD (Macmillan, 1978)...£20
FATHOM FIVE (Macmillan, 1979) £20
THE SCARECROWS (Chatto & Windus, 1981) £15
BREAK OF DARK (Chatto & Windus, 1982) £15
FUTURETRACK 5 (Kestrel, 1983) £15
THE HAUNTING OF CHAS McGILL (Macmillan, 1983)...£15
THE CATS OF SEROSTER (Macmillan, 1984)...£10
THE CHILDREN OF THE BLITZ: Memoirs of Wartime Childhood. Edited by Robert Westall (Viking, 1985) £10
RACHEL AND THE ANGEL (Macmillan, 1986) £10
URN BURIAL (Viking Kestrel, 1987) £10
ROSALIE (Macmillan, 1987) £10
GHOSTS AND JOURNEYS (Macmillan, 1988) £10
GHOST ABBEY (Macmillan, 1988)..£10
THE CREATURE IN THE DARK (Blackie, 1988) £10
BLITZCAT (Macmillan, 1989) £10

A WALK ON THE WILD SIDE (Methuen, 1989) £10
OLD MAN ON A HORSE (Blackie, 1989)...£10
ECHOES OF WAR (Viking Kestrel, 1989) £10
CAT! (Viking Kestrel, 1989) £10
THE CALL (Viking Kestrel, 1989) £10
IF CATS COULD FLY (Methuen, 1990) £10
STORMSEARCH (Blackie, 1990) £10
THE PROMISE (Macmillan, 1990) £10
KINGDOM BY THE SEA (Methuen 1990)..£10
YAXLEY'S CAT (Macmillan, 1991) £10
THE CHRISTMAS CAT (Methuen, 1991) £10
THE CHRISTMAS GHOST (Methuen, 1992) £10
GULF (Methuen, 1992) £10
FEARFUL LOVERS (Macmillan, 1992)..£10
THE STONES OF MUNCASTER CATHEDRAL (Viking, 1993) £10
A PLACE FOR ME (Macmillan, 1993) £10
THE WHEATSTONE POND (Viking, 1993) £10
FALLING INTO GLORY (Methuen, 1993)...£10
A TIME OF FIRE (Macmilan, 1994)..£10
NIGHTMARE (Methuen, 1995) £10
CHILDREN OF THE BLITZ (Macmillan, 1995) £10

WESTERMAN, Percy F.

British author. Born: Percy Francis Westerman in 1876. Served with the RAF during the First World War. Wrote well over 100 novels, but is probably best known for those featuring the pilot, Colin Standish. Voted the most popular boys' author in Britain in the late 1930s. Died: 1959.

Prices are for books in Very Good condition with dustjackets where applicable.

A LAD OF GRIT (illustrated by Edward S. Hodgson) (Blackie, 1909 [1908]) £75
THE WINNING OF THE GOLDEN SPURS (Nisbet, 1911) £75
THE YOUNG CAVALIER: A Story of the Civil Wars (illustrated by Gordon Browne) (The Scout Library, 1909) £75
THE WINNING OF GOLDEN SPURS (Nisbet, 1911) £75
THE QUEST OF THE 'GOLDEN HOPE': A Seventeenth Century Story of Adventure (illustrated by Frank E. Wiles)
  (Blackie, 1912) £75
THE FLYING SUBMARINE (illustrated by John de Walton) (Nisbet, 1912) £55
CAPTURED AT TRIPOLI: A Tale of Adventure (illustrated by Charles M. Sheldon) (Blackie, [1912]) £55
THE SEA MONARCH (illustrated by E.S. Hodgson) (A. & C. Black, 1912) £55
THE SCOUTS OF SEAL ISLAND (illustrated by Ernest Prater) (Black, 1913) £50
THE RIVAL SUBMARINES (illustrated by C. Fleming Williams) (Partridge, [1913]) £55
THE STOLEN CRUISER (Jarrold, [1913])...£55
UNDER KING HENRY'S BANNERS (illustrated by John Campbell) (Pilgrim Press, 1913) £75
WHEN EAST MEETS WEST: A Story of the Days of Agincourt (illustrated by C. Padday) (Blackie, [1914]) £55
THE SEA-GIRT FORTRESS: A Story of Heligoland (illustrated by W.E. Wigfull) (Blackie, [1914]) ...£50
THE SEA SCOUTS OF THE 'PETREL' (illustrated by Ernest Prater) (A. & C. Black, 1914) £50
THE LOG OF A SNOB (illustrated by W. Edward Wigfull) (Chapman & Hall, 1914) £80
'GAINST THE MIGHT OF SPAIN: A Story of the Days of the Great Armada (illustrated by Saville Lumley)
  (Pilgrim Press, [1914]) £75
BUILDING THE EMPIRE: A Story of the North-West Frontier (Jarrold, [1914]) £45
THE DREADNOUGHT OF THE AIR (Partridge, [1914])...£55
THE DISPATCH-RIDERS (Blackie, [1915]) £55
THE FIGHT FOR CONSTANTINOPLE: A Story of the Gallipoli Peninsula (Blackie, [1915])..............£55
THE NAMELESS ISLAND: A Story of Some Modern Robinson Crusoes (Pearson, 1915) £45
A SUB OF THE R.N.R.: A Story of the Great War (S.W. Partridge & Co., [1915]) £55
ROUNDING UP THE RAIDER: A Naval Story of the Great War (illustrated by E.S. Hodgson) (Blackie & Son, [1916]) £55
THE SECRET BATTLEPLANE (Partridge, [1916]) £55
THE TREASURES OF THE 'SAN PHILIPO' (Boy's Own Paper, [1916]) £45
A WATCH-DOG OF THE NORTH SEA: A Naval Story of the Great War (Partridge, [1917]) £55
DEEDS OF PLUCK AND DARING IN THE GREAT WAR (Blackie, [1917])......................................£55
TO THE FORE WITH THE TANKS! (illustrated by Dudley Tennant) (Partridge, [1918]) £55
UNDER THE WHITE ENSIGN: A Naval Story of the Great War (Blackie, [1918]) £55
THE FRITZ STRAFERS: A Story of the Great War (Partridge, [1918]) £55
BILLY BARCROFT R.N.A.S.: A Story of the Great War (Partridge [1918]) £55
A LIVELY BIT OF THE FRONT: A Tale (illustrated by Wal Paget) (Blackie, [1918]) £55
THE SECRET CHANNEL AND OTHER STORIES OF THE GREAT WAR (A. & C. Black, 1918) £55
THE SUBMARINE HUNTERS: A Story (Blackie, [1918]) £55
WITH BEATTY OFF JUTLAND: A Romance of the Great Sea Fight (Blackie, [1918])........................£55
WILMSHURST OF THE FRONTIER FORCE: A Story of the Conquest of German East Africa (Partridge, [1918]) £55
A SUB AND A SUBMARINE (Blackie, [1919]) £55
WINNING HIS WINGS: A Story of the R.A.F. (illustrated by E.S. Hodgson) (Blackie, [1919]) £55
THE THICK OF THE FRAY AT ZEEBRUGE, APRIL 1918 (illustrated by W.E. Wigfull) (Blackie, [1919]) £55

A Lad of Grit was the first of many stirring boys' adventures to come from the prolific pen of Percy F. Westerman.

*The pictorial front board of '*Gainst the Might of Spain*. Very Good copies in the scarce dustjacket are valued at £75.*

'MIDST ARCTIC PERILS (Pearson, 1919) £45
THE AIRSHIP 'GOLDEN HIND' (Partridge, [1920]) £45
THE MYSTERY SHIP: A Naval Story of the Great War (Partridge, [1920]) £55
THE SALVING OF THE 'FUSI YAMA' (illustrated by E.S. Hodgson) (Blackie, [1920]) £25
SEA SCOUTS ALL (illustrated by Charles Pears) (Blackie, [1920])...£25
SEA SCOUTS ABROAD (illustrated by Charles Pears) (Blackie, [1921]) £25
THE THIRD OFFICER (illustrated by E.S. Hodgson) (Blackie, [1921]) £45
SEA SCOUTS UP-CHANNEL (illustrated by C.M. Padday) (Blackie, [1922])............................£25
THE WIRELESS OFFICER (illustrated by W.E. Wigfull) (Blackie, [1922]).................................£25
THE WAR OF THE WIRELESS WAVES (illustrated by W. E. Wightman) (Humphrey Milford, 1923) ...£25
THE PIRATE SUBMARINE (Nisbet, [1923]) £45
A CADET OF THE MERCANTILE MARINE (illustrated by W. Edward Wigfull) (Blackie, 1923) ...£25
CLIPPED WINGS (illustrated by E.S. Hodgson) (Blackie, [1923])..£25
THE MYSTERY OF STOCKMERE SCHOOL (Partridge, [1924])...£45
SINCLAIR'S LUCK: A Story of Adventure in East Africa (Partridge, [1924])............................£25
CAPTAIN CAIN (Nisbet, [1924]) £45
THE GOOD SHIP 'GOLDEN EFFORT' (illustrated by W.E. Wigfull) (Blackie, [1924]) £25
THE TREASURE OF THE SACRED LAKE (Pearson, [1924]) £25
UNCONQUERED WINGS (illustrated by E.S. Hodgson) (Blackie, [1924]) £25
CLINTON'S QUEST (illustrated by R.B. Ogle) (Pearson, 1925) £25
EAST IN THE 'GOLDEN GAIN' (illustrated by Rowland Hilder) (Blackie, [1925]) £25
THE BOYS OF THE 'PUFFIN' (illustrated by G.W. Goss) (Partridge, 1925) £25
THE BUCCANEERS OF BOYA (illustrated by William Rainey) (Blackie, [1925])......................£25
THE SEA SCOUTS OF THE 'KESTREL' (Seeley, 1926 [1925]) £25
ANNESLEY'S DOUBLE (Blackie: 'Black's Boy's and Girl's Library' series, 1926) £25
KING OF KILBA (Ward Lock, 1926) £25
THE LUCK OF THE 'GOLDEN DAWN' (illustrated by Rowland Hilder) (Blackie, [1926])............£25
THE RIDDLE OF THE AIR (illustrated by Rowland Hilder) (Blackie, [1926]) £25
THE TERROR OF THE SEAS (Ward Lock, 1927) £25
MYSTERY ISLAND (Humphrey Milford, [1927]) £40
CAPTAIN BLUNDELL'S TREASURE (illustrated by J. Cameron) (Blackie, [1927]) £25
CHUMS OF THE 'GOLDEN VANITY' (illustrated by Rowland Hilder) (Blackie, [1927]) £25

WESTERMAN, Percy F.

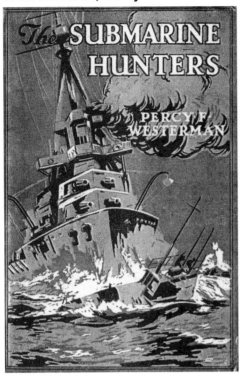

Westerman flew the flag during the First World War with morale-boosting novels like **The Submarine Hunters** (1918).

He took to the air in 1919 with **Winning His Wings**, now valued at £55 in Very Good condition with the dustjacket.

HIS FIRST SHIP (Blackie, [1936]) £25
MIDSHIPMAN RAXWORTHY (Blackie, [1936]) £25
RINGED BY FIRE (Blackie, [1936])..£25
TIRELESS WINGS (Blackie, [1936]) £25
WINGED MIGHT (Blackie, 1937)..£25
UNDER FIRE IN SPAIN (illustrated by Ernest Prater) (Blackie, 1937) £40
THE LAST OF THE BUCCANEERS (Blackie, 1937) £25
HAUNTED HARBOUR (illustrated by John de Walton) (Blackie, [1937]) £25
HIS UNFINISHED VOYAGE (illustrated by D.L. Mays) (Blackie, [1937]) £25
MIDSHIPMAN WEBB'S TREASURE (illustrated by D.L. Mays) (Blackie, 1937)...........£25
CADET ALAN CARR (illustrated by D.L. Mays) (Blackie, 1938).....................................£25
STANDISH GETS HIS MAN (illustrated by W.E. Wigfull) (Blackie, 1938) £25
STANDISH LOSES HIS MAN (illustrated by W.E. Wigfull) (Blackie, [1939])................£25
IN EASTERN SEAS (Blackie, [1939]) £25
THE BULLDOG BREED (illustrated by E. Boye Uden) (Blackie, [1939]) £25
AT GRIPS WITH THE SWASTIKA (illustrated by Leo Bates) (Blackie, 1940) £25
EAGLES' TALONS (Blackie, 1940) £25
IN DANGEROUS WATERS (Blackie, [1940]) £25
WHEN THE ALLIES SWEPT THE SEAS (illustrated by J.C.B. Knight) (Blackie, [1940]) £20
STANDISH PULLS IT OFF (Blackie, [1940]) £25
THE WAR — AND ALAN CARR (illustrated by E. Boye Uden) (Blackie, 1940)............£25
WAR CARGO (Blackie, [1941]) £25
SEA SCOUTS AT DUNKIRK (Blackie, 1941) £25
STANDISH HOLDS ON (Blackie, 1941) £25
FIGHTING FOR FREEDOM (Blackie, 1941) £25
ALAN CARR IN THE NEAR EAST (Blackie, [1942]) £25
DESTROYER'S LUCK (Blackie, [1942]) £25
ON GUARD FOR ENGLAND (illustrated by J.C.B. Knight) (Blackie, [1942]) £25
SECRET FLIGHT (Blackie, [1942]) £25
WITH THE COMMANDOS (illustrated by S. Van Abbé) (Blackie, [1943]) £20
SUB-LIEUTENANT JOHN CLOCHE (illustrated by H. Pym) (Blackie, [1943])............£25
ALAN CARR IN THE ARCTIC (illustrated by E. Boye Uden) (Blackie, [1943]) £25
COMBINED OPERATIONS (illustrated by S. Van Abbé) (Blackie, [1944]) £20
"ENGAGE THE ENEMY CLOSELY" (illustrated by Terence Cuneo) (Blackie, 1944)....£30
SECRET CONVOY (illustrated by Terence Cuneo) (Blackie, [1944]) £30
ALAN CARR IN COMMAND (illustrated by Terence Cuneo) (Blackie, [1945]) £30
ONE OF THE MANY (illustrated by Ellis Silas) (Blackie, [1945]) £20
OPERATIONS SUCCESSFULLY EXECUTED (illustrated by S. Drigin) (Blackie, [1945]) £25
BY LUCK AND PLUCK (illustrated by Terence T. Cuneo) (Blackie, [1946]) £30
RETURN TO BASE (illustrated by Leslie A. Wilcox) (Blackie, [1946])..........................£25
SQUADRON LEADER (illustrated by Terence Cuneo) (Blackie, [1946]) £30
UNFETTERED MIGHT (illustrated by S. Jezzard) (Blackie, [1947]) £15
TRAPPED IN THE JUNGLE (illustrated by A.S. Forrest) (Blackie, [1947])..................£15
THE PHANTOM SUBMARINE (illustrated by J.C.B. Knight) (Blackie, [1947]) £15
THE 'GOLDEN GLEANER' (illustrated by M. Mackinlay) (Blackie, [1948])..................£20
FIRST OVER (illustrated by Ellis Silas) (Blackie, [1948]) £15
THE MYSTERY OF THE KEY (illustrated by Ellis Silas) (Blackie, [1948]) £15
MISSING, BELIEVED LOST (illustrated by Will Nickless) (Blackie, [1949])................£15
CONTRABAND (illustrated by A. Barclay) (Blackie, [1949]) £15
BEYOND THE BURMA ROAD (illustrated by Victor Bertoglio) (Blackie, [1949]) £15
SABARINDA ISLAND (illustrated by A. Barclay) (Blackie, [1950]) £15
THE MYSTERY OF NIX HALL (illustrated by D.C. Eyles) (Blackie, [1950]) £15
BY SEA AND AIR: Two Stories of Adventure (contains 'Midshipman Doughty' and 'Forced Landing';
    edited and adapted for school reading) (Blackie, 1950) £15
DESOLATION ISLAND (illustrated by W. Gale) (Blackie, [1950]) £15
HELD TO RANSOM (illustrated by Ellis Silas) (Blackie, 1951) £15
THE ISLE OF MYSTERY (illustrated by Philip) (Blackie, [1951]) £15
WORKING THEIR PASSAGE (illustrated by Ellis Silas) (Blackie, 1951) £20
SABOTAGE! (illustrated by Ellis Silas) (Blackie, [1952]) £15
ROUND THE WORLD IN THE 'GOLDEN GLEANER' (illustrated by Jack Matthew) (Blackie, [1952])............£20
DANGEROUS CARGO (illustrated by W. Gale) (Blackie, [1952]) £15
BOB STRICKLAND'S LOG (illustrated by Jack Matthew) (Blackie, [1953])................£15
THE MISSING DIPLOMAT (illustrated by R.G. Campbell) (Blackie, [1953]) £15
ROLLING DOWN TO RIO (illustrated by R.G. Campbell) (Blackie, [1953]) £20
WRESTED FROM THE DEEP (illustrated by Robert Johnston) (Blackie, [1954]) £15
A MIDSHIPMAN OF THE FLEET (illustrated by P.A. Jobson) (Blackie, [1954]) £15
THE JU-JU HAND (Blackie, [1954]) £25
THE DARK SECRET (illustrated by Victor J. Bertoglio) (Blackie, [1954]) £15
DAVENTRY'S QUEST (illustrated by P.A. Jobson) (Blackie, 1955) £15
THE LURE OF THE LAGOON (illustrated by E. Kearon) (Blackie, 1955)......................£15

The original American edition of E.B. White's **Charlotte's Web**, published by Harper in 1952.

"SEA SCOUTS ALERT!" (illustrated by G. Graham) (Blackie, 1955) £15
HELD IN THE FROZEN NORTH (illustrated by Edward Osmond) (Blackie, 1956) £15
THE MYSTERY OF THE "SEMPIONE" (illustrated by P.B. Batchelor) (Blackie, 1957) £15
JACK CRADDOCK'S COMMISSION (illustrated by Edward Osmond) (Blackie, [1958])..£15
MISTAKEN IDENTITY (illustrated by Robert Johnston) (Blackie, [1959])..£20

WHITE, E.B.

American author. Born: Elwyn Brooks White in 1899. A regular contributor to *New Yorker*, he also wrote a handful of children's books, of which *Stuart Little* (1945) is the best-known. There have been two film versions. Died: 1985.

Prices are for books in Very Good condition with dustjackets.

STUART LITTLE (illustrated by Garth Williams) (Harper, U.S., 1945) £300
STUART LITTLE (illustrated by Garth Williams) (Hamish Hamilton, 1946) £120
CHARLOTTE'S WEB (illustrated by Garth Williams) (Harper, U.S., 1952)...£300
CHARLOTTE'S WEB (illustrated by Garth Williams) (Hamish Hamilton, 1952) £60

THE SECOND TREE FROM THE CORNER (Harper, U.S., 1954) £15
THE SECOND TREE FROM THE CORNER (Hamish Hamilton, 1954) £10
TRUMPET OF THE SWAN (Harper, U.S., 1970) £30
TRUMPET OF THE SWAN (illustrated by Edward Frascino) (Hamish Hamilton, 1970) £20

WHITE, T.H.

British author. Born: Terence Hanbury White in Bombay in 1906. Studied at Cheltenham College and Cambridge University, subsequently teaching English as Stowe School. Best-known for the Arthurian tetralogy, *The Once and Future King* (1958). His 1947 children's novel, *Mistress Masham's Repose*, is an unusual sequel to *Gulliver's Travels*. Died: 1964.

Prices are for books in Very Good condition with dustjackets.

THE SWORD IN THE STONE (Collins, 1938)...£425
THE WITCH IN THE WOOD (Collins, 1940) £400
THE ILL-MADE KNIGHT (illustrated by the author) (Collins, 1941) £400
MISTRESS MASHAM'S REPOSE (Cape, 1947) £70
THE ELEPHANT AND THE KANGAROO (Cape, 1948) £50
THE GOSHAWK (Cape, 1951) £75
THE MASTER: An Adventure Story (Cape, 1957) £40
THE ONCE AND FUTURE KING (contains the first three titles and 'The Candle in the Wind') (Collins, 1958) £150
THE GODSTONE AND THE BLACKYMOR (illustrated by Edward Ardizzone) (Cape, 1959).....................£40
THE BOOK OF MERLYN (illustrated by Trevor Studley) (University of Texas Press, U.S., 1977) £25

WIGGIN, Kate Douglas

American author. Born: Kate Douglas Smith in Philadelphia in 1856. Trained as a kindergarten teacher, and wrote her first children's book, *The Story of Patsy* (1883), to raise money for the movement. Her 1903 novel, *Rebecca of Sunnybrook Farm*, provided Mary Pickford with one of her most famous roles in 1918. Died: 1923.

Prices are for books in Very Good condition.

THE STORY OF PATSY (Privately printed, U.S., 1883)...£1,000
THE STORY OF PATSY (Gay & Bird, 1889) £150
THE BIRDS' CHRISTMAS CAROL (Murdock, U.S., 1887) £950

*The **Once and Future King** brings together T.H. White's first three 'Arthur' novels, plus the story, 'Candle in the Wind'.*

*T.H. White's 1959 tale, **The Godstone and the Blackymor**, was illustrated by the very collectable artist, Edward Ardizzone.*

THE BIRDS' CHRISTMAS CAROL (Gay & Bird, 1891) £150
A SUMMER IN A CAÑON: A Californian Story (Houghton Mifflin, U.S., 1890) £650
A SUMMER IN A CAÑON: A Californian Story (Gay & Bird, 1896) £150
TIMOTHY'S QUEST: A Story (Houghton Mifflin, U.S., 1892) £400
TIMOTHY'S QUEST (Gay & Bird, 1893 [1892]) £150
A CATHEDRAL COURTSHIP AND PENELOPE'S ENGLISH EXPERIENCES (Gay & Bird, 1893) £300
POLLY OLIVER'S PROBLEM: A Story for Girls (Houghton Mifflin, U.S., 1893) £150
POLLY OLIVER'S PROBLEM: A Story for Girls (Gay & Bird, 1894) £75
THE VILLAGE WATCH TOWER and Other Tales (Gay & Bird, 1895) £125
MARM LISA (Chapters I-X) (Gay & Bird, [1896]) £100
PENELOPE'S PROGRESS (Watt, 1897) £225
PENELOPE'S EXPERIENCES IN SCOTLAND (Gay & Bird, 1898) £175
PENELOPE'S EXPERIENCES IN ENGLAND (illustrated by C.E. Brock) (Houghton Mifflin, U.S., 1900) ... £125
PENELOPE'S ENGLISH EXPERIENCES (illustrated by C.E. Brock) (Houghton Mifflin, U.S., 1900) £125
PENELOPE'S IRISH EXPERIENCES (Gay & Bird, 1901) £125
THE DIARY OF A GOOSE GIRL (illustrated by C.A. Shepperson) (Gay & Bird, 1902) £125
HALF-A-DOZEN HOUSEKEEPERS: A Story for Girls (Kelly, [1903]) £60
HALF-A-DOZEN HOUSEKEEPERS: A Story for Girls (illustrated by Mills Thompson) (Gay & Bird, [1903]) ... £50
REBECCA OF SUNNYBROOK FARM (Houghton Mifflin, U.S., 1903) £200
ROSE O' THE RIVER (illustrated by George Wright) (Constable, U.S., 1905) £60
THE OLD PEABODY PEW: A Christmas Romance of a Country Church (illustrated by Alice Barber Stephens)
(Constable, [1907]) £50
NEW CHRONICLES OF REBECCA (Houghton Mifflin, U.S., 1907) £125
SUSANNA AND SUE (Houghton Mifflin, U.S., 1909) £40
ROBINETTA (with Mary Findlater, Jane Findlater and Allan McAulay) (Gay & Hancock, 1911) £35
MOTHER CAREY (Hodder & Stoughton, [1911]) £55
NEW CHRONICLES OF REBECCA OF SUNNYBROOK FARM (Hodder & Stoughton, [1912]) £60
A CHILD'S JOURNEY WITH DICKENS (Houghton Mifflin, U.S., 1912) £40
THE STORY OF WAITSTILL BAXTER (illustrated by H M Brett) (Hodder & Stoughton, [1913]) £40
BLUEBEARD: A Musical Fantasy (Harper, U.K./U.S., 1914) £45
PENELOPE'S POSTSCRIPTS (Hodder & Stoughton, 1915) £60
THE ROMANCE OF A CHRISTMAS CARD (Hodder & Stoughton, [1916]) £50
LADIES-IN-WAITING (Hodder & Stoughton, [1919]) £40
CREEPING JENNY and Other New England Stories (Houghton Mifflin, U.S., 1924) £35
TWILIGHT STORIES: More Tales for the Story Hour (Houghton Mifflin, U.S., 1925) £35
MOTHER CAREY'S CHICKENS (play; with Nora Archibald Smith) (Samuel French:
'Standard Library' edition, U.K./U.S., [1925]) £8
REBECCA OF SUNNYBROOK FARM (play) (Samuel French: 'Acting' edition, [1932]) £10

WILDE, Oscar

Irish author. Born: Oscar Fingal O'Flahertie Wills Wilde in 1854. The great playwright wrote a handful of
Hans Andersen-style fairy stories for children, collected under the title *The Happy Prince and Other Tales*
in 1888. A later collection, *A House of Pomegranates*, is not a children's book, but is aimed at an adult
readership. Died: 1900.

Prices are for books in Very Good condition (with dustjackets after 1950).

THE HAPPY PRINCE and Other Tales (illustrated by Walter Crane and G. Jacomb-Hood) (David Nutt, 1888) £750
THE HAPPY PRINCE and Other Tales (edition limited to 75 copies signed by the author and publisher)
(David Nutt, 1888) £3,300
THE HAPPY PRINCE and Other Tales (illustrated by Charles Robinson) (Duckworth, 1913) £250
THE HAPPY PRINCE and Other Tales (illustrated by Charles Robinson; De Luxe edition: limited to 250 copies signed by the
artist; vellum binding) (Duckworth, 1913) £1,000
A HOUSE OF POMEGRANATES (illustrated by Charles Ricketts and C.H. Shannon) (Osgood & McIlvaine, 1891) £750
A HOUSE OF POMEGRANATES (illustrated by Jessie M. King) (Methuen, 1915) £500
THE HAPPY PRINCE and A HOUSE OF POMEGRANATES: The Complete Fairy Stories of Oscar Wilde
(illustrated by Philippe Jullian) (Duckworth, 1952) £30
THE SELFISH GIANT (illustrated by Michael Foreman) (Kaye & Ward, 1978) £20

WILDER, Laura Ingalls

American author. Born: Laura Ingalls in 1867. Best known for the semi-autobiographical 'Little House'
books, which were based on her childhood experiences. The first novel in the series, *Little House in the
Big Woods*, was published in 1932, when Wilder was 65 years old. The books have become well-known in
Britain thanks to the television series, *Little House on the Prairie*. Died: 1957.

Prices are for books in Very Good condition with dustjackets where applicable.

LITTLE HOUSE IN THE BIG WOODS (illustrated by Helen Sewell) (Harper, U.S., 1932) £300
LITTLE HOUSE IN THE BIG WOODS (illustrated by Garth Williams) (Methuen, 1956) £150
FARMER BOY (illustrated by Helen Sewell) (Harper, U.S., 1933) £250
FARMER BOY (illustrated by Garth Williams) (Lutterworth Press, 1965) £40
LITTLE HOUSE ON THE PRAIRIE (illustrated by Helen Sewell) (Harper, U.S., 1935) £300

LITTLE HOUSE ON THE PRAIRIE (illustrated by Garth Williams) (Methuen, 1957) £150
ON THE BANKS OF PLUM CREEK (illustrated by Helen Sewell and Mildred Boyle) (Harper, U.S., 1937) £250
ON THE BANKS OF PLUM CREEK (illustrated by Garth Williams) (Methuen, 1958) £50
BY THE SHORES OF SILVER LAKE (illustrated by Helen Sewell and Mildred Boyle) (Harper, U.S., 1939) £250
BY THE SHORES OF SILVER LAKE (illustrated by Garth Williams) (Lutterworth Press, 1961) £30
THE LONG WINTER (illustrated by Helen Sewell and Mildred Boyle) (Harper, U.S., 1940) £250
THE LONG WINTER (illustrated by Garth Williams) (Lutterworth Press, 1961) £30
LITTLE TOWN ON THE PRAIRIE (illustrated by Helen Sewell and Mildred Boyle) (Harper, U.S., [1941]) £250
LITTLE TOWN ON THE PRAIRIE (illustrated by Garth Williams) (Lutterworth Press, 1963) £30
THESE HAPPY GOLDEN YEARS (illustrated by Helen Sewell and Mildred Boyle) (Harper, U.S., 1943).................£250
THESE HAPPY GOLDEN YEARS (illustrated by Garth Williams) (Lutterworth Press, 1964) £30
THE FIRST FOUR YEARS (illustrated by Garth Williams; epilogue by Rose Wilder) (Harper, U.S., 1971) £35
THE FIRST FOUR YEARS (illustrated by Garth Williams; epilogue by Rose Wilder) (Lutterworth Press, 1973)........£20
THE FIRST FOUR YEARS (illustrated by Garth Williams; epilogue by Rose Wilder; paperback) (Puffin, 1978) £10
WEST FROM HOME (Harper & Row, U.S., 1974) £35

WILDSMITH, Brian

British illustrator. Born: Penistone, Yorkshire, in 1930. He illustrated *The Oxford Book of Poetry for Children* (1960) and the 1981 edition of *Arabian Nights.* He won the Kate Greenaway Medal for *Brian Wildsmith's ABC* (1962) and produced a series of picture books based on fables by La Fontaine (1963 onwards).

Prices are for books in Very Good condition with dustjackets where applicable.

Books Written and Illustrated by Brian Wildsmith

TALES FROM THE ARABIAN NIGHTS (OUP, 1961) £25
BRIAN WILDSMITH'S ABC (OUP, 1962) £30
BRIAN WILDSMITH'S BIRDS (OUP, 1963) £30
THE LION AND THE RAT by Jean de La Fontaine (OUP, 1963) £25
THE NORTH WIND AND THE SUN by Jean de La Fontaine (OUP, 1964) £25
1 2 3 (OUP, 1964) £20
THE RICH MAN AND THE SHOE-MAKER by Jean de La Fontaine (OUP, 1965) £25
THE HARE AND THE TORTOISE by Jean de La Fontaine (OUP, 1966) £25
BRIAN WILDSMITH'S WILD ANIMALS (OUP, 1968)...£20
BRIAN WILDSMITH'S FISHES (OUP, 1969) £20
BRIAN WILDSMITH'S PUZZLES (OUP, 1970) £20
BRIAN WILDSMITH'S CIRCUS (OUP, 1970) £20
LITTLE WOOD DUCK (OUP, 1972) £20
THE TWELVE DAYS OF CHRISTMAS by Jean de La Fontaine (illustrated by Brian Wildsmith) (OUP, 1972) £25
WHAT THE MOON SAW (OUP, 1978) £10
HUNTER AND HIS DOG (OUP, 1979) £10
ANIMAL GAMES (OUP, 1980) £10
ANIMAL HOMES (OUP, 1980) £10
ANIMAL SHAPES (OUP, 1980) £10
ANIMAL TRICKS (OUP, 1980) £10
PROFESSOR NOAH'S SPACESHIP (OUP, 1980) £10
SEASONS (OUP, 1980)..£20
DAISY (OUP, 1984) £20
THE TUNNEL (OUP, 1993) £30

Books Illustrated by Brian Wildsmith

THE OXFORD BOOK OF POETRY FOR CHILDREN (OUP, 1963)...£35
FOLLOW MY BLACK PLUME by Geoffrey Trease (Macmillan, 1963) £30
THE KNIGHTS OF KING MIDAS by Paul Berna (paperback) (Penguin, 1964) £5
A THOUSAND FOR SICILY by Geoffrey Trease (Macmillan, 1964) £30
CHILD'S GARDEN OF VERSES by R.L. Stevenson (OUP, 1966) £20
BLUE BIRD by Maurice Maeterlinck (OUP, 1976) £20

WILLARD, Barbara

British author. Born: Sussex, 1909. Has written many adult works as well as more than fifty children's books, of which the 'Mantlemass' novels are the best known. Died: 1994.

Prices are for books in Very Good condition with dustjackets.

SNAIL AND THE PENNITHORNES (illustrated by Geoffrey Fletcher) (Epworth Press, 1957) £25
SNAIL AND THE PENNITHORNES NEXT TIME (illustrated by Geoffrey Fletcher) (Epworth Press, 1958) £20
THE HOUSE WITH ROOTS (illustrated by Robert Hodgson) (Constable, [1959]) £15
SON OF CHARLEMAGNE (illustrated by Emil Weiss) (Heinemann, 1960) £15
SNAIL AND THE PENNITHORNES AND THE PRINCESS (illustrated by Geoffrey Fletcher) (Epworth Press, 1960) £20
THE DIPPERS AND JO (illustrated by Jean Harper) (Hamish Hamilton, 1960) £15
EIGHT FOR A SECRET (illustrated by Lewis Hart) (Constable, [1960]) £15
THE PENNY PONY (illustrated by Juliette Palmer) (Hamish Hamilton, 1961) £15

IF ALL THE SWORDS IN ENGLAND (illustrated by Robert M. Sax) (Burns & Oates, 1961) £15
STOP THE TRAIN! (illustrated by Jean Harper) (Hamish Hamilton, 1961).. £12
THE SUMMER WITH SPIKE (illustrated by Anne Linton) (Constable, [1961]) £12
DUCK ON A POND (illustrated by Mary Rose Hardy) (Constable, [1962]) £12
HETTY (illustrated by Pamela Mara) (Constable, [1962]) £12
THE BATTLE OF WEDNESDAY WEEK (illustrated by Douglas Hall) (Constable: 'Young Books' series, [1963]) £12
THE DIPPERS AND THE HIGH-FLYING KITE (illustrated by Maureen Eckersley) (Hamish Hamilton, 1963) £12
THE SUDDENLY GANG (illustrated by Lynne Hemmant) (Hamish Hamilton, 1963) £12
THE PRAM RACE (illustrated by Constance Marshall) (Hamish Hamilton, 1964) £12
A DOG AND A HALF (illustrated by Jane Paton) (Hamish Hamilton, 1964) £12
THREE AND ONE TO CARRY (illustrated by Douglas Hall) (Constable: 'Young Books' series, [1964]) £12
AUGUSTINE CAME TO KENT (illustrated by Hans Guggenheim) (World's Work, 1964) £12
THE WILD IDEA (illustrated by Douglas Bissett) (Hamish Hamilton, 1965) £12
CHARITY AT HOME (illustrated by Douglas Hall) (Constable: 'Young Books' series, [1965]) £12
SURPRISE ISLAND (illustrated by Jane Paton) (Hamish Hamilton, 1966) £12
THE RICHLEIGHS OF TANTAMOUNT (illustrated by C. Walter Hodges) (Constable, 1966)... £12
THE GROVE OF GREEN HOLLY (illustrated by Gareth Floyd) (Constable, 1967) £15
THE PET CLUB (illustrated by Lynne Hemmant) (Hamish Hamilton, 1967) £12
TO LONDON! TO LONDON! (illustrated by Antony Maitland) (Longman, 1968) £20
HURRAH FOR ROSIE! (illustrated by Gareth Floyd) (Hutchinson, 1968) £12
ROYAL ROSIE (illustrated by Gareth Floyd) (Hutchinson, 1968) £12
THE FAMILY TOWER (Constable: 'Young Books' series, [1968]) £12
THE TOPPLING TOWERS (Longman, 1969) £12
THE POCKET MOUSE (illustrated by Mary Russon) (Hamish Hamilton, 1969) £12
JUNIOR MOTORIST: The Driver's Apprentice (with Frances Howell; non-fiction; illustrated by Ionicus) (Collins, 1969) £12
CHICHESTER AND LEWES (non-fiction; illustrated by Graham Humphreys) (Longman, 1970).. £12
THE LARK AND THE LAUREL (illustrated by Gareth Floyd) (Longman, 1970) £30
PRISCILLA PENTECOST (illustrated by Doreen Roberts) (Hamish Hamilton, 1970) £12
THE REINDEER SLIPPERS (illustrated by Tessa Jordan) (Hamish Hamilton, 1970) £12
THE SPRIG OF BROOM (illustrated by Paul Shardlow) (Longman, 1971) £20
A COLD WIND BLOWING (Longman, 1972) £20
THE DRAGON BOX (illustrated by Tessa Jordan) (Hamish Hamilton, 1972) £12
JUBILEE! (illustrated by Hilary Abrahams) (Heinemann, 1973) £12

TARKA THE OTTER
HIS JOYFUL WATER-LIFE AND DEATH
IN THE COUNTRY OF THE TWO RIVERS

by Henry Williamson

WITH AN INTRODUCTION BY
THE HON. SIR JOHN FORTESCUE, K.C.V.O.

ILLUSTRATED BY
C. F. Tunnicliffe

London : G. P. PUTNAM'S SONS : *New York*

*The opening spread of the first illustrated edition of Henry Williamson's **Tarka the Otter**, which features plates by C.F. Tunnicliffe.*

THE IRON LILY (Longman, 1973) £20
HARROW AND HARVEST (Kestrel, 1974) £20
HAPPY FAMILIES. Edited by Barbara Willard (anthology) (Hamilton, 1974) £12
THE GIANT'S FEAST by Max Bollinger (illustrated by Monika Laimgruber; translated by Barbara Willard)
   (Hamish Hamilton, 1975) £15
FIELD AND FOREST. Edited by Barbara Willard (illustrated by Faith Jaques) (Kestrel, 1975) £15
CONVENT CAT (illustrated by Bunchu Iguchi; translated by Barbara Willard) (Hamish Hamilton 1975) £15
THE MILLER'S BOY (illustrated by Gareth Floyd) (Kestrel, 1976) £12
BRIDESMAID (illustrated by Jane Paton) (Hamish Hamilton, 1976) £12
THE ELDEST SON (Kestrel, 1977) £12
THE COUNTRY MAID (Hamish Hamilton, 1978) £12
THE GARDENER'S GRANDCHILDREN (illustrated by Gordon King) (Kestrel, 1978) £10
SPELL ME A WITCH (illustrated by Phillida Gili) (Hamish Hamilton, 1979) £10
A FLIGHT OF SWANS (Kestrel, 1980) £15
THE KEYS OF MANTLEMASS (Kestrel, 1981) £25
SUMMER SEASON (Julia MacRae, 1981) £10
FAMOUS ROWENA LAMONT (Hardy, 1983) £10
THE QUEEN OF THE PHARISEES' CHILDREN (Julia MacRae, 1983) £10
SMILEY TIGER (illustrated by Laszelo Acs) (Julia MacRae, 1984) £10
NED ONLY (Julia MacRae, 1985) £10

WILLIAMS, Kit
British illustrator, best known for his unique visual puzzle-book, *Masquerade* (1979). The book — which was the idea of the publisher, Tom Maschler — contained clues to a hidden treasure, which was eventually found in 1982.

Prices are for books in Very Good condition.

MASQUERADE (boards; issued without dustjacket) (Cape, 1979) £20
UNTITLED (title can be found by solving clues concealed within the text and illustrations; boards; issued without dustjacket)
   (Cape, 1984) £15
OUT OF ONE EYE: The Art of Kit Williams (issued with dustjacket) (Cape, 1986) £15

WILLIAMSON, Henry
British author. Born: London, 1895. Studied at Colfe's Grammar School, Lewisham, and served with the Bedfordshire Regiment during the First World War, subsequently settling in North Devon. Completed two major series of novels, the 'Flax of Dreams' and 'Chronicle of Ancient Sunlight' sequences, but is best-known for his animals books, notably *Tarka the Otter* (1927) and *Salar the Salmon* (1935). Died: 1977.

Prices are for books in Very Good condition with dustjackets.

TARKA THE OTTER (private printing for subscribers only; limited to 100 copies, signed by the author) (Putnam, 1927) £400
TARKA THE OTTER (first trade edition; limited to 1,000 copies) (Putnam, 1927) £220
TARKA THE OTTER (first unlimited edition) (Putnam, 1927) £80
TARKA THE OTTER (first illustrated edition; illustrated by C.F. Tunnicliffe) (Putnam, 1932) £40
THE LONE SWALLOWS and Other Essays of Boyhood and Youth (illustrated by C.F. Tunnicliffe) (Putnam, 1933) £40
THE OLD STAG and Other Hunting Stories (illustrated by C.F. Tunnicliffe) (Putnam, 1933) £40
THE STAR-BORN (illustrated by C.F. Tunnicliffe) (Faber, 1933) £40
THE PEREGRINE'S SAGA (illustrated by C.F. Tunnicliffe) (Putnam, 1934) £60
SALAR THE SALMON (illustrated by C.F. Tunnicliffe) (Faber, 1935) £60
SALAR THE SALMON (illustrated in colour by C.F. Tunnicliffe) (Putnam, 1936) £60
SCRIBBLING LARK (Faber, 1949) £20
THE SCANDAROON (illustrated by Ken Lilly) (Macdonald, 1972) £15
THE HENRY WILLIAMSON ANIMAL SAGA (anthology) (Macdonald/Jane's, 1974) £15

WODEHOUSE, P.G.
British author. Born: Pelham Grenville Wodehouse in Guildford in 1881. Studied at Dulwich College, subsequently working in a Hong Kong bank before becoming a freelance writer. Began his career contributing school stories to *Captain* magazine, later producing a handful of novels in the genre. The last of these, *Mike* (1909), includes the first appearance of the character, Psmith, who later featured in a number of adult novels. Died: 1975.

Prices are for books in Very Good condition (with dustjackets after 1930).

THE POTHUNTERS (silver chalice on front cover) (A. & C. Black, 1902) £2,000
THE POTHUNTERS (pictorial cover) (A. & C. Black, 1902) £800
A PREFECT'S UNCLE (illustrated by R. Noel Pocock) (A. & C. Black, 1903) £750
TALES OF ST AUSTIN'S (illustrated by R. Noel Pocock) (A. & C. Black, 1903) £1,500
THE GOLD BAT (illustrated by T.M.R. Whitwell) (A. & C. Black, 1904) £950
WILLIAM TELL TOLD AGAIN (with J.W. Houghton; illustrated by P. Dadd) (A. & C. Black, 1904) £600
THE HEAD OF KAY'S (illustrated by T.M.R. Whitwell; without advertising supplement) (A. & C. Black, 1905) £1,250
THE HEAD OF KAY'S (illustrated by T.M.R. Whitwell; with advertising supplement) (A. & C. Black, 1905) £1,000

THE WHITE FEATHER (illustrated by W. Townend) (A. & C. Black, 1907) £800
MIKE: A Public School Story (illustrated by T.M.R. Whitwell; without advertising supplement) (A. & C. Black, 1909) £1,800
MIKE: A Public School Story (illustrated by T.M.R. Whitwell; with advertising supplement) (A. & C. Black, 1910) £1,100
ENTER PSMITH (revised version of second half of 'Mike'; issued with dustjacket) (A. & C. Black, 1935) £145
ENTER PSMITH (as 'Mike and Smith'; issued with dustjacket) (Herbert Jenkins, 1953) £125
MIKE AT WRYKYN (revised version of first half of 'Mike'; issued with dustjacket) (Herbert Jenkins, 1953) £125

WOOD, Lawson

British illustrator. Born: Highgate, London, in 1878, the grandson of the landscape painter, L.J. Wood.
Studied at the Slade School and Heatherley's, serving in the Royal Flying Corps during the Great War. Wood
was Pearson's chief artist for six years, and also contributed to the *Graphic* and *Illustrated London News*.
Died: 1957.

Prices are for books in Very Good condition.

THE BOW-WOW BOOK by John C. Kernahan (illustrated by L. Wood and L. Raven-Hill) (Nisbet, 1912) £100
A BASKET OF PLUMS by R. Waylett (Gale & Polden, [1916]) £80
A BOX OF CRACKERS by R. Waylett (Gale & Polden, [1916]) £80
THE 'MR' BOOKS (Warne, [1916]) ....each £40
'SPLINTERS' (Duckworth, [1916]) £65
THE MR AND MRS BOOKS (Warne, [1918]) ....each £20
THE 'MRS' BOOKS (Warne, [1920]) ....each £20
RUMMY TALES: A Series of Illustrated Children's Books (Warne, [1920]) ....each £20
THE 'RUMMY TALES' PAINTING BOOK (Warne, [1921]) £30
RUMMY TALES: A Series of Illustrated Booklets for Children (Warne, [1922]) ....each £20
THE NOO-ZOO TALES: A Series of illustrated Children's Books (Warne, [1922]) ....each £20
'BOOK TOYS' SERIES by Lawson Wood (Valentine, [1925-]) ....each £35
THE 'LAWSON WOOD' COLOUR BOOK SERIES (Partridge, [1925] ....each £20
JOLLY RHYMES by Lawson Wood (Nelson, [1926]) £40
THE SCOT 'SCOTCHED' by Lawson Wood (Newnes, [1927]) £60
THE LAWSON WOOD NURSERY RHYME BOOK (board book) (Nelson, [c.1930]) £75
LAWSON WOOD'S FUN FAIR by Lawson Wood (Arundel, [1931]) £100
THE OLD NURSERY RHYMES (Nelson, [1933]) £120
GRAN'POP'S ANNUAL ([Dean], [1935-]) ....each £75
A BEDTIME PICTURE BOOK (Birn, [1943]) £50
GRAN 'POP'S BOOK OF FUN (Birn, [1943]) £60
MERRY MONKEYS (Birn, [1946]) £35
MISCHIEF MAKERS (Birn, 1946) £25
POPULAR GRAN'POP (Birn, 1946) £40
LAWSON WOOD'S ANNUAL ([Dean], [1951-52]) ....each £40

WYSS, J.D.

Swiss author. Born: Johann David Wyss in Switzerland in 1743. Served as a chaplain in the Swiss army,
writing his famous story, *The Swiss Family Robinson*, for the entertainment of his four sons. One of them,
Johann Rudolf Wyss, was responsible for the story's publication in 1813, an English version — translated
by William Godwin and published by his wife, Mary — appearing the following year. Died: 1818.

Prices are for books in Very Good condition.

THE FAMILY ROBINSON CRUSOE (translated by William Godwin; two volumes) (M.J. Godwin, 1814) ....the set £3,000
THE SWISS FAMILY ROBINSON (second edition; two volumes) (M.J. Godwin, 1818) ....the set £1,750
SWISS FAMILY ROBINSON (translated by J. Lovell) (London, [1869]) £250
THE SWISS FAMILY ROBINSON (translated by W.H. Davenport Adams; introduction by C. Nodier) (London, 1870 [1869]) £125
THE SWISS FAMILY ROBINSON (translated by Mrs H.B. Paull) (London, [1877]) £85
THE SWISS FAMILY ROBINSON (Routledge, [1885]) £70
THE SWISS FAMILY ROBINSON. Edited with Notes by A. Gardiner (J. Heywood, 1886) £60
THE SWISS FAMILY ROBINSON (translated by Mrs H.B. Paull) (Warne: 'Chandos Classics' series, [1890]) £185
THE SWISS FAMILY ROBINSON (illustrated by J. Finnemore; translated by E.A. Brayley Hodgetts) (Newnes, 1897 [1896]) £60
THE SWISS FAMILY ROBINSON (Blackie, 1905) £30
THE SWISS FAMILY ROBINSON (illustrated by Charles Folkard) (Dent, 1910) £25
THE SWISS FAMILY ROBINSON. Edited by W.H.G. Kingston (illustrated by Ernest Prater;
    introduction by Walter Jerrold) (Nister/Dutton, U.S.: 'Children's Classics' series, [1910]) £45
THE SWISS FAMILY ROBINSON (illustrated by Gordon Browne) (Cassell, [1910]) £35
THE CHILDREN'S SWISS FAMILY ROBINSON. Adapted by F.H. Lee (illustrated by Honor C. Appleton) (Harrap, 1938)...........£25
THE SWISS FAMILY ROBINSON (illustrated by Mervyn Peake) (Heirloom Library, 1950) £15

OLD Mother Goose, when
She wanted to wander,
Would ride through the air
On a very fine gander.

'Old Mother Goose' as depicted by British illustrator, Lawson Wood, in his **Nursery Rhyme Book** from the early 1930s. Wood served in the Royal Flying Corps during the Great War, which might have helped him with the composition of this plate!

Y

YONGE, Charlotte M.

British author. Born: Otterbourne, near Winchester, in 1823. The author of over 150 works, she is best known for her 'Langley' books and *The Heir of Redclyffe* (1853) . Died: 1901.

Prices are for books in Good condition.

'Aunt Charlotte's Stories'

AUNT CHARLOTTE'S STORIES OF ENGLISH HISTORY FOR THE LITTLE ONES (Marcus Ward, 1873) £40
AUNT CHARLOTTE'S STORIES OF BIBLE HISTORY (Marcus Ward, 1875) £40
AUNT CHARLOTTE'S STORIES OF GREEK HISTORY (Marcus Ward, 1876) £40
AUNT CHARLOTTE'S STORIES OF ROMAN HISTORY (Marcus Ward, 1877) £40
AUNT CHARLOTTE'S STORIES OF GERMAN HISTORY (Marcus Ward, 1878) £40
AUNT CHARLOTTE'S STORIES OF AMERICAN HISTORY (Marcus Ward, 1883) £40
AUNT CHARLOTTE'S STORIES OF FRENCH HISTORY (Marcus Ward, 1884) £40
AUNT CHARLOTTE'S STORIES OF BIBLE HISTORY FOR YOUNG DISCIPLES (John C. Winston, 1909) £60

Others

LANGLEY SCHOOL (Macmillan, 1850) £150
THE HEIR OF REDCLYFFE (Macmillan, 1853) £300
THE LITTLE DUKE (Parker, 1854) £250
HEARTSEASE, or The Brother's Wife (Parker, 1854)...£75
THE LANCES OF LYNWOOD (Parker, 1855)..£75
THE HISTORY OF SIR THOMAS THUMB (Constable, 1855) £75
THE DAISY CHAIN, or Aspirations (Parker, 1856) £100
DYNEVOR TERRACE, or The Clue of Life (Parker, 1857) £100
PIGEON PIE: A Tale of Roundhead Times (Mozley, 1860)..£100
THE TRIAL: More Links of the Daisy Chain (Macmillan, 1864)..£200
THE DOVE IN THE EAGLE'S NEST(two volumes) (Macmillan, 1866)..the set £200
THE CHAPLET OF PEARLS (two volumes) (Macmillan, 1868)...the set £150
A BOOK OF WORTHIES (Macmillan, 1869)..£75
THE CAGED LION (Macmillan, 1870) £75
LADY HESTOR, or Ursula's Narrative (Macmillan, 1870)...£75
THE PILLARS OF THE HOUSE, or Under Wode, Under Road (four volumes) (Macmillan, 1873) ....the set £150
WOMANKIND (Mozley & Smith, 1876) £100
A MAN OF OTHER DAYS (two volumes) (Hurst & Blackett, 1877) ....the set £50
THE STORY OF THE CHRISTIANS AND MOORS IN SPAIN (Macmillan, 1878) £60
MAGNUM BONUM, or Mother Carey's Brood (three volumes) (Macmillan, 1879) ....the set £180
BYWORDS: Tales Old and New (Macmillan, 1880)..£45
UNKNOWN TO HISTORY: A Story of the Captivity of Mary of Scotland (two volumes) (Macmillan, 1882) ....the set £100
STRAY PEARLS, Memoirs of Margaret de Ribaumont Viscontess of Bellaise (illustrated by W.J. Hennessy)
    (two volumes) (Macmillan, 1883)...the set £100
THE ARMOURER'S PRENTICES (two volumes) (Macmillan, 1884) ....the set £150
THE TWO SIDES OF THE SHIELD (two volumes) (Macmillan, 1885) ....the set £250
CHANTRY HOUSE (two volumes) (Macmillan, 1886)..the set £120
THE PRINCE AND THE PAGE: A Story of the Last Crusade (illustrated by Marguerite de Angeli)
    (Macmillan, 1886)..£50
UNDER THE STORM, or Steadfast's Change (National Society Depository, 1887)..£40
BEACHCROFT AT ROCKSTONE (two volumes) (Macmillan, 1888) ....the set £200
MORE BYWORDS (Macmillan, 1890)..£35
THE CONSTABLE'S TOWER (National Society Depository, 1891) £35
GRISLY GRISELL, or the Laidly Lady of Whitburn (two volumes) (Macmillan, 1893) ....the set £140
A TALE OF THE CHEDDAR CAVES ONE HUNDRED YEARS AGO (Wells Clare Son & Co, 1891) £35
THE RELEASE OF CAROLINE'S FRENCH KINDRED (Macmillan, 1896) £35
AN OLD WOMAN'S OUTLOOK IN A HAMPSHIRE VILLAGE (Macmillan, 1897) £30
FOUNDED ON PAPER, or Up Hill and Down Hill Between the Two Jubilees (National Society Depository, 1898) £40
MODERN BROODS, or Developments Unlooked For (Macmillan, 1900)...£35
A BOOK OF GOLDEN DEEDS (illustrated by W. Rainey) (SW Partridge, 1914)..£15
LITTLE LUCY'S WONDERFUL GLOBE (illustrated by Anne Merriman Peck) (Harper, 1927) £25

*The frontispiece from **Aunt Charlotte's Stories of English History for the Little Ones** (1873) by Charlotte M. Yonge.*

GRADING YOUR BOOK

Below are the Standard Conditions for grading secondhand books and their dustjackets. The five basic conditions accepted by collectors all over the world are listed here, together with a description of what each one means.

Mint

This means that the book is in perfect condition. It is complete with its dustjacket and is impossible to distinguish from a new copy.

DUSTJACKET: as new.

Fine

The book appears to be in excellent condition. Closer examination, however, will show evidence of ownership and storage. There may also be a small inscription to or by the previous owner, but generally the book is in near perfect condition.

DUSTJACKET: as new, but with very slight rubbing on corners.

Very Good

Slightly less than Fine condition. Apart from slight foxing or fading, the book has no faults.

DUSTJACKET: clean with excellent colouring, but with slight rubbing to most edges and corners.

Good

It is obvious that the book is secondhand. However, apart from minor faults, it must always be assumed that books in Good condition are complete in all respects, unless described otherwise.

DUSTJACKET: fairly clean with almost perfect colouring, but suffering from marks, slight creasing and other signs of wear. Most of the edges are rubbed or have very small tears in them.

Poor

A book in this category is in really bad condition. It may be warped, the preliminary pages may be missing, and the spine irreparably damaged. The text is complete but the book is really only suitable to read.

DUSTJACKET: tatty and grubby, and may well be marked, creased or torn.

READY RECKONER OF PRICES

This Ready Reckoner will help you work out the value of a book in any condition. For example, if you have a book which we value at £10 in Fine condition, but which is only in Good condition, you can read across the appropriate line and find the correct value of your book – in this case, £5. Please note that Poor condition books worth less than £10 in Fine condition are virtually worthless to collectors. However, Poor condition books may be worth many times more if they contain intact, well-preserved illustrations.

Mint	Fine	Very Good	Good	Poor
10,000	8,000	6,000	3,000	500
5,000	4,000	3,000	1,500	250
2,000	1,500	1,000	500	60
1,000	800	600	300	40
750	600	450	200	30
500	400	300	150	20
200	180	150	80	10
150	135	125	70	8
100	90	75	40	5
75	65	55	30	4
50	45	40	20	3
40	35	30	18	2.50
30	27	22	13	2
25	22	18	10	1.50
20	17	15	8	1
15	13	11	7	1
12	10	8	5	–
10	8	6.50	4	–
9	7	5.75	3.50	–
8	6	4.50	2.50	–
7	5	3.75	2	–
6	4.50	3.50	1.50	–
5	4	3	1	–
4	3.50	2.50	50p	–
3	2.50	2	50p	–
2	1.75	1.30	–	–